STRUCTURED BASIC AND PROGRAM DESIGN

Margaret McRitchie

Holt, Rinehart and Winston of Canada, Limited

Toronto

Canadian Cataloguing in Publication Data
McRitchie, Margaret
Structured BASIC and program design

Includes index.
ISBN 0-03-921985-2

1. BASIC (Computer program language). 2. IBM
Personal Computer - Programming. I. Title.

QA76.73.B3M27 1989 005.13'3 C89-094347-8

Illustrations of a computer system and keyboards courtesy of International Business Machines Corporation

Publisher: Scott Duncan
Editorial Assistant: Sarah Duncan
Publishing Services Manager: Karen Eakin
Cover Design: Zena Povse/Dan Kewley
Typesetting and Assembly: True to Type Inc.
Printing and Binding: Webcom Limited

Printed in Canada
1 2 3 4 5 94 93 92 91 90

PREFACE

Programming has changed dramatically over the last few years. At first, little thought was given on how programs should be written, the main goal was to produce the output required. Today, the development of software has become a major industry. Keeping down the costs of writing and maintaining the programs that make up the software is now of prime importance. Programs must be written in such a way that they can be easily understood not only by those who write the programs, but by those who may be asked to modify the programs at a later date. The emphasis now is on easy-to-read, well-organized programs.

The central focus of this book is to teach good programming techniques. Applying these techniques not only facilitates programming, it produces programs that are easy to understand and simple to maintain. To enable students to produce such programs, heavy emphasis is placed on program design and structured programming.

Students are shown how to design a program as early as Chapter Three shortly after being introduced to computers. Each chapter, from Chapter Three through to Chapter Fourteen, includes a section on program design. In each of these sections, a problem is solved by first designing the program and then coding the program from the design. Two methods of designing are illustrated for each problem: the structure chart and pseudocode.

Structured programming is discussed in detail in Chapter Five immediately after students have learned how to enter data into the computer. It is here that the three control structures (sequence, decision, and looping) are explained. Emphasis is placed on program modularization. Students are shown how to develop a program module by module. They must ensure that:

1. Modules are well planned.
2. The best choice of a control structure is selected for a particular operation.
3. Programs are documented and styled in a manner that enhances clarity.

The GOTO statement is used sparingly. Its use is restricted to two specific functions: (a) to introduce the student to a simple loop and (b) to verify keyed-in data. Immediately after students become familiar with a loop, they move on to the more structured WHILE/WEND loop. A FOR/NEXT loop is discussed later on in the book.

The concept of files is introduced after students have become familiar with the three control structures and after they have used these structures in a number of programs. It is in Chapter Seven where they learn how to create a sequential data file and how to retrieve and update records. From this chapter through to Chapter 14 (with the exception of the chapter on two-dimensional arrays), students use sequential data files.

Random access files are introduced in Chapter 15. Here, students are shown how a random access file can be created, how records can be added to and deleted from a file, and how records can be updated. In particular, students are asked to devise formulas to retrieve records from random access files. Each formula must use one of the fields in a random access file as the base. When the value of the field is keyed in, the formula produces the number of the record desired. The formulas are relatively simple. The primary purpose of this chapter is to show students how to produce programs that retrieve and update files in a truly random access fashion.

Report generation and control breaks are given special consideration. Reports must be centred vertically and horizontally on the screen and must be attractively displayed with the main heading centred horizontally and with column headings centred over the columns. The concept of a multi-page report is explained. Each page must be numbered and must begin with headings. Printing must be controlled to produce specific top and bottom margins. Reports with and without page totals are discussed, as well as reports that contain control breaks and groups totals. Programs that produce such reports are listed in Chapter 9. Students can use these programs as guides to solve the programming problems at the end of the chapter.

The maintenance of programs is stressed through the use of three often-used business applications. These are:

1. A payroll application based on hours of work per week. This application is used as a sample to introduce students to programming and to introduce many of the concepts discussed in the book.

2. An accounts receivable application. This application is assigned as a programming problem in a number of chapters. The application begins with the creation of one account and, after the updating of several accounts, ends with the printing of a form letter addressed to specific customers. The form letter and the customers' addresses must be retrieved from two separate data files.

3. An inventory application. This application is actually a project started after students become familiar with sequential files and then maintained in subsequent chapters. The project begins with the creation of several inventory accounts and ends with a menu-driven program. Since each assignment requires more work than a normal programming problem, we suggest that more than one student work on each project.

The last chapter involves a major project in which most of the concepts learned in the book are applied to the development of a payroll software package. This is a large piece of work requiring several teams of programmers each headed by a team leader. The project gives students valuable experience in working in groups as well as serving as a tool to review the majority of topics covered in this book.

The book can be used by beginners and by those who already have some knowledge of BASIC. Advanced topics such as two-dimensional arrays, multi-page reports with control breaks, and pointers (for which a program was designed in Chapter 12) are explained in detail. If time is a factor, these topics can be bypassed without seriously disrupting the flow of learning. A few problems may have to be omitted and some projects modified so that the above concepts are not included in the programs. For instance, rather than produce a report with page totals and control breaks, the program for a project can simply produce an attractively centred report without these features.

There is a sufficient number of programming problems at the end of a chapter to allow the instructor (or the student) to choose the ones to be solved. The problems progress from simple to difficult making it possible for the latter problems to be used as "bonus" problems.

Students are strongly urged to write programs module by module. After designing a program, a student keys the first module into the computer, then saves and tests the module. If there is an error, the module must be debugged and resaved. The second module is appended to the first and the combined modules are saved. The two modules are tested and, if necessary, debugged and resaved. This continues until all the tasks are performed.

When students develop programs by modules, there is little hesitancy in tackling a problem since the first few modules are often similar to those of previous programs. Students are usually amazed at the ease by which they can write a complex and lengthy program and are unaware of its length until the entire program is listed.

To aid a student in program writing, a number of often-used programs and subroutines are developed throughout the book. After the concepts in a module have been explained, a student is encouraged to save the module on his/her own diskette and thus build up a library of frequently used files. Subroutines must be saved in ASCII format so that they can be merged with a program in memory. The subroutines have been standardized in such a way that little or no modifications are required. The often-used files are listed by name and by line number in Appendix B.

Students create data files starting in Chapter Seven. To facilitate programming, a diskette is available on which we have stored the majority of the data files needed for the programming problems in Chapters Eight through to Fifteen. The frequently used files mentioned above are also stored on the diskette. The files stored on the diskette are listed in Appendix C.

In the dynamic world of computers, few things remain the same. So it is with DOS and with BASIC. As this book was being written, new versions of DOS and new versions of BASIC were issued. A few of the facts and features mentioned in the book may not apply to your version of DOS or BASIC. If in doubt, please consult your manual.

Acknowledgments

First and foremost, my thanks to the many students who tested the material in the manuscript. Grateful appreciation is given as well to the reviewers who contributed their valuable ideas and suggestions throughout the development of the book. I wish to thank, also, the staff at Computerland, Winnipeg, who provided me access to the latest equipment.

Gratitude is extended as well to the staff involved with the book at Holt, Rinehart and Winston: Scott Duncan, Publisher; Sarah Duncan, Editorial Assistant; and Karen Eakin, Publishing Services Manager for all their help. I am especially grateful to Karen for her superb job in transforming the manuscript into its final product, for her cooperation, and for her devotion to the project. Thanks, also, to the staff at True to Type Inc. for their skillful drawings.

Finally, a special thank you to my husband, Robert, for his patience and understanding.

Margaret McRitchie

Publisher's Note to Instructors and Students

This text book is a key component of your course. If you are the instructor of this course, you undoubtedly considered a number of texts carefully before choosing this as the one that will work best for your students and you. The authors and publishers of this book spent considerable time and money to ensure its high quality, and we appreciate your recognition of this effort and accomplishment.

If you are a student, we are confident that this text will help you to meet the objectives of your course. You will also find it helpful after the course is finished, as a valuable addition to your personal library. So hold on to it.

As well, please don't forget that photocopying copyright work means the authors lose royalties that are rightfully theirs. This loss will discourage them from writing another edition of this text or other books, because doing so will simply not be worth their time and effort. If this happens, we all lose—students, instructors, authors, and publishers.

And since we want to hear what you think about this book, please be sure to send us the stamped reply card at the end of this text. This will help us to continue publishing high-quality books for your courses.

TABLE OF CONTENTS

Four—Entering Data, Writing and Saving Programs

Five—Structured Programming and Program Design

Six—Decision Structures

Seven—Sequential Files

Eight—Generating Reports

Eleven—Strings

Twelve—One-Dimensional Arrays

Fourteen—Other Topics

Fifteen—Random Access Files

Sixteen—Project

1

AN INTRODUCTION TO COMPUTERS

Objectives

This brief introduction to computers will familiarize you with the following:

- Computer hardware and software
- The fundamental units of a computer system
- The internal structure of a microcomputer
- Mass storage of information
- Diskettes

Contents

1.1 Computer Hardware

The Fundamental Units of a Computer System

The computer is an electronic device that uses stored data and stored instructions to generate results. Data are unorganized items or facts upon which the computer operates to produce the results. Examples of data items are employee names, hours of work, and students' scores. We give the computer the instructions that tell it what to do with the data. The set of instructions, which is called a program, must be written in a manner that the computer understands. The program is used to enter the data into the computer and to tell the computer what to do with the data and how to display the results it obtains.

The term computer hardware refers to those components of a computer system which are physical. There are five such physical components:

1. The Central Processing Unit (CPU) which is composed of the Control Unit and the Arithmetic-Logic Unit.
2. Internal memory.
3. A device, such as a disk drive, used to store data and information externally.

4. An input device such as the keyboard.
5. An output device such as the monitor (screen) and the printer.

Figure 1-1 illustrates schematically the components of a computer system.

FIGURE 1-1 COMPONENTS OF A COMPUTER SYSTEM

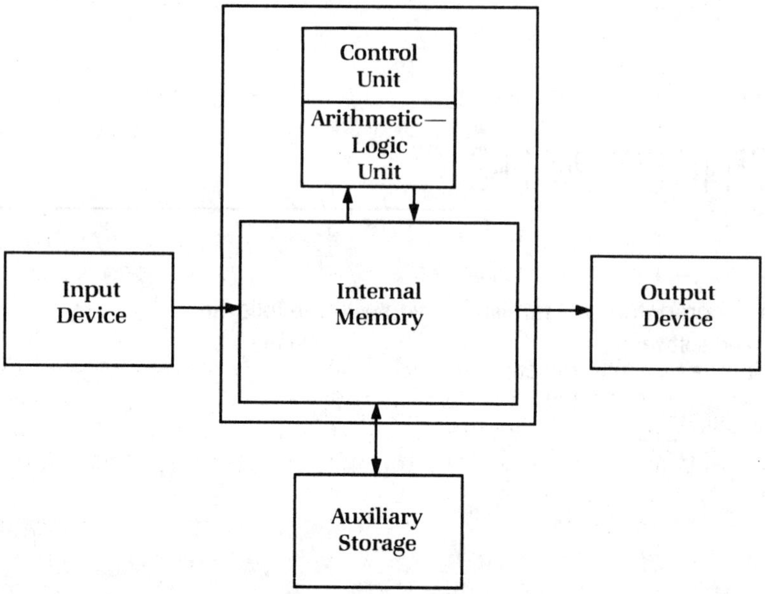

We will first discuss the internal structure of a microcomputer (the system unit which consists of the microprocessor unit and internal memory) then follow this with a brief explanation of the external devices.

The Internal Structure of a Microcomputer

The Microprocessor Unit (MPU) The heart of a microcomputer consists of a tiny silicon chip called the microprocessor. In spite of its minuscule size, this component incorporates all the functions of a traditional Central Processing Unit. The features that make microcomputers different from other computer systems are their reduced cost and size brought about by the microprocessor. The cost of a processor is presently one of the least expensive components in a microcomputer, while its compactness has reduced the size of a microcomputer to such an extent that a computer can now be held in one hand. Another important aspect of the microprocessor is its programmability, a feature that makes it so versatile it is often considered a peripheral to other equipment, such as pocket calculators, digital watches, microwave ovens, and video games.

The microprocessor includes the following units:

The Arithmetic and Logical Unit (ALU). This unit contains the circuitry that performs the arithmetic operations of addition, subtraction, multiplication, and division. It also performs logical operations, such as comparing two values.

The Control Unit (CU). This unit directs and coordinates all the activities of the computer. It retrieves, interprets, and executes the instructions stored in the computer's memory. It controls the activities of the ALU and functions in conjunction with the input/output devices.

Internal Memory The memory of a microcomputer system comes in the form of specialized memory chips. Two of the several types of memory are: **R**andom **A**ccess **M**emory (RAM), in which data and information can be stored and from which they can be read; and **R**ead **O**nly **M**emory (ROM), from which information can only be read. We cannot store data or information in ROM. Programs and frequently used instructions are written permanently into ROM by the manufacturer. Unfortunately, anything stored in RAM is lost when the computer is turned off, while that stored in ROM is permanent and always available.

Memory in a computer is organized into units called bytes. Each byte is capable of holding one character: digit, letter, space, or special symbol. A byte consists of eight bits (**b**inary dig**its**). A character is stored electronically as a series of bits. Each bit is either on or off depending on the character stored. On paper, we represent a bit that is on by the digit 1, a bit that is off by the digit Ø. We draw a stroke through a stand-alone zero to distinguish it from the letter O.

Many computers combine bytes into words. A word may consist of 4, 8, 16, or 32 bits. A four-bit word is called a nibble. A 16-bit word consists of two bytes, a 32-bit word consists of four bytes. A microcomputer may possess an 8-bit processor, a 16-bit processor, or a 32-bit processor. Four-bit processors are normally used in such items as calculators and timers.

The storage capacity of a microcomputer is usually measured in K bytes or in megabytes. K represents Kilo. One K is 2^{10} (1024) bytes. A megabyte is 2^{20} (1,048,576) bytes. Not all of this memory is available to the user. A small amount is taken up as ROM and a small amount is used as a work space by the computer.

The External Devices

Input/Output Devices. Input/output devices provide the means by which people can communicate with the computer. The devices must be interfaced (connected) with the computer. The usual input device is a keyboard, while typical output devices are video monitors and printers.

Mass Storage. Since the internal memory of a microcomputer is limited, large quantities of data and information must be stored on external storage media. Any part of this storage can be retrieved and placed in internal memory whenever it is needed. Thus, data and information can be transferred between external storage media and internal memory. This external storage is referred to as auxiliary storage. An external device, usually a disk drive, contains a read/write head which reads or writes information. The drive must be attached to the computer and is controlled by instructions issued from the computer.

Drives interfaced with the computer may be enclosed in separate cabinets or they may be installed within the computer's cabinet. Data and information are written either on a diskette or on a hard disk. A hard disk can store a much greater amount of data and information than a diskette. A diskette can be removed from a drive, the hard disk is fixed.

Diskettes

Two types of diskettes commonly used in microcomputers are available. One is sealed in a hard jacket and is 3 1/2 inches in diameter, the other is sealed in a plastic jacket and is 5 1/4 inches in diameter. The jackets protect the diskettes from scratches and contamination and must never be removed. Inside the jackets, the diskettes spin freely. The diskettes are coated with ferromagnetic material on which data and information can be stored.

Both types of diskettes should be handled with care. However, greater care must be taken with the diskette sealed in a plastic jacket since this jacket offers less protection. Your manual or the paper envelope that comes with the plastic-covered diskette should list a number of diskette-handling precautions. Figures 1-2 and 1-3 illustrate the diskettes.

Diskettes are divided into concentric bands called tracks. Tracks are divided into sectors. The diskettes are spun by the disk drive which is equipped with a reading and recording head. As the diskette spins inside its jacket, the read/write head seeks the information it must read or finds a place in which to write new information. Figure 1-4 illustrates tracks and sectors on a diskette. Diskettes are either single-sided or double-sided. The computer writes to and reads from only one side of a single-sided diskette but uses both sides of a double-sided diskette.

It is possible to overwrite information stored on a diskette. The old information is now destroyed. Sometimes accidental overwrites or erasures occur. If you wish to protect what is stored on a diskette, you must cover the write-protect notch on the 5 1/4 inch diskette and open the write-protect window on the 3 1/2 inch diskette. Although you will not be able to write to a diskette that is write-protected, you can still read information from the diskette.

On the 5 1/4 inch diskette, the write-protect notch is the large notch on the edge of the diskette opposite the label. Cover the notch with one of the removable tabs that come with the diskettes. Only the supplied tabs should be used. Other materials, such as masking tape or transparent tape may not provide sufficient protection.

FIGURE 1-2 5 1/4 INCH DISKETTE

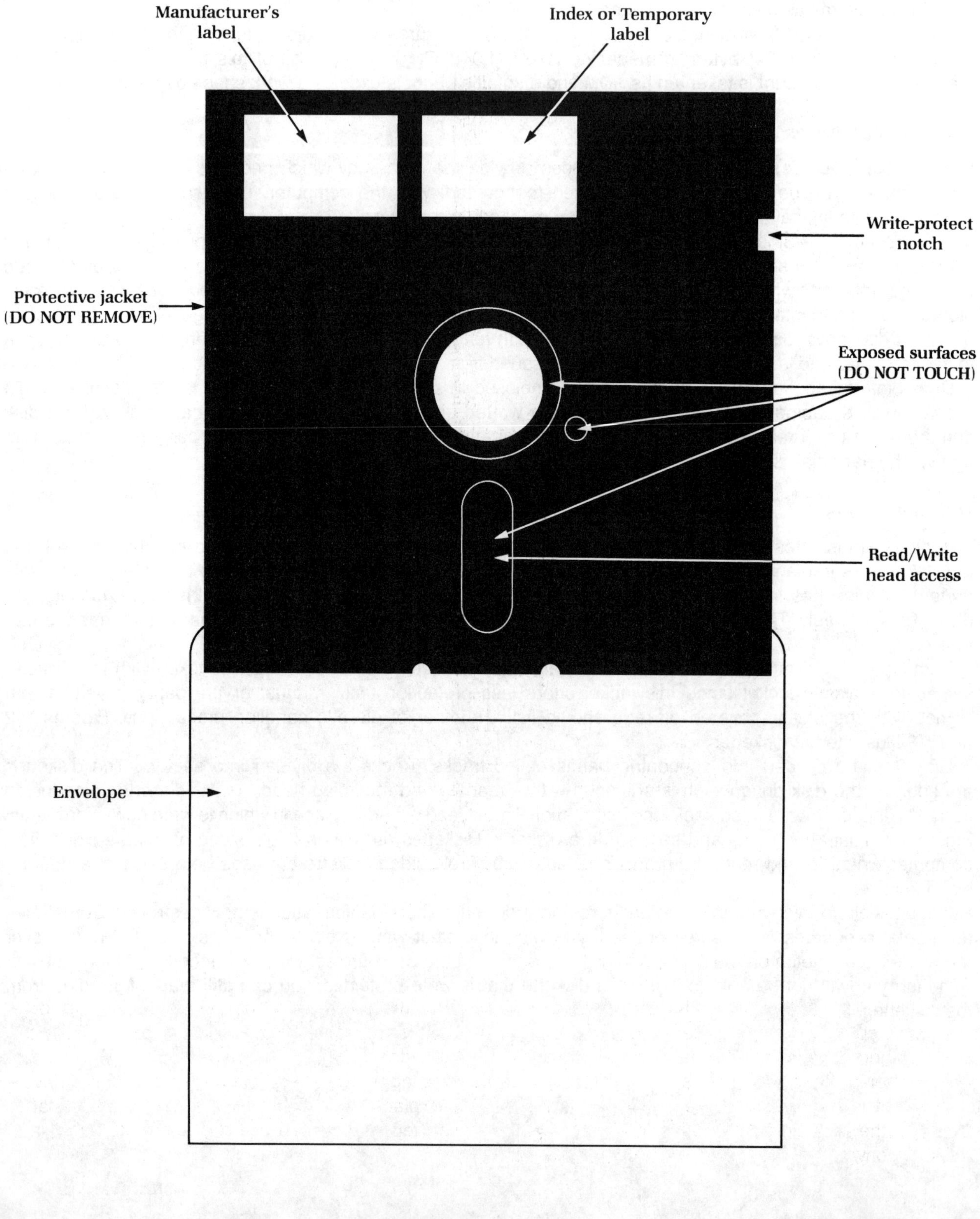

FIGURE 1-3 3 1/2 INCH DISKETTE

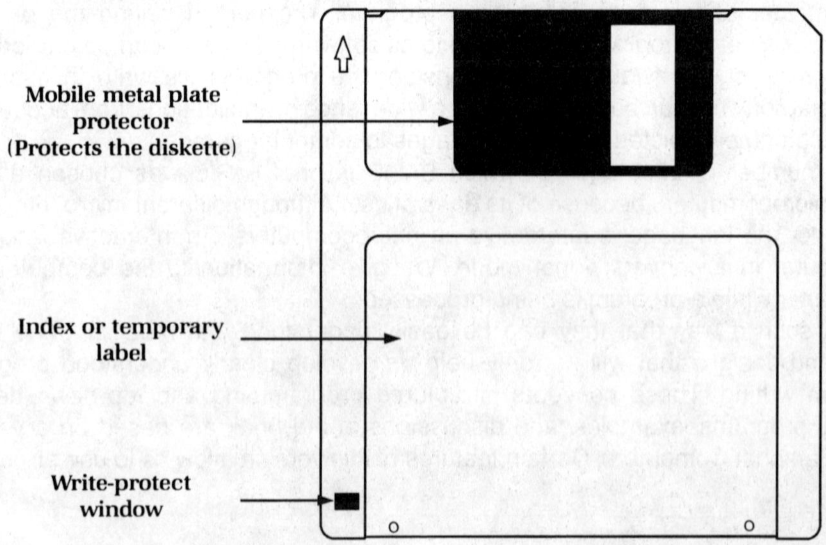

FIGURE 1-4 TRACKS AND SECTORS ON A DISKETTE

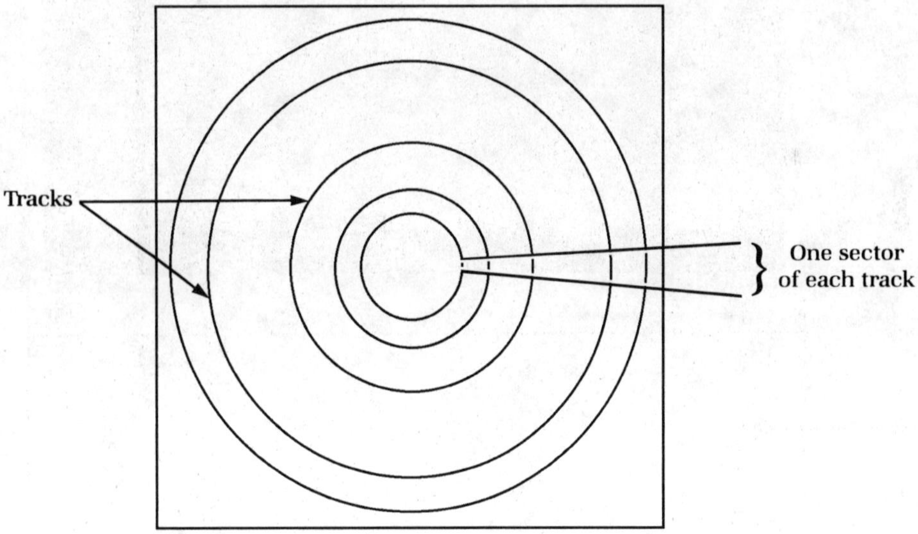

On the 3 1/2 inch diskette, the write-protect window is on the reverse side of the diskette in the lower right-hand corner. To write protect the diskette, slide the plastic tab so that the window is open. Close the window when you wish to write data and information on the diskette.

Two other precautionary measures must be noted. Never remove a diskette from its drive until the drive's in-use light is off. And, with the 5 1/4 inch diskette, always place the diskette in its paper envelope after removing the diskette from a drive. It should also be mentioned that we will use the terms "diskette" and "disk" synonymously.

1.2 Computer Software

A computer cannot function unless it receives explicit instructions telling it what to do. This series of instructions, written in a manner that the computer understands, is called a program. The person writing the program is called a programmer. A program, or a set of programs, is referred to as software. Software can be categorized into user-written software and commercial software. We will consider the programs we write in this book as user-written software. Commercial software can be purchased for a wide range of applications: from accounting systems to word processing, from computer assisted learning packages to computer games.

Programs can be written in a number of languages of which BASIC is one. BASIC was chosen as one of the languages to implement in microcomputers because of its ease of use. Although different microcomputers may use different versions of BASIC, the language is interactive on microcomputers. An interactive language allows us to work with the computer in a conversational mode. We give information to the computer and receive information from the computer while a program is being processed.

Programs should be written in such a way that they can be easily understood and modified. The focus of this book is to use concepts and designs that will not only help us develop clearly understood programs but will ease the task of program writing. These concepts, structured programming and top-down design, are explained in Chapter Five. All programs, examples, and discussions in the book are based on a version of BASIC implemented in the IBM Personal Computers. Certain features of this version allow us to use structured techniques.

Chapter Summary

1. A computer is an electronic device that uses stored data and stored instructions to generate results. Data are the unorganized facts upon which the computer operates to produce results. We must supply the computer with the data and with the instructions.
2. The five fundamental units of a computer system are:
   (a) The Central Processing Unit (CPU) which is composed of the Control Unit and the Arithmetic-Logic Unit.
   (b) Internal memory.
   (c) A device, such as a disk drive, used to store data and information externally.
   (d) An input device such as the keyboard.
   (e) An output device such as the monitor (screen) and the printer.
3. The internal structure of a microcomputer consists of the microprocessor and internal memory.
4. The microprocessor includes the following units:
   (a) The Arithmetic and Logical Unit which performs arithmetic and logical operations.
   (b) The Control Unit which supervises the activities of the computer and functions in conjunction with the input/output devices. It retrieves, interprets, and executes instructions stored in the computer's memory.
5. Two types of internal memory are:
   (a) **R**andom **A**ccess **M**emory (RAM) to which data and information can be written and from which they can be read.
   (b) **R**ead **O**nly **M**emory (ROM) from which information can only be read.
6. Memory in a computer is organized into units called bytes. Each byte is capable of holding one character.
7. A byte consists of eight bits (**b**inary dig**its**). A character is stored electronically as a series of bits. Each bit is either on or off depending on the character stored.
8. Many computers combine bytes into words. A word may consist of 4, 8, 16, or 32 bits. A 16-bit word consists of two bytes, a 32-bit word consists of four bytes.
9. The storage capacity of a microcomputer is usually measured in K bytes or megabytes. K represents Kilo. One K is 2^{10} (1024) bytes, a megabyte is 2^{20} (1,048,576) bytes.
10. Input/output devices such as keyboards, video monitors, and printers provide the means by which people can communicate with a computer.
11. Large quantities of data and information can be stored on external storage media such as hard disks and diskettes. This type of storage is referred to as auxiliary storage. An external device, usually a disk drive, contains a read/write head which reads or writes the data and information. The drive is controlled by instructions issued from the computer.
12. A diskette is a circular, plastic disk coated with ferromagnetic material on which data and information can be stored. The diskette is protected by either a hard jacket or a plastic jacket. The size of the hard-covered diskette commonly used in microcomputers is 3 1/2 inches in diameter, the size of the plastic-covered diskette commonly used in microcomputers is 5 1/4 inches in diameter.
13. A diskette is divided into concentric bands called tracks; the tracks are divided into sectors.
14. A series of instructions that tells the computer what to do is called a program. A program, or a set of programs, is referred to as software.
15. An interactive language allows an individual to work with the computer in a conversational mode while a program is being processed.
16. We will be using concepts known as structured programming and top-down design to develop and to write easy-to-understand programs.

Questions for Review

1. What five physical components do most computer systems possess?
2. Name the two main components of a microprocessor and state the functions of each.
3. Give the definition and purpose of
   (a) RAM,
   (b) ROM.
4. (a) What is a byte?
   (b) What does a byte consist of?
   (c) How many bytes does one character (digit, letter, space, symbol) require?
   (d) What is a word?
5. When representing storage capacity in a microcomputer, what does the acronym K represent? How many bytes are there in 1K?
6. Name three external devices used by a computer.
7. What is an interactive language?

2

AN INTRODUCTION TO IBM PERSONAL COMPUTERS

Objectives

In this chapter, you will learn how to operate the IBM personal computers, specifically the IBM Personal Computer (IBM PC) and the IBM Personal System/2 (IBM PS/2). You will learn how to prepare the computer for use and how to use a number of specific keys on two types of keyboards. You will also become familiar with some of the commands that tell the computer what to do.

Contents

2.1 An Overview of an IBM Personal Computer System

The Components

The basic components of an IBM personal computer system are illustrated in Figure 2-1.

FIGURE 2-1 AN IBM PERSONAL COMPUTER SYSTEM

The cabinet of this computer houses the internal processor, the internal memory, and two disk drives. The keyboard is one of the ways by which we will be entering values into the computer. We will also be using a disk drive to enter values. The monitor and printer provide the means by which we obtain the results of processing. All units; that is, the disk drives, the keyboard, the monitor, and the printer must be connected to the internal processor.

The Disk Drives

When a computer has two disk drives, we call the drive on the left drive A and the one on the right drive B. Throughout the book, dialogue concerning disk drives applies to an IBM personal computer system with two drives.

The Keyboard

There are several types of keyboards for the IBM personal computers. Two of these are the standard keyboard and the enhanced keyboard. The keyboards are similar to the keyboard of an ordinary typewriter, however, both have additional keys to accommodate the extra functions supported by a computer. As keys are introduced in the chapter, refer to the appropriate diagram to locate their positions.

FIGURE 2-2 THE STANDARD IBM PERSONAL COMPUTER KEYBOARD

SOURCE: BASIC-IBM Personal Computer Hardware Reference Library P. 2-8 (6025010-5/82)

FIGURE 2-3 THE ENHANCED IBM PERSONAL COMPUTER KEYBOARD

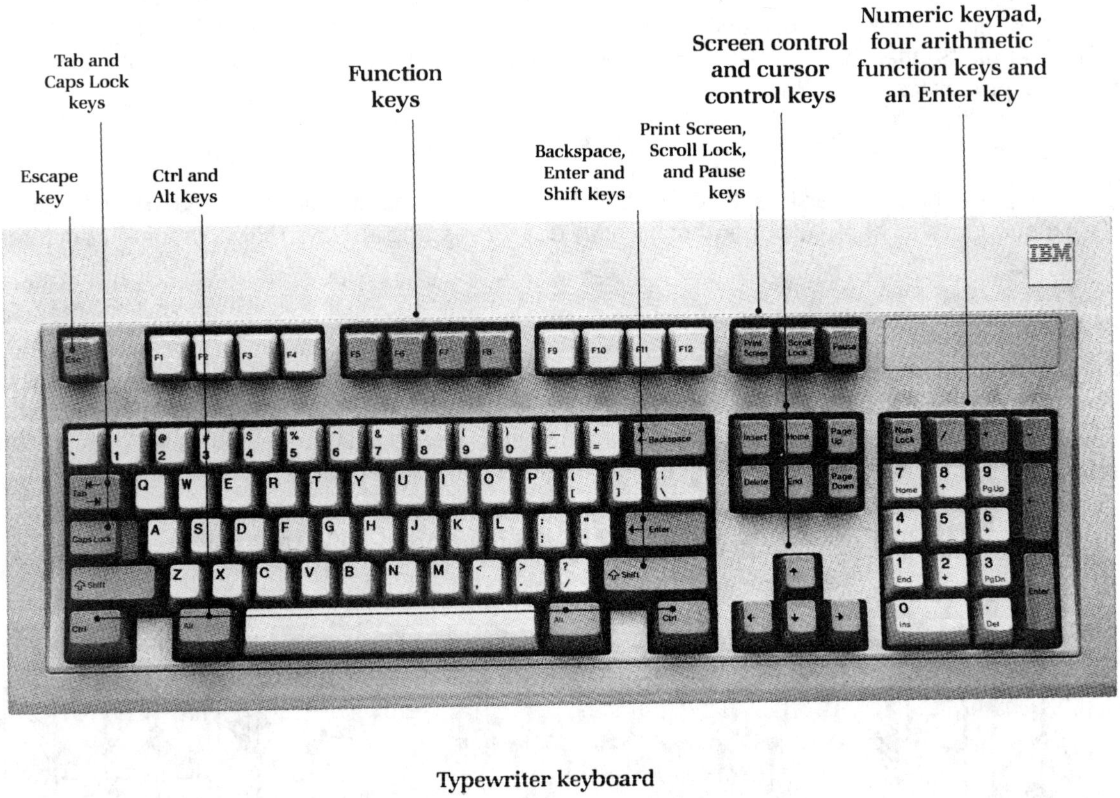

The Monitor

The monitor, which is similar to a TV screen, displays each character as it is typed into the computer. For example, when we type an A, the A appears on the screen. The monitor also displays a program stored in memory and the program's results when we ask the computer for these. Material displayed on the screen is called "soft" copy.

In addition, the computer displays messages and prompts to help us with our programs. These displays often tell us what to do and where to look for an error if we make one. The screen we will be using has 25 rows and 80 columns. The top row is considered row one, the left-most column is considered column one.

The Printer

Whereas the display on the screen is called "soft" copy, the material printed on paper is called "hard" copy. Page widths and printer widths vary. One common width is 80 characters. Our discussions on hard copy relate to an 80-column page.

2.2 The DOS Operating System

An Overview of the Disk Operating System

In order to write information on disk and to retrieve information from disk, we must first load the Disk Operating System (DOS) into memory. DOS is a collection of programs stored on a diskette. The programs perform a number of tasks, such as storing and handling information on disk, processing programs, and enabling us to use the system devices, such as the disk drives and the printer.

Loading DOS into the computer is discussed in Section 2.4. Let us first become familiar with some of the commands offered by DOS.

DOS Commands

The Disk Operating System supports a number of commands which you will find useful as you progress through the book. In this chapter, we will merely discuss the purpose of some of the commands. How each can be used is explained in detail in Appendix D.

(a) FORMAT
Before a diskette can be used, it must be changed to a format that is acceptable to DOS. This is performed by the FORMAT command which divides the diskette into the tracks and sectors required by the system. We refer to this operation as formatting the diskette. **WARNING: If you format a diskette that already has information stored on it, the FORMAT command will destroy this information.** Thus, if some or all of the information is needed, it must first be copied to another diskette. See commands DISKCOPY and COPY.

(b) DIR
Related information stored on disk is stored as a separate entity called a file. Each file must have a unique name. We refer to the name of a file as its filename. The DIR command lists the filenames of the files stored on a diskette.

(c) DISKCOPY
DISKCOPY copies the contents of one diskette to another diskette. If the second diskette is unformatted, the command will format the diskette as it copies. **If the second diskette contains information, the information on the second diskette will be destroyed.**

(d) COPY
The COPY command copies one or more files rather than the entire contents of a diskette. Optionally, the file copied can be given a different name.

(e) RENAME
RENAME changes the name of a file. It does not make a copy of the file.

(f) ERASE
The ERASE command removes a file from a diskette.

2.3 Useful Keys

Before we load DOS into the computer, we should be familiar with the following keys.

The Enter Key

As mentioned earlier, each character typed on the keyboard is displayed on the screen. The Enter key, marked [← Enter] on the enhanced keyboard and [←┘] on the standard keyboard sends the typed information to the computer's memory.

The Shift Keys

Both keyboards have two shift keys (⇧). When a shift key is depressed in combination with a desired key, the two keys produce either a capital letter or the character shown in the upper portion of a keytop. Shift/r produces **R**, shift/4 produces **$**.

The Caps Lock Key

The Caps Lock key is similar, although not quite the same, as the corresponding key on a typewriter. It switches letters from upper case to lower case and vice versa. Pressing the key gives uppercase letters, pressing it again gives lowercase letters. The Caps Lock key operates only on the letter keys. It does not shift the numeric keys nor the special symbol keys.

The Backspace Key

The Backspace key, marked [← Backspace] on the enhanced keyboard and [←] on the standard keyboard, can be used to correct a typing error before the typed line is sent to the computer's memory. The key erases one character from the screen each time the key is pressed; erasing characters in a right-to-left direction. After you reach the error, type the correct character, then retype the characters erased. Other methods of correcting errors are explained in Chapter Three.

The Combination Ctrl, Alt, and Del Keys

Holding down the Ctrl, Alt, and Del keys simultaneously is one of the ways to bring up the Disk Operating System. Bringing up the system is discussed in the next section; the individual functions of the Ctrl, Alt, and Del keys are explained in Section 2.6 and in Chapter Three.

The Cursor Movement Keys

The blinking underscore on the screen is called a cursor. It marks the current print position on the screen. We can move the cursor in any direction. On both the enhanced keyboard and the standard keyboard, the cursor movement keys are on the numeric keypad. The enhanced keyboard has an additional bank of keys dedicated to cursor movement. This keypad is in the lower portion of the keyboard.

↑	Cursor up. Moves the cursor up one line.
↓	Cursor down. Moves the cursor down one line.
→	Cursor right. Moves the cursor to the right by one position. If the cursor goes over the right edge of the screen, it drops down to the next line at the left edge of the screen.
←	Cursor left. Moves the cursor to the left by one position. If the cursor goes over the left edge of the screen, it moves up to the previous line at the right edge of the screen.
End	Moves the cursor to the position immediately after the last character in a line.
Home	Places the cursor in the top left-hand corner of the screen.

2.4 Bringing Up the System

Loading DOS

Loading DOS into the computer is referred to as "booting" up the system. There are two ways we can boot up the system. The method chosen depends on whether the computer is on or off.

If the computer is off, insert the DOS diskette in drive A. Close the drive door. Switch on the external devices (monitor, printer), then switch on the computer. This is referred to as a "cold" boot.

If the computer is on, insert the DOS diskette in drive A and close the drive door. Press down the Ctrl and Alt keys. As you hold down these keys, press the Del key. We refer to this method of booting DOS as a "warm" boot.

After DOS has been booted, the computer may ask for a new date and time. A date and time have already been assigned to DOS, however, you may wish to update this information.

Entering the Date and Time

Suppose we wish to enter 08-26-2099 (August 26, 2099) as the date and 09:15:46 (hour, minutes, seconds) as the time. To enter the date, we must key in the month, day, and year all separated by either hyphens or slashes. To enter the time, we must key in the hour, minutes, and seconds separated by colons. The entries shaded below illustrate how the date and time can be typed in.

FIGURE 2-4 ENTERING THE DATE AND TIME

```
Current date is Tue  1-01-1980
Enter new date (mm-dd-yy): 08-26-2099          Press Enter
Current time is  0:00:05.21
Enter new time: 09:15:46            Press Enter


The IBM Personal Computer DOS
Version x.xx (C)Copyright International Business Machines Corp 19xx, 19xx
             (C)Copyright Microsoft Corp 19xx, 19xx

A>_
```

The prompt A> is a system response. This is the DOS prompt indicating that the computer is under the control of DOS. The A signifies that the computer is operating out of drive A. At this point, drive A is called the default drive since no drive has yet been specified. The blinking underscore is the cursor.

The year must fall in the range 1980 to 2099. A leading zero may be omitted from any value and the year may be entered as a two-digit number. For example, we may enter the date February 7, 2099 as 2-7-99. Furthermore, we may omit the entire procedure by pressing Enter twice. This action defaults the date and time to that first assigned to DOS.

Loading BASIC

Before we can key in a program, the computer must be in the BASIC system. We will be using a version of BASIC called BASICA. Since BASICA is part of DOS, we must first load DOS into memory. We then type BASICA after the DOS prompt and press Enter. BASICA can be typed in either uppercase or lowercase letters.

```
A>BASICA
```

The dialogue asking for the date and time disappears from the screen and the computer displays, at the top of a cleared screen, the version of BASIC just loaded and the number of bytes free.

FIGURE 2-5 LOADING BASICA

```
The IBM Personal Computer Basic
Version Ax.xx Copyright IBM Corp. 19xx, 19xx
xxxxx Bytes free

OK
_
```

The letter A following the word "Version" denotes Advanced BASIC. The prompt OK is a system response. Whereas A> is the DOS prompt indicating that the computer is under the control of DOS, OK is the BASIC prompt indicating that the computer is under the control of BASIC.

2.5 BASIC Commands and Ctrl/Home Keys

A number of BASIC commands are used each time we key in a program. These commands are explained below. Although a command may be typed in either uppercase or lowercase letters, throughout the text we will use upper case. After typing a command, press Enter.

Clearing the Computer's Memory

Any program stored in the computer's memory must be erased before you type in a new program. If a former program is not cleared from memory, some or all of its instructions may be included in the program currently being typed. To erase a previous program, type NEW. NEW does not clear the screen; it clears the internal memory and any work space in memory.

```
NEW    ←—— Press Enter
OK
_
```

Clearing internal memory after a cold boot or after a warm boot is not required. However, it is a good habit to adopt.

Clearing the Screen

Although not necessary, you should clear the screen of extraneous material before typing a program into the computer. Your screen can be cleared in one of two ways. Both ways do not erase a program from memory.

(a) Hold down the Ctrl key as you press the Home key. In addition to clearing the screen, the command places the cursor in the top left-hand corner of the screen.

(b) Type CLS and press Enter. This command clears the screen and places the BASIC prompt, followed by the cursor, in the top left-hand corner of the screen.

Listing a Program Stored in Memory

Each line of a BASIC program is numbered. To display an entire program currently stored in memory, type LIST. An example is given below.

```
LIST  ←—— Press Enter
2010 PRINT
2020 PRINT "A Computer Program"
2030 PRINT
2040 PRINT "Written in BASIC"
2050 END
OK
_
```

If your program more than fills the screen, the top lines scroll off the screen before you have a chance to examine them. This can be a problem if you want to view these lines. There are two solutions. Either freeze the lines you wish to examine (this is called a scroll lock) or list only a segment of your program. To scroll lock the lines of your program on the standard keyboard, hold down the Ctrl key and press the Num Lock key as your program is being listed. On the enhanced keyboard, press only the Pause key. To continue the listing, press any key except a number of special keys such as a Shift key, the Ins key, or the Break key.

You can list a segment of your program in a number of ways. These are given below. Note that a space must be left between LIST and a line number.

`LIST 2020`	Displays only line 2020.
`LIST 2000-3000`	Displays lines 2000 to 3000 inclusive.
`LIST -3000`	Displays all lines up to and including line 3000.
`LIST 3000-`	Displays all lines from 3000 to the end of the program.

Processing a Program

To execute (process) a program, type RUN and press Enter. BASIC will process the instructions and display an error message when it detects an error. The error message attempts to tell you what is wrong. Here is what happens when you RUN the program shown above.

```
LIST
2010 PRINT
2020 PRINT "A Computer Program"
2030 PRINT
2040 PRINT "Written in BASIC"
2050 END
OK
RUN  ←—— Press Enter

A Computer Program

Written in BASIC
OK
_
```

The results of the program; that is, the lines displayed after the command RUN, are followed by the BASIC prompt OK and the cursor. One last comment. A program need not be LISTed before the program is executed.

Exercises

Boot up the system, bring up BASICA, then key in the above program. After typing each line, press the Enter key. Perform the following:

1. RUN the program.
2. Clear the screen, then list the program.
3. List lines 2010 to 2030 inclusive.
4. List line 2020 only.
5. Clear the program from memory. Clear the screen and list the program. The program should not appear on your screen since it has been erased from memory.

2.6 Other Useful Keys

A number of keys are available that ease the task of typing in and executing a program. These are the function keys, the ALT key, the Num Lock key, the Ctrl key, and the Pause key.

The Function Keys

The keys labeled F1 through F10 located on the left side of the standard keyboard and on the top row of the enhanced keyboard are the function keys. These keys are meant to reduce the number of keystrokes required to execute common tasks. Frequently used commands, such as LIST and RUN, have been assigned to the keys. For instance, instead of typing LIST we can press Function key F1 and the command LIST appears on the screen. We can complete the LIST command by entering a line number (or line numbers), then pressing Enter. Or, we can simply press Function key F1, press Enter and a listing of our program will be displayed on the screen.

There is no need to press the Enter key for a function key command such as RUN. We simply press F2 and the program in memory is executed. Function key F1, which gives us LIST, allows us to append line numbers. Hence, the need to press Enter.

The commands assigned to the ten function keys are displayed on line 25 of the screen and are collectively called the function key display. The display may be erased by typing KEY OFF. Line 25 can now be used. KEY OFF does not disable these function keys. To restore the function key display, type KEY ON.

The function keys are known as "soft keys" which means we can assign our own sequence of characters (up to 15) to a key. When the key is depressed, the characters assigned to it are displayed. The sequence of characters must be enclosed in quotation marks when assigned to a function key. The quotation marks are referred to as delimiters. Since a quotation mark is used here for a special purpose, it may not be used as one of the characters in the assigned sequence. It should be noted that the keys F11 and F12 on the enhanced keyboard have been added to provide greater flexibility in other applications.

To assign characters to a function key, we must use the command **KEY n,"characters"** where n represents a function key number and "characters" represents a sequence of characters. The sequence is assigned to Function key n. For example, KEY 1,"STOP" assigns STOP to Function key 1. The keys revert to their original functions when the system is rebooted.

The Alt Key

The Alt key gives us a short cut in typing a number of reserved words. A reserved word has a special meaning to BASIC and cannot be used for any purpose other than the one intended. To display a reserved word, we simply hold down the Alt key and type the first letter of the word. For example, instead of typing PRINT, we hold down the Alt key and press a P. PRINT will be displayed on the screen. Listed below are some of the reserved words that can be typed in this manner. The letter associated with each word is also given.

C	COLOR	N	NEXT
D	DELETE	O	OPEN
E	ELSE	P	PRINT
F	FOR	R	RUN
I	INPUT	T	THEN
K	KEY	U	USING
L	LOCATE	V	VAL

The Num Lock Key

Both keyboards have a numeric keypad that can be used in either cursor control mode or in calculator mode. Cursor control mode allows us to move the cursor up, down, right, or left. We can shift the mode to calculator mode by pressing the Num Lock key. The keys now produce the digits zero through nine and the decimal point. Pressing Num Lock again returns the keypad to cursor control mode.

The Ctrl Key

The Ctrl key, when pressed with another key or keys produces a particular function not otherwise available. We have already learned that Ctrl-Alt-Del boots up the system and that Ctrl-Home clears the screen and places the cursor in the top left-hand corner of the screen. Here, we discuss two more combinations. Additional combinations will be explained as we need them.

Ctrl-Break—the combination interrupts the execution of a program. On the standard keyboard, the Break key is the key with the words Scroll Lock on its top and Break on its front. On the enhanced keyboard, the key has Pause on its keytop and Break on its front. To resume execution, type CONT and press Enter.

Ctrl-Num Lock (used on the standard keyboard)—places the computer into a temporary halt. The keys temporarily halt the listing of a program on the screen, the printing of a program on the printer, the execution of a program, and the listing of filenames (the names of files stored on a diskette). To resume activity, press any key except one of the special keys, such as a Shift key, the Ins key, or the Break key.

The Pause Key (used on the enhanced keyboard)

Similar to the Ctrl-Num Lock combination on the standard keyboard, the Pause key places the computer into a temporary halt for the listing, printing, and execution of a program and for the listing of filenames. To resume activity, press any key except the ones mentioned above.

Exercises

1. Change Function key 2 from RUN to CLS. Press the key. Change its command back to RUN.
2. Change Function key 8 from TROFF to any sequence of characters (up to 15). Press the key. Change its command back to TROFF.
3. Erase the function key display. Restore the display.
4. Experiment with the Alt key using some of the reserved words.
5. Experiment with the Num Lock key. First move the cursor in different directions, then change the mode to calculator mode and produce the digits zero through nine. Shift the mode back to cursor control.

Summary of DOS Commands

COPY	Copies one or more files.
DIR	Lists the names of the files stored on a diskette.

DISKCOPY	Copies the contents of one diskette to another diskette.
ERASE	Removes a file from a diskette.
FORMAT	Divides a diskette into the tracks and sectors required by DOS.
RENAME	Changes the name of a file.

Summary of Special Keys

Alt	Used with the first letter of a number of reserved words to display the word on the screen.
Backspace	Erases a character from the screen each time the key is pressed. This is performed before the line currently being typed is sent to the computer's memory.
Caps Lock	Switches letters from upper case to lower case and vice versa.
Ctrl	Used with other keys to produce particular functions not otherwise available. A summary of Ctrl and key combinations is given below.
Cursor Movement Keys	Used to move the cursor one position left, right, up or down.
End	Moves the cursor to the position immediately after the last character of a line.
Enter	Enters typed information into the computer's memory.
Function Keys	Frequently used commands are assigned to the function keys. Users may assign their own sequence of characters (up to 15) to the keys.
Home	Places the cursor in the top left-hand corner of the screen.
Num Lock	Shifts the numeric keypad from cursor control mode to calculator mode and vice versa.
Pause	Used on the enhanced keyboard. Places the computer into a temporary halt. To resume activity, press any key except a number of special keys, such as a Shift key, the Ins key, the Break key.
Shift	When depressed with a desired key, produces a capital letter or the special character shown in the upper portion of a keytop.

Summary of CTRL-Key Combinations

Ctrl-Alt-Del	Boots up DOS.
Ctrl-Break	Interrupts execution of a program. To resume execution, type CONT.
Ctrl-Home	In addition to clearing the screen, places the cursor in the top left-hand corner of the screen.
Ctrl-Num Lock	Used on the standard keyboard to perform the same function as the Pause key on the enhanced keyboard.

Summary of BASIC Commands

CLS	Clears the screen and places the BASIC prompt, followed by the cursor, in the top left-hand corner of the screen.

CONT	Resumes execution of a program.
KEY OFF	Erases the function key display.
KEY ON	Restores the function key display.
KEY n,"chrs"	Assigns up to 15 characters to a function key. The letter n represents a function key number, "chrs" represents a sequence of characters. The sequence must be enclosed in quotation marks.
LIST	Displays a program or a program segment on the screen.
NEW	Clears internal memory.
RUN	Executes (processes) a program.

Chapter Summary

1. The basic components of an IBM personal computer system are the internal processor and internal memory, the disk drive(s), the keyboard, the monitor, and the printer.
2. When a computer has two disk drives, the drive on the left is called drive A, the one on the right is called drive B.
3. There are several types of keyboards for the IBM personal computers. Two of these are the standard keyboard and the enhanced keyboard. The enhanced keyboard has a number of additional keys.
4. Material displayed on the monitor is referred to as "soft copy", material printed by the printer is referred to as "hard copy".
5. The Disk Operating System (DOS) is a collection of programs stored on a diskette. The programs perform a number of tasks, such as storing and handling information on disk, processing programs, and enabling us to use the system devices.
6. Related information stored on disk is stored as a file. Each file must have a unique name which is referred to as a filename.
7. Before we key in a program, DOS and BASICA (a version of BASIC) must be loaded into the computer. Loading DOS is called "booting" up the system. DOS may ask for a new date and time, after which BASICA must be loaded into the computer.
8. The prompt A> indicates that the system is in DOS operating out of drive A, the prompt OK indicates that the system is in BASIC.
9. Any program in memory must be erased before a new program is typed. If a former program is not cleared from memory, some or all of its instructions may be included in the new program.
10. Although not necessary, you should clear the screen before typing a program into the computer.
11. If a program more than fills the screen, the top lines scroll off the screen before they can be examined. To view these lines, either freeze the lines you wish to examine or list only a segment of your program.
12. As BASIC executes (processes) a program, it prints an error message when it detects an error. The error message attempts to tell you what is wrong.

Questions and Exercises

1. What is meant by "soft" copy? "Hard" copy?
2. State several functions of DOS.
3. What is the purpose of the FORMAT command? What precaution must be taken before you use the command?
4. What is the difference between the DISKCOPY and COPY commands?
5. What is the purpose of the Enter key?
6. What is the DOS prompt? The BASIC prompt?
7. State two ways by which the screen can be cleared.
8. Why must a program be cleared from memory before a new program is typed?
9. Does clearing the screen also clear memory? Does clearing memory clear the screen?
10. Boot up DOS, load BASICA, and type the following program into the computer.

```
2010 PRINT
2020 PRINT "BRINGING UP THE SYSTEM"
2030 PRINT
```

```
2040 PRINT "Loading DOS"
2050 PRINT "Loading BASICA"
2060 END
```

(a) Clear the screen.
(b) Use function key F1 to display line 2020.
(c) Use function key F1 to display all lines from 2020 to the end of the program.
(d) Use function key F2 to execute the program.
(e) Clear the screen. Erase the program from memory, then list the program.

3

AN INTRODUCTION TO PROGRAMMING

Objectives

Now that you are familiar with the features of an IBM personal computer, it is time to learn how to solve problems on the computer. In this chapter, you will learn how to develop a program in an organized, step-by-step manner and how to use the statements (instructions) explained in the chapter to write the program. Essentially, you will learn how to:

- Design a program.
- Enter values into the computer.
- Write programs that use arithmetic operations on values entered into the computer.
- Make corrections in programs.
- Produce a hard copy of your program and its output.

Contents

3.1 Program Development and Top-Down Design

Program Development

Problems must be solved in an organized and systematic manner. This organized method is referred to as program development. At no time should you proceed directly to program coding after being presented with a problem. Coding a program means translating a set of instructions into a computer language.

Before we discuss the development of a program, it is necessary that you be familiar with the terms input and output. Input is another term for data. Recall that data are the unorganized facts or items entered into the computer and upon which the computer must operate to obtain the results. The results, and any data displayed along with the results, are collectively called output.

Problem solving involves a number of steps of which program coding is only one. Although details vary from programmer to programmer, the steps usually followed are the ones listed below.

1. Understand the problem thoroughly. This means that you must:

   (a) Be provided with the input needed to solve the problem and ensure that the input can produce the output.
   (b) Understand the processing that must be done.
   (c) Be provided with a rough layout of the output.

2. Design an overall plan for the program. First, break down the problem into major tasks. The major tasks may include the following:

   Enter the date and print the headings.
   Enter the data.
   Perform the calculations and print the results.

   Break down each major task into more detailed tasks. Each expansion is considered a component (a module). To design a program, some programmers use structure charts, others use pseudocode, some use both. A structure chart graphically portrays a program. Pseudocode is a method of writing instructions in short English phrases so that they resemble program instructions. This set of instructions is called an algorithm.

3. Code the program. Coding sheets are often available, some designed specifically for a particular language. If a program is not too complex, the coding step is sometimes omitted and each module is typed directly into the computer as explained in Step 4.

4. Type the first module into the computer and save the module on disk. Test the module by RUNning it. Correct any errors then resave the module if errors have been corrected. Type the second module into the computer, appending it to the first. Save and test the combined modules. Continue in this manner until all tasks have been performed. The mechanics of breaking down a problem into modules, linking the modules, and saving the modules on disk are explained later on in the book.

5. Check the results for accuracy. When the program is complete and the expected output is produced, obtain a "hard" copy of the program and output. If important enough, a copy should be placed in the vault.

6. Prepare support material. Include such items as a detailed description of the program, the language and computer used, any operating instructions, and any program restrictions.

Top-Down Design

In Step 2 above, we mentioned that an overall problem should be broken down into major tasks, then each major task broken down into more refined tasks. If one of these latter tasks is too complex, it must be broken down into more detailed tasks. This breakdown is referred to as top-down design. Many beginning programmers dislike the time spent in designing. Instead, they start the overall program by keying program instructions into the computer hoping that somehow the solution will appear. Invariably, it does not and the programmer is left with an undecipherable mess. The time spent in designing a program, then developing it module by module is often less than the time it takes to find errors in a poorly written program. Before a programmer keys a detailed module into the computer, most errors, if not all, have been detected.

Suppose we wish to write a program that calculates an employee's net pay. Our program must enter the date into the computer, print the headings, enter the master data (such as the employee's name, address, and telephone number), enter data from the employee's timecards, perform the calculations, and print the results. Figure 3-1 illustrates a structure chart, Figure 3-2 illustrates pseudocode.

FIGURE 3-1 STRUCTURE CHART

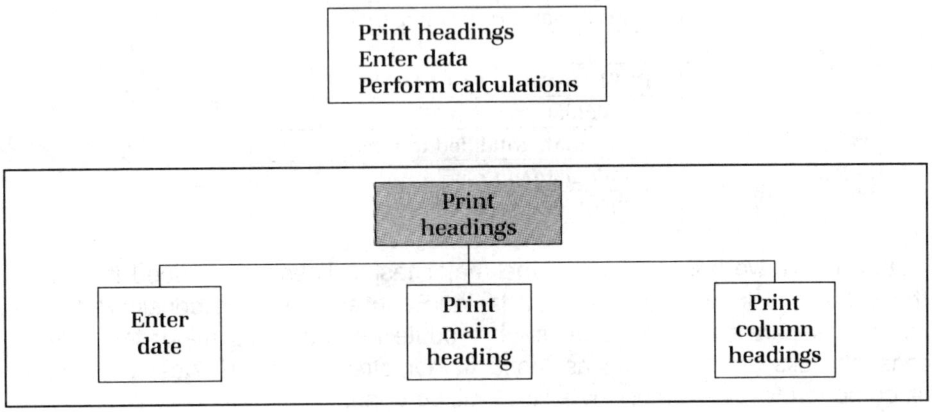

Figure 3-1 Continued

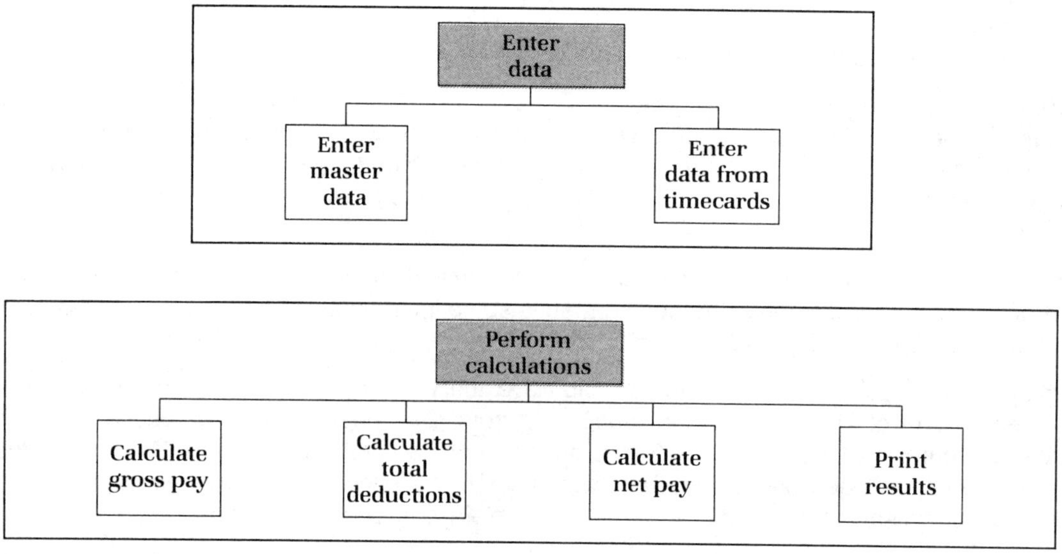

We start our design by listing the major tasks. We now expand the first major task; that is, task **Print headings** by breaking it down into the three detailed tasks Enter date, Print main heading, and Print column headings. Each task is placed in its own box. The boxes are aligned horizontally and lines are drawn to connect the upper box with the boxes below. Note that the description inside each box states what will be done. No reference is made as to how the instruction will be carried out. We have now completed module **Print headings**. The procedure continues with the breakdown of major task **Enter Data** and the breakdown of major task **Perform calculations** thus creating two more modules. Figure 3-2 illustrates pseudocode.

FIGURE 3-2 PSEUDOCODE

MAJOR TASKS
- Print headings
- Enter data
- Perform calculations

PRINT HEADINGS
- Enter date
- Print main heading
- Print column headings

ENTER DATA
- Enter master data
- Enter data from timecards

PERFORM CALCULATIONS
- Calculate gross pay
- Calculate total deductions
- Calculate net pay
- Print results

As in our structure chart, we begin by listing the major tasks. These are placed in a box. We then break down each of these three tasks into more refined tasks. Each expansion is considered a module and each module is placed in a separate box. We start each module by stating its major task, then list the detailed tasks. Descriptions of tasks are the same as those in our structure chart. Again, no mention is made as to how a task will be performed. We simply state what will be done.

3.2 Characteristics of Data

Types of Data

Data can be categorized into two broad classifications: numeric data and string data. Numeric data items are those values upon which we can perform arithmetic calculations. String data items are those values upon which we cannot perform arithmetic calculations.

Numeric data items are, therefore, numbers. A number may be preceded by a positive sign or a negative sign. If no sign precedes the number, the number is assumed to be positive. A number cannot include special characters, such as the dollar sign in $126.94 or the comma in 123,456.

A string data item may include letters of the alphabet, digits, spaces, and special characters such as periods, parentheses, question marks, and commas. We refer to a string data item as a string since it consists of a string of characters. The length of a string may range from zero to 255 characters. A string must often be enclosed in quotation marks ("). The quotation marks are not considered part of the string. When a string is enclosed in quotation marks, the string may not contain a quotation mark as one of its characters. **Smith,John**, **786-1234**, and **06/26/99** are examples of strings.

Types of Numbers

Programs can manipulate numeric values of three types. These are integers, single-precision numbers, and double-precision numbers. The three classifications are explained below.

Integer numbers are whole numbers that lie between -32768 and 32767 inclusive. An integer needs two bytes of memory. Examples of integers are:

Ø -600 10001 -12345 32767

A single-precision number is a number that does not fall into the integer classification. In other words, the number either contains a decimal point or it exceeds the range for integers. Up to seven digits are stored and printed but only the first six digits are accurate. A single-precision number needs four bytes of memory. Examples of single-precision numbers are:

1234567 -42.859 852614.7 -1.026 .000067

A double-precision number consists of eight or more digits with a maximum of 16 digits stored and printed. The first 15 digits are accurate. A double-precision number needs eight bytes of memory. Examples of double-precision numbers are:

12345678 -21.3649157 .00015394 123456789000000

Exercises

State the precision of each of the numbers shown below.

1. 32767
2. 32768
3. 49612000
4. 93.1485267
5. -4.36182
6. .008917

3.3 Variables

Variable Names

Values that remain the same, such as 126.94 and Brown,Darryl, are referred to as "constants". While they do have a place in a BASIC program, programs can be made more flexible with the use of variables. A variable is a symbol that represents a number or a string stored in the memory of the computer. We can think of a variable as an address that designates a location in storage. Variable QUANTITY could represent the location that stores the value 6. We consider the value of QUANTITY to be 6. Whenever we reference variable QUANTITY, we are actually gaining access to the number stored in QUANTITY. A variable can represent only one value at a time. What makes a variable so useful is that its value can be changed. We simply assign a different value to the variable.

There are two broad categories of variables: numeric and string. Numeric variables can store only numbers, string variables can store only strings. If a number is assigned to a string variable, the number is considered a string and no arithmetic calculations can be performed on this number.

A variable name may consist of 1 to 40 characters. The first character must be a letter of the alphabet, the remaining characters may be letters, digits or periods. However, a string variable must end with a dollar sign ($). QUANTITY is a numeric variable, ENAME$ is a string variable.

We may not use a reserved word as a variable name. Recall that a reserved word has a special meaning to BASIC and cannot be used for any other purpose. For instance, we cannot use NEW as a variable name. We can, however, use a reserved word as part of a variable name as in NEW.STOCK. And, we may not start a variable name with FN. FN signals a call to a user-defined function. A user-defined function is discussed in Chapter Fourteen.

When choosing a variable, we should select one that best describes the value it stores. In this respect, complete variable names such as DEPOSIT and ADDRESS$ more clearly tell us what the variables store than do such names as D and A$.

Types of Variables

We have already learned that appending a dollar sign ($) to a variable name designates the variable as a string variable. The dollar sign is called a type indicator. We can also specify the precision of a numeric variable by appending a type indicator to the variable name. These type indicators are:

% Integer
Examples: SCORE%, COUNT.EMPLOYEES%, ACCOUNT.NUMBER%

! Single-precision
Examples: AVERAGE!, TOTAL.PENSION!, RATE!

Double-precision
Examples: E#, TOTAL.WAGES#, MAXIMUM#

A numeric variable with no type indicator defaults to single-precision. For example, AMOUNT.OF.INTEREST is a single-precision variable. This example also shows that a variable name may contain more than one period. (It may also end with a period.)

In making our decision concerning the type of numeric variable to use, we must be aware of the tradeoffs. An integer requires fewer bytes of memory and less time in calculations but it is the least precise. A double-precision number is the most precise but it requires the most memory and the greatest amount of time in calculations. Programmers of business programs are less concerned about memory and time than they are about precision. Since single-precision gives accuracy of six digits, 999999 is the highest single-precision number that is accurate, while the highest accurate dollar value is $9999.99. To preserve accuracy, we must use double-precision variables to store numbers greater than 999999 and to store dollar amounts greater than $9999.99.

In addition to specifying precision, a type indicator creates a new variable. (An exception is the ! indicator appended to a variable name. N and N! are considered the same variable.) N%, N!, N# and N$ are four distinct variables. Forgetting to append a %, a #, or a $ to a variable creates a single-precision variable and may produce erroneous results. And, one last note. Adding a type indicator to a reserved word does not make the word a legal variable. For example, LIST is a reserved word; LIST$ is an illegal variable.

Exercises

Identify the invalid variable names in the list below. Modify each invalid name to make it valid.

1. AMOUNT.DUE
2. 4.EMPLOYEES
3. LIST.NAME$
4. TELEPHONE$.NO
5. RAN
6. NEW$
7. N
8. NAME.&.ADDRESS$
9. A7!

3.4 BASIC Statements

A program is made up of statements. Some of these statements tell the computer what to do, others are explanatory remarks that help a reader understand the program. Each statement starts with a line number. Four statements are discussed below.

The LET Statement

Before a program is executed, BASIC places zeros in numeric variables and null strings (no characters) in string variables. One of the ways by which we can assign values to variables is by means of the LET statement (usually referred to as the assignment statement). Three other statements that perform a similar function; the READ statement, the INPUT statement, and the INPUT # statement; will be discussed in Chapters Four and Seven. Here is an example of a LET statement.

```
2020 LET HOURS = 38
```

The equal sign is called the assignment operator. The space before and the space after the assignment operator are optional. We insert spaces only to increase clarity. In the above example, the assignment operator assigns 38 to variable HOURS. Thus, the zero initially stored in hours is replaced by 38. HOURS must be a numeric variable.

We can also use the LET statement to assign a string to a string variable. The statement

```
2010 LET ENAME$ = "Darryl Brown"
```

assigns **Darryl Brown** to ENAME$. The null string initially stored in ENAME$ is replaced by Darryl Brown. ENAME$ must be a string variable. We inserted an "E" in ENAME$ since NAME is a reserved word. Recall that adding a type indicator to a reserved word does not give us a valid variable. A string assigned to a string variable by means of the assignment statement must be enclosed in quotation marks. The quotation marks are not stored.

A value and the variable to which the value is assigned must correspond in type, otherwise, BASIC displays a Type mismatch error message. Each of the following will cause an error message.

```
               2070 LET NUMBER$ = 50
BASIC displays: Type mismatch in 2070
               2080 LET STREET.NO = "134"
BASIC displays: Type mismatch in 2080
```

In the first example, we are attempting to assign a number to a string variable. In the second example, we are trying to assign a string to a numeric variable. A statement such as 2090 LET TEN$ = "10" stores the number as a string, making the number unusable in arithmetic calculations.

The assignment statement can also be written without the reserved word LET. In the statement

```
2020 HOURS = 38
```

38 is assigned to HOURS just as it was in 2020 LET HOURS = 38. We will use LET in this chapter, however, starting in Chapter Four the word will be omitted.

The PRINT Statement

Values assigned to variables can be displayed on the screen by means of PRINT statements. Suppose we wish to examine the contents of our two variables ENAME$ and HOURS. The PRINT statements that display these values are given below.

```
2040 PRINT ENAME$
2050 PRINT HOURS
```

The output displayed on the screen will be:

```
Darryl Brown
 38
```

Line 2040 instructs BASIC to print the contents of variable ENAME$, line 2050 instructs BASIC to print the contents of variable HOURS. Note that the number 38 is indented by one space. This is because BASIC leaves a space before a positive number. When a number is negative, the space is filled with a minus sign.

The above output tells us very little. It does not identify Darryl Brown nor the number 38. The following PRINT statements clarify the output.

```
2040 PRINT "Employee name: ";ENAME$      (Trailing space)
2050 PRINT "Hours worked:";HOURS         (No trailing space)
```

Output:

```
Employee name: Darryl Brown
Hours worked: 38
```

Employee name:b̸ (the symbol b̸ denotes a space) and **Hours worked:** are called strings, just as the name stored in ENAME$ is called a string. All consist of a "string" of characters. Strings in PRINT statements must be enclosed in quotation marks.

The trailing space in the string **Employee name:b̸** is needed since BASIC leaves no space before or after a string. After BASIC prints this string, the semicolon in the PRINT statement causes the cursor; that is, the print element, to stay on the same output line but to move to the next print position. (In Section 3.10 we learn that a comma moves the cursor to a different position on the output line.) BASIC now prints **Darryl Brown**. In line 2050, we leave no trailing space in the string **Hours worked:** since BASIC automatically leaves a space before a positive number. BASIC also leaves a space after any number; positive or negative.

There are other ways by which we can insert spaces between printed strings. Here are two more examples. Assume values have been assigned to the variables.

```
2060 PRINT NAME1$; " and ";NAME2$      (Leading space, Trailing space)
```

Output:

```
Brian and Susan
```

In line 2060, we inserted a leading space and a trailing space in the string "and" (" and ").

```
2070 PRINT NAME1$;"   ";NAME2$      (A string of three spaces)
```

Output:

```
Brian   Susan
```

In line 2070, we constructed a string of three spaces between the variables.

A PRINT statement with no strings or variables following the reserved word PRINT gives us a blank line. We will refer to this PRINT statement as a "blank" PRINT.

```
2030 PRINT
```

One last comment. BASIC does not store a number's insignificant leading or trailing zeros when such a number is assigned to a variable. Therefore, the leading and trailing zeros are not displayed when the value of the variable is printed. Examine the following statements and the output.

```
2010 LET NUMBER1 = 132.00
2020 LET NUMBER2 = 01.20
2030 PRINT "First number:";NUMBER1
2040 PRINT "Second number:";NUMBER2
```

Output:

```
First number: 132
Second number: 1.2
```

The END Statement

The END statement terminates program execution. The statement may be omitted at the end of a program since no further statements exist. However, it is good programming practice to place an END statement at the end of every program.

```
2090 END
```

The REM Statement

The REM (remark) statement is not an instruction but an explanatory remark inserted in a program to help a reader understand what is going on. BASIC does not execute a REM statement, however, it does display the statement when the program is listed. We use REM statements to state the purpose of the program, to define the variables, to describe major routines, and to explain statements or logic that may be obscure to the reader. Clarifying a program by REM statements is referred to as program documentation.

A REM statement consists of a line number followed by REM and the explanatory remark. REM informs BASIC that the remark is to be ignored during program execution. The version of BASIC we will be using allows us to replace REM with an apostrophe ('). Examples of REM statements are shown below.

```
1000 REM EMPLOYEE HOURS        M. MCRITCHIE        JAN 4
1000 'EMPLOYEE HOURS          M. MCRITCHIE        JAN 4
```

The first statement uses the word REM, the second statement uses the apostrophe. Both REM statements give the name of the program, the name of the programmer, and the date the program was written. Throughout the book, we will be using the apostrophe rather than the word REM.

REM statements may be stand-alone statements as the ones above or they may trail other statements. However, only the apostrophe REM can trail. Here are two examples.

```
2010 LET ENAME$ = "Darryl Brown"       'Assign values
2020 LET HOURS = 38                    'to variables
```

Normally, we place descriptive remarks opposite statements that need clarification. The assignment statements above are self-explanatory. We have appended REM statements only to illustrate their use.

More on LISTing a Program

A warning before we go on to a sample program. BASIC may append a type indicator to a number when a program is listed. Examine the following programs and their listings.

A program keyed in as:

```
2010 LET NUMBER = 46825
2020 PRINT NUMBER
2030 END
```

is LISTed as:

```
2010 LET NUMBER = 46825!
2020 PRINT NUMBER
2030 END
```

A program keyed in as:

```
2010 LET NUMBER = 123456789
2020 PRINT NUMBER
2030 END
```

is LISTed as:

```
2010 LET NUMBER = 123456789#
2020 PRINT NUMBER
2030 END
```

When the programs are listed, BASIC appends an exclamation mark (!) to 46825 since the number is a single-precision number and a number sign (#) to 123456789 since this number is a double-precision number.

Exercises

1. State the errors, if any, in the following assignment statements. Make the necessary corrections.

   (a) `2010 LET NAME$ = "John Smith"`
   (b) `2020 LET NUMBER = 1,2`
   (c) `2030 LET ADDRESS$ = 123 Main St.`
   (d) `2040 LET MONTH = "January"`
   (e) `2050 LET NUMBER$ = "23"`
   (f) `2060 LET B = C`

2. If the values of A, B, and C are initially 1, 2, and 3 respectively for each of the following program segments, what will their values be after execution of each segment?

   (a)
   ```
   2040 LET C = A
   2050 LET A = B
   2060 LET B = C
   ```
   (b)
   ```
   2040 LET A = C
   2050 LET B = A
   2060 LET C = B
   ```

3. What is the output of the following program?

   ```
   2010 LET MONTH$ = "July"
   2020 LET DAY = 31
   2030 PRINT
   2040 PRINT MONTH$;DAY;"(The end of the fiscal year.)"
   2050 END
   ```

3.5 A Sample Program

A BASIC Program

Let us now incorporate the statements learned so far into a BASIC program, then discuss the general features of a program. The program listed below enters data into the computer and prints the data.

```
1000 'EMPLOYEE HOURS                    M. MCRITCHIE                      JAN 4
1002 '*************************************************************************
1004 '              THIS PROGRAM ENTERS AN EMPLOYEE'S NAME AND
1006 '              HOURS OF WORK THEN PRINTS THE NAME AND HOURS
1008 '*************************************************************************
1010 'ENAME$ - EMPLOYEE NAME
1020 'HOURS  - HOURS OF WORK
2000 '*************************************************************************
2002 '                          ENTER AND PRINT DATA
2004 '*************************************************************************
2010  LET ENAME$ = "Darryl Brown"
```

```
2020 LET HOURS = 38
2030 PRINT
2040 PRINT "Employee name: ";ENAME$
2050 PRINT "Hours worked:";HOURS
2060 END
RUN
```

```
Employee name: Darryl Brown
Hours worked: 38
```

The program is decomposed into two blocks of line numbers: lines 1000 to 1020 which document the program and lines 2000 to 2060 which document the routine that follows, enter the data, and produce the output. The breakdown, documentation, and styling of programs are discussed in detail in Chapter Five.

Note that we no longer display the BASIC prompt OK after a program listing and after the program's output. Note, also, the blank line following the word RUN. This was produced by the blank PRINT in line 2030.

General Features of a BASIC Program

1. Programs consist of statements. Each statement starts with a line number and ends with the depression of the Enter key.
2. Each statement may contain a maximum of 255 characters which includes the line number, the spaces, the instruction, and the Enter command. BASIC ignores all characters exceeding the 255-character maximum.
3. When a statement contains more than 80 characters, the additional characters are displayed on the next screen line. The Enter key must be depressed at the end of the statement (not at the end of a screen line) to transmit the statement to memory.
4. When a statement contains exactly 80 characters, the cursor drops down to the next screen line after the 80th character is typed. Although the cursor is positioned on the next screen line, the Enter key must be depressed to send the statement to memory.
5. Line numbers must be positive integers that range from Ø to 65529 inclusive. Each line number must be greater than the previous number by a value such as 5 or 10 to allow for the insertion of additional statements. We increased line numbers by two when highlighting program descriptions and routine descriptions and by ten elsewhere. At least one space should follow a line number. If no space is left, BASIC inserts a space when the program is listed.
6. Unless BASIC is told otherwise, statements are always executed according to line number, from lowest to highest.
7. Programs are made up of executable and nonexecutable statements. An executable statement is an instruction, such as, 2050 PRINT "Hours worked:"; HOURS. A nonexecutable statement is not an instruction, for example, a REM statement.
8. Statements may be typed in upper case, lower case, or a combination of the two. BASIC converts all letters to upper case, except letters in REM statements, letters enclosed in quotation marks, and letters in DATA statements. DATA statements are explained in Chapter Four.

Exercises

1. What is the maximum number of characters allowed in a statement?
2. Why must the Enter key be pressed at the end of each statement?
3. State two rules that must be observed concerning line numbers.
4. State four reasons why REM statements are used in programs.

5. Key in the program below as shown. List the program. All lowercase letters will be converted to uppercase letters except those within the REM statement and those enclosed within the quotation marks.

```
2000 'An example of statements typed in upper case and lower case
2010 print
2020 print "Programming in BASIC"
2030 end
```

3.6 The Difference Between a Statement and a Command

Now that you are familiar with both statements and commands, it is important that the difference between the two be understood. Let us use the instruction CLS as an example. Recall that CLS clears the screen. The instruction can be used as a command or as a statement. When you type CLS without a line number, you are telling the computer to clear the screen immediately. When you type CLS with a line number (say, 2010 CLS), you are telling the computer to store the instruction in memory. The screen will be cleared when you later tell the computer to RUN (execute) the statement. In other words, you consciously make an instruction a command or a statement by excluding or including the line number. An instruction without a line number is a command, an instruction with a line number is a statement.

3.7 Editing a Line

Editing a line means making changes in the line. Often an error is realized as a line is being typed. There are various ways to edit a line. They are actually easier to do than to read. Most of the corrections use the cursor movement keys so make sure the numeric keypad is in the cursor control mode. In the illustrations of keys given below, the digits over the arrows are the digits shown on the keytops.

Correcting a Character

Three ways are:

1. Press the Cursor Left key (4 ←) until the cursor is under the incorrect character, then type the correct character. To reposition the cursor immediately after the last character in the line, press the Cursor Right key (6 →) until the cursor is positioned where desired or press the End key. The End key moves the cursor to the position immediately after the line's last character.
2. Holding down the Ctrl key and pressing the Cursor Left key moves the cursor in blocks of characters rather than one character at a time. Use these keys when the first character of a block is incorrect. For example, if you typed MIST 2120 instead of LIST 2120, hold down the Ctrl key as you press the Cursor Left key twice to move the cursor under the M, then change the M to L.
3. We explained how the backspace key can be used to correct an error. The key erases one character each time you press the key. Characters are erased in a right-to-left direction. If the incorrect character is not the last character in the line, all characters up to the error will be erased as you backspace to the error. For an error within a line, method one discussed above may be faster. This way, there is no need to retype characters after an error has been corrected.

Deleting a Character

To delete a character, place the cursor under the character to be deleted, then press the Del key. Move the cursor to the position immediately after the last character in the line by pressing the Cursor Right key or the End key as explained above.

Inserting Characters

To insert characters, move the cursor to the position where the characters must be inserted. Press the Ins key which places you in the Insert mode and changes the shape of the cursor from an underscore to a box. Type the additional characters. The typed characters start at the cursor and the former characters from the cursor on move to the right. After inserting the characters, move the cursor to the position immediately after the line's last character. Insert mode is turned off when you press a cursor movement key, the End key, the Enter key, or repress the Ins key.

Erasing a Line or a Portion of a Line

To erase the line you are currently typing, press the Esc key. The entire line will be erased. Do not press Enter. The Esc key may be pressed at any point in the line.

To erase a portion of the line you are currently typing, position the cursor under the first character to be erased. Hold down the Ctrl key as you press the End key. The character under which the cursor is positioned and all characters to the right of the cursor will be erased.

Exercises

1. Key in the following line. Do not press Enter after typing the line. Change PRIMT to PRINT.

```
2120 PRIMT "A BASIC Program"
```

2. Key in the following line. Do not press Enter.

```
2180 PRINT "Hi, Alan"
```

   (a) Delete the comma. Do not press Enter.
   (b) Insert another l in the name Alan.

3.8 Editing a Program

Making corrections in a program is referred to as editing a program. Sometimes we do not detect an error until the entire program has been keyed in. The error is now in the computer's memory. Other than the Esc key, we can use the keys discussed in the previous section to correct an error in memory. However, an additional task must be performed when we correct an error in a program. We must first gain access to the statement in which the error resides.

Accessing a Statement

A statement may be accessed in a number of ways.

We can move the cursor to the statement by using one or several of the Cursor movement keys. If there is more than one statement to edit, we correct all the errors; then move the cursor to the first edited statement and press Enter repeatedly until the end of the program is reached. The cursor need not be positioned at the end of a statement before we press the Enter key. However, we must ensure that Enter is pressed for each corrected statement.

We can type LIST, the line number of the statement to be edited, then press Enter. The computer will display the statement specified. Or we can type EDIT, the statement's line number, and press Enter. The computer displays the statement with the cursor placed under the first digit of the line number.

Making Corrections

After accessing the statement in which an error resides, the error can be corrected by following the instructions previously given for line editing. In addition to correcting a line, it may be necessary to edit a program in several other ways. The editing features discussed below are normally performed beneath a program listing.

1. Inserting a statement.

   Recall that statements should be typed into the computer in line number order. However, you can insert a forgotten statement or an extra statement by typing the appropriate line number, the statement, then pressing Enter. BASIC will insert the statement in proper sequence. Study the example given on the following page.

Type the statement to be inserted at the end of the program

```
2010 PRINT
2020 PRINT "Structured"
2030 END

2025 PRINT "Programming"  <—— Press Enter
```

BASIC inserts the statement in proper sequence.

```
2010 PRINT
2020 PRINT "Structured"
2025 PRINT "Programming"
2030 END
```

2. Deleting a statement.

   Type the line number of the statement, then press Enter. The statement will be deleted from memory. Suppose we wish to delete statement 2030 from the program given below.

Type the line number of the statement to be deleted at the end of the program

```
2010 PRINT
2020 PRINT "BASIC"
2030 PRINT "Programs"
2040 END
2030  <—— Press Enter
```

BASIC deletes the statement from the program

```
2010 PRINT
2020 PRINT "BASIC"
2040 END
```

We can also delete one statement or several consecutive statements by using the DELETE command.

`DELETE`	Deletes the entire program.
`DELETE 2040`	Deletes line 2040.
`DELETE 2030-2060`	Deletes lines 2030 to 2060 inclusive.
`DELETE -2040`	Deletes all lines up to and including line 2040.
`DELETE 2040-`	Deletes all lines from 2040 to the end of the program.

Care must be exercised when using the DELETE command, particularly DELETE without a line number. **This form of DELETE erases the entire program from memory.** Although we can use the DELETE command to erase a program, NEW is normally used. The Esc key cannot be used to delete a statement from memory since Esc merely erases the statement from the screen.

3. Replacing a statement.

   Type the line number of the existing statement, the new statement, and press Enter. The new statement will replace the old one. Another method is to move the cursor to the beginning of the statement and type the new statement over the old one. The line number need not be retyped. Make sure any extra characters left over from the old statement are erased. Do this by pressing the Del key. Press Enter.

Changing a Line Number

Care must be taken when altering line numbers in a program. When a line number is changed, the statement is duplicated. One statement starts with the former line number, the other statement starts with the new line number. Unless the duplication is needed, you should delete the statement with the former line number.

Interrupting Execution

You may wish to interrupt execution of a program when you realize the output is incorrect. As mentioned on page 18, you can interrupt execution by holding down the Ctrl key as you press the Break key. Execution stops and the computer prints **Break in xxxx** where xxxx is the line number where the break occurred. To resume execution, type CONT and press Enter.

It was also mentioned that you can halt execution temporarily by pressing the Ctrl-Num Lock keys simultaneously on the standard keyboard or pressing the Pause key on the enhanced keyboard. To resume execution, press any key except one of the special keys, such as a Shift key, the Ins key, or the Break key.

Exercises

Clear the screen and the computer's memory. Key in the following program, then change the program as indicated in each exercise. If you wish, RUN the program after each change. Be sure to RUN the program in Exercise Five.

```
2010 LET NUMBER = 1
2020 PRINT
2030 WHILE NUMBER <= 8
2040    PRINT NUMBER
2050    LET NUMBER = NUMBER + 1
2060 WEND
2070 END
```

1. In Statement 2030, change the number 8 to 4.
2. Delete statement 2020. List the program. Statement 2020 should be deleted.
3. Insert the statement 2035 PRINT. List the program. Notice how the inserted statement has been placed in proper sequence.
4. Replace statement 2040 with 2040 PRINT "Number:";NUMBER. List the program.
   After the above changes, your program should look like this:

```
2010 LET NUMBER = 1
2030 WHILE NUMBER <= 4
2035    PRINT
2040    PRINT "Number:";NUMBER
2050    LET NUMBER = NUMBER + 1
2060 WEND
2070 END
```

5. Change statement 2030 to be: 2030 WHILE NUMBER <> Ø. List and RUN the program. Notice that the output never stops. Interrupt program execution. Resume program execution, then interrupt it once more. Try both the break and the temporary halt.

3.9 Arithmetic Operators

Arithmetic Operators and their BASIC Symbols

Numbers are operated on by arithmetic operators which must be written in a manner that BASIC understands. Examine the following list.

Operation	*Symbol in BASIC*
Exponentiation	^
Multiplication	*
Division	/
Addition	+
Subtraction	−

As in algebra, the operators follow an order of precedence. The order is discussed in the next unit.

The Order of Precedence

An arithmetic expression is a grouping of numbers and variables connected by arithmetic operators. Performing the arithmetic operations in an expression is referred to as evaluating the expression. When two or more arithmetic operators appear in an expression, the order of precedence is as follows:

First, BASIC operates on the exponents in the order in which they appear. For example, 2^3^4 = 8^4 = 4096. Secondly, BASIC performs multiplication and division in the order in which the operators appear. For example, 9 / 3 * 4 = 3 * 4 = 12. Lastly, BASIC performs addition and subtraction in the order in which the operators appear. For example, 3 + 4 − 1 = 7 − 1 = 6.

Also, as in algebra, we can use parentheses to group values. BASIC executes the operations within the parentheses first, starting with the innermost pair of parentheses, moving outwards to the second innermost pair, then to the third innermost pair, etc. Here is an example.

```
2*(4+(6/3+7)-10)
        9

2*(4+9-10)
      3
```

BASIC now multiplies two by three. Notice that square brackets are not used.

When there are two sets of parentheses, one following the other, BASIC clears the parentheses in a left-to-right order. In the following example, BASIC executes the first set of parentheses before executing the second.

```
(2+8)/(7-2)
10/(7-2)
10/5
```

Ten is now divided by five.

Parentheses can alter the normal order of execution. For instance:

2+(3*4) = 14 but (2+3)*4 = 20

Two expressions are evaluated below to illustrate how BASIC applies the above rules.

```
1. (2^3^2+5)/(2^3-5)+7
   (8^2+5)/(2^3-5)+7
   (64+5)/(2^3-5)+7
   69/(2^3-5)+7
   69/(8-5)+7
   69/3+7
   23+7
   30
```

```
2. 15-(2^3-2*(3*(7-5)-5))
   15-(2^3-2*(3*2-5))
   15-(2^3-2*(6-5))
   15-(2^3-2*1)
   15-(8-2*1)
   15-(8-2)
   15-6
   9
```

Converting from Algebra to BASIC

When writing BASIC programs, we must often convert algebraic expressions to BASIC. Here are several examples.

	Algebra	*BASIC*
(a)	2+3(6-4)	2+3*(6-4)
(b)	$\frac{2+6}{4}$	(2+6)/4
(c)	$\frac{8}{3-1}$	8/(3−1)

(d) $\frac{4*8}{2*5}$ (4*8)/(2*5)

(e) $\frac{6+(5-2)^2}{3+4}$ 6+(5−2)^2/(3+4)

(f) $\frac{(7-3)^3+8^2-4}{5+2}$ ((7−3)^3+8^2−4)/(5+2)

In algebra, we assume multiplication as in 3(6-4). In BASIC, we must specify each operation explicitly. Thus, 3(6-4) in algebra must be expressed as 3*(6-4) in BASIC. Note that an expression representing a numerator or a denominator must be enclosed in parentheses when written in BASIC. In example (b), the numerator (2+6) must be enclosed in parentheses. If it is not, BASIC divides 4 into 6, then adds 2 to the result. In example (c), the denominator (3-1) must be enclosed in parentheses, otherwise BASIC divides 3 into 8, then subtracts one. The same principle applies to (d). Here, both the numerator and the denominator must be enclosed in parentheses. In (e), only $(5-2)^2$ is divided by (3+4) while in (f) all of the numerator is divided by (5+2).

In BASIC, we use the LET statement (the assignment statement) to assign the result of an evaluated expression to a variable. The first two expressions above would be incorporated in BASIC statements in the following manner:

```
2010 LET A = 2+3*(6-4)
2020 LET B = (2+6)/4
```

More often than not, the expression on the right-hand side of the assignment operator contains variables. These variables must be assigned values before they are used, otherwise, they contain zeros, placed there by BASIC before the program is executed. The following example calculates gross pay after values have been assigned to HOURS and RATE.

```
2010 LET HOURS = 38
2020 LET RATE = 9.54
2030 LET GROSS.PAY = HOURS*RATE
```

As mentioned earlier, leading and trailing zeros in numbers are not stored. Suppose we expect the result of an expression to contain a two-digit decimal fraction. If the last digit in the fraction is zero or the last two digits are zeros, BASIC does not print these zeros as in 371.6 and in 371.

Exercises

1. Evaluate the following BASIC expressions by hand, then RUN each expression on the computer and compare the output with your manually calculated answer.

   (a) 9−9/3+1
   (b) 10+3^2^2+6/(10−8)+3
   (c) 6*3−(8/2^2)/(6−4)
   (d) 16−(2*(9/3+1)−4)+2
   (e) 7−(2*(3*(8/4-1)+2)−6)+5
   (f) 9−(9/3+1)/(7*2−12)+3

2. Convert the following algebraic expressions to BASIC.

   (a) $\frac{6}{2} + 4(9-3)$
   (b) $\frac{6}{4-2} + \frac{4^2-8}{3}$
   (c) $\frac{6+2}{4-2} + \frac{8-(5+4)}{7}$
   (d) $\frac{3^2+6}{9-5} + \frac{10-4}{3}$
   (e) $\frac{(3+2)^2-4^3+6}{5-3}$
   (f) $\frac{3^2-4(12-(7+3)+9)+5^2}{7-1}$

3.10 Using Commas to Separate Items in PRINT Statements

Business reports often contain columns of items separated by spaces. Although there are more elegant ways to separate items (we will learn these methods later on), at this point we will separate these items by using commas in our PRINT statements.

An output line is divided into five zones with 14 character positions in each zone. When we separate items in a PRINT statement with commas, BASIC prints the first item starting in position 1, the second item starting in position 15, the third item starting in position 29, etc.

Suppose we want to print the headings NAME, HOURS, and GROSS PAY with the employee name, hours of work, and gross pay beneath the headings. Shown below is a program segment that prints the output just described. Assume that values have previously been assigned to the variables. The numbers above the output are column numbers. They are not displayed on the screen but are shown here merely to indicate where the printing of each item begins.

```
2040 PRINT "NAME","HOURS","GROSS PAY"
2050 PRINT
2060 PRINT ENAME$,HOURS,GROSS.PAY
```

Output:

```
         10        20        30
1234567890123456789012345678901234567
NAME          HOURS         GROSS PAY

Darryl Brown   38            362.52
```

The output line beneath the column headings is called a detail line. Line 2040 prints the column headings while line 2060 prints the detail line. Items in both PRINT statements are separated by commas. The blank PRINT in line 2050 gives a blank line between the headings and the detail line. Note the period in variable GROSS.PAY. We will be inserting a period in many of our variables in order to obtain descriptive variable names.

The headings start in columns 1, 15, and 29. In the detail line, number 38 starts in column 16 and number 362.52 starts in column 30. This is because BASIC leaves a space before a positive number.

We can also use a combination of commas and semicolons in PRINT statements to separate items. This is illustrated below.

```
2080 PRINT "Name: ";ENAME$,"Hours:";HOURS
```

Output:

```
         10        20        30
1234567890123456789012345678901234567
Name: Darryl Brown          Hours: 38
```

The semicolons cause Darryl Brown and b̸38 to be printed in the positions immediately after the respective strings. In this example, the comma causes the cursor to move to the third zone since Darryl Brown occupies a portion of zone two. Thus, Hours: 38 starts in column 29.

Exercises

Write program segments that produce the outputs shown below. Assume the values in the detail lines have been assigned to variables. Print the values of these variables.

1.

```
         10        20        30        40
1234567890123456789012345678901234567890
MONTH              ASSETS           LIABILITIES

December            67000            41000
```

2.
```
SALES REPORT

ARTICLE          NUMBER SOLD     VALUE

Printer           8               4219.84
```

3.
```
Sales: 9450    Commission: 1417.52
```

3.11 Producing a Hard Copy

We mentioned on page 25 that it would be wise to produce a hard copy of a program and its output. To obtain a listing of the program on the printer, simply type LLIST and press Enter. To obtain a copy of the output, change all PRINT statements to LPRINT statements. If you wish to send output to the printer and display the output on the screen, use both PRINT statements and LPRINT statements. The program below directs output to the screen and to the printer.

```
2010 LET ENAME$ = "Darryl Brown"
2020 LET HOURS = 38
2030 PRINT
2035 LPRINT
2040 PRINT "Employee name: ";ENAME$
2045 LPRINT "Employee name: ";ENAME$
2050 PRINT "Hours worked:";HOURS
2055 LPRINT "Hours worked:";HOURS
2060 END
```

A simple method to code the above LPRINT statements is to make copies of the PRINT statements. For example, to change the PRINT statement in line 2040 to an LPRINT statement, type 2045 over 2040 and place an L in front of PRINT. The rest of the statement remains the same. Press Enter.

Another method you can use to produce a hard copy of the program and its output is to hold down one of the shift keys as you press the PrtSc key on the standard keyboard or just the Print Screen key on the enhanced keyboard. The computer directs whatever is displayed on the screen to the printer. This method of printing is not recommended for a program listing or an output that more than fills the screen as the program or output must be listed and printed by the screenful. However, it works quite well for a short program or output. With the cursor under the last line to be sent to the printer, press Enter as many times as necessary to scroll away extraneous material displayed at the top of the program or output, then direct the remaining material on the screen to the printer as explained above.

3.12 Program Design

Let us now use the concepts learned in this chapter to design and develop a program. Both a structure chart and pseudocode are given. The designs are slightly different from those shown on pages 25 and 26 since the program there had additional tasks. Here is the problem we are about to solve.

Darryl Brown, an employee of the ABC Computer Company, receives $9.54 for each hour of work. If Mr. Brown worked 38 hours last week, what was his gross pay? What would be his net pay if his payroll deductions amounted to $80.49? Your program should produce the following output.

```
         10        20        30        40        50        60
123456789012345678901234567890123456789012345678901234567890123

PAYROLL REPORT

NAME           HOURS          GROSS PAY      DEDUCTIONS     NET PAY

Darryl Brown    38             362.52         80.49          282.03
```

Formulas:

Gross Pay = Hours of Work × Rate of Pay
Net Pay = Gross Pay − Deductions

FIGURE 3-3 STRUCTURE CHART

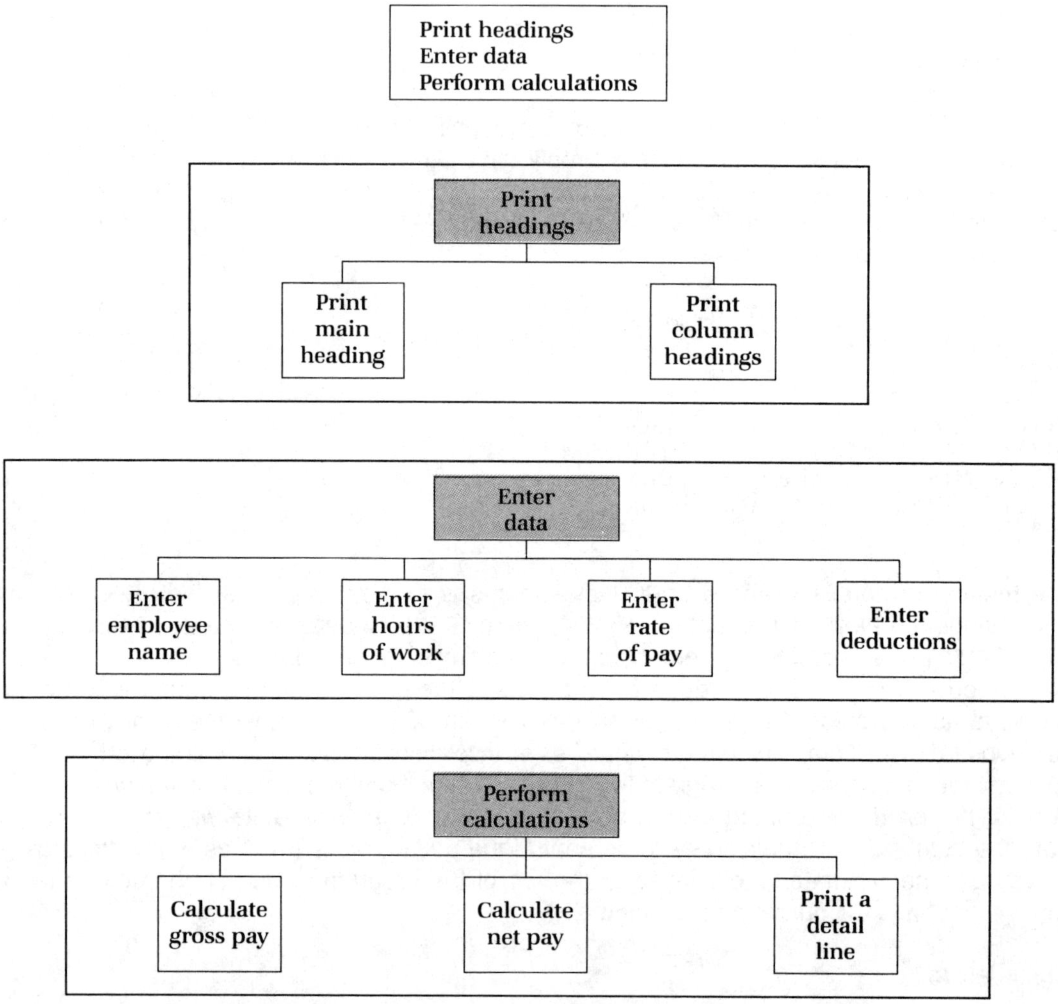

FIGURE 3-4 PSEUDOCODE

MAJOR TASKS
- Print headings
- Enter data
- Perform calculations

PRINT HEADINGS
- Print main heading
- Print column headings

ENTER DATA	
Enter employee name	ENAME$
Enter hours of work	HOURS
Enter rate of pay	RATE
Enter deductions	DEDUCTIONS

PERFORM CALCULATIONS	
Calculate gross pay	GROSS.PAY
Calculate net pay	NET.PAY
Print a detail line	

Note that we include variables in the above design. We list the variables as they are needed. For instance, ENAME$ was listed when we realized that a variable was needed for the employee name.

We now code the program and key it into the computer. We test the program by RUNning it. Recall that each expansion in our designs is considered a module. Later on, when we have learned a few more BASIC instructions, we will key in and test a program module by module.

Here is the program.

```
1000 'NET PAY                             M. MCRITCHIE                      JAN 13
1002 '*********************************************************************
1004 '           THIS PROGRAM CALCULATES THE NET PAY FOR ONE EMPLOYEE
1006 '*********************************************************************
1010 'ENAME$       - EMPLOYEE NAME
1020 'HOURS        - HOURS OF WORK
1030 'RATE         - RATE OF PAY
1040 'DEDUCTIONS - DEDUCTIONS
1050 'GROSS.PAY    - GROSS PAY
1060 'NET.PAY      - NET PAY
2000 '*********************************************************************
2002 '              ENTER AND PROCESS THE DATA, PRODUCE THE OUTPUT
2004 '*********************************************************************
2010  PRINT
2020  PRINT "PAYROLL REPORT"
2030  PRINT
2040  PRINT "NAME","HOURS","GROSS PAY","DEDUCTIONS","NET PAY"
2050  PRINT
2060  LET ENAME$ = "Darryl Brown"
2070  LET HOURS = 38
2080  LET RATE = 9.54
2090  LET DEDUCTIONS = 80.49
2100  LET GROSS.PAY = HOURS*RATE
2110  LET NET.PAY = GROSS.PAY-DEDUCTIONS
2120  PRINT ENAME$,HOURS,GROSS.PAY,DEDUCTIONS,NET.PAY
2130  END
```

As in the sample program listed on page 32, the statements in the 1000 block of line numbers document the program and define the variables. The statements in the 2000 block of line numbers document the routine that follows, print the headings, enter the data, perform the calculations, and print the detail line.

Summary of BASIC Statements

END Terminates execution of a program.

```
2130 END
```

LET Assigns a value to a variable. The reserved word LET is optional.

```
2060 LET ENAME$ = "John Smith"      2060 ENAME$ = "John Smith"
```

LPRINT Directs output to the printer.

```
2055 LPRINT "Hours worked:";HOURS
```

PRINT Displays output on the screen.

```
2120 PRINT ENAME$,HOURS,GROSS.PAY,DEDUCTIONS,NET.PAY
```

REM A comment statement used to document a program. A nonexecutable statement. REM may be expressed as an apostrophe.

```
1050 'GROSS.PAY - GROSS PAY
2110 LET NET.PAY = GROSS.PAY-DEDUCTIONS      'Calculate net pay
```

Summary of BASIC Commands

DELETE Deletes one statement, several statements, or an entire program from memory.

```
DELETE       DELETE 2010-2050
```

EDIT Displays the statement specified.

```
EDIT 2110
```

LLIST Lists a program or a program segment in memory on the printer.

```
LLIST        LLIST 1000-2000
```

Summary of Special Keys

Del	Erases the character above the cursor.
Esc	Erases a line from the screen but not from memory.
Ins	Sets and unsets the insert mode of operation. Allows characters to be inserted.
Print Screen	Used on the enhanced keyboard. Directs whatever is displayed on the screen to the printer.
Shift-PrtSc	Used on the standard keyboard to direct whatever is displayed on the screen to the printer.

Summary of CTRL-Key Combinations

Ctrl-Cursor Left	Moves the cursor to the left in blocks of characters.
Ctrl-End	Erases all characters from the cursor to the end of the line.

Chapter Summary

1. Problems must be solved in an organized and systematic manner. This involves the following steps.
   (a) Understand the problem.
   (b) Design an overall plan for the program. Do this by breaking down the problem into major tasks, then breaking down each of these tasks into more refined tasks. An expansion of a major task is considered a module.
   (c) Code (write) the program.
   (d) Key in and test the program module by module. Testing means RUNning a module or modules on the computer. Program segments should be saved on disk as the program is being developed.
   (e) Check the results for accuracy. Save the final version on disk and produce a hard copy of the program and its output.
   (f) Prepare support material.
2. Breaking down an overall problem into major tasks then breaking down each major task into more refined tasks is referred to as top-down design.
3. A program can be designed graphically (the portrayal is called a structure chart), or it can be written in short English phrases (referred to as pseudocode).
4. Data can be categorized into two broad classifications: numeric data and string data.
5. Numeric data items are numbers; string data items, called strings, may consist of letters of the alphabet, digits, spaces, and special characters. The length of a string may range from zero to 255 characters.
6. Numbers are classified into three categories:
   (a) Integer. Whole numbers that range from -32768 to 32767 inclusive.
   (b) Single-precision. Does not fall into the integer range or contains a decimal.
   (c) Double-precision. Consists of eight or more digits with a maximum of 16 digits.
7. A variable is a symbol that represents a number or a string stored in the computer's memory. There are two broad categories of variables: numeric and string.
8. A variable name may consist of 1 to 40 characters. The first character must be a letter of the alphabet, the remaining characters may be letters, digits, or periods. A string variable must end with a dollar sign ($).
9. A reserved word must not be used as a variable name. However, a reserved word may form part of a variable name.
10. A numeric variable name may end with a type indicator to specify precision. The type indicators are % (integer), ! (single-precision), and # (double-precision).
11. With the exception of the ! indicator, a type indicator appended to a variable name creates a new variable.
12. The assignment (LET) statement performs two important functions:
    (a) It assigns a number or a string to a variable.
    (b) It assigns the result of an evaluated expression to a variable.
13. When a string is assigned to a variable by an assignment statement, the string must be enclosed in quotation marks.
14. When items in a PRINT statement are separated by semicolons, the items are printed closely spaced.
15. Strings in a PRINT statement must be enclosed in quotation marks.
16. A PRINT statement with no list of items to print leaves a blank line.
17. Programs consist of statements. Each statement starts with a line number and ends with the depression of the Enter key.
18. Line numbers must be positive integers that range from Ø to 65529 inclusive.

19. Unless BASIC is told otherwise, statements are always executed according to line number, from lowest to highest.

20. Statements may be typed in upper case, lower case, or a combination of the two. BASIC converts all letters to upper case, except letters in REM statements, letters enclosed in quotation marks, and letters in DATA statements.

21. An instruction without a line number is a command, an instruction with a line number is a statement.

22. (a) We can insert a statement in a program by typing the statement's line number, the statement, then pressing Enter.
    (b) We can delete a statement from a program by typing its line number and pressing Enter. To delete several statements, we use the DELETE command.
    (c) We can replace a statement in a program by reusing its line number for the new statement.

23. Algebraic equations must be converted to BASIC when incorporated in a program. The BASIC arithmetic operators are ^ (exponentiation), * (multiplication), / (division), + (addition), and − (subtraction).

24. Operations within a statement are executed in a specific order referred to as the order of precedence. The order is as follows:
    (a) Exponentiation.
    (b) Multiplication and division, whichever appears first.
    (c) Addition and subtraction, whichever appears first.
    As in algebra, parentheses are used to group values.

25. An output line is divided into five zones with 14 character positions in each zone. When items in a PRINT statement are separated by commas, BASIC prints the items in consecutive zones, one item per zone.

Questions and Exercises

1. What is meant by top-down design?

2. What is meant by a "string"? What types of characters may a string contain?

3. Which of the following are valid strings and which are not? If a string is invalid, state why.

    (a) "Enter yes or no"
    (b) "Employee's name?"
    (c) "Susan replied, "I'll meet you on Tuesday."
    (d) "123"

4. How would the following numbers be displayed by the computer?

    (a) 125.00
    (b) 48.09
    (c) 012.45
    (d) .063480

5. State the precision of each of the constants shown below (integer, single-precision, or double-precision).

    (a) 12345
    (b) 67.394
    (c) 34128593
    (d) −2639841
    (e) 42.968512
    (f) −32768
    (g) Ø
    (h) −1.823194
    (i) .00000615

6. What is a variable?

7. Which of the following variables are invalid and why are they invalid?

    (a) 1A
    (b) B+2
    (c) "C"
    (d) Z9
    (e) $S
    (f) C.4
    (g) DELETE%
    (h) XYZ

8. Identify the errors, if any, in the statements shown below. Make the necessary corrections.

(a) `2010 LET B$ = BASIC`
(b) `2020 LET 4Z = 4`
(c) `2030 LET CITY$ = "Roxvale"`
(d) `2040 LET S1 = S+2`
(e) `2050 LET NUMBER% = 12`
(f) `2060 LET A/B = C`
(g) `2070 "END"`
(h) `65529 End of processing`
(i) `2080 LET AMOUNT = PRINCIPAL(1+RATE/100)^YEARS`
(j) `2090 PRINT "Name of student:";SNAME$`
(k) `2100 PRINT "Scores:";SCORE1;SCORE2;SCORE3`
(l) `2110 PRINT "NAME";"ADDRESS";"TELEPHONE NUMBER"`

Output:

```
NAME                ADDRESS            TELEPHONE NUMBER
```

9. Write PRINT statements that produce the following:

(a)
```
NAME       SALE     COMMISSION
```

Leave seven spaces between NAME and SALE, leave five spaces between SALE and COMMISSION.

(b)
```
Monday and Tuesday
```

Assume the strings Monday and Tuesday have been assigned to variables.

(c)
```
Parts produced: 40   42   46
Total parts:    128
Wages:          256
```

10. Write a short program that copies a value stored in location B and places it in location A. Print out the values of both A and B along with strings to identify the values.

11. Evaluate the following BASIC expressions, first by hand then on the computer.

(a) 3+16/(2^2^2)−6/3
(b) 8+12/4*(2^3+7)/5
(c) (3^2+5)/(2+5)+6
(d) 3+4/2+(8−(4+2))^2
(e) 6+4*3*(9/(6-3)−2)−7
(f) 30−(2*(8/4+3*(7−5)+5))

12. Convert the following algebraic equations to BASIC expressions.

(a) $\frac{8}{2}-3(6+4)$
(b) $\frac{9}{4-2}+\frac{3+4}{5+2}$
(c) $\frac{3^2}{6+3}+\frac{(8-3)^2}{4}$
(d) $8^3-(3(2+5)^2-4)$
(e) $\frac{4+6-3(5-2)^2}{7}+\frac{6}{5+1}$
(f) $\frac{8-(3(6-2)+4)}{9-2}$

13. What would be the output from the following program? Why does the program produce such output?

```
2010 LET PRICE = 199.95
2020 LET TOTAL.COST = PRICE+(PRICE*TAX/100)
2030 LET TAX = 6
2040 PRINT "Price:";PRICE,"Total cost:";TOTAL.COST
2050 END
```

Programming Problems

Design and write programs for the following problems. If required, make a hard copy of each program and its output.

1. An employee in a furniture factory is paid according to the number of pieces produced. Find the total number of pieces produced in 8 hours if the production was 6 pieces per hour.

RUN

```
HOURS          PIECES          TOTAL PIECES

 8              6               48
```

2. Convert 77°F to degrees Celsius. The conversion formula is as follows.
$$C = \frac{5}{9}(F-32)$$

RUN

```
Fahrenheit: 77
Celsius: 25
```

3. A retailer purchases shoes at a total cost of $2000 and sells them for $3100. Operating expenses amount to $500. Write a program that finds the profit before expenses are paid (gross profit) and the profit after expenses are paid (net profit). Align the numbers as shown.

RUN

```
Sales:         3100
Cost:          2000
Gross Profit:  1100
Expenses:       500
Net Profit:     600
```

4. Suppose you own 5 bonds each having a par value of $1000. If the interest rate is 9%, what will be your annual interest income?

RUN

```
QUANTITY       PAR VALUE       INTEREST

 5              1000            450
```

5. Assume you are working in the furniture department of a store and that you receive a basic salary of $100 a week and a commission of 15% based on sales. If you sold $2200 worth of furniture last week, how much commission did you receive? What was your income for the week?

RUN

```
SALARY         SALES           COMMISSION     TOTAL INCOME

 100            2200            330            430
```

6. Design and write a program that produces the Accounts Receivable account shown below. The account has a previous balance of $342.16. On September 21, the store made a sale of goods amounting to $460.32 to the customer and received a payment of $242.85. Find the new balance. Assign all values to variables including the account number, the customer's name, and the dates. Do not use DATE$ as

the variable for a date since DATE$ is a reserved word. You may use DATE1$ and DATE2$ to store the two dates. Note: the value under the heading DEBIT represents the amount of the sale, the value under the heading CREDIT represents the payment received.

To print the first balance under the heading BALANCE, code three commas in your PRINT statement between the variable for the date and the variable for the balance. The three commas move the cursor three zones after BASIC prints the date.

```
RUN
```

```
Account number: 391

Name: Jennifer Ross

DATE            DEBIT           CREDIT          BALANCE

Sept. 19                                         342.16
Sept. 21        460.32          242.85           559.63
```

Solutions for Exercises

3.2 Characteristics of Data

1. Integer
2. Single precision
3. Double precision
4. Double precision
5. Single precision
6. Single precision

3.3 Variables

1. Nothing is wrong.
2. A variable must not begin with a digit.

   EMPLOYEES.4
3. Nothing is wrong.
4. The dollar sign must be placed at the end of the variable name.

   TELEPHONE.NO$
5. Nothing is wrong.
6. A reserved word must not be used as a variable even when a type indicator is appended to the word.

   NEWS$
7. Nothing is wrong.
8. A special character must not be used in a variable name.

   NAME.ADDRESS$
9. Nothing is wrong.

3.4 BASIC Statements

1. (a) NAME is a reserved word, thus NAME$ is an invalid variable name.

```
2010 LET ENAME$ = "John Smith"
```

(b) Only one value may be assigned to a variable.

```
2020 LET NUMBER1 = 1
2025 LET NUMBER2 = 2
```

(c) The string must be enclosed in quotation marks.

```
2030 LET ADDRESS$ = "123 Main St."
```

(d) The variable must be a string variable.

```
2040 LET MONTH$ = "January"
```

(e) If the number is not intended to be used in arithmetic calculations, then nothing is wrong.

(f) Nothing is wrong.

2. (a)

```
2040 LET C = A
     C     = 1
2050 LET A = B
     A     = 2
2060 LET B = C
     B     = 1
```

(b)

```
2040 LET A = C
     A     = 3
2050 LET B = A
     B     = 3
2060 LET C = B
     C     = 3
```

3.

```
RUN
July 31 (The end of the fiscal year.)
```

3.5 A Sample Program

1. The maximum number of characters allowed in a statement is 255. This includes the line number, the spaces, the instruction, and the Enter command.
2. The Enter key must be pressed at the end of each statement to transmit the statement to memory.
3. Line numbers must be positive integers that lie in the range Ø to 65529 inclusive.
4. REM statements are used to state the purpose of a program, to define variables, to describe routines, and to comment on statements.

3.9 Arithmetic Operators

1. (a) 7
   (b) 97
   (c) 17
   (d) 14
   (e) 8
   (f) 10

2. (a) 6/2+4*(9−3)
   (b) 6/(4−2)+(4^2−8)/3
   (c) (6+2)/(4−2)+(8−(5+4))/7
   (d) (3^2+6)/(9−5)+(10−4)/3
   (e) ((3+2)^2−4^3)/(5−3)+6
   (f) (3^2−4*(12−(7+3)+9))/(7−1)+5^2

3.10 Using Commas to Separate Items in PRINT Statements

1.

```
2010 PRINT "MONTH","ASSETS","LIABILITIES"
2020 PRINT
2030 PRINT MONTH$,ASSETS,LIABILITIES
```

2.

```
2010 PRINT "SALES REPORT"
2020 PRINT
2030 PRINT "ARTICLE","NUMBER SOLD","VALUE"
2040 PRINT
2050 PRINT ARTICLE$,NUMBER.SOLD,VALUE
```

3.

```
2010 PRINT "Sales:";SALES,"Commission:";COMMISSION
```

4

ENTERING DATA, WRITING AND SAVING PROGRAMS

Objectives

In Chapter Three, you learned how to assign values to variables by means of the assignment statement. In this chapter, you will learn two other ways to assign values to variables: (a) by READing values into variables using the READ and DATA statements and (b) by INPUTing values into variables using the INPUT statement. You will learn how to code a routine that must be executed repetitively, how to detect errors in programs, how to save programs on a diskette, and how to load and delete programs from the diskette. Furthermore, you will become familiar with the terms file, record, and field.

Contents

4.1 The READ and DATA Statements

Assigning Values to Variables

In this section, you will learn how to assign values to variables by using the READ statement. The READ statement must always be accompanied by one or more DATA statements. Examine the following two statements. The hyphens indicate additional statements.

```
2010 READ SNAME$,SALES1,SALES2,SALES3
----
2080 DATA "Thomas Reid",825,942,895
```

The DATA statement supplies the data. BASIC places the data items listed in the DATA statement into a data pool; a special area of memory. The items are placed in the data pool in the same order as they appear in the DATA statement. When the computer encounters a READ statement, the items in the data pool are assigned to the variables listed in the READ statement. A data pointer within the data pool keeps track of the items as they are being assigned.

In the above example, BASIC places the data items Thomas Reid, 825, 942, and 895 in a data pool and sets the data pointer at Thomas Reid. The READ statement assigns Thomas Reid to SNAME$ and the data pointer moves to the next item (825). The READ statement assigns 825 to SALES1 and the data pointer moves to item 942. This continues until all the data items have been assigned to the variables. The procedure is equivalent to:

```
SNAME$ = "Thomas Reid"
SALES1 = 825
SALES2 = 942
SALES3 = 895
```

The data pointer is now positioned immediately after the last item in the data pool. A statement following the READ can access one of the data items by referencing the appropriate variable name. For example, a reference to variable SALES3 accesses the number 895.

A number of rules must be observed when we use the READ and DATA statements. These rules are listed below.

General Rules that Apply to the READ and DATA Statements

1. A READ statement must be accompanied by at least one DATA statement.

2. The variables in the READ statement and the values in the DATA statement must be separated by commas.

3. The DATA statement must have at least the same number of values as the READ statement has variables. There must be a one-to-one correspondence between the values and the variables.

```
2010 READ N$,S1,S2,S3             'Same number of values as variables
---------                         'Same order
2090 DATA "Jim",85,87,89          'Same type
```

Excess data is either read by subsequent READ statements or ignored if there are no other READ statements in the program. Insufficient data causes the error message **Out of DATA in xxxx** where xxxx is the line number of the READ statement.

When an attempt is made to read a string into a numeric variable, BASIC prints **Syntax error in xxxx** where xxxx is the line number of the DATA statement. When a number is read into a string variable, the number is considered a string and no arithmetic operations can be performed on this number.

4. A program may contain several DATA statements for one READ statement. Several DATA statements are usually used when the READ statement is executed repetitively. (We will learn repetitive processing in Section 4.4.) The commas in the DATA statements should be lined up so that the data items can be easily identified. The styling has no impact on the program. A block of data statements is illustrated below.

```
2080 DATA "Thomas Reid"    ,825,942,895
2090 DATA "Irene Anderson",913,864,893
2100 DATA "Erin Froese"    ,958,831,867
```

5. Although DATA statements may be placed anywhere in a program, it is best to place them together as shown above. In this chapter, we will place DATA statements just before the END statement. In subsequent chapters, we will place DATA statements near the end of the program segment in which the READ statement resides.

6. A string in a DATA statement need not be enclosed in quotation marks unless the string includes a comma, a colon, a leading space, or a trailing space. However, it is good programming practice to enclose all strings in DATA statements within quotation marks.

Exercises

1. Identify the errors, if any, in the statements below. Make the necessary corrections.

(a)
```
2010 READ A,B,C
2090 DATA 17;39;42.89
```

(b)
```
2010 READ A,B,C
2090 DATA,21.41,84,67.05
```

(c)
```
2010 READ N,N$
2090 DATA "Terri",49.58
```

(d)
```
2010 READ M$,Y
2090 DATA "July",2000
```

(e)
```
2010 READ N,D
2090 DATA 67,"10/15/2000"
```

(f)
```
2010 READ N$,T$
2090 DATA "Brenda","649-3157"
```

2. What output does the following program produce?

```
2010 STORE$ = "Buy-Rite Shoes"
2020 READ SALE1,SALE2,SALE3
2030 TOTAL.SALES = SALE1+SALE2+SALE3
2040 PRINT
2050 PRINT STORE$
2060 PRINT "Total sales for three months:";TOTAL.SALES
2070 DATA 15000,12000,16000
2080 END
```

4.2 The INPUT Statement

Assigning Values to Variables

Values assigned to variables by the assignment statement and by the READ and DATA statements form part of the program. In many business applications, data items must be keyed in as the program is being executed. Thus, the values do not become part of the program. Each time the program is executed, new values can be typed in.

The INPUT statement takes one or more values from the keyboard during program execution. The program should display a question or a statement to which the user of the program must respond by typing in a number or a string. This interaction between the user and the computer is called "user interface". The program allowing this interaction is referred to as an interactive program. Note: Hereafter, we will refer to a user of a program simply as the "user."

Two general forms of the INPUT statement are given below.

```
(a)  xxxx INPUT variable,variable,......
(b)  xxxx INPUT "prompt";variable,variable,......
```

In (a), INPUT may be followed by one or more variables. In (b), INPUT is followed by a question or a statement each of which is called a prompt. The prompt is followed by a semicolon or a comma and one or more variables.

A number of sample programs and program segments are listed below.

Sample Programs and Program Segments that Use the INPUT Statement

1. Suppose we want to assign a sales amount of 8500 to a variable by means of the INPUT statement. Here is what happens when we key in and RUN the following program.

```
2010 PRINT
2020 INPUT SALE
2030 END
RUN
```

```
?
```

When the computer encounters the INPUT statement, it displays a question mark and waits for us to type in a number and press Enter.

```
RUN
```

```
? 8500    ←— Type in 8500 and press Enter.
```

The shaded entry indicates a response to an INPUT statement. After we press Enter, BASIC assigns the number 8500 to variable SALE. If we want to change the value of SALE from 8500 to 8700, we simply RUN the program once more. Again, the computer displays a question mark and waits for us to type in a number and press Enter.

```
RUN
```

```
? 8700
```

2. The question mark gives no indication as to the type of data we must key in. In the program below, the computer displays a question referred to as a prompt.

```
2010 PRINT
2020 INPUT "What is the sales amount";SALE  ←— Variable to which the
2030 END              ↑                ↑          keyed-in value is assigned
RUN                 Prompt         Semicolon
```

```
What is the sales amount? 9400   ←— Keyed-in value
      ↑                  ↑
    Prompt         Question mark
                   followed by a space
```

The prompt **What is the sales amount** in line 2020 must be enclosed in quotation marks and may be followed by either a comma or a semicolon. The prompt may be in upper case, lower case, or a combination of the two. Throughout the book, we will use upper/lower case.

Statement 2020 prints the prompt, a question mark, and a space. The semicolon produces the question mark and the space. (The effect of a comma is discussed on page 56.) The space is always printed regardless of the type of value keyed in; numeric or string. We must now type in the sale.

A prompt should clearly indicate the kind of data we must key in. In other words, the prompt should be "user friendly". Notice that it explicitly asks for a sales amount.

3. The following program uses only one INPUT statement to assign several data items to variables. Note the user-friendly prompt.

```
2010 PRINT
2020 INPUT "What are the three sales amounts";SALE1,SALE2,SALE3
2030 END
RUN
```

```
What are the three sales amounts? 8500,8700,8200
```

The variables in the INPUT statement and the values keyed in during program execution must be separated by commas. As with the READ and DATA statements, there must be a one-to-one correspondence between the values keyed in and the variables listed in the INPUT statement (same number of values as variables, same order, same type). Insufficient data or an attempt to assign a string to a numeric variable causes the error message **?Redo from start**. BASIC redisplays the prompt and we are given another chance to type in the correct data. Here is an example.

```
3030 INPUT "What is your score";SCORE
RUN
```

```
What is your score? 85%
?Redo from start
What is your score?
```

BASIC is expecting a numeric value. When we key in a string, such as 85%, BASIC gives us another chance to type in a value. We can either type in the proper score or break out of the INPUT mode. To break out of INPUT, we simply press Ctrl-Break.

4. Strings and numbers can be assigned to variables by using one INPUT statement. The program below allows us to enter a string and two numbers.

```
2010 PRINT
2020 INPUT "Name and two scores";SNAME$,SCORE1,SCORE2
2030 END
RUN
```

```
Name and two scores? Cindy Ellis,85,79
```

A string typed in response to an INPUT statement is normally not enclosed in quotation marks. However, if the string contains a comma, a leading space, or a trailing space, we must enclose the string in quotation marks. As with the assignment statement and the READ and DATA statements, a number assigned to a string variable by an INPUT statement is considered a string and cannot be used in arithmetic operations.

5. In some programs, we may wish to display a multi-line prompt. To produce such a prompt, PRINT statements are used in addition to the INPUT statement. Examine the following program segment.

```
2010 PRINT
2020 PRINT "This program calculates an employee's gross pay"
2030 INPUT "Do you wish to continue (y/n)";RESPONSE$
RUN
```

```
This program calculates an employee's gross pay
Do you wish to continue (y/n)? y
```

6. Some prompts, such as, **Please enter your name**, should not end with a question mark. To suppress the question mark, we use a comma rather than a semicolon after the prompt. This is illustrated in the program segment below.

```
2010 PRINT
2020 PRINT "Enter your first name and last name"
2030 PRINT "separated by a space (e.g. John Smith)"
2040 INPUT "Please enter your name--",SNAME$
                  ↑                  ↑
                Prompt             Comma
```

```
RUN

Enter your first name and last name
separated by a space (e.g. John Smith)
Please enter your name--Audrey Davies
```

Not only does the comma suppress the question mark, it leaves no space before a keyed-in value; numeric or string. Thus, we separate the prompt and the keyed-in value by hyphens, spaces, or some other characters. We will use hyphens in our programs.

The program segment below enters a numeric value.

```
2010 PRINT
2020 INPUT "Please enter the sales amount--",SALES
RUN

Please enter the sales amount--2500
```

Exercises

1. Identify the errors, if any, in the statements and responses shown below. Make the necessary corrections.

```
(a) 2010 INPUT,"What is your name";YNAME$
(b) 2020 INPUT "Commission--",COMMISSION
(c) 2030 INPUT "Hours";HOURS
    RUN

    Hours? H

(d) 2040 INPUT "Enter the salary--";SALARY
    RUN

    Enter the salary--2000

(e) 2050 INPUT "Name";ENAME$
    RUN

    Name? Brown,Susan

(f) 2060 INPUT "Address",ADDRESS
    RUN

    Address? 123 Main Street

(g) 2070 INPUT Telephone No.;T$
    RUN

    Telephone No.? 352-4961
```

2. From the output given below each program, fill in the missing lines. Remember, DATE$ is a reserved word, therefore, do not use DATE$ as a variable in exercise (b).

(a)
```
2010 PRINT
2020
2030
2040 COMMISSION = TOTAL.SALES*RATE/100
2050 PRINT "Commission:";COMMISSION
2060 END
RUN
```
```
Rate of commission? 15
Total sales? 2400
Commission: 360
```

(b)
```
2010 PRINT
2020
2030
2040 END
RUN
```
```
Enter date (month and day, e.g. September 30)
Please enter the date--May 16
```

4.3 A Sample Program

Let us now examine a program that uses both the INPUT statement and the READ and DATA statements to enter values into the computer. The program finds the commission for one salesperson.

```
1000 'COMMISSION                                     M. MCRITCHIE                    FEB 4
1002 '*********************************************************************************
1004 '       THIS PROGRAM CALCULATES THE COMMISSION FOR ONE SALESPERSON
1006 '*********************************************************************************
1010 'RATE          - RATE OF COMMISSION
1020 'SNAME$        - SALESPERSON'S NAME
1030 'SALE          - AMOUNT OF A SALE
1040 'COMMISSION - COMMISSION
2000 '*********************************************************************************
2002 '               ENTER AND PROCESS THE DATA, PRODUCE THE OUTPUT
2004 '*********************************************************************************
2010  READ RATE
2020  PRINT
2030  PRINT "Enter the salesperson's first name and last name separated"
2040  PRINT "by a space (e.g. John Smith). Enter the sales amount."
2050  PRINT
2060  INPUT "Name";SNAME$
2070  INPUT "Sale";SALE
2080  COMMISSION = SALE*RATE/100
2090  PRINT "Commission:";COMMISSION
2100  DATA 15
2110  END
RUN
```
```
Enter the salesperson's first name and last name separated
by a space (e.g. John Smith). Enter the sales amount.

Name? John Smith
Sale? 1000
Commission: 150
```

Line 2010 reads in the rate. Lines 2030 and 2040 display instructions that tell the user what values to key in and how they must be typed. Lines 2060 and 2070 allow the user to key in the salesperson's name and the sales amount. Line 2080 calculates the commission while line 2090 prints the commission. Note that we place the DATA statement near the end of the program.

The program processes data for just one salesperson. Most programs process data for several people. Before we can develop such a program, let us learn how to process statements repetitively.

4.4 Processing Statements Repetitively

Sequential Processing

Our previous programs used sequential processing. A statement was executed, then the next statement was executed, then the next, etc. until BASIC reached the end of the program. This is illustrated in the following program which finds the commission for each of three sales amounts.

```
2010 READ RATE
2020 PRINT
2030 INPUT "Sale";SALE
2040 COMMISSION = SALE*RATE/100
2050 PRINT "Commission:";COMMISSION
2060 INPUT "Sale";SALE
2070 COMMISSION = SALE*RATE/100
2080 PRINT "Commission:";COMMISSION
2090 INPUT "Sale";SALE
2100 COMMISSION = SALE*RATE/100
2110 PRINT "Commission:";COMMISSION
2120 DATA 15
2130 END
RUN
```

```
Sale? 1000
Commission: 150
Sale? 2000
Commission: 300
Sale? 3000
Commission: 450
```

Line 2010 reads in the rate. The program now takes a sales amount from the keyboard, calculates the commission, then prints the commission. These three operations are performed for two more sales. Three statements are needed for each sale processed. We have indicated the repetitions by brackets.

It is possible to simplify the program by writing the three statements just once and then asking BASIC to process the set of instructions several times. In other words, we are creating a loop. A loop is a sequence of statements that is executed over and over. However, before we learn how to create and control a loop, let us first become familiar with two control statements: the GOTO statement and the IF/THEN statement. A control statement alters or controls a sequence of instructions.

The GOTO Statement

The GOTO statement causes an unconditional and immediate transfer of control to another statement. The jump can be backwards to a former statement or forwards to a statement further on in the program. For instance, the statement

```
2060 GOTO 2030
```

transfers control to statement 2030. Execution resumes starting at statement 2030.

Before we examine a program that uses the GOTO statement, a word of caution is in order. Because the GOTO is simple to use, it invites abuse. The indiscriminate use of the GOTO statement makes a program extremely difficult to read and is one of the main reasons for the switch to structured programming. Structured programming is explained in the next chapter. We discuss the GOTO here in order to introduce a loop. After this chapter, the statement will be used sparingly; in fact, in many programs it is eliminated entirely.

Here is how a loop can be created by using a GOTO statement.

```
2010 READ RATE
2020 PRINT
2030   INPUT "Sale";SALE
2040   COMMISSION = SALE*RATE/100
2050   PRINT "Commission:";COMMISSION
2060   GOTO 2030
2070 DATA 15
2080 END
RUN
```

```
Sale? 1000
Commission:  150
Sale? 2000
Commission:  300
Sale? 3000
Commission:  450
Sale?
Break in 2030
```

Line 2010 reads in the rate. Line 2030 requests a sales amount, line 2040 calculates the commission, and line 2050 prints the commission. The GOTO statement in line 2060 transfers control back to line 2030. Statements 2030, 2040, and 2050 are re-executed. When BASIC encounters the GOTO statement again, control is transferred back to line 2030 and statements 2030, 2040, and 2050 are executed once more. Note that the loop starts in line 2030 and that we place the READ statement outside the loop. There is no point reading the rate repeatedly, once is sufficient.

You have probably realized by now there is a problem with this loop. The computer keeps asking for a sale. Execution never stops since BASIC is unable to reach the END statement. In fact, we halted execution manually by pressing Ctrl-Break. Let us now find out how to control this loop.

The IF/THEN Statement

We can control the above loop by using an IF/THEN statement. There is much to be said about an IF/THEN, however, at this point we will use the statement in its simplest form. The general form of an IF/THEN statement is

IF a certain condition is true **THEN** do a particular task

The condition mentioned in the IF part of the IF/THEN statement is actually a relational expression which consists of two values separated by a relational operator. The relational operator compares the two values. An IF/THEN statement is given below. In this example, the relational operator is the equal sign. BASIC supports a number of relational operators. These will be discussed in later chapters.

```
2040 IF SALE = -1 THEN 2100
```

If the condition in the IF part is true, BASIC executes the THEN part of the IF/THEN statement. In this case, control transfers to the statement numbered 2100. If the condition is false, BASIC drops down to the statement following the IF.

To control the loop in the program listed above, let us incorporate this IF/THEN statement in the program.

```
2010 READ RATE
2020 PRINT
2030 INPUT "Sale";SALE
2040   IF SALE = -1 THEN 2100
2050   COMMISSION = SALE*RATE/100
2060   PRINT "Commission:";COMMISSION
2070   INPUT "Sale";SALE
2080   GOTO 2040
2090 DATA 15
2100 END
RUN
```

```
Sale? 1000
Commission: 150
Sale? 2000
Commission: 300
Sale? 3000
Commission: 450
Sale? -1
```

The loop starts with line 2040. All statements within the loop; that is, statement 2040 through to statement 2080 should be indented at least two spaces to highlight the loop. Just before the loop, we code an INPUT statement that assigns a value to SALE. SALE must be assigned a value before it can be compared with -1 in line 2040.

In line 2040, BASIC compares the value of SALE with -1. If the value of SALE is equal to -1, the condition (the relationship) in the IF/THEN statement is true and control transfers to line 2100, the END statement. If the value of SALE is not equal to -1, the condition is false. BASIC ignores the THEN part of the IF/THEN statement and, instead, drops through to the statement after the IF.

The value -1 that we compare with SALE is called a trailer value or flag. This item is usually some illogical value for the program being written. It is entered as the last value and thus signals the end of the data. Each time a value is entered, a test is made to determine whether or not the value is the trailer value. If the value just entered is not the trailer value, BASIC executes the statements within the loop; if it is the trailer value, BASIC transfers out of the loop.

Note that we INPUT another sale inside the loop (line 2070). If we do not code this statement, the GOTO must transfer control back to the INPUT statement in line 2030. Testing and transferring control is no longer performed in a statement at the top of the loop.

```
2010 READ RATE
2020 PRINT
2030    INPUT "Sale";SALE
2040    IF SALE = -1 THEN 2090
2050    COMMISSION = SALE*RATE/100
2060    PRINT "Commission:";COMMISSION
2070    GOTO 2030
2080 DATA 15
2090 END
```

We will code the routine in the manner shown on page 59 so that logic is the same as that of another loop: the WHILE/WEND loop discussed in Chapter Five. This loop also performs a test and transfers control by means of a statement located at the top of the loop.

As mentioned also on page 59, the equal sign in an IF/THEN statement is a relational operator. It does not have the same meaning as the equal sign in an assignment statement. Examine the following statements:

```
3020 DAYS = 5
3030 IF DAYS = -1 THEN 3100
```

In line 3020, the equal sign is an assignment operator. Here, it assigns 5 to DAYS. In line 3030, the equal sign is a relational operator. In this statement, it compares the value of DAYS with the constant −1. As with the assignment operator, we leave a space before and a space after the relational operator for the sake of clarity.

Exercises

1. What happens when BASIC executes the following GOTO statement?

```
3010 GOTO 3010
```

2. Write a program segment that finds simple interest on each of four investments. INPUT an investment (a principal). The formula that finds simple interest is as follows:

$$\text{Interest} = \text{Principal} \times \text{Rate}/100 \times \text{Time}$$

Read in the rate and the time. Express the time in years. Display an appropriate prompt in your INPUT statement. Use the IF/THEN . . . GOTO combination to form and control a loop. Choose your own data.

4.5 A Sample Program

We will now modify the program on page 57 so that it calculates the commissions for several salespeople.

```
1000 'COMMISSION                              M. MCRITCHIE                    FEB 6
1002 '**************************************************************************
1004 '      THIS PROGRAM CALCULATES COMMISSIONS FOR SEVERAL SALESPEOPLE
1006 '**************************************************************************
1010 'RATE          - RATE OF COMMISSION
1020 'SNAME$        - SALESPERSON'S NAME
1030 'SALE          - AMOUNT OF A SALE
1040 'COMMISSION - COMMISSION
2000 '**************************************************************************
2002 '              ENTER AND PROCESS THE DATA, PRODUCE THE OUTPUT
2004 '**************************************************************************
2010  READ RATE
2020  PRINT
2030  PRINT "Enter the salesperson's first name and last name separated"
2040  PRINT "by a space (e.g. John Smith). Enter the sales amount."
2050  PRINT
2060  INPUT "Name";SNAME$
2070    IF SNAME$ = "End" THEN 2150
2080    INPUT "Sale";SALE
2090    COMMISSION = SALE*RATE/100
2100    PRINT "Commission:";COMMISSION
2110    PRINT
2120    INPUT "Name";SNAME$
2130    GOTO 2070
2140  DATA 15
2150  END
RUN
```

```
Enter the salesperson's first name and last name separated
by a space (e.g. John Smith). Enter the sales amount.

Name? Ellen Hughes
Sale? 1000
Commission: 150

Name? Bruce Duncan
Sale? 2000
Commission: 300

Name? Shirley Wiebe
Sale? 3000
Commission: 450

Name? End
```

Note the relationship in the IF/THEN statement. Here, we must compare SNAME$ with a string since SNAME$ is a string variable in which a string is stored. We have chosen End as our trailer value. End must be enclosed in quotation marks. As long as a value stored in SNAME$ is not equal to End, the statements inside the loop are executed. The loop terminates when the user types in End.

4.6 Error Detection

Types of Errors

The process of finding and correcting errors in a program is called debugging a program. There are three types of errors.

1. Syntax errors.
2. Run-time errors.
3. Program logic errors.

Violations of language rules cause syntax errors. A typing error, such as misspelling a reserved word (PRIMT instead of PRINT) is an example of a syntax error. Other examples are a missing line number, a missing operator, mismatched parentheses, and an expression instead of a variable placed on the left-hand side of the assignment operator. BASIC detects the error and, for most of these errors, prints out an error message. An example of a syntax error message might be **Syntax error in 2030** where 2030 is the line number of the statement in which the error resides. Following the error message, BASIC displays the incorrect statement.

Careless coding usually causes run-time errors. Examples of run-time errors are insufficient data, a reference to a non-existent statement, and assigning the wrong type of constant to a variable. BASIC detects run-time errors and tells us what is wrong, such as **Out of DATA in 2060** or **Undefined line number in 2040**.

Logic errors appear when a RUN produces no output at all, or the results are obviously incorrect, or the results are reasonable, but incorrect. Logic errors are the most difficult to find. Incorrect calculations, incorrect data, transferring to a wrong statement, and an incorrect sequence of statements are examples of errors in logic.

A Program with an Error

Suppose a course is offered over two semesters. Students are tested three times in the first semester and twice in the second. The following program was written to calculate the final mark.

```
2010 NO.TESTS1 = 3
2020 SCORE1 = 78
2030 SCORE2 = 81
2040 SCORE3 = 84
2050 TOTAL1 = SCORE1+SCORE2+SCORE3
2060 SEMESTER1 = TOTAL1/NO.TESTS1
2070 SCORE4 = 82
2080 SCORE5 = 80
2090 TOTAL2 = SCORE4+SCORES
2100 SEMESTER2 = TOTAL2/NO.TESTS2
2110 FINAL.MARK = (SEMESTER1+SEMESTER2)/2
2120 PRINT "The final mark is:";FINAL.MARK
2130 END
```

When we RUN the program, the computer displays:

```
Division by zero

The final mark is: 8.507059E+37
```

The final mark is displayed in exponential form. BASIC converts numbers that are very large or very small to this form. Our concerns here are these: Why does the computer give us the error message **Division by zero** and why is the final mark as large as shown when the program operates on much lower numbers? We do have one clue. We know that the error must occur in one of the statements where division takes place. Here are three methods we can use to track down the error.

Using the PRINT Statement to Detect an Error

One of the simplest ways to detect a hard-to-find error is to print out the values of those variables where we think the error may lie. Let us see what happens when we print out the values of SEMESTER1 and SEMESTER2 immediately after statements 2060 and 2100 where divisions occur. The program and its output will look as follows.

```
2010 NO.TESTS1 = 3
2020 SCORE1 = 78
2030 SCORE2 = 81
2040 SCORE3 = 84
2050 TOTAL1 = SCORE1+SCORE2+SCORE3
2060 SEMESTER1 = TOTAL1/NO.TESTS1
2065 PRINT "At line 2065, the mark for Semester 1 is:";SEMESTER1
2070 SCORE4 = 82
2080 SCORE5 = 80
2090 TOTAL2 = SCORE4+SCORE5
2100 SEMESTER2 = TOTAL2/NO.TESTS2
2105 PRINT "At line 2105, the mark for Semester 2 is:";SEMESTER2
2110 FINAL.MARK = (SEMESTER1+SEMESTER2)/2
2120 PRINT "The final mark is:";FINAL.MARK
2130 END
RUN
At line 2065, the mark for Semester 1 is: 81
Division by zero

At line 2105, the mark for Semester 2 is: 1.701412E+38
The final mark is: 8.507059E+37
```

BASIC prints out the mark for Semester 1. Nothing is wrong with statement 2060 because no error message appeared before line 2065 was executed. The error message must be caused by the next statement that divides. This is statement 2100. Here, BASIC attempts to divide TOTAL2 by zero, but cannot. (Since no value was assigned to NO.TESTS2, the variable contains a zero.) The system divides TOTAL2 by a number that is as near to zero as it can possibly approach; for example, TOTAL2/.0000001. Thus, large values are produced for SEMESTER2 and FINAL.MARK.

Using the STOP Statement to Detect an Error

Halting a program by means of the STOP statement is another debugging technique. This allows us to print out the values of those variables we wish to examine. To continue execution, we type CONT.

Let us experiment by replacing the PRINT statements in lines 2065 and 2105 of the previous program with the word STOP. Our output will look like the one shown below the program. Comments to the right of the output explain what is going on.

```
2010 NO.TESTS1 = 3
2020 SCORE1 = 78
2030 SCORE2 = 81
2040 SCORE3 = 84
2050 TOTAL1 = SCORE1+SCORE2+SCORE3
2060 SEMESTER1 = TOTAL1/NO.TESTS1
2065 STOP
2070 SCORE4 = 82
2080 SCORE5 = 80
2090 TOTAL2 = SCORE4+SCORE5
2100 SEMESTER2 = TOTAL2/NO.TESTS2
2105 STOP
2110 FINAL.MARK = (SEMESTER1+SEMESTER2)/2
2120 PRINT "The final mark is:";FINAL.MARK
2130 END
RUN
Break in 2065              — Caused by the instruction STOP in line 2065
OK
PRINT SEMESTER1            — We key in PRINT SEMESTER1
 81
OK
CONT                       — We key in CONT
Division by zero           — BASIC prints an error message
```

```
Break in 2105                           — Caused by the instruction STOP in line 2105
OK
PRINT SEMESTER2                         — We key in PRINT SEMESTER2
 1.701412E+38
OK
CONT                                    — We key in CONT
The final mark is: 8.507059E+37         — BASIC prints the final mark
OK
```

Notice that the PRINT and CONT instructions in the output do not start with line numbers. The instructions are executed immediately and are considered commands. The error message is printed after BASIC prints the value of SEMESTER1, but before the break message caused by STOP in line 2105. This indicates that the error occurred in statement 2100.

Using TRON and TROFF to Detect an Error

The IBM personal computers support a trace mechanism that lists the line numbers of every statement executed where the trace is active. The instructions we must use are TRON (TRace ON) and TROFF (TRace OFF). TRON turns on the trace mechanism, TROFF turns it off.

The TRON and TROFF instructions may or may not be used as commands. Again, let us experiment using the program above. First, we will use TRON and TROFF as statements, then use them as commands. If we change the instruction in line 2065 to TRON and the instruction in line 2105 to TROFF, the trace mechanism will start in line 2065 and end in line 2105. Here is the output.

```
RUN
[2070][2080][2090][2100]Division by zero

[2105]The final mark is: 8.507059E+37
```

The first number in square brackets indicates that statement 2070 is the first statement executed after TRON turns on the trace mechanism. The bracketed numbers following [2070] indicate that statements 2080, 2090, and 2100 have also been executed. After displaying [2100], the computer prints the error message **Division by zero**. The bracketed number [2105] informs us that statement 2105 has been executed. This is the statement that turns off the trace mechanism (2105 TROFF). The PRINT statement in line 2120 produces the output: The final mark is: 8.507059E+37. Line numbers [2110], [2120], and [2130] are not shown since the trace mechanism was turned off in line 2105. Because the computer prints the error message immediately after displaying [2100], it is likely that the error occurred in statement 2100.

To use TRON and TROFF as commands, type TRON under the program, type RUN and, following the output, type TROFF. The display is given below.

```
TRON
OK
RUN
[2010][2020][2030][2040][2050][2060][2070][2080][2090][2100]Division by zero

[2110][2120]The final mark is: 8.507059E+37
[2130]
OK
TROFF
```

This time, every line number is displayed since the trace mechanism starts at the beginning of the program and traces through the entire program.

The debugging instructions PRINT, STOP, TRON, and TROFF can be used in any combination desired. After all errors have been found and corrected, all debugging instructions should be removed from the program.

Exercise

Trace the execution of the following program using one of the tracing methods discussed above. (Try several methods if you wish to experiment.) The program contains one error. Its data and output are correct.

```
2010 READ NO.SHARES,INITIAL.PRICE,CURRENT.PRICE,NO.SOLD
2020 CURRENT.VALUE = NO.SHARES*CURRENT.PRICE
2030 PROFIT = CURRENT.PRICE-INITIAL.PRICE*NO.SOLD
2040 PRINT
2050 PRINT "Profit:";PROFIT
2060 DATA 20,58,67,5
2070 END
RUN

Profit: 45
```

4.7 Saving, Loading, and Deleting Programs

The Concept of Storing Information on Disk

The first thing we should do after typing a program into the computer is to save the program on disk. We should do this even before we RUN the program. There is nothing more aggravating than to accidentally lose a program by a power failure or by inadvertently typing NEW or turning off the computer before the program is saved. At other times, we may wish to save an incomplete program, then finish the program at a later date. Thus, we should know how to save a program on disk, how to load a program from disk, how to find out which programs are stored on the disk, and how to delete programs no longer needed on disk.

We will refer to the diskette storing our programs as our BASIC diskette. It is important that the distinction between the DOS diskette and our BASIC diskette be understood. The DOS diskette holds the Disk Operating System. The BASIC diskette is the diskette on which we store the programs we develop and any data we may need. Methods of storing data are explained in later chapters.

As we mentioned in Chapter Two, before anything can be saved on a new diskette, the diskette's surface must be arranged in tracks and sectors acceptable to DOS. This is known as initializing or formatting a diskette. Refer to Appendix D for instructions in formatting your BASIC diskette. We also mentioned that any reference to disk drives applies to an IBM personal computer system with two drives. Therefore, to access information on a diskette, we must place the DOS diskette in drive A and our BASIC diskette in drive B. Recall that drive A is the drive on the left, drive B is the one on the right.

Any information stored on disk is stored as a file. A file is a collection of related items. We consider a program on disk a file since it consists of related pieces of information. In the next section, we will be discussing a file of data items. A program stored on disk is called a program file, a set of related data items stored on disk is called a data file.

Filenames

Each file must be saved under a unique filename which must conform to the rules listed below.

1. A filename may consist of two parts. The first part is called the name, the second part is called the extension. The name and extension must be separated by a period. The name should indicate what is stored on the diskette. For example, if the file is a program that calculates net pay, we could use the name NET-PAY. A name may contain a maximum of eight characters.

   The extension is optional, however, we strongly urge that an extension be used. It should indicate the type of file stored, such as BAS for a BASIC program and DAT for a data file. Thus, the filename for our net pay program would be NET-PAY.BAS. An extension may contain a maximum of three characters.

2. Letters, digits, and many special characters may be used in the filename. The examples in this book use letters, digits, and hyphens.

3. No space may be inserted in a filename. Examples of legal and illegal filenames are given below.

Legal Filenames	*Illegal Filenames*	
GROSSPAY.BAS	COMMISSION.BAS	COMMISSION contains more than 8 characters.
PROB2-1.BAS		
6FINAL	NET PAY.BAS	NET PAY contains a space.

The SAVE, LOAD, KILL, and FILES Commands

SAVE, LOAD, KILL, and FILES are the BASIC commands we can use to handle our program files. The commands may be typed in either uppercase or lowercase letters. Since our BASIC diskette resides in drive B, each command must be followed by B, the drive specification. A colon must follow the drive specification. Except for the FILES command, the filename must be specified next. The drive specification, the colon, and the filename must all be enclosed in quotation marks. An example of a command is given below.

```
Command       Filename
   ↓              ↓
 SAVE "B:NET-PAY.BAS"  ←——  Drive specification, colon, filename
       ↑                    enclosed in quotation marks
       |
     Drive
     specification
```

1. The SAVE Command

We use the SAVE command to save a program on disk. Three examples are given below.

	The SAVE Command	*Filename under which the file is stored*
(a)	SAVE "B:NET-PAY.BAS"	NET-PAY.BAS
(b)	SAVE "B:DISCOUNT"	DISCOUNT.BAS
(c)	SAVE "B:NET-PAY.ONE"	NET-PAY.ONE

The files in (a) and (c) are two distinct files since their extensions differ. If no extension is specified, as in (b), BASIC adds the extension BAS. **If we save a file under the name of an existing file, the SAVE command overwrites the existing file and thus destroys this file**. Care must be exercised when choosing a filename.

2. The LOAD Command

The LOAD command retrieves any file saved by the SAVE command. When a file is LOADed, a program in memory is replaced by the file retrieved from disk. **Therefore, it is important that we first save a program already in memory (if the program is needed later) before we load a file**. The following commands retrieve the files SAVEd in #1 above.

```
(a) LOAD "B:NET-PAY.BAS"     or   LOAD "B:NET-PAY"
(b) LOAD "B:DISCOUNT.BAS"    or   LOAD "B:DISCOUNT"
(c) LOAD "B:NET-PAY.ONE"
```

When we load a file, the extension BAS is optional as illustrated in examples (a) and (b). If the extension is something other than BAS, as in (c), we must specify the extension.

3. The KILL Command

The KILL command deletes a file from disk. The following KILL commands delete the files SAVEd in #1.

```
(a) KILL "B:NET-PAY.BAS"
(b) KILL "B:DISCOUNT.BAS"
```

(c) `KILL "B:NET-PAY.ONE"`

Unlike the SAVE and LOAD commands, we must specify the extension in every filename.

4. The FILES Command

The FILES command lists the names of the files stored on our BASIC diskette. We simply type FILES "B:" and press Enter. The system displays the filenames as well as the number of free bytes remaining on the diskette.

If the names more than fill up the screen, we can scroll lock a segment of the listing by holding down the Ctrl key as we press the Num Lock key on the standard keyboard or press the Pause key on the enhanced keyboard. To resume the listing, we press any key except a Shift key, the Ins key, or the Break key. Here is a sample listing.

```
FILES "B:"
B:\
NET-PAY .BAS        DISCOUNT.BAS        NET-PAY .ONE
 295864 Bytes free
```

Exercises

1. Place a newly formatted diskette in drive B.
2. After loading BASICA, key in the following program.

```
2010 PRINT
2020 PRINT "BASIC PROGRAMMING"
2030 END
```

3. Save the program on disk, then examine the contents of the diskette.
4. Erase the program from memory and type LIST to ensure that it has been erased. LOAD the program stored on disk, then list and execute the program.
5. Delete the program from disk and from memory. Examine the contents of the diskette once more. The program should be deleted from the diskette.

4.8 Files, Records, and Fields

A set of related data items is considered a file. The file of data can be broken down into records each of which can be further broken down into fields. It is important that the terms file, record, and field be understood. Suppose the ABC Computer Company has four employees. To calculate the employees' wages and to produce a payroll report, the accounting department needs each employee's name, rate of pay, hours of work, and payroll deductions. The information relating to the four employees make up a file.

A file

Name	*Rate*	*Hours*	*Tax*	*Dues*	*Pension*
Darryl Brown	9.54	38	74.57	2.25	3.67
Ellen Miller	8.87	39	72.14	2.25	3.42
Lorne Hayes	9.88	42	79.84	2.25	4.15
Andrea Jones	10.04	47	85.26	2.25	6.31

A file is divided into records. In the above file, the information concerning one employee is a record. There are four records in the file.

A record

Darryl Brown	9.54	38	74.57	2.25	3.67
Ellen Miller	8.87	39	72.14	2.25	3.42
Lorne Hayes	9.88	42	79.84	2.25	4.15
Andrea Jones	10.04	47	85.26	2.25	6.31

A record is subdivided into fields. There are six fields in each record.

A field

Darryl Brown	9.54	38	74.57	2.25	3.67
Ellen Miller	8.87	39	72.14	2.25	3.42

Lorne Hayes	9.88	42	79.84	2.25	4.15
Andrea Jones	10.04	47	85.26	2.25	6.31

Let us now design a program that uses the concepts of file, record, and field. We will use the above file as our data.

4.9 Program Design

The program we will design is an extension to the one designed in Chapter Three. Here, we process records for four employees rather than one. The records are read into the computer by the READ statement. Furthermore, a date is INPUTed and total payroll deductions are calculated. The program produces the following output.

```
         10        20        30        40        50        60
123456789012345678901234567890123456789012345678901234567890123

Enter the date (month and day, e.g. September 30)
Date? October 17

PAYROLL REPORT
Week Ending October 17

NAME            HOURS           GROSS PAY       DEDUCTIONS      NET PAY

Darryl Brown    38               362.52          80.49           282.03
Ellen Miller    39               345.93          77.81           268.12
Lorne Hayes     42               414.96          86.24           328.72
Andrea Jones    47               471.88          93.82           378.06
```

FIGURE 4-1 STRUCTURE CHART

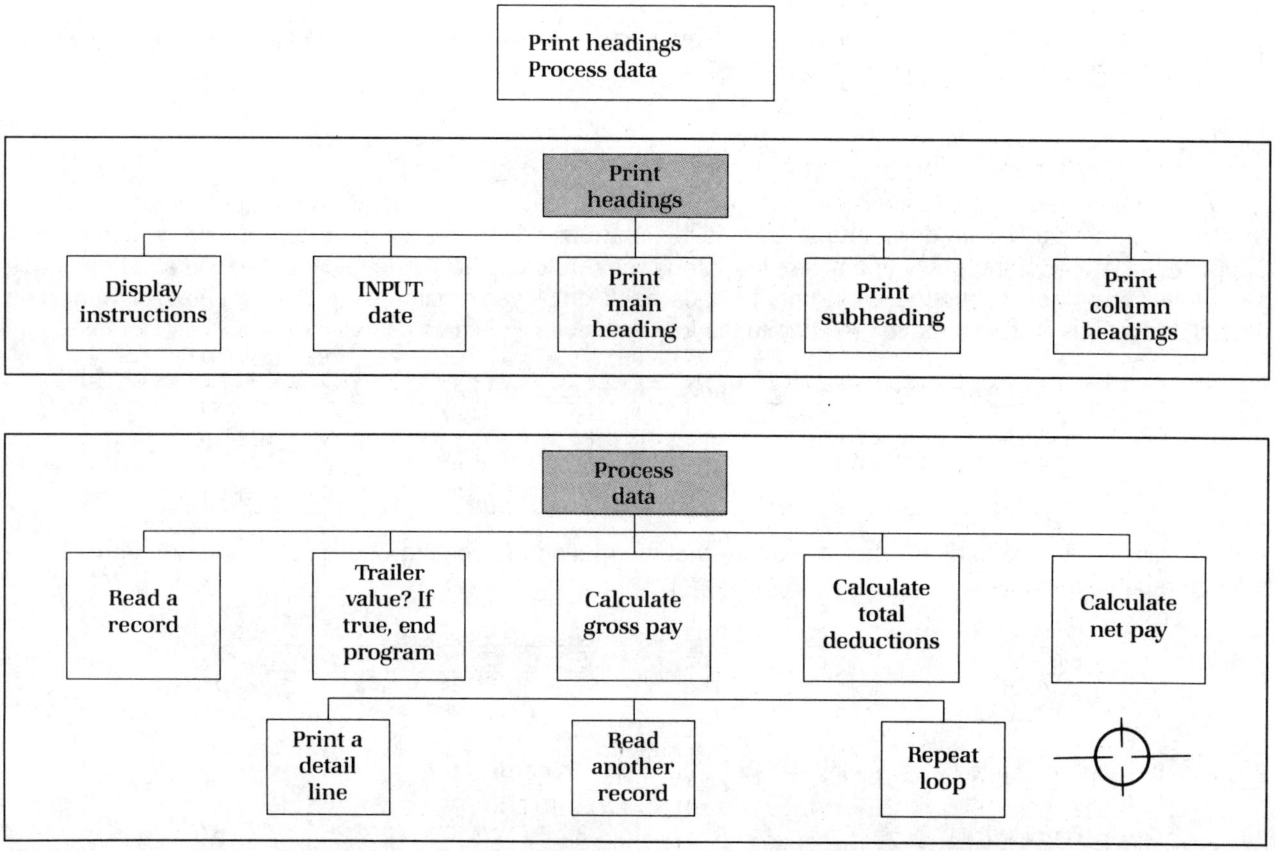

Because of the many instructions under PROCESS DATA, two rows of boxes are drawn.

FIGURE 4-2 PSEUDOCODE

MAJOR TASKS
Print headings
Process data

PRINT HEADINGS	
Display instructions	
INPUT date	DATE1$
Print main heading	
Print subheading	
Print column headings	

PROCESS DATA	
Read a record	ENAME$,RATE,HOURS,INCOME.TAX,UNION,PENSION
Trailer value?	
If true, end program	
If false:	
Calculate gross pay	GROSS.PAY
Calculate total deductions	DEDUCTIONS
Calculate net pay	NET.PAY
Print a detail line	
Read another record	
Repeat loop	

Here is the program listing.

```
1000 'NET PAY                         M. MCRITCHIE                        FEB 15
1002 '***********************************************************************
1004 '    THIS PROGRAM CALCULATES THE NET PAY FOR EACH OF SEVERAL EMPLOYEES
1006 '***********************************************************************
1010 'DATE1$       - DATE
1020 'ENAME$       - EMPLOYEE NAME
1030 'RATE         - RATE OF PAY
1040 'HOURS        - HOURS OF WORK
1050 'INCOME.TAX - INCOME TAX DEDUCTION
1060 'UNION        - UNION DUES
1070 'PENSION      - PENSION DEDUCTION
1080 'GROSS.PAY  - GROSS PAY
1090 'DEDUCTIONS - TOTAL DEDUCTIONS
1100 'NET.PAY      - NET PAY
2000 '***********************************************************************
2002 '               ENTER AND PROCESS THE DATA, PRODUCE THE OUTPUT
2004 '***********************************************************************
2010  PRINT
2020  PRINT "Enter the date (month and day, e.g. September 30)"
2030  INPUT "Date";DATE1$
2040  PRINT
2050  PRINT "PAYROLL REPORT"
2060  PRINT "Week Ending ";DATE1$
2070  PRINT
2080  PRINT "NAME","HOURS","GROSS PAY","DEDUCTIONS","NET PAY"
2090  PRINT
2100  READ ENAME$,RATE,HOURS,INCOME.TAX,UNION,PENSION
2110    IF ENAME$ = "End of file" THEN 2230
2120    GROSS.PAY = HOURS*RATE
2130    DEDUCTIONS = INCOME.TAX+UNION+PENSION
2140    NET.PAY = GROSS.PAY-DEDUCTIONS
2150    PRINT ENAME$,HOURS,GROSS.PAY,DEDUCTIONS,NET.PAY
2160    READ ENAME$,RATE,HOURS,INCOME.TAX,UNION,PENSION
2170    GOTO 2110
2180  DATA "Darryl Brown",9.54 ,38,74.57,2.25,3.67
2190  DATA "Ellen Miller",8.87 ,39,72.14,2.25,3.42
```

```
2200   DATA "Lorne Hayes" ,9.88 ,42,79.84,2.25,4.15
2210   DATA "Andrea Jones",10.04,47,85.26,2.25,6.31
2220   DATA "End of file" ,0,0,0,0,0
2230   END
```

Now that we are printing more than one detail line, the output is beginning to resemble a report. In Chapter Eight, reports will be centred so that they are attractively displayed on the screen.

To terminate the program, one of the fields in a record must be tested for the trailer value. Any field can be tested, we chose the name field. We used **End of file** as our trailer value. Data statement 2220 contains this trailer value. Values for the remaining fields must also be included in this DATA statement. We used Ø for each of the remaining fields. This entire record is called a trailer record and must be the last record read into the computer.

The READ statement, the IF/THEN statement, and DATA statement 2220 are redisplayed below so you can readily see the relationships among the statements. In the DATA statement, **"End of file" ,Ø,Ø,Ø,Ø,Ø** is the trailer record, **End of file** is the trailer value.

```
2100 READ ENAME$,RATE,HOURS,INCOME.TAX,UNION,PENSION
2110 IF ENAME$ = "End of file" THEN 2230
2220 DATA "End of file" ,0,0,0,0,0
```

The trailer value in the IF/THEN statement and the trailer value in the trailer record must be identical.

Summary of BASIC Statements

DATA — Creates a data pool for a READ statement.

```
2180 DATA "Darryl Brown",9.54,38,74.57,2.25,3.67
```

GOTO — Transfers control to the line specified.

```
2170 GOTO 2110
```

IF/THEN — If the condition in the IF is true, executes the instruction following THEN. If the condition is false, BASIC drops down to the next statement.

```
2110 IF ENAME$ = "End of file" THEN 2230
```

INPUT — Allows a user to enter data through the keyboard as the program is being executed.

```
2070 INPUT "NAME";ENAME$  or  2070 INPUT "Enter a name--",ENAME$
```

READ — Assigns the data items in the data pool to variables.

```
2100 READ ENAME$,RATE,HOURS,INCOME.TAX,UNION,PENSION
```

STOP — Halts program execution and displays a Break message.

```
2065 STOP
```

Summary of BASIC Commands

FILES — Lists the names of the files stored on a diskette.

```
FILES "B:"
```

KILL — Deletes from disk the file specified.

```
KILL "B:NET-PAY.BAS"
```

LOAD Retrieves the named file from disk, puts it into memory.

```
LOAD "B:NET-PAY.BAS"
```

SAVE Saves the program in memory on disk under the filename specified.

```
SAVE "B:NET-PAY.BAS"
```

TROFF Turns off the trace mechanism.

```
2105 TROFF
```

TRON Turns on the trace mechanism.

```
2065 TRON
```

Chapter Summary

1. The READ statement provides another method by which values may be assigned to variables. The READ statement must be accompanied by at least one DATA statement which supplies the data.
2. The DATA statement creates a data pool. The READ statement assigns the values in the data pool to the variables listed in the READ statement.
3. The variables in the READ statement and the values in the DATA statement must be separated by commas.
4. There must be a one-to-one correspondence between the variables in the READ statement and the values in the DATA statement.
5. Although DATA statements may be placed anywhere in a program, it is best to place them together, preferably near the end of the program segment in which the READ statement resides.
6. A string in a DATA statement need not be enclosed in quotation marks unless the string contains a comma, a colon, a leading space, or a trailing space. However, it is good programming practice to enclose all strings in DATA statements within quotation marks.
7. Interaction between a user and the computer is called "user interface". The program allowing this interaction is referred to as an interactive program.
8. When the computer encounters the INPUT statement, it displays a question mark and then waits for the user to type in a value.
9. An interactive program should display a prompt that indicates the type of data to be entered. The prompt must be "user friendly"; that is, it must let the user know exactly what to key in and how it must be typed.
10. The prompt in an INPUT statement may be followed by a semicolon or a comma. When we use a semicolon, a question mark and a space follow the prompt displayed on the screen. When we use a comma, the question mark and the space are suppressed.
11. One INPUT statement can assign several values to variables. There must be a one-to-one correspondence between the values keyed in and the variables listed in the INPUT statement.
12. A string, typed in response to an INPUT statement, need not be enclosed in quotation marks unless the string contains a comma, a leading space, or a trailing space.
13. In this book, a string, assigned to a variable, is enclosed in quotation marks when:
    (a) The string is assigned to a variable by the assignment statement.
    (b) The string is listed in a DATA statement.
    (c) The string, typed in response to an INPUT statement, contains a comma, a leading space, or a trailing space.
14. Sequential processing is the execution of statements one after the other until the end of the program is reached.
15. The GOTO statement causes a break in sequential processing by transferring control to another statement in the program.
16. A loop is a sequence of statements that is executed over and over.
17. A trailer value is some illogical value for the program being written. It signals the end of the data.
18. An IF/THEN statement can control a loop by testing a variable for a trailer value. If the value just entered is not the trailer value, BASIC executes the statements within the loop; if it is the trailer value, BASIC transfers out of the loop.
19. There are three types of errors:
    (a) Syntax errors (violations of language rules).
    (b) Run-time errors (usually careless coding).
    (c) Program logic errors (errors in logic).

20. To detect an error in a program, we can use:
    (a) The PRINT statement to print the values of specific variables.
    (b) The STOP statement to allow us to insert instructions during program execution.
    (c) The trace facilities TRON and TROFF.
21. A program should be saved on disk immediately after it is typed into the computer. Should the program be inadvertently lost from memory, it can be easily retrieved from disk by the LOAD command.
22. Any information stored on disk is stored as a file. A file is a collection of related items. A program stored on disk is called a program file, a set of related data items stored on disk is called a data file.
23. Each file must be saved under a unique filename which must conform to a number of rules.
24. A data file can be broken down into records, a record can be further broken down into fields.

Questions and Exercises

1. Identify the errors, if any, in the following statements. Make the necessary corrections.

(a)
```
2010 READ X,Y,Z
2090 DATA 2.5,4,6.7,8
```
(b)
```
2010 READ X,Y,Z
2090 DATA 2,8.15
```
(c)
```
2010 READ M$;W$
2090 DATA "Monday","Wednesday"
```
(d)
```
2010 READ 10.2,4,89
2090 DATA X,Y,Z
```
(e)
```
2010 READ T$,T
2090 DATA "TAX",T
```
(f)
```
2010 READ X,Y,Z
2090 DATA 10,10,10
```
(g)
```
2010 READ C$,P
2090 DATA "Roxvale";15000
```
(h)
```
2010 READ SALES
2090 DATA 2,000.00
```

2. The two programs listed below produce unexpected results. What output does the computer print when you RUN each program? Why does the computer produce the results that it does? Supply your own data in response to the INPUT statements.

(a)
```
2010 PRINT
2020 INPUT "Please enter the retail price--",PRICE
2030 TAX = PRICE*RATE/100
2040 PRINT
2050 PRINT "The sales tax is:";TAX
2060 END
```
(b)
```
2010 PRINT
2020 PRINT "Student's name";SNAME$
2030 INPUT "Student's score";SCORE
2040 PRINT
2050 PRINT SNAME$;"    ";SCORE
2060 END
```

3. Identify the errors in the statements and responses shown below. Make the necessary corrections.

(a)
```
2010 PRINT "Are there more names to sort?"
2020 INPUT "Enter y or n--",RESPONSE
RUN
```
```
Are there more names to sort?
Enter y or n--[y]
```
(b)
```
2010 INPUT "Enter the depositor's name";DNAME$
RUN
```
```
Enter the depositor's name--[Roslyn Peters]
```

(c)
```
2010 INPUT "Current expenses";EXPENSES
RUN
```

```
Current expenses? $1500
```

(d)
```
2010 INPUT "Do you wish to try again (y/n)",RESPONSE$
RUN
```

```
Do you wish to try again (y/n)? y
```

4. Code statements that produce the following prompts.

(a) `What is the rate of commission? 15`
(b) `Invalid response. Enter TRUE or FALSE--TRUE`
(c) `Would you like another question (y/n)? n`

5. Indicate the errors in the programs shown below. Make the necessary corrections then RUN each program.

(a)
```
2010 READ NUMBER.TESTS
2020 READ SNAME$,SCORE1,SCORE2,SCORE3
2030   IF SNAME$ = "End of file" THEN 2060
2040   TOTAL.SCORE = SCORE1+SCORE2+SCORE3
2050   AVERAGE.SCORE = TOTAL.SCORE/NUMBER.TESTS
2060   PRINT
2070   PRINT "Name:";SNAME$
2080   PRINT "Scores:";SCORE1;SCORE2;SCORE3
2090   PRINT "Average score:";AVERAGE.SCORE
2100   READ SNAME$,SCORE1,SCORE2,SCORE3
2110 DATA "Edward Hull",66,74,82
2120 DATA "Jody Reimer",74,82,69
2130 DATA "Alan Penner",84,80,85
2140 END
```

(b)
```
2010 PRINT
2020 PRINT "Number of hours",HOURS
2030 INPUT "Rate of pay, deductions",RATE,DEDUCTIONS
2040 GROSS.PAY = HOURS*RATE
2050 NET.PAY = GROSS.PAY-DEDUCTION
2060 PRINT
2070 PRINT "Gross pay:";GROSS.PAY
2080 PRINT "Net pay:";NET.PAY
2090 END
```

6. What is a loop?

7. What is a trailer value? How is it used to terminate the entering of data into a computer?

8. Each of the following contains a syntax error, a run-time error, or a logic error. State the category of each error.

(a) `2010 A+B = C`

(b) `2010 M = "Michelle"`

(c)
```
2010 PRINT A,B
2020 READ A,B
2030 DATA 7,12
```

(d) `S = T+1`

(e) An incorrect formula

(f)
```
2010 DATA 4,9
2020 READ A,B,C
```

(g) `2010 INPUT "Two names";N1,N2`

9. A salesperson receives a commission of 5% on the first $3000 of sales and 8% on the excess. In addition, the salesperson receives a salary of $200. Assume the salesperson's total sales amounts to $5000. Debug the following program so that it produces the output shown. The program contains an error in logic.

```
2010 READ BASE,RATE1,RATE2,SALARY,SALES
2020 COMMISSION1 = BASE*RATE1/100
2030 COMMISSION2 = (SALARY-BASE)*RATE2/100
2040 INCOME = COMMISSION1+COMMISSION2+SALARY
2050 PRINT
2060 PRINT "Income:";INCOME
```

```
2070 DATA 3000,5,8,200,5000
2080 END
RUN
```

```
Income: 510
```

10. Identify the errors, if any, in the following filenames. Make the necessary corrections. State the name under which each file is stored (include those corrected).

(a) `QUEST-1`
(b) `QUESTION.BAS1`
(c) `PROB 4A.BAS`
(d) `INPUTT.BAS`
(e) `8.BAS`
(f) `8`

11. Identify the errors in the following commands. Make the necessary corrections.

(a) `SAVE 'B:NET-PAY'`
(b) `LOAD "B:PAYROLL".BAS`
(c) `KILL "B:SALES"`

12. What is a file, a record, a field? Use examples in your definitions.

Programming Problems

Design and code programs for the following problems. A shaded value indicates a response to an INPUT statement. You should save each program on disk and, if required, make a hard copy of the program and its output.

1. A clothing store is offering a discount of 20% on any item purchased during the month of May. Barbara Taylor, a regular customer, purchases a coat originally priced at $180.95. What is the discount on the coat? What is the reduced price of the coat?

```
RUN
```

```
Enter the customer's first name and last name
separated by a space (e.g. John Smith)
Enter the original price

Please enter the customer's name--Barbara Taylor
Original price? 180.95

Discount: 36.19
Reduced price: 144.76
```

2. Suppose you started your first job at age 25 and intend to retire at age 65. What would be the total number of working hours in your lifetime if:

(a) Each year consists of 365 days (no leap years).
(b) You have 130 non-working days in a year. This includes weekends, statutory holidays, and 15 days vacation.
(c) You work seven hours per day.

Formulas:

Number of Years of Work = Retirement Age − Age when Starting

Number of Working Days in a Year = Number of Days in a Year − Number of Non-working Days in a Year

Total Number of Hours = Number of Years of Work × Number of Working Days in a Year × Number of Working Hours per Day

```
RUN
```

```
Age when starting work? 25
Retirement age? 65
```

```
Years of work: 40
Working days per year: 235
Total hours: 65800
```

3. Small disbursements (payments) in a business office are usually paid out of a petty cash fund. In one particular office, such a fund started with $30. If payments of $10.31 and $6.45 were made, what was the total amount paid out? How much cash remains in the fund? Do not use a loop.

```
RUN

Amount of the fund: 30
Please enter the payments
? 10.31
? 6.45

Total payments: 16.76
Remaining cash: 13.24
```

4. Modify the program for Problem 4 in Chapter Three so that you find the interest income from each of four bonds. Assume the values of the bonds are $500, $1000, $5000, and $10 000 and the interest rate is 9%. You will need a loop in this program.

```
RUN

Customer's name? [          ]  <---- Key in your name.

PAR VALUE      INTEREST

 500           45
 1000          90
 5000          450
 10000         900
```

5. A householder's consumption of electricity for the months of January, February, and March is shown below:

Data:

January,1050
February,988 — Month, kilowatt-hours
March,842

If the consumption charge is 3.5 cents per kilowatt-hour, what was the cost of electricity for each month?

```
RUN

Enter the customer's name in lower case (e.g. John Smith)
Customer's name? Rodney Lockhart

ELECTRICITY CONSUMPTION      Rodney Lockhart

MONTH           HOURS        COST

January         1050          36.75
February        988           34.58
March           842           29.47
```

6. Find the amount of increase and the percent of increase in the yearly traveling expenses for each of three salespeople. Compare this year's expenses with those of last year for each salesperson. In the output, 19XX represents a year.

Data:

Earl Reid,8000,8500
Terri Morton,9000,9459 — Name, expenses last year, expenses this year
Jerry Ingram,10400,10868

Formulas:

Increase = Expenses This Year − Expenses Last Year

$$\text{Percent Increase} = \frac{\text{Increase}}{\text{Expenses Last Year}} \times 100$$

RUN

```
Enter the month and year, e.g. September 19XX
Date? July 19XX

EXPENSE REPORT
For Year Ending July 19XX

NAME            LAST YEAR      THIS YEAR      INCREASE       PERCENT

Earl Reid       8000           8500           500            6.25
Terri Morton    9000           9459           459            5.1
Jerry Ingram    10400          10868          468            4.5
```

7. Modify the program for Problem 6 in Chapter Three so that you create three Accounts Receivable accounts. Use the READ and DATA statements to read the records each of which consists of an account number, the customer's name, a credit limit, the date of the last transaction, and the balance due. We consider these records our master file. Enter the current transaction (the date of the transaction, the amount sold, and the payment received) through the keyboard. If there is no sale or payment, enter zero for each. Separate two accounts with a row of hyphens. The master file and the transaction data are given below.

After a record is read and tested for a trailer value, display the record on the screen. In this way, a user of your program will know which account is being updated. Later on, when you have more BASIC at your disposal, you will be able to write a program that searches for a specific account, then allows the user to enter transactions for that account.

This program will be continually modified throughout the book. Therefore, you must save each modified version as well as make a hard copy of each program and its output. To obtain a hard copy of an account scroll away material before the account, and direct the output to the printer (Shift/PrtSc or Print Screen depending on your keyboard). RUN the program again to obtain the output for the next account. In Chapter Eight, you will learn how to freeze an account on the screen so that it can be examined and printed.

Master File:

31001,Diane Fraser,1000,Nov. 12,342.16
31002,Derek Andrews,1000,Nov. 17,821.44 — Account number, customer's name, credit limit, date of last transaction, balance due
31003,Lee Harris,1000,Nov. 21,531.27

Current Transactions:

Account Number	*Date*	*Sale*	*Payment Received*
31001	Nov. 14	$ 59.21	$ 0.00
31002	Nov. 20	532.95	316.52
31003	Nov. 23	0.00	531.27

Partial Output:

```
Transaction for the following account:

 31001    Diane Fraser   Balance on Nov. 12: 342.16   Credit limit: 1000

Enter transaction (date, sale, payment)--Nov. 14,59.21,0

Account number: 31001

Name: Diane Fraser

DATE              DEBIT             CREDIT            BALANCE

Nov. 12                                               342.16
Nov. 14           59.21             0                 401.37
--------------------------------------------------------------

Transaction for the following account:

 31002    Derek Andrews   Balance on Nov. 17: 821.44   Credit limit: 1000

Enter transaction (date, sale, payment)--Nov. 20,532.95,316.52

Account number: 31002

Name: Derek Andrews

DATE              DEBIT             CREDIT            BALANCE

Nov. 17                                               821.44
Nov. 20           532.95            316.52            1037.87
--------------------------------------------------------------
```

Solutions for Exercises

4.1 The READ and DATA Statements

1. (a) The values in the DATA statement must be separated by commas, not semicolons.

```
2090 DATA 17,39,42.89
```

(b) No comma must be placed after the reserved word DATA.

```
2090 DATA 21.41,84,67.05
```

(c) A string must be assigned to a string variable, a number should be assigned to a numeric variable. Either switch the variables or switch the data items.

```
2010 READ N$,N                      or       2010 READ N,N$
2090 DATA "Terri",49.58                      2090 DATA 49.58,"Terri"
```

(d) Nothing is wrong.

(e) Variable D must be a string variable.

```
2010 READ N,D$
```

(f) Nothing is wrong.

2. RUN

```
Buy-Rite Shoes
Total sales for three months: 43000
```

4.2 The INPUT Statement

1. (a) No comma must be coded after the reserved word INPUT.

```
2010 INPUT "What is your name";YNAME$
```

(b) Nothing is wrong.

(c) The item keyed in after the prompt must be a number, not a variable.

```
Hours? 40
```

(d) The prompt in line 2040 must be followed by a comma.

```
2040 INPUT "Enter the salary--",SALARY
```

(e) In the name keyed in, either the comma must be omitted or the name must be enclosed in quotation marks.

```
Name? Brown Susan
```

or

```
Name? "Brown,Susan"
```

(f) The prompt in line 2060 must be followed by a semicolon. The variable must be a string variable.

```
2060 INPUT "Address";ADDRESS$
```

(g) The prompt in the INPUT statement must be enclosed in quotation marks.

```
2070 INPUT "Telephone No.";T$
```

2. (a)

```
2020 INPUT "Rate of commission";RATE
2030 INPUT "Total sales";TOTAL.SALES
```

(b)

```
2020 PRINT "Enter date (month and day, e.g. September 30)"
2030 INPUT "Please enter the date--",DATE1$
```

4.4 Processing Statements Repetitively

1. BASIC is in an infinite loop. The statement continuously transfers control to itself.

2.

```
2010 READ RATE,TIME
2020 PRINT
2030 INPUT "Principal";PRINCIPAL
2040   IF PRINCIPAL = -1 THEN 2110
2050   INTEREST = PRINCIPAL*RATE/100*TIME
2060   PRINT "Interest:";INTEREST
2070   PRINT
2080   INPUT "Principal";PRINCIPAL
2090   GOTO 2040
2100 DATA 9,4
2110 END
```

4.6 Error Detection

The error exists in line 2030. Insert parentheses as follows:

```
2030 PROFIT = (CURRENT.PRICE-INITIAL.PRICE)*NO.SOLD
```

5

STRUCTURED PROGRAMMING AND PROGRAM DESIGN

Objectives

From this chapter, you will learn how to break down a problem into modules. You will learn how to design each module, how to combine the modules to form a complete program, and how to style and document the program. You will become familiar with the term "control structure" and understand that programs are made up of three control structures: the sequence structure, the selection structure, and the loop structure. And, you will learn a different way to repeat instructions by using the WHILE/WEND loop.

Contents

5.1 Structured Programming

Introduction

The memories of early computers were very limited. To conserve memory, programs had to be short and concise which made them difficult to read. It was difficult, also, to find errors and to modify programs at a later date. As a new science, programming was then in its infancy.

Since the appearance of the first computers, prices of computers have decreased while, at the same time, the salaries of programmers have risen. It soon became apparent that programs were becoming expensive to develop because of the amount of time spent on debugging programs that had been poorly written in terms of today's methods and priorities.

In addition, the development and maintenance of software was becoming a major part of the computing industry. A software package may consist of one or several programs. Software maintenance refers to its upkeep; that is, the modification of its program or programs. Software is updated for various reasons some of which are: to reflect new trends, to incorporate improved techniques, to include new product lines, and to include additional customers.

Keeping down the cost of software maintenance is now of prime importance. Thus, it is essential that programmers spend more time planning and designing easily understood programs that can be maintained with a minimal amount of effort. The major task of program development is now program design.

The older approach in developing a program is being replaced by a method known as structured programming. The emphasis in structured programming is on well-organized, clear, and logical steps. Structured programming should include the features discussed below.

Modules

A program should be broken down into a hierarchy of modules. Each module performs a specific function. A utility module describes the purpose of the program and defines the variables. The main module calls upon submodules to perform the tasks and, depending on the program, allows the user to call the submodules as often as desired. A submodule performs a specific task. If a task in one of the submodules is too complex, the submodule may call a lower module to perform a more detailed task.

Suppose we wish to break down the net pay program written in Chapter Four. In addition to the utility module and the main module, we could include a module that INPUTs the date, one that prints the headings, one that takes in the data, and another that performs the calculations and prints the results. Each module must be well designed and all modules must be combined in such a way that the program remains clear and simple.

A program comprised of modules is simpler to develop and modify. Since each module performs a unique task, modules can be developed separately. Furthermore, when the program needs modification, only a particular module (or a group of related modules) requires change.

Control Structures

A block of statements that governs the flow of control in a program is known as a control structure. There are three elementary control structures. We can use one of these structures or combinations of the three to solve any programming problem. The three control structures are shown in Figure 5-1.

FIGURE 5-1 CONTROL STRUCTURES

The sequence structure.

One instruction follows another.

```
PRINT HEADINGS
   Display instructions
   INPUT date
   Print main heading
   Print subheading
   Print column headings
```

The loop structure.

A sequence of instructions that is repeated as long as a particular condition exists.

```
PERFORM CALCULATIONS
  INPUT sale
    Sale = Trailer value? If true, end loop
    Calculate commission
    Print commission
    INPUT sale
    Repeat loop
```

The selection (decision) structure.

Selects one of two alternatives depending on a certain condition.

```
PERFORM CALCULATIONS
  INPUT sale
  If sale is greater than 500 then rate = 15
     else rate = 12
  Calculate commission
  Print commission
```

We are already familiar with the first two control structures. The selection structure is slightly different than the one we used in Chapter Four. Here, BASIC selects one of two alternatives depending on whether the condition in the IF part of the statement is true or false. We will be discussing this structure in the next chapter.

If a program contains modules, the modules themselves are made up of one or more of the above structures. Each structure must have a single entry point and a single exit point. Entry must be at the beginning of the structure, exit must be at the end of the structure.

Documentation and Writing Style

It is important that we use REM statements to clarify a program. This clarification is a form of program documentation called internal documentation. The other form of documentation, called external documentation, consists of support material prepared outside the program. External documentation is discussed in Chapter Fourteen.

A program well documented by REM statements is easier to modify should the program require change at a later date. Recall that BASIC does not execute a REM statement, however, it does display the statement when the program is listed. As mentioned in Chapter Three, we use REM statements to state the purpose of the program, to define the variables, to describe major routines, and to comment on statements or logic that may be obscure to the reader.

The style in which a program is written is also important in structured programming. The style must be such that it improves program readability. REM statements can be centred between rows of asterisks (or some other symbol) while other statements may be highlighted by indenting them several spaces. Methods used to document and style a program vary, different organizations and instructors set different standards. Still, the main goal in structured programming is to reduce the complexity of programs and thus increase their clarity.

Reducing complex programs to a series of less complex and manageably-sized modules improves readability. However, structured programming is not merely a process of segmenting a program into modules. It is an analysis and design process that starts with the analysis of the problem. Structured programming is a composite skill that includes the following aspects of programming.

1. Well planned modules.
2. The best choice of a control structure for a particular operation.
3. Simple linkages between all parts of a program.
4. Documentation and a style of coding that enhances clarity.

Exercises

1. What is meant by software maintenance?
2. State two reasons for modularizing a program.
3. What are the three control structures?
4. What important concept must be incorporated in a control structure?
5. What is structured programming?

5.2 Program Modularizing

A Sample Program

The program designed in Chapter Four is rewritten below in modularized form. Since we are not yet familiar with the WHILE/WEND loop, just one record will be processed. The program is broken down into six modules, each beginning with a descriptive comment enclosed in two rows of asterisks. These modules are:

1. The utility module.
2. The main module.
3. The module that INPUTs the date.
4. The module that prints the headings.
5. The module that reads a record.
6. The module that performs the calculations and prints the detail line.

We will refer to the main module as our main routine and to submodules as subroutines. The program begins with the utility module. This is followed by the main routine which calls three subroutines: the subroutine that INPUTs the date, the subroutine that prints the headings, and the subroutine that reads a record. Subroutine READ A RECORD calls the subroutine that performs the calculations and prints the detail line.

Between a calling module and the called module there must be a two-way communication link. This link is obtained by a GOSUB statement which calls a subroutine and a RETURN statement which returns control to the calling module. The GOSUB and RETURN statements are explained in detail beneath the program listing.

```
1000 'NET PAY                          M. MCRITCHIE                         MAR 3
1002 '*********************************************************************
1004 '          THIS PROGRAM CALCULATES THE NET PAY FOR ONE EMPLOYEE
1006 '*********************************************************************
1010 'DATE1$       - DATE
1020 'ENAME$       - EMPLOYEE NAME
1030 'RATE         - RATE OF PAY
1040 'HOURS        - HOURS OF WORK
1050 'INCOME.TAX - INCOME TAX DEDUCTION
1060 'UNION        - UNION DUES
1070 'PENSION      - PENSION DEDUCTION
1080 'GROSS.PAY    - GROSS PAY
1090 'DEDUCTIONS - TOTAL DEDUCTIONS
1100 'NET.PAY      - NET PAY
2000 '*********************************************************************
2002 '                                  MAIN ROUTINE
2004 '*********************************************************************
2010   GOSUB 3000                    'INPUT data
2020   GOSUB 4000                    'Print headings
2030   GOSUB 5000                    'Read a record
2040   END
3000 '*********************************************************************
3002 '                               INPUT DATA (DATE)
3004 '*********************************************************************
3010   PRINT
3020   PRINT "Enter the date (month and day, e.g. September 30)"
```

```
3030  INPUT "Date";DATE1$
3040  RETURN
4000 '*********************************************************************
4002 '                            PRINT HEADINGS
4004 '*********************************************************************
4010  PRINT
4020  PRINT "PAYROLL REPORT"
4030  PRINT "Week Ending ";DATE1$
4040  PRINT
4050  PRINT "NAME","HOURS","GROSS PAY","DEDUCTIONS","NET PAY"
4060  PRINT
4070  RETURN
5000 '*********************************************************************
5002 '                            READ A RECORD
5004 '*********************************************************************
5010  READ ENAME$,RATE,HOURS,INCOME.TAX,UNION,PENSION
5020  GOSUB 6000              'Perform calculations
5030  DATA "Darryl Brown",9.54,38,74.57,2.25,3.67
5040  RETURN
6000 '*********************************************************************
6002 '                         PERFORM CALCULATIONS
6004 '*********************************************************************
6010  GROSS.PAY = HOURS*RATE
6020  DEDUCTIONS = INCOME.TAX+UNION+PENSION
6030  NET.PAY = GROSS.PAY-DEDUCTIONS
6040  PRINT ENAME$,HOURS,GROSS.PAY,DEDUCTIONS,NET.PAY
6050  RETURN
65529 'End of program listing
RUN
```

```
Enter the date (month and day, e.g. September 30)
Date? October 17

PAYROLL REPORT
Week Ending October 17

NAME            HOURS            GROSS PAY       DEDUCTIONS      NET PAY

Darryl Brown    38               362.52          80.49           282.03
```

Note that the modules are numbered in blocks of line numbers, in multiples of 1000. The line numbers in the utility module are in the 1000 block, the line numbers in the main routine are in the 2000 block, etc. This serves to highlight the separateness of the modules. The program ends with the REM statement **65529 'End of program listing**. We use line number 65529 as this is the highest line number allowed in BASIC.

The GOSUB and RETURN Statements

To call a subroutine, we use the instruction **GOSUB** xxxx where xxxx is the line number of the first statement in the called subroutine. GOSUB is an abbreviated form of GO to SUBroutine. The main routine must end with an END statement and each subroutine must end with a RETURN statement. RETURN causes BASIC to return to the statement immediately following the GOSUB that referenced the subroutine. The sequence of statements that interfaces (links) the main routine with Subroutine INPUT DATA is illustrated in Figure 5-2.

FIGURE 5-2 INTERFACING MODULES

```
 ----
 2010  GOSUB 3000        'INPUT data ---------+
>2020  GOSUB 4000        'Print headings      |
 2030  GOSUB 5000        'Read a record       |
 2040  END                                    |
 3000 '****************************************<
 3002 '                INPUT DATA (DATE)
 3004 '****************************************
 ----
 3040   RETURN
```

GOSUB 3000 in the main routine calls the subroutine that begins with line 3000. This is Subroutine INPUT DATA. BASIC breaks away from the main routine and executes this subroutine. When BASIC encounters the RETURN statement in line 3040, it returns to the main routine, specifically to line 2020, the statement following the GOSUB that called Subroutine INPUT DATA. Thus, a link between the main routine and Subroutine INPUT DATA has been established.

The main routine now calls Subroutine PRINT HEADINGS. BASIC executes this subroutine and returns to statement 2030 in the main routine. This is a GOSUB statement that calls Subroutine READ A RECORD. When BASIC returns from this subroutine, statement 2040 is executed. This is the END statement which ends the program.

It is important that the main routine ends with an END statement and that each subroutine ends with a RETURN. Suppose we left out 2040 END. After executing subroutines 3000, 4000, and 5000 and returning to the main routine, BASIC would drop into Subroutine INPUT DATA and execute it once more. When it encounters the RETURN statement in Subroutine INPUT DATA, BASIC would display the error message **RETURN without GOSUB in 3040**. The message is displayed because, this time, the subroutine has not been called. Something similar happens when we do not end a subroutine with a RETURN. BASIC drops into the next subroutine instead of returning to the calling module. The above error message would not be printed since BASIC is already within a call.

The program on page 84 illustrates that we can call a subroutine from another subroutine. Statement 5020 in Subroutine READ A RECORD calls Subroutine PERFORM CALCULATIONS. When BASIC encounters RETURN in line 6050, it returns to line 5030 of Subroutine READ A RECORD then drops down to line 5040. This is a RETURN statement which returns control to the main routine.

There is one more item that must be pointed out. Except for a particular type of variable in a user-defined function, variables in a BASIC program are global. User-defined functions are discussed in Chapter Fourteen. This means that variables can be referenced by any module. Although a subroutine is considered a discrete unit, the values it uses can be shared by the main routine and by all other subroutines. Thus, if the value of a variable changes in a module, the change is reflected in any module that references the variable. We must exercise care when changing the value of a variable, since the change may cause an unexpected result in another module when both modules use the same variable.

Documenting and Styling a Program

As mentioned earlier, standards for documentation and writing style are usually determined by the organization for whom programming is done. The documentation and the writing style of the program on page 84 are merely examples. However, all programs must include documentation which may be any or all of the following:

1. A brief description of the program.
2. A variable dictionary in which variables are defined.
3. A brief description of each module.
4. Comments that explain statements or logic that may be obscure to the reader.

In our program, the entire utility module is made up of REM statements. We reserve lines 1000 to 1009 to name and describe the program. The first statement gives the name of the program, the name of the author, and the date the program was written. A brief description of the program follows. To highlight the description, we enclose the documentation in two lines of asterisks. You may wish to use some other styling feature. Notice that the description is centred. The remaining statements in the utility module define the variables used in the program. The variables are listed in order of use starting with DATE1$ in line 1010. Some programmers list them in alphabetical order. The list is referred to as a variable dictionary.

Each of the remaining modules begins with a brief description centred between two rows of asterisks. When a subroutine is called, we append a REM to the GOSUB statement in order to identify the called subroutine. Recall that only an "apostrophe" REM may trail a statement. The documentation of a subroutine is illustrated below. The subroutine we chose is Subroutine READ A RECORD in which a GOSUB statement calls another subroutine.

```
5000 '**********************************************************************
5002 '                            READ A RECORD
5004 '**********************************************************************
5010  READ ENAME$,RATE,HOURS,INCOME.TAX,UNION,PENSION
5020  GOSUB 6000                  'Perform calculations
5030  DATA "Darryl Brown",9.54,38,74.57,2.25,3.67
5040  RETURN
```

Although the program processes just one record, it serves to illustrate several features of structured programming: program modularization, documentation and writing style. These concepts are especially important, not only now in this program, but later on when programs become larger and more complex. Programs written in this manner are much easier to develop, to understand, and to modify.

Program Maintenance

Programs, particularly those in commercial software packages, rarely remain the same. New product lines, new customers, new techniques to solve the same problem, a new model of computer are some of the reasons why programs must be changed. Recall that updating programs is referred to as program maintenance. Program maintenance is now a major part of the computer software industry. Hence, it is important that programs be written in such a way that they can be easily modified. Using structured programming techniques to develop a program helps reduce the time and effort spent in maintaining the program. Usually, only a particular module or a number of related modules needs to be changed.

An example of program maintenance is the NET PAY program first designed in Chapter Three. The program is continually updated by the inclusion of currently learned concepts. This process is also applied to the Accounts Receivable program started in Chapter Three. Another exercise in program maintenance will be a project which begins in Chapter Seven after you have learned how to store data on disk. The project is based on an inventory problem.

Exercises

1. Briefly explain the communication link between a calling module and the called module (subroutine).
2. What is a global variable?
3. What is the purpose of a utility module?
4. Identify the errors in the following program segments. Make the necessary corrections.

(a)
```
2000 'MAIN ROUTINE
2010   GOSUB 3000                      'Print headings
2020   GOSUB 4000                      'Read data
3000 'SUBROUTINE PRINT HEADINGS
3010   PRINT
3020   PRINT "MONTH","DAY","YEAR"
3030   PRINT
3040   RETURN
```

(b)
```
4000 'SUBROUTINE READ DATA
4010   READ SALES,COST,EXPENSES
4020   GOSUB 5000                      'Perform calculations
4030   DATA 50000,30000,5000
```

(c)
```
5000 'SUBROUTINE PERFORM CALCULATIONS
5010   INTEREST = PRINCIPAL*RATE/100*TIME
5020   PRINT PRINCIPAL,RATE,TIME,INTEREST
5030   END
```

5. In addition to income tax, union dues, and pension fees, a medical insurance payment in the amount of $12.45 must also be deducted from an employee's gross pay. Modify Subroutine READ A RECORD and Subroutine PERFORM CALCULATIONS on page 85 to reflect this change.

5.3 The WHILE/WEND Loop

Let us now learn a different loop structure: the WHILE/WEND loop. Listed below is the loop structure we used in Chapter Four, alongside it is the WHILE/WEND loop.

The IF/THEN . . . GOTO Loop

```
2010 READ RATE
2020 PRINT
```

The WHILE/WEND Loop

```
2010 READ RATE
2020 PRINT
```

```
2030 INPUT "Sale";SALE
2040   IF SALE = -1 THEN 2100
2050   COMMISSION = SALE*RATE/100
2060   PRINT "Commission:";COMMISSION
2070   INPUT "Sale";SALE
2080   GOTO 2040
2090 DATA 15
2100 END
RUN
```

```
Sale? 1000
Commission: 150
Sale? 2000
Commission: 300
Sale? 3000
Commission: 450
Sale? -1
```

```
2030 INPUT "Sale";SALE
2040 WHILE SALE <> -1
2050   COMMISSION = SALE*RATE/100
2060   PRINT "Commission:";COMMISSION
2070   INPUT "Sale";SALE
2080 WEND
2090 DATA 15
2100 END
RUN
```

```
Sale? 1000
Commission: 150
Sale? 2000
Commission: 300
Sale? 3000
Commission: 450
Sale? -1
```

We will first trace through the logic of the WHILE/WEND loop and then compare the two loop structures.

The WHILE/WEND loop must begin with a WHILE statement and end with a WEND statement. Inside the loop, we place the statements that need to be executed several times. These are indicated above by a bracket. The statements are considered the body of the loop and are indented at least two spaces to highlight the loop.

The WHILE statement contains the condition. As in the IF/THEN statement, the condition is either true or false. As long as the condition is true, the statements inside the loop are executed. The WEND statement transfers control back to the WHILE statement thus forming a loop. When the condition in the WHILE statement becomes false, BASIC drops out of the loop and executes the statement following the WEND. If the condition is false initially, the body of the loop is bypassed entirely.

In line 2010, we read in a rate. Line 2030 allows us to key in the first sale, 1000, making the value of SALE equal to 1000. The INPUT statement that accepts this value must be placed before the loop so that SALE contains a data item before BASIC enters the loop. BASIC now enters the WHILE/WEND loop.

The WHILE statement compares the value of SALE with -1, our trailer value. The symbol "<>", which means "is not equal to", is the relational operator. We leave a space before and a space after the operator for the sake of clarity. Since SALE is not equal to -1, the condition in the WHILE statement is true and BASIC executes the three statements inside the loop. The third statement within the loop (line 2070) allows us to key in another sale. We now type in 2000. The WEND statement transfers control back to the WHILE. Again, the value of SALE is compared with -1. Since SALE (whose value is now 2000) is not equal to -1, BASIC re-executes the statements inside the loop.

This procedure continues until we key in a -1. As in the program that uses the IF/THEN . . . GOTO structure, the trailer value must be some illogical value for the program being written and is entered as the last value to signal the end of the data. When the WHILE statement compares SALE (whose value is now -1) with -1, the values are equal. Because the condition in the WHILE statement is false, BASIC drops out of the loop and executes the END statement in line 2100.

In the IF/THEN . . . GOTO structure, the GOTO statement gives us a very simple tool to create a loop. We simply transfer control to a previous statement. Because of its simplicity, we chose this type of loop to introduce you to the concept of looping. However, the loop requires an exit point and this is why we inserted the IF/THEN statement.

Let us now compare the two loop structures. The IF statement in the IF/THEN . . . GOTO loop is similar to the WHILE statement in the WHILE/WEND loop. Both statements terminate the loop when SALE is equal to -1. The GOTO and WEND statements also perform similar functions. Both transfer control to a control statement. The GOTO statement transfers control to the IF/THEN, the WEND statement transfers control to the WHILE.

Both structures follow the structured programming rule: one entry point, one exit. Since we wish to minimize the use of the GOTO statement, we will use the WHILE/WEND loop wherever possible. Another loop structure that needs no GOTO statement will be introduced in Chapter Ten.

As with the IF/THEN statement, the WHILE statement can compare strings. Suppose we are assigning names to ENAME$, one name at a time inside a WHILE/WEND loop, and suppose we use "End" as our trailer value.

The WHILE statement will now be

```
2040 WHILE ENAME$ <> "End"
```

The trailer value End must be enclosed in quotation marks. If our data consists of records and each record contains several fields, we must choose one of the fields as our comparison field. Assume each record contains an employee's name, rate of pay, hours of work, income tax deduction, union dues, and pension deduction. If we choose the name field as our comparison field and "End of file" as our trailer value, the WHILE statement will be

```
2040 WHILE ENAME$ <> "End of file"
```

Exercise

Write a program segment that INPUTs four records each of which consists of a student's name and three scores. Find the average score for each student. Assign the number of tests to a variable. Use a WHILE/WEND loop. Use the following formula to find the total score:

Total Score = Score 1 + Score 2 + Score 3

5.4 Comparing An Unstructured Program with a Structured Program

Two programs are written below; the first unstructured, the second structured. Both programs INPUT a rate of pay and read in three records each of which contains an employee's name, the number of pieces produced, and the payroll deductions. The programs find the gross pay and the net pay for each employee. The output produced by both programs is as follows:

```
Rate of pay? 9.24

Lee Butler     452.76          44.73          408.03
Brian Lewis    471.24          47.99          423.25
Ann Morton     489.72          54.93          434.79
```

The Unstructured Program

```
1000 PRINT
1010 INPUT "Rate of pay";RATE
1020 PRINT
1030 READ ENAME$,PIECES,DEDUCTIONS
1040 GOTO 1090
1050 GROSS.WAGES = PIECES*RATE
1060 NET.WAGES = GROSS.WAGES-DEDUCTIONS
1070 PRINT ENAME$,GROSS.WAGES,DEDUCTIONS,NET.WAGES
1080 GOTO 1030
1090 IF ENAME$ = "End of file" THEN 1150
1100 GOTO 1050
1110 DATA "Lee Butler" ,49,44.73
1120 DATA "Brian Lewis",51,47.99
1130 DATA "Ann Morton" ,53,54.93
1140 DATA "End of file", 0,0
1150 END
```

The Structured Program

```
1000 'PIECE WORK                          M. MCRITCHIE                          Mar 14
1002 '*************************************************************************
1004 '              THIS PROGRAM FINDS NET WAGES BASED ON PIECE WORK
1006 '*************************************************************************
```

```
1010 'RATE         - RATE OF PAY
1020 'ENAME$       - EMPLOYEE NAME
1030 'PIECES       - NUMBER OF PIECES PRODUCED
1040 'DEDUCTIONS   - DEDUCTIONS
1050 'GROSS.WAGES  - GROSS WAGES
1060 'NET.WAGES    - NET WAGES
2000 '*******************************************************************
2002 '                         MAIN ROUTINE
2004 '*******************************************************************
2010  GOSUB 3000                    'INPUT data
2020  GOSUB 4000                    'Read data
2030  END
3000 '*******************************************************************
3002 '                      INPUT DATA (RATE)
3004 '*******************************************************************
3010  PRINT
3020  INPUT "Rate of pay";RATE
3030  PRINT
3040  RETURN
4000 '*******************************************************************
4002 '                         READ DATA
4004 '*******************************************************************
4010  READ ENAME$,PIECES,DEDUCTIONS
4020  WHILE ENAME$ <> "End of file"
4030    GOSUB 5000                            'Perform calculations
4040    READ ENAME$,PIECES,DEDUCTIONS
4050  WEND
4060  DATA "Lee Butler" ,49,44.73
4070  DATA "Brian Lewis",51,47.99
4080  DATA "Ann Morton" ,53,54.93
4090  DATA "End of file", 0, 0
4100  RETURN
5000 '*******************************************************************
5002 '                     PERFORM CALCULATIONS
5004 '*******************************************************************
5010  GROSS.WAGES = PIECES*RATE
5020  NET.WAGES = GROSS.WAGES-DEDUCTIONS
5030  PRINT ENAME$,GROSS.WAGES,DEDUCTIONS,NET.WAGES
5040  RETURN
65529 'End of program listing
```

The unstructured program is more difficult to read. There are several reasons:

1. The program is not modularized.
2. There is no documentation.
3. The indiscriminate use of the GOTO statement makes it difficult to follow the logic and to find the loop.
4. The program is not styled.

The structured program is longer than the unstructured one, the result of modularization and documentation. However, the structured program is easier to understand. In our programs, we give program clarity first priority. You will find this particularly helpful when it comes to maintaining a program.

Exercise

Rewrite the following program in structured form.

```
1000 PRINT
1010 GOTO 1080
1020 PRINT
1030 IF PRINCIPAL = -1 THEN 1130
```

```
1040 INTEREST = PRINCIPAL*RATE/100*YEARS
1050 NEW.PRINCIPAL = PRINCIPAL+INTEREST
1060 GOTO 1100
1070 PRINT
1080 INPUT "Principal, rate, years";PRINCIPAL,RATE,YEARS
1090 GOTO 1030
1100 PRINT "Interest:";INTEREST
1110 PRINT "New principal:";NEW.PRINCIPAL
1120 GOTO 1070
1130 END
RUN
```

```
Principal, rate, years? 1000,10,2
Interest: 200
New principal: 1200

Principal, rate, years? 1000,9,2
Interest: 180
New principal: 1180

Principal, rate, years? -1,0,0
```

5.5 Program Design

Let us now modify the program on page 84 so that it processes more than one record. We will be using a WHILE/WEND loop. Here is the problem once more.

The ABC Computer Company employs four people. Write a program that produces a payroll report entitled PAYROLL REPORT. Find each employee's gross pay, total payroll deductions, and net pay. INPUT the month and day and display the date in a subheading; such as, Week Ending October 17. The data is given below.

Data:

Darryl Brown,9.54,38,74.57,2.25,3.67
Ellen Miller,8.87,39,72.14,2.25,3.42
Lorne Hayes,9.88,42,79.84,2.25,4.15
Andrea Jones,10.04,47,85.26,2.25,6.31

— Employee name, rate of pay, hours of work, income tax deduction, union dues, pension deduction

Your program must produce the following output.

```
         10        20        30        40        50        60
123456789012345678901234567890123456789012345678901234567890123

Enter the date (month and day, e.g. September 30)
Date? October 17

PAYROLL REPORT
Week Ending October 17

NAME            HOURS           GROSS PAY       DEDUCTIONS      NET PAY

Darryl Brown     38              362.52          80.49           282.03
Ellen Miller     39              345.93          77.81           268.12
Lorne Hayes      42              414.96          86.24           328.72
Andrea Jones     47              471.88          93.82           378.06
```

FIGURE 5-3 STRUCTURE CHART

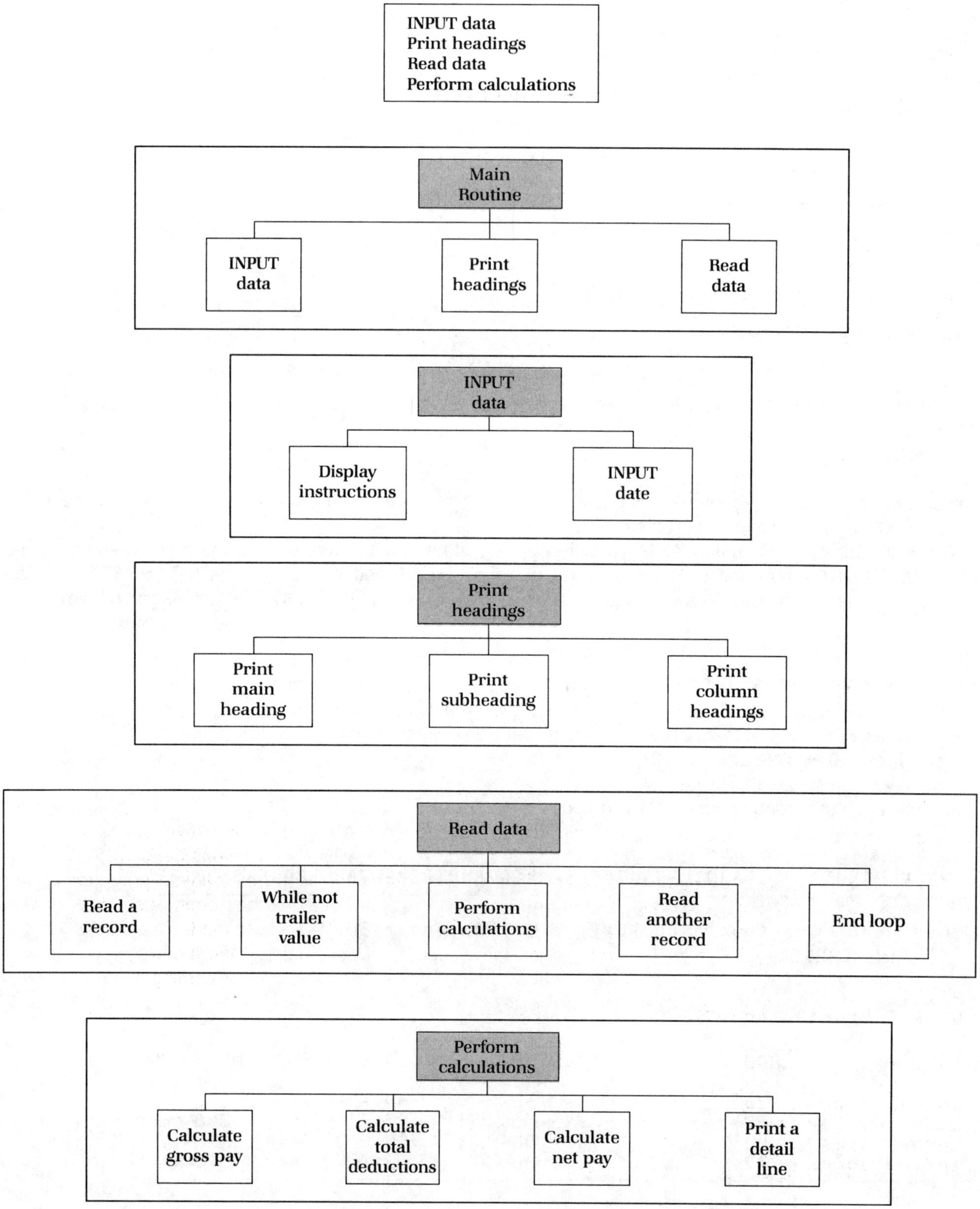

FIGURE 5-4 PSEUDOCODE

MAJOR TASKS	
INPUT data	
Print headings	
Read data	
Perform calculations	

MAIN ROUTINE	
INPUT data	(subroutine)
Print headings	(subroutine)
Read data	(subroutine)

INPUT DATA	
Display instructions	
INPUT date	DATE1$

PRINT HEADINGS	
Print main heading	
Print subheading	
Print column headings	

READ DATA	
Read a record	ENAME$,RATE,HOURS,INCOME.TAX,UNION,PENSION
While not trailer value	
Perform calculations	(subroutine)
Read another record	
End loop	
Data records	

PERFORM CALCULATIONS	
Calculate gross pay	GROSS.PAY
Calculate total deductions	DEDUCTIONS
Calculate net pay	NET.PAY
Print a detail line	

In both modes of design, each extension is considered a module. Note that the list of tasks in the Main Routine does not include Perform calculations as this module is called from module Read data.

We will now develop the program module by module. The output for each intermediate program is given beneath a listing. An intermediate program is one in which the current module has been appended to those already typed and tested. Intermediate programs become longer and longer as more modules are appended.

As a beginning programmer, it is strongly urged that you develop programs by the module. It is also wise to save each intermediate program. After you have gained some experience in programming, you may decide to type in and test more than one module at a time.

THE MAIN ROUTINE

```
1000 'NET PAY                          M. MCRITCHIE                        MAR 16
1002 '***********************************************************************
1004 '   THIS PROGRAM CALCULATES THE NET PAY FOR EACH OF SEVERAL EMPLOYEES
1006 '***********************************************************************
1010 'DATE1$      - DATE
```

```
1020 'ENAME$       - EMPLOYEE NAME
1030 'RATE         - RATE OF PAY
1040 'HOURS        - HOURS OF WORK
1050 'INCOME.TAX - INCOME TAX DEDUCTION
1060 'UNION        - UNION DUES
1070 'PENSION      - PENSION DEDUCTION
1080 'GROSS.PAY   - GROSS PAY
1090 'DEDUCTIONS - TOTAL DEDUCTIONS
1100 'NET.PAY      - NET PAY
2000 '*********************************************************************
2002 '                                  MAIN ROUTINE
2004 '*********************************************************************
2010  GOSUB 3000                    'INPUT data
2020  GOSUB 4000                    'Print headings
2030  GOSUB 5000                    'Read data
2040  END
3000 'SUBROUTINE INPUT DATA
3010   PRINT "INPUT data"
3020   RETURN
4000 'SUBROUTINE PRINT HEADINGS
4010   PRINT "Print headings"
4020   RETURN
5000 'SUBROUTINE READ DATA
5010   PRINT "Read data"
5020   RETURN
65529 'End of program listing
RUN
```

```
INPUT data
Print headings
Read data
```

After describing the program, we key in the variable dictionary. We can either scan through our structure chart and name variables as we come across instructions that require variables or find the names in our pseudocode.

Notice that we must append skeleton subroutines to the main routine, one for GOSUB 3000, another for GOSUB 4000, and the third for GOSUB 5000. If we do not include statements 3000, 4000, and 5000 in our program, a RUN would produce the error message **Undefined line number in xxxx** where xxxx is the line number of a GOSUB statement. Of course, we must end each skeleton subroutine with a RETURN.

Immediately after keying in the module and the skeleton subroutines, we must save the program on disk. Should our program be inadvertently destroyed or if we did not have time to continue, there is no need for concern when the program is safely stored. To save the program, let us use filename MAIN.BAS (for main routine). Our save command will be SAVE "B:MAIN.BAS". Suppose we did not have time to continue and that we saved the program and turned off the computer. Our program is lost from memory. Since we saved the program on disk, we can retrieve the program by using the command LOAD "B:MAIN.BAS".

If you did not obtain the above output, debug your program and resave the modified version under the same filename. Using the same filename in your SAVE command causes the former file to be overwritten. The output serves as a reminder that we have at least three more modules to key in and test. The skeleton subroutines produce these reminders.

Let us now append module INPUT data to the program developed so far.

INPUT DATA

```
3000 '*********************************************************************
3002 '                              INPUT DATA (DATE)
3004 '*********************************************************************
3010  PRINT
3020  PRINT "Enter the date (month and day, e.g. September 30)"
3030  INPUT "Date";DATE1$
3040  RETURN
RUN
```

```
Enter the date (month and day, e.g. September 30)
Date? October 17
Print headings
Read data
```

We have created a specific subroutine to INPUT data, in this case we INPUT the date. Any data entered by means of the INPUT statement should be keyed in before a report is printed, otherwise the prompts and the keyed-in data may be interspersed with the lines of the report. In many of our programs that print reports, values will be entered through the keyboard. It will be a simple matter to code these INPUT statements in a subroutine set aside for this purpose.

The reminder "INPUT data" in our previous output is replaced by the instruction and the prompt for the date. The reminder is replaced because the PRINT statement in the skeleton subroutine has been replaced by the PRINT and INPUT statements of the above module. Notice that our program continues to display "Print headings" and "Read data" as reminders that these modules must still be keyed in.

We now have three modules stored in the computer: the utility module, the main routine, and Subroutine INPUT DATA all linked together to form an intermediate program. Let us save this intermediate program on disk under filename INPUTT.BAS. It is a good idea to save each intermediate program under a new filename in case we need a former one. When the program is completely written, we can clean up our BASIC diskette by removing all intermediate programs.

PRINT HEADINGS

```
4000 '**************************************************************************
4002 '                              PRINT HEADINGS
4004 '**************************************************************************
4010  PRINT
4020  PRINT "PAYROLL REPORT"
4030  PRINT "Week Ending ";DATE1$
4040  PRINT
4050  PRINT "NAME","HOURS","GROSS PAY","DEDUCTIONS","NET PAY"
4060  PRINT
4070  RETURN
RUN
```

```
Enter the date (month and day, e.g. September 30)
Date? October 17

PAYROLL REPORT
Week Ending October 17

NAME          HOURS          GROSS PAY     DEDUCTIONS     NET PAY

Read data
```

The reminder "Print headings" in our previous output is replaced by the actual headings. The only reminder left is "Read data". Save this intermediate program under filename PRINTT.BAS.

READ DATA

```
5000 '**************************************************************************
5002 '                                READ DATA
5004 '**************************************************************************
5010  READ ENAME$,RATE,HOURS,INCOME.TAX,UNION,PENSION
5020  WHILE ENAME$ <> "End of file"
5030    GOSUB 6000                          'Perform calculations
5040    READ ENAME$,RATE,HOURS,INCOME.TAX,UNION,PENSION
5050  WEND
5060  DATA "Darryl Brown",9.54 ,38,74.57,2.25,3.67
5070  DATA "Ellen Miller",8.87 ,39,72.14,2.25,3.42
5080  DATA "Lorne Hayes" ,9.88 ,42,79.84,2.25,4.15
5090  DATA "Andrea Jones",10.04,47,85.26,2.25,6.31
5100  DATA "End of file" ,0,0,0,0,0
5110  RETURN
6000 'SUBROUTINE PERFORM CALCULATIONS
6010   PRINT "Perform calculations"
6020   RETURN
```

RUN

```
Enter the date (month and day, e.g. September 30)
Date? October 17

PAYROLL REPORT
Week Ending October 17

NAME           HOURS          GROSS PAY      DEDUCTIONS     NET PAY

Perform calculations
Perform calculations
Perform calculations
Perform calculations
```

As before, we must save our program. Suggested filename: READD.BAS. The reminder "Read data" in our previous output is replaced by the reminder "Perform calculations" displayed four times. BASIC displays this message more than once since the GOSUB that calls skeleton Subroutine PERFORM CALCULATIONS is coded inside a WHILE/WEND loop. Thus, the subroutine is called and the message is displayed until the READ statement encounters the trailer record.

PERFORM CALCULATIONS

```
6000 '***********************************************************************
6002 '                          PERFORM CALCULATIONS
6004 '***********************************************************************
6010  GROSS.PAY = HOURS*RATE
6020  DEDUCTIONS = INCOME.TAX+UNION+PENSION
6030  NET.PAY = GROSS.PAY-DEDUCTIONS
6040  PRINT ENAME$,HOURS,GROSS.PAY,DEDUCTIONS,NET.PAY
6050  RETURN
```

Output will be as shown on page 91. Since this is the last module to write, we have completed the program. As with all the intermediate programs, the program must be saved. A common practice is to use the name of the program as the filename. We could save the program under filename NET-PAY.BAS. The results and any statements that affect the results must now be examined. For instance, we must make certain we keyed in the right data, used the right formulas, and printed the values of the right variables. If changes are made, we must resave the program.

We should also make a hard copy of the program by using the LLIST command and a hard copy of its output by changing all PRINT statements to LPRINT.

Here is the complete program listing.

```
1000 'NET PAY                          M. MCRITCHIE                     MAR 16
1002 '***********************************************************************
1004 '    THIS PROGRAM CALCULATES THE NET PAY FOR EACH OF SEVERAL EMPLOYEES
1006 '***********************************************************************
1010 'DATE1$      - DATE
1020 'ENAME$      - EMPLOYEE NAME
1030 'RATE        - RATE OF PAY
1040 'HOURS       - HOURS OF WORK
1050 'INCOME.TAX  - INCOME TAX DEDUCTION
1060 'UNION       - UNION DUES
1070 'PENSION     - PENSION DEDUCTION
1080 'GROSS.PAY   - GROSS PAY
1090 'DEDUCTIONS  - TOTAL DEDUCTIONS
1100 'NET.PAY     - NET PAY
2000 '***********************************************************************
2002 '                             MAIN ROUTINE
2004 '***********************************************************************
2010  GOSUB 3000                      'INPUT data
2020  GOSUB 4000                      'Print headings
2030  GOSUB 5000                      'Read data
2040  END
```

```
3000 '**********************************************************************
3002 '                              INPUT DATA (DATE)
3004 '**********************************************************************
3010  PRINT
3020  PRINT "Enter the date (month and day, e.g. September 30)"
3030  INPUT "Date";DATE1$
3040  RETURN
4000 '**********************************************************************
4002 '                                PRINT HEADINGS
4004 '**********************************************************************
4010  PRINT
4020  PRINT "PAYROLL REPORT"
4030  PRINT "Week Ending ";DATE1$
4040  PRINT
4050  PRINT "NAME","HOURS","GROSS PAY","DEDUCTIONS","NET PAY"
4060  PRINT
4070  RETURN
5000 '**********************************************************************
5002 '                                     READ DATA
5004 '**********************************************************************
5010  READ ENAME$,RATE,HOURS,INCOME.TAX,UNION,PENSION
5020  WHILE ENAME$ <> "End of file"
5030    GOSUB 6000                             'Perform calculations
5040    READ ENAME$,RATE,HOURS,INCOME.TAX,UNION,PENSION
5050  WEND
5060  DATA "Darryl Brown",9.54 ,38,74.57,2.25,3.67
5070  DATA "Ellen Miller",8.87 ,39,72.14,2.25,3.42
5080  DATA "Lorne Hayes" ,9.88 ,42,79.84,2.25,4.15
5090  DATA "Andrea Jones",10.04,47,85.26,2.25,6.31
5100  DATA "End of file" ,0,0,0,0,0
5110  RETURN
6000 '**********************************************************************
6002 '                             PERFORM CALCULATIONS
6004 '**********************************************************************
6010  GROSS.PAY = HOURS*RATE
6020  DEDUCTIONS = INCOME.TAX+UNION+PENSION
6030  NET.PAY = GROSS.PAY-DEDUCTIONS
6040  PRINT ENAME$,HOURS,GROSS.PAY,DEDUCTIONS,NET.PAY
6050  RETURN
65529 'End of program listing
```

One of the advantages in breaking down a program into modules is the ease in pinpointing errors. If there is a syntax error, our prime suspect is a statement in the latest module developed. If we obtain an incorrect result after executing Subroutine PERFORM CALCULATIONS, the error is probably an error in logic and may lie in either the previous module or in the current module. Even with this type of error, we can pin the error down to one or two modules. There is no need to trace through the entire program.

An advantage in numbering our modules in blocks of line numbers is the simple way by which we can examine a module. We just list the module by its line number range. For instance, if we wish to examine Subroutine PRINT HEADINGS, we type LIST 4000-5000.

One final task remains. We should clean up our BASIC diskette by using the KILL command to delete all intermediate programs. The final version is all we need.

Throughout the book, we will be saving programs and data on disk. Eventually, our BASIC diskette will become full. When this occurs, BASIC displays either **Disk full** or **Too many files**. At this point, we must save our files on another diskette.

Summary of BASIC Statements

GOSUB — Transfers control to the statement specified by the line number following GOSUB.

```
2010 GOSUB 3000
```

RETURN — Returns control to the calling module, specifically to the statement immediately after the calling GOSUB.

```
3040 RETURN
```

WHILE First statement of a WHILE/WEND loop. The loop continues as long as the condition in the WHILE statement is true.

```
5020 WHILE ENAME$ <> "End of file"
```

WEND Last statement of a WHILE/WEND loop. Transfers control back to the WHILE statement.

```
5050 WEND
```

Chapter Summary

1. A program can be broken down into a hierarchy of modules. Each module performs a specific task.
2. A utility module describes the purpose of the program and lists and defines the variables. The main module calls the submodules, the submodules perform specific tasks.
3. A block of statements that governs the flow of control in a program is known as a control structure.
4. There are three elementary control structures:
   (a) A sequence of instructions. (A sequence structure)
   (b) A sequence of instructions that is repeated. (A loop structure)
   (c) A selection based on a test. (A decision structure)
5. A control structure must have a single entry point and a single exit point.
6. The clarification of a program by REM statements is referred to as internal documentation. External documentation refers to support material prepared outside the program.
7. Structured programs include the following aspects of programming:
   (a) Well planned modules.
   (b) The best choice of a control structure for a particular operation.
   (c) Simple linkages between all parts of a program.
   (d) Documentation and a style of coding that enhances clarity.
8. The main module is called the main routine.
9. GOSUB and RETURN statements provide the communication link between a calling module and the called module. The called module is called a subroutine.
10. The main routine must end with an END statement, each subroutine must end with a RETURN statement.
11. Except for a particular type of variable in a user-defined function, variables in a program are global. This means that variables can be referenced by any module.
12. Program maintenance refers to a program's upkeep. Programs, particularly those in commercial software packages, must be continually updated.
13. The statements within a WHILE/WEND loop are executed as long as a condition in the WHILE statement remains true. When the condition becomes false, BASIC drops out of the loop and executes the statement following the WEND.

Questions and Exercises

1. Briefly explain the concept of main module and associated submodules.
2. What is meant by the term "control structure"?
3. What is meant by internal documentation of a program?
4. What is meant by external documentation of a program?
5. What is the purpose of the RETURN statement?
6. Why must the main routine end with an END statement and each subroutine end with a RETURN?
7. Why must care be exercised when changing the value of a global variable?
8. Identify the errors in the following program segments.

(a)
```
4000 'SUBROUTINE ENTER DATA
4010   RATE = 8
4020   READ ITEM1,ITEM2,ITEM3
4030   DATA 32.15,46.21,18.26
```

```
      4040    RETURN
      4050    GOSUB 5000            'Process data
```

(b)
```
3000 'SUBROUTINE PRINT HEADINGS
3010    PRINT
3020    PRINT "EMPLOYEE DATA"
3030    PRINT
3040    PRINT "NAME","ADDRESS","TELEPHONE NUMBER"
3050    GOSUB 3000
3060    RETURN
```

9. Suppose the RETURN statement is omitted in the last subroutine of a program. Can the program be executed? If the program does RUN, is there any possibility of an error?

10. Explain briefly the execution of a WHILE/WEND loop.

11. Design and code a subroutine that reads four records each of which contains the name of an article just purchased, the quantity purchased, the unit price, and the delivery charge. Call a subroutine that calculates and prints the total cost. Code only a skeleton routine for the subroutine that calculates and prints. Use a WHILE/WEND loop in the subroutine that reads. Provide your own data.

Programming Problems

Develop programs for the following problems using the design in Section 5.5 as your guide. Break down each program into modules. A shaded value in an output shown indicates a response to an INPUT statement. Note that dollar amounts are not rounded off to the nearest cent. Use the WHILE/WEND loop in any program that needs a loop structure.

1. Develop a modularized program for Problem 5 in Chapter Four. INPUT the consumption charge and the customer's name. Read in the months and the kilowatt-hours. The data is given in the output below.

```
RUN

Enter the consumption charge per kilowatt-hour
Enter the customer's name in lower case (e.g. John Smith)

Consumption charge per kilowatt-hour? 3.5
Customer's name? Rodney Lockhart

ELECTRICITY CONSUMPTION      Rodney Lockhart

MONTH           HOURS           COST

January          1050            36.75
February         988             34.58
March            842             29.47
```

2. Members of a local community club sold tickets to a baseball game for two days prior to the game. The price of a ticket was $2.25. Find the amount of money collected by each of the following members.

Data:

Susan Bates,12,14
Fred Dawson,13,15 — Name of member, number of tickets sold each day
Diana Lee,16,14

Use the INPUT statement to assign the two days (month and day for each) to two variables. INPUT the price of a ticket. Read in the name of each member and the number of tickets sold by each member each day.

RUN

```
Enter the days of the sale (e.g. June 18,June 19)
Enter the price per ticket

Days tickets sold? May 14,May 15
Price? 2.25

TICKETS SOLD
For the two days May 14 and May 15

NAME           TICKETS        COLLECTED

Susan Bates     26             58.5
Fred Dawson     28             63
Diana Lee       30             67.5
```

3. Interest on an investment is often based on the principal plus the interest of a previous period. This means you are actually receiving interest on interest. Interest calculated this way is called compound interest and the final principal is known as the compound amount. The formula for finding the compound amount is as follows:

$$\text{Compound Amount} = \text{Principal}(1+\text{Rate of Interest}/100)^{\text{Period of Time}}$$

Find the compound amount on each of the following investments:

Data:

2000,0.5,2
3100,9,4 — Principal, rate of interest, number of years
4200,9.5,5

RUN

```
Enter the customer's name in upper case (e.g. JOHN SMITH)
Name? TERRI BURTON

INVESTMENTS: TERRI BURTON

PRINCIPAL      RATE           YEARS          AMOUNT

 2800           8.5            2              3296.23
 3100           9              4              4375.904
 4200           9.5            5              6611.803
```

4. A car purchased for $12 000 was traded in on a new vehicle after seven years of use. An amount of $3000 was offered for the old car. How much did the car depreciate? What percentage of the purchase price was the depreciation? INPUT all data. Call Subroutine PERFORM CALCULATIONS from the main routine. Do not use a loop in your program.

Formulas:

Depreciation = Purchase Price − Trade-in Allowance

$$\text{Percentage} = \frac{\text{Depreciation}}{\text{Purchase Price}} \times 100$$

RUN

```
Purchase price of the car? 12000
Trade-in allowance? 3000

The depreciation is: 9000
The percentage of depreciation is 75 percent
```

5. Develop a program that calculates the principal needed to yield a desired amount of interest for a specific number of years at a rate of interest that is noncompounding. Your program must perform calculations for more than one principal. INPUT all data. Hint: Consider carefully where you should call Subroutine PERFORM CALCULATIONS.

Formula:

$$\text{Principal} = \frac{\text{Interest}}{\text{Rate}/100 \times \text{Years}}$$

RUN

```
Enter the interest, rate, and period of time in years

Interest, rate, years? 600,8,3
Principal: 2500

Interest, rate, years? 1500,9.25,5
Principal: 3243.243

Interest, rate, years? -1,0,0
```

6. Modify the Accounts Receivable program for Problem 7 in Chapter Four by modularizing the program. Use the following subroutines. Hint: The main routine calls only Subroutine READ AND INPUT DATA.

READ AND INPUT DATA	—	Reads and prints a record from the master file. INPUTs a transaction. Calls the subroutine that performs the calculations.
PERFORM CALCULATIONS	—	Calculates the new balance and calls the subroutine that prints the account.
PRINT ACCOUNT	—	Prints the account.

Your output should be the same as the one shown on page 78.

Solutions for Exercises

5.1 Structured Programming

1. Software maintenance refers to the updating of the program or programs that make up the software.
2. A modularized program is easier to develop and simpler to modify.
3. The three control structures are:

   (a) A sequence of instructions. (A sequence structure)
   (b) A sequence of instructions that is repeated. (A loop structure)
   (c) A selection based on a test. (A decision structure)

4. A control structure must have a single entry point and a single exit point. The entry must be at the beginning of the structure, the exit must be at the end of the structure.

5. Structured programming includes the following features:

   (a) Well planned modules.
   (b) The best choice of a control structure for a particular operation.
   (c) Simple linkages between all parts of a program.
   (d) Documentation and a style of coding that enhances clarity.

5.2 Program Modularizing

1. The instruction GOSUB xxxx in the calling module calls the subroutine whose first statement is numbered xxxx. A RETURN statement in the subroutine returns control to the statement immediately following the GOSUB that called the subroutine.

2. A global variable is one that can be referenced by any module in a program.

3. A utility module is used to name the program, to display the name of the programmer and the date the program was written, to state the purpose of the program, and to define the variables.

4. (a) The main routine must end with an END statement.

```
2000 'MAIN ROUTINE
2010   GOSUB 3000          'Print headings
2020   GOSUB 4000          'Read data
2030   END
```

   (b) A RETURN statement is missing.

```
4040 RETURN
```

   (c) The subroutine must end with RETURN, not END.

```
5030 RETURN
```

5. In Subroutine READ A RECORD, the READ and DATA statements (lines 5010 and 5030) must now be:

```
5010 READ ENAME$,RATE,HOURS,INCOME.TAX,UNION,PENSION,MEDICAL
5030 DATA "Darryl Brown",9.54,38,74.57,2.25,3.67,12.45
```

   In Subroutine PERFORM CALCULATIONS, line 6020 must be changed to:

```
6020 DEDUCTIONS = INCOME.TAX+UNION+PENSION+MEDICAL
```

5.3 The WHILE/WEND Loop

```
2010 NUMBER.TESTS = 3
2020 PRINT
2030 INPUT "Name and scores";SNAME$,SCORE1,SCORE2,SCORE3
2040 WHILE SNAME$ <> "End of file"
2050   TOTAL.SCORE = SCORE1+SCORE2+SCORE3
2060   AVERAGE.SCORE = TOTAL.SCORE/NUMBER.TESTS
2070   PRINT "Name: ";SNAME$,"Average:";AVERAGE.SCORE
2080   PRINT
2090   INPUT "Name and scores";SNAME$,SCORE1,SCORE2,SCORE3
2100 WEND
```

5.4 Comparing an Unstructured Program with a Structured Program

```
1000 'SIMPLE INTEREST                    M. MCRITCHIE                    MAR 14
1002 '*********************************************************************
1004 '                  THIS PROGRAM CALCULATES SIMPLE INTEREST
1006 '*********************************************************************
1010 'PRINCIPAL      - PRINCIPAL
1020 'RATE           - RATE OF INTEREST
1030 'YEARS          - NUMBER OF YEARS
1040 'INTEREST       - AMOUNT OF INTEREST
1050 'NEW.PRINCIPAL  - NEW PRINCIPAL
```

```
2000 '************************************************************************
2002 '                              MAIN ROUTINE
2004 '************************************************************************
2010  GOSUB 3000                    'INPUT data
2020  END
3000 '************************************************************************
3002 '                  INPUT DATA (PRINCIPAL, RATE, YEARS)
3004 '************************************************************************
3010  PRINT
3020  INPUT "Principal, rate, years";PRINCIPAL,RATE,YEARS
3030  WHILE PRINCIPAL <> -1
3040    GOSUB 4000                  'Perform calculations
3050    PRINT
3060    INPUT "Principal, rate, years";PRINCIPAL,RATE,YEARS
3070  WEND
3080  RETURN
4000 '************************************************************************
4002 '                           PERFORM CALCULATIONS
4004 '************************************************************************
4010  INTEREST = PRINCIPAL*RATE/100*YEARS
4020  NEW.PRINCIPAL = PRINCIPAL+INTEREST
4030  PRINT "Interest:";INTEREST
4040  PRINT "New principal:";NEW.PRINCIPAL
4050  RETURN
65529 'End of program listing
```

6

DECISION STRUCTURES

Objectives

From this chapter you will learn how to use the IF statement to make a decision. BASIC actually supports two forms of IF statements: the IF/THEN and the IF/THEN/ELSE. The IF/THEN either performs the task following the word THEN or ignores the task depending on the condition in the IF. We used this form of IF in Chapter Four to control a loop. The IF/THEN/ELSE provides a choice between two alternatives. For instance, an employee receives overtime pay only if the number of hours of work is greater than the regular hours, otherwise, the employee receives no overtime pay.

You will also learn how to create a decision structure that offers multiple alternatives. Furthermore, you will learn how to use logical operators to combine conditions.

Contents

6.1 The IF/THEN Statement

General Form

In Chapter Four, we used the IF/THEN statement to control a loop. There, we transferred control to the END statement when the condition in the IF/THEN statement was true. In this chapter, we will either execute a statement or transfer control when the condition is true. Essentially, the general form of the IF/THEN statement is as follows:

IF a certain condition is true **THEN** do a particular task.

As mentioned in Chapter Four, the condition in the IF part of the IF/THEN statement is actually a relational expression which consists of two values separated by a relational operator. The relational operator compares the two values. Let us quickly review a relational expression using the following example.

```
IF MEAL > 6.00
```

The symbol ">", which means "is greater than", is our relational operator. We already know two such operators: "=" which means "is equal to" and "<>" which means "is not equal to". A complete list follows.

Values on both sides of the operator may be expressed as constants, variables, or BASIC expressions. The above example uses a variable and a constant. The following example uses a variable and an expression.

```
IF DEPRECIATION > CURRENT.VALUE/NO.YEARS
```

BASIC evaluates the expression before making the comparison.

Executing an IF/THEN Statement

Let us complete the IF that checks the cost of a meal.

```
6020 IF MEAL > 6.00 THEN SALES.TAX = MEAL*RATE/100
```

The logic in this statement is as follows. If the cost of the meal is greater than $6.00, the condition (the relationship) in the IF/THEN is true and BASIC executes the statement following the word THEN. Thus, the sales tax is calculated. Execution continues with the statement following the IF/THEN. If the cost of the meal is $6.00 or less, the condition is false. BASIC ignores the statement after THEN and, instead, drops through to the statement after the IF. Regardless of the condition in the IF/THEN (whether the condition is true or false) BASIC continues with the statement following the IF/THEN.

A list of relational operators, along with their meanings, is given below.

Relational Operator	*Meaning*
=	is equal to
>	is greater than
>=	is greater than or equal to
<	is less than
<=	is less than or equal to
<>	is not equal to

Recall that the above equal sign is a relational operator and does not have the same meaning as it does when used in an assignment statement.

Exercises

1. Code IF/THEN statements for the following.
   (a) If B is not equal to Ø, divide A by B and assign the result to C.
   (b) If A is less than 10, find the product of A and B and assign the result to C.
   (c) If B is positive, call Subroutine 7000.
   (d) If a score is greater than or equal to 50, print "Passed".
   (e) If the number of miles is less than 500, calculate the rental of a car by multiplying the number of miles by a rate and adding a service charge.
2. State whether the condition in each of the following IF/THEN statements is true or false. If the condition is true, process the THEN part of the IF statement. Assume that A=2, B=3, C=6, D=8, and E=12 for each problem.
   (a) `6020 IF A*B = C/2 THEN PRINT C/2`
   (b) `6030 IF E/C+A > B THEN F = A+B`
   (c) `6040 IF D-B <> C+4 THEN PRINT "Not equal"`
   (d) `6050 IF B*A/C >= 1 THEN F = B*A/C`
   (e) `6060 IF A+E/B <= C/A THEN F = C/A`

6.2 A Multi-Statement IF/THEN

An Unstyled IF/THEN

The IF/THEN statements in the previous section consisted of just one statement following the word THEN. More often than not, multiple tasks must be performed when the condition in the IF is true. In these situations, the word THEN must be followed by several statements.

So far, each numbered line in our programs contains only one statement. (We will call these lines BASIC lines.) It is possible to place several statements in a BASIC line by separating the statements with colons (:). The statements within the line are not numbered, only the line is numbered. Although this style of coding is not encouraged, we do make an exception when it comes to the IF. Here is an example of a multi-statement IF/THEN.

```
6020 IF NO.YEARS > 5 THEN INTEREST.RATE = 9 : INTEREST = INVESTMENT*INTEREST.RAT
E/100
```

The THEN part of the IF is followed by two statements separated by a colon. The two statements are:

```
INTEREST.RATE = 9
INTEREST = INVESTMENT*INTEREST.RATE/100
```

We mentioned earlier that a screen line is capable of holding 80 characters and that a BASIC line may contain a maximum of 255 characters. These maximums include the Enter command at the end of the line. The above IF/THEN consists of more than 80 characters but less than 255. Since the IF/THEN contains more characters than can be placed on a screen line, the extra characters wrap around the screen and continue on the next screen line starting in the left-most position. This position is directly under the first digit of a line number. It should be noted that lengthy lines can occur in other BASIC statements, not just in an IF/THEN.

If there are many such BASIC lines, the line numbers will be obscured by the characters wrapped around the screen. We can style lengthy lines so that line numbers remain clearly visible. Let us find out how this can be done using the above IF. Here, we will highlight not only the line number but also the reserved word IF.

Styling a Multi-Statement IF/THEN

The style used in coding a multi-statement IF/THEN is a matter of choice. We will illustrate two methods. You may wish to develop a style of your own.

Example One:

```
6020 IF NO.YEARS > 5 THEN INTEREST.RATE = 9 :
        INTEREST = INVESTMENT*INTEREST.RATE/100
```

Example Two:

```
6020 IF NO.YEARS > 5
        THEN INTEREST.RATE = 9 :
        INTEREST = INVESTMENT*INTEREST.RATE/100
```

As in the unstyled IF/THEN, each of the above examples is actually one BASIC line numbered 6020. The THEN part is followed by the same two statements:

```
INTEREST.RATE = 9
INTEREST = INVESTMENT*INTEREST.RATE/100
```

In Example One, we break up the IF/THEN between the two statements. After keying in INTEREST.RATE = 9 and the colon, we hold down the space bar which enters spaces. The spaces will eventually wrap around the screen and continue on the next screen line. We continue entering spaces until the cursor is passed the word IF, then we key in the second statement. In this way, the word IF is clearly visible. Since the spaces count, this example is longer than the unstyled IF/THEN. Although Example One seems to be broken up into parts, it is important to understand that this multi-statement IF/THEN is still one BASIC line made up of statements and inserted spaces. The Enter key is not pressed until the very end.

In Example Two, we break up the IF/THEN in two places: after the number 5 and between the two statements following THEN. As in Example One, we hold down the space bar where we wish to break up the IF/THEN and continue holding down the space bar until the cursor reaches the desired position in the next screen line. We then continue typing our BASIC line. Note that Example Two is longer than Example One because of the additional spaces. However, Example Two is still one BASIC line.

Rather than holding down the space bar to enter spaces, we can hold down the Ctrl key and press Enter. This inserts spaces from the character just typed to the end of the screen line. BASIC places the cursor in the left-most position of the next line. We now hold down the space bar until we reach the desired position whereupon we resume typing our BASIC line.

The 255 characters allowed in a BASIC line give us a little over three screen lines. Remember, the term "characters" includes the spaces we insert to style the line and the Enter command at the end of the line. When an IF/THEN statement consists of more than 255 characters, a subroutine must be called.

Although styling an IF/THEN promotes clarity, it does use extra memory because of the inserted spaces. If insufficient memory is a problem due to a lengthy program, the IF/THEN statement should be left unstyled.

Exercises

For each of the exercises below, assume that values are already assigned to variables.

1. Code a multi-statement IF/THEN to determine the net income of a taxpayer. If the taxpayer has a number of dependents, your statement must:

   (a) Calculate the deduction by multiplying the number of dependents by $700.
   (b) Calculate the net income by subtracting the deduction from the total income.

2. Code an IF/THEN statement that calls a subroutine when the age of a piece of equipment is greater than one year. In addition to coding the IF statement, code the subroutine. The subroutine must perform the following:

   (a) Find the depreciation by multiplying the equipment's previous value by the rate of depreciation.
   (b) Find the current value by subtracting the depreciation from the previous value.
   (c) Print the depreciation and the current value on two separate lines.

6.3 The IF/THEN/ELSE Statement

General Form

The IF/THEN statement discussed in Section 6.1 provided an option: either do something or do not do something. In many programs, a selection must be made from two tasks. In this situation, we use the IF/THEN/ELSE statement which has the general form:

IF a certain condition is true **THEN** do a particular task **ELSE** do a different task.

If the condition in the IF/THEN/ELSE is true, BASIC performs the THEN part; if the condition is false, BASIC performs the ELSE part. An example of an IF/THEN/ELSE statement is as follows:

```
6020 IF NO.YEARS <= 5 THEN INTEREST.RATE = 7 ELSE INTEREST.RATE = 9
```

If the number of years is less than or equal to 5 (the condition is true), the interest rate is 7%. If the number of years is greater than 5 (the condition is false), the interest rate is 9%. Upon execution of the IF/THEN/ELSE statement, BASIC continues with the statement following the IF.

Styling an IF/THEN/ELSE

As with the multi-statement IF/THEN, the style used to code a multi-statement IF/THEN/ELSE is a matter of preference. One style is shown below.

```
6020 IF DEPOSIT <= 500
        THEN CURRENT.ACCOUNT = CURRENT.ACCOUNT+DEPOSIT : PRINT CURRENT.ACCOUNT
        ELSE SAVINGS.ACCOUNT = SAVINGS.ACCOUNT+DEPOSIT : PRINT SAVINGS.ACCOUNT
```

We must insert spaces to complete a screen line and insert spaces before the reserved words THEN and ELSE. These spaces are entered in the manner explained previously.

When an IF/THEN/ELSE statement contains more than 255 characters, we have two choices. We can

1. Call a subroutine for either alternative (or subroutines for both) when an alternative contains more than 255 characters.

2. Divide the IF/THEN/ELSE into two IF/THEN statements when each alternative contains less than 255 characters.

   Examples are given on the following page.

An IF/THEN/ELSE that Calls a Subroutine

```
6020 IF SALES <= BASE THEN COMMISSION = SALES*RATE1/100 :
        PRINT "Name: ";ENAME$,"Sales:";SALES,"Commission:";COMMISSION
        ELSE GOSUB 7000

7000 'SUBROUTINE SALES > BASE
7010   EXCESS = SALES-BASE
7020   COMMISSION1 = BASE*RATE1/100
7030   COMMISSION2 = EXCESS*RATE2/100
7040   COMMISSION = COMMISSION1+COMMISSION2
7050   PRINT "Name: ";ENAME$,"Sales:";SALES,"Excess sales:";EXCESS
7060   PRINT "Commission on base:";COMMISSION1,"Commission on excess:";
       COMMISSION2
7070   PRINT "Total commission:";COMMISSION
7080   RETURN
```

If the sales are less than or equal to a base amount, commission is calculated on the sales. If the sales are greater than a base amount, Subroutine 7000 is called to calculate the commission on the base sales, the commission on the excess sales, the total commission, and to print the results. For this alternative, we must call a subroutine because the length of the alternative exceeds 255 characters.

Note the styling of the PRINT statement in line 7060. Here, we start COMMISSION2 under the "P" of PRINT to keep the line numbers visible. A line division must never occur within a string (that is, between quotation marks) as the inserted spaces become part of the string.

Using Two IF/THEN Statements

Suppose only the salesperson's name, sales, excess sales, and commission need to be printed in the ELSE alternative. This reduces the length of the ELSE alternative to less than 255 characters. (The entire IF still contains more than 255 characters.) Rather than call a subroutine, we will divide the IF/THEN/ELSE statement into two IF/THEN statements. This is illustrated below.

```
6020 IF SALES <= BASE THEN COMMISSION = SALES*RATE1/100 :
        PRINT "Name: ";ENAME$,"Sales:";SALES,"Commission:";COMMISSION
6030 IF SALES > BASE THEN EXCESS = SALES-BASE : COMMISSION = (BASE*RATE1/100)
        + (EXCESS*RATE2/100) : PRINT "Name: ";ENAME$,"Sales:";SALES,
        "Excess sales:";EXCESS,"Commission:";COMMISSION
```

Wherever possible, try to keep the logic within the decision structure rather than call a subroutine. Since we combined formulas to obtain the total commission (the other commissions were not required) and since the number of PRINT statements is reduced, the number of characters in the ELSE alternative is now less than 255. Thus, we are able to write the ELSE alternative as a separate IF. Keeping the logic within the decision structure, rather than calling a subroutine, often makes the structure easier to understand. In fact, you may prefer to divide a lengthy and complex IF/THEN/ELSE statement into two IF/THEN statements even when the statement contains less than 255 characters.

Exercises

1. Code IF statements for the following.

   (a) If an inventory count indicates more than ten items in stock, print the number of items in stock; otherwise, print a warning that additional items must be ordered.

   (b) If the number of days on a business trip is less than or equal to three, print the number of days and the regular fare. Otherwise, calculate a 20% discount on the regular air fare; calculate the reduced fare; and print the number of days, the regular fare, the discount, and the reduced fare.

2. Evaluate the following IF/THEN/ELSE statements. Assume that A=3, B=5, C=2, D=6, and E=15 for each problem.

   (a) `6020 IF B*2 = E/B THEN G = D*C ELSE G = D*A`

   (b) `6030 IF D*C/A <= A THEN G = A*B ELSE G = D-E/B`

(c) `6040 IF A+B*C <> E+C THEN G = E-A ELSE G = A+B*C`
(d) `6050 IF D/C+B > E-C THEN G = A*B ELSE G = D/A`
(e) `6060 IF A*B <= E THEN G = A*B ELSE G = D/A`

6.4 Comparing Strings

In a number of programs in Chapters Four and Five, we controlled a loop by comparing two strings. The example below controls a WHILE/WEND loop.

```
5020 WHILE ENAME$ <> "End of file"
```

BASIC uses the ordering of the alphabet to compare strings. Thus, the letter A is less than the letter B, the letter B is less than the letter C, etc. When BASIC compares two strings, it compares one character from one string with one character from the other string moving in a left-to-right direction on both strings until a difference is found. It should be noted that BASIC differentiates between uppercase letters and lowercase letters. More will be said on this in Chapter Eleven.

Examine the following comparisons. The results, with comments, are shown to the right. The READ statement in line 5020 assigns names to the variables.

```
5020 READ NAME1$,NAME2$,NAME3$,NAME4$
5030 DATA "Jansen","Browne","Lindsay","Phillips"
```

1.	`NAME1$ = "Janzen"`	`"Jansen" = "Janzen"` False, s is not equal to z.
2.	`NAME2$ > "Brown"`	`"Browne" > "Brown"` True. Since no character follows Brown, Browne is considered to be greater.
3.	`"Lindsey" < NAME3$`	`"Lindsey" < "Lindsay"` False, e is not less than a.
4.	`"Phillips" <> NAME4$`	`"Phillips" <> "Phillips"` False. The strings are the same.
5.	`"Allan" >= "Alan"`	`"Allan" >= "Alan"` True, l is greater than a.
6.	`NAME2$ < NAME1$`	`"Browne" < "Jansen"` True, B is less then J.

Notice that a string in a relational expression must be enclosed in quotation marks. Here is an example of an IF statement that compares two strings.

```
6030 IF NAME1$ = "Janzen" THEN PRINT NAME1$
```

Exercises

State whether the following relational expressions are true or false. Strings are assigned to the variables by the READ statement in line 5020.

```
5020 READ NAME1$,NAME2$,NAME3$,DESIGN$
5030 DATA "Frederick","Krueger","Lynn","Top-down design"
```

1. `NAME1$ < "Fredrick"`
2. `"Krueger" <> NAME2$`
3. `NAME2$ <= NAME3$`
4. `NAME3$ >= "Lynne"`
5. `DESIGN$ = "Top down design"`

6.5 Logical Operators

Until now, we have been using arithmetic operators (*, /, +, −) and relational operators (=, >, >=, <, <=, <>) in our decision statements. Sometimes a decision may depend on more than one condition. For example, in order to qualify for student employment, an applicant must be a student and must be willing to work full time throughout the summer months. The combined conditions form a compound condition. To combine two or more conditions, we must use logical operators. The operators are: AND, OR, and NOT.

The AND Operator

Here are two examples of IF statements that use the AND operator. Example (a) uses the AND operator in an IF/THEN statement, example (b) uses the AND operator in an IF/THEN/ELSE statement.

(a) IF the applicant is a student AND employed throughout the summer
    THEN Print the student's name :
    Print "Under the student employment program."

(b) IF the number of days > 3 AND the number of days <= 30
    THEN assign the reduced fare to a variable : Print the number of days and the reduced fare
    ELSE assign the regular fare to a variable : Print the number of days and the regular fare

Since the IF part contains more than one condition, we will refer to this part of the statement as the entire expression. If such a statement uses an AND operator, the entire expression is true only if the condition before the operator and the condition after the operator are true. If one of the conditions is false, the expression is considered to be false. In the first example, the entire expression is true if the applicant is a student AND employed throughout the summer. In the second example, the expression is true if a traveler is away more than 3 days AND not more than 30 days.

The OR Operator

The following example uses the OR operator.

IF an employee's age >= 65 OR the years of employment >= 35
    THEN Print the employee's name : Print "Entitled to full pension."
    ELSE Print the employee's name : Print "Not entitled to full pension."

The entire expression is true if one (or both) of the conditions on either side of the OR operator is true. The expression is false only if both conditions are false. In this example, the expression is true if (a) the employee is 65 years of age or older or (b) the employee worked for 35 years or more or (c) both conditions are true.

The NOT Operator

The example shown below illustrates the NOT operator.

IF NOT (cloudy OR rainy) THEN go on a picnic

The relationship within the parentheses is evaluated. If the condition is false, the NOT operator changes the condition to true and the entire expression is considered to be true. If the condition within the parentheses is true, the NOT operator changes the condition to false and the entire expression is considered to be false.

The above expression is equivalent to:

IF sunny THEN go on a picnic

Thus, expressions can often be changed so that the NOT operator need not be used.

A Sample IF Statement

The IF statement below illustrates how a compound condition can be coded in BASIC. It is written for algorithm (b) shown on page 112.

```
5040 IF DAYS > 3 AND DAYS <= 30
     THEN FARE = 184 : PRINT "Days:";DAYS,"Reduced fare:";FARE
     ELSE FARE = 394 : PRINT "Days:";DAYS,"Regular fare:";FARE
```

Multiple Logical Operators in an IF Statement

Most of our decision statements so far have had just one logical operator. An exception is the example which uses both the NOT and the OR operators. Occasions will arise when we must use several logical operators in an IF statement. Here is an example.

```
6030 IF MILES > 500 OR DAYS > 3 OR MONTH$ = "January"
     THEN DISCOUNT = 25
     ELSE DISCOUNT = 0
```

If one of the conditions on either side of an OR operator is true, the discount is $25, otherwise the discount is zero.

Any combination of AND, OR, and NOT operators may be used in an IF statement. An example is given in the next unit.

The Order of Precedence for Operators

When arithmetic, relational, and logical operators are used in one statement, BASIC executes the arithmetic operators first in the order of precedence, then the relational operators in the order in which they appear, and finally the logical operators in the order NOT, AND, OR. Examine the following statement.

```
6040 IF A > B AND A = C OR B*2 = D THEN PRINT A ELSE PRINT B
```

The order of operations in the above statement would be *, >, =, =, AND, OR. Suppose A=3, B=4, C=3 and D=8. The result from each evaluation is as follows:

B*2	A > B	A = C	B*2 = D	A > B AND A = C
8	3 > 4	3 = 3	8 = 8	False AND True
	False	True	True	False

A > B AND A = C OR B*2 = D
False OR True
True

Since the final condition is true, BASIC prints the value of A.

Parentheses may be used to alter the normal order of operations. Suppose the IF statement is changed as follows:

```
6040 IF A > B AND (A = C OR B*2 = D) THEN PRINT A ELSE PRINT B
```

BASIC evaluates the compound condition within the parentheses first. Using the values given above, the result within the parentheses is True. It then evaluates A > B AND the result in the parentheses. The final condition is false as shown below.

A > B AND (True)
False AND True
False

This time, BASIC prints the value of B.

Logical Operators in a WHILE Statement

Logical operators may also be used in a WHILE statement to control a WHILE/WEND loop. On the following page, examine the skeleton loop (the periods indicate statements).

```
6010 WHILE DAYS > 3 AND DAYS <= 30
6020    ....
6030    ....
6040 WEND
```

In this example, the statements inside the loop are executed as long as both conditions in the WHILE statement are true. When one of the conditions becomes false, the loop terminates.

Exercises

1. Identify the errors, if any, in the statements shown below. Assume that values have been assigned to variables prior to each statement. Make the necessary corrections.

```
(a) 6010 IF A = B AND IF A = C THEN D = A+B ELSE D = A+C
(b) 6020 IF A/B = C OR A*B = C THEN PRINT C
(c) 6030 IF A = B AND A < B THEN C = A*B ELSE C = B-A
(d) 6040 IF A = C OR A < B AND A > B THEN D = A+B+C
(e) 6050 IF (A = C OR A < B) AND A > B THEN PRINT B ELSE PRINT C
(f) 6060 WHILE ENAME$ <> "Smith" OR "Jones"
```

2. State whether the result of the entire expression in each of the following statements is true or false. Assume that A=1, B=2, C=3, and D=4.

```
(a) 6010 IF B > C OR C < D THEN E = B
(b) 6020 IF D/B = B AND A*B = B THEN E = A+B ELSE E = A+D
(c) 6030 IF NOT (A*C = C AND A*B = D) THEN PRINT C ELSE PRINT D
(d) 6040 IF A > B OR A = C AND B*2 = D THEN E = B*2 ELSE E = C*3
(e) 6050 IF (A > B OR A = C) AND B*2 = D THEN PRINT A/C
(f) 6060 WHILE B*2 > C AND C < D
```

3. Code an IF/THEN/ELSE statement that checks the number of students registered in a course. If there are between 8 and 30 students inclusive, print the number of students; otherwise, print the number of students and the message: Invalid number of students.

Sample output for valid number of students:

```
 26 students in the course
```

Sample output for invalid number of students:

```
 31 students
Invalid number of students
```

6.6 Multiple Alternatives

The IF statement offers, at the most, two alternatives. Often a decision must be made from more than two possibilities. In this chapter, we will illustrate two ways of writing a decision structure that involves more than two alternatives. Another structure, the CASE structure, will be explained in Chapter Fourteen.

The Multiple IF Statement

When a decision must be made from multiple alternatives and each alternative is fairly short (say, one or two statements), we can combine the IF's in one statement. Here is an example.

Suppose $1000 is invested with a trust and loan company. Interest rates vary depending on the number of years the amount is invested.

```
6040 IF YEARS <= 5 THEN RATE = 6.5 ELSE IF YEARS <= 10 THEN RATE = 8
        ELSE IF YEARS <= 12 THEN RATE = 10.5
```

Note that the words ELSE and IF must appear before each condition except the first. If the value of YEARS is less than or equal to 5, the first condition is true, therefore, 6.5 is assigned to RATE. If the value of YEARS is greater than 5 but less than or equal to 10, the first condition is false, therefore, BASIC proceeds to the second condition. Since this condition is true, 8 is assigned to RATE. If the value of YEARS is greater than 10 but less than or equal to 12, the first two conditions are false. BASIC proceeds to the third condition where 10.5 is assigned to RATE. If no conditions are true, the entire expression is false and BASIC drops down to the next statement.

Multiple IF/THEN's

Each alternative in the multiple IF above performed just one task. When a number of tasks must be performed in each alternative and the number of alternatives is relatively small, say four at the most, it is better to use multiple IF/THEN'S. As already mentioned, we will discuss the CASE structure later on in the book when the structure is needed. The CASE structure can handle many alternatives. Each alternative, in turn, may consist of any number of statements.

In the example below, each alternative requires several statements. There are three alternatives. Since there are three alternatives, we will use three IF/THEN statements. We could use the multiple IF and call a subroutine for each alternative, however, we mentioned earlier that we will attempt to keep the logic within the decision structure.

Suppose a firm offers its employees the following pay schedule:

Hours: 39 or less	No overtime pay
Hours between 40 and 45 inclusive:	Overtime pay based on time and a half
Hours over 45:	Overtime pay based on double time

A regular work week is 39 hours, the base for double time is 45 hours. For our program segment, previous statements have assigned values to REGULAR.HOURS, BASE.DOUBLE, RATE, and HOURS.WORK. Let us assume that the rate of pay is $10.00.

```
6010 IF HOURS.WORK <= 39 THEN REGULAR.PAY = HOURS.WORK*RATE :
        OVERTIME.HALF = 0 :
        OVERTIME.DOUBLE = 0
6020 IF HOURS.WORK>39 AND HOURS.WORK<=45 THEN REGULAR.PAY=REGULAR.HOURS*RATE :
        OVERTIME.HALF = (HOURS.WORK-REGULAR.HOURS)*RATE*1.5 :
        OVERTIME.DOUBLE = 0
6030 IF HOURS.WORK > 45 THEN REGULAR.PAY = REGULAR.HOURS*RATE :
        OVERTIME.HALF = (BASE.DOUBLE-REGULAR.HOURS)*RATE*1.5 :
        OVERTIME.DOUBLE = (HOURS.WORK-BASE.DOUBLE)*RATE*2
```

If an employee worked 39 hours or less, BASIC executes the first alternative. The employee receives no overtime pay.

If an employee worked more than 39 hours but not more than 45, BASIC executes the second alternative. Note the use of the relational operator AND. This employee receives regular pay and overtime pay at time and a half. Suppose the employee worked 42 hours. Calculations are as follows:

Regular pay = 39×10.00
Overtime pay at time and a half = $(42 - 39) \times 10.00 \times 1.5$

If an employee worked more than 45 hours, BASIC executes the third alternative. This employee receives regular pay, overtime pay at time and a half, and overtime pay at double time. Suppose the employee worked 47 hours. The following calculations will occur.

Regular pay = 39×10.00
Overtime pay at time and a half = $(45 - 39) \times 10.00 \times 1.5$
Overtime pay at double time = $(47 - 45) \times 10.00 \times 2$

Following the decision structure, statements would be coded to perform the calculations and to print a detail line. The entire program is designed in Section 6.9.

Exercise

Code a multiple IF statement for the following conditions.

If a score is less than 50, the grade is F.
If a score is less than 58, the grade is D.
If a score is less than 70, the grade is C.
If a score is less than 80, the grade is B.
if a score is less than 90, the grade is A.
if a score is less than 101, the grade is A+

6.7 A Decision Within a Decision

The last form of decision structure to learn is one in which we must make a second decision after making a first. Let us start off with an example.

A community club charges a lower rate for shareholders than it does for nonshareholders. Furthermore, within each category, a family rate is lower than an individual rate. One member is charged three-quarters of the individual fee and each additional member is charged $20.00 less than the individual fee. The accounting department requires a listing of the registrants and their fees. The following formulas are used.

Individual Fee = Rate for shareholder or nonshareholder.

Family Fee = Individual Fee × .75 + (Number of Family Members − 1) × (Individual Fee − 20)

Assume RATE1 is the rate for shareholders, RATE2 is the rate for nonshareholders, NUMBER stores the number of members in a family and STATUS$ is assigned either S (for shareholder) or N (for nonshareholder). Here is how this structure could be coded.

```
6010 IF STATUS$ = "S" THEN RATE = RATE1 ELSE RATE = RATE2
6020 IF NUMBER > 1
        THEN FEE = RATE*.75+(NUMBER-1)*(RATE-20)
        ELSE FEE = RATE
```

Line 6010 makes the first decision: Is the registrant a shareholder or a nonshareholder? If STATUS$ is equal to "S", the rate for shareholders is assigned to RATE, if STATUS$ is not equal to "S", the rate for non-shareholders is assigned to RATE.

Line 6020 makes the second decision: Is the applicant registering as an individual or as a family? If there is more than one person registering, the fee will be the family rate; if there is only one person registering, the fee will be the individual rate.

In a decision structure where we must make a second decision after making a first, it is often possible to find a common variable that can be used in the calculations. In the above example, we used RATE as our common variable. After finding whether or not the registrant is a shareholder, we assigned the appropriate rate to our common variable, then used this variable to calculate the fee.

By assigning a rate to a common variable, we have avoided the repetition of code. If we had not assigned each rate to RATE, it would be necessary to use RATE1 to calculate the fee for a shareholder (for both family and individual) and RATE2 to calculate the fee for a nonshareholder (for both family and individual).

Here is another example.

A manufacturer is clearing out a line of goods by offering retailers a trade discount of 15%. Furthermore, the manufacturer is offering an additional discount of 5% on the same line of goods if the quantity purchased is greater than 100 items. The merchandise is identified by the code number 4J1267. Assume variables have been assigned values. Variable T.RATE represents the trade discount rate (15%), variable Q.RATE represents the quantity discount rate (5%).

```
6000 'SUBROUTINE PROCESS DATA
6010   IF CODE$ = "4J1267" THEN GOSUB 6200 ELSE DISCOUNT = 0
6015   'Subroutine 6200 calculates a discount
6020   PRICE = VALUE-DISCOUNT
6030   PRINT
6040   PRINT "Value:";VALUE,"Discount:";DISCOUNT,"Price:";PRICE
6050   RETURN
```

```
6200 'SUBROUTINE CALCULATE DISCOUNT
6210    IF QUANTITY > 100
           THEN DISCOUNT = VALUE * (T.RATE+Q.RATE)/100
           ELSE DISCOUNT = VALUE * T.RATE/100
6220    RETURN
```

In this decision structure, our common variable is DISCOUNT. Line 6010 makes the first decision. Did the retailer purchase the merchandise in question? If the code is 4J1267, we call a subroutine to calculate a discount; if the code is not 4J1267, we assign zero to DISCOUNT.

Subroutine 6200 makes the second decision. Is the quantity purchased greater than 100 items? If it is, the discount includes both a trade discount and a quantity discount. If the quantity purchased is 100 items or less, the discount is only the trade discount.

In the above decision structure, we call a subroutine to calculate the discount for a retailer who purchases the merchandise coded 4J1267. A subroutine should be called, otherwise, the IF statement may contain more than 255 characters. Furthermore, the subroutine contains an IF/THEN/ELSE. Inserting an IF/THEN/ELSE within another makes the overall IF statement complex and difficult to read. Although we suggested that decisions should be kept within the decision structure wherever possible, in this case the logic is easier to follow when the two IF/THEN/ELSE's are separated by placing the second in a subroutine.

When control returns to the calling module from Subroutine 6200, BASIC calculates the price of the merchandise and prints a detail line. Note that we used the common variable DISCOUNT in line 6020. At this point the discount may be zero, it may be just a trade discount, or it may include both a trade discount and a quantity discount.

Exercise

Code a decision structure that makes the following decisions.

If a student's grade point average is greater than 3.5, determine whether or not the student has been involved in more than two extra curricular activities. If the number of extra curricular activities is more than two, the student receives a scholarship of $1000; otherwise, the student receives a scholarship of $800. If the student's grade point average is less than or equal to 3.5, the student receives no scholarship.

After all decisions have been made, print the student's name, grade point average, and the amount of the scholarship.

6.8 Editing Data

When data is keyed in during program execution, errors are often detected as the values are being typed. This kind of error is easily corrected by backspacing to the error and making the correction. However, when the user realizes that an error has been made after the Enter key has been pressed, the incorrect data is now in memory. If the program has no data editing features, the user's only alternative is to start over and key in the data once more.

The example below allows a user to correct a date that has been incorrectly typed and sent to memory.

```
3040 INPUT "Date";DATE1$
3050 INPUT "Is the date correct (y/n)";RESPONSE$
3060 IF RESPONSE$ <> "y" AND RESPONSE$ <> "Y"
        THEN INPUT "Re-enter the date--",DATE1$ : GOTO 3050
```

Statement 3040 allows the user to key in the date. The INPUT statement in line 3050 asks the user if the date is correct. Line 3060 checks the user's response. If the response is not "y" and not "Y", the user is given the opportunity to retype the date.

The GOTO statement transfers control back to line 3050 which redisplays the question "Is the date correct (y/n)?". Again, line 3060 checks the response and allows the user to type the date once more if the response is not "y" or "Y". The GOTO statement transfers control. The process continues until the user responds with "y" or "Y". At that point, BASIC drops down to the statement following line 3060.

Note that the response can be a lowercase letter or an uppercase letter (BASIC differentiates between lowercase and uppercase letters) and that the logical operator must be AND and not OR. Suppose we used the OR operator.

```
3060 IF RESPONSE$ <> "y" OR RESPONSE$ <> "Y"
        THEN INPUT "Re-enter the date--",DATE1$ : GOTO 3050
```

The user keys in the correct date, then responds to "Is the date correct (y/n)?" with an uppercase "Y". The first condition in the above IF is true since "Y" is not equal to "y". This makes the entire expression true causing the prompt "Re-enter the date--" to appear on the screen. Yet, the user keyed in the correct date. The result is the same when the user keys in a lowercase "y".

Data should be verified in any data entry program. This is just good programming practice. Besides checking a response, other verification techniques exist. Two are given below.

The limit test:

```
3040 INPUT "Number of employees";NO.EMPLOYEES
3050 IF NO.EMPLOYEES > 12
        THEN PRINT "Number of employees must not be greater than 12" :
        GOTO 3040
```

The range test:

```
3040 INPUT "Rate of pay";RATE
3050 IF RATE < 5.00 OR RATE > 15.00
        THEN PRINT "The rate must be between $5.00 and $15.00 inclusive" :
        GOTO 3040
```

6.9 Program Design

Let us now design the program whose decision structure was explained on page 115. The program updates (maintains) the program designed in Chapter Five by verifying keyed-in data and including overtime pay. Here is the problem once more.

A firm offers its employees the following pay schedule:

Hours: 39 or less	No overtime pay
Hours between 40 and 45 inclusive:	Overtime pay based on time and a half
Hours over 45:	Overtime pay based on double time

A regular work week is 39 hours, the base for double time is 45 hours. For each employee, income tax, union dues, and a pension deduction are deducted from the gross pay. We are to find the gross pay, the total deductions, and the net pay for each employee.

Data:

Darryl Brown,9.54,38,74.57,2.25,3.67
Ellen Miller,8.87,39,72.14,2.25,3.42
Lorne Hayes,9.88,42,79.84,2.25,4.15
Andrea Jones,10.04,47,85.26,2.25,6.31

— Employee name, rate of pay, hours of work, income tax deduction, union dues, pension deduction

Formulas:

Regular Pay:

(a) For employees with no overtime:
Hours of Work × Rate of Pay

(b) For employees with overtime:
Regular Hours × Rate of Pay

Overtime pay based on time and a half:

(a) For employees with no double time:
(Hours of Work − Regular Hours) × Rate of pay × 1.5

(b) For employees with double time:
(Base for Double Time − Regular Hours) × Rate of Pay × 1.5

Overtime pay based on double time:

(Hours of work − Base for Double Time) × Rate of Pay × 2

Gross Pay = Regular Pay + Overtime Pay at Time and a Half + Overtime Pay at Double Time
Total Deductions = Income Tax Deduction + Union Dues + Pension Deduction
Net Pay = Gross Pay − Total Deductions

The program will produce the following output:

```
         10        20        30        40        50        60
123456789012345678901234567890123456789012345678901234567890123

Enter date (month and day), regular hours, base for double time
Date, hours? October 17,39,45
Are the entries correct (y/n)? y

PAYROLL REPORT
Week Ending October 17

NAME           HOURS          GROSS PAY      DEDUCTIONS      NET PAY

Darryl Brown   38              362.52          80.49          282.03
Ellen Miller   39              345.93          77.81          268.12
Lorne Hayes    42              429.78          86.24          343.54
Andrea Jones   47              522.08          93.82          428.26
```

FIGURE 6-1 STRUCTURE CHART

INPUT data
Print headings
Read data
Perform calculations

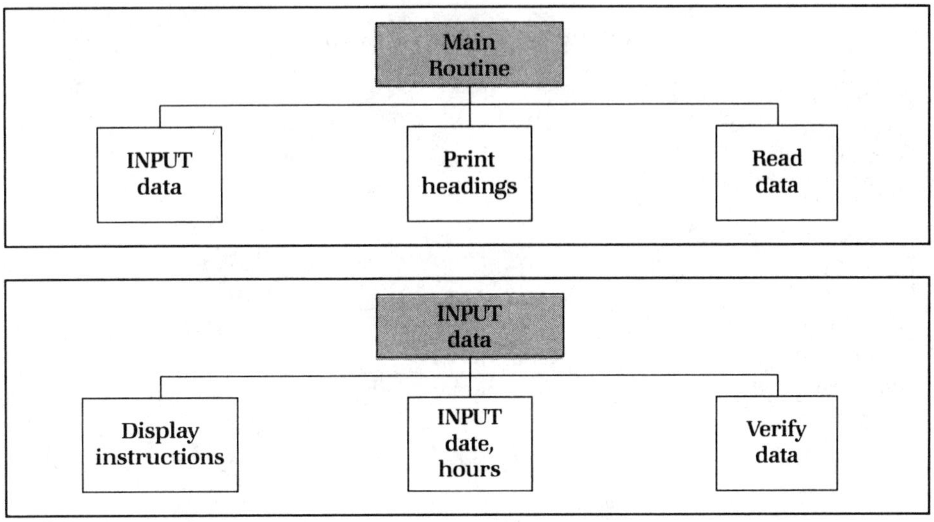

Figure 6-1 Continued

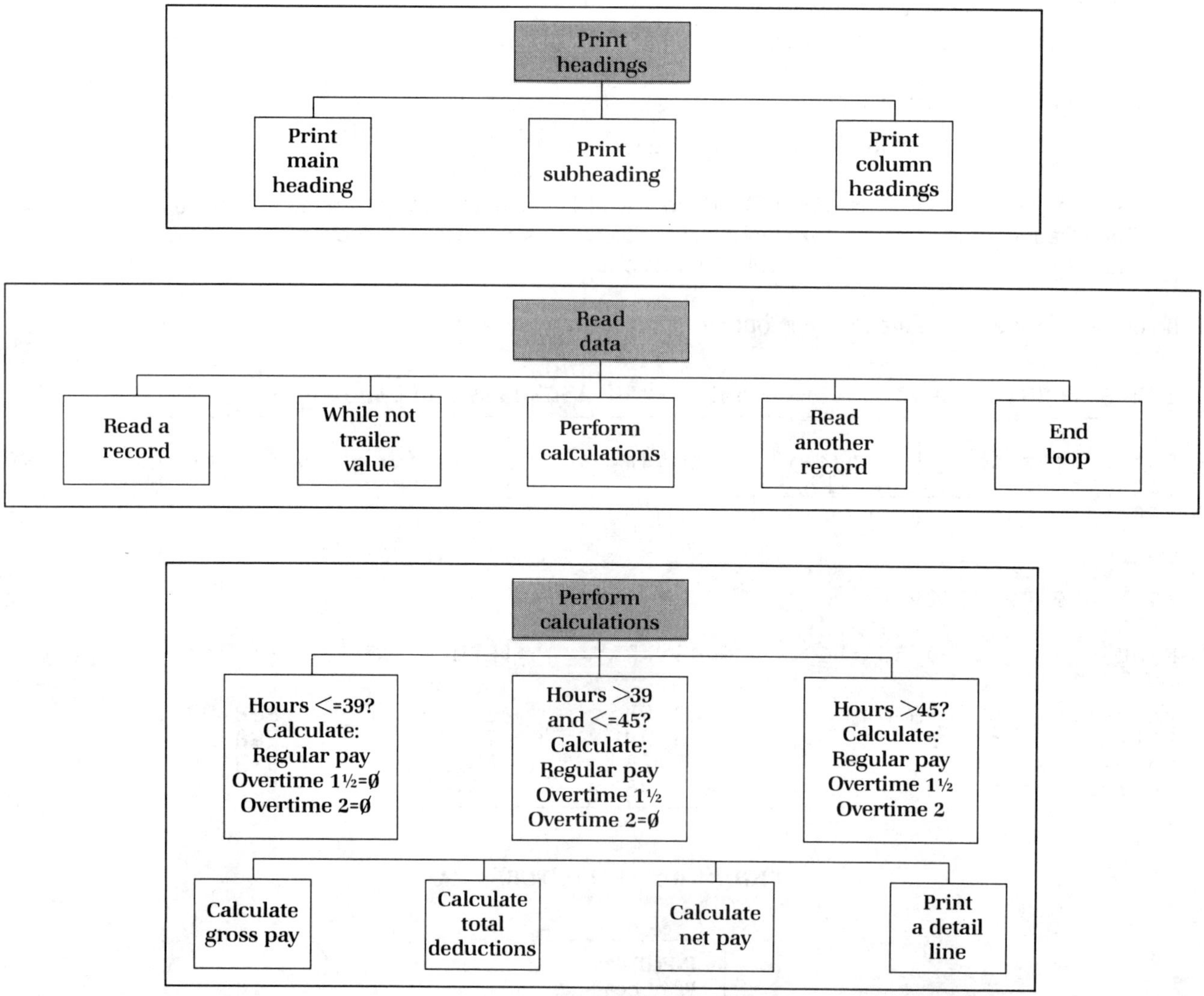

In the above chart, the notation Overtime 1½ represents overtime pay at time and a half while the notation Overtime 2 means overtime pay at double time.

FIGURE 6-2 PSEUDOCODE

MAJOR TASKS
INPUT data
Print headings
Read data
Perform calculations

MAIN ROUTINE	
INPUT data	(subroutine)
Print headings	(subroutine)
Read data	(subroutine)

INPUT DATA	
Display instructions	
INPUT date, hours	DATE1$,REGULAR.HOURS,BASE.DOUBLE
Verify data	RESPONSE$

PRINT HEADINGS
Print main heading
Print subheading
Print column headings

READ DATA	
Read a record	ENAME$,RATE,HOURS.WORK,INCOME.TAX,UNION,PENSION
While not trailer value	
Perform calculations	(subroutine)
Read another record	
End loop	
Data records	

PERFORM CALCULATIONS	
Hours of work <= 39?	
Calculate regular pay	REGULAR.PAY
Overtime pay at time and a half = Ø	OVERTIME.HALF
Overtime pay at double time = Ø	OVERTIME.DOUBLE
Hours of work > 39 and <= 45?	
Calculate regular pay	
Calculate overtime pay at time and a half	
Overtime pay at double time = Ø	
Hours of work > 45?	
Calculate regular pay	
Calculate overtime pay at time and a half	
Calculate overtime pay at double time	
Calculate gross pay	GROSS.PAY
Calculate total deductions	DEDUCTIONS
Calculate net pay	NET.PAY
Print a detail line	

THE MAIN ROUTINE

```
1000 'NET PAY                       M. MCRITCHIE                     APR 18
1002 '*********************************************************************
1004 ' THIS PROGRAM CALCULATES NET PAY FOR EACH OF SEVERAL EMPLOYEES. THE PAY
1006 ' SCHEDULE INCLUDES OVERTIME PAY AT TIME AND A HALF AND AT DOUBLE TIME.
1008 '*********************************************************************
1010 'DATE1$          - DATE
1020 'REGULAR.HOURS   - REGULAR HOURS
1030 'BASE.DOUBLE     - BASE HOURS FOR DOUBLE TIME
1040 'RESPONSE$       - USER'S RESPONSE (y/n)
1050 'ENAME$          - EMPLOYEE NAME
1060 'RATE            - RATE OF PAY
1070 'HOURS.WORK      - HOURS OF WORK
1080 'INCOME.TAX      - INCOME TAX DEDUCTION
1090 'UNION           - UNION DUES
1100 'PENSION         - PENSION DEDUCTION
1110 'REGULAR.PAY     - REGULAR PAY
1120 'OVERTIME.HALF   - OVERTIME PAY AT TIME AND A HALF
```

```
1130 'OVERTIME.DOUBLE - OVERTIME PAY AT DOUBLE TIME
1140 'GROSS.PAY       - GROSS PAY
1150 'DEDUCTIONS      - TOTAL DEDUCTIONS
1160 'NET.PAY         - NET PAY
2000 '**************************************************************************
2002 '                              MAIN ROUTINE
2004 '**************************************************************************
2010  GOSUB 3000                      'INPUT data
2020  GOSUB 4000                      'Print headings
2030  GOSUB 5000                      'Read data
2040  END
3000 'SUBROUTINE INPUT DATA
3010   PRINT "INPUT data"
3020   RETURN
4000 'SUBROUTINE PRINT HEADINGS
4010   PRINT "Print headings"
4020   RETURN
5000 'SUBROUTINE READ DATA
5010   PRINT "Read data"
5020   RETURN
65529 'End of program listing
RUN
```

```
INPUT data
Print headings
Read data
```

INPUT DATA

```
3000 '**************************************************************************
3002 '                        INPUT DATA (DATE AND HOURS)
3004 '**************************************************************************
3010  PRINT
3020  PRINT "Enter date (month and day), regular hours, base for double time"
3030  INPUT "Date, hours";DATE1$,REGULAR.HOURS,BASE.DOUBLE
3040  INPUT "Are the entries correct (y/n)";RESPONSE$
3050  IF RESPONSE$ <> "y" AND RESPONSE$ <> "Y"
        THEN INPUT "Re-enter the data--",DATE1$,REGULAR.HOURS,BASE.DOUBLE :
        GOTO 3040
3060  RETURN
RUN
```

```

Enter date (month and day), regular hours, base for double time
Date, hours? October 17,39,46
Are the entries correct (y/n)? n
Re-enter the data--October 17,39,45
Are the entries correct (y/n)? y
Print headings
Read data
```

Note the prompt displayed when the response to "Are the entries correct (y/n)?" is "n".

PRINT HEADINGS

```
4000 '**************************************************************************
4002 '                            PRINT HEADINGS
4004 '**************************************************************************
4010  PRINT
4020  PRINT "PAYROLL REPORT"
4030  PRINT "Week Ending ";DATE1$
4040  PRINT
4050  PRINT "NAME","HOURS","GROSS PAY","DEDUCTIONS","NET PAY"
4060  PRINT
4070  RETURN
```

RUN

```
Enter date (month and day), regular hours, base for double time
Date, hours? October 17,39,45
Are the entries correct (y/n)? y

PAYROLL REPORT
Week Ending October 17

NAME             HOURS            GROSS PAY     DEDUCTIONS     NET PAY

Read data
```

READ DATA

```
5000 '******************************************************************
5002 '                              READ DATA
5004 '******************************************************************
5010  READ ENAME$,RATE,HOURS.WORK,INCOME.TAX,UNION,PENSION
5020  WHILE ENAME$ <> "End of file"
5030    GOSUB 6000                     'Perform calculations
5040    READ ENAME$,RATE,HOURS.WORK,INCOME.TAX,UNION,PENSION
5050  WEND
5060  DATA "Darryl Brown",9.54 ,38,74.57,2.25,3.67
5070  DATA "Ellen Miller",8.87 ,39,72.14,2.25,3.42
5080  DATA "Lorne Hayes" ,9.88 ,42,79.84,2.25,4.15
5090  DATA "Andrea Jones",10.04,47,85.26,2.25,6.31
5100  DATA "End of file" ,0,0,0,0,0
5110  RETURN
6000 'SUBROUTINE PERFORM CALCULATIONS
6010   PRINT "Perform calculations"
6020   RETURN
RUN
```

```
Enter date (month and day), regular hours, base for double time
Date, hours? October 17,39,45
Are the entries correct (y/n)? y

PAYROLL REPORT
Week Ending October 17

NAME             HOURS            GROSS PAY     DEDUCTIONS     NET PAY

Perform calculations
Perform calculations
Perform calculations
Perform calculations
```

PERFORM CALCULATIONS

```
6000 '******************************************************************
6002 '                         PERFORM CALCULATIONS
6004 '******************************************************************
6010  IF HOURS.WORK <= 39 THEN REGULAR.PAY = HOURS.WORK*RATE :
          OVERTIME.HALF = 0 :
          OVERTIME.DOUBLE = 0
6020  IF HOURS.WORK>39 AND HOURS.WORK<=45 THEN REGULAR.PAY=REGULAR.HOURS*RATE :
          OVERTIME.HALF = (HOURS.WORK-REGULAR.HOURS)*RATE*1.5 :
          OVERTIME.DOUBLE = 0
```

```
6030  IF HOURS.WORK > 45 THEN REGULAR.PAY = REGULAR.HOURS*RATE :
         OVERTIME.HALF = (BASE.DOUBLE-REGULAR.HOURS)*RATE*1.5 :
         OVERTIME.DOUBLE = (HOURS.WORK-BASE.DOUBLE)*RATE*2
6040  GROSS.PAY = REGULAR.PAY+OVERTIME.HALF+OVERTIME.DOUBLE
6050  DEDUCTIONS = INCOME.TAX+UNION+PENSION
6060  NET.PAY = GROSS.PAY-DEDUCTIONS
6070  PRINT ENAME$,HOURS.WORK,GROSS.PAY,DEDUCTIONS,NET.PAY
6080  RETURN
```

The output is shown on page 119. Here is the complete program listing.

```
1000 'NET PAY                          M. MCRITCHIE                    APR 18
1002 '*********************************************************************
1004 ' THIS PROGRAM CALCULATES NET PAY FOR EACH OF SEVERAL EMPLOYEES. THE PAY
1006 ' SCHEDULE INCLUDES OVERTIME PAY AT TIME AND A HALF AND AT DOUBLE TIME.
1008 '*********************************************************************
1010 'DATE1$            - DATE
1020 'REGULAR.HOURS     - REGULAR HOURS
1030 'BASE.DOUBLE       - BASE HOURS FOR DOUBLE TIME
1040 'RESPONSE$         - USER'S RESPONSE (y/n)
1050 'ENAME$            - EMPLOYEE NAME
1060 'RATE              - RATE OF PAY
1070 'HOURS.WORK        - HOURS OF WORK
1080 'INCOME.TAX        - INCOME TAX DEDUCTION
1090 'UNION             - UNION DUES
1100 'PENSION           - PENSION DEDUCTION
1110 'REGULAR.PAY       - REGULAR PAY
1120 'OVERTIME.HALF     - OVERTIME PAY AT TIME AND A HALF
1130 'OVERTIME.DOUBLE   - OVERTIME PAY AT DOUBLE TIME
1140 'GROSS.PAY         - GROSS PAY
1150 'DEDUCTIONS        - TOTAL DEDUCTIONS
1160 'NET.PAY           - NET PAY
2000 '*********************************************************************
2002 '                              MAIN ROUTINE
2004 '*********************************************************************
2010  GOSUB 3000                   'INPUT data
2020  GOSUB 4000                   'Print headings
2030  GOSUB 5000                   'Read data
2040  END
3000 '*********************************************************************
3002 '                     INPUT DATA (DATE AND HOURS)
3004 '*********************************************************************
3010  PRINT
3020  PRINT "Enter date (month and day), regular hours, base for double time"
3030  INPUT "Date, hours";DATE1$,REGULAR.HOURS,BASE.DOUBLE
3040  INPUT "Are the entries correct (y/n)";RESPONSE$
3050  IF RESPONSE$ <> "y" AND RESPONSE$ <> "Y"
         THEN INPUT "Re-enter the data--",DATE1$,REGULAR.HOURS,BASE.DOUBLE :
         GOTO 3040
3060  RETURN
4000 '*********************************************************************
4002 '                            PRINT HEADINGS
4004 '*********************************************************************
4010  PRINT
4020  PRINT "PAYROLL REPORT"
4030  PRINT "Week Ending ";DATE1$
4040  PRINT
4050  PRINT "NAME","HOURS","GROSS PAY","DEDUCTIONS","NET PAY"
4060  PRINT
4070  RETURN
5000 '*********************************************************************
5002 '                              READ DATA
5004 '*********************************************************************
5010  READ ENAME$,RATE,HOURS.WORK,INCOME.TAX,UNION,PENSION
5020  WHILE ENAME$ <> "End of file"
5030    GOSUB 6000                          'Perform calculations
5040    READ ENAME$,RATE,HOURS.WORK,INCOME.TAX,UNION,PENSION
```

```
5050  WEND
5060  DATA "Darryl Brown",9.54 ,38,74.57,2.25,3.67
5070  DATA "Ellen Miller",8.87 ,39,72.14,2.25,3.42
5080  DATA "Lorne Hayes" ,9.88 ,42,79.84,2.25,4.15
5090  DATA "Andrea Jones",10.04,47,85.26,2.25,6.31
5100  DATA "End of file" ,0,0,0,0,0
5110  RETURN
6000 '*****************************************************************
6002 '                       PERFORM CALCULATIONS
6004 '*****************************************************************
6010  IF HOURS.WORK <= 39 THEN REGULAR.PAY = HOURS.WORK*RATE :
         OVERTIME.HALF = 0 :
         OVERTIME.DOUBLE = 0
6020  IF HOURS.WORK>39 AND HOURS.WORK<=45 THEN REGULAR.PAY=REGULAR.HOURS*RATE :
         OVERTIME.HALF = (HOURS.WORK-REGULAR.HOURS)*RATE*1.5 :
         OVERTIME.DOUBLE = 0
6030  IF HOURS.WORK > 45 THEN REGULAR.PAY = REGULAR.HOURS*RATE :
         OVERTIME.HALF = (BASE.DOUBLE-REGULAR.HOURS)*RATE*1.5 :
         OVERTIME.DOUBLE = (HOURS.WORK-BASE.DOUBLE)*RATE*2
6040  GROSS.PAY = REGULAR.PAY+OVERTIME.HALF+OVERTIME.DOUBLE
6050  DEDUCTIONS = INCOME.TAX+UNION+PENSION
6060  NET.PAY = GROSS.PAY-DEDUCTIONS
6070  PRINT ENAME$,HOURS.WORK,GROSS.PAY,DEDUCTIONS,NET.PAY
6080  RETURN
65529 'End of program listing
```

Because the program in Chapter Five was modularized, it was fairly easy to update the program. We simply modified the utility module, Subroutine INPUT DATA, and Subroutine PERFORM CALCULATIONS. The other modules remained the same.

Summary of BASIC Statements

IF/THEN — If the condition in the IF is true, executes one or more statements following the word THEN.

```
6020 IF MEAL > 6.00 THEN SALES.TAX = MEAL*RATE/100
```

IF/THEN/ELSE — If the condition in the IF is true, executes one or more statements following the word THEN. If the condition is false, executes one or more statements following the word ELSE.

```
6020 IF NO.YEARS <= 5 THEN INTEREST.RATE = 7 ELSE INTEREST.RATE = 9
```

Summary of Special Keys

Ctrl-Enter — Completes a screen line with spaces, then positions the cursor in the left-most position of the next screen line.

Chapter Summary

1. An IF statement makes a decision. There are basically two forms of IF statements:
   (a) An IF/THEN which decides whether or not a task will be performed.
   (b) An IF/THEN/ELSE which selects one task from a choice of two.
2. An IF statement contains a relational expression which consists of two values separated by a relational operator. The relational operator compares the two values. The relational operators are = (equal to), > (greater than), >= (greater than or equal to), < (less than), <= (less than or equal to), and <> (not equal to).
3. A numbered line may contain more than one statement. The statements must be separated by colons.
4. The IF/THEN and both alternatives of the IF/THEN/ELSE may contain several statements.
5. When a statement contains more than 80 characters, the extra characters wrap around the screen and continue in the left-most column of the next screen line.
6. An IF statement longer than 80 characters should be styled in such a way that its line number is not obscured by the wrapped-around characters. This is accomplished by breaking up the statement into several screen lines.
7. When an IF/THEN statement contains more than 255 characters, a subroutine must be called.
8. When an IF/THEN/ELSE statement contains more than 255 characters, the statement can be coded in one of two ways:
   (a) A subroutine must be called for either alternative when an alternative contains more than 255 characters.
   (b) The IF/THEN/ELSE can be divided into two IF/THEN statements when each alternative contains less than 255 characters.
9. Wherever possible, we should try to keep the logic of a decision structure within the structure rather than call a subroutine.
10. BASIC uses the ordering of the alphabet to compare strings.
11. A logical operator combines two conditions. Three such operators are AND, OR, and NOT.
12. Multiple logical operators may be used in an IF statement. An example:

```
6040 IF A > B AND A = C OR B*2 = D THEN PRINT A ELSE PRINT B
```

13. When arithmetic, relational and logical operators are used in one statement, BASIC executes the arithmetic operators first in the order of precedence, then the relational operators in the order in which they appear, and finally the logical operators in the order NOT, AND, OR. Parentheses may be used to alter the normal order of operations.
14. Logical operators may also be used in a WHILE statement. For example:

```
6010 WHILE DAYS > 3 AND DAYS <= 30
```

15. Two ways to write a decision structure that involves more than two alternatives are:
    (a) Using a multiple IF statement
    (b) Using multiple IF/THEN's
16. In a decision structure where we must make a second decision after making a first, it is often possible to find a common variable. This common variable is then used in calculations.
17. Data entry programs should contain data editing features to give a user the opportunity to correct a keyed-in value. Some of the verification tests are:
    (a) The response test
    (b) The limit test
    (c) The range test

Questions and Exercises

1. Give an example of each of the following statements and explain how BASIC evaluates each one.
   (a) An IF/THEN statement.
   (b) An IF/THEN/ELSE statement.

2. When must an IF statement call a subroutine?

3. Identify the errors in the following IF statements. Assume values have been assigned to the variables. Make the necessary corrections.

   (a) The IF statement must print the values of A and B in ascending order.

```
6020 IF A < B THEN PRINT A,B ELSE PRINT A,B
```

   (b) The IF statement must print a name only if the last name is Smith.

```
6020 IF LAST$ = Smith THEN PRINT FIRST$
```

   (c) The IF statement must print the account number and "is overdrawn" if the account is tagged with an "O" (for Overdrawn); otherwise the account number and the current balance must be printed.

```
6020 IF ACCOUNT = "O"
     THEN PRINT "Account number";NUMBER;"is overdrawn"
     ELSE PRINT "Account number:";NUMBER,"Balance:";BALANCE
```

4. State whether the result of each of the following IF statements is true or false. Assume that A = 2, B = 4, C = 6, and D = 8.

```
(a) 6020 IF B > C OR B > A THEN E = A+B ELSE E = A-B
(b) 6030 IF B > C AND B > A THEN PRINT A*B
(c) 6040 IF D/B = A AND B/A = A THEN E = B/A ELSE E = D/B
(d) 6050 IF NOT (C-B < A OR B+C < D) THEN PRINT A+B+C
(e) 6060 IF B < C OR C > D AND D = A*3 THEN E = B/C ELSE E = B*C
(f) 6070 IF (B < C OR C > D) AND D = A*3 THEN E = B/C ELSE E = B*C
```

5. Use WHILE/WEND loops for the following exercises. Use the READ and DATA statements to enter data into the computer. Supply your own data.

   (a) Print the names of five students, their scores and whether or not each passed a test just given. A passing score is 50 or greater. Sample output line:

```
Davis             52          Passed
```

   (b) A bank charges senior citizens (65 years of age or older) no service charge for cashing checks; otherwise the bank charges $.15 for each check cashed. Print the customer's account number, the number of checks cashed, and the service charge for each of four customers. Display appropriate messages. A sample output line is given below.

```
Account number: 21034     Number of checks: 5     Service charge: .75
```

6. Identify the errors in the following routine. Make the necessary corrections. Assume values have been assigned to variables.

```
6010 IF CODE = L AND AREA.CODE = 412
        THEN BILL = RENTAL
        ELSE LONG.DISTANCE = MINUTES*RATE BILL = RENTAL+LONG DISTANCE
6020 PRINT BILL
```

Programming Problems

Design and code programs for the following problems. Note: A year is expressed as 19XX. Verify all data keyed in during program execution.

1. Design and code a program that prints the names and faculties of only graduate students. The code G in the data given below denotes Graduate, U represents Undergraduate. Save your program as it is needed for Problem 2.

   Data:

   Edwards,Science,G
   Haines,Medicine,G
   Hall,Commerce,U
   Barton,Commerce,G — Student's name, faculty, code
   Peters,Science,U
   Lindsay,Commerce,G
   Adams,Arts,G
   Palmer,Music,U
   Ross,Science,G

```
RUN

Please enter the year--19XX
Is the year correct (y/n)? y

GRADUATE STUDENTS
Year: 19XX

NAME            FACULTY

Edwards         Science
Haines          Medicine
Barton          Commerce
Lindsay         Commerce
Adams           Arts
Ross            Science
```

2. Modify the program for Problem 1 so that it prints the names and faculties of graduate students in Science and Commerce only. Your IF statement must not only check for a graduate student but must also check whether the student is in Science or in Commerce.

```
RUN

Please enter the year--19XX
Is the year correct (y/n)? y

GRADUATE STUDENTS IN SCIENCE AND COMMERCE
Year: 19XX

NAME            FACULTY

Edwards         Science
Barton          Commerce
Lindsay         Commerce
Ross            Science
```

3. A company pays its sales personnel 12% commission on sales up to and including $5000 and 15% on sales in excess of $5000. The $5000 is referred to as the base. Find the amount of commission

for each salesperson shown in the data below. Calculate a commission in an IF/THEN/ELSE statement. Save your program. It is needed for a problem in Chapter Seven.

Data:

James Kelly,5839
Tom Powell,4987 — Name of salesperson, amount of sales
Joan Friesen,6025
Leslie Dale,5000

Formulas:

(a) Sales <= Base
Commission = Sales x Rate on Base/100
(b) Sales > Base
Commission = Base x Rate on Base/100 + (Sales−Base) x Rate on Excess/100

RUN

```
Enter month and day as the date, e.g. September 30
Enter date, base, regular rate, excess rate--August 19,5000,12,15
Are the entries correct (y/n)? y

COMMISSION REPORT
Week Ending August 19

NAME            SALES           COMMISSION

James Kelly      5839            725.85
Tom Powell       4987            598.44
Joan Friesen     6025            753.75
Leslie Dale      5000            600
```

4. Write a program for the problem presented on page 116 and for which a decision structure was discussed. Here is the problem once more.

A community club charges a lower rate for shareholders than it does for nonshareholders. Furthermore, within each category, a family rate is lower than an individual rate. One member is charged three-quarters of the individual fee and each additional member is charged $20.00 less than the individual fee. The individual fee for a shareholder is $340, the individual fee for a nonshareholder is $400. The following formulas are used.

Individual Fee = $340 or $400 depending on whether the registrant is a shareholder or a nonshareholder.

Family Fee = Individual Fee × .75 + (Number of Family Members − 1) × (Individual Fee − 20)

The accounting department requires a listing of the registrants and their fees. In the data given below, S denotes shareholder, N means nonshareholder. The number of members in a family includes the registrant.

Data:

Johnson,S,3
Payne,N,2
Rodgers,S,2 — Name, code for type of registrant,
Adams,S,1 number of people applying
Harrison,N,3
Neumann,N,1

```
RUN

Enter starting year, ending year, rates--[19XX,19XX,340,400]
Are the entries correct (y/n)? [y]

COMMUNITY CLUB MEMBERS
For Winter Season 19XX to 19XX

NAME            STATUS         NUMBER         FEE

Johnson         S              3              895
Payne           N              2              680
Rodgers         S              2              575
Adams           S              1              340
Harrison        N              3              1060
Neumann         N              1              400
```

5. A retailer purchases six microcomputers at a total cost of $8500. The terms of sale are 5/10,2/30,n/60 which has the following meanings.

(a) A discount of 5% is offered if the invoice is paid within 10 days from the date of the invoice.
(b) A discount of 2% is offered if the invoice is paid within 30 days from the date of the invoice.
(c) No discount is given if the invoice is paid after 30 days from the date of the invoice. The invoice must be paid within 60 days.

Read in the rates (5, 2, Ø) as one record. Use a multiple IF statement to determine the rate to use. The rate depends on the number of days within which the invoice was paid. Calculate the discount, if any, and the net price.

Sample Output:

```
Purchase price, days? [8500,10]
Are the entries correct (y/n)? [y]

Purchase price: 8500            Rate: 5
Discount: 425                   Net price: 8075
```

6. Write a program that prints an interest table for various types of bonds. The rate of interest depends on the type of bond (municipal, corporate, or government) and, for some types of bonds, on the period of time. Codes are used to differentiate the types of bonds. A code of M denotes a municipal bond, a code of C denotes a corporate bond, and a code of G means a government bond. The interest rates are given below.

Municipal Bond: 7.5%

Corporate Bond		*Government Bond*	
<= 5 years	> 5 years	<= 5 years	> 5 years
8%	9%	9.5%	10%

Data:

C,5000,7
M,3000,5
G,7000,9 — Type of bond, value, number of years
G,6000,5
M,2000,3
C,4000,5

Formula:

Interest = Value of Bond × Number of Years × Rate of Interest/100

Determine the type of bond (municipal, corporate, or government). Assign the appropriate rate to a common variable, say RATE. If the type of bond is M merely assign the municipal rate to RATE. If the type of bond is C or G, check the number of years before assigning the appropriate rate to RATE. Hint: Use three IF statements. For corporate and government bonds, use a multiple IF statement for each type of bond (see page 114 for a multiple IF). Each multiple IF statement should contain compound conditions using the AND operator. Following the decision structure, calculate the interest using the common variable RATE as the rate of interest. Print a detail line.

RUN

```
Enter municipal rate, corporate rates (2), government rates (2)
Rates? 7.5,8,9,9.5,10
Are the rates correct (y/n)? y

INTEREST TABLE FOR VARIOUS TYPES OF BONDS

TYPE          RATE           VALUE          YEARS          INTEREST

C             9              5000           7              3150
M             7.5            3000           5              1125
G             10             7000           9              6300
G             9.5            6000           5              2850
M             7.5            2000           3              450
C             8              4000           5              1600
```

7. The president of a large transfer company must decide whether the company should branch out into interstate trucking or remain local. Furthermore, at each level, he must decide whether the company should purchase a truck and hire an employee or hire a leased operator who already owns a truck. All decisions are based on a ten-year period. In the data given below, an employee's salary and the maintenance on the company owned truck are yearly costs, the number of miles for a leased operator are miles per month. Do not verify data. In Chapter Eight, you will learn how to verify data entered by more than one INPUT statement.

Interstate

Salaried Employee		*Leased Operator*	
Truck	— $150 000	Miles	— 3200
Maintenance on Truck	— 40 000	Rate per mile	— $2.25
Salary	— 30 000		

Local

Salaried Employee		*Leased Operator*	
Truck	— $ 75 000	Miles	— 1700
Maintenance on Truck	— 5 000	Rate per mile	— $1.95
Salary	— 27 000		

Formulas:

Salaried employee:
Cost = Cost of Truck + (Maintenance on Truck + Salary) × 10

Leased operator:
Cost = (Miles × Rate per Mile) × 12 × 10

RUN

```
Interstate or local trucking? Enter I or L--I
Employee or leased operator? Enter E or O--E
Cost of truck,maintenance,salary for interstate employee? 150000,40000,30000

HIRING AN EMPLOYEE

AREA           TRUCK           MAINTENANCE     SALARY          TEN-YEAR COST

I               150000          40000           30000           850000
```

Another RUN should produce:

```
Interstate or local trucking? Enter I or L--L
Employee or leased operator? Enter E or O--O
Miles, rate per mile for local leased operator? 1700,1.95

HIRING A LEASED OPERATOR

AREA           RATE            MILES           TEN-YEAR COST

L               1.95            1700            397800
```

The ten year cost for a leased operator and interstate trucking is $864,000; the cost for a salaried employee and local trucking is $395,000.

In the subroutine that processes the data, use four IF/THEN statements each with a compound condition that checks the area and the type of trucker. Each statement must display a prompt asking the user for particular costs and must allow the user to key in these costs. An example of such a statement is as follows:

```
4010 IF AREA$ = "I" AND TRUCKER$ = "E"
     THEN INPUT "Cost of truck,maintenance,salary for interstate employee";
     TRUCK,MAINTENANCE,SALARY : GOSUB 5000         'Salaried employee
```

The subroutine calculates the cost and prints the report.

The four IF/THEN statements must make decisions from four combinations of choices. These combinations are:

(a) Interstate trucking and salaried employee
(b) Interstate trucking and leased operator
(c) Local trucking and salaried employee
(d) Local trucking and leased operator

8. One of the fields in the Accounts Receivable master file is a credit limit. For example, the record for account number 31002 contains the following fields:

31002,Derek Andrews,1000,Nov. 17,821.44

The value 1000 following the name is the credit limit. Modify the Accounts Receivable program so that it checks the final balance of each account to determine whether or not the customer has exceeded the credit limit. If the credit limit has been exceeded, display "Credit limit of xxxx dollars exceeded by xx.xx" at the bottom of the account. (xxxx represents the credit limit and xx.xx represents the amount by which the customer has exceeded the limit.) Account number 31002 is shown on the following page.

```
Transaction for the following account:

 31002   Derek Andrews   Balance on Nov. 17: 821.44   Credit limit: 1000

Enter transaction (date, sale, payment)--Nov. 20,532.95,316.52
Are the entries correct (y/n)? y

Account number: 31002

Name: Derek Andrews

DATE          DEBIT          CREDIT          BALANCE

Nov. 17                                       821.44
Nov. 20        532.95         316.52          1037.87

Credit limit of 1000 dollars exceeded by 37.87
-------------------------------------------------
```

Solutions for Exercises

6.1 The IF/THEN Statement

1. (a) `6010 IF B <> 0 THEN C = A/B`
   (b) `6020 IF A < 10 THEN C = A*B`
   (c) `6030 IF B > 0 THEN GOSUB 7000`
   (d) `6040 IF SCORE >= 50 THEN PRINT "Passed"`
   (e) `6050 IF MILES < 500 THEN RENTAL = MILES*RATE+SERVICE.CHARGE`

2. (a) False.
   (b) True. F = 5
   (c) True. Prints Not equal
   (d) True. F = 1
   (e) False

6.2 A Multi-Statement IF/THEN

1.
```
6020 IF NO.DEPENDENTS > 0
        THEN DEDUCTION = NO.DEPENDENTS*700 :
        NET.INCOME = TOTAL.INCOME-DEDUCTION
```

2.
```
6020 IF AGE > 1 THEN GOSUB 7000       'Calculate current value

7000 'SUBROUTINE CALCULATE CURRENT VALUE
7010   DEPRECIATION = PREVIOUS.VALUE*RATE/100
7020   CURRENT.VALUE = PREVIOUS.VALUE-DEPRECIATION
7030   PRINT "Depreciation:";DEPRECIATION
7040   PRINT "Current value:";CURRENT.VALUE
7050   RETURN
```

6.3 The IF/THEN/ELSE Statement

1. (a)
```
6020 IF INVENTORY.COUNT > 10
        THEN PRINT "Current stock:";INVENTORY.COUNT
        ELSE PRINT "Out of stock. Please reorder."
```
   (b)
```
6020 IF NO.DAYS <= 3 THEN PRINT NO.DAYS,REGULAR.FARE
6030 IF NO.DAYS > 3 THEN DISCOUNT = REGULAR.FARE*DISCOUNT.RATE/100 :
        REDUCED.FARE = REGULAR.FARE-DISCOUNT :
        PRINT NO.DAYS,REGULAR.FARE,DISCOUNT,REDUCED.FARE
```

2. (a) G = 18
   (b) G = 3
   (c) G = 12
   (d) G = 2
   (e) G = 15

6.4 Comparing Strings

1. True
2. False
3. True
4. False
5. False

6.5 Logical Operators

1. (a) The reserved word IF must be coded only once in an IF statement.

   `6010 IF A = B AND A = C THEN D = A+B ELSE D = A+C`

   (b) Nothing is wrong.

   (c) A cannot be both equal to B and less than B.

   `6030 IF A = B OR A < B THEN C = A*B ELSE C = B-A`

(d) In the AND condition, A cannot be both less than B and greater than B.

```
6040 IF (A = C OR A < B) AND A > B THEN D = A+B+C
```

(e) Nothing is wrong.

(f) A value and an operator must be coded before "Jones".

```
6060 WHILE ENAME$ <> "Smith" OR ENAME$ <> "Jones"
```

2. (a) True (d) False
(b) True (e) False
(c) True (f) True

3.
```
6040 IF NO.STUDENTS >= 8 AND NO.STUDENTS <= 30
        THEN PRINT NO.STUDENTS;"Students in the course"
        ELSE PRINT NO.STUDENTS;"Students" : PRINT "Invalid number of students"
```

6.6 Multiple Alternatives

```
6020 IF SCORE<50 THEN GRADE$="F" ELSE IF SCORE<58 THEN GRADE$="D"
        ELSE IF SCORE<70 THEN GRADE$="C" ELSE IF SCORE<80 THEN GRADE$="B"
        ELSE IF SCORE<90 THEN GRADE$="A" ELSE IF SCORE<101 THEN GRADE$="A+"
```

6.7 A Decision Within a Decision

```
6000 'SUBROUTINE PROCESS DATA
6010    IF GRADE.POINT > 3.5 THEN GOSUB 6200 ELSE SCHOLARSHIP = 0
6015       'Subroutine 6200 determines the amount of the scholarship
6020    PRINT SNAME$,GRADE.POINT,SCHOLARSHIP
6030    RETURN
6200 'SUBROUTINE GRADE.POINT > 3.5
6210    IF EXTRA.CURRICULAR > 2
           THEN SCHOLARSHIP = 1000
           ELSE SCHOLARSHIP = 800
6220    RETURN
```

7

SEQUENTIAL FILES

Objectives

In the previous chapters, we assigned values to variables by the assignment statement, the READ and DATA statements, and the INPUT statement. All data items were stored internally and used only by the program that stored the items. In this chapter, you will learn how to store data externally on disk so that the data can be retrieved and used by other programs.

BASIC supports two methods of storing data on disk. One method uses sequential files, the other uses random access files. This chapter focuses on sequential files. We will discuss random access files in Chapter Fifteen.

Contents

Questions and Exercises

Programming Problems

Project

7.1 Defining Files

In Chapter Four, we defined a file as a collection of related items. A file may consist of a program, a set of related data items, or it may consist of text such as a form letter. A program stored on disk is called a program file, a file of data stored on disk is called a data file. Text, such as the form letter, is called a text file.

A data file can be divided into records, each record can be subdivided into fields. Until now, most of our programs entered records into the computer by the READ and DATA statements. Records can also be entered by the INPUT statement. The assignment statement can enter only one value. Unfortunately, all data entered into the computer by one of these methods cannot be shared by other programs. The values can be used only by the program that enters the values. Furthermore, the data items are not permanent. When we clear the program from memory, the data disappears along with the program.

Ideally, the data items should be set apart from the program so that:

1. The data items can be shared by other programs.
2. The data items are permanent and can be stored for long periods of time.
3. A large quantity of data items can be stored, ready for use. The quantity stored is often more than internal memory can hold at any one time.

To be able to take advantage of the above features, we must store the data externally. Although other types of storage media exist, we will store data on our BASIC diskette. The INPUT statement will be used to take values from the keyboard and place them in memory. We will then transfer the values from memory to our BASIC diskette.

BASIC uses two types of data files: sequential files and random access files. In a sequential file, records are stored and retrieved sequentially, one record after the other. Thus, if we wish to retrieve the sixth record, we must retrieve the five records preceding the sixth. Reading can start only at the beginning of a sequential file. Furthermore, to change an item in a sequential file, we must read and rewrite the entire file.

In a random access file, we can store and access records in any order. If we wish to retrieve the sixth record, we can do so directly without having to retrieve the five preceding records. However, to access a specific record, we must let DOS know the exact location of the record in the file.

What are the advantages and disadvantages of sequential and random access files? In a sequential data file, even if a few records need to be changed, all records must be read from the file. After the required records have been updated, all records must be written to the same file or to another file. Consequently, records may be updated periodically, perhaps once a month or once a week. Depending on the updating schedule, records may remain out of date for too long a period of time. However, programs using sequential files are relatively simple to write. There is no need to know where records are stored in the file since they are read and written sequentially. Furthermore, DOS does most of the work for us.

Programs using random access files are more difficult to write. To be able to access a record directly, we are given greater control over the transfer of records to and from the data file. We tell DOS where to store a specific record and where it can be found. This control requires more tasks in our programs. The main advantage of a random access file is the speed by which we can access a specific record. Since we can access a record directly, retrieving a record from a random access file is much faster than retrieving one from a sequential file. Furthermore, since all records need not be retrieved, all records need not be rewritten to a random access file after a record has been updated. A record can be retrieved, updated, then stored in the same location of the same file. Because a record is more readily accessible, a random access file is more likely to be kept up-to-date than a sequential file.

In business applications, sequential files are often used when all records must be retrieved and held in memory for processing. An example of such an application is the sorting of the records. All records must be in memory before they can be sorted. On the other hand, many applications require the direct retrieval of a specific record. Asking a customer in a bank to wait for his account to be found as the computer searches through all the preceding accounts is hardly considered practical. This is when random access files prove to be most useful.

Exercises

1. Why should data items be stored externally? State three reasons.
2. Explain briefly the difference between a sequential file and a random access file.
3. State the advantages and disadvantages of sequential and random access files.

7.2 Creating a Sequential Data File

A Sample Program

Let us store the following file on disk as a sequential data file.

Darryl Brown,9.54,38,74.57,2.25,3.67 Ellen Miller,8.87,39,72.14,2.25,3.42 Lorne Hayes,9.88,42,79.84,2.25,4.15 Andrea Jones,10.04,47,85.26,2.25,6.31	—	Employee name, rate of pay, hours of work, income tax deduction, union dues, pension deduction

Although it is not possible to write a routine that can create any data file, we have standardized the routine as much as possible by using a common prompt (Record), by displaying no instructions, and by omitting the variable dictionary. You should save the program on disk since many of its statements can be used to create other data files. Suggested filename: CREATE1.BAS. Throughout the book, we will be saving a number of frequently used programs and subroutines. We refer to these files as our library files.

To create a sequential data file, leave the DOS diskette in drive A and place your BASIC diskette in drive B. Load up DOS and BASICA, then key in the following program. The file-handling statements OPEN, WRITE #, and CLOSE are explained beneath the output.

```
1000 'CREATE SEQUENTIAL FILE                  M. MCRITCHIE            MAY 4
1002 '*********************************************************************
1004 ' THIS PROGRAM CREATES A SEQUENTIAL DATA FILE. ALL RECORDS ARE SIMILAR.
1006 '*********************************************************************
2010  OPEN "B:EMPLOYE1.DAT" FOR OUTPUT AS #1
2020  PRINT
2030  INPUT "Record";ENAME$,RATE,HOURS.WORK,INCOME.TAX,UNION,PENSION
2040  WHILE ENAME$ <> "End of file"
2050    INPUT "Is the record correct (y/n)";RESPONSE$
2060    IF RESPONSE$ <> "y" AND RESPONSE$ <> "Y"
          THEN INPUT "Re-enter the record--",ENAME$,RATE,HOURS.WORK,
          INCOME.TAX,UNION,PENSION : GOTO 2050
2070    WRITE #1, ENAME$,RATE,HOURS.WORK,INCOME.TAX,UNION,PENSION
2080    PRINT
2090    INPUT "Record";ENAME$,RATE,HOURS.WORK,INCOME.TAX,UNION,PENSION
2100  WEND
2110  CLOSE #1
2120  END
RUN
```

```
Record? Darryl Black,9.54,38,74.57,2.25,3.67
Is the record correct (y/n)? n
Re-enter the record--Darryl Brown,9.54,38,74.57,2.25,3.67
Is the record correct (y/n)? y

Record? Ellen Miller,8.87,39,72.14,2.25,3.42
Is the record correct (y/n)? y

Record? Lorne Hayes,9.88,42,79.84,2.25,4.15
Is the record correct (y/n)? y

Record? Andrea Jones,10.04,47,85.26,2.25,6.31
Is the record correct (y/n)? y

Record? End of file,0,0,0,0,0
```

The employee names keyed in are not enclosed in quotation marks, since no name in our file contains a comma, a leading space, or a trailing space. However, the string constant in the WHILE statement must be enclosed in quotation marks. Note that we have a small loop within the WHILE/WEND loop: the loop that verifies our keyed-in data.

A trailer record must be keyed in after all records have been entered. The record terminates the WHILE/WEND loop. The trailer record is not written to the data file. When the trailer record is keyed in, its first field, End of file, is assigned to ENAME$. The WHILE statement compares ENAME$ with End of file. Since ENAME$ is equal to End of file, the condition in the WHILE statement is false. BASIC drops out of the loop, thus bypassing the WRITE # statement which writes data to a sequential data file. Hence, the trailer record is not sent to the file.

The OPEN Statement

The OPEN statement opens a data file by creating a communication link between the file and the program. The OPEN statement must specify the following:

1. The drive in which the data file resides.
2. The name of the file. The name must conform to the rules applied to filenames as outlined on page 65. We include a digit in the name so that a similar name can be used later on. When we create a file whose filename is EMPLOYE2.DAT, the contents of EMPLOYE1.DAT will not be destroyed since EMPLOYE2.DAT is a distinct and separate file. Note that we use DAT as the extension to differentiate a data file from a program file. (We use BAS as the extension when we store a program.)

   The drive specification and filename must be enclosed in quotation marks. They must be separated by a colon.
3. The mode of access. OUTPUT specifies the writing of data to a sequential file. **If an existing file is opened in OUTPUT mode, the OPEN statement destroys the contents of the existing file.**
4. The file number. Subsequent file-handling statements will reference the data file by its number rather than by its name as do WRITE #1 in line 2070 and CLOSE #1 in line 2110.

   The maximum number of files we may open by default is three. Thus, the file number may be 1, 2, or 3. We can change this maximum by using the /F: option when loading BASICA. For instance, BASICA/F:6 allows six files to be open at any one time. Fifteen is the maximum number of files we can open when BASICA is loaded with the /F: option.

The WRITE # Statement

The WRITE # statement writes data to a sequential file, in this case to file #1. The file number must be followed by a comma. In our program, file #1 is associated with data file EMPLOYE1.DAT because of the OPEN statement we used. Each time the computer encounters the WRITE # statement in line 2070, the values stored in the six variables listed in the statement are placed as a record in data file EMPLOYE1.DAT. We will refer to these variables as program variables. It should be noted that the WRITE # statement places quotation marks around strings and inserts commas between the data items.

Throughout our discussions on data files, we will be using the terms transfer, move and send. It is important to realize that values do not literally move from one storage area to another. Copies of the values are placed in the storage areas specified. When we say a value is transferred from a program variable to a data file, the value remains in the memory location designated by the variable. A copy of the value is placed in the data file.

It is possible to examine a sequential data file by using the DOS command TYPE. The command merely displays the contents of a data file on the screen; it does not allow you to use the data. Section 7.3 explains how data can be retrieved from disk so that the values can be used in BASIC statements. Refer to Appendix D for instructions in how to use the TYPE command. Caution: Since TYPE is a DOS command, DOS must be loaded into the computer before TYPE can be used. **Loading DOS destroys any program in memory, therefore, you must first save your program.**

The CLOSE Statement

The CLOSE statement closes the communication link between the program and the data file. The number sign (#) before the file number is optional. It should be noted that the END statement not only terminates execution but also closes a data file. Hence, the CLOSE statement is actually not needed in the program. However, it is good programming practice to explicitly close a data file.

At the end of a sequential data file, DOS stores an EOF (end-of-file) character, placed there when the file is created. This EOF character signals the end of the data file and is useful when we retrieve the contents of the file.

Exercises

1. What is the purpose of the OPEN statement?
2. What must an OPEN statement specify?
3. Suppose an existing data file is opened in OUTPUT mode. What, if anything, happens to the contents of the file?
4. What is the maximum number of files that can be open by default? How can this be changed?
5. What is the purpose of the CLOSE statement?
6. Create the following data file. Name the file SALES1.DAT. This file will be used in a subsequent exercise.

   SALES1.DAT
   Marion Evans,6000
   Stanley Doerksen,6400 — Salesperson's name, amount of sales
   Anne Peterson,6300
   Norm Loewen,6100

7.3 Recalling Data from a Data File

A Sample Program

Unlike the DOS command TYPE which merely allows us to examine a data file, the following program allows us to use the data it retrieves from a file. Here we simply print the records. The program retrieves the records stored in sequential file EMPLOYE1.DAT. The OPEN and WHILE statements differ slightly from those in the program on page 139, the INPUT # statement in line 2040 is new. Read the program then study the dialogue given below the output. Save the program. Suggested filename: RETRIEV1.BAS

```
1000 'RETRIEVE DATA (SEQUENTIAL FILE)              M. MCRITCHIE               May 8
1002 '************************************************************************
1004 '        THIS PROGRAM RETRIEVES DATA FROM A SEQUENTIAL DATA FILE
1006 '************************************************************************
2010  OPEN "B:EMPLOYE1.DAT" FOR INPUT AS #1
2020  PRINT
2030  WHILE NOT EOF(1)
2040    INPUT #1, ENAME$,RATE,HOURS.WORK,INCOME.TAX,UNION,PENSION
2050    PRINT ENAME$;RATE;HOURS.WORK;INCOME.TAX;UNION;PENSION
2060  WEND
2070  CLOSE #1
2080  END
RUN
```

```
Darryl Brown 9.54   38   74.57   2.25   3.67
Ellen Miller 8.87   39   72.14   2.25   3.42
Lorne Hayes 9.88   42   79.84   2.25   4.15
Andrea Jones 10.04   47   85.26   2.25   6.31
```

The OPEN Statement

As in the program on page 139, the OPEN statement must specify the drive and filename enclosed in quotation marks, the mode of access, and the file number. Unlike the OPEN statement in our former program, the mode of access here is INPUT because we want to retrieve the data. The file number need not be the same number used when we created the file, however, since this is the first and only file opened in the above program, we have numbered it #1.

Another Method to Terminate a WHILE/WEND Loop

When data file EMPLOYE1.DAT was created, we did not keep track of the number of records stored. Storing ended when we keyed in our trailer record. Nor is it necessary to know the number of records in the file when we retrieve its contents. BASIC provides us with an EOF function that detects the end-of-file character. Remember, an end-of-file character is placed at the end of a sequential file when the file is created.

In line 2030, EOF represents End Of File, the number in parentheses specifies the number of the file. In this case, the number must be #1 since we numbered our file #1 in the OPEN statement. If we had numbered our file #2, we would use EOF(2). We use EOF in our WHILE statement in the form NOT EOF(1). As long as the end-of-file character is NOT detected, the loop continues. When DOS detects the EOF character, the loop terminates.

The INPUT # Statement

The INPUT # statement retrieves data items from a sequential file and assigns the values to program variables (variables used in a program). In our program, the data is recalled from file #1, that is, from our file EMPLOYE1.DAT. The file number in the INPUT # statement must be followed by a comma. Each time the computer encounters our INPUT # statement, a record's six fields are transferred from the file to the six program variables listed in the statement. Because the INPUT # statement has been placed inside the WHILE/WEND loop, records are retrieved until the EOF character is encountered.

Although not necessary, we chose the same variables used when we created the file. Note that the variable types must correspond with the values. For example, the first variable must be a string variable since a name is assigned to this variable.

Recall that the READ statement transfers values from a *data pool* to program variables. The INPUT # statement also transfers values but in this case from a *data file* to program variables. When a data file is opened in either INPUT or OUTPUT mode, a file pointer is automatically positioned at the beginning of the file. The pointer keeps track of the records in the data file in the same manner as a data pool pointer keeps track of the data in a data pool. After records have been written to a data file or read from a data file, the data file pointer is positioned immediately after the last record in the file. Since the operations performed by a READ statement and by an INPUT # statement are almost the same, we will refer to the retrieval of data from a data file as a "read".

Exercises

1. State the difference in execution between the following OPEN statements:

   (a) `2010 OPEN "B:EMPLOYE1.DAT" FOR OUTPUT AS #1`
   (b) `2010 OPEN "B:EMPLOYE1.DAT" FOR INPUT AS #1`

2. How does NOT EOF(2) in a WHILE statement control the WHILE/WEND loop?
3. What statement transfers values from a data file to program variables?
4. What is the purpose of a data file pointer?
5. Modify the program on page 141 so that it retrieves and prints the contents of data file SALES1.DAT created for the exercise on the same page.

7.4 Creating a Data File with Different Records

The Concept of Different Records

So far, our data files contain records with similar fields. For instance, each record in our file EMPLOYEE1.DAT consists of the following fields: Name, Rate of Pay, Hours of Work, Income Tax Deduction, Union Dues, Pension Deduction.

Each employee pays $2.25 for union dues. Since the union dues are the same for all employees, let us remove this deduction from each record and create another record that contains just a union dues field. All records in the file are no longer the same. One record contains just the union dues, each of the remaining records contains the rest of the fields. We will refer to the union dues record as a "special record" and to the remaining records as "data records".

The one-field record must be handled apart from the data records, either before the WHILE/WEND loop or after the loop. We will process this special record before the loop.

The program CREATE1.BAS, which creates a sequential file, must be modified. Our new version of CREATE1.BAS creates the file given below. EMPLOYE2.DAT is the name of our data file. The program should be saved on disk. Suggested filename: CREATE2.BAS

EMPLOYE2.DAT	
2.25	— Union dues
Darryl Brown,9.54,38,74.57,3.67	— Employee name, rate of pay, hours of work, income tax deduction, pension deduction
Ellen Miller,8.87,39,72.14,3.42	
Lorne Hayes,9.88,42,79.84,4.15	
Andrea Jones,10.04,47,85.26,6.31	

The Program

```
1000 'CREATE SEQUENTIAL FILE                          M. MCRITCHIE                 MAY 10
1002 '*******************************************************************************
1004 ' THIS PROGRAM CREATES A SEQUENTIAL FILE THAT CONTAINS DIFFERENT RECORDS
1006 '*******************************************************************************
2010  OPEN "B:EMPLOYE2.DAT" FOR OUTPUT AS #1
2020  PRINT
2030  INPUT "Union dues";UNION
2040  INPUT "Are the union dues correct (y/n)";RESPONSE$
2050  IF RESPONSE$ <> "y" AND RESPONSE$ <> "Y"
         THEN INPUT "Re-enter the union dues--",UNION : GOTO 2040
2060  WRITE #1, UNION
2070  PRINT
2080  INPUT "Record";ENAME$,RATE,HOURS.WORK,INCOME.TAX,PENSION
2090  WHILE ENAME$ <> "End of file"
2100     INPUT "Is the record correct (y/n)";RESPONSE$
2110     IF RESPONSE$ <> "y" AND RESPONSE$ <> "Y"
            THEN INPUT "Re-enter the record--",ENAME$,RATE,HOURS.WORK,
            INCOME.TAX,PENSION : GOTO 2100
2120     WRITE #1, ENAME$,RATE,HOURS.WORK,INCOME.TAX,PENSION
2130     PRINT
2140     INPUT "Record";ENAME$,RATE,HOURS.WORK,INCOME.TAX,PENSION
2150  WEND
2160  CLOSE #1
2170  END
```

Partial Output:

```
Union dues? [2.25]
Are the union dues correct (y/n)? [y]

Record? [Darryl Brown,9.54,38,74.57,3.67]
Is the record correct (y/n)? [y]
```

The last record keyed in must be a trailer record such as **End of file,0,0,0,0**. The record for union dues is entered, verified, and written to the file in lines 2030 to 2060 inclusive. As with CREATE1.BAS, the first data record is entered just before the loop. Inside the loop, the record is verified and written to the file (lines 2100 to 2120 inclusive). In line 2140, another data record is entered. The WEND statement in line 2150 returns control to the WHILE and the entire process of verifying, writing, and entering a data record is repeated until the trailer value "End of file" is assigned to ENAME$.

Exercises

1. Modify the above program so that it creates the following data file. The data file will be used in Exercise 2 below and in the exercise on page 146.

   SALES2.DAT
   12 — Rate of commission

Marion Evans,6000
Stanley Doerksen,6400 — Salesperson's name, amount of sales
Anne Peterson,6300
Norm Loewen,6100

2. Modify the program RETRIEV1.BAS listed on page 141 so that it retrieves and prints the records in data file SALES2.DAT. Hint: You must read and print the rate of commission before the WHILE/WEND loop begins. Save the modified program. Suggested filename: RETRIEV2.BAS

7.5 Updating a Data File

Information in a data file rarely stays the same. Records are often changed to reflect the latest information. Changing records in a data file is referred to as updating the file. In this chapter, we will update every data record. Later on, you will learn how to update only specific records. Regardless of the number of records that must be changed, all the records in a sequential file must be retrieved. The records, of which some or all may be updated, can be written back to the same file or written to a new file.

A program that updates a data file requires two modes of OPEN. One OPEN statement opens the original file for an INPUT to read records from the file. The other OPEN statement opens either the same file (which must first be closed after records have been read and updated) or it opens a new file. This OPEN statement must open the file for an OUTPUT to write records to the file. In the program given below, we write records to a new file. In Chapter 12, you will learn how to write records to the same file after records have been updated.

Suppose all employees, whose records are stored in data file EMPLOYE2.DAT, receive a 10% increase in their hourly rates of pay. Furthermore, changes must be made to their income tax and pension deductions. The new data for each employee is as follows.

Name	*Rate of Pay*	*Income Tax*	*Pension*
Darryl Brown	10.49	82.03	4.04
Ellen Miller	9.76	79.35	3.76
Lorne Hayes	10.87	87.82	4.57
Andrea Jones	11.04	93.79	6.94

Here is the program.

```
1000 'UPDATE SEQUENTIAL FILE                    M. MCRITCHIE                 MAY 12
1002 '*********************************************************************
1004 '                THIS PROGRAM UPDATES A SEQUENTIAL DATA FILE
1006 '*********************************************************************
1010 'UNION       - UNION DUES
1020 'ENAME$      - EMPLOYEE NAME
1030 'RATE        - RATE OF PAY
1040 'HOURS.WORK  - HOURS OF WORK
1050 'INCOME.TAX  - INCOME TAX DEDUCTION
1060 'PENSION     - PENSION DEDUCTION
2000 '*********************************************************************
2002 '                              MAIN ROUTINE
2004 '*********************************************************************
2010  OPEN "B:EMPLOYE2.DAT" FOR INPUT AS #1
2020  OPEN "B:EMPLOYE3.DAT" FOR OUTPUT AS #2
2030  GOSUB 3000                          'Update data file
2040  CLOSE #1,#2
2050  END
3000 '*********************************************************************
3002 '                            UPDATE DATA FILE
3004 '*********************************************************************
3010  INPUT #1, UNION
3020  WRITE #2, UNION
3030  WHILE NOT EOF(1)
3040    PRINT
3050    INPUT #1, ENAME$,RATE,HOURS.WORK,INCOME.TAX,PENSION
3060    PRINT ENAME$;RATE;HOURS.WORK;INCOME.TAX;PENSION
```

```
3070      INPUT "Enter new rate of pay, income tax and pension deductions--",
          RATE,INCOME.TAX,PENSION
3080      INPUT "Are the entries correct (y/n)";RESPONSE$
3090      IF RESPONSE$ <> "y" AND RESPONSE$ <> "Y"
               THEN INPUT "Re-enter the data--",RATE,INCOME.TAX,PENSION : GOTO 3080
3100      WRITE #2, ENAME$,RATE,HOURS.WORK,INCOME.TAX,PENSION
3110    WEND
3120    RETURN
65529 'End of program listing
```

Partial Output:

```
Darryl Brown 9.54  38  74.57  3.67
Enter new rate of pay, income tax and pension deductions--10.49,82.03,4.04
Are the entries correct (y/n)? y

Ellen Miller 8.87  39  72.14  3.42
Enter new rate of pay, income tax and pension deductions--9.76,79.35,3.76
Are the entries correct (y/n)? y
```

We must first open the two data files; the original file for INPUT and a new file for OUTPUT. We use data file EMPLOYE2.DAT as our original file and EMPLOYE3.DAT as our new file. EMPLOYE2.DAT is numbered file #1, EMPLOYE3.DAT is numbered file #2. Remember, we stored union dues as a special record in file EMPLOYE2.DAT. Since all records must be read, we must read the union dues (line 3010). Line 3020 writes the record to file EMPLOYE3.DAT.

Inside the WHILE/WEND loop, line 3050 reads a data record (these records are all similar) from our original file and line 3060 displays the record on the screen. Line 3070 allows us to key in the new rate of pay, new income tax deduction, and new pension deduction. Lines 3080 and 3090 give us a chance to correct any error in the data just keyed in and line 3100 writes the record to the new file, EMPLOYE3.DAT.

Even though we intend to change only three fields in each data record, we must read an entire record (five fields) from the original file. After the desired fields have been updated, we must write the entire record to the new file. We do these tasks record by record. Each updated record will contain the original name and hours of work and the new rate of pay, new income tax deduction, and new pension deduction. The original and updated records for Darryl Brown are shown below.

Original record:	Darryl Brown,9.54,38,74.57,3.67
Updated record:	Darryl Brown,10.49,38,82.03,4.04

Suppose we wish to display the updated file in the same program that changed the records. Our main routine must be modified in the following manner:

```
2000 '*********************************************************************
2002 '                          MAIN ROUTINE
2004 '*********************************************************************
2010   OPEN "B:EMPLOYE2.DAT" FOR INPUT AS #1
2020   OPEN "B:EMPLOYE3.DAT" FOR OUTPUT AS #2
2030   GOSUB 3000                    'Update data file
2040   CLOSE #1,#2
2050   OPEN "B:EMPLOYE3.DAT" FOR INPUT AS #2
2060   GOSUB 4000                    'Read updated file
2070   CLOSE #2
2080   END
```

After calling the subroutine that updates the data file, then closing both the original file and the updated file, we open the updated file for an INPUT (line 2050). This repositions the data file pointer from the end of the updated file to the beginning of the file. We number the file #2 since we gave it this number when we opened the file for an OUTPUT. However, we can just as well number the file 1, 2, or 3. In line 2060, we call the subroutine that reads the updated file. Line 2070 closes the file.

To read the updated data file, we use a modified version of RETRIEV2.BAS as a subroutine. The subroutine is given below. Note that we read all the records but choose to display only the updated records and not the union dues.

```
4000 '***********************************************************************
4002 '                           READ UPDATED FILE
4004 '***********************************************************************
4010  INPUT #2, UNION
4020  PRINT
4030  WHILE NOT EOF(2)
4040    INPUT #2, ENAME$,RATE,HOURS.WORK,INCOME.TAX,PENSION
4050    PRINT ENAME$;RATE;HOURS.WORK;INCOME.TAX;PENSION
4060  WEND
4070  RETURN
```

Exercise

Update data file SALES2.DAT created for the exercise on page 143 by changing the sales for each salesperson to that shown below. Store the updated file under filename SALES3.DAT. In the same program, read all records from the updated file but display only the updated records on the screen. Use the main routine on page 145 as a guide and code a subroutine similar to the one listed above to read the updated file. The update routine is given on page 144. Remember to customize all routines so they can be used for files SALES2.DAT and SALES3.DAT.

Name	*Sale*
Marion Evans	6400
Stanley Doerksen	6200
Anne Peterson	6700
Norm Loewen	6600

7.6 BASIC Commands for Handling Data Files

Of the four BASIC commands used to handle program files in Chapter Four (SAVE, LOAD, KILL, and FILES), only the last two can be used with data files. We cannot SAVE or LOAD data files. We can, however, use KILL to delete a data file from disk and FILES to list data files (the command lists all files). Examples of the two commands are given below.

```
KILL "B:ACCOUNTS.DAT"
FILES "B:"
```

A sample listing obtained by the FILES command could be:

```
FILES "B:"
B:\
NET-PAY .BAS      CREATE1 .BAS      EMPLOYE1.DAT      RETRIEV1.BAS
CREATE2 .BAS      EMPLOYE2.DAT      RETRIEV2.BAS      EMPLOYE3.DAT
 318536 Bytes free
```

Exercises

1. Display the contents of your BASIC diskette on the screen.
2. Delete the data files created for the exercises in this chapter. The files were named SALES1.DAT, SALES2.DAT and SALES3.DAT.

7.7 Program Design

The program designed below maintains (updates) the one designed in Chapter Six. The former program will be changed as follows:

1. The data will be read from a data file.
2. The former union dues will be read as a special record.

Because our program is modularized, we simply modify the modules involved; namely, the Main Routine where a data file will be opened and closed, and Subroutine READ DATA FILE where records will be read from a data file. Records will be read from file EMPLOYE3.DAT which is given below.

```
EMPLOYE3.DAT
2.25                                   — Union dues
Darryl Brown,10.49,38,82.03,4.04       — Employee name, rate of pay, hours of
Ellen Miller,9.76,39,79.35,3.76          work, income tax deduction, pension
Lorne Hayes,10.87,42,87.82,4.57          deduction
Andrea Jones,11.04,47,93.79,6.94
```

The program will produce the following output.

```
         10        20        30        40        50        60
1234567890123456789012345678901234567890123456789012345678901234

Enter date (month and day), regular hours, base for double time
Date, hours? October 17,39,45
Are the entries correct (y/n)? y

PAYROLL REPORT
Week Ending October 17

NAME            HOURS           GROSS PAY       DEDUCTIONS      NET PAY

Darryl Brown    38              398.62          88.32           310.3
Ellen Miller    39              380.64          85.36           295.28
Lorne Hayes     42              472.845         94.64           378.205
Andrea Jones    47              574.08          102.98          471.1
```

FIGURE 7-1 STRUCTURE CHART

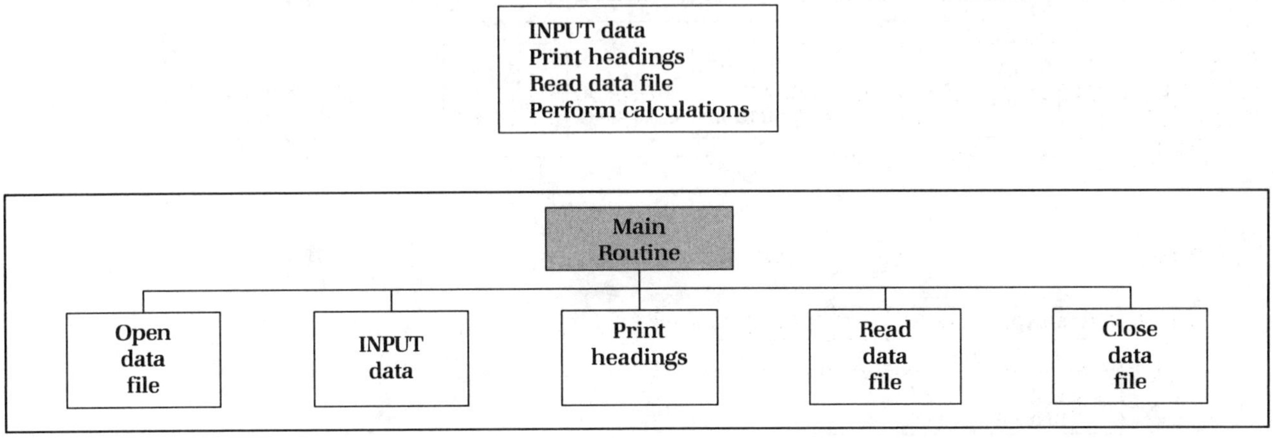

Figure 7-1 Continued

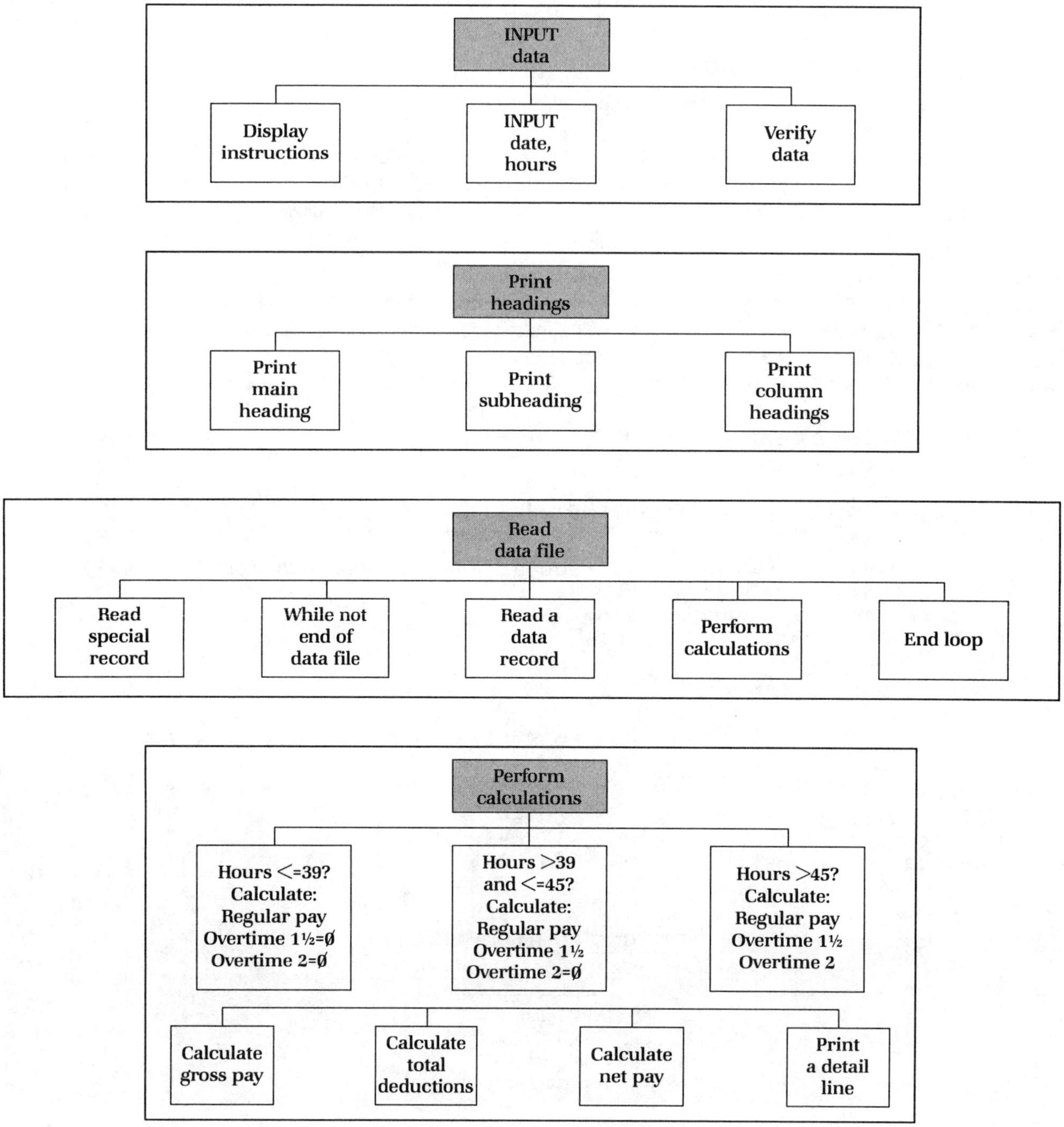

FIGURE 7-2 PSEUDOCODE

MAJOR TASKS
INPUT data
Print headings
Read data file
Perform calculations

MAIN ROUTINE	
Open data file	
INPUT data	(subroutine)
Print headings	(subroutine)
Read data file	(subroutine)
Close data file	

INPUT DATA	
Display instructions	
INPUT date, hours	DATE1$,REGULAR.HOURS,BASE.DOUBLE
Verify data	RESPONSE$

PRINT HEADINGS
Print main heading
Print subheading
Print column headings

READ DATA FILE	
Read special record	UNION
While not end of data file	
Read a data record	ENAME$,RATE,HOURS.WORK,INCOME.TAX,PENSION
Perform calculations	(subroutine)
End loop	

PERFORM CALCULATIONS	
Hours of work <= 39?	
Calculate regular pay	REGULAR.PAY
Overtime pay at time and a half = Ø	OVERTIME.HALF
Overtime pay at double time = Ø	OVERTIME.DOUBLE
Hours of work > 39 and <= 45?	
Calculate regular pay	
Calculate overtime pay at time and a half	
Overtime pay at double time = Ø	
Hours of work > 45?	
Calculate regular pay	
Calculate overtime pay at time and a half	
Calculate overtime pay at double time	
Calculate gross pay	GROSS.PAY
Calculate total deductions	DEDUCTIONS
Calculate net pay	NET.PAY
Print a detail line	

Since you are now familiar with modularization and with the outputs obtained from intermediate programs, we will simply list the entire program. However, we strongly urge you to develop all programs module by module.

```
1000 'NET PAY                          M. MCRITCHIE                       MAY 16
1002 '*********************************************************************
1004 '  THIS PROGRAM READS EMPLOYEE RECORDS FROM A DATA FILE AND CALCULATES
1006 '  THE NET PAY FOR EACH EMPLOYEE. THE PAY SCHEDULE INCLUDES OVERTIME
1007 '  PAY AT TIME AND A HALF AND AT DOUBLE TIME.
1008 '*********************************************************************
1010 'DATE1$            - DATE
1020 'REGULAR.HOURS     - REGULAR HOURS
1030 'BASE.DOUBLE       - BASE HOURS FOR DOUBLE TIME
1040 'RESPONSE$         - USER'S RESPONSE (y/n)
```

```
1050 'UNION             - UNION DUES
1060 'ENAME$            - EMPLOYEE NAME
1070 'RATE              - RATE OF PAY
1080 'HOURS.WORK        - HOURS OF WORK
1090 'INCOME.TAX        - INCOME TAX DEDUCTION
1100 'PENSION           - PENSION DEDUCTION
1110 'REGULAR.PAY       - REGULAR PAY
1120 'OVERTIME.HALF     - OVERTIME PAY AT TIME AND A HALF
1130 'OVERTIME.DOUBLE   - OVERTIME PAY AT DOUBLE TIME
1140 'GROSS.PAY         - GROSS PAY
1150 'DEDUCTIONS        - TOTAL DEDUCTIONS
1160 'NET.PAY           - NET PAY
2000 '*******************************************************************
2002 '                              MAIN ROUTINE
2004 '*******************************************************************
2010  OPEN "B:EMPLOYE3.DAT" FOR INPUT AS #1
2020  GOSUB 3000                    'INPUT data
2030  GOSUB 4000                    'Print headings
2040  GOSUB 5000                    'Read data file
2050  CLOSE #1
2060  END
3000 '*******************************************************************
3002 '                        INPUT DATA (DATE AND HOURS)
3004 '*******************************************************************
3010  PRINT
3020  PRINT "Enter date (month and day), regular hours, base for double time"
3030  INPUT "Date, hours";DATE1$,REGULAR.HOURS,BASE.DOUBLE
3040  INPUT "Are the entries correct (y/n)";RESPONSE$
3050  IF RESPONSE$ <> "y" AND RESPONSE$ <> "Y"
        THEN INPUT "Re-enter the data--",DATE1$,REGULAR.HOURS,BASE.DOUBLE :
        GOTO 3040
3060  RETURN
4000 '*******************************************************************
4002 '                              PRINT HEADINGS
4004 '*******************************************************************
4010  PRINT
4020  PRINT "PAYROLL REPORT"
4030  PRINT "Week Ending ";DATE1$
4040  PRINT
4050  PRINT "NAME","HOURS","GROSS PAY","DEDUCTIONS","NET PAY"
4060  PRINT
4070  RETURN
5000 '*******************************************************************
5002 '                              READ DATA FILE
5004 '*******************************************************************
5010  INPUT #1, UNION
5020  WHILE NOT EOF(1)
5030    INPUT #1, ENAME$,RATE,HOURS.WORK,INCOME.TAX,PENSION
5040    GOSUB 6000                  'Perform calculations
5050  WEND
5060  RETURN
6000 '*******************************************************************
6002 '                           PERFORM CALCULATIONS
6004 '*******************************************************************
6010  IF HOURS.WORK <= 39 THEN REGULAR.PAY = HOURS.WORK*RATE :
        OVERTIME.HALF = 0 :
        OVERTIME.DOUBLE = 0
6020  IF HOURS.WORK>39 AND HOURS.WORK<=45 THEN REGULAR.PAY=REGULAR.HOURS*RATE :
        OVERTIME.HALF = (HOURS.WORK-REGULAR.HOURS)*RATE*1.5 :
        OVERTIME.DOUBLE = 0
6030  IF HOURS.WORK > 45 THEN REGULAR.PAY = REGULAR.HOURS*RATE :
        OVERTIME.HALF = (BASE.DOUBLE-REGULAR.HOURS)*RATE*1.5 :
        OVERTIME.DOUBLE = (HOURS.WORK-BASE.DOUBLE)*RATE*2
6040  GROSS.PAY = REGULAR.PAY+OVERTIME.HALF+OVERTIME.DOUBLE
6050  DEDUCTIONS = INCOME.TAX+UNION+PENSION
6060  NET.PAY = GROSS.PAY-DEDUCTIONS
6070  PRINT ENAME$,HOURS.WORK,GROSS.PAY,DEDUCTIONS,NET.PAY
6080  RETURN
65529 'End of program listing
```

Data file EMPLOYE3.DAT is opened for an INPUT (line 2010) since we wish to read records from this file. Subroutine INPUT DATA allows the user to key in the date, the regular hours and the base for double time. Lines 3040 and 3050 give the user the opportunity to correct an entry.

Since the first record in data file EMPLOYE3.DAT is different from the other records in the file, this record must be read before BASIC enters the WHILE/WEND loop which starts in line 5020. The WHILE statement checks for the end-of-file character, line 5030 reads a data record from the file and line 5040 calls Subroutine PERFORM CALCULATIONS to calculate an employee's net pay.

Summary of BASIC Statements

CLOSE — Closes the communication link between a program and a data file.

```
2050 CLOSE #1
```

INPUT # — Retrieves data items from a sequential data file and assigns the values to variables.

```
5030 INPUT #1, ENAME$,RATE,HOURS.WORK,INCOME.TAX,PENSION
```

OPEN — Opens a data file by creating a communication link between the file and the program.

```
2010 OPEN "B:EMPLOYE3.DAT" FOR INPUT AS #1
```

WRITE # — Writes values to a sequential data file.

```
3120 WRITE #1, ENAME$,RATE,HOURS.WORK,INCOME.TAX,PENSION
```

Summary of BASIC Functions

EOF(n) — Detects the end-of-file character at the end of a sequential data file. The "n" specifies the number of the file.

```
5020 WHILE NOT EOF(1)
```

Summary of Library Files

CREATE1.BAS	Creates a sequential data file of similar records.
CREATE2.BAS	Creates a sequential data file in which one record differs from the others.
RETRIEV1.BAS	Retrieves data stored in a sequential data file. All records are similar.
RETRIEV2.BAS	Retrieves data stored in a sequential file. One record differs from the others.

Chapter Summary

1. A collection of related items is referred to as a file. A program stored on disk is called a program file, a set of related data items stored on disk is called a data file.
2. Data items should be set apart from a program so that:
   (a) The data items can be shared by other programs.
   (b) The data items are permanent.
   (c) A large quantity of data items can be stored.
3. To take advantage of the above features, we must store the data externally. BASIC uses two types of data files: sequential files and random access files.
4. In a sequential data file, records are stored and retrieved sequentially. To access a specific record in a sequential file, all preceding records must first be retrieved.
5. In a random access file, records may be stored and retrieved in any order. However, to access a specific record, BASIC must know the exact location of the record in the file.
6. An OPEN statement that opens a sequential file must specify the drive in which the data file resides, the filename, the mode of access, and the file number.
7. When the mode of access is OUTPUT, records can be written to a sequential file. **If an existing file is opened in OUTPUT mode, the OPEN statement destroys the contents of the file.**
8. Following the OPEN statement, all subsequent file-handling statements must reference a data file by its number rather than by its name.
9. The WRITE # statement sends the values of the variables listed in the statement to the data file.
10. Values do not literally move from program variables to the data file, copies of the values are placed in the data file.
11. DOS places an EOF (end-of-file) character at the end of a sequential file when the file is created. The EOF character marks the end of the file.
12. When a program reads records from a sequential file, the mode of access in the OPEN statement must be INPUT.
13. The EOF character can be detected by means of the EOF function. When the function is used in the form NOT EOF(1) in a WHILE statement, the loop continues as long as the end-of-file character is not detected. When the EOF character is detected, the loop terminates. The number 1 in EOF(1) specifies the file number.
14. The INPUT # statement reads values from a sequential file and assigns the values to the variables listed in the INPUT # statement.
15. When one record is not the same as the remaining records in a file, the record must be processed outside the WHILE/WEND loop that processes the remaining records.
16. Changing information in a data file is referred to as updating the file.
17. To update records in a sequential file, all records must be retrieved. After a record has been read and updated, it can be written either to the same file or written to a new file. The program must have two modes of OPEN: one for INPUT, the other for OUTPUT.
18. If we wish to read an updated file in the same program that changed the original file, we must first close the updated file, then reopen the file for an INPUT.
19. Only the file-handling commands KILL and FILES can be used with data files.

Questions and Exercises

1. What is a data file?
2. State one application of a sequential file and one application of a random access file.

3. Write OPEN statements for the following:
   (a) Open file NAMES.DAT to write records to the file.
   (b) Open file NAMES.DAT to read records from the file.

4. Code statements that perform the following. A record consists of a student's name, a course name, the course number.
   (a) Write a record to a sequential file.
   (b) Read a record from the sequential file.

5. What does DOS place at the end of a sequential file? What is the purpose of this marker?

6. The READ statement and the INPUT # statement perform almost the same operation. In what way are they different?

7. Write Subroutine READ DATA FILE that reads records from sequential file PRICE.DAT given below. Use a WHILE/WEND loop for records that are similar. Call a subroutine that performs the calculations but do not code the subroutine.

   PRICE.DAT
   40 — Rate of markup
   Desk,384.95
   Chair,99.50 — Item, list price
   File cabinet,285.98

8. Why are two OPEN statements needed in a program that updates records?

9. Identify the errors, if any, in the following program. Make the necessary corrections.

```
2010 OPEN "B:MASTER1.DAT FOR INPUT AS #1
2020 OPEN "B:MASTER2.DAT FOR OUTPUT AS #2
2030 WHILE NOT EOF(2)
2040   PRINT
2050   INPUT #2, ENAME$,ADDRESS$,TELEPHONE$
2060   PRINT ENAME$,ADDRESS$,TELEPHONE$
2070   INPUT "Enter new address and telephone number--";ADDRESS$,TELEPHONE$
2080   INPUT "Are the entries correct (y/n)",RESPONSE$
2090   IF RESPONSE = "y" AND RESPONSE$ = "Y"
          THEN INPUT "Re-enter the data--";ADDRESS$,TELEPHONE$
2100   WRITE #2, ADDRESS$,TELEPHONF$
2110 WEND
2120 CLOSE #1,#2
2130 END
```

10. Identify the errors in the following commands.

    (a) `LOAD "B:GROSS.PAY.BAS"`
    (b) `KILL "B:SCORES"`
    (c) `LOAD "B:NAMES.DAT"`
    (d) `FILES B`
    (e) `SAVE "B:TAXES.DAT"`

11. Create a data file named SALES.DAT using the data given below.

Name	*Amount of Sales*
Debra Hayes	405,321,345
Wayne Keeler	385,297,340
Melvin Braun	416,326,389

12. Modify program RETRIEV1.BAS listed on page 141 so that the program retrieves the records stored in data file SALES.DAT. Display the contents of the file on the screen.

```
RUN

Debra Hayes     405          321          345
Wayne Keeler    385          297          340
Melvin Braun    416          326          389
```

13. Delete data file SALES.DAT from your BASIC diskette. Use the FILES command to ensure that the file has been deleted.

Programming Problems

Design and code programs for the following problems. Create data files by customizing either library file CREATE1.BAS or library file CREATE2.BAS. **Pay special attention to the OPEN statement in these files. The filename must be changed; otherwise, the new data will replace the contents of an existing file.** Also, you may find it necessary to change the condition in the WHILE statement.

For most problems, a data filename is given along with the data. Remember, results are not rounded off to the nearest cent nor to the nearest whole number. Rounding off numbers will be discussed in the next chapter.

1. The program for Problem 3 in Chapter Five found the compound amounts on several investments. In this problem, produce a table that displays the years and compound amounts for a particular investment (principal) and a particular rate of interest. The principal and the rate of interest must be keyed in by the user. Investments are for periods of 1, 5, 7, 10, and 15 years. Store the years in a data file; one year per record. Suggested filename: YEARS.DAT. The table produced below is based on a $1000 investment bearing interest at 9 1/4%. Use the following formula to find the compound amount.

$$\text{Compound Amount} = \text{Principal}(1+\text{Rate of Interest}/100)^{\text{Period of Time}}$$

Sample Output:

```
Enter the principal and interest rate--[1000,9.25]
Are the entries correct (y/n)? [y]

COMPOUND INTEREST TABLE
Principal: 1000
Interest Rate: 9.25

YEARS          COMPOUND AMOUNT

 1               1092.5
 5               1556.35
 7               1857.591
 10              2422.225
 15              3769.828
```

2. Often, a manufacturer offers a discount to a retailer when merchandise is purchased in large quantities. Suppose a retailer qualifies for such a discount. What amount of discount would the retailer receive on each of the purchases shown below if the discount rate is 6%? What would be the reduced value of each purchase?

PURCHAS1.DAT
25,Rain coats,116.85
30,Jackets,98.45 — Quantity, item, unit price
35,Slacks,59.98

Formulas:

Value of Purchase = Quantity × Unit Price
Discount = Value of Purchase × Rate of Discount/100
Reduced Value = Value of Purchase − Discount

```
RUN
Date, rate of discount? March 8,6
Are the entries correct (y/n)? y

FASHION DESIGNS
Date of Purchase: March 8

QUANTITY        ITEM            VALUE           DISCOUNT        REDUCED VALUE

 25             Rain coats      2921.25         175.275         2745.975
 30             Jackets         2953.5          177.21          2776.29
 35             Slacks          2099.3          125.958         1973.342
```

3. Update data file PURCHAS1.DAT by changing the quantity and the unit price of each item to those shown below. Write the updated records to a new data file. Suggested filename: PURCHAS2.DAT. Read and print the contents of both data files.

Quantity	*Item*	*Unit Price*
20	Rain coats	$96.85
26	Jackets	84.55
31	Slacks	49.98

In your main routine (use the one listed on page 145 as a guide), open PURCHAS1.DAT for INPUT and PURCHAS2.DAT for OUTPUT. Call a subroutine to update PURCHAS1.DAT. Remember, after all records in a data file have been processed, the data file pointer is positioned immediately after the last record in the file. An OPEN statement moves the pointer back to the beginning of the file. Thus, you must close both files, then reopen the files for INPUT before you call the subroutines that read and print the files. Following the GOSUB statements that call these subroutines, close both files.

Note that PURCHAS1.DAT does not have a special record. Therefore, lines 3010 and 3020 must be omitted from Subroutine UPDATE DATA FILE listed on page 144. Use separate subroutines to print the files. In each subroutine, print the appropriate headings then read and print the records of the file in a WHILE/WEND loop. The subroutines should produce the following output.

```
ORIGINAL STOCK

QUANTITY        ITEM            UNIT PRICE
 25             Rain coats       116.85
 30             Jackets          98.45
 35             Slacks           59.98

CURRENT STOCK

QUANTITY        ITEM            UNIT PRICE
 20             Rain coats       96.85
 26             Jackets          84.55
 31             Slacks           49.98
```

4. Employees of Howard Electronics Ltd. are paid by the hour. The employees' timecards show the following starting times and leaving times for May 27.

Name	*Starting Time*	*Leaving Time*
Norman Hall	8:00 a.m.	5:00 p.m.
Andrew Janzen	9:00 a.m.	4:00 p.m.
Sheri Logan	8:00 a.m.	4:00 p.m.

(a) Find the total hours of work for each employee. All employees have a one-hour lunch period from 12:00 noon to 1:00 p.m.
(b) Find the wages for each employee.

TIMECARD.DAT
12,1 — Noon, one p.m.
Norman Hall,12.68,8,5
Andrew Janzen,12.97,9,4 — Employee name, rate of pay, starting time, leaving time
Sheri Logan,12.74,8,4

RUN

```
Enter the date (month and day, e.g. September 30) May 27
Is the date correct (y/n)? y

REPORT ON HOURS AND WAGES
May 27

NAME            HOURS          WAGES

Norman Hall     8               101.44
Andrew Janzen   6               77.82
Sheri Logan     7               89.18
```

5. Rewrite the program for Problem 3, Chapter Six. For your current program, INPUT the date and read the remaining data from a data file. The data file is given below. Verify the date. Except for the prompt asking for the date and the data editing display, your output should be the same as the one given on page 129. Save your program as it is needed for a problem in Chapter Eight.

SALES4.DAT
5000,12,15 — Base, rate on base, rate on excess
James Kelly,5839
Tom Powell,4987 — Name of salesperson, amount of sales
Joan Friesen,6025
Leslie Dale,5000

6. A bank offers two types of accounts: Checking accounts and Savings accounts. No interest is given on Checking accounts, the following interest rates are applied to Savings accounts.

Balance	*Interest Rate*
< \$500	4%
>= \$500 and < \$1000	4.5%
>= \$1000 and < \$3000	5%
>= \$3000 and < \$5000	5.5%
>= \$5000	6%

Write a program that calculates the amount in each savings account at the end of one year if interest is compounded monthly. Assume each depositor makes no deposits or withdrawals. Use the following formula.

$$\text{Compound Amount} = \text{Balance}(1+\text{Rate}/(100\times 12))^{12}$$

ACCOUNTS.DAT
4,4.5,5,5.5,6 — Rates of interest
3487,Tim Lewis,327.18,C
4312,Cathy Enns,1248.21,S
4593,Len Ross,419.26,S — Account number, name of depositor, account balance, type of account (C for checking, S for savings)
4217,Terri Lowe,821.42,S
4859,Lloyd Cyr,4085.31,S
4125,Susan Hull,6849.57,S

Use IF/THEN statements to check the type of account. If the account is a checking account, merely assign zero to a common variable, say RATE. If the account is a savings account, check the balance and assign the appropriate rate to RATE. An example of an IF/THEN statement for a savings account is given below.

```
6030 IF TYPE$ = "S" AND (BALANCE >= 500 AND BALANCE < 1000) THEN RATE = RATE2
```

RUN

```
Enter month--November
Is the month correct (y/n)? y

ACCOUNT BALANCES
For the Month of November

NUMBER          NAME            BALANCE         RATE        NEW BALANCE

 3487           Tim Lewis        327.18          0           327.18
 4312           Cathy Enns      1248.21          5          1312.072
 4593           Len Ross         419.26          4           436.3412
 4217           Terri Lowe       821.42          4.5         859.1556
 4859           Lloyd Cyr       4085.31          5.5        4315.754
 4125           Susan Hull      6849.57          6          7272.037
```

7. Write two programs. One creates an Accounts Receivable file, the other updates the file and prints the accounts.

(a) The records of your Accounts Receivable file in former programs were read into the computer by means of READ and DATA statements. Create a master data file on disk. Each record must consist of an account number; the customer's name, address, telephone number, and credit limit; the date of the last transaction; and the balance due. The file is given below. Suggested filename: AR1.DAT. Leave two spaces between the street address and the city, between the city and the province, and between the province and the postal code.

Save the program that creates this data file. You will need the program in Chapter Nine where it will be modified to append additional records to the file. Suggested filename: CREATEAR.BAS

```
AR1.DAT
31001,Diane Fraser,367 River Road  Anycity  ZZ  M3L 4S8,339-8542,1000,Nov. 12,342.16
31002,Derek Andrews,493 Aster Bay  Anycity  ZZ  M3L 2T6,489-1613,1000,Nov. 17,821.44
31003,Lee Harris,584 Horwood Avenue  Anycity  ZZ  M3L 5V7,667-3421,1000,Nov. 21,531.27
```

(b) Write a program that performs the following for each account: (a) reads a record from the master file and displays specific fields on the screen (b) INPUTS a transaction into the computer and verifies the data (c) finds the new balance (d) updates the record in the data file (e) displays the account on the screen. The transactions are as follows:

Account Number	*Date*	*Sale*	*Payment*
31001	Nov. 14	$ 59.21	$ 0.00
31002	Nov. 20	532.95	316.52
31003	Nov. 23	0.00	531.27

As in the previous programs, enter the transactions through the keyboard. Do not determine if a customer has exceeded the credit limit. In addition to the account number, customer's name, previous balance, transaction, and new balance print the customer's address and telephone number on the account.

Write the updated records to a new file. Suggested filename: AR2.DAT. Open this file in the main routine for an OUTPUT. An updated record must consist of the account number; the customer's name, address, telephone number, and credit limit; and the new date and new balance. Do not use the update routine given on page 144. Update the accounts as you did in the former Accounts Receivable programs, simply by keying in a transaction and calculating the new balance. Write an updated record to the new file in Subroutine PERFORM CALCULATIONS immediately after calculating the new balance.

Note: It is important that you save each Accounts Receivable program as each program is to be modified in a subsequent chapter.

Partial Output:

```
Transaction for the following account:

 31001    Diane Fraser   Balance on Nov. 12: 342.16    Credit limit: 1000

Enter transaction (date, sale, payment)--Nov. 14,59.21,0
Are the entries correct (y/n)? y

Account number: 31001

Name: Diane Fraser
Address: 367 River Road  Anycity  ZZ  M3L 4S8
Telephone number: 339-8542

DATE            DEBIT           CREDIT          BALANCE

Nov. 12                                          342.16
Nov. 14          59.21            0              401.37
------------------------------------------------------
```

Project

This is the first version of a program that must be updated in many of the remaining chapters. In order to maintain the program, each version must be saved. Since the project requires more work than a programming problem, we suggest that at least two people be involved. The last project at the end of the book requires a team of programmers.

Here is the initial problem.

The accounting department of a department store has decided to computerize its inventory records. Stock must be numbered by department; for instance, the stock number of any item stored in the housewares department must start with an H, the stock number of any item stored in the furnishings department must start with an F. The manager of the accounting department has asked you to write two programs:

1. The first creates the data file.
2. The second updates all inventory accounts.

Creating the Data File

Although there are more departments and more items within each department, create a data file of at least ten records divided among three departments. Each record must contain the stock number, the department name, the item, the minimum stock allowed, the date of the last transaction, and the balance on hand. A partial data file named INVENT1.DAT is given below.

```
INVENT1.DAT
H001,Housewares,Flatware (stainless steel),3,Dec. 31,6
H002,Housewares,Flatware (silver plate),3,Dec. 31,5
H003,Housewares,Flatware (silver),3,Dec. 31,3
F001,Furnishings,Sofa (contemporary),3,Dec. 31,5
F002,Furnishings,Sofa (French),2,Dec. 31,4
F003,Furnishings,Sofa (Italian),2,Dec. 31,4
```

The minimum amount of stock in each housewares record represents the number of place settings.

Updating Inventory Accounts

The Main Routine

Open data file INVENT1.DAT for INPUT and data file INVENT2.DAT for OUTPUT. Call a subroutine that reads records from INVENT1.DAT and INPUTs transactions. Close both files.

Subroutine READ DATA FILE AND INPUT DATA

In a WHILE/WEND loop, read a record from file INVENT1.DAT and display the record on the screen. (See the output below.) INPUT a transaction. The transaction must include the date of the transaction, the quantity ordered, and the quantity sold. In each of three accounts, enter a transaction that will cause a balance that is less than the minimum allowed. Call a subroutine that calculates the new balance and writes the updated record to the new file. End the loop.

Subroutine PERFORM CALCULATIONS AND WRITE TO NEW FILE

Calculate the new balance. Write the stock number, the department, the item, the minimum stock allowed, the new date, and the new balance to data file INVENT2.DAT. An updated account has now been stored in the file. Call a subroutine that prints the account.

Subroutine PRINT ACCOUNT

Print the account as shown below. Determine whether or not the stock has been depleted below its minimum. If it has, display a warning beneath the account that more stock must be ordered.

```
Transaction for the following account:

H003  Housewares  Flatware (silver)  Balance on Dec. 31: 3   Min: 3

Enter the transaction (date, amount ordered, amount sold)--Jan. 5,0,1
Are the entries correct (y/n)? y

Stock number: H003

Department: Housewares
Item: Flatware (silver)

DATE              ORDERED           SOLD              BALANCE

Dec. 31                                               3
Jan. 5            0                 1                 2

Insufficient stock. Please reorder.
----------------------------------------------------------
```

Solutions for Exercises

7.1 Defining Files

1. Data items should be stored externally so that:

   (a) The data items can be shared by other programs.
   (b) The data items are permanent.
   (c) A large quantity of data items can be stored.

2. A sequential file stores data sequentially, one data item after the other. To access a particular item, all items preceding the one desired must be retrieved. In a random access file, items may be stored and retrieved in any order. There is no need to retrieve all items preceding the one desired.

3. To update records in a sequential file, all records must be read from the file and then written to an output file even if only a few records must be updated. Consequently, records are often updated periodically and may remain out of date for too long a period of time. However, programs using sequential files are relatively simple to write.

   Updating records in a random access file is much faster since a specific record can be retrieved directly. Thus, a random access file is more likely to be kept up-to-date. However, programs using random access files are more difficult to write.

7.2 Creating a Sequential Data File

1. The OPEN statement opens a data file by creating a communication link between the file and the program.

2. An OPEN statement must specify the drive in which the data file resides, the filename, the mode of access, and the file number.

3. When an existing file is opened in OUTPUT mode, the OPEN statement destroys the contents of this file.

4. The maximum number of files that can be open by default is three. This can be changed by the /F: option when loading BASICA.

5. The CLOSE statement closes the communication link between the program and the data file.

Exercise 6

```
1000 'CREATE FILE SALES1.DAT                    M. MCRITCHIE                    MAY 5
1002 '*************************************************************************
1004 '    THIS PROGRAM CREATES FILE SALES1.DAT. ALL RECORDS ARE THE SAME.
1006 '*************************************************************************
2010  OPEN "B:SALES1.DAT" FOR OUTPUT AS #1
2020  PRINT
2030  INPUT "Record";SNAME$,SALES
2040  WHILE SNAME$ <> "End of file"
2050    INPUT "Is the record correct (y/n)";RESPONSE$
2060    IF RESPONSE$ <> "y" AND RESPONSE$ <> "Y"
           THEN INPUT "Re-enter the record--",SNAME$,SALES : GOTO 2050
2070    WRITE #1, SNAME$,SALES
2080    PRINT
2090    INPUT "Record";SNAME$,SALES
2100  WEND
2110  CLOSE #1
2120  END
```

7.3 Recalling Data from a Data File

1. `2010 OPEN "B:EMPLOYE1.DAT" FOR OUTPUT AS #1`

   Opens the file EMPLOYE1.DAT for the writing of data to the file.

```
2010 OPEN "B:EMPLOYE1.DAT" FOR INPUT AS #1
```

Opens the file EMPLOYE1.DAT for the reading (retrieval) of data from the file.

2. NOT EOF(2) in a WHILE statement controls the WHILE/WEND loop by checking for the end-of-file character in file #2. As long as the end-of-file character is NOT detected, the loop continues. When the end-of-file character is detected, the loop terminates.
3. The INPUT # statement transfers values from a data file to program variables.
4. The data file pointer keeps track of the records in a data file as the records are being processed.

Exercise 5

```
1000 'RETRIEVE FILE SALES1.DAT                          M. MCRITCHIE                   MAY 9
1002 '*****************************************************************************
1004 '                  THIS PROGRAM RETRIEVES FILE SALES1.DAT
1006 '*****************************************************************************
2010  OPEN "B:SALES1.DAT" FOR INPUT AS #1
2020  PRINT
2030  WHILE NOT EOF(1)
2040    INPUT #1, SNAME$,SALES
2050    PRINT SNAME$;SALES
2060  WEND
2070  CLOSE #1
2080  END
```

7.4 Creating a Data File with Different Records

Exercise 1

```
1000 'CREATE FILE SALES2.DAT                          M. MCRITCHIE                   MAY 11
1002 '*****************************************************************************
1004 ' THIS PROGRAM CREATES DATA FILE SALES2.DAT. CONTAINS DIFFERENT RECORDS.
1006 '*****************************************************************************
2010  OPEN "B:SALES2.DAT" FOR OUTPUT AS #1
2020  PRINT
2030  INPUT "Rate of commission";RATE
2040  INPUT "Is the rate correct (y/n)";RESPONSE$
2050  IF RESPONSE$ <> "y" AND RESPONSE$ <> "Y"
         THEN INPUT "Re-enter the rate--",RATE : GOTO 2040
2060  WRITE #1, RATE
2070  PRINT
2080  INPUT "Record";SNAME$,SALES
2090  WHILE SNAME$ <> "End of file"
2100    INPUT "Is the record correct (y/n)";RESPONSE$
2110    IF RESPONSE$ <> "y" AND RESPONSE$ <> "Y"
           THEN INPUT "Re-enter the record--",SNAME$,SALES : GOTO 2100
2120    WRITE #1, SNAME$,SALES
2130    PRINT
2140    INPUT "Record";SNAME$,SALES
2150  WEND
2160  CLOSE #1
2170  END
```

Exercise 2

```
1000 'RETRIEVE FILE SALES2.DAT                        M. MCRITCHIE                   MAY 12
1002 '*****************************************************************************
1004 '              THIS PROGRAM RETRIEVES DATA FILE SALES2.DAT
1006 '*****************************************************************************
2010  OPEN "B:SALES2.DAT" FOR INPUT AS #1
2020  INPUT #1, RATE
2030  PRINT
2040  PRINT RATE
2050  WHILE NOT EOF(1)
```

```
2060     INPUT #1, SNAME$,SALES
2070     PRINT SNAME$;SALES
2080   WEND
2090   CLOSE #1
2100   END
```

7.5 Updating a Data File

```
1000 'UPDATE SALES2.DAT                        M. MCRITCHIE                    MAY 13
1002 '**********************************************************************
1004 '         THIS PROGRAM UPDATES DATA FILE SALES2.DAT AND DISPLAYS THE
1006 '                      UPDATED RECORDS ON THE SCREEN
1008 '**********************************************************************
1010 'RATE       - RATE OF COMMISSION
1020 'SNAME$     - SALESPERSON'S NAME
1030 'SALES      - AMOUNT OF SALES
1040 'RESPONSE$ - USER'S RESPONSE (y/n)
2000 '**********************************************************************
2002 '                               MAIN ROUTINE
2004 '**********************************************************************
2010  OPEN "B:SALES2.DAT" FOR INPUT AS #1
2020  OPEN "B:SALES3.DAT" FOR OUTPUT AS #2
2030  GOSUB 3000                    'Update data file
2040  CLOSE #1,#2
2050  OPEN "B:SALES3.DAT" FOR INPUT AS #2
2060  GOSUB 4000                    'Read updated file
2070  CLOSE #2
2080  END
3000 '**********************************************************************
3002 '                            UPDATE SALES2.DAT
3004 '**********************************************************************
3010  INPUT #1, RATE
3020  WRITE #2, RATE
3030  WHILE NOT EOF(1)
3040    PRINT
3050    INPUT #1, SNAME$,SALES
3060    PRINT SNAME$;SALES
3070    INPUT "Enter new sales--";SALES
3080    INPUT "Are the sales correct (y/n)";RESPONSE$
3090    IF RESPONSE$ <> "y" AND RESPONSE$ <> "Y"
           THEN INPUT "Re-enter the sales--",SALES : GOTO 3080
3100    WRITE #2, SNAME$,SALES
3110  WEND
3120  RETURN
4000 '**********************************************************************
4002 '                           READ UPDATED FILE
4004 '**********************************************************************
4010  INPUT #2, RATE
4020  PRINT
4030  WHILE NOT EOF(2)
4040    INPUT #2, SNAME$,SALES
4050    PRINT SNAME$;SALES
4060  WEND
4070  RETURN
65529 'End of program listing
```

7.6 BASIC Commands for Handling Data Files

1. ```
   FILES "B:"
   ```

2. ```
   KILL "B:SALES1.DAT"
   KILL "B:SALES2.DAT"
   KILL "B:SALES3.DAT"
   ```

8

GENERATING REPORTS

Objectives

Until now, our only method of arranging output has been by means of commas or semicolons in PRINT statements. Although we produced a report, little attention was given to the details that make a report attractive and easy to read. Centring the report horizontally and vertically on a cleared screen, placing dollar signs before dollar amounts, rounding off dollar amounts to two decimal places, inserting commas in numbers, and aligning numbers at decimal points make reports easier to understand. Arranging output is referred to as formatting or editing the output. Discussed in this chapter are a variety of features which can be used to generate attractive and easy-to-read reports. These include:

- The TAB function
- The PRINT USING statement
- The CLS command
- The STRING$ function
- The LOCATE statement

In addition, you will learn how to:

- Use the LINE INPUT statement to enter strings that contain commas
- Edit data by the screenful
- Freeze a display on the screen
- Merge a library file with a program in memory
- Use counters and accumulators
- Produce summaries at the end of reports
- Print on preprinted forms

Contents

8.1 Centring Output

Layout Charts

Now that we have learned how to produce reports, let us format these reports so that they are attractive and easy to read. We will first concentrate on centring a report vertically and horizontally then discuss such matters as inserting dollar signs and commas in numbers, rounding off numbers, aligning decimal points, and protecting dollar amounts with asterisks.

The program developed in Chapter Seven produced the following report.

```
PAYROLL REPORT
Week Ending October 17

NAME            HOURS           GROSS PAY       DEDUCTIONS      NET PAY


Darryl Brown    38               398.62          88.32           310.3
Ellen Miller    39               380.64          85.36           295.28
Lorne Hayes     42               472.845         94.64           378.205
Andrea Jones    47               574.08          102.98          471.1
```

We will format the report so that it looks as follows. Remember, the numbers above the report are column numbers.

```
         10        20        30        40        50        60        70        80
12345678901234567890123456789012345678901234567890123456789012345678901234567890
                                PAYROLL REPORT

                             Week Ending October 17
         ===========================================================================
               NAME              HOURS        GROSS        DEDUCTIONS        NET
         ===========================================================================
         Darryl Brown             38          $398.62      $ 88.32          $310.30
         Ellen Miller             39          $380.64      $ 85.36          $295.28
         Lorne Hayes              42          $472.85      $ 94.64          $378.21
         Andrea Jones             47          $574.08      $102.98          $471.10
```

Planning the layout of a report is a time-consuming but necessary task. To lighten the job, we will use a layout chart. The sample chart in Figure 8-1 plans the layout of the report given above.

FIGURE 8-1 LAYOUT CHART

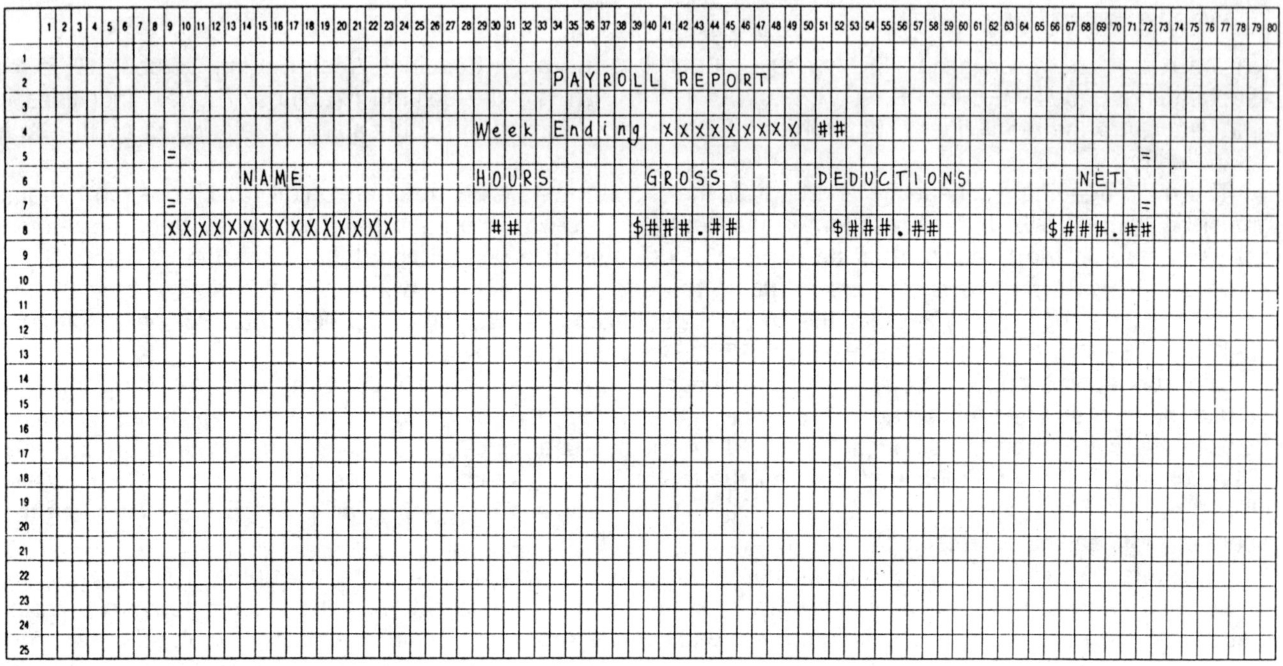

The layout chart consists of 25 rows and 80 columns; the number of rows and the number of columns on the screen. The report should be planned before programming begins. Actual headings can be centred on the layout chart since headings are often decided upon before the program is written. In a business environment, a programmer usually plans only one detail line. The detail line is filled in with X's to represent strings and with number signs (#) to represent numbers. The longest detail line is the one formatted.

Although not normal business practice, the uncentred layouts (rough layouts) given for the programming problems in this book will list all detail lines along with calculated results. The intent is to help you with the formatting task and to supply you with the results of a program.

Let us now find out how to centre reports vertically and horizontally. We will use the above report in our discussions.

Centring a Report Vertically

In a vertically centred report, the spacing at the top of the report must be the same as the spacing at the bottom. (We may be out by one screen line.) To obtain the spacing, we count the number of lines in the report, subtract this number from 25, and divide the difference by 2.

The above report contains ten lines. We subtract 10 from 25 and divide the difference (15) by 2. When the division is not exact, we drop the fraction. Thus, seven blank lines should be left at the top of the report which means that our report must start on line 8. To position the first line of the report, we use the LOCATE statement. For this report, the statement should look as follows:

```
4020 LOCATE 8
```

The statement must be placed before the PRINT statements that print the report. We can use the LOCATE statement to designate a column as well as a screen line. 4020 LOCATE 8,34 positions the cursor on line 8 in column 34. However, in all of our programs, we will use the LOCATE statement to designate only a screen line. It should be noted that LOCATE is a screen-control statement. It has no effect on output sent to the printer.

If output exceeds the 25 lines available on the screen, we do not centre the output vertically, but simply start the display near the top of the screen. To view the output, we must interrupt the display by pressing the Ctrl-Num Lock keys or the Pause key depending on the keyboard. In the next chapter, we will discuss the printing of output that requires more than one page when output is sent to the printer.

Centring a Report Horizontally

In the report shown on page 165, PAYROLL REPORT is the main heading, Week Ending October 17 is the subheading, and NAME, HOURS, GROSS, DEDUCTIONS, NET are the column headings. The last four lines in the report are the detail lines. That portion of the report following the subheading is referred to as the body of the report.

The main heading, subheading, and body of the report must be centred horizontally. Each column heading must be centred over the longest item in the column. To centre the main heading, we subtract the number of characters in the heading from the number of columns in a screen line, then divide the difference by 2. PAYROLL REPORT has 14 characters including the space between the words. We subtract 14 from 80 and divide the difference (66) by 2. When the division is not exact, the fraction is dropped. Thus, 33 spaces precede PAYROLL REPORT. This means that PAYROLL REPORT must start in column 34.

The subheading and the body of the report are centred in a similar manner. When a heading includes a month, as does the subheading in this report, it may be a good idea to format for the longest-named month. This is especially significant when the month is keyed in by a user, since the length is unknown to the programmer. The subheading may be slightly off centre if the month is not September as illustrated on page 165. However, this problem will be rectified in Chapter Eleven where we use a string-handling function in a statement that centres any heading automatically.

To centre the body of the report, we must work with the longest item in each column. This may include a column heading. Since we do not always know the number of characters in the longest name in a report; let us set aside 15 positions for a name. For each of the remaining items in a detail line; that is, the hours of work, gross pay, deductions, and net pay, we will use the number of positions allotted in the report on page 165. In actual practice, a programmer would estimate the maximum number of positions required by each field.

Let us now construct the longest line in our report. The b̸'s represent blanks that fill up the name field, the underscores represent spaces between the columns.

Darryl Brownb̸b̸b̸_____HOURS_____$398.62_____DEDUCTIONS_____$310.30

Note that the longest item in each column may or may not be a column heading. While HOURS and DEDUCTIONS are the longest items in their respective columns, the amounts $398.62 and $310.30 are both longer than their headings. To centre the above line, we count the number of characters in the line including the spaces between the columns. There are 64 characters. We subtract 64 from 80 and divide the difference (16) by 2. Thus, eight spaces must precede each row of equal signs and each detail line.

Each of the column headings must now be centred over its items. For example, to centre NAME over the names, we count the number of characters in NAME and subtract the number (4) from 15, the number of positions allotted to a name. We then divide the difference by 2. Thus, NAME is indented by 5 spaces. We use a similar process to centre a column heading that is longer than the longest item beneath it.

The layout chart can be considered the most refined level of design in the formatting of a report. We simply type the routine into the computer directly from our layout chart. In the next two sections, we will learn how to print an item so that it starts at a specific column.

Exercise

On a layout chart, centre the following report and its headings horizontally. Set aside 15 positions for each name. Centre the column headings over the columns.

```
SALES AND COMMISSION REPORT

For Month of August
============================================
NAME                SALES            COMMISSION
============================================
Hugh Chalmers       $3,146.95        $472.04
Shirley Dalton      $3,584.16        $537.62
Ross Gallagher      $3,719.32        $557.90
```

8.2 Tabulating to a Specific Column

Library Functions

Before we begin our discussion on tabulating, you should first be familiar with the term "library function". BASIC has a number of built-in functions that are written directly into the language. These are prewritten routines that we may call upon to perform specific operations, such as finding the square root of a number. The function returns one value. To call a library function, we must code its name along with the value upon which the function must operate. This value, called the argument, must follow the function name and must be enclosed in parentheses. The argument may be expressed as a constant, a variable, a library function, an arithmetic expression, or a string. Any variable used in the argument must first be assigned a value.

Let us use the square root function as an example. The function is accessed by SQR(X), where SQR is the name of the function and X is the argument. No space may be left between the name SQR and the left parenthesis. The function may be called from an assignment statement, a PRINT statement, or an IF statement. The three statements are illustrated below.

```
4040 SQUARE.ROOT = SQR(X)
4050 PRINT SQR(X)
4060 IF SQR(X) = Y THEN PRINT SQR(X)
```

We will make frequent use of the many library functions offered by BASIC. The TAB function is one of these.

The TAB Function

The TAB function gives us greater flexibility in the horizontal centring of items than does the comma or semicolon. Similar to the setting of tab stops on a typewriter, it instructs the computer to override a print zone and skip to a specific column before an item is printed. A number of examples are given below.

1. The following statement tabulates to column 34 before printing a string. The statement prints the main heading of the report shown on page 165.

```
4050 PRINT TAB(34) "PAYROLL REPORT"
```

Output:

```
1234567890123456789012345678901234
                                 PAYROLL REPORT
```

The argument of the TAB function specifies the column in which printing must begin. TAB(34) instructs BASIC to print PAYROLL REPORT starting in column 34.

2. More than one TAB function may be used in a PRINT statement. Here, we print the column headings of our report.

```
4090 PRINT TAB(14) "NAME"; TAB(29) "HOURS"; TAB(40) "GROSS"; TAB(51)
     "DEDUCTIONS"; TAB(68) "NET"
```

Output:

```
12345678901234567890123456789012345678901234567890123456789012345678901234567890
             NAME           HOURS      GROSS      DEDUCTIONS       NET
```

Semicolons separate the fields. The space following a semicolon and the space following an argument are inserted for clarity. We can break up a lengthy PRINT statement by inserting spaces where we wish the division to occur, then continue the statement on the next screen line (as we did with a lengthy IF statement in Chapter Six). The statement should continue just beyond the line number to keep the number clearly visible. The division must not take place within a string since the inserted spaces become part of the string.

3. The TAB function can be used to print numbers.

```
4070 PRINT TAB(8) 153; TAB(28) -153
```

Output:

```
123456789012345678901
        153       -153
```

When the number is positive, the tabbed column, in this case column 8, contains a space for the assumed plus sign.

4. We can use the TAB function to position strings and dollar amounts on one output line. In the example below, the numbers are assigned to variables.

```
4030 PRICE = 150.45
4040 TAX = 18.03
4050 PRINT "Price"; TAB(8) "$"; PRICE; TAB(21) "Tax"; TAB(26) "$"; TAX
```

Output:

```
12345678901234567890123456789012
| Price   $ 150.45        Tax   $ 18.03|
```

Note that it is unnecessary to tabulate to an amount that follows a dollar sign since the semicolon positions an item immediately after a previously printed item. However, BASIC leaves a space between the dollar sign and the positive amount for the assumed plus sign.

Exercises

1. Code PRINT statements with TAB functions to produce the following. Use constants in your PRINT statements for exercises (a) to (d) inclusive. Use constants for the column headings in exercises (e) and (f) but variables for the detail lines. Assume that the data items for the detail lines have already been assigned to the variables.

(a)
```
1234567890123456
|  67         -49|
```

(b)
```
1234567890123456789
|         August  23|
```

(c)
```
1234567890123456789012
| Commission    $ 263.42|
```

(d)
```
1234567890123456789012
| CUSTOMER
|    NAME          BALANCE|
```

(e)
```
12345678901234567890123456789012345
|        MONTH         K HOURS         CHARGE|
|
|        March           684          $ 28.25|
```

(f)
```
12345678901234567890123456789012
|       NAME OF          TOTAL AMOUNT|
|     SALESPERSON            SOLD    |
|
|     Andrews, W.          $ 485.26  |
```

2. What will be printed by the following PRINT statements? Indicate the column number where each printed field begins.

(a)
```
4040 HOURS = 40
4050 RATE = 9.54
4060 PRINT TAB(12) "HOURS"; TAB(23) "RATE"
4070 PRINT TAB(12) HOURS; TAB(22) RATE
```

(b)
```
4040 ENAME$ = "Harrison"
4050 SALARY = 580.25
4060 PRINT TAB(14) ENAME$; TAB(31) "$"; SALARY
```

(c)
```
4040 YEARS = 36
4050 AMOUNT = 1500
4060 INTEREST = 482.67
4070 PRINT TAB(7) "YEARS"; TAB(17) "AMOUNT"; TAB(30) "INTEREST"
4080 PRINT
4090 PRINT TAB(7) YEARS; TAB(17) "$"; AMOUNT; TAB(30) "$"; INTEREST
```

8.3 The PRINT USING Statement

Features Provided by a PRINT USING Statement

Although the TAB function is a convenient tool often used to centre headings, it leaves much to be desired when it comes to formatting detail lines. Many features that would be helpful in centring detail lines are either not available or difficult to implement with the TAB function. A statement that provides a number of additional features is the PRINT USING statement. With the PRINT USING we can:

1. Align whole numbers in a column.
2. Align decimal numbers at decimal points.
3. Round off a number and print insignificant zeros to the right of the decimal point.

4. Print a dollar sign before a number.
5. Print commas within a number.
6. Protect an amount by printing asterisks to the left of the number.
7. Print a minus sign after a number.
8. Print a percent sign after a number.

As with the TAB function, we can use the PRINT USING statement to position strings.

The Two Forms of PRINT USING

The PRINT USING statement comes in two forms. Both forms reference an image which edits the output line. One form of PRINT USING includes the image, the other form references a string variable to which the image is assigned. The two types of PRINT USING statements are illustrated below. Although a whole number is printed in each example, both forms can print decimal numbers and strings. The editing of decimal numbers and strings is explained later on in this section.

1. In the following PRINT USING statement, the image is coded within the statement. The underscores represent spaces.

Edit field

```
4020 NUMBER = 123
4030 PRINT USING "__###"; NUMBER
```

Print instruction — Image

The PRINT USING instruction is followed by the image which is enclosed in quotation marks. In this example, the image consists of two spaces and a series of number signs. Each number sign positions one digit of the number. The series of number signs is called the edit field. The PRINT USING instruction tells BASIC to print the value of NUMBER using the image given to format the output line. Thus, BASIC leaves two spaces, then prints 123. Note that the image and the variable are separated by a semicolon. The space following the semicolon is inserted for clarity. The value to be printed may also be expressed as a constant, a numeric expression, or a library function. The output line edited by the above PRINT USING statement is shown below.

```
4020 NUMBER = 123
4030 PRINT USING "__###"; NUMBER
```

Edited line: `__123`

If we wish to print more than one value in a PRINT USING statement, we must create more than one edit field in the image. The number of edit fields should correspond with the number of values to be printed. We may have more edit fields than values, but not less.

```
4020 READ NUMBER1,NUMBER2,NUMBER3
4030 DATA 1234,123,9
4040 PRINT USING "___####___###___#"; NUMBER1,NUMBER2,NUMBER3
```

Edited line: `___1234___123___9`

2. In the PRINT USING statement shown below, the image is assigned to a string variable and the PRINT USING instruction references the string variable.

```
4020 READ NUMBER1,NUMBER2,NUMBER3
4030 DATA 1234,123,9
4040 F$ = "___####___###___#"
4050 PRINT USING F$; NUMBER1,NUMBER2,NUMBER3
```

Edited line: `___1234___123___9`

The PRINT USING instruction tells BASIC to use the image assigned to F$ to edit the output line. Variable F$ in the PRINT USING statement must be followed by a semicolon and at least one variable, constant, numeric expression, or library function. This program segment produces the same output line as the one produced by the preceding example.

Which form of PRINT USING statement should be used? Generally, we will use the PRINT USING that references the variable storing the image when the image must be used more than once. When an image is used only once, we will use the PRINT USING that includes the image.

Inserting Commas in a Whole Number

To obtain commas in whole numbers greater than 999, we must place commas in the edit fields. BASIC inserts the commas where they are normally written in a number; that is, every three digits moving from right to left. In the examples below, we use images assigned to string variables.

Edit Field	*Unedited Value*	*Edited Value*
F$ = "#,###,###"	1234567	1,234,567
F$ = "#######,,"	1234567	1,234,567
F$ = "########,"	1234	1,234
	123456	123,456
	-123456	-123,456
	12345670	%12,345,670

Three ways of inserting commas are shown above. In the first edit field, we place commas in the positions where they would normally be written in the edited number. In the second edit field, we place two commas to the right of the number. Commas may be placed anywhere in the edit field *except* in the first position. The third edit field is particularly interesting. Although only one comma is coded in the edit field, BASIC will insert two commas (or as many as are needed) in the edited number. However, extra number signs must be included in the edit field to accommodate the extra commas.

Several other points should be noted. When we code an edit field larger than the number, BASIC leaves spaces to the left of the number. Thus, an extra number sign or an extra comma in the edit field is replaced by a space. When we code an edit field smaller than the number, BASIC prints a % sign immediately to the left of the number. The percent sign is printed in the first position of the edit field with the number taking up more positions than those reserved. When a number is negative, the edit field must reserve a position for the minus sign.

Editing Decimal Numbers

Editing decimal numbers involves a number of additional features. Study the following examples.

Edit Field		*Unedited Value*	*Edited Value*
F$ = "####.##"	(a)	2345.67	2345.67
	(b)	45.67	45.67
	(c)	2345.6	2345.60
	(d)	12345.67	%12345.67
	(e)	2345.675	2345.68
	(f)	2345.674	2345.67
	(g)	.67	0.67
	(h)	-345.67	-345.67

The number 2345.67 in (a) uses all the positions in the edit field. When the edit field reserves too many positions for the integer part of a number as in (b), spaces are placed to the left of the number. When the edit field reserves too many positions for the decimal part of a number as in (c), trailing zeros are placed to the right of the number.

An insufficient number of positions for the integer part of a number produces a percent sign (%) before the number with the number taking up more positions than those reserved. An insufficient number of positions for the decimal part of the number as in (e) and (f) rounds off the number. When the number is a decimal fraction as in (g) and positions are reserved for the integer part, a zero and spaces are placed to the left of the decimal point. And, as with whole numbers, the edit field must reserve a position for the minus sign when a number is negative.

Inserting Commas in a Decimal Number

As with whole numbers, commas can be inserted in a decimal number in various ways. Examine the following.

Edit Field	Unedited Value	Edited Value
F$ = "##,###,###.##"	12345678.9	12,345,678.90
	1234.9	1,234.90
F$ = "########,,.##"	12345678.9	12,345,678.90
	1234.9	1,234.90
F$ = "#########,.##"	12345678.9	12,345,678.90
	1234.9	1,234.90

Each edit field produces the same output. In the first edit field, commas are coded in positions where they would normally appear in a number. In the second edit field, each comma may be coded anywhere to the left of the decimal point, except in the first position of the edit field. The third edit field illustrates that only one comma may be coded in the field, however, extra number signs are needed to accommodate extra commas. Spaces replace unused commas and number signs to the left of the decimal point and are placed to the left of the edited number.

Printing Trailing Minus Signs

In a business report, a minus sign is usually printed to the right of a number to indicate that the number is negative. To obtain the trailing minus sign, we code a trailing minus sign in the edit field. Note that the minus sign is replaced by a space when the number is positive.

Edit Field	Unedited Value	Edited Value
F$ = "######,.##-"	-123456.78	123,456.78-
	-123.78	123.78-
	-1.5	1.50-
	-.8	0.80-
	123.78	123.78

Preceding a Number with a Dollar Sign

The PRINT USING statement can be used to print floating dollar signs before dollar amounts. The dollar sign is referred to as a floating dollar sign because its position depends on the length of the number.

Edit Field	Unedited Value	Edited Value
F$ = "$$####,.##"	.025	$0.03
	12.342	$12.34
	1234.567	$1,234.57
	12345.6	$12,345.60

Placing two dollar signs in the left-most positions of an edit field produces one dollar sign immediately to the left of the edited number. Each dollar sign in an edit field reserves one position. One of the dollar signs produces the floating dollar sign, the other dollar sign is replaced by a digit.

All PRINT USING features discussed so far apply to edit fields that contain dollar signs. This includes rounding off numbers, inserting commas, inserting trailing minus signs, and inserting spaces and zeros when the edit field is longer than the number.

Protecting Dollar Amounts with Asterisks

Asterisks can be printed immediately to the left of a dollar amount to protect the amount.

Edit Field	Unedited Value	Edited Value
F$ = "**###,.##"	.025	****0.03

Edit Field	Unedited Value	Edited Value
	12.342	***12.34
	1234.567	*1,234.57
	12345.6	12,345.60
F$ = "**$###,.##"	.025	*****$0.03
	12.342	****$12.34
	1234.567	*$1,234.57
	12345.6	$12,345.60

Two asterisks in the left-most positions of an edit field fill any spaces to the left of an edited number with asterisks. Each asterisk in the edit field reserves one position. Two asterisks and a dollar sign in the left-most positions of the edit field produce a dollar sign immediately to the left of the edited number and asterisks in the remaining positions to the left of the dollar sign. All PRINT USING features previously discussed apply to edit fields that contain asterisks.

Editing Strings

As with numeric data, strings may be edited by coding the image in the PRINT USING statement or by assigning the image to a string variable. The two forms are shown below. The underscores in the image represent spaces.

1. Image coded in a PRINT USING statement.

```
4010 S$ = "PROGRESS REPORT"
4020 PRINT USING "\_____________\"; S$
```

2. Image assigned to a string variable.

```
4010 S$ = "PROGRESS REPORT"
4020 F$ = "\_____________\"
4030 PRINT USING F$; S$
```

Each of the above examples produces PROGRESS REPORT. The backward slash (\) is used to edit string data. The first backward slash reserves a position for the first character of the string, the second backward slash reserves a position for the last character of the string. The spaces between the backward slashes reserve positions for the remaining characters. Other examples of string editing are given below.

Edit Field		*Unedited Value*	*Edited Value*
F$ = "_____________\"	(a)	PROGRESS REPORTING	PROGRESS REPORT
	(b)	PROGRESS	PROGRESS
F$ = "\\"	(a)	PROGRESS	PR
		MS	MS
F$ = "!"	(a)	PROGRESS REPORTING	P
		M	M

An edited string is left-justified. This means that the first character of the string is printed in the left-most position of the field with the remaining characters following. In the examples marked (a), an insufficient number of positions has been reserved for each string. Thus, the right-most characters with no reserved positions are truncated (discarded). When an edit field is longer than the string, spaces are placed to the right of the string as illustrated in example (b).

The second edit field shows that the minimum number of characters we can edit with backward slashes is two, since the edit field must contain two backward slashes. To edit one character, we must use the exclamation mark (!) as shown by the third edit field.

Other Examples

1. The PRINT USING statement given on the following page uses the image shown to edit the detail lines of our report on page 165. Our illustration edits the first detail line, however, each detail line would be edited in a similar manner.

```
F$ = "________\_____________\______##_______$###.##______$###.##_______$###.##"

                 Darryl Brown             38      $398.62     $ 88.32       $310.30

PRINT USING F$; ENAME$,           HOURS.WORK, GROSS.PAY, DEDUCTIONS,      NET.PAY
```

The image begins with eight spaces. The set of backward slashes reserves positions for the 15 characters in a name. Since Darryl Brown consists of only 12 characters, spaces are inserted in the extra positions to the right of the name. The name field is followed by six spaces. The next edit field edits the hours. This field is followed by seven spaces. The next three edit fields edit the dollar amounts for the gross pay, the deductions, and the net pay. Spaces separate the fields. The PRINT USING statement lists five variables.

2. We can print a percent sign (%) to the right of a number by placing a percent sign in the right-most position of the number's edit field. Furthermore, we can code a string directly in the image.

```
4010 RATE = 12.31
4020 PRINT USING "______The rate is ##.##%"; RATE
```

Output:

```
1234567890123456789012345
      The rate is 12.31%
```

3. The following program aligns the whole numbers 1234, 123, 12 and 1 in a column.

```
4010 F$ = "____####,"
4020 READ NUMBER
4030 WHILE NUMBER <> -1
4040   PRINT USING F$; NUMBER
4050   READ NUMBER
4060 WEND
4070 DATA 1234,123,12,1,-1
4080 END
```

Output:

```
123456789
    1,234
      123
       12
        1
```

4. The program listed below rounds off and aligns the decimal numbers .042, 139.246, and 8493.16. Furthermore, the edit field contains asterisks, a dollar sign, and a comma.

```
4010 F$ = "____**$###,.##"
4020 READ NUMBER
4030 WHILE NUMBER <> -1
4040   PRINT USING F$; NUMBER
4050   READ NUMBER
4060 WEND
4070 DATA .042,139.246,8493.16,-1
4080 END
```

Output:

```
12345678901234
    *****$0.04
    ***$139.25
    *$8,493.16
```

5. We may include the TAB function in a PRINT USING statement. However, it is best to restrict its use to a PRINT USING that contains an image in order to keep the editing in one statement. A PRINT USING statement with the TAB function is illustrated below.

```
6030 PRINT TAB(27) USING "Total sales______$####,.##"; TOTAL.SALES
```

6. We can direct output to the printer by changing PRINT USING to LPRINT USING.

Exercises

Use READ and DATA statements to enter data into the computer.

1. Write program segments to produce the outputs shown below. Code each image within a PRINT USING statement.

   (a) Print the numbers 485, −94, and 163.98 as shown.

```
123456789012345678901234567890
   485       -94       163.98
```

   (b) Insert commas in the numbers 1234, 123456, and 1234567.

```
123456789012345678901234567890123
  1,234     123,456     1,234,567
```

   (c) Print the strings and the amounts as shown below. Code the strings in the image; do not assign the strings to variables.

```
123456789012345678901234567890123456789012345678901234567
    Principal    $16,925.00          Payment    $196.55
```

   (d) Print the two lines given below. Code the strings in the image.

```
123456789012345678901234567890123456789012345678901234567890123456789012
                                   Total sales                 $3,496.00
                                   Average sales           $     874.00
```

2. Write programs similar to those shown on page 174 to produce the following outputs. Assign the image to a string variable.

   (a) Round off the numbers .048, 67.237, and 2185.36 to two decimal places and print a floating dollar sign before each number.

```
123456789012345
          $0.05
         $67.24
      $2,185.36
```

   (b) Protect the above dollar amounts by coding an image that inserts one or more asterisks before each amount.

```
123456789012345
     *****$0.05
     ****$67.24
     *$2,185.36
```

3. What output will each of the following program segments produce? Indicate the column number where each printed field begins.

   (a)

```
4010 READ NAME1$,GRADE,COURSE$,COURSE.NO
4020 DATA "Smith,James",12,"Data Processing",302
4030 F$ = "__\__________\___##_____\_______________\___###"
4040 PRINT USING F$; NAME1$,GRADE,COURSE$,COURSE.NO
```

(b)
```
4010 READ NAME1$,BATS,HITS
4020 DATA "Peters",49,15
4030 F$ = "_____\____\_____Bats___##_____Hits___##"
4040 PRINT USING F$; NAME1$,BATS,HITS
```

(c)
```
4010 BILLS = 5
4020 TOTAL = 89.42
4030 PRINT TAB(19) USING "Number of bills_______#"; BILLS
4040 PRINT TAB(19) USING "Total expenses______$##.##"; TOTAL
```

4. Prepare a report from the information shown below. Use the PRINT USING statement to print the detail line and the TAB function in a PRINT statement to edit the remaining lines. Enter the data for the detail line by the READ and DATA statements.

```
12345678901234567890123456789012345678901234567890123456
                      ACCOUNT BALANCE

        NUMBER               NAME                   BALANCE

          263               Glen Miles              $1,023.68
```

8.4 Other Editing Features

Clearing the Screen

Output should be displayed on a screen that is cleared of all extraneous material. To clear the screen, we use the CLS command introduced in Chapter Two. (CLS represents CLear Screen.) CLS clears the screen and places the BASIC prompt and the cursor in the top left-hand corner of the screen. The command does not erase the function key display. This is erased by the command KEY OFF.

The CLS command can be coded as a statement; for example, 4010 CLS. When the CLS statement is placed before a PRINT statement, the information printed by the PRINT statement will be displayed on a cleared screen.

The STRING$ Function

The STRING$ function returns a string of any desired character. Suppose we wish to print a row of 26 equal signs. We can call the STRING$ function in one of two ways:

(a)
```
4020 S$ = STRING$(26,"=")
4030 PRINT S$
```
or (b)
```
4020 PRINT STRING$(26,"=")
```

The STRING$ function requires two arguments. The first argument specifies the number of characters; the second argument specifies the character desired. The character must be enclosed in quotation marks.

We will be using the STRING$ function to produce rows of equal signs in order to highlight column headings and to produce leaders (periods) between items. The program segment listed below illustrates how we can use the STRING$ function to produce an attractive report.

```
         10        20        30        40        50        60        70        80
12345678901234567890123456789012345678901234567890123456789012345678901234567890
                                       CURRENT ORDER
                                  ==========================
                                    ITEM               PRICE
                                  ==========================
                                  Diskettes ..........  $7.98
                                  Ribbons   ..........  $9.95
                                  Binder    ..........  $4.50
```

```
4030 S1$ = STRING$(26,"=")
4040 S2$ = STRING$(10,".")
4050 F$ = "_________________________\_______\_\________\_$#.##"
4060 CLS
4070 PRINT TAB(34) "CURRENT ORDER"
4080 PRINT TAB(28) S1$
4090 PRINT TAB(30) "ITEM"; TAB(49) "PRICE"
4100 PRINT TAB(28) S1$

5030 PRINT USING F$; ITEM$,S2$,PRICE
```

The PRINT USING statement would be coded in another module and placed within a loop. In line 4030, twenty-six equal signs are assigned to S1$; in line 4040, ten periods are assigned to S2$. The first string field in the image reserves positions for the item, the second string field reserves positions for the ten leaders, the numeric field sets aside positions for the price. Lines 4080 and 4100 print the equal signs. The PRINT USING statement prints the item, the ten leaders stored in S2$, and the price.

Checking the Horizontal Centring of an Output Line

To ensure that your output is centred horizontally, print a row of 80 numbers (the numbers 1234567890 eight times) just after a LOCATE. This is illustrated below.

```
4010  CLS
4020  LOCATE 8
4025  PRINT "1234567890123456789012345678901234567890123456789012345678901234567
8901234567890"
```

This row of numbers will be printed across the screen. By using these numbers, you can tell at a glance whether or not the number of spaces to the left of an output line is the same as the number of spaces to the right. (You can be out by one space.) Here is an example.

```
12345678901234567890123456789012345678901234567890123456789012345678901234567890
                                 PAYROLL REPORT

                         Week Ending September 30, 19XX
        ================================================================
             NAME           HOURS      GROSS       DEDUCTIONS         NET
        ================================================================
```

We can readily see that **PAYROLL REPORT** is centred horizontally since there are 33 spaces to the left of the heading and 33 spaces to the right of it. Similarly, there are 25 spaces to the left of **Week Ending September 30, 19XX** and 25 spaces to the right. The rows of equal signs can be checked in a similar manner. When your program is error-free, you must delete the PRINT statement that prints the row of numbers.

Let us now use the concepts learned so far to format the report given on page 165.

Subroutine Format Report and Print Headings

```
4000 '*****************************************************************
4002 '                      FORMAT REPORT AND PRINT HEADINGS
4004 '*****************************************************************
4010  CLS
4020  LOCATE 8
4025  PRINT "1234567890123456789012345678901234567890123456789012345678901234567
8901234567890"
4030  S$ = STRING$(64,"=")
4040  F$ = "________\_____________\______##_______$###.##______$###.##_______$##
#.##"
4050  PRINT TAB(34) "PAYROLL REPORT"
4060  PRINT
4070  PRINT TAB(26) "Week Ending ";DATE1$
4080  PRINT TAB(9) S$
4090  PRINT TAB(14) "NAME"; TAB(29) "HOURS"; TAB(40) "GROSS"; TAB(51)
      "DEDUCTIONS"; TAB(68) "NET"
4100  PRINT TAB(9) S$
4110  RETURN
```

Line 4010 clears the screen and line 4020 locates the row. Line 4030 assigns 64 equal signs to S$ while line 4040 creates the image and assigns it to F$. The statements in lines 4050 to 4100 print the headings, a blank line, and the equal signs. Line 4025 must be deleted when the program produces the desired output.

Exercises

1. What will be the output from each of the following? Indicate the column number where each printed field begins.

(a)
```
4010 S$ = STRING$(12,".")
4020 PRINT S$
```

(b)
```
4010 S$ = STRING$(12,".")
4020 PRINT TAB(15) S$
```

(c)
```
4010 S$ = STRING$(20,"=")
4020 PRINT TAB(4) S$
```

(d)
```
4010 S$ = STRING$(15,"*")
4020 PRINT TAB(10) S$
```

2. Produce the following report. Use the STRING$ function to obtain the equal signs and the leaders. Assign the name and the number of parts produced to variables.

```
        10        20        30        40        50        60        70        80
12345678901234567890123456789012345678901234567890123456789012345678901234567890

                                ==============================
                                  NAME        NUMBER PRODUCED
                                ==============================
                                Armstrong ......... 161
```

8.5 Other Useful Features

The LINE INPUT Statement

When we key in a string in response to an INPUT statement and the string contains a comma, the string must be enclosed in quotation marks. If the string is not enclosed in quotation marks, the comma acts as a separator. BASIC considers the string as two values and two variables would be needed.

So far, we have restricted our string responses to those that do not include commas. For example, a date did not include a year. To enter a string that contains a comma without having to enclose the string in quotation marks, we use the LINE INPUT statement. LINE INPUT reads the entire line, including the comma, as one string. In this way, we can assign a date; such as, October 17, 19XX to one variable. The statement accepts a maximum of 254 characters. Shown below is a LINE INPUT statement that accepts a string which contains a comma.

```
3030 PRINT TAB(15) "Enter month, day and year (e.g. September 30, 19XX)
3040 LINE INPUT "______________Please enter the date--";DATE1$
RUN
```

```
Enter month, day and year (e.g. September 30, 19XX)
Please enter the date--October 17, 19XX
```

The prompt may be followed by either a semicolon or a comma. Unlike the INPUT statement, LINE INPUT does not differentiate between the two. LINE INPUT produces no question mark nor does it leave a space before a keyed-in value. If we wish to display a question mark and a space, we must code these as trailing characters in a prompt.

```
3030 PRINT TAB(15) "Enter month, day and year (e.g. September 30, 19XX)
3040 LINE INPUT "______________Date? ";DATE1$
RUN
```

```
Enter month, day and year (e.g. September 30, 19XX)
Date? October 17, 19XX
```

The LINE INPUT statement has two restrictions:

1. We can enter only one value.
2. The value must be type string.

To store a one-field record on disk and the field contains a comma, we simply use the WRITE # statement we have been using all along. Suppose we wish to store a file of names on disk and each name must be stored in the following manner: Last name, a comma, first name; such as Smith,John. Since the name contains a comma, we should use the LINE INPUT statement to assign the name to a variable so that the user need not enclose the name in quotation marks when keying it in. We then use the WRITE # statement to send the name to disk. The entire field, including the comma, will be stored on disk. The program below stores names that contain commas.

```
1000 'CREATE NAMES.DAT                  M. MCRITCHIE                  JUNE 10
1002 '***********************************************************************
1004 '          THIS PROGRAM CREATES A FILE OF NAMES IN WHICH
1006 '                    EACH NAME CONTAINS A COMMA
1008 '***********************************************************************
2010  OPEN "B:NAMES.DAT" FOR OUTPUT AS #1
2020  PRINT
2030  LINE INPUT "Name? ";ENAME$
2040  WHILE ENAME$ <> "End of file"
2050    INPUT "Is the name correct (y/n)";RESPONSE$
2060    IF RESPONSE$ <> "y" AND RESPONSE$ <> "Y"
          THEN LINE INPUT "Re-enter the name--",ENAME$ : GOTO 2050
2070    WRITE #1, ENAME$
2080    PRINT
2090    LINE INPUT "Name? ";ENAME$
2100  WEND
2110  CLOSE #1
2120  END
```

Note that we must use LINE INPUT in line 2060 to re-enter a name as well as in lines 2030 and 2090. To read the names from the file, we would use the INPUT # statement as we did in previous programs.

Editing Data by the Screenful

Until now, our programs used just one INPUT statement to accept data keyed in during program execution. For example, the program designed in Chapter Seven used one INPUT statement to accept the date, the regular hours, and the base for double time. An IF/THEN . . . GOTO loop verified the keyed-in data.

Suppose we use two statements to accept the data: a LINE INPUT to accept the date and an INPUT to accept the hours. Rather than verify data immediately after each statement, we will call a subroutine that verifies the data after it has all been keyed in. Let us use the statements below to enter the date and the hours into the computer.

```
3030 PRINT TAB(11) "Enter month, day and year (e.g. September 30, 19XX)"
3040 LINE INPUT "__________Date? ";DATE1$
3050 PRINT
3060 INPUT "__________Enter the regular hours and the base for double time--",
     REGULAR.HOURS,BASE.DOUBLE
3070 GOSUB 10000                        'Verify data
3080 RETURN
```

We now use the following subroutine to verify the data.

```
10000 '**********************************************************************
10002 '         VERIFY DATA (DATE, REGULAR HOURS, BASE FOR DOUBLE TIME)
10004 '**********************************************************************
10010  PRINT
10020  PRINT USING "The date is \_______________\";DATE1$
10030  INPUT "Is the date correct (y/n)";RESPONSE$
10040  IF RESPONSE$ <> "y" AND RESPONSE$ <> "Y"
         THEN LINE INPUT "Re-enter the date--",DATE1$ : GOTO 10030
```

```
10050   PRINT
10060   PRINT USING "The regular hours and base for double time are ## and ##";
        REGULAR.HOURS,BASE.DOUBLE
10070   INPUT "Are the hours correct (y/n)";RESPONSE$
10080   IF RESPONSE$ <> "y" AND RESPONSE$ <> "Y"
           THEN INPUT "Re-enter the hours--",REGULAR.HOURS,BASE.DOUBLE :
           GOTO 10070
10090   RETURN
```

Sample Output:

```
          Enter month, day and year (e.g. September 30, 19XX)
          Date? October 31, 19XX

          Enter the regular hours and the base for double time--39,45

The date is October 31, 19XX
Is the date correct (y/n)? n
Re-enter the date--October 17, 19XX
Is the date correct (y/n)? y

The regular hours and base for double time are 39 and 45
Are the hours correct (y/n)? y
```

After all items have been keyed in, the GOSUB statement in line 3070 calls the subroutine that verifies the data. In line 10020, we redisplay the date. If the user keys in an "n" in response to "Is the date correct (y/n)?" (line 10030), line 10040 gives the user the opportunity to key in the correct date. We use LINE INPUT as we did in line 3040 since the date includes a comma. When the correct date has been keyed in and the user responds to statement 10030 with a "y", we redisplay the hours in line 10060. In lines 10070 and 10080, we verify the hours in a manner similar to the verification of the date.

Note that we redisplay keyed-in data even though, in this program, it remains on the screen. Occasions arise when the amount of data keyed in is so great that part of the display scrolls off the screen. In the event that keyed-in data can no longer be seen, the original entries should be redisplayed. Verifying data by the screenful is possible when the statements that input the data are consecutive. When one INPUT (or LINE INPUT) statement lies inside a loop and others lie outside the loop, the data keyed in within the loop must be verified separately.

You should save Subroutine VERIFY DATA on disk. However, it must be saved in ASCII format, a format that stores one character per byte. Saved in this manner, we can merge the subroutine with a program in memory. We will refer to the saved subroutine as an ASCII file. Section 8.6 explains how we can save a subroutine in ASCII format and how we can merge the subroutine with a resident program.

The INKEY$ Function

The INKEY$ function accepts one character from the keyboard and assigns the character to a string variable. A sample statement is shown below.

```
11030 K$ = INKEY$
```

Although the INKEY$ function and the INPUT and LINE INPUT statements seem to perform similar operations, there are differences between the function and the statements. The following features apply to the INKEY$ function.

1. The INKEY$ function can accept only one character.
2. The variable to which the character is assigned must be a string variable.
3. The Enter key is not depressed after a character is keyed in.

4. BASIC displays neither a question mark nor the typed-in character.
5. If no key is pressed, BASIC assigns the null string to the string variable; that is, nothing is assigned to the variable. BASIC then proceeds to the next statement.

Item 5 reveals that the INKEY$ function does not halt a program as do the INPUT and LINE INPUT statements. To give us time to press a key, the INKEY$ function must be placed in a loop. Examine the following subroutine.

```
11000 '***********************************************************************
11002 '                          FREEZE DISPLAY
11004 '***********************************************************************
11010  PRINT
11020  PRINT "Press any key to continue"
11030  K$ = INKEY$
11040  WHILE K$ = ""
11050    K$ = INKEY$
11060  WEND
11070  RETURN
```

Line 11030 assigns the null string to K$. The WHILE statement in line 11040 tests for the null string. Since nothing is stored in K$, BASIC proceeds to statement 11050. Here, a second INKEY$ function gives us another chance to press a key. The WEND statement transfers control back to line 11040. As long as no key is pressed, the loop continues. As soon as we press a key, the loop breaks since K$ no longer equals the null string.

The above routine is particularly useful when we wish to freeze a display on the screen. If the PRINT statements that print a display are followed by a clear screen instruction, the display vanishes so quickly it cannot be seen. Thus, Subroutine FREEZE DISPLAY must be called between the group of statements that prints the display and the statement that clears the screen. The display remains on the screen until a key is pressed. Any key may be depressed except a number of special keys, such as the CTRL key, the ALT key, and a SHIFT key.

As with the subroutine that verifies data, you should save this subroutine in ASCII format. Directions in how to save in ASCII are given in Section 8.6.

Exercises

1. Identify the errors in the following statements. Make the necessary corrections.

```
(a) 3010 LINE INPUT "Enter three scores--";SCORE1,SCORE2,SCORE3
(b) 3020 INPUT "What is your answer",ANSWER$
(c) 3030 LINE INPUT "What is your telephone number";TELEPHONE$
(d) 3040 INPUT "Enter month and year separated by a comma--";DATE1$
(e) 3050 INPUT "Enter amount of deposit--";DEPOSIT
```

2. Customize Subroutine VERIFY DATA so that it verifies the data INPUTted by the following statements. Verify by the screenful.

```
3030 LINE INPUT "______Enter customer's name (e.g. Smith,John)--",CNAME$
3040 INPUT "______Enter the telephone number--",TELEPHONE$
3050 GOSUB 10000                            'Verify data
```

3. What happens when the following program segment is executed? State the reason for the result. What change should be made in the program to rectify the error?

```
11010 PRINT
11020 PRINT "Press any key to continue"
11030 K$ = INKEY$
11040 WHILE K$ = " "
11050   K$ = INKEY$
11060 WEND
11070 PRINT K$
11080 END
```

8.6 Saving and Merging Subroutines

The SAVE Command

As we write more programs, a number of subroutines will be used quite frequently. Subroutine VERIFY DATA on page 179 and Subroutine FREEZE DISPLAY on page 181 are examples of often-called modules. Rather than keying in the subroutine each time it is needed, we can save the subroutine on disk, then retrieve the module whenever we need it in a program. Some of the subroutines may require customizing. You experienced this in Exercise 2 on page 181 where you customized Subroutine VERIFY DATA by changing variables and prompts.

As mentioned on page 180, the subroutine must be saved in ASCII format so that it can be merged with a program in memory. To save the module in this format, we simply append a comma and an A to our SAVE command following the filename. For example, the command below saves Subroutine VERIFY DATA in ASCII format.

```
SAVE "B:VERIFY.ASC",A
```

B specifies the drive, VERIFY.ASC is the filename, and the trailing letter A saves the file in ASCII format. The extension ASC differentiates this file from the other files on our diskette. Our library files are now identified in the following manner:

NET-PAY.BAS	The extension BAS identifies a program file.
EMPLOYE1.DAT	The extension DAT identifies a data file.
VERIFY.ASC	The extension ASC identifies an ASCII file.

Save Subroutine VERIFY DATA under filename VERIFY.ASC and Subroutine FREEZE DISPLAY under filename FREEZE.ASC. Make sure both are saved in ASCII format.

The MERGE Command

To merge an ASCII file with a program in memory, we use the MERGE command, such as

```
MERGE "B:VERIFY.ASC"
```

B specifies the drive, VERIFY.ASC is the filename. Unlike the LOAD command, MERGE does not destroy a program in memory, but, instead, merges an ASCII file with the program in memory.

Our ASCII files are restricted in two ways:

1. The line numbers of an ASCII file must be different than the line numbers of the program with which the file will be merged. **If any line numbers are the same, the lines from the file will replace the corresponding lines in the program.**
2. The line numbers of an ASCII file must be different than those of another ASCII file. The ASCII files in this book have line numbers in blocks of 1000. Subroutine VERIFY DATA has line numbers in the 10 000 block, Subroutine FREEZE DISPLAY has line numbers in the 11 000 block. The filenames, their block numbers, and the pages where the files can be found are listed in Appendix B.

8.7 Producing Summaries

A business report often displays a total or a count. The total may be the total wages earned, the total commissions paid, the total pensions deducted. The count may be the number of employees working during a particular week. This additional information is usually printed as a summary at the bottom of a report. Let us find out how a count and a total can be obtained. Assume that data is read from our data file EMPLOYE3.DAT.

EMPLOYE3.DAT	
2.25	— Union dues
Darryl Brown,10.49,38,82.03,4.04	
Ellen Miller,9.76,39,79.35,3.76	— Employee name, rate of pay, hours of work,
Lorne Hayes,10.87,42,87.82,4.57	income tax deduction, pension deduction
Andrea Jones,11.04,47,93.79,6.94	

In order to trace through the logic without transferring to a subroutine, we will place the statement that counts and the one that totals in Subroutine READ DATA FILE. In the majority of programs later on in the book, the statements will be placed in Subroutine PERFORM CALCULATIONS.

A Counter

A counter is actually a variable which is increased by one each time something occurs. For example, we may wish to count the number of employees in our data file. The following subroutine counts the employees as the data records are being read.

```
5000 'SUBROUTINE READ DATA FILE AND COUNT EMPLOYEES
5010    COUNT.EMPLOYEES = Ø
5020    INPUT #1, UNION
5030    WHILE NOT EOF(1)
5040      INPUT #1, ENAME$,RATE,HOURS.WORK,INCOME.TAX,PENSION
5050      COUNT.EMPLOYEES = COUNT.EMPLOYEES+1
5060    WEND
5070    RETURN
```

When a value is assigned to a variable for the first time, it is said that the variable has been initialized. Although BASIC sets a non-initialized numeric variable to zero and a non-initialized string variable to the null string, we will explicitly initialize variables with these values. Here, we initialize our counter, COUNT.EMPLOYEES, to zero before counting begins. Thus, the counter must be initialized before the loop. Statement 5050 keeps track of the number of data records read. Notice that we use a variable name that identifies the items we are counting: COUNT.EMPLOYEES which represents "count the employees". Let us trace through the logic of the count routine.

The first time BASIC passes through the WHILE/WEND loop, the value of COUNT.EMPLOYEES becomes 1.

```
5050 COUNT.EMPLOYEES = COUNT.EMPLOYEES+1
                     = Ø+1
                     = 1
```

The result (1) replaces the Ø in COUNT.EMPLOYEES. The second time BASIC passes through the loop, the value of COUNT.EMPLOYEES becomes 2.

```
5050 COUNT.EMPLOYEES = COUNT.EMPLOYEES+1
                     = 1+1
                     = 2
```

COUNT.EMPLOYEES continues to be increased in this manner until the end-of-file character is reached. The value of COUNT.EMPLOYEES, which will eventually be 4, can then be printed in the summary of a report along with an appropriate comment. An example of such a PRINT statement is shown below.

```
6020 PRINT TAB(26) USING "Number of employees:__##";COUNT.EMPLOYEES
```

An Accumulator

As with a counter, an accumulator is a variable. However, an accumulator is increased by various amounts, not always by 1. Here is the subroutine once more, this time with an accumulator that finds the total amount of pension deducted from the employees.

```
5000 'SUBROUTINE READ DATA FILE, COUNT AND ACCUMULATE
5010    COUNT.EMPLOYEES = Ø
5020    TOTAL.PENSION = Ø
5030    INPUT #1, UNION
5040    WHILE NOT EOF(1)
5050      INPUT #1, ENAME$,RATE,HOURS.WORK,INCOME.TAX,PENSION
5060      COUNT.EMPLOYEES = COUNT.EMPLOYEES+1
5070      TOTAL.PENSION = TOTAL.PENSION+PENSION
5080    WEND
5090    RETURN
```

Our accumulator is TOTAL.PENSION. We name the accumulator by preceding PENSION with the word TOTAL. As with our counter, we initialize TOTAL.PENSION to zero before the loop begins. Here is how the total pension is found.
The first time BASIC passes through the loop, the value of TOTAL.PENSION becomes 4.04.

```
5070 TOTAL.PENSION = TOTAL.PENSION+PENSION
                   = Ø + 4.04
                   = 4.04
```

The result (4.04) replaces the Ø in TOTAL.PENSION. The second time BASIC passes through the loop, the value of TOTAL.PENSION becomes 7.80.

```
5070 TOTAL.PENSION = TOTAL.PENSION+PENSION
                   = 4.04 + 3.76
                   = 7.80
```

TOTAL.PENSION continues to accumulate the values of PENSION until the end-of-file character is reached. The total, which will eventually be 19.31, can then be printed in the summary of a report. An example of such a PRINT statement is shown below.

```
6030 PRINT TAB(26) USING "Total pension:_______$###.##";TOTAL.PENSION
```

An accumulator may also be used to total calculated results. In this case, the accumulator must follow the statement that performs the calculation.

Exercise

Write a subroutine that reads the following data file and performs the tasks listed below.

PARTS1.DAT
Julie Galloway,49
Arthur Knowles,50 — Name of employee, number of parts produced
Helen Janzen,51

(a) Find the number of employees.

(b) Find the total number of parts produced.

(c) Print the name of each employee and the number of parts produced by each employee.

(d) Print the number of employees and the total number of parts produced. Use PRINT USING statements. Code descriptive strings along with the results. (These statements would normally be placed in a subroutine that prints a summary.)

8.8 Sending Output to the Printer

Much of the output produced by business programs is directed to the printer. In many cases, the output is printed on preprinted forms. Only variable output is sent to the printer. The preprinted forms are chain fed to the printer and must be aligned exactly so that output is properly positioned. The following subroutine prints a check on an assumed preprinted form.

```
3000 'SUBROUTINE ENTER DATA AND PRINT CHECK
3010   CLS
3020   LOCATE 11
3030   READ CHECK.NO,DATE1$,PAYEE$,AMOUNT,DOLLARS,CENTS
3040   PRINT TAB(50) CHECK.NO
3045   LPRINT TAB(50) CHECK.NO
3050   PRINT TAB(51) DATE1$
3055   LPRINT TAB(51) DATE1$
3060   PRINT
3065   LPRINT
3070   PRINT TAB(24) USING "\______________________\______________**#####.##";
       PAYEE$,AMOUNT
```

```
3075    LPRINT TAB(24) USING "\______________________\______________**#####.##";
        PAYEE$,AMOUNT
3080    PRINT TAB(30) USING "**#####DOLLARS.##CENTS";DOLLARS,CENTS
3085    LPRINT TAB(30) USING "**#####DOLLARS.##CENTS";DOLLARS,CENTS
3090    DATA 142,"06/18/XX","XYZ Department Store",124.07
3100    DATA 124,.07
3110    RETURN
```

The output directed to the printer is shown below in bold face.

```
         10        20        30        40        50        60        70        80
12345678901234567890123456789012345678901234567890123456789012345678901234567890

                                        Check number: 142
                                                Date: 06/18/XX
          To the
          order of        XYZ Department Store                      $****124.07
                       The sum of****124DOLLARS.07CENTS
```

Notice that we display the output on the screen as well as print the output on the form. For debugging purposes, it is wise to obtain the desired output first on the screen. After you are satisfied with the results, you can direct the output to the printer by making copies of PRINT and PRINT USING statements (for example, we typed 3045 over line number 3040) and changing PRINT to LPRINT and PRINT USING to LPRINT USING.

Programs that send output to the printer should display a message on the screen to inform the user when processing is done. The message should be displayed only on the screen and not sent to the printer. In programs that send output to the printer, we will append the following statements to our main routine. The line numbers will vary with each program.

```
2080 PRINT
2090 PRINT "End of processing"
2100 END
```

Exercise

Address labels produced by a computer are printed on blank forms, usually two or three blank labels positioned side by side and adhered to paper that fits the printer being used. Write a program that prints three labels as shown below. Use the READ and DATA statements to enter the data. To enter three names, assign the names to three variables, such as NAME1$, NAME2$, NAME3$. Do the same for the street addresses, the cities/provinces, and the postal codes. Direct the output to the screen as well as to the printer.

```
         10        20        30        40        50        60        70        80
12345678901234567890123456789012345678901234567890123456789012345678901234567890

Mr. John Smith                Mrs. Doris Moore              Mr. Russell Knight
123 Main Street               1394 Harcourt Street          498 Ashberry Drive
Anycity  ZZ                   Anycity  ZZ                   Mytown  XX
M3L 6S7                       M3L 1R4                       N6Y 3A2
```

8.9 Program Design

We will now modify our NET PAY program designed in previous chapters so that it incorporates most of the concepts learned in this chapter. The concepts incorporated will be:

1. Formatting the report by means of the TAB function, the PRINT USING statement, the LOCATE statement, and the STRING$ function.
2. Using the LINE INPUT statement to enter a date that includes a comma.
3. Editing data by the screenful.
4. Using a counter and an accumulator.

5. Merging an ASCII file with our program in memory.
6. Producing a summary.

We will be reading data file EMPLOYE3.DAT which contains the following records:

EMPLOYE3.DAT	
2.25	— Union dues
Darryl Brown,10.49,38,82.03,4.04	— Employee name, rate of pay, hours of work, income tax deduction, pension deduction
Ellen Miller,9.76,39,79.35,3.76	
Lorne Hayes,10.87,42,87.82,4.57	
Andrea Jones,11.04,47,93.79,6.94	

As with the program designed in Chapter Seven, our program will calculate overtime pay based on time and a half and on double time. In addition, it will produce the summary shown in the rough layout below.

Rough Layout of the Output:

```
                                                            (cleared screen)
        Enter month, day and year (e.g. September 30, 19XX)
        Date? October 17, 19XX

        Enter the regular hours and the base for double time--39,45

 The date is October 17, 19XX
 Is the date correct (y/n)? y

 The regular hours and base for double time are 39 and 45
 Are the hours correct (y/n)? y

                                                            (cleared screen)
      PAYROLL REPORT

      Week Ending October 17, 19XX
      ===============================================================
      NAME                 HOURS      GROSS        DEDUCTIONS    NET
      ===============================================================
      Darryl Brown         38         $398.62      $ 88.32       $310.30
      Ellen Miller         39         $380.64      $ 85.36       $295.28
      Lorne Hayes          42         $472.85      $ 94.64       $378.21
      Andrea Jones         47         $574.08      $102.98       $471.10

      Totals                          $1,826.18    $371.30       $1,454.89

      Number of employees             4
      Average number of hours        42
      Total income tax deduction      $342.99
      Total union dues                $  9.00
      Total pension deduction         $ 19.31
```

Layout Chart:

We will assume there are 15 characters to the longest name.

FIGURE 8-2 LAYOUT CHART

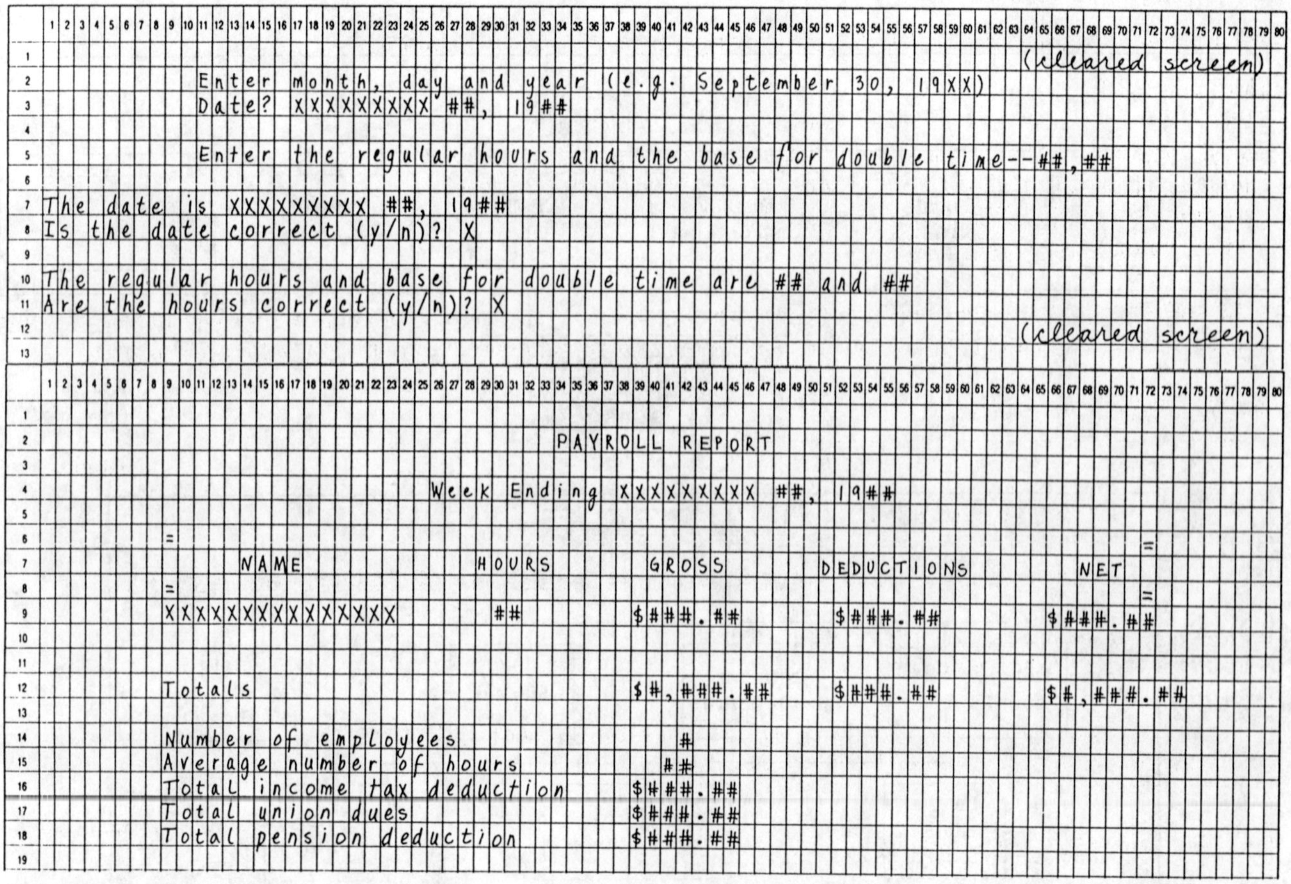

Remember, we consider a layout chart the most refined level of design. Therefore, we do not break down Subroutine FORMAT REPORT AND PRINT HEADINGS in our designs. The statements are typed directly into the computer from the layout chart. Nor do we list, in our designs, all the PRINT statements needed in the summary. We code these statements from the layout chart.

FIGURE 8-3 STRUCTURE CHART

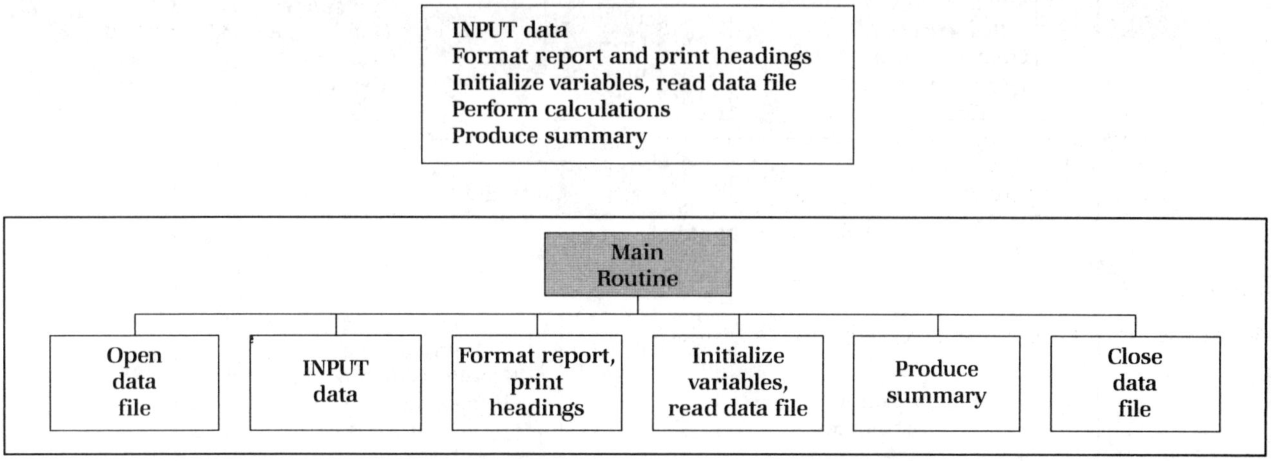

Figure 8-3 Continued

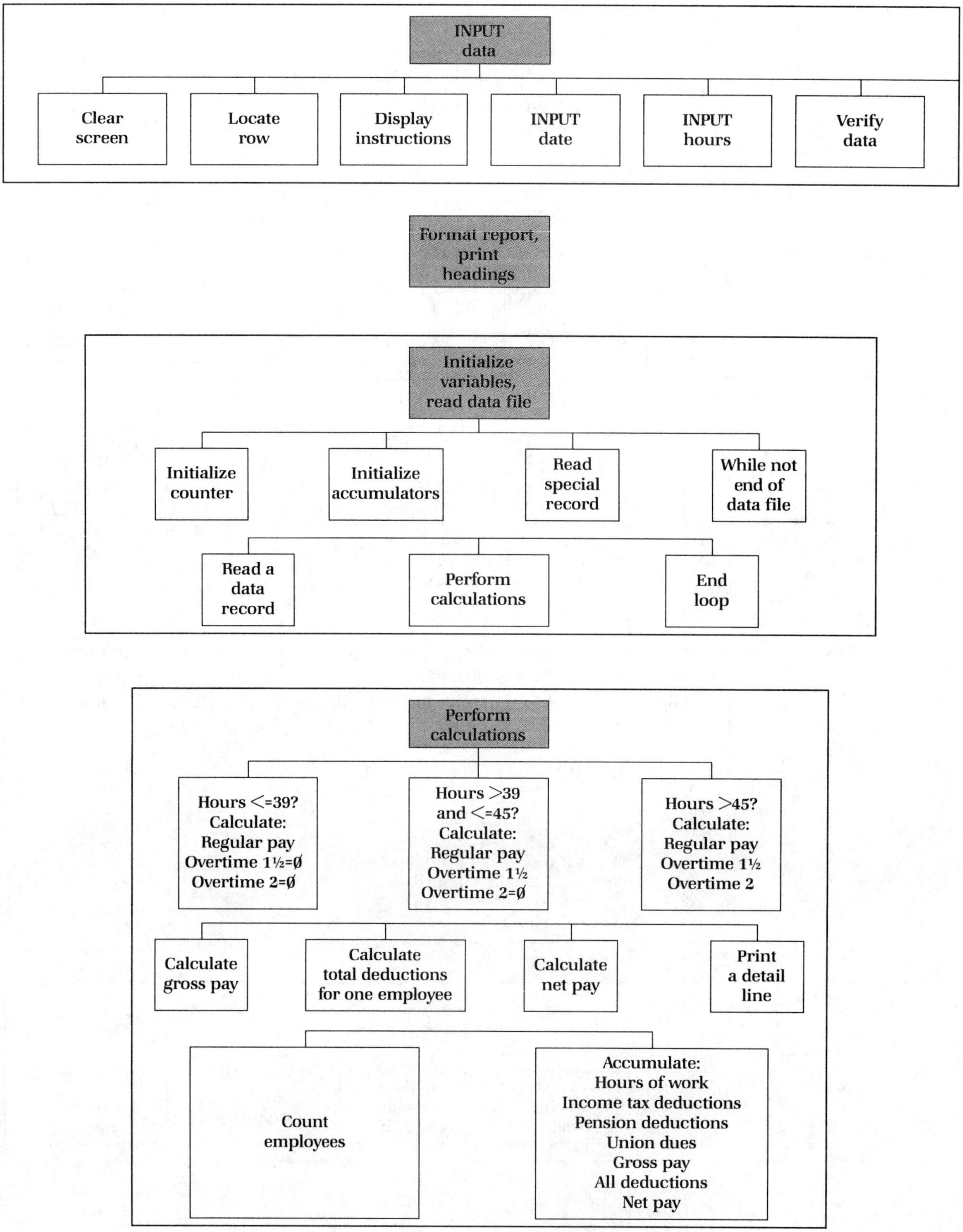

Figure 8-3 Continued

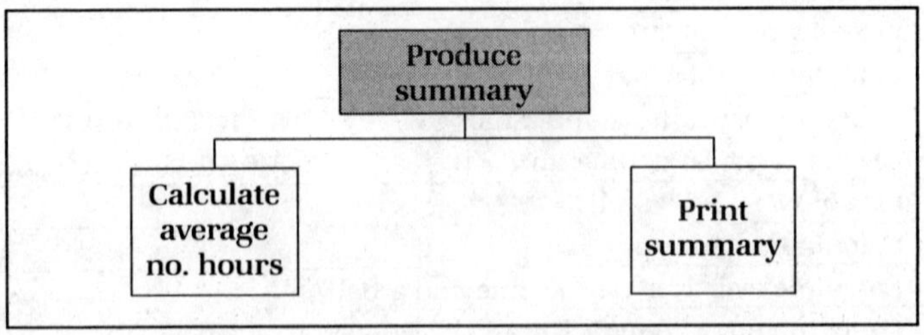

FIGURE 8-4 PSEUDOCODE

MAJOR TASKS
INPUT data
Format report and print headings
Initialize variables, read data file
Perform calculations
Produce summary

MAIN ROUTINE	
Open data file	
INPUT data	(subroutine)
Format report and print headings	(subroutine)
Initialize variables, read data file	(subroutine)
Produce summary	(subroutine)
Close data file	

INPUT DATA	
Clear screen	
Locate row	
Display instructions	
INPUT date	DATE1$
INPUT hours	REGULAR.HOURS,BASE.DOUBLE
Verify data	(merged subroutine)

FORMAT REPORT AND PRINT HEADINGS

INITIALIZE VARIABLES, READ DATA FILE	
Initialize counter	COUNT.EMPLOYEES
Initialize accumulators	TOTAL.HOURS.WORK,TOTAL.INCOME.TAX,TOTAL.PENSION,
	TOTAL.UNION.DUES,TOTAL.GROSS.PAY,
	TOTAL.DEDUCTIONS,TOTAL.NET.PAY
Read special record	UNION
While not end of data file	
Read a data record	ENAME$,RATE,HOURS.WORK,INCOME.TAX,PENSION
Perform calculations	(subroutine)
End loop	

Figure 8-4 Continued

PERFORM CALCULATIONS	
Hours of work <= 39?	
Calculate regular pay	REGULAR.PAY
Overtime pay at time and a half = Ø	OVERTIME.HALF
Overtime pay at double time = Ø	OVERTIME.DOUBLE
Hours of work > 39 and <= 45?	
Calculate regular pay	
Calculate overtime pay at time and a half	
Overtime pay at double time = Ø	
Hours of work > 45?	
Calculate regular pay	
Calculate overtime pay at time and a half	
Calculate overtime pay at double time	
Calculate gross pay	GROSS.PAY
Calculate total deductions	
for one employee	DEDUCTIONS
Calculate net pay	NET.PAY
Print a detail line	
Count employees	
Accumulate:	
Hours of work	
Income tax deductions	
Pension deductions	
Union dues	
Gross pay	
All deductions	
Net pay	

PRODUCE SUMMARY	
Calculate average number of hours	AVERAGE.HOURS
Print summary	

```
1000 'NET PAY                        M. MCRITCHIE                    June 15
1002 '*******************************************************************
1004 '                  THIS PROGRAM PRODUCES A PAYROLL REPORT
1006 '*******************************************************************
1010 'DATE1$             - DATE
1020 'REGULAR.HOURS      - REGULAR HOURS
1030 'BASE.DOUBLE        - BASE HOURS FOR DOUBLE TIME
1040 'RESPONSE$          - USER'S RESPONSE (y/n)
1050 'S$                 - EQUAL SIGNS
1060 'F$                 - IMAGE OF A DETAIL LINE
1070 'COUNT.EMPLOYEES    - COUNTS EMPLOYEES
1080 'TOTAL.HOURS.WORK   - TOTAL HOURS OF WORK
1090 'TOTAL.INCOME.TAX   - TOTAL INCOME TAX DEDUCTIONS
1100 'TOTAL.PENSION      - TOTAL PENSION DEDUCTIONS
1110 'TOTAL.UNION.DUES   - TOTAL UNION DUES
1120 'TOTAL.GROSS.PAY    - TOTAL GROSS PAY
1130 'TOTAL.DEDUCTIONS   - TOTAL DEDUCTIONS
1140 'TOTAL.NET.PAY      - TOTAL NET PAY
1150 'UNION              - UNION DUES
1160 'ENAME$             - EMPLOYEE NAME
1170 'RATE               - RATE OF PAY
1180 'HOURS.WORK         - HOURS OF WORK
1190 'INCOME.TAX         - INCOME TAX DEDUCTION
1200 'PENSION            - PENSION DEDUCTION
1210 'REGULAR.PAY        - REGULAR PAY
```

```
1220 'OVERTIME.HALF      - OVERTIME PAY AT TIME AND A HALF
1230 'OVERTIME.DOUBLE    - OVERTIME PAY AT DOUBLE TIME
1240 'GROSS.PAY          - GROSS PAY
1250 'DEDUCTIONS         - DEDUCTIONS FOR ONE EMPLOYEE
1260 'NET.PAY            - NET PAY
1270 'AVERAGE.HOURS      - AVERAGE NUMBER OF HOURS OF WORK
2000 '***********************************************************
2002 '                          MAIN ROUTINE
2004 '***********************************************************
2010  OPEN "B:EMPLOYE3.DAT" FOR INPUT AS #1
2020  GOSUB 3000                    'INPUT data
2030  GOSUB 4000                    'Format report and print headings
2040  GOSUB 5000                    'Initialize, read data file
2050  GOSUB 7000                    'Produce summary
2060  CLOSE #1
2070  END
3000 '***********************************************************
3002 '                    INPUT DATA (DATE AND HOURS)
3004 '***********************************************************
3010  CLS
3020  LOCATE 5
3030  PRINT TAB(11) "Enter month, day and year (e.g. September 30, 19XX)"
3040  LINE INPUT "__________Date? ";DATE1$
3050  PRINT
3060  INPUT "__________Enter the regular hours and the base for double time--",
      REGULAR.HOURS,BASE.DOUBLE
3070  GOSUB 10000                    'Verify data (date and hours)
3080  RETURN
4000 '***********************************************************
4002 '                   FORMAT REPORT AND PRINT HEADINGS
4004 '***********************************************************
4010  CLS
4020  LOCATE 4
4030  S$ = STRING$(64,"=")
4040  F$ = "________\______________\______##_______$###.##______$###.##_______$##
#.##"
4050  PRINT TAB(34) "PAYROLL REPORT"
4060  PRINT
4070  PRINT TAB(26) "Week Ending ";DATE1$
4080  PRINT TAB(9) S$
4090  PRINT TAB(14) "NAME"; TAB(29) "HOURS"; TAB(40) "GROSS"; TAB(51)
      "DEDUCTIONS"; TAB(68) "NET"
4100  PRINT TAB(9) S$
4110  RETURN
5000 '***********************************************************
5002 '                    INITIALIZE, READ DATA FILE
5004 '***********************************************************
5010  COUNT.EMPLOYEES = 0
5020  TOTAL.HOURS.WORK = 0
5030  TOTAL.INCOME.TAX = 0
5040  TOTAL.PENSION = 0
5050  TOTAL.UNION.DUES = 0
5060  TOTAL.GROSS.PAY = 0
5070  TOTAL.DEDUCTIONS = 0
5080  TOTAL.NET.PAY = 0
5090  INPUT #1, UNION
5100  WHILE NOT EOF(1)
5110    INPUT #1, ENAME$,RATE,HOURS.WORK,INCOME.TAX,PENSION
5120    GOSUB 6000                  'Perform calculations
5130  WEND
5140  RETURN
6000 '***********************************************************
6002 '                         PERFORM CALCULATIONS
6004 '***********************************************************
6010  IF HOURS.WORK <= 39 THEN REGULAR.PAY = HOURS.WORK*RATE :
         OVERTIME.HALF = 0 :
         OVERTIME.DOUBLE = 0
```

```
6020  IF HOURS.WORK>39 AND HOURS.WORK<=45 THEN REGULAR.PAY=REGULAR.HOURS*RATE :
         OVERTIME.HALF = (HOURS.WORK-REGULAR.HOURS)*RATE*1.5 :
         OVERTIME.DOUBLE = 0
6030  IF HOURS.WORK > 45 THEN REGULAR.PAY = REGULAR.HOURS*RATE :
         OVERTIME.HALF = (BASE.DOUBLE-REGULAR.HOURS)*RATE*1.5 :
         OVERTIME.DOUBLE = (HOURS.WORK-BASE.DOUBLE)*RATE*2
6040  GROSS.PAY = REGULAR.PAY+OVERTIME.HALF+OVERTIME.DOUBLE
6050  DEDUCTIONS = INCOME.TAX+PENSION+UNION
6060  NET.PAY = GROSS.PAY-DEDUCTIONS
6070  PRINT USING F$; ENAME$,HOURS.WORK,GROSS.PAY,DEDUCTIONS,NET.PAY
6080  COUNT.EMPLOYEES = COUNT.EMPLOYEES+1
6090  TOTAL.HOURS.WORK = TOTAL.HOURS.WORK+HOURS.WORK
6100  TOTAL.INCOME.TAX = TOTAL.INCOME.TAX+INCOME.TAX
6110  TOTAL.PENSION = TOTAL.PENSION+PENSION
6120  TOTAL.UNION.DUES = TOTAL.UNION.DUES+UNION
6130  TOTAL.GROSS.PAY = TOTAL.GROSS.PAY+GROSS.PAY
6140  TOTAL.DEDUCTIONS = TOTAL.DEDUCTIONS+DEDUCTIONS
6150  TOTAL.NET.PAY = TOTAL.NET.PAY+NET.PAY
6160  RETURN
7000 '*****************************************************************************
7002 '                               PRODUCE SUMMARY
7004 '*****************************************************************************
7010  AVERAGE.HOURS = TOTAL.HOURS.WORK/COUNT.EMPLOYEES
7020  PRINT
7030  PRINT TAB(9) USING "Totals________________________$####,.##____$###.##____
___$####,.##"; TOTAL.GROSS.PAY,TOTAL.DEDUCTIONS,TOTAL.NET.PAY
7040  PRINT
7050  PRINT TAB(9) USING "Number of employees______________##";COUNT.EMPLOYEES
7060  PRINT TAB(9) USING "Average number of hours_________##";AVERAGE.HOURS
7070  PRINT TAB(9) USING "Total income tax deduction____$###.##";
      TOTAL.INCOME.TAX
7080  PRINT TAB(9) USING "Total union dues______________$###.##";
      TOTAL.UNION.DUES
7090  PRINT TAB(9) USING "Total pension deduction_______$###.##";TOTAL.PENSION
7100  RETURN
10000 '****************************************************************************
10002 '                        VERIFY DATA (DATE AND HOURS)
10004 '****************************************************************************
10010  PRINT
10020  PRINT USING "The date is \________________\";DATE1$
10030  INPUT "Is the date correct (y/n)";RESPONSE$
10040  IF RESPONSE$ <> "y" AND RESPONSE$ <> "Y"
          THEN LINE INPUT "Re-enter the date--",DATE1$ : GOTO 10030
10050  PRINT
10060  PRINT USING "The regular hours and base for double time are ## and ##";
       REGULAR.HOURS,BASE.DOUBLE
10070  INPUT "Are the hours correct (y/n)";RESPONSE$
10080  IF RESPONSE$ <> "y" AND RESPONSE$ <> "Y"
          THEN INPUT "Re-enter the hours--",REGULAR.HOURS,BASE.DOUBLE :
          GOTO 10070
10090  RETURN
65529 'End of program listing
```

The Output:

(cleared screen)

```
        10        20        30        40        50        60        70        80
12345678901234567890123456789012345678901234567890123456789012345678901234567890

          Enter month, day and year (e.g. September 30, 19XX)
          Date? October 17, 19XX

          Enter the regular hours and the base for double time--39,45

The date is October 17, 19XX
Is the date correct (y/n)? y

The regular hours and base for double time are 39 and 45
Are the hours correct (y/n)? y
```

(cleared screen)

```
                         PAYROLL REPORT

                   Week Ending October 17, 19XX
  ================================================================
       NAME             HOURS       GROSS      DEDUCTIONS      NET
  ================================================================
  Darryl Brown            38      $398.62     $ 88.32      $310.30
  Ellen Miller            39      $380.64     $ 85.36      $295.28
  Lorne Hayes             42      $472.85     $ 94.64      $378.21
  Andrea Jones            47      $574.08     $102.98      $471.10

  Totals                          $1,826.18   $371.30      $1,454.89

  Number of employees               4
  Average number of hours          42
  Total income tax deduction      $342.99
  Total union dues                $   9.00
  Total pension deduction         $  19.31
```

Remember, Subroutine VERIFY DATA must be merged with the program. Since the subroutine was initially written for this program, it need not be customized. For a different program, the prompts and the variables probably need to be changed. Note that the average number of hours is calculated in the summary after the accumulator for the total hours and the counter for the number of employees have been assigned their final values.

Summary of BASIC Statements

CLS — Clears the screen and places the BASIC prompt and the cursor in the top left-hand corner of the screen.

```
4010 CLS
```

LINE INPUT — Assigns an entire string (up to 255 characters including commas) to a string variable. The string is entered through the keyboard. Prints no question mark.

```
3040 LINE INPUT "Enter month and year separated by a comma--";DATE1$
```

LOCATE r,c — Positions the cursor on a desired screen line and column. The parameter r represents the row, the parameter c represents the column. An option is to specify only the row.

```
4020 LOCATE 8,21   or   4020 LOCATE 8
```

LPRINT USING — Directs output to the printer using format specified by an image. The image may be coded in the statement or assigned to a string variable referenced by LPRINT USING.

```
5030 LPRINT USING " ###"; NUMBER   or   5020 F$ = " ###"
                                        5030 LPRINT USING F$; NUMBER
```

PRINT USING — Similar to the LPRINT USING statement. Displays the output on the screen.

```
5030 PRINT USING " \      \"; ENAME$   or   5020 F$ = " \      \"
                                            5030 PRINT USING F$; ENAME$
```

Summary of BASIC Functions

INKEY$ — Accepts one character from the keyboard.

```
11030 K$ = INKEY$
```

STRING$(n,"c") — Returns a string of a desired character. The symbol n represents the number of characters, the symbol c represents the character desired.

```
4030 S$ = STRING$(26,"=")
```

TAB(n) — Tabulates to a specific column before an item is printed. The symbol n represents the number of a column. May be used in PRINT, LPRINT, PRINT USING, and LPRINT USING statements.

```
5040 PRINT TAB(10) RATE       5060 PRINT TAB(10) USING "\       \"; MONTH$
5050 LPRINT TAB(10) "NAME"    5070 LPRINT TAB(20) USING "$####,.##"; SALES
```

Summary of BASIC Commands

MERGE — Merges an ASCII file saved on disk with a program in memory.

```
MERGE "B:VERIFY.ASC"
```

SAVE — When a comma and an A are appended to the SAVE command, the file is saved in ASCII format.

```
SAVE "B:VERIFY.ASC",A
```

Summary of Library Files

FREEZE.ASC — Freezes a display on the screen.

VERIFY.ASC — Verifies keyed-in data by the screenful.

Chapter Summary

1. Planning an output that is attractive and easy-to-read is referred to as formatting or editing the output.
2. Reports should be centred vertically and horizontally on the screen. The report must first be planned on a layout chart which consists of 25 rows and 80 columns.
3. The LOCATE statement is used to centre output vertically.
4. All parts of a report should be centred. The heading and subheading should be centred horizontally, column headings should be centred over their items, and a summary (if any) should be displayed attractively at the bottom of the report.
5. A library function is a prewritten routine that performs a specific operation. The routine is written directly into the BASIC language and returns just one result.
6. A library function is called by coding its name and the value upon which the function is to operate. This value is referred to as the argument and must be enclosed in parentheses.
7. A PRINT statement may contain multiple TAB functions to position strings and numbers.
8. The image for a PRINT USING statement may be coded within the PRINT USING statement or it may be assigned to a string variable.
9. When the image is assigned to a string variable, one or several subsequent PRINT USING statements may reference the string variable.
10. A series of number signs (#) in an edit field designates positions for the digits of a numeric item.
11. Commas can be inserted in a number by placing commas in the edit field where they would normally appear in the number. An alternative is to place one or more commas in the right-most position(s) of the field for a whole number or to the left of the decimal point for a decimal number. A comma should not occupy the first position of a numeric edit field.
12. Placing a trailing minus sign in a numeric edit field produces a trailing minus sign in a negative number. The minus sign is replaced by a space when the number is positive.
13. Placing two dollar signs in the left-most positions of a numeric edit field produces one dollar sign immediately to the left of the edited number. The dollar sign is referred to as a floating dollar sign.
14. Two asterisks in the left-most positions of a numeric edit field fill the spaces to the left of the edited number with asterisks.
15. Two asterisks and a dollar sign in the left-most positions of a numeric edit field produce a dollar sign immediately to the left of the edited number and asterisks in the remaining positions to the left of the dollar sign.
16. To reserve positions for a string, two backward slashes are used; one for the first character of the string and another for the last character. The spaces between the backward slashes reserve positions for the remaining characters of the string.
17. An exclamation mark is used to edit a one-character string.
18. Strings may be coded directly in an image.
19. A percent sign (%) can be printed to the right of a number by coding a percent sign in the right-most position of the number's edit field.
20. A CLS instruction coded in a statement clears the screen when the statement is executed.
21. Characters produced by a STRING$ function can be used to highlight the headings of a report. The function may also be used to produce leaders (periods) between items.
22. The LINE INPUT statement can be used to enter a string that contains commas. The string need not be enclosed in quotation marks when keyed in.
23. We can edit data by the screenful by calling a "verification" subroutine after all items have been keyed in.

24. When statements that print a display are followed by a clear screen instruction, the display vanishes so quickly it cannot be seen. Subroutine FREEZE DISPLAY must be called between the group of statements that prints the display and the statement that clears the screen.

25. Any frequently called subroutine should be stored on disk in ASCII format (one character per byte). When saved in this manner, the subroutine can later be merged with a program in memory by means of the MERGE command.

26. Counters and accumulators are often used to obtain results printed in a summary. A counter is a variable that keeps track of the number of times a particular transaction occurs. An accumulator is a variable that accumulates numeric values to attain a total.

27. Many business programs direct output to the printer, often to preprinted forms such as checks and invoices.

Questions and Exercises

1. (a) What is a library function?
   (b) How is a library function called?
   (c) Give three statements from which a library function may be called.

2. (a) What is an argument in BASIC?
   (b) State five ways by which an argument may be expressed.

3. What output will each of the following program segments produce? Indicate the column number where each printed field begins.

(a)
```
4020 PIECES = 39
4030 RATE = 2.55
4040 PRINT TAB(12) "PIECES"; TAB(23) "RATE"
4050 PRINT TAB(13) PIECES; TAB(22) RATE
```

(b)
```
4010 READ PURCHASE,BALANCE
4020 DATA 64.89,185.07
4030 PRINT TAB(2) "PURCHASE"; TAB(12) "$"; PURCHASE; TAB(24) "BALANCE";
     TAB(33) "$"; BALANCE
```

4. Code PRINT statements with TAB functions to produce the following. Assume that the data items for detail lines have already been assigned to variables.

(a)
```
12345678901234567890123456789012345
         DEPOSIT    WITHDRAWAL    BALANCE

         625.43        125.43         500
```

(b)
```
12345678901234567890123456789012345678901234567890123
          NAME OF                  AMOUNT OF
          CUSTOMER                 PURCHASE

         Davidson, L.                $ 63.45
```

(c) Centre the following name and address vertically and horizontally on a cleared screen. Assume each of the following has been assigned to a variable: (a) the name (b) the number and street (c) the city and province, and (d) the postal code.

```
Mr. John Smith
123 Main Street
Anycity  ZZ
M3L 6S7
```

(d) Display the program description given below centred vertically and horizontally on a cleared screen. Use any line length.

```
This program calculates the amount of interest on a charge
account. The account number and the number of days for which
interest is charged must be entered by the user.
```

5. What output lines will the following statements produce?

```
6020 PRINT TAB(10) USING "Sales:__________$#####,.##";SALES
6030 PRINT TAB(10) USING "Commission:_____$#####,.##";COMMISSION
```

(a) for SALES = 34610.42 and COMMISSION = 3461.04
(b) for SALES = 5219 and COMMISSION = 521
(c) for SALES = 395.21 and COMMISSION = 39.52

6. Use PRINT USING statements to produce the following. Assign all degrees to variables. Assign the images to string variables and reference these variables in your PRINT USING statements. Code the strings in the images.

```
Degrees Fahrenheit:    50   55   60   65   70
Degrees Celsius:       10   13   16   18   21
```

7. Reproduce the output above but this time code the images in the PRINT USING statements.

8. Write programs to produce the following outputs. In each program, assign the image to a string variable. Use the READ and DATA statements to enter the values into the computer. Use a WHILE/WEND loop.

(a) Align the decimal points and insert commas (where necessary) for the numbers .07, 382.94, and 3184.25.

```
12345678901234
          0.07
        382.94
      3,184.25
```

(b) Round off the numbers .067, 143.581, and 4160.23 to two decimal places and place a floating dollar sign before each number.

```
12345678901234
         $0.07
       $143.58
     $4,160.23
```

(c) Protect the dollar amounts in Exercise (b) by coding an image that inserts one or more asterisks before each amount.

```
12345678901234
*****$0.07
***$143.58
*$4,160.23
```

9. Write a program that prints the following report. Use the STRING$ function to produce the equal signs and the leaders. Use a PRINT USING statement to print the detail line. Do not document the program since this is simply an exercise in centring.

```
         10        20        30        40        50        60        70        80
12345678901234567890123456789012345678901234567890123456789012345678901234567890
                         ================================
                             ITEM                 INVENTORY
                         ================================
                         Printer ribbons ............ 18
```

10. Use INPUT or LINE INPUT statements to produce the following. In exercise (a), use one variable.

(a) `Enter last name, first name separated by a comma--Smith,John`
(b) `What is your telephone number? 467-1593`
(c) `What is your address? 498 Treehern Drive,Anycity  ZZ,M3L 4R3`
(d) `Enter amount received--125.98`

Programming Problems

Write programs for the following problems. Centre reports vertically and horizontally on a cleared screen. Centre instructions and prompts horizontally and centre column headings over columns. Do not centre prompts produced by a verification routine or by a merged subroutine. A date in the heading of a report must be keyed in by the user. Your programs must give the user the opportunity to correct all keyed-in data. Wherever possible, allow the user to verify data by the screenful. The prompts for entering and verifying data are given for the first two problems. Use these as guides for the remaining problems.

Unless instructed otherwise, assume that the maximum number of characters in a name or in the name of an item is 15. Refer to the rough layout of each report for the number of characters in the other fields. Create data files on disk for the first seven problems.

1. Write a program that lists a householder's expenses for the month of November, then produces the summary shown in the rough layout. Count the number of invoices for the month and find the total amount of expenses for the month. In the subroutine that produces the summary, find the total number of invoices and the total expenses to date. To find these totals, add the number of previous invoices (28) to your counter and the total amount of these invoices ($626.13) to your accumulator.

HOUSE.DAT

28,626.13	— Number of invoices and total expenses since the beginning of the year
Telephone,12.25	
Water,8.24	— Type of expense, amount of expense for the month
Heat (Gas),40.89	
Lights,18.95	

Rough Layout of the Output:

```
                                                        (cleared screen)
          Enter month and year (e.g. September, 19XX)
          Date? [November, 19XX]

Is the date correct (y/n)? [y]

                                                        (cleared screen)
              HOUSEHOLD EXPENSES

              November, 19XX
              ==================================
              EXPENSE ITEM                AMOUNT
              ==================================
              Telephone                   $12.25
              Water                       $ 8.24
              Heat (Gas)                  $40.89
              Lights                      $18.95

              Number of invoices               4
              Total for November, 19XX     $ 80.33
              Number of invoices to date      32
              Total expenses to date       $706.46
```

2. Modify the program for Problem 5 in Chapter Seven as follows:
   (a) Rather than read (from a data file) the base sales, the rate of commission on the base sales, and the rate of commission on the excess sales, allow the user to key in these values.
   (b) Change the instructions and the prompts to those shown in the rough layout on page 200.
   (c) Allow the user to verify data by the screenful. Merge Subroutine VERIFY DATA with your program and customize the subroutine.
   (d) Find the total sales and the total commission. Print these results in Subroutine PRODUCE SUMMARY. Hint: Your statement that accumulates the commissions must be placed after the statement that calculates a commission.

Here is the problem once more.

A company pays its sales personnel 12% commission on sales up to and including $5000 and 15% on sales in excess of $5000. The $5000 is referred to as the base. Find the amount of commission for each salesperson shown in the data file below. Calculate a commission in an IF/THEN/ELSE statement. Change your former data file to the following.

SALES5.DAT
James Kelly,5839
Tom Powell,4987 — Name of salesperson, amount of sales
Joan Friesen,6025
Leslie Dale,5000

Formulas:

(a) Sales <= Base
Commission = Sales × Rate on Base/100
(b) Sales > Base
Commission = Base × Rate on Base/100 + (Sales−Base) × Rate on Excess/100

Rough Layout of the Output:

```
                                                        (cleared screen)
      Enter month, day and year (e.g. September 30, 19XX)
      Date? [August 19, 19XX]

      Enter base, regular rate, excess rate--[5000,12,15]

   The date is August 19, 19XX
   Is the date correct (y/n)? [y]

   The base, regular rate, excess rate are $5,000.00,12%,15%
   Are the entries correct (y/n)? [y]

                                                        (cleared screen)
       COMMISSION REPORT

       Week Ending August 19, 19XX
       ===============================================
       NAME                SALES               COMMISSION
       ===============================================
       James Kelly         $5,839.00           $725.85
       Tom Powell          $4,987.00           $598.44
       Joan Friesen        $6,025.00           $753.75
       Leslie Dale         $5,000.00           $600.00

       Totals              $21,851.00          $2,678.04
```

3. An electronics company keeps a record of its monthly telephone expenses. In addition to the long distance charges given below for the month of December, the company pays a monthly rental of $39.25. Use two statements to INPUT the date and the monthly rental. Verify the data by the screenful. Although the report lists only four long distance calls, in reality the company makes many more. Produce a report that displays the following.

   (a) The cities and the respective long distance charges.
   (b) The monthly rental.
   (c) The total long distance charges.
   (d) The amount due.
   (e) The number of long distance calls.
   (f) The average long distance charge.

   PHONE.DAT
   Washington,10.32
   Ottawa,12.67 — City, long distance charge
   Canberra,37.26
   London,31.94

   Formulas:

   Amount Due = Monthly Rental + Total Long Distance Charge

   $$\text{Average Long Distance Charge} = \frac{\text{Total Long Distance Charge}}{\text{No. of Long Distance Calls (the counter)}}$$

   Calculate the amount due and the average long distance charge in the subroutine that produces the summary. Display the summary on a cleared screen. Hint: You must call Subroutine FREEZE DISPLAY from your main routine before you call the subroutine that produces the summary. Otherwise, the CLS instruction in the summary removes the display of cities and charges so quickly you will not be able to view them. Remember to merge Subroutine FREEZE DISPLAY with your program. For many of the remaining problems in this book, we will no longer remind you to merge an ASCII file with your program.

Rough Layout of the Report:

```
                                                        (cleared screen)
                 TELEPHONE EXPENSE
                 December, 19XX

                 LONG DISTANCE CHARGES
                 ================================
                 CITY                      CHARGE
                 ================================
                 Washington                $10.32
                 Ottawa                    $12.67
                 Canberra                  $37.26
                 London                    $31.94

  Press any key to continue
                                                        (cleared screen)
        SUMMARY OF TELEPHONE EXPENSES--December, 19XX

             Monthly rental                       $ 39.25
             Total long distance charge           $ 92.19
             Amount due                           $131.44

             Number of long distance calls           4
             Average long distance charge         $ 23.05
```

4. A department store, opening a new branch in a suburban shopping centre, is offering a 15% discount on any purchase made during opening day at its new store. A customer purchases the items listed below. What is the total amount of the purchase? What is the reduced amount? If a sales tax of 6% is added to the reduced amount, what is the amount of the customer's bill? All data required by the program is stored in a data file.

BILL.DAT
15,6 — Rate of discount, rate of sales tax
Shoes,54.90
Sports jacket,63.80 — Item purchased, price
Dress shirt,21.50

Formulas:

Discount = Total Purchase × Rate of Discount/100
Reduced Amount = Total Purchase − Discount
Sales Tax = Reduced Amount × Rate of Sales Tax/100
Amount of Bill = Reduced Amount + Sales Tax

Use the STRING$ function to produce the leaders. Positions for the leaders must be reserved not only in the image that edits the detail lines but also in the PRINT USING statements that print the summary. Find the discount, the reduced amount, the sales tax, and the amount due in the subroutine that produces the summary.

```
MEN'S FASHIONS
======================================
ITEM                      RETAIL PRICE
======================================
Shoes            ......... $ 54.90
Sports jacket    ......... $ 63.80
Dress shirt      ......... $ 21.50

Total purchase   ......... $140.20
Discount         ......... $ 21.03
Reduced amount   ......... $119.17
Sales tax        ......... $  7.15
Amount due       ......... $126.32
```

5. The club members listed below sold tickets to a local baseball game. The price of each ticket was $2.50. Find the amount of money collected by each member, the total number of tickets sold, the total amount of money collected, and the average number of tickets sold. The price of a ticket is to be keyed in by the user.

   In addition to a counter that counts the members, you will need two accumulators; one to accumulate the number of tickets sold by each member and the other to accumulate the amounts collected. Find the average in the subroutine that produces the summary.

   TICKETS.DAT
   Susan Fraser,14
   Michael Hansen,15 — Member's name, number of tickets sold
   Tracy Edwards,13

   Formula:

   $$\text{Average Number Sold} = \frac{\text{Total Number Sold}}{\text{Number of Members (a counter)}}$$

```
TICKET SALES
===============================================
NAME                  TICKETS SOLD    COLLECTED
===============================================
Susan Fraser              14          $ 35.00
Michael Hansen            15          $ 37.50
Tracy Edwards             13          $ 32.50

Totals                    42          $105.00
Average number sold       14
```

6. On October 12 Frank Martin, a retailer of appliances, purchased the items listed below. Find the extended cost of each item. In addition to the cost of the appliances, Mr. Martin is charged $125.00 for delivery. Use two statements to INPUT the date and the delivery charge. As a summary, display the cost of the appliances, the delivery charge, and the total cost which includes the delivery charge. Allow a maximum of 10 characters to the name of an appliance.

   APPLIANC.DAT
   5,Washer,489.95
   7,Oven,786.45 — Quantity, item, unit price
   6,Range,521.98

   Formula:

   Extended Cost = Quantity × Unit Price

```
PURCHASE ON OCTOBER 12, 19XX
=====================================================
QUANTITY      ITEM            UNIT PRICE       COST
=====================================================
5             Washer          $489.95          $2,449.75
7             Oven            $786.45          $5,505.15
6             Range           $521.98          $3,131.88

Cost of appliances                             $11,086.78
Delivery                                       $   125.00
Total cost                                     $11,211.78
```

7. Employees working in a machine shop are paid on a piece-work basis. For the first 180 pieces produced, the employees receive $2.85 for each piece. For pieces in excess of 180, the employees receive $3.45 for each piece. Consider 180 as the base.

   Write a program that produces the weekly report given on page 204. Use one statement to INPUT the date and another to INPUT the base, the regular rate, and the excess rate.

PIECES.DAT

1.95	— Union dues
Henry Richards,174,82.15,3.27	
Judy Miller,180,94.57,5.26	— Name, pieces produced, income tax deduction, pension deduction
Ellen Wilson,186,98.23,7.34	
Carl Foster,187,99.87,7.93	

Formulas:

Pieces produced <= base:
Regular Pay = Pieces Produced × Regular Rate
Excess Pay = Ø

Pieces produced > base:
Regular Pay = Base × Regular Rate
Excess Pieces = Pieces Produced − Base
Excess Pay = Excess Pieces × Excess Rate

General Formulas:

Gross Pay = Regular Pay + Excess Pay
Deductions = Income Tax Deduction + Union Dues + Pension Deduction
Net Pay = Gross Pay − Deductions

Use two IF/THEN statements in your decision structure; one to perform the calculations when the number of pieces produced is less than or equal to the base and the other to perform the calculations when the number of pieces produced is greater than the base. Following the decision structure, process the general formulas and find the total pieces, the total excess pieces, the total gross pay, the total deductions, and the total net pay. Use accumulators to find these totals.

In the subroutine that produces the summary, use the following formulas to calculate the total regular pieces, the total regular pay, and the total excess pay.

(a) Total Regular Pieces = Total Pieces−Total Excess Pieces
(b) Total Regular Pay = Total Regular Pieces × Regular Rate
(c) Total Excess Pay = Total Excess Pieces × Excess Rate

```
       PAYROLL ON PIECE WORK

       Week Ending January 31, 19XX
       ================================================================
       NAME                   PIECES      GROSS          DEDUCTIONS     NET
       ================================================================
       Henry Richards         174         $495.90        $ 87.37        $408.53
       Judy Miller            180         $513.00        $101.78        $411.22
       Ellen Wilson           186         $533.70        $107.52        $426.18
       Carl Foster            187         $537.15        $109.75        $427.40

TOTALS:

       Regular pieces         714          Regular pay    $2,034.90
       Excess pieces           13          Excess pay     $    44.85
       Pieces produced        727          Gross pay      $2,079.75

                                           Deductions     $   406.42
                                           Net pay        $1,673.33
```

8. Modify the program written for Problem 7 in Chapter Seven as indicated below. The program updates Accounts Receivable file AR1.DAT. and writes the records to file AR2.DAT.

(a) Display the prompts for each transaction on a cleared screen.

(b) Produce accounts similar to the one shown below. Each account must be centred on a cleared screen.

Just before the RETURN statement in the subroutine that prints an account, call Subroutine FREEZE DISPLAY. Remember to save your program.

Partial Output:

```
                                                                    (cleared screen)
     Transaction for the following account:

     31001    Diane Fraser    Balance on Nov. 12: 342.16    Credit limit: 1000

     Enter transaction (date, sale, payment)--Nov. 14,59.21,0

Are the entries correct (y/n)? y
                                                                    (cleared screen)
       Account number 31001
       *************************************************************
       * NAME: Diane Fraser                               TELEPHONE *
       * ADDRESS: 367 River Road  Anycity  ZZ  M3L 4S8     339-8542  *
       *------------------------------------------------------------*
       * DATE            ITEM           DEBIT     CREDIT     BALANCE  *
       *------------------------------------------------------------*
       * Nov. 12         Balance                          $  342.16 *
       * Nov. 14                        $ 59.21   $ 0.00  $  401.37 *
       *                                                            *
       *                                                            *
       *                                                            *
       *                                                            *
       *                                                            *
       *                                                            *
       *************************************************************

Press any key to continue
```

Project

Modify the inventory program written in Chapter Seven as follows:

1. Display the prompts for each transaction on a cleared screen. The prompts for stock number F003 are given below.

(cleared screen)

```
Transaction for the following account:

F003  Furnishings  Sofa (Italian)  Balance on Dec. 31: 4   Min: 2

Enter the transaction (date, amount ordered, amount sold)--Jan. 6,0,3

Are the entries correct (y/n)? y
```

2. Produce inventory accounts similar to the Accounts Receivable accounts of Problem 8 above. Display each account on a cleared screen.
3. If the balance in an account is less than the minimum number of items allowed, display a warning beneath the account.
4. Count the number of inventory accounts whose balances are below the minimum and display this count, centred vertically and horizontally, on a cleared screen. Hint: Consider the display a summary.
5. End your output with "End of processing".
6. Remember to save your program.

   The inventory account for stock number F003 could look as follows.

(cleared screen)

```
          Stock number F003
          ****************************************************************
          * DEPARTMENT: Furnishings                                      *
          * ITEM: Sofa (Italian)                            Minimum: 2   *
          *--------------------------------------------------------------*
          * DATE                         ORDERED        SOLD     BALANCE *
          *--------------------------------------------------------------*
          * Dec. 31                                                4     *
          * Jan. 6                          0             3        1     *
          *                                                              *
          *                                                              *
          *                                                              *
          *                                                              *
          *                                                              *
          *                                                              *
          ****************************************************************
                        Insufficient stock. Please reorder.

Press any key to continue
```

   Your summary could be:

(cleared screen)

```
                        Number of accounts under the minimum: 6

End of processing
```

Solutions for Exercises

8.1 Centring Output

FIGURE 8-5 LAYOUT CHART

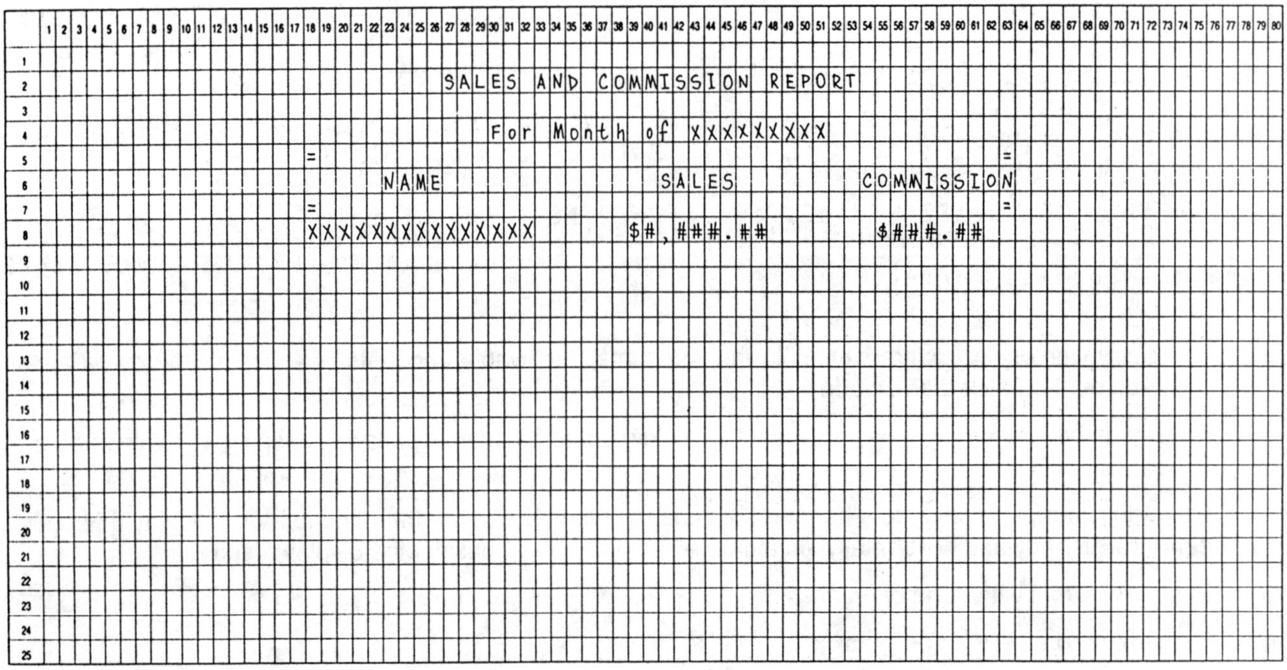

8.2 Tabulating to a Specific Column

1. (a)
```
4010 PRINT TAB(3) 67; TAB(14) -49
```
(b)
```
4010 PRINT TAB(10) "August"; TAB(17) 23
```
(c)
```
4010 PRINT TAB(2) "Commission"; TAB(15) "$"; 263.42
```
(d)
```
4010 PRINT TAB(2) "CUSTOMER"
4020 PRINT TAB(4) "NAME"; TAB(16) "BALANCE"
```
(e)
```
4010 PRINT TAB(7) "MONTH"; TAB(17) "K HOURS"; TAB(30) "CHARGE"
4020 PRINT
4030 PRINT TAB(7) MONTH$; TAB(18) K.HOURS; TAB(29) "$"; CHARGE
```
(f)
```
4010 PRINT TAB(7) "NAME OF"; TAB(21) "TOTAL AMOUNT"
4020 PRINT TAB(5) "SALESPERSON"; TAB(25) "SOLD"
4030 PRINT
4040 PRINT TAB(5) SNAME$; TAB(23) "$"; SALES
```

2. (a)
```
12345678901234567890123456
           HOURS      RATE
            40        9.54
```
(b)
```
1234567890123456789012345678901234567890123456789012345678
                     Harrison           $ 580.25
```
(c)
```
1234567890123456789012345678901234567890123456789012345678901234567
         YEARS          AMOUNT              INTEREST

          36            $ 1500              $ 482.67
```

8.3 The PRINT USING Statement

1. (a)
```
4010 READ NUMBER1,NUMBER2,NUMBER3
4020 DATA 485,-94,163.98
4030 PRINT USING "____###_______###_______###.##"; NUMBER1,NUMBER2,NUMBER3
```
(b)
```
4010 READ NUMBER1,NUMBER2,NUMBER3#
4020 DATA 1234,123456,1234567
4030 PRINT USING "__####,_____######,_____#######,,"; NUMBER1,NUMBER2,
     NUMBER3#
```
(c)
```
4010 READ PRINCIPAL,PAYMENT
4020 DATA 16925,196.55
4030 PRINT USING "___Principal__$#####,.##_______Payment__$###.##";
     PRINCIPAL,PAYMENT
```
(d)
```
4010 READ SALES,AVERAGE.SALES
4020 DATA 3496,874
4030 PRINT TAB(26) USING "Total sales______$####,.##"; SALES
4040 PRINT TAB(26) USING "Average sales_____$####,.##"; AVERAGE.SALES
```

2. (a)
```
4010 F$ = "______$$###,.##"
4020 READ NUMBER
4030 WHILE NUMBER <> -1
4040 PRINT USING F$; NUMBER
4050 READ NUMBER
4060 WEND
4070 DATA .048,67.237,2185.36,-1
4080 END
```
(b)
```
4010 F$ = "_____**$###,.##"
```

3. (a)
```
1234567890123456789012345678901234
  Smith,James    12      Data Processing   302
```
(b)
```
1234567890123456789012345678901234567890
    Peters       Bats    49      Hits    15
```
(c)
```
1234567890123456789012345678901234567890
                      Number of bills        5
                      Total expenses    $89.42
```

4.
```
4010 READ NUMBER,NAME1$,BALANCE
4020 F$ = "_______###________\________\_________$####,.##"
4030 PRINT TAB(19) "ACCOUNT BALANCE"
4040 PRINT
4050 PRINT TAB(7) "NUMBER"; TAB(22) "NAME"; TAB(39) "BALANCE"
4060 PRINT
4070 PRINT USING F$; NUMBER,NAME1$,BALANCE
4080 DATA 263,"Glen Miles",1023.68
4090 END
```

8.4 Other Editing Features

1. (a)
```
123456789012
.............
```
(b)
```
12345678901234567890123456
             .............
```
(c)
```
12345678901234567890123
   ====================
```
(d)
```
123456789012345678901234
         ***************
```

2.
```
4010 NAME1$ = "Armstrong"
4020 NUMBER = 161
4030 CLS
4040 S1$ = STRING$(29,"=")
4050 S2$ = STRING$(9,".")
4060 F$ = "_________________________\_______\_\_______\_###"
4070 PRINT TAB(26) S1$
4080 PRINT TAB(28) "NAME"; TAB(40) "NUMBER PRODUCED"
4090 PRINT TAB(26) S1$
4100 PRINT USING F$; NAME1$,S2$,NUMBER
4110 END
```

8.5 Other Useful Features

1. (a) LINE INPUT must be changed to INPUT since LINE INPUT can accept only one value and that value must be a string. Furthermore, the prompt must be followed by a comma in order to suppress the question mark.

```
3010 INPUT "Enter three scores--",SCORE1,SCORE2,SCORE3
```

(b) The prompt is a question, therefore, it must be followed by a semi-colon in order to obtain a question mark after **What is your answer.**

```
3020 INPUT "What is your answer";ANSWER$
```

(c) The prompt should be followed by a question mark and a space or LINE INPUT should be replaced by INPUT.

```
3030 LINE INPUT "What is your telephone number? ";TELEPHONE$
3030 INPUT "What is your telephone number";TELEPHONE$
```

(d) INPUT must be changed to LINE INPUT since the string assigned to DATE1$ contains a comma.

```
3040 LINE INPUT "Enter month and year separated by a comma--";DATE1$
```

(e) The semicolon following the prompt must be changed to a comma to suppress the question mark.

```
3050 INPUT "Enter amount of deposit--",DEPOSIT
```

Exercise 2

```
10000 '************************************************************************
10002 '                         VERIFY DATA (NAME AND TELEPHONE NUMBER)
10004 '************************************************************************
10010  PRINT
10020  PRINT USING "The customer's name is \_____________\"; CNAME$
10030  INPUT "Is the name correct (y/n)";RESPONSE$
10040  IF RESPONSE$ <> "y" AND RESPONSE$ <> "Y"
           THEN LINE INPUT "Re-enter the name--";CNAME$ : GOTO 10030
10050  PRINT
10060  PRINT USING "The telephone number is \______\"; TELEPHONE$
10070  INPUT "Is the number correct (y/n)";RESPONSE$
10080  IF RESPONSE$ <> "y" AND RESPONSE$ <> "Y"
       THEN INPUT "Re-enter the number--",TELEPHONE$ : GOTO 10070
10090  RETURN
```

3. The computer prints only the prompt. Line 11030 assigns the null string to K$. In line 11040, the WHILE statement tests K$ for a space. Since K$ contains the null string (no characters), the condition is false and control transfers to the statement following the WEND statement. The PRINT statement in line 11070 prints the null string and, therefore, produces no output. The WHILE statement must compare K$ with the null string.

```
11040 WHILE K$ = ""
```

8.7 Producing Summaries

```
4000 'SUBROUTINE READ DATA FILE, COUNT EMPLOYEES, ACCUMULATE PARTS
4010   COUNT.EMPLOYEES = 0
4020   TOTAL.PARTS = 0
4030   WHILE NOT EOF(1)
4040     INPUT #1, ENAME$,PARTS
4050     COUNT.EMPLOYEES = COUNT.EMPLOYEES+1
4060     TOTAL.PARTS = TOTAL.PARTS+PARTS
4070     PRINT TAB(5) "Employee name: ";ENAME$; TAB(40) "Number of parts:";
         PARTS
4080   WEND
4090   PRINT
4100   PRINT TAB(14) USING "Number of employees_______###"; COUNT.EMPLOYEES
4110   PRINT TAB(14) USING "Total parts produced______###"; TOTAL.PARTS
4120   RETURN
```

8.8 Sending Output to the Printer

```
1000 'LABELS                       M. MCRITCHIE                        JUNE 13
1002 '**********************************************************************
1004 '  THIS PROGRAM PRINTS ADDRESS LABELS ON THE SCREEN AND TO THE PRINTER
1006 '**********************************************************************
1010 'NAME1$,NAME2$,NAME3$          - NAMES
1020 'STREET1$,STREET2$,STREET3$ - STREET ADDRESSES
1030 'CITY.PROVINCE1$,CITY.PROVINCE2$,CITY.PROVINCE3$
1040 '                              - CITIES AND PROVINCES
1050 'POSTAL1$,POSTAL2$,POSTAL3$ - POSTAL CODES
2000 '**********************************************************************
2002 '                              MAIN ROUTINE
2004 '**********************************************************************
2010  GOSUB 3000                   'Read data and print labels
2020  PRINT
2030  PRINT "End of processing"
2040  END
3000 '**********************************************************************
3002 '                       READ DATA AND PRINT LABELS
3004 '**********************************************************************
3010  CLS
3020  LOCATE 11
3030  READ NAME1$,STREET1$,CITY.PROVINCE1$,POSTAL1$
3040  READ NAME2$,STREET2$,CITY.PROVINCE2$,POSTAL2$
3050  READ NAME3$,STREET3$,CITY.PROVINCE3$,POSTAL3$
3060  PRINT TAB(2) NAME1$; TAB(28) NAME2$; TAB(54) NAME3$
3065  LPRINT TAB(2) NAME1$; TAB(28) NAME2$; TAB(54) NAME3$
3070  PRINT TAB(2) STREET1$; TAB(28) STREET2$; TAB(54) STREET3$
3075  LPRINT TAB(2) STREET1$; TAB(28) STREET2$; TAB(54) STREET3$
3080  PRINT TAB(2) CITY.PROVINCE1$; TAB(28) CITY.PROVINCE2$;
      TAB(54) CITY.PROVINCE3$
3085  LPRINT TAB(2) CITY.PROVINCE1$; TAB(28) CITY.PROVINCE2$;
      TAB(54) CITY.PROVINCE3$
3090  PRINT TAB(2) POSTAL1$; TAB(28) POSTAL2$; TAB(54) POSTAL3$
3095  LPRINT TAB(2) POSTAL1$; TAB(28) POSTAL2$; TAB(54) POSTAL3$
3100  DATA "Mr. John Smith","123 Main Street","Anycity  ZZ","M3L 6S7"
3110  DATA "Mrs. Doris Moore","1394 Harcourt Street","Anycity  ZZ","M3L 1R4"
3120  DATA "Mr. Russell Knight","498 Ashberry Drive","Mytown  XX","N6Y 3A2"
3130  RETURN
65529 'End of program listing
```

9

MULTI-PAGE REPORTS

Objectives

In Chapter Eight, you learned how to produce attractive, easy-to-read reports, many with summaries below the reports. In this chapter, you will learn how to:

- Print the current date and time in the heading of a report.
- Print a multi-page report with specific top and bottom margins on each page and with headings printed at the beginning of each page.
- Print a multi-page report with page totals (totals of columns) at the bottom of each page.
- Print group totals; for example, the total sales for each department in a store.
- Produce summary reports.

Contents

9.1 Printing the Current Date and Time in Reports

Headings of a report often include the date to inform the reader when the report was printed. The time may also be useful to indicate whether the report was printed at the start or at the end of a day. Recall that we set the date and time when we load up DOS. To retrieve the date, we use the function DATE$; to retrieve the time, we use the function TIME$. The time is always current; retrieved from a constantly changing internal clock.

The following routine prints the date, then prints the time continuously. The periods in the output denote additional output lines.

```
3000 PRINT
3010 PRINT "The date is: ";DATE$
3020 PRINT
3030 WHILE TIME$ <> ""
3040    PRINT "The time is: ";TIME$
3050 WEND
3060 END
RUN
```

```
The date is: 03-24-19XX

The time is: 09:30:16
The time is: 09:30:16
The time is: 09:30:16
The time is: 09:30:17
... .... ... ........
```

The date is of the form month, day, year; the time is of the form hour, minutes, seconds. The following statement prints the date and time as a heading.

```
3050 PRINT TAB(12) USING "Date printed:_\________\____________________Time:_\___
___\";DATE$,TIME$
```

Sample Output:

```
Date printed: 03-24-19XX                    Time: 09:57:49
```

Rather than print the values of DATE$ and TIME$, we can assign their values to variables, then use the variables in PRINT statements. The significance of this concept rests with TIME$. By assigning its value to a variable, say T$, we can retain the current value of TIME$. Whereas the value of TIME$ keeps changing, the value of T$ remains constant. The following statements assign the current values of DATE$ and TIME$ to variables.

```
3010 D$ = DATE$
3020 T$ = TIME$
```

9.2 A Multi-Page Report

In actual business applications, reports are often longer than one page. If our printer prints six lines to an inch and a page is 11 inches in length, we can print 66 lines on the page. However, we should leave a one-inch top margin and a one-inch bottom margin. This leaves us with 54 rows for the detail lines (66-6-6 = 54).

Reports are usually printed on continuously form-fed paper. Upon filling a page, our programs must reposition the paper to the top of the next page. Each page of the report should begin with headings. Suppose our headings require five lines. We are now left with 49 rows for the detail lines (54-5 = 49).

In this section, we will be discussing multi-page reports of two types: one without page totals and the other with page totals. Page totals are the totals of amounts that are usually listed by columns on each page of a report. A page total is not carried forward to the next page. Although each program listed in this section produces a two-page report, each program is capable of producing as many pages as are required. The number of pages printed depends on the number of records read from a data file and the amount of information printed in the report.

A Report Without Page Totals

The program below produces a report that lists departments by number, the names of the employees in each department, and the number of parts produced by each employee. Each record in the data file consists of a department number, an employee's name, and the number of parts produced by the employee.

```
1000 'MULTI-PAGE REPORT                   M. MCRITCHIE                 JULY 7
1002 '*******************************************************************
1004 '           THIS PROGRAM PRODUCES A MULTI-PAGE PRODUCTION REPORT
1006 '*******************************************************************
1010 'S$          - EQUAL SIGNS
1020 'F$          - IMAGE OF A DETAIL LINE
1030 'PAGE        - PAGE NUMBER
1040 'ROW         - ROW NUMBER
1050 'DEPT.NUMBER - DEPARTMENT NUMBER
1060 'ENAME$      - EMPLOYEE NAME
1070 'PARTS       - PARTS PRODUCED BY ONE EMPLOYEE
2000 '*******************************************************************
2002 '                             MAIN ROUTINE
2004 '*******************************************************************
2010  OPEN "B:PARTS.DAT" FOR INPUT AS #1
2020  GOSUB 3000                   'Format report
2030  GOSUB 4000                   'Read data file and print report
2040  CLOSE #1
2050  END
3000 '*******************************************************************
3002 '                            FORMAT REPORT
3004 '*******************************************************************
3010  S$ = STRING$(43,"=")
3020  F$ = "____________________####________\____________\______####"
3030  PAGE = 1
3040  GOSUB 3500                   'Print headings
3050  RETURN
3500 '*******************************************************************
3502 '                            PRINT HEADINGS
3504 '*******************************************************************
3510  LPRINT CHR$(12); CHR$(10); CHR$(10); CHR$(10); CHR$(10)
3520  LPRINT TAB(13) DATE$; TAB(32) "PRODUCTION REPORT"; TAB(63) "Page"; PAGE
3530  LPRINT TAB(19) S$
3540  LPRINT TAB(19) "DEPARTMENT"; TAB(37) "EMPLOYEE"; TAB(55) "PARTS"
3550  LPRINT TAB(21) "NUMBER"; TAB(39) "NAME"; TAB(54) "PRODUCED"
3560  LPRINT TAB(19) S$
3570  RETURN
4000 '*******************************************************************
4002 '                   READ DATA FILE AND PRINT REPORT
4004 '*******************************************************************
4010  ROW = 5
4020  WHILE NOT EOF(1)
4030    INPUT #1, DEPT.NUMBER,ENAME$,PARTS
4040    IF ROW >= 54 THEN PAGE = PAGE+1 : GOSUB 3500 : ROW = 5
4045       'Subroutine 3500 prints headings
4050    LPRINT USING F$; DEPT.NUMBER,ENAME$,PARTS
4060    ROW = ROW+1
4070  WEND
4080  RETURN
65529 'End of program listing
```

Partial Output:

```
         10        20        30        40        50        60        70        80
12345678901234567890123456789012345678901234567890123456789012345678901234567890
```

```
06-17-19XX          PRODUCTION REPORT               Page 1
           ===========================================
           DEPARTMENT        EMPLOYEE          PARTS
             NUMBER            NAME           PRODUCED
           ===========================================
              1263      Paterson,Gerald          38
              1263      Kelly,Susan              42
              1263      Owen,Fred                41
              1263      Thompson,John            37
              1263      Law,Barbara              42
              1263      Nicholson,Tracy          40
              1263      Jones,Henry              39
              ....      ...............          ..
              5894      Shaw,Jim                 43
              5894      Warren,Erica             39
              5894      Snider,Susan             42
```

```
06-17-19XX          PRODUCTION REPORT               Page 2
           ===========================================
           DEPARTMENT        EMPLOYEE          PARTS
             NUMBER            NAME           PRODUCED
           ===========================================
              5894      Newman,Tom               40
              6785      Conway,Glen              43
              6785      Berry,Edith              37
              6785      Armstrong,Roy            38
              6785      Barrett,Arnold           40
              6785      Connors,Merle            41
              6785      Law,Thomas               43
              6785      Norton,Ken               37
              6785      Russell,Glenda           40
```

The row of periods in the output indicates additional detail lines to make up the 49 detail lines allotted to a page.

Subroutine FORMAT REPORT AND PRINT HEADINGS used in previous programs is divided into two subroutines: one to format the report and the other to print the headings. Subroutine FORMAT REPORT is executed only once, Subroutine PRINT HEADINGS is executed each time headings must be printed.

In Subroutine FORMAT REPORT, we assign equal signs to S$, create an image for the detail lines, and assign 1 to PAGE. We then call Subroutine 3500 to print the headings.

Line 3510 in Subroutine PRINT HEADINGS causes the computer to skip to a new page and leave a one-inch top margin. CHR$(12), which represents "form feed", tells the computer to skip to a new page. CHR$(10), which represents "line feed", tells the computer to proceed to the next line. CHR$ is a library function; its purpose will be explained in detail in Chapter Eleven. The number of CHR$(10) functions required to produce the one-inch top margin depends on the printer and on the position of the top edge of the paper in the printer. Here, only four CHR$(10) functions were needed. Line 3520 prints the date, the heading PRODUCTION REPORT, and the page number. The remaining statements in the subroutine print the equal signs and the column headings.

In Subroutine READ DATA FILE AND PRINT REPORT, we assign 5 to ROW since the heading has used 5 of the 54 rows allotted to a page. After a record is read from the data file, we check the row number. If ROW is greater than or equal to 54, we increase PAGE by 1, call Subroutine PRINT HEADINGS to print headings on the next page, and reassign 5 to ROW. ROW will now keep track of the rows on the new page. Line 4050 prints a detail line. Since a row has just been filled with a detail line, we increase ROW by 1 in line 4060.

Note that we check ROW for "equal to 54 and greater than 54" in line 4040. If ROW is equal to 54, the 54 rows allotted to a page have been filled. We have added "greater than" in order to be consistent with subsequent programs where ROW is increased by 2 when a total is printed.

Testing a program that prints the output to the printer and that fills several pages each with 54 lines can be a formidable task. To simplify the job, use less data, print to the screen rather than to the printer, and reduce the number of rows to a page. You could print, for example, 15 lines on a page. It will also be necessary to call Subroutine FREEZE DISPLAY; otherwise, the computer skips to a new page on the screen before you have a chance to examine the previous page. In the program above, the GOSUB statement that calls Subroutine FREEZE DISPLAY should be coded in the IF statement in line 4040, immediately after the word THEN.

After testing the program and correcting any errors, change the PRINT statements to LPRINT statements, change the maximum number of lines on a page to 54, increase the contents of the data file, and delete the statement GOSUB 11000 and the Subroutine FREEZE DISPLAY.

A Report With Page Totals

Page totals are often printed at the bottom of each page of a report with a grand total printed at the end of the report. The program on page 213 is modified to include this additional information. The modified version listed below also calculates and displays the average number of parts produced.

```
1000 'MULTI-PAGE REPORT                 M. MCRITCHIE                  JULY 9
1002 '*********************************************************************
1004 '    THIS PROGRAM PRODUCES A MULTI-PAGE PRODUCTION REPORT. THE REPORT
1006 '    INCLUDES PAGE TOTALS AND A SUMMARY.
1008 '*********************************************************************
1010 'S$                - EQUAL SIGNS
1020 'F$                - IMAGE OF A DETAIL LINE
1030 'PAGE              - PAGE NUMBER
1040 'ROW               - ROW NUMBER
1050 'COUNT.EMPLOYEES   - COUNTS THE EMPLOYEES
1060 'PAGE.TOTAL        - PAGE TOTAL
1070 'GRAND.TOTAL       - TOTAL PARTS PRODUCED
1080 'DEPT.NUMBER       - DEPARTMENT NUMBER
1090 'ENAME$            - EMPLOYEE NAME
1100 'PARTS             - PARTS PRODUCED BY ONE EMPLOYEE
2000 '*********************************************************************
2002 '                            MAIN ROUTINE
2004 '*********************************************************************
2010  OPEN "B:PARTS.DAT" FOR INPUT AS #1
2020  GOSUB 3000                   'Format report
2030  GOSUB 4000                   'Read data file and process data
2040  GOSUB 6000                   'Produce summary
2050  CLOSE #1
2060  END
3000 '*********************************************************************
3002 '                           FORMAT REPORT
3004 '*********************************************************************
3010  S$ = STRING$(43,"=")
3020  F$ = "________________________####________\_____________\______####"
3030  PAGE = 1
3040  GOSUB 3500                  'Print headings
3050  RETURN
3500 '*********************************************************************
3502 '                           PRINT HEADINGS
3504 '*********************************************************************
3510  LPRINT CHR$(12); CHR$(10); CHR$(10); CHR$(10); CHR$(10)
3520  LPRINT TAB(13) DATE$; TAB(32) "PRODUCTION REPORT"; TAB(63) "Page"; PAGE
3530  LPRINT TAB(19) S$
3540  LPRINT TAB(19) "DEPARTMENT"; TAB(37) "EMPLOYEE"; TAB(55) "PARTS"
3550  LPRINT TAB(21) "NUMBER"; TAB(39) "NAME"; TAB(54) "PRODUCED"
3560  LPRINT TAB(19) S$
3570  RETURN
4000 '*********************************************************************
4002 '                  READ DATA FILE AND PROCESS DATA
4004 '*********************************************************************
4010  ROW = 5
4020  COUNT.EMPLOYEES = 0
4030  PAGE.TOTAL = 0
4040  GRAND.TOTAL = 0
4050  WHILE NOT EOF(1)
4060    INPUT #1, DEPT.NUMBER,ENAME$,PARTS
```

```
4070    IF ROW = 52 THEN GOSUB 5000      'Print page total, accumulate totals
4080    IF ROW >= 54 THEN PAGE = PAGE+1 : GOSUB 3500 : ROW = 5
4090    COUNT.EMPLOYEES = COUNT.EMPLOYEES+1
4100    PAGE.TOTAL = PAGE.TOTAL+PARTS
4110    LPRINT USING F$; DEPT.NUMBER,ENAME$,PARTS
4120    ROW = ROW+1
4130  WEND
4140  RETURN
5000 '************************************************************************
5002 '                    PRINT PAGE TOTAL, ACCUMULATE TOTALS
5004 '************************************************************************
5010  LPRINT
5020  LPRINT TAB(24) USING "Total parts on page ##_________####";
      PAGE,PAGE.TOTAL
5030  ROW = ROW+2
5040  GRAND.TOTAL = GRAND.TOTAL+PAGE.TOTAL
5050  PAGE.TOTAL = 0
5060  RETURN
6000 '************************************************************************
6002 '                              PRODUCE SUMMARY
6004 '************************************************************************
6010  GRAND.TOTAL = GRAND.TOTAL+PAGE.TOTAL      'Add page total on last page
6020  LPRINT
6030  LPRINT TAB(24) USING "Total parts on page ##_________####";
      PAGE,PAGE.TOTAL                   'Print page total on last page
6040  LPRINT
6050  LPRINT TAB(13) USING "Total number of parts produced:__________________###
#";GRAND.TOTAL
6060  LPRINT TAB(13) USING "Average number of parts produced by ## employees:__#
#";COUNT.EMPLOYEES,GRAND.TOTAL/COUNT.EMPLOYEES
6070  RETURN
65529 'End of program listing
```

Partial Output:

```
         10        20        30        40        50        60        70        80
12345678901234567890123456789012345678901234567890123456789012345678901234567890

         06-21-19XX          PRODUCTION REPORT               Page 1
                ===========================================
                DEPARTMENT        EMPLOYEE             PARTS
                  NUMBER            NAME              PRODUCED
                ===========================================
                   1263           Paterson,Gerald          38
                   1263           Kelly,Susan              42
                   1263           Owen,Fred                41
                   1263           Thompson,John            37
                   1263           Law,Barbara              42
                   1263           Nicholson,Tracy          40
                   1263           Jones,Henry              39
                   ....           ...............          ..
                   4231           Mitchell,Debra           40
                   5894           Pruden,Frank             38
                   5894           Shaw,Jim                 43

                      Total parts on page  1             1888
```

```
06-21-19XX         PRODUCTION REPORT                    Page 2
               ==========================================
               DEPARTMENT         EMPLOYEE          PARTS
                 NUMBER             NAME           PRODUCED
               ==========================================
                  5894          Warren,Erica           39
                  5894          Snider,Susan           42
                  5894          Newman,Tom             40
                  6785          Conway,Glen            43
                  6785          Berry,Edith            37
                  6785          Armstrong,Roy          38
                  6785          Barrett,Arnold         40
                  6785          Connors,Merle          41
                  6785          Law,Thomas             43
                  6785          Norton,Ken             37
                  6785          Russell,Glenda         40

                    Total parts on page  2            440

Total number of parts produced:                          2328
Average number of parts produced by 58 employees:          40
```

The IF statement in line 4070 determines whether or not the row number is 52. If it is, we transfer control to Subroutine 5000 where we print a blank line on row 53 and the page total on row 54. In line 5030, we increase ROW by two since two more rows have just been filled. We add the page total to our grand total accumulator in line 5040. In line 5050, we set PAGE.TOTAL to zero. This accumulator is now ready to total the numbers of parts that will be listed on the next page.

If ROW is not equal to 52, we check to see if ROW is greater than or equal to 54, (line 4080). Remember, 54 is the maximum number of rows allotted to a page. If ROW is greater than or equal to 54, we increase PAGE by 1, call the subroutine that prints the headings on the next page, and reset ROW to 5 since the headings use up five rows. We now count the employee, add the number of parts just read to our page accumulator, and print a detail line (lines 4090 to 4110). In line 4120, we increase the row number by one since a detail line has just been printed.

Rather than skip to a new page in Subroutine READ DATA FILE AND PROCESS DATA by the statement

```
4080 IF ROW >= 54 THEN PAGE = PAGE+1 : GOSUB 3500 : ROW = 5
```

we could have coded the statement in Subroutine PRINT PAGE TOTAL, ACCUMULATE TOTALS following line 5050. In fact, since this subroutine is called when ROW = 52 and since the subroutine prints two more rows, there is no need to code the IF part that compares ROW with 54. We can skip immediately to a new page.

```
5055 PAGE = PAGE+1 : GOSUB 3500 : ROW = 5
```

To maintain consistency in our programs, we will leave statement 4080 in Subroutine READ DATA FILE AND PROCESS DATA. Here, we must compare ROW with 54; otherwise, each detail line will be printed on a new page.

Note that, in the summary, we must add the page total of the last page to GRAND.TOTAL and print this page total. If the last page is only partially filled when the last data record is read from the data file, Subroutine PRINT PAGE TOTAL, ACCUMULATE TOTALS will not be called as ROW is not equal to 52. Because the EOF character has been detected, control drops out of the loop and RETURNs to the main routine where Subroutine PRODUCE SUMMARY is called. Since the page total of the last page has not yet been added to GRAND.TOTAL nor has it yet been printed, these tasks must be performed in Subroutine PRODUCE SUMMARY.

The same problem exists when the last page is filled with 52 printed rows and the last record has been read. After this detail line is printed and ROW is increased to 52, the WEND statement transfers control to the WHILE. Since the EOF character has been detected, the condition in the WHILE is false. Control RETURNs to the main routine which calls Subroutine PRODUCE SUMMARY. Therefore, statement 4070 has been bypassed. As with the page total of a partially filled last page, the page total of this last page has not yet been added to GRAND.TOTAL nor has it been printed. The tasks must be performed in Subroutine PRODUCE SUMMARY.

In other words, Subroutine PRODUCE SUMMARY must add the page total of the last page to GRAND.TOTAL and print this page total regardless whether the page is partially filled or filled with the maximum number of rows allotted to the headings and the detail lines.

Exercises

1. What would be the output from the program listed on page 213, if the program were modified as follows?
   (a) Subroutines FORMAT REPORT and PRINT HEADINGS are combined into one subroutine. (Lines 3040 and 3050 are deleted.)
   (b) The IF statement in line 4040 calls Subroutine 3000.
2. What would be the output from the program listed on page 215 if statements 4070 and 4080 were placed after the statement that increases the row counter? (Statement 4070 determines whether or not a page total should be printed; statement 4080 determines whether or not printing should start on a new page.)

9.3 Group Totals

Often, a total must be found for a group of items that has something in common. In our last two programs, we retrieved data from a file that contains the records of employees who work in various departments. Departments differ by number. The first department is numbered 1263, the second may be numbered 2485, the third may be numbered 3967, etc. A list of all employees working in one department is considered a group, a list of all employees working in another department is considered another group. The item of similarity in each group is the department number. This item is called a control value.

A listing of the groups must be ordered, usually from the lowest numbered group to the highest. Figure 9-1 illustrates groups and their order. We have staggered the groups so they can be easily seen. (Actually, our data file contains more groups and more employees in each group than are given below.)

FIGURE 9-1 CONTROL GROUPS

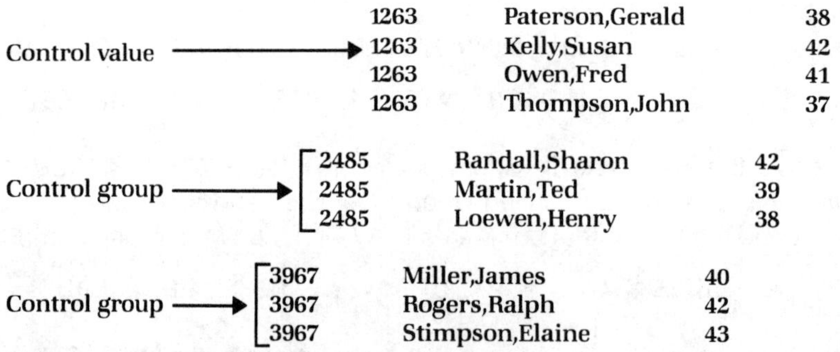

In our example, a department number is our control value. A group with the same control value is called a control group. What we would like to find is the total number of parts produced by employees in each department. Each total is referred to as a group total. Furthermore, accumulating the group totals gives us the total number of parts produced by all employees.

Recall that our two previous programs stored a department number in DEPT.NUMBER. To find a group total, we must let the computer know where one control group ends and where another starts. This is determined in the following manner.

After a record is read and the necessary tasks performed, we copy the control value stored in DEPT.NUMBER into another variable, say HOLD. The control value of the next record is read into DEPT.NUMBER. Thus, HOLD stores the control value of the previous record while DEPT.NUMBER stores the control value of the record just read. We compare the two variables. If their values are the same, we are in the same control group and must add the number of parts just read to our group accumulator. If the values are different, we are in the next control group. We must print the value of our accumulator which gives us the total number of parts produced by the group just processed. Furthermore, we will add this total to the accumulator for group totals. The accumulator will eventually give us the total number of parts produced by all employees.

Here is the program that performs the operations.

```
1000 'GROUP TOTALS                    M. MCRITCHIE                      JULY 12
1002 '***********************************************************************
1004 '    THIS PROGRAM PRODUCES A MULTI-PAGE PRODUCTION REPORT. THE TOTAL
1006 '    PRODUCTION FOR EACH DEPARTMENT IS PRINTED AS A GROUP TOTAL.
1008 '    A SUMMARY IS PRINTED AT THE END OF THE REPORT.
1009 '***********************************************************************
1010 'S$              - EQUAL SIGNS
1020 'F1$             - IMAGE OF A DETAIL LINE
1030 'F2$             - IMAGE FOR A DEPARTMENT TOTAL
1040 'PAGE            - PAGE NUMBER
1050 'ROW             - ROW NUMBER
1060 'HOLD            - HOLDS A CONTROL VALUE (DEPARTMENT NUMBER)
1070 'COUNT.EMPLOYEES - COUNTS THE EMPLOYEES
1080 'DEPT.TOTAL      - TOTAL PARTS PRODUCED IN A DEPARTMENT
1090 'GRAND.TOTAL     - TOTAL PARTS PRODUCED IN ALL DEPARTMENTS
1100 'DEPT.NUMBER     - DEPARTMENT NUMBER
1110 'ENAME$          - EMPLOYEE NAME
1120 'PARTS           - PARTS PRODUCED BY ONE EMPLOYEE
2000 '***********************************************************************
2002 '                               MAIN ROUTINE
2004 '***********************************************************************
2010  OPEN "B:PARTS.DAT" FOR INPUT AS #1
2020  GOSUB 3000                    'Format report
2030  GOSUB 4000                    'Read data file and process data
2040  GOSUB 6000                    'Produce summary
2050  CLOSE #1
2060  END
3000 '***********************************************************************
3002 '                              FORMAT REPORT
3004 '***********************************************************************
3010  S$ = STRING$(43,"=")
3020  F1$ = "_____________________####________\_____________\______####"
3030  F2$ = "______________________________________________________####*"
3040  PAGE = 1
3050  GOSUB 3500                    'Print headings
3060  RETURN
3500 '***********************************************************************
3502 '                              PRINT HEADINGS
3504 '***********************************************************************
3510  LPRINT CHR$(12); CHR$(10); CHR$(10); CHR$(10); CHR$(10)
3520  LPRINT TAB(13) DATE$; TAB(32) "PRODUCTION REPORT"; TAB(63) "Page"; PAGE
3530  LPRINT TAB(19) S$
3540  LPRINT TAB(19) "DEPARTMENT"; TAB(37) "EMPLOYEE"; TAB(55) "PARTS"
3550  LPRINT TAB(21) "NUMBER"; TAB(39) "NAME"; TAB(54) "PRODUCED"
3560  LPRINT TAB(19) S$
3570  RETURN
4000 '***********************************************************************
4002 '                    READ DATA FILE AND PROCESS DATA
4004 '***********************************************************************
4010  ROW = 5
4020  HOLD = 0
4030  COUNT.EMPLOYEES = 0
4040  DEPT.TOTAL = 0
4050  GRAND.TOTAL = 0
4060  WHILE NOT EOF(1)
4070    INPUT #1, DEPT.NUMBER,ENAME$,PARTS
4080    IF DEPT.NUMBER <> HOLD AND HOLD <> 0 THEN GOSUB 5000
4090    IF ROW >= 54 THEN PAGE = PAGE+1 : GOSUB 3500 : ROW = 5
4100    COUNT.EMPLOYEES = COUNT.EMPLOYEES+1
4110    DEPT.TOTAL = DEPT.TOTAL+PARTS
4120    LPRINT USING F1$; DEPT.NUMBER,ENAME$,PARTS
4130    ROW = ROW+1
4140    HOLD = DEPT.NUMBER
4150  WEND
4160  GOSUB 5000                    'Print total for last group
4170  RETURN
```

```
5000 '*************************************************************************
5002 '                     PRINT GROUP TOTAL, ACCUMULATE TOTALS
5004 '*************************************************************************
5010  LPRINT USING F2$; DEPT.TOTAL
5020  LPRINT
5030  ROW = ROW+2
5040  GRAND.TOTAL = GRAND.TOTAL+DEPT.TOTAL
5050  DEPT.TOTAL = 0
5060  RETURN
6000 '*************************************************************************
6002 '                              PRODUCE SUMMARY
6004 '*************************************************************************
6010  LPRINT TAB(13) USING "Total number of parts produced:__________________###
#";GRAND.TOTAL
6020  LPRINT TAB(13) USING "Average number of parts produced by ## employees:__#
#";COUNT.EMPLOYEES,GRAND.TOTAL/COUNT.EMPLOYEES
6030  RETURN
65529 'End of program listing
```

Partial Output:

```
         10        20        30        40        50        60        70        80
12345678901234567890123456789012345678901234567890123456789012345678901234567890

            06-26-19XX        PRODUCTION REPORT              Page 1
                  ===========================================
                  DEPARTMENT         EMPLOYEE          PARTS
                    NUMBER             NAME           PRODUCED
                  ===========================================
                     1263          Paterson,Gerald       38
                     1263          Kelly,Susan           42
                     1263          Owen,Fred             41
                     1263          Thompson,John         37
                     1263          Law,Barbara           42
                     1263          Nicholson,Tracy       40
                     1263          Jones,Henry           39
                     1263          Muir,Cathy            41
                     1263          Taylor,Michael        43
                     1263          Ginter,William        41
                                                        404*

                     2485          Randall,Sharon        42
                     ....          ...............       ..
                     2485          Baxter,Helen          38
                                                        516*

                     ....          ...............       ..
                     4231          Parks,Ralph           39

            06-26-19XX        PRODUCTION REPORT              Page 2
                  ===========================================
                  DEPARTMENT         EMPLOYEE          PARTS
                    NUMBER             NAME           PRODUCED
                  ===========================================
                     4231          Janzen,Terry          41
                     4231          Mitchell,Debra        40
                                                        483*

                     ....          ...............       ..
                     6785          Russell,Glenda        40
                                                        319*

            Total number of parts produced:                   2328
            Average number of parts produced by 58 employees:   40
```

Line 4020 initializes HOLD to zero. When the first record is read from the data file (line 4070), DEPT.NUMBER will be storing the first control value. The IF statement in line 4080 consists of a compound condition. The first test compares DEPT.NUMBER with HOLD. Since DEPT.NUMBER contains the first control value and HOLD contains a zero, their values are not equal. The first condition is, therefore, true. To prevent control from transferring to the subroutine that prints a group total, we add a second condition to the IF statement. The test compares HOLD with zero. Since HOLD is equal to zero, the second condition is false. This makes the entire expression in the IF statement false. Thus, BASIC does not transfer to Subroutine 5000. Instead, execution continues with the next statement.

In lines 4090 to 4130, we compare ROW with 54, count an employee, add the number of parts just read to our group accumulator, print a detail line, and increase the row counter by one. Line 4140 places the control value of the record just processed in HOLD. The loop is repeated. Another record is read and its control value assigned to DEPT.NUMBER. In line 4080, we again compare the control value in DEPT.NUMBER with the value stored in HOLD. Remember, HOLD now contains the control value of the former record, DEPT.NUMBER contains the control value of the record just read. If the values are equal, we are still in the same control group and the current record is processed. These operations continue until a different control value is read.

When the values of DEPT.NUMBER and HOLD are not equal, the control value of the next group has just been read. The IF statement in line 4080 calls Subroutine 5000. The subroutine prints the group total for the group just processed and adds this total to our grand total accumulator. After BASIC returns from the subroutine, the new record is processed (lines 4090 to 4130). Line 4140 assigns the control value of this record to HOLD and the loop is repeated.

Each time BASIC passes through the WHILE/WEND loop, a control value just read and assigned to DEPT.NUMBER is compared with the value stored in HOLD. BASIC either branches to Subroutine 5000 if the values in DEPT.NUMBER and HOLD are not the same or it executes the remaining statements in the loop if the values are the same. The loop continues until the last record is read and processed.

It was mentioned on page 212 that we should leave a one-inch top margin and a one-inch bottom margin on printed reports. To obtain the one-inch top margin, we used four CHR$(10) functions following the CHR$(12) function in an LPRINT statement. Recall that CHR$(12) means "form feed", CHR$(10) means "line feed".

Generally, the spacing in the top margin should remain one inch. We may vary the spacing in the bottom margin depending on whether or not a group total is to be printed. A detail line should never be printed in the one-inch bottom margin. However, it is considered proper to print a group total in the bottom margin rather than print the total alone on the next page. This keeps the group total on the same page as its group.

To ensure that a detail line is not printed in the bottom margin, we compare the row number with 54 in line 4090. If ROW is greater than or equal to 54, the next detail line will be printed on the next page. The row number is not checked when we print a group total. Line 4080 compares DEPT.NUMBER with HOLD and if their values are different, we transfer to Subroutine 5000 to print a group total without first checking ROW. Thus, the group total is printed on the same page as its group.

One last comment. Notice the instruction GOSUB 5000 following the WHILE/WEND loop. The subroutine prints a group total and adds this total to our grand total accumulator. The subroutine must be called when the values of DEPT.NUMBER and HOLD are the same after the last record has been read or when their values are different but there is only one record in the last group.

Exercise

What would be the output from the program listed on page 219 if statements 4080 and 4090 were placed after the statement that increases the row counter? (Statement 4080 determines whether or not a group total should be printed; statement 4090 determines whether or not printing should start on a new page.)

9.4 Program Design

The programs presented so far in this chapter all print detail lines. Often management requires a report that prints only the total of each control group with an appropriate description. For instance, a report may list the total parts produced by each department or the total sales made by each department. Detail lines, such as the parts produced by each employee or the sales made by each salesperson would not be printed. This type of report is considered a group summary report.

Only minor changes need to be made to the program that prints both detail lines and group totals. In the program on page 219, we simply delete the statement that creates the image for a detail line (line 3020), the statement that prints a detail line (line 4120), and the statement that increases a row number after a detail line has been printed (line 4130). We should also modify the statement that prints a group total and modify the image needed to print this total. Immediately after a group total is printed we must increase the row number by one. It may also be necessary to change the headings. The program designed below incorporates these changes.

Rough Layout of the Output:

```
06-26-19XX        PRODUCTION REPORT        PAGE 1
=================================
DEPARTMENT         TOTAL PRODUCED
=================================
1263               404
2485               516
3967               404
4231               483
5894               202
6785               319

Total number of parts produced: 2328
Average number of parts produced by 58 employees: 40
```

FIGURE 9-2 LAYOUT CHART

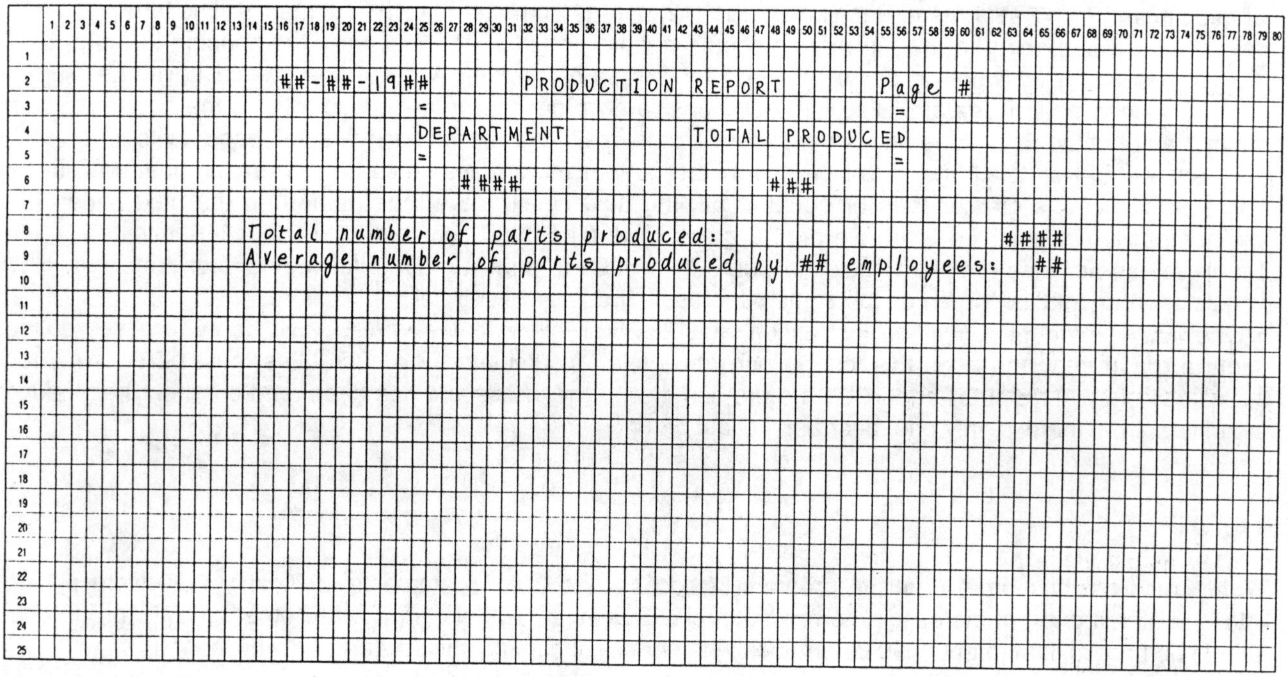

Although we normally do not design the module that formats a report and prints the headings, we will include this routine in our designs to show how the tasks are shared between two modules.

FIGURE 9-3 STRUCTURE CHART

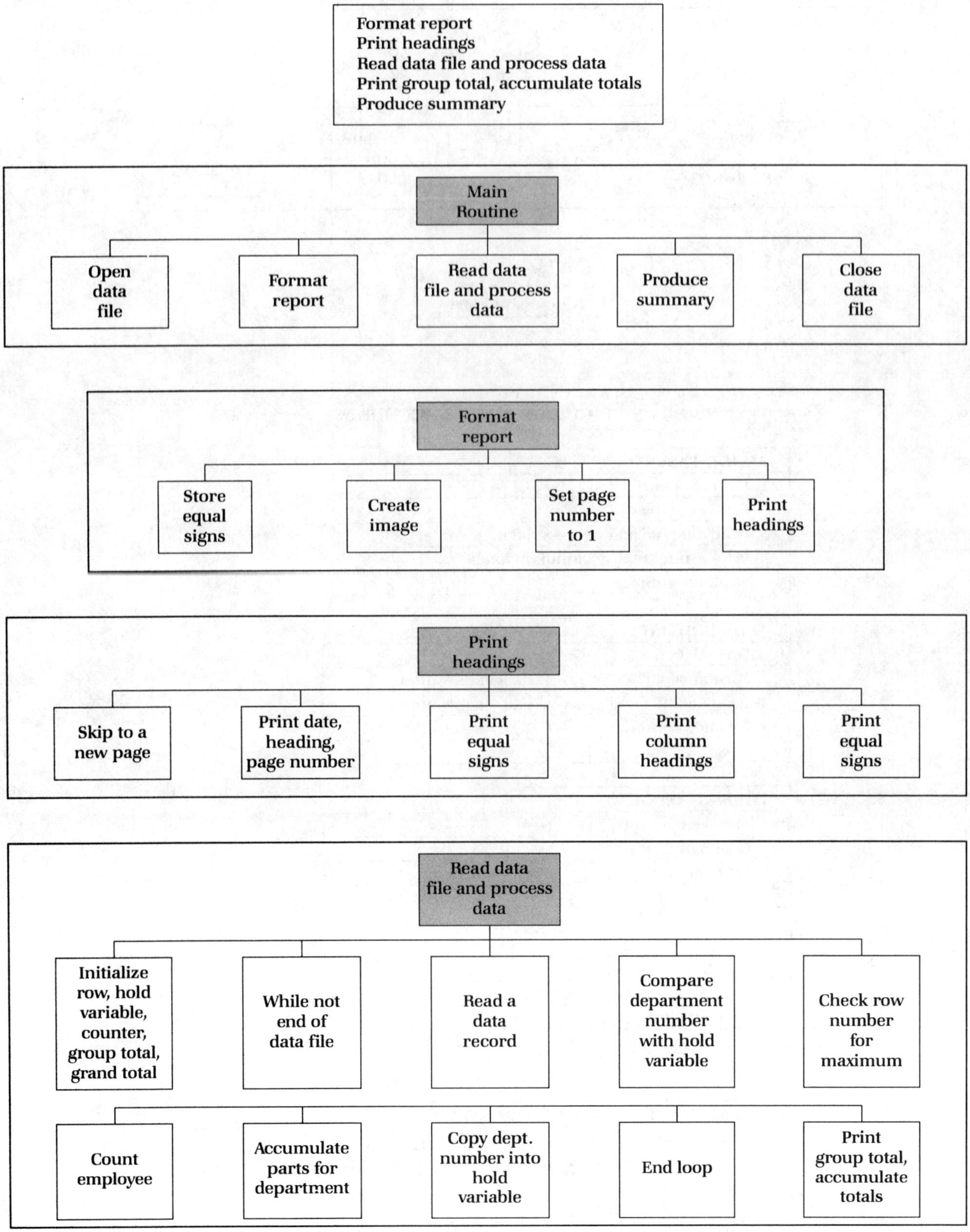

Figure 9-3 Continued

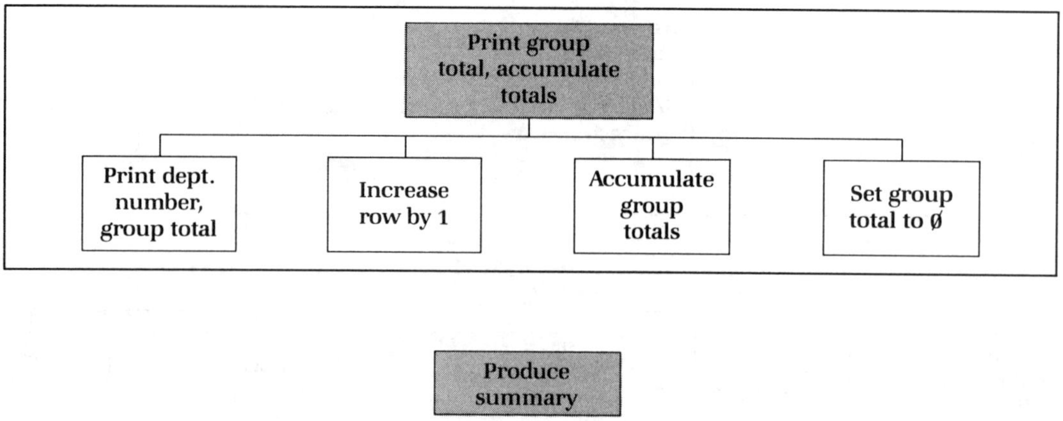

FIGURE 9-4 PSEUDOCODE

MAJOR TASKS
Format report
Print headings
Read data file and process data
Print group total, accumulate totals
Produce summary

MAIN ROUTINE	
Open data file	
Format report	(subroutine)
Read data file and process data	(subroutine)
Produce summary	(subroutine)
Close data file	

FORMAT REPORT	
Store equal signs	S$
Create image	F$
Set page number to 1	PAGE
Print headings	(subroutine)

PRINT HEADINGS
Skip to a new page
Print date, heading, page number
Print equal signs
Print column headings
Print equal signs

READ DATA FILE AND PROCESS DATA	
Initialize:	
Row, hold variable, counter,	ROW,HOLD,COUNT.EMPLOYEES
group total, grand total	DEPT.TOTAL,GRAND.TOTAL
While not end of data file	
Read a data record	DEPT.NUMBER,ENAME$,PARTS
Compare department number	
with hold variable	
Check row number for maximum	

Count employee
Accumulate parts for department
Copy department number into
hold variable
End loop
Print group total, accumulate totals

PRINT GROUP TOTAL, ACCUMULATE TOTALS

Print department number, group total
Increase row by 1
Accumulate group totals
Set group total to zero

PRODUCE SUMMARY

```
1000 'GROUP SUMMARY REPORT                    M. MCRITCHIE                JULY 15
1002 '**********************************************************************
1004 '           THIS PROGRAM PRINTS A GROUP SUMMARY REPORT FOR
1006 '           THE NUMBER OF PARTS PRODUCED IN EACH DEPARTMENT
1008 '**********************************************************************
1010 'S$              - EQUAL SIGNS
1020 'F$              - IMAGE FOR A GROUP TOTAL
1030 'PAGE            - PAGE NUMBER
1040 'ROW             - ROW NUMBER
1050 'HOLD            - HOLDS A CONTROL VALUE (DEPARTMENT NUMBER)
1060 'COUNT.EMPLOYEES - COUNTS THE EMPLOYEES
1070 'DEPT.TOTAL      - TOTAL PARTS PRODUCED IN A DEPARTMENT
1080 'GRAND.TOTAL     - TOTAL PARTS PRODUCED IN ALL DEPARTMENTS
1090 'DEPT.NUMBER     - DEPARTMENT NUMBER
1100 'ENAME$          - EMPLOYEE NAME
1110 'PARTS           - PARTS PRODUCED BY ONE EMPLOYEE
2000 '**********************************************************************
2002 '                              MAIN ROUTINE
2004 '**********************************************************************
2010  OPEN "B:PARTS.DAT" FOR INPUT AS #1
2020  GOSUB 3000                 'Format report
2030  GOSUB 4000                 'Read data file and process data
2040  GOSUB 6000                 'Produce summary
2050  CLOSE #1
2060  END
3000 '**********************************************************************
3002 '                             FORMAT REPORT
3004 '**********************************************************************
3010  S$ = STRING$(32,"=")
3020  F$ = "____________________________####_________________###"
3030  PAGE = 1
3040  GOSUB 3500                 'Print headings
3050  RETURN
3500 '**********************************************************************
3502 '                             PRINT HEADINGS
3504 '**********************************************************************
3510  LPRINT CHR$(12); CHR$(10); CHR$(10); CHR$(10); CHR$(10)
3520  LPRINT TAB(16) DATE$; TAB(32) "PRODUCTION REPORT"; TAB(55) "Page"; PAGE
3530  LPRINT TAB(25) S$
3540  LPRINT TAB(25) "DEPARTMENT"; TAB(43) "TOTAL PRODUCED"
3550  LPRINT TAB(25) S$
3560  RETURN
4000 '**********************************************************************
4002 '                   READ DATA FILE AND PROCESS DATA
4004 '**********************************************************************
4010  ROW = 5
4020  HOLD = 0
4030  COUNT.EMPLOYEES = 0
4040  DEPT.TOTAL = 0
```

```
4050  GRAND.TOTAL = 0
4060  WHILE NOT EOF(1)
4070    INPUT #1, DEPT.NUMBER,ENAME$,PARTS
4080    IF DEPT.NUMBER <> HOLD AND HOLD <> 0 THEN GOSUB 5000
4090    IF ROW >= 54 THEN PAGE = PAGE+1 : GOSUB 3500 : ROW = 5
4100    COUNT.EMPLOYEES = COUNT.EMPLOYEES+1
4110    DEPT.TOTAL = DEPT.TOTAL+PARTS
4120    HOLD = DEPT.NUMBER
4130  WEND
4140  GOSUB 5000                    'Print total for last group
4150  RETURN
5000 '*******************************************************************
5002 '                  PRINT GROUP TOTAL, ACCUMULATE TOTALS
5004 '*******************************************************************
5010  LPRINT USING F$; HOLD,DEPT.TOTAL
5020  ROW = ROW+1
5030  GRAND.TOTAL = GRAND.TOTAL+DEPT.TOTAL
5040  DEPT.TOTAL = 0
5050  RETURN
6000 '*******************************************************************
6002 '                           PRODUCE SUMMARY
6004 '*******************************************************************
6010  LPRINT
6020  LPRINT TAB(14) USING "Total number of parts produced:__________________###
#";GRAND.TOTAL
6030  LPRINT TAB(14) USING "Average number of parts produced by ## employees:__#
#";COUNT.EMPLOYEES,GRAND.TOTAL/COUNT.EMPLOYEES
6040  RETURN
65529 'End of program listing
```

The Output:

```
         10        20        30        40        50        60        70        80
12345678901234567890123456789012345678901234567890123456789012345678901234567890
              06-26-19XX      PRODUCTION REPORT      Page 1
                        ================================
                        DEPARTMENT          TOTAL PRODUCED
                        ================================
                           1263                  404
                           2485                  516
                           3967                  404
                           4231                  483
                           5894                  202
                           6785                  319

              Total number of parts produced:                 2328
              Average number of parts produced by 58 employees:  40
```

Our detail line consists of the department number and the number of parts produced in that department. Note that we must print the value of HOLD and not the value of DEPT.NUMBER in line 5010. The number of the department just processed has been copied into HOLD while DEPT.NUMBER stores the number of the next department.

Summary of BASIC Functions

DATE$ Retrieves the date.

```
3030 PRINT "The date is: ";DATE$
```

TIME$ Retrieves the current time in string form.

```
3040 PRINT "The time is: ";TIME$
```

Chapter Summary

1. The DATE$ and TIME$ functions are often used in a program to indicate when the output was printed.
2. Each page of a multi-page report should have a one-inch top margin and a one-inch bottom margin. When output must continue on a new page, the program must reposition the paper to the top of the new page, then leave the one-inch top margin.
3. Each page of a report should begin with headings.
4. CHR$(12), which represents "form feed", instructs BASIC to skip to a new page. CHR$(10), which represents "line feed", instructs BASIC to proceed to the next line.
5. To obtain the one-inch bottom margin, we must increase a row counter each time a line is printed. After each increase, the row counter must be checked for the maximum number of lines allotted to a page.
6. Page totals are often printed at the bottom of each page of a report with a grand total printed at the end of the report. The row counter must be checked to determine when a page total is to be printed. The total should be placed one inch from the bottom of a page.
7. Frequently, a total must be found for a group of items that have something in common. The group is called a control group, the item of similarity is called a control value, and the total of a group is called a group total.
8. To obtain a group total, BASIC must know where one control group ends and where another starts. This is determined by comparing the control value of a record just read with the control value of the previous record. The latter control value must be saved in a "hold" variable. If the values are the same, processing for the group continues. If the values are different, the group total for the control group just processed is printed.
9. A detail line should never be printed in the one-inch bottom margin. However, it is considered proper to print a group total in the bottom margin, rather than print the total alone on the next page.
10. Often, a report must be produced that consists of group totals without the detail lines. The report is referred to as a group summary report.

Programming Problems

Test all programs first on the screen. Allow 15 rows to a page. When the desired output is obtained, change the maximum number of rows to 54 and print to the printer. Remember to call Subroutine FREEZE DISPLAY when printing to the screen, then delete the subroutine when printing to the printer.

1. Using the program on page 219 as a guide, write a program that produces a monthly sales and commission report for the furniture department of a store. The amount of each sale, along with the number of the salesperson who made the sale, is stored in a data file.

   Sample data file: (the periods indicate further records)

   ```
   SALES6.DAT
   164,1523.95 — Salesperson number (3 digits), amount of sale (<= 9,999.99)
   164,949.40
   ...,.....
   164,1012.89
   164,686.15
   231,852.67
   231,1242.95
   ...,.......
   ```

The records are stored in numeric order by salesperson number. Calculate the commission earned on each sale. The rate of commission is 15%. Each detail line must display the salesperson's number, the amount of a sale, and the commission earned on the sale.

Your program must print group totals for the sales and the commissions. Should a group listing end at the bottom of a page, print its group totals in the bottom margin, not on the next page. Your program must also produce, on a separate page, a summary that displays the total sales, the total commission earned, and the top salesperson of the month. Hint: To print the summary on a new page and leave a one-inch top margin, use the CHR$(12) and CHR$(10) functions in Subroutine PRODUCE SUMMARY as you did in Subroutine PRINT HEADINGS. Print a page number on each page, including the summary page. Sample output is shown below. Save your program as it is needed for the next two problems.

```
04-12-19XX     SALES AND COMMISSION REPORT        Page 1
         ========================================
         SALESPERSON          SALES        COMMISSION
         ========================================
             164           $1,523.95       $228.59
             164           $  949.40       $142.41
             ...           .........       .......
             164           $1,012.89       $151.93
             164           $  686.15       $102.92

         Totals            $16,650.49      $2,497.57

             231           $  852.67       $127.90
             231           $1,242.95       $186.44
             ...           .........       .......
```

Your summary page should look as follows:

```
                  SUMMARY OF SALES AND COMMISSIONS          Page 3
                             04-12-19XX

                  Total sales:              $84,002.53
                  Total commission:         $12,600.38

Salesperson of the month:    Salesperson 467 with sales of $17,220.05
```

To determine the salesperson of the month, compare a salesperson's total sales with a variable, say LARGEST, which initially contains a zero. If a salesperson's total sales is greater than LARGEST, store his/her total sales in LARGEST and store this salesperson's number (currently stored in HOLD) in another variable, say TOP.SALESPERSON. Do this comparison for each salesperson. Perform this routine in the subroutine that prints and accumulates group totals. After all records have been processed, print the values of TOP.SALESPERSON and LARGEST in the summary.

2. Modify the program for Problem 1 so that it produces a group summary report. On one output line, print the salesperson's number, the group total for the sales and the group total for the commissions for that salesperson. A sample output line is shown below.

```
04-12-19XX     SALES AND COMMISSION REPORT        Page 1
         ========================================
         SALESPERSON          SALES        COMMISSION
         ========================================
             164           $16,650.49      $2,497.57
```

On a separate page, print the summary of sales and commissions and the top salesperson of the month as in the former program.

3. Modify your program for Problem 1 in the following manner:

(a) Start each new group on a new page. Do not assume that each group listing fills one page. One group listing may require less than one page, another may require several pages.

(b) Print the number of the salesperson in the heading rather than as an item in a detail line.

Sample Output:

```
Salesperson: 164          04-12-19XX          Page  1

             SALES AND COMMISSION REPORT
             ===========================
               SALES            COMMISSION
             ===========================
             $1,523.95            $228.59
             $   949.40           $142.41
             .........            .......
             $1,012.89            $151.93
             $   686.15           $102.92

Totals       $16,650.49          $2,497.57
```

```
Salesperson: 231          04-12-19XX          Page  2

             SALES AND COMMISSION REPORT
             ===========================
               SALES            COMMISSION
             ===========================
             $   852.67           $127.90
             $1,242.95            $186.44
             .........            .......
```

The summary on the last page remains unchanged.

To print the number of the first salesperson before printing his/her sales as a group, read the first record in Subroutine FORMAT REPORT then call the subroutine that prints the headings. In Subroutine PRINT HEADINGS, print the salesperson's number that has just been read, the date, and the page number. Print this line just before the main heading. Use a PRINT USING statement.

The record just read must now be processed in Subroutine READ DATA FILE AND PROCESS DATA. Since the first statement in the WHILE/WEND loop normally reads a record, your first record will be destroyed. Thus, it is necessary that you set up a counter to keep track of the records being read.

Just before the WHILE statement that checks for the end-of-file character, initialize a counter to one. This statement signifies that the first record has been read. The first statement inside the loop must check the counter. If the counter is equal to one, by-pass the INPUT # statement that reads a record. Sample statement: xxxx IF I = 1 THEN xxxx. I is the counter and xxxx following the word THEN is the line number of the first statement after the INPUT # statement. This first statement and those following must process the record just read. (Refer to your program for Problem 1 for statements that process a record.) Remember to increase the counter before the WEND statement.

Skip to a new page after printing the group totals in Subroutine PRINT AND ACCUMULATE GROUP TOTALS. Your statement must ensure that BASIC has not detected the end-of-file character. The statement could look as follows:

```
xxxx IF NOT EOF(1) THEN PAGE = PAGE+1 : GOSUB 3500 : ROW = 6
```

Place the statement just before the RETURN statement in this subroutine. If you do not check for the EOF character, the headings for the last salesperson will be reprinted.

Save your program and produce a hard copy. The program can be used as a guide for the Accounts Receivable program in Problem 4 and for a problem in Chapter 14.

4. The Accounts Receivable file, AR2.DAT, contains three records. Increase the number of records by at least seven. To add records to the existing file, modify the CREATE program used to create the original file (the program should be stored under filename CREATEAR.BAS) by changing the mode of access to APPEND. APPEND moves the data file pointer to the end of the file so that additional records can be added. Your OPEN statement should look as follows:

```
2010 OPEN "B:AR2.DAT" FOR APPEND AS #1
```

The accounts in file AR2.DAT are numbered in the following manner. The digit 1 in each number specifies a credit limit of $1000.

31001,31002,31003 (Credit limit of $1000)

Number the appended accounts as follows:

32001,32002,32003,32004 (Credit limit of $2000)
33001,33002,33003 (Credit limit of $3000)

At least four accounts should have balances over the credit limit. Examples of two records are shown below.

32001,Fred Gardiner,194 Linden Street Mytown XX N6Y 2B4,998-1452,2000,
Nov. 6,1432.25
32002,Jodi Morrison,315 Clare Blvd. Mytown XX N6Y 7C3,842-5813,2000,
Nov. 8,2162.49

Each record consists of an account number; the customer's name, address, telephone number, and credit limit; the date of the last transaction; and the balance due. Leave two spaces between the street address and the city, between the city and the province, and between the province and the postal code.

Use the program written for Problem 3 as a guide to list the accounts in each credit limit category. Print the listing of each category on a new page. In an IF statement, determine whether or not a customer has overextended his/her credit limit, find the overextended amount, and accumulate these amounts. Your statement could look as follows:

```
4110 IF BALANCE > LIMIT THEN OVER = BALANCE-LIMIT :
        TOTAL.OVER = TOTAL.OVER+OVER
```

where BALANCE is the balance in the account, OVER is a customer's overextended amount, and TOTAL.OVER accumulates the overextended amounts for that particular limit. Place this IF statement in Subroutine READ DATA FILE AND PROCESS DATA. For each credit limit category, print the amount overextended by customers in that category (value of TOTAL.OVER). A summary page must display the total amount overextended in all credit limits. Output for one category and the partial output for a second are given below.

```
 Limit: $1,000.00        11-30-19XX         Page  1

              ACCOUNTS RECEIVABLE REPORT
=====================================================
ACCOUNT NUMBER              NAME              BALANCE
=====================================================
    31001            Diane Fraser          $   401.37
    31002            Derek Andrews         $1,037.87
    31003            Lee Harris            $     0.00

Over the limit                             $    37.87
```

```
 Limit: $2,000.00        11-30-19XX         Page  2

              ACCOUNTS RECEIVABLE REPORT
=====================================================
ACCOUNT NUMBER              NAME              BALANCE
=====================================================
    32001            Fred Gardiner         $1,432.25
    32002            Jodi Morrison         $2,162.49
    .....          ................        .........
```

Your summary page could display the following:

```
               TOTAL OVEREXTENDED AMOUNT         Page  4
                      11-30-19XX

Total amount exceeding the credit limits     $1,133.54
```

Project

Combine the inventory program developed in Chapter Eight with the Accounts Receivable program written for Problem 4 above. Customize the Accounts Receivable program so that it handles inventory accounts. The program in Chapter Eight updates INVENT1.DAT, stores the updated records in INVENT2.DAT and displays each inventory account on the screen. Your Problem 4 program (which must be customized for this project) must list the inventory of each department on a new page and print, beneath each department's inventory list, the number of accounts whose balances are less than the minimum. A summary on the last page must display the total number of inventory accounts with balances less than the minimum.

Use GOSUB statements to combine the programs. Update the inventory accounts first, (display each account on the screen after it is updated), then group list the inventories by department. Thus, your main routine must:

1. Open INVENT1.DAT for INPUT to read the old file.
2. Open INVENT2.DAT for OUTPUT to write the updated records to the file.
3. Call a subroutine that reads the old file, INPUTS a transaction, and calls another subroutine to perform the calculations and to write the updated record to the new file. This latter subroutine, in turn, calls a subroutine to print the account.
4. Close the two files.
5. Open the new file for INPUT.
6. Call a subroutine that formats the inventory report.
7. Call a subroutine that reads the new file and processes the data for the group listing.
8. Call a subroutine that produces the summary.
9. Close the new file.

An inventory account is given in Chapter Eight, on page 205. A group listing for the inventory of one department is given below.

```
          Department: Furnishings          01-15-19XX          Page  2

                           INVENTORY REPORT
          ==========================================================
          STOCK NO.               ITEM               MINIMUM   BALANCE
          ==========================================================
            F001      Sofa (contemporary)               3          1
            F002      Sofa (French)                     2          2
            F003      Sofa (Italian)                    2          1

          Number of accounts under the minimum          2

Press any key to continue
```

The summary page could look as follows:

```
        NUMBER OF ACCOUNTS UNDER THE MINIMUM   Page  4
                     01-15-19XX

Total number of accounts under the minimum  6
```

Find the total in the subroutine that group prints the accounts.

Write a separate program that lists only those accounts with balances less than the minimum. List the accounts by department, each department listing on a new page. From your previous program, delete the following modules:

1. The module that updates an account.
2. The module that performs calculations and writes a record to a new file.
3. The module that prints the account.
4. The module that produces the summary.

Modify the modules needed in your previous program to group print the inventory. You must omit the statement that prints a detail line and the one that increases the row. Instead, the IF statement that checks for a minimum balance must print an output line similar to the ones shown below, then increase row by 1. Also, the statement that compares a department name with your control value must cause BASIC to skip to a new page if the values are not the same rather than call a subroutine to print a total. The page of accounts with balances less than the minimum for the furnishings department could look as follows:

```
          Department: Furnishings      01-15-19XX         Page  2

                              INVENTORY REPORT
          ==========================================================
          STOCK NO.               ITEM               MINIMUM   BALANCE
          ==========================================================
            F001        Sofa (contemporary)             3          1
            F003        Sofa (Italian)                  2          1

Press any key to continue
```

Save this latter program. Part of it can be used for the project in Chapter Fourteen.

Solutions for Exercises

9.2 A Multi-Page Report

1. Each page would be numbered Page 1.

2. The output will be the same as the output for the program on page 215. Suppose record 47 is the last record printed on page 1. Here is how the two programs differ in coding but produce the same output. Only relevant statements from the WHILE/WEND loop are listed.

Program on Page 215	*Modified Program*
Read record 47	Read record 47
Print record 47	Print record 47
Increase row (ROW now equals 52)	Increase row (ROW now equals 52)
Read record 48	Call subroutine to print total
Call subroutine to print total	Read record 48
Print record 48 on new page	Print record 48 on new page

It does not matter whether record 48 is read first and then the subroutine is called to print the total or the subroutine is called first and then record 48 is read since a record is not printed on the next page until both operations have been performed.

9.3 Group Totals

In the modified program, the last record in a group listing is actually the first record of the following control group. Furthermore, the number of parts for this record is included in the previous group total.

Program on Page 219	*Modified Program*
Read next record	Read next record
Compare new control value and HOLD	Print the record just read
Print the record just read	Increase row
Increase row	Compare new control value and HOLD
HOLD = control value just read	HOLD = control value just read

The program on page 219 checks for a new control value before printing a record. The modified version prints a record before checking a control value. Thus, in the modified version, the first record of the next group is printed in the current group.

10

LOOP STRUCTURES

Objectives

Our first encounter with a loop was in Chapter Four where we used an IF/THEN . . . GOTO combination to create and control a loop. Recall that a loop is a sequence of instructions that is repeated. We then used a WHILE/WEND loop. Although this loop was used for several reasons, we applied it mainly in the creation and reading of data files.

In this chapter, you will learn a third loop structure: the FOR/NEXT loop. In addition, you will become familiar with nested loops, that is, a loop within a loop and with the RESTORE statement that allows you to read data from a data pool more than once.

Contents

Questions and Exercises

Programming Problems

10.1 The WHILE/WEND Loop

Before we discuss FOR/NEXT loops, let us review a WHILE/WEND loop and discover another use for this loop.

Review of the WHILE/WEND Loop

```
5010 WHILE NOT EOF(1)
5020   INPUT #1, ENAME$
5030   PRINT ENAME$
5040 WEND
```

The two statements within the WHILE/WEND loop (lines 5020 and 5030) are executed as long as the condition in the WHILE statement is true. BASIC returns control to the WHILE statement each time it encounters the WEND statement, thus creating a loop. When the condition in the WHILE statement is false, the loop terminates and control transfers to the statement following the WEND. The condition in the WHILE statement above checks for an end-of-file character at the end of a sequential file. As long as the EOF character is not encountered, BASIC executes statements 5020 and 5030. When the EOF character is encountered, the loop terminates.

Processing a Program Repeatedly

So far, our main routine allows a user to process a program just once. If the user wishes to execute several routines in the program a number of times, the complete program must be re-executed each time. A more efficient method of re-executing the required modules is to place the GOSUB statements that call the modules within a WHILE/WEND loop.

Although there are other ways to ask a user if a procedure is to be repeated, we will illustrate two. One method uses a prompt within a WHILE/WEND loop, the other uses a prompt in Subroutine FREEZE DISPLAY.

Displaying a Prompt Within a WHILE/WEND Loop

Examine the following program segment.

```
2000 'MAIN ROUTINE
2010   OPEN "B:NAMES.DAT" FOR INPUT AS #1
2020   GOSUB 3000                    'Read data file
2030   RESPONSE$ = "y"
2040   WHILE RESPONSE$ = "y" OR RESPONSE$ = "Y"
2050     GOSUB 4000                  'INPUT data
2060     GOSUB 5000                  'Format table and print headings
2070     GOSUB 6000                  'Perform calculations
2080     PRINT
2090     INPUT "Do you wish to produce another table (y/n)";RESPONSE$
2100     IF RESPONSE$ <> "y" AND RESPONSE$ <> "Y" AND RESPONSE$ <> "n" AND
         RESPONSE$ <> "N" THEN PRINT "Invalid response. Enter y or n." :
         GOTO 2090
2110   WEND
2120   CLOSE #1
2130   END
```

Note that the data file must be opened and read before the loop begins. If the OPEN statement is placed inside the loop, BASIC displays the error message **File already open** when the loop is re-executed. If the GOSUB statement that calls Subroutine 3000 is placed inside the loop, BASIC reads the data file then performs one of the following when the loop is re-executed:

(a) Displays the error message **Input past end** if the EOF function is not used to detect the end-of-file character. Execution terminates.

(b) Displays no error message but performs no further read operation if the EOF function is used to detect the end-of-file character. Execution is not terminated.

We assume that the user wishes to process the program at least once. Therefore, we assign "y" to RESPONSE$. As long as RESPONSE$ is equal to "y" or "Y", the loop continues. Inside the loop we call Subroutines 4000, 5000, and 6000, and display the prompt "Do you wish to produce another table?". The INPUT statement allows the user to key in "y" or "n". If the response is "y" or "Y", the statements within the loop are executed once more. If the response is "n" or "N", the entire expression in the WHILE statement is false and the loop terminates. Following the loop, line 2120 closes the file, line 2130 ends the program.

In line 2100 we check for a valid response. If the keyed-in value is not "y", "Y", "n", or "N", the response is invalid and the user is asked to key in the response once more. If we omitted the "n" or "N" check in our verification, a keyed-in "n" or "N" would transfer control back to line 2090 instead of ending the loop. When this editing feature is included, a keyed-in "n" or "N" causes the entire expression in the IF statement to be false. BASIC drops down to the WEND statement which transfers control to the WHILE. Since the value of RESPONSE$ is not "y" or "Y", both conditions in the WHILE statement are false. The loop terminates and the program ends.

Displaying a Prompt in Subroutine FREEZE DISPLAY

If your program calls Subroutine FREEZE DISPLAY, the prompt in the subroutine can be changed to "Press any key to continue, press 'q' to quit." The WHILE statement in the main routine can now use the typed-in character to control the loop. A sample main routine and Subroutine FREEZE DISPLAY are given below.

```
2000 'MAIN ROUTINE
2010   OPEN "B:SALES.DAT" FOR INPUT AS #1
2020   GOSUB 3000                    'Display instructions
2030   GOSUB 4000                    'Read data file
2040   GOSUB 11000                   'Freeze display
2050   WHILE QUIT$ <> "q" AND QUIT$ <> "Q"
2060     GOSUB 5000                  'Perform calculations
2070     GOSUB 11000                 'Freeze display
2080   WEND
2090   CLOSE #1
2100   END
11000 'SUBROUTINE FREEZE DISPLAY
11010   PRINT
11020   PRINT "Press any key to continue, press 'q' to quit"
11030   K$ = INKEY$
11040   WHILE K$ = ""
11050     K$ = INKEY$
11060     QUIT$ = K$
11070   WEND
11080   RETURN
```

Subroutine FREEZE DISPLAY is called before the WHILE/WEND loop to freeze the instructions on the screen. The user may press any key to continue or "q" to quit. Line 11060 assigns the typed-in character to QUIT$. The WHILE statement in the main routine checks the value of QUIT$. As long as its value is not "q" or "Q", the loop continues. When the user types in a "q", the loop terminates and the program ends. Note that Subroutine FREEZE DISPLAY is also called from within the WHILE/WEND loop, this time to freeze the results on the screen.

If Subroutine FREEZE DISPLAY is not called before the WHILE/WEND loop in the main routine, a value must be assigned to QUIT$. Let us assign the null string to the variable. The statement, which must be coded before the WHILE statement, should look as follows:

```
2040 QUIT$ = ""
```

Exercises

Write WHILE statements that cause WHILE/WEND loops to continue as long as:

1. RESPONSE$ is not equal to "true".
2. CODE is less than or equal to 7.

3. RESPONSE$ is not equal to "yes" and not equal to "YES".

4. NUMBER is greater than 100 or less than 200.

10.2 The FOR/NEXT Loop

Comparing a WHILE/WEND Loop With a FOR/NEXT Loop

Before we begin our discussions on FOR/NEXT loops, let us first compare a WHILE/WEND loop with a FOR/NEXT loop.

The WHILE/WEND loop

```
5010 WHILE NOT EOF(1)
5020    INPUT #1, ENAME$
5030    PRINT ENAME$
5040 WEND
```

The FOR/NEXT loop

```
5010 FOR I = 1 TO 3 STEP 1
5020    INPUT #1, ENAME$
5030    PRINT ENAME$
5040 NEXT I
```

In the WHILE/WEND loop, the WHILE statement marks the beginning of the loop, the WEND statement marks the end of the loop. In the FOR/NEXT loop, the FOR statement marks the beginning of the loop, the NEXT statement marks the end of the loop. In our structures above, the body of the loop (the two statements inside the loop) is the same.

The main difference between the two loops is the method used to terminate a loop. The WHILE/WEND loop is performed as long as the condition in the WHILE statement remains true. When the condition becomes false, the loop terminates. The FOR/NEXT loop is performed a specific number of times; in the above example exactly three times. Thus, the FOR/NEXT loop is often referred to as a counting loop.

Let us now find out how the FOR/NEXT loop operates.

The FOR Statement

```
5010   FOR   I          =   1              TO   3            STEP 1
             ↑              ↑                   ↑                 ↑
          Control       Initial value       Test value      Step value
          variable
```

The control variable acts as a counter. The initial value is the first value assigned to the control variable, the test value sets a limit to the control variable, and the step value is the amount by which the control variable increases each time BASIC passes through the loop. If the step value is omitted, the increment is assumed to be 1. The initial value, the test value, and the step value are called the parameters of the loop.

The NEXT Statement

A FOR statement must be accompanied by a NEXT statement.

```
5040 NEXT I
```

The reserved word NEXT increases the control variable by the amount specified by the step value, then transfers control to the statement following the FOR. Execution of the loop continues until the value of the control variable is greater than the test value. Using the following program segment in our discussions, here is how the FOR and NEXT statements work together.

```
5010 FOR I = 1 TO 3 STEP 1
5020    INPUT #1, ENAME$
5030    PRINT ENAME$
5040 NEXT I
RUN
John Smith
Leslie Brown
Andre Fraser
```

The first time the loop is executed, I is set to 1. BASIC executes lines 5020 and 5030. When BASIC encounters the NEXT statement, I is increased by one. The value of I is now 2. Since the value of I is not greater than 3, BASIC executes statements 5020 and 5030 once more. NEXT increases I to 3. Since I is not greater than 3, statements 5020 and 5030 are executed again. NEXT increases I to 4. Now that I is greater than 3, the loop terminates and control drops down to the statement following NEXT. The statements inside the loop have been executed three times.

Note that the control variable is not compared with the test value the first time BASIC executes the loop. This means that the loop is executed at least once.

As well as controlling a loop, the control variable can also be used inside the loop. It can either be printed or used in calculations and in comparisons. However, its value must not be changed inside the loop as this change will interfere with its automatic increments.

Variations of the FOR Statement

The following statements illustrate additional features of the FOR.

1. The initial value and the step value need not always be one. Furthermore, we can use variables and expressions to represent the initial value, the test value, and the step value.

```
5010 FOR I = A TO B STEP C
5010 FOR I = 2 TO A+8 STEP 2
```

2. Zero or a negative number may be used as the initial value and the test value.

```
5010 FOR I = Ø TO 24 STEP 4
5010 FOR I = -10 TO Ø STEP 2
5010 FOR I = -21 TO -3 STEP 3
```

3. The values in the FOR statement may be fractions. The example below also shows that the control variable need not eventually equal the test value. The values of I will be 0.5, 1.5, 2, and 2.5. The first value greater than the test value stops the loop. This will be value 2.5.

```
5010 FOR I = 0.5 TO 2.3 STEP 0.5
```

Care must be exercised when using some fractional increments. An increment of 0.1 is likely to be troublesome since its storage in the computer is not exact whereas that of 0.5 is exact. We can circumvent the problem by using whole numbers in the FOR statement, such as 7 instead of 0.07, 10 instead of 0.10, and 1 instead of 0.01. Then, in a statement that uses the control variable, we divide the control variable by 100.

Here is an example:

```
5010 FOR RATE = 7 TO 10 STEP 1
5020    DIVIDENDS = AMOUNT*RATE/100
5030    PRINT DIVIDENDS
5040 NEXT RATE
```

The first time line 5020 is executed, AMOUNT will be multiplied by 0.07, the second time by 0.08, the third time by 0.09. The last time line 5020 is executed, AMOUNT will be multiplied by 0.10.

4. The step value may be negative. In the following example, the loop is executed six times; when I is equal to 10, 8, 6, 4, 2, and Ø. The loop continues until the value of the control variable is less than the test value.

```
5010 FOR I = 10 TO Ø STEP -2
```

Exercises

1. State the errors, if any, in the following FOR statements. Make the necessary corrections.

```
(a) 5010 FOR I = -20 TO -5 STEP 3
(b) 5010 FOR I = 25 TO 5 STEP 5
(c) 5010 FOR I = 0.5 TO 4.5 STEP -0.5
(d) 5010 FOR I = -42 TO Ø STEP 7
(e) 5010 FOR I = Ø TO -42 STEP 7
```

2. What values will the control variable take on in each of the following FOR statements? Do not include the value that terminates the loop.

```
(a) 5010 FOR I = 35 TO 48 STEP 3
(b) 5010 FOR I = 0.5 TO 3.0 STEP 0.5
(c) 5010 FOR I = 14 TO 0 STEP -2
(d) 5010 FOR I = -8 TO 8 STEP 3
(e) 5010 FOR I = J TO J*5+3 STEP 6      where J = 7
```

3. How many times will the loop be performed for each of the following FOR statements?

```
(a) 5010 FOR I = 12 TO 28 STEP 3
(b) 5010 FOR I = 1 TO 8 STEP 2
(c) 5010 FOR I = 8 TO 1 STEP -2
```

4. What is the output from each of the following?

(a)
```
5010 PRINT
5020 A = 4
5030 FOR I = 2 TO 13 STEP 3
5040   A = A+I
5050   PRINT I,A
5060 NEXT I
```

(b)
```
5010 PRINT
5020 FOR I = 6 TO -6 STEP -2
5030   J = I^2
5040   PRINT J;
5050 NEXT I
```

10.3 A Sample Program

We will now incorporate, in a sample program, the concepts learned in the last two sections. The user will be able to process the program as many times as desired. The FOR/NEXT loop generates the data; no data will be read from a data file or supplied by data statements.

The program produces a payroll table. The user must key in the minimum hours of work, the maximum hours of work, and the rate of pay. The minimum hours of work will be used as the initial value in the FOR statement, the maximum hours of work will be used as the test value. Inside the FOR/NEXT loop, we will calculate the gross pay and print a detail line.

```
1000 'PAYROLL TABLE                     M. MCRITCHIE                    AUG 3
1002 '*********************************************************************
1004 '                    THIS PROGRAM PRODUCES A PAYROLL TABLE
1006 '*********************************************************************
1010 'RESPONSE$ - USER'S RESPONSE (y/n)
1020 'MINIMUM   - MINIMUM HOURS OF WORK
1030 'MAXIMUM   - MAXIMUM HOURS OF WORK
1040 'RATE      - RATE OF PAY
1050 'S$        - EQUAL SIGNS
1060 'F$        - IMAGE OF A DETAIL LINE
1070 'HOURS     - CONTROL VARIABLE
1080 'GROSS.PAY - GROSS PAY
2000 '*********************************************************************
2002 '                              MAIN ROUTINE
2004 '*********************************************************************
2010   RESPONSE$ = "y"
2020   WHILE RESPONSE$ = "y" OR RESPONSE$ = "Y"
2030     GOSUB 3000                  'INPUT data
2040     GOSUB 4000                  'Format table and print headings
2050     GOSUB 5000                  'Generate and process data
2060     PRINT
2070     INPUT "Do you wish to produce another table (y/n)";RESPONSE$
2080     IF RESPONSE$ <> "y" AND RESPONSE$ <> "Y" AND RESPONSE$ <> "n" AND
            RESPONSE$ <> "N" THEN PRINT "Invalid response. Enter y or n." :
            GOTO 2070
2090   WEND
2100   END
```

```
3000 '**********************************************************************
3002 '                              INPUT DATA (HOURS, RATE)
3004 '**********************************************************************
3010  CLS
3020  LOCATE 10
3030  INPUT "_____________Minimum hours, maximum hours, rate of pay";
      MINIMUM,MAXIMUM,RATE
3040  PRINT
3050  INPUT "Are the entries correct (y/n)";RESPONSE$
3060  IF RESPONSE$ <> "y" AND RESPONSE$ <> "Y"
         THEN INPUT "Re-enter the hours and the rate of pay--",
         MINIMUM,MAXIMUM,RATE : GOTO 3050
3070  RETURN
4000 '**********************************************************************
4002 '                         FORMAT TABLE AND PRINT HEADINGS
4004 '**********************************************************************
4010  CLS
4020  LOCATE 4
4030  S$ = STRING$(26,"=")
4040  F$ = "____________________________##_______________$###.##"
4050  PRINT TAB(34) "PAYROLL TABLE"
4060  PRINT
4070  PRINT TAB(32) USING "RATE OF PAY: $#.##";RATE
4080  PRINT TAB(28) S$
4090  PRINT TAB(28) "HOURS"; TAB(45) "GROSS PAY"
4100  PRINT TAB(28) S$
4110  RETURN
5000 '**********************************************************************
5002 '                            GENERATE AND PROCESS DATA
5004 '**********************************************************************
5010  FOR HOURS = MINIMUM TO MAXIMUM
5020     GROSS.PAY = HOURS*RATE
5030     PRINT USING F$; HOURS,GROSS.PAY
5040  NEXT HOURS
5050  RETURN
65529 'End of program listing
```

The Output:

(cleared screen)

```
         10        20        30        40        50        60        70        80
12345678901234567890123456789012345678901234567890123456789012345678901234567890
             Minimum hours, maximum hours, rate of pay? 35,45,9.54

Are the entries correct (y/n)? y
```

(cleared screen)

```
                                 PAYROLL TABLE

                               RATE OF PAY: $9.54
                           ==========================
                           HOURS            GROSS PAY
                           ==========================
                            35               $333.90
                            36               $343.44
                            37               $352.98
                            38               $362.52
                            39               $372.06
                            40               $381.60
                            41               $391.14
                            42               $400.68
                            43               $410.22
                            44               $419.76
                            45               $429.30

Do you wish to produce another table (y/n)?
```

As long as the user responds to "Do you wish to produce another table (y/n)?" with "y" or "Y", the main routine calls subroutines 3000, 4000, and 5000. When the user responds with "n" or "N", the program ends.

Subroutine INPUT DATA allows the user to key in the minimum and maximum hours of work and the rate of pay. Suppose the user keys in 35 and 45 as the range for the hours of work. The two variables MINIMUM and MAXIMUM, to which the values are assigned, are used as the initial value and the test value in the FOR statement in line 5010. This means that the control variable HOURS takes on the values 35 to 46 inclusive, in increments of one. Each of the values is a number of hours of work. Thus, data is being generated by the FOR/NEXT loop. Note, however, that the statements within the loop are not executed when the value of HOURS becomes 46 since 46 exceeds the test value of 45.

Inside the loop, we use the control variable HOURS to calculate the gross pay. The first time the loop is executed, the value of HOURS is 35, the second time, HOURS is 36. The value of HOURS increases by one until it becomes 46, at which time the loop terminates.

10.4 Nested FOR/NEXT Loops

The Concept of Nested FOR/NEXT Loops

Occasions often arise when we must place one FOR/NEXT loop inside another. The loops are referred to as being nested. Suppose we wish to read and print the scores for 30 students. We need two loops: an outer loop to keep track of the students, an inner loop to keep track of each student's scores. This is illustrated in the structure below.

```
5020 FOR STUDENT = 1 TO 30
5030    INPUT #1, SNAME$
5040    PRINT SNAME$
5050    FOR TEST = 1 TO 4
5060      INPUT #1, SCORE
5070      PRINT SCORE
5080    NEXT TEST
5090 NEXT STUDENT
```

Note that the loop for the scores is nested entirely within the loop for the students. Let us trace through the logic of the above structure.

In line 5020, the value 1 is assigned to STUDENT. This means the structure will be processing the scores for the first student. In line 5050, BASIC encounters the test loop. This inner loop reads and prints four scores. Since the structure is currently working with student number one, the inner loop will be reading and printing the scores for the first student. Figures 10-1 and 10-2 illustrate the logic for two passes through the outer loop using skeleton structures in which only FOR and NEXT statements are coded.

FIGURE 10-1

```
5020 FOR STUDENT = 1 TO 30
5030    ----
5040    ----
5050    FOR TEST = 1 TO 4        STUDENT = 1      While STUDENT = 1, the test
5060    ----                     TEST = 1,2,3,4   loop goes through its cycle
5070    ----                                      4 times.
5080    NEXT TEST
5090 NEXT STUDENT
```

In line 5020, number 1 is assigned to STUDENT. BASIC executes lines 5030 and 5040. It then encounters the test loop which it executes four times. When the inner loop is complete, control drops down to line 5090 where NEXT STUDENT increases STUDENT to 2. Control transfers to line 5030.

FIGURE 10-2

```
5020 FOR STUDENT = 1 TO 30
5030    ----
5040    ----
5050    FOR TEST = 1 TO 4
5060    ----
5070    ----
5080    NEXT TEST
5090 NEXT STUDENT
```

STUDENT = 2
TEST = 1,2,3,4

TEST reverts to 1 at the beginning of the inner loop.

The scores for student number two will now be processed. When BASIC encounters the test loop, it reassigns 1 to TEST and proceeds to execute, once again, the inner loop four times. Since the structure is currently working with student number two, the inner loop will be reading and printing the four scores for the second student. (See lines 5060 and 5070 in our complete sample program.) NEXT STUDENT in line 5090 increases STUDENT to 3. The scores for student number three will now be processed.

Execution of the structure continues until the scores for all 30 students have been read and printed. Note that for each outer loop, the inner loop is performed four times. This means that the inner loop is executed 30 x 4 = 120 times.

A Sample Subroutine

A modified version of the subroutine listed on page 242 is given below. Here, we use a test value of 3 in line 5020 in order to process the scores for only three students rather than 30. We also insert two PRINT statements and append a semicolon at the end of the PRINT statement in line 5070. Let us find out what output the module produces. The module reads the following data file.

SCORES1.DAT
Wayne Ferguson — Student's name
85,74,89,82 — Student's scores
Debbie Smith
76,64,67,79
Sharon Palmer
89,93,98,86

```
5010 PRINT
5020 FOR STUDENT = 1 TO 3
5030    INPUT #1, SNAME$
5040    PRINT SNAME$
5050    FOR TEST = 1 TO 4
5060       INPUT #1, SCORE
5070       PRINT SCORE;
5080    NEXT TEST
5090    PRINT
5100 NEXT STUDENT
5110 RETURN
RUN
```

```
Wayne Ferguson
 85   74   89   82
Debbie Smith
 76   64   67   79
Sharon Palmer
 89   93   98   86
```

Line 5030 reads a student's name from the data file, line 5040 prints the name. Inside the inner loop, line 5060 reads a student's score, line 5070 prints the score. The trailing semicolon in line 5070 causes the print element to stay on the same output line but to move to the next print position. Thus, the next score will be printed on the same line. After the inner loop is complete, the four scores will be printed on one output line.

The PRINT statement in line 5090 does not print a blank line. Instead, it causes the print element to drop down to the next line where the next student's name will be printed. Since the PRINT statement that prints a student's name (line 5040) does not end with a semicolon, only the name is printed on the output line.

Finding a Total

Suppose we wish to calculate and print the average score for each student. Before finding the average, we must accumulate the scores for each student. Here is a subroutine that performs these operations.

```
5010 PRINT
5020 FOR STUDENT = 1 TO 3
5030   INPUT #1, SNAME$
5040   PRINT SNAME$
5050   TOTAL.SCORE = 0
5060   FOR TEST = 1 TO 4
5070     INPUT #1, SCORE
5080     TOTAL.SCORE = TOTAL.SCORE+SCORE
5090     PRINT SCORE;
5100   NEXT TEST
5110   AVERAGE = TOTAL.SCORE/4
5120   PRINT "  Average:";AVERAGE
5130   PRINT
5140 NEXT STUDENT
5150 RETURN
RUN
```

```
Wayne Ferguson
 85  74  89  82   Average: 82.5

Debbie Smith
 76  64  67  79   Average: 71.5

Sharon Palmer
 89  93  98  86   Average: 91.5
```

TOTAL.SCORE is our accumulator. In line 5050, we set TOTAL.SCORE to zero. The student's scores are accumulated in the inner loop. This total is then used in line 5110 to find an average. It is particularly important that TOTAL.SCORE be set to zero between the two FOR statements. After the inner loop is complete and control transfers back to the beginning of the outer loop to read another student's name, the accumulator must be reset to zero. Coding the statement between the two FOR statements resets the accumulator just before BASIC enters the inner loop to read and accumulate the scores for the next student.

The average is calculated and printed immediately after the inner loop has totaled a student's scores but before control transfers back to the beginning of the structure to process the data for the next student. Since a semicolon trails the PRINT statement in line 5090, the average will be printed on the same output line as the scores.

Exercises

1. Identify the errors, if any, in the program segments shown below.

(a)
```
5010 FOR I = 5 TO 14 STEP 3
5020   FOR J = 4 TO 1 STEP 1
5030     PRINT J;
5040   NEXT J
5050 NEXT I
```

(b)
```
5010 FOR I = 1 TO 16
5020   FOR J = 1 TO I
5030     K = J+I
5040     PRINT K;
5050   NEXT J
5060   PRINT
5070 NEXT I
```

(c)
```
5010 FOR I = 3 TO 12 STEP 3
5020   FOR J = 5 TO 20 STEP 5
5030     PRINT J;
5040   NEXT J
5050   PRINT
5060   FOR K = 1 TO 6
5070     PRINT K;
5080   NEXT K
5090 NEXT I
```

(d)
```
5010 FOR I = 3 TO 7 STEP 2
5020   FOR J = 1 TO 4
5030     PRINT J;
5040   NEXT I
5050 NEXT J
```

2. What will be the value of TOTAL.HOURS in the following program segment?

```
5010 TOTAL.HOURS = 0
5020 FOR EMPLOYEE = 1 TO 3
5030    READ ENAME$
5040    FOR DAY = 1 TO 5
5050       READ HOURS
5060       TOTAL.HOURS = TOTAL.HOURS+HOURS
5070    NEXT DAY
5080    PRINT TOTAL.HOURS
5090 NEXT EMPLOYEE
5100 DATA "Brown"  ,8,8,7,7,8
5110 DATA "Davis"  ,7,8,8,7,7
5120 DATA "Jansen",8,7,7,8,8
```

Modify the above program segment so that it prints the total hours for each employee.

3. What is the output of each of the following programs?

(a)
```
5010 FOR I = 1 TO 3
5020    PRINT
5030    PRINT "I =";I
5040    FOR J = 1 TO 6 STEP 2
5050       PRINT "J =";J,
5060    NEXT J
5070    PRINT
5080 NEXT I
5090 END
```

(b)
```
5010 PRINT
5020 N = 12
5030 FOR I = N TO 1 STEP -1
5040    FOR J = 1 TO I STEP 1
5050       PRINT "*";
5060    NEXT J
5070    PRINT
5080 NEXT I
5090 END
```

10.5 General Rules that Apply to FOR/NEXT Loops

1. To maintain structured programming, each FOR/NEXT loop must have a single entry point and a single exit point.
2. The control variable must be numeric. In addition to serving as a counter, the control variable may be used inside the loop as data. Thus, a FOR/NEXT loop can generate data. However, the value of the control variable should not be changed within the loop as this change interferes with its automatic increments.
3. There may be any number of statements inside the loop, including none. A FOR/NEXT loop such as

```
5020 FOR I = 1 TO 500
5030 NEXT I
```

is often used to delay processing or to allow messages and instructions to remain on the screen long enough so that the material can be read.

4. If the step value is omitted, BASIC assumes the value to be 1.
5. When the step value is positive, the loop continues until the value of the control variable exceeds the test value. When the step value is negative, the loop continues until the value of the control variable is less than the test value.
6. No transfer must be made to a statement within a FOR/NEXT loop from a point outside the loop. The loop can be entered only by means of the FOR statement.
7. No transfer should be made out of a FOR/NEXT loop before the loop is complete as this violates the single entry, single exit rule of structured programming. A FOR/NEXT loop is used normally as a counting loop. To transfer out of a loop based on a certain condition, a WHILE/WEND loop should be used.
8. A program may contain several levels of loops.

```
┌─FOR I = 1 TO 3
│     —
│ ┌─FOR J = 1 TO 4
│ │     —
```

(continued on page 246)

```
        FOR K = 1 TO 8
          —
        NEXT K
          —
    NEXT J
      —
NEXT I
```

9. A program may contain several inner loops nested inside one outer loop.

```
FOR I = 1 TO 4
  —
  FOR J = 1 TO 5
    —
  NEXT J
  —
  FOR K = 1 TO 3
    —
  NEXT K
  —
NEXT I
```

10. A loop may not cross over (overlap) another loop.

Permitted

```
FOR I = 1 TO 4
  —
  FOR J = 1 TO 6
    —
    FOR K = 1 TO 3
      —
    NEXT K
    —
  NEXT J
  —
NEXT I
```

Not permitted

```
FOR I = 1 TO 4
  —
  FOR J = 1 TO 6
    —
    FOR K = 1 TO 3
      —
    NEXT J
    —
  NEXT K
  —
NEXT I
```

10.6 The RESTORE Statement

In Chapter Four, we learned that data items entered into the computer by the READ and DATA statements are placed in a data pool, then assigned to the variables listed in the READ statement. A pointer keeps track of the items in the data pool. After all the items have been assigned to variables, the pointer is positioned immediately after the last item in the data pool.

Suppose a subroutine, called from a main routine, enters data into the computer by the READ and DATA statements. If a user wishes to produce more than one report or table, the data items must be reread for each output. Recall that our programs can now process modules as often as a user desires.

A problem arises when a READ statement must be re-executed. Since the data pointer is now positioned after the last item in the data pool, any attempt to reread the items will cause an out of data error. We can solve this problem by using a RESTORE statement. RESTORE sets the pointer back to the beginning of the data pool making it possible for items to be reread. Here is a sample subroutine that uses this technique.

```
5000 'SUBROUTINE READ DATA
5010   FOR R = 1 TO 4
5020     READ RATE
5030     COMMISSION = SALES*RATE/100
5040     PRINT USING F$; SALES,COMMISSION
5050   NEXT R
5060   RESTORE
5070   DATA 12,15,18,20
5080   RETURN
```

After the FOR/NEXT loop reads the four data items, the RESTORE statement in line 5060 sets the data pointer back to the first item in the data pool. When the subroutine is called again, the FOR/NEXT loop rereads the four data items. Again, the RESTORE statement resets the data pointer to the beginning of the pool. It should be noted that the data pointer can be moved to the beginning of the data pool regardless of its position at the time of the RESTORE.

Exercises

What output will each of the following programs produce?

(a)

```
5010 READ A,B
5020 PRINT
5030 PRINT "A =";A,"B =";B
5040 READ P,Q,R
5050 PRINT "P =";P,"Q =";Q,"R =";R
5060 DATA 3,6,9,12,15
5070 END
```

(b)

```
5010 READ A,B
5020 PRINT
5030 PRINT "A =";A,"B =";B
5040 RESTORE
5050 READ P,Q,R
5060 PRINT "P =";P,"Q =";Q,"R =";R
5070 DATA 3,6,9,12,15
5080 END
```

10.7 Program Design

A manufacturer of windows and doors would like a table showing the production costs of two types of doors: cedar doors and steel doors. The cost of each door depends on the following factors:

1. The width of the door. The width varies from 28 inches to 36 inches. To keep the table reasonably short, our program will increase each width by two inches.
2. The cost of the material based on the cost per square inch. The doors are coded 1 for cedar and 2 for steel. To find the cost per square inch, the manufacturer uses the following formula: Code × .05 + .02.
3. The height of the door. The height of each door is 78 inches.
4. The labor. The hourly wage is $9.45 per hour, the number of hours to produce a door varies. The number of hours will be keyed in by the user.

DOORS.DAT
9.45 — Rate of pay
78,28,36 — Height, minimum width, maximum width

Rough Layout of the Output:

```
                                                        (cleared screen)
                 Number of hours to produce a door? [4]

Are the hours correct (y/n)? [y]

                                                        (cleared screen)
             COSTS FOR PRODUCING CEDAR AND STEEL DOORS
             ===========================
             WIDTH                  COST
             ===========================
                   CEDAR DOORS
             28                  $190.68
             30                  $201.60
             32                  $212.52
             34                  $223.44
             36                  $234.36
                   STEEL DOORS
             28                  $299.88
             30                  $318.60
             32                  $337.32
             34                  $356.04
             36                  $374.76

Do you wish to produce another table (y/n)?
```

FIGURE 10-3 LAYOUT CHART

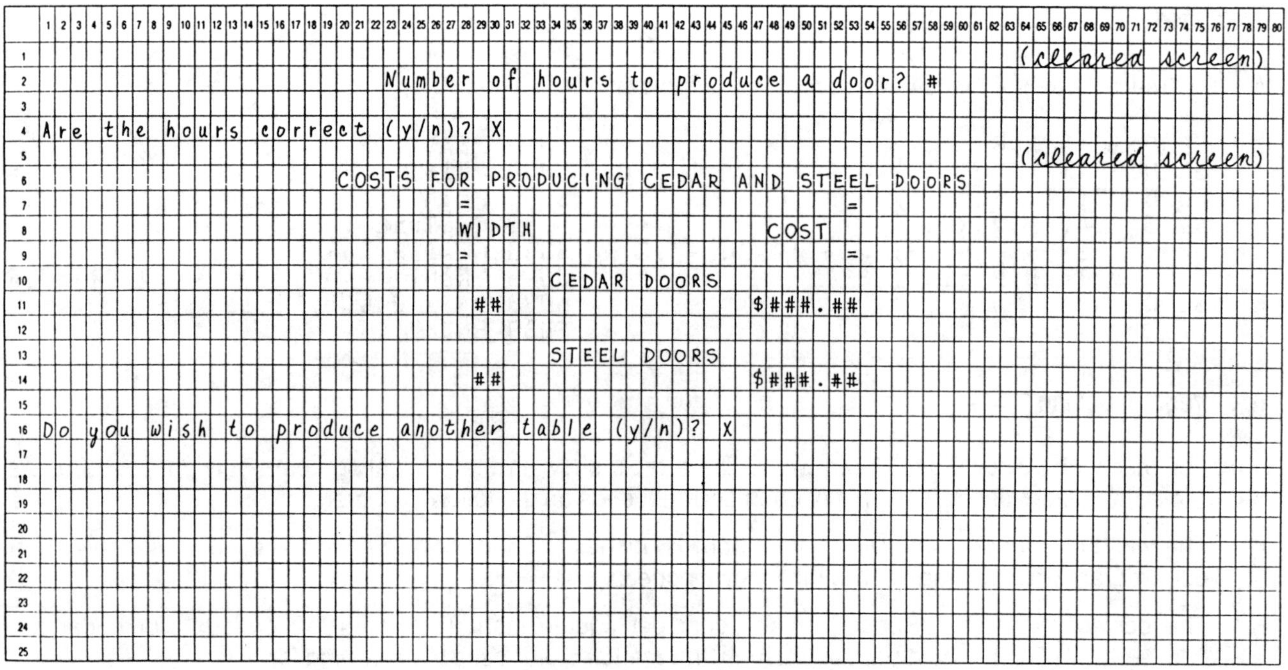

FIGURE 10-4 STRUCTURE CHART

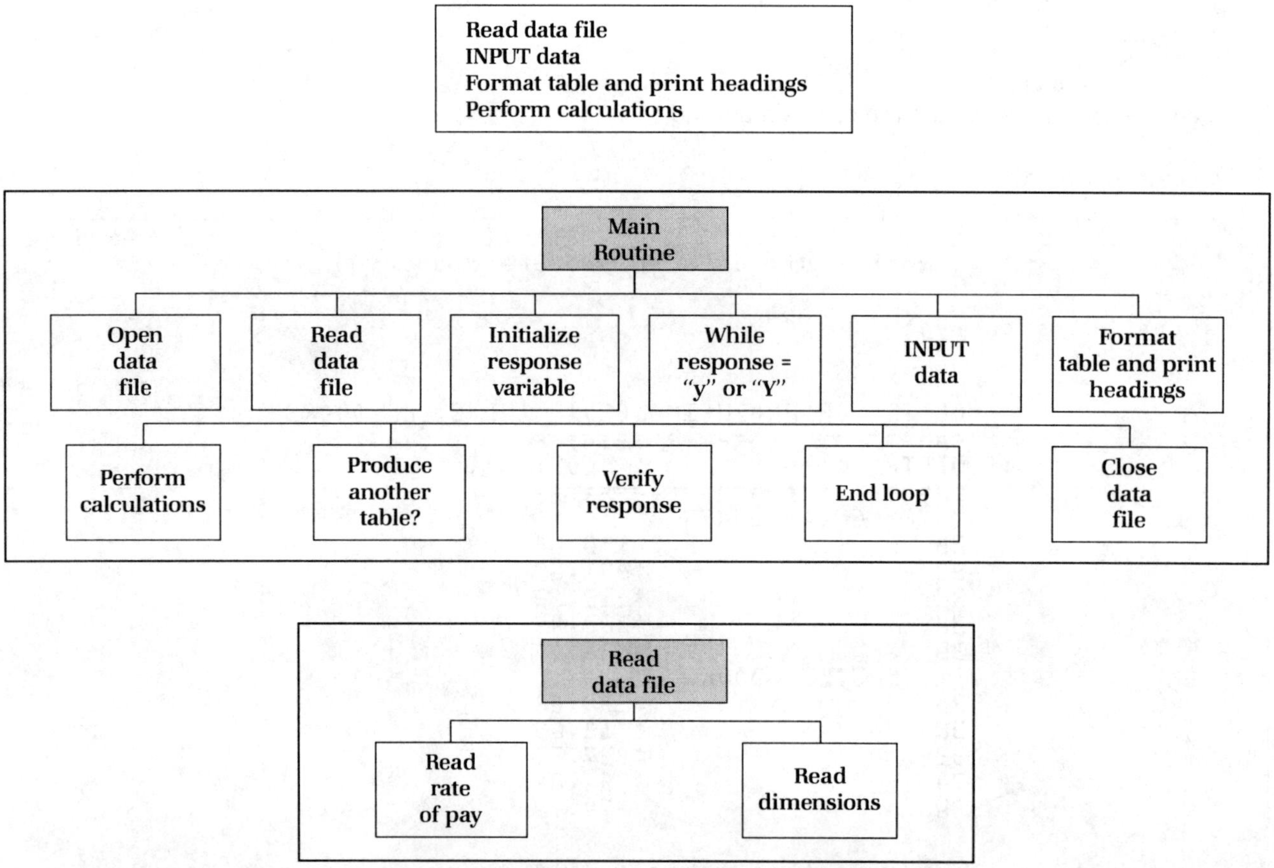

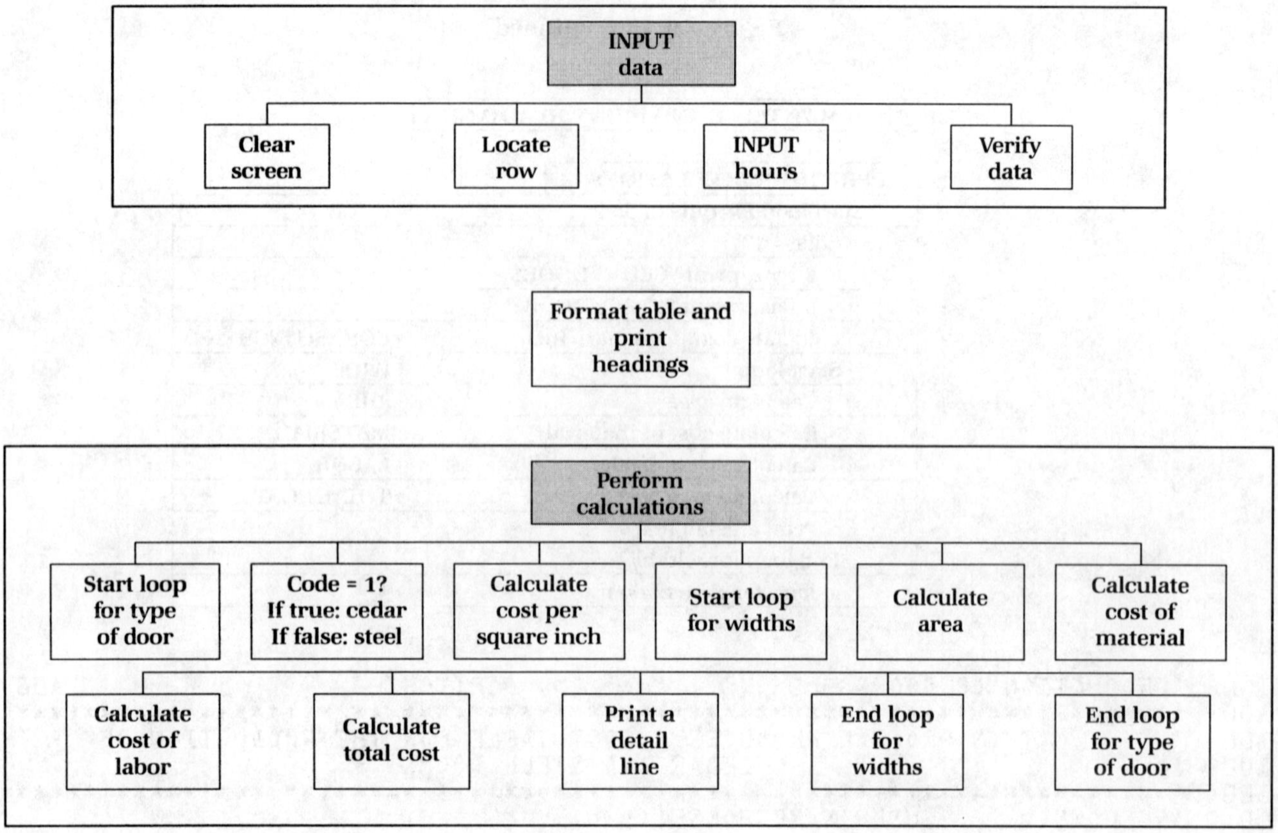

FIGURE 10-5 PSEUDOCODE

MAJOR TASKS
Read data file
INPUT data
Format table and print headings
Perform calculations

MAIN ROUTINE	
Open data file	
Read data file	(subroutine)
Initialize "response" variable	RESPONSE$
While response is "y" or "Y"	
INPUT data	(subroutine)
Format table and print headings	(subroutine)
Perform calculations	(subroutine)
Produce another table?	
Verify response	
End loop	
Close data file	

READ DATA FILE	
Read rate of pay	RATE
Read dimensions	HEIGHT,MINIMUM,MAXIMUM

INPUT DATA	
Clear screen	
Locate row	
INPUT hours	HOURS
Verify data	

Figure 10-5 Continued

FORMAT TABLE AND PRINT HEADINGS	

PERFORM CALCULATIONS	
Start loop for type of door	CODE
Code = 1?	
If true, print "CEDAR DOORS"	
If false, print "STEEL DOORS"	
Calculate cost per square inch	COST.SQ.INCH
Start loop for widths	WIDE
Calculate area	AREA
Calculate cost of material	MATERIAL
Calculate cost of labor	LABOR
Calculate total cost	TOTAL.COST
Print a detail line	
End loop for widths	
End loop for type of door	

```
1000 'PRODUCTION OF DOORS                M. MCRITCHIE                  AUG 12
1002 '****************************************************************************
1004 '         THIS PROGRAM PRODUCES A COST TABLE FOR THE PRODUCTION OF
1006 '                         CEDAR AND STEEL DOORS
1008 '****************************************************************************
1010 'RESPONSE$     - USER'S RESPONSE (y/n)
1020 'RATE          - RATE OF PAY
1030 'HEIGHT        - HEIGHT OF A DOOR
1040 'MINIMUM       - MINIMUM WIDTH
1050 'MAXIMUM       - MAXIMUM WIDTH
1060 'HOURS         - NUMBER OF HOURS TO PRODUCE ONE DOOR
1070 'S$            - EQUAL SIGNS
1080 'F$            - IMAGE OF A DETAIL LINE
1090 'CODE          - TYPE OF DOOR. CONTROL VARIABLE FOR OUTER LOOP.
1100 'COST.SQ.INCH  - COST OF MATERIAL PER SQUARE INCH
1110 'WIDE          - WIDTH OF A DOOR. CONTROL VARIABLE FOR INNER LOOP.
1120 'AREA          - AREA
1130 'MATERIAL      - COST OF MATERIAL
1140 'LABOR         - COST OF LABOR
1150 'TOTAL.COST    - COST OF MATERIAL AND LABOR
2000 '****************************************************************************
2002 '                            MAIN ROUTINE
2004 '****************************************************************************
2010  OPEN "B:DOORS.DAT" FOR INPUT AS #1
2020  GOSUB 3000                    'Read data file
2030  RESPONSE$ = "y"
2040  WHILE RESPONSE$ = "y" OR RESPONSE$ = "Y"
2050    GOSUB 4000                  'INPUT data
2060    GOSUB 5000                  'Format table and print headings
2070    GOSUB 6000                  'Perform calculations
2080    PRINT
2090    INPUT "Do you wish to produce another table (y/n)";RESPONSE$
2100    IF RESPONSE$ <> "y" AND RESPONSE$ <> "Y" AND RESPONSE$ <> "n" AND
          RESPONSE$ <> "N" THEN PRINT "Invalid response. Enter y or n." :
          GOTO 2090
2110  WEND
2120  CLOSE #1
2130  END
```

```
3000 '************************************************************************
3002 '                             READ DATA FILE
3004 '************************************************************************
3010  INPUT #1, RATE
3020  INPUT #1, HEIGHT,MINIMUM,MAXIMUM
3030  RETURN
4000 '************************************************************************
4002 '                           INPUT DATA (HOURS)
4004 '************************************************************************
4010  CLS
4020  LOCATE 10
4030  INPUT "______________________Number of hours to produce a door";HOURS
4040  PRINT
4050  INPUT "Are the hours correct (y/n)";RESPONSE$
4060  IF RESPONSE$ <> "y" AND RESPONSE$ <> "Y"
         THEN INPUT "Re-enter the hours--",HOURS : GOTO 4050
4070  RETURN
5000 '************************************************************************
5002 '                    FORMAT TABLE AND PRINT HEADINGS
5004 '************************************************************************
5010  CLS
5020  LOCATE 4
5030  S$ = STRING$(26,"=")
5040  F$ = "____________________________##_______________$###.##"
5050  PRINT TAB(20) "COSTS FOR PRODUCING CEDAR AND STEEL DOORS"
5060  PRINT TAB(28) S$
5070  PRINT TAB(28) "WIDTH"; TAB(48) "COST"
5080  PRINT TAB(28) S$
5090  RETURN
6000 '************************************************************************
6002 '                          PERFORM CALCULATIONS
6004 '************************************************************************
6010  FOR CODE = 1 TO 2
6020    IF CODE = 1
           THEN PRINT TAB(34) "CEDAR DOORS"
           ELSE PRINT TAB(34) "STEEL DOORS"
6030    COST.SQ.INCH = CODE*.05+.02
6040    FOR WIDE = MINIMUM TO MAXIMUM STEP 2
6050      AREA = HEIGHT*WIDE
6060      MATERIAL = AREA*COST.SQ.INCH
6070      LABOR = HOURS*RATE
6080      TOTAL.COST = MATERIAL+LABOR
6090      PRINT USING F$; WIDE,TOTAL.COST
6100    NEXT WIDE
6110  NEXT CODE
6120  RETURN
65529 'End of program listing
```

(cleared screen)

```
         10        20        30        40        50        60        70        80
12345678901234567890123456789012345678901234567890123456789012345678901234567890
                    Number of hours to produce a door? [4]

Are the hours correct (y/n)? [y]
```

(cleared screen)

```
                 COSTS FOR PRODUCING CEDAR AND STEEL DOORS
                      ==========================
                      WIDTH                COST
                      ==========================
                            CEDAR DOORS
                       28                 $190.68
                       30                 $201.60
                       32                 $212.52
                       34                 $223.44
                       36                 $234.36
                            STEEL DOORS
                       28                 $299.88
                       30                 $318.60
                       32                 $337.32
                       34                 $356.04
                       36                 $374.76

Do you wish to produce another table (y/n)?
```

Summary of BASIC Statements

FOR — Used with a NEXT statement to execute a sequence of statements a specific number of times. Contains a control variable, an initial value, a test value and a step value.

```
5010 FOR EMPLOYEE = 1 TO 15 STEP 1
```

NEXT — Marks the end of a FOR/NEXT loop. Increases or decreases the control variable in the FOR by the amount specified by the step value then transfers control to the statement following the FOR.

```
5080 NEXT EMPLOYEE
```

RESTORE — Resets the data pointer in the data pool.

```
5090 RESTORE
```

Chapter Summary

1. A program can be processed as often as desired by having, inside a WHILE/WEND loop, GOSUB statements that call the required modules. The modules are re-executed when a user responds with a "y" or a "Y" to an INPUT statement within the WHILE/WEND loop or when the user presses any key (except perhaps a "q" for "quit") in response to a statement in Subroutine FREEZE DISPLAY.
2. Two statements create and control a FOR/NEXT loop; the FOR statement and the NEXT statement.
3. The FOR statement contains a control variable, an initial value, a test value, and a step value. The control variable acts as a counter, the initial value is the first value assigned to the control variable, the test value sets a limit to the control variable, and the step value is the amount by which the control variable is increased or decreased.
4. If the step value is omitted, BASIC assumes the value to be 1.
5. When the step value is positive, the loop continues until the value of the control variable exceeds the test value. When the step value is negative, the loop continues until the value of the control variable is less than the test value.
6. When the loop is complete, control drops down to the statement following the NEXT statement.
7. The initial value, test value, and step value may be represented by numeric constants, numeric variables, or numeric expressions.
8. The control variable must be numeric. In addition to serving as a counter, the control variable may be used inside the loop. However, its value should not be changed inside the loop.
9. There may be any number of statements inside a FOR/NEXT loop including none.
10. No transfer must be made to a statement within a FOR/NEXT loop from a point outside the loop. Furthermore, no transfer should be made out of a FOR/NEXT loop before the loop is complete. In other words, a FOR/NEXT loop must have a single entry point and a single exit point.
11. When one loop is placed inside another, the loops are said to be nested.
12. Each time BASIC executes the outer loop, the control variable of the inner loop is reset to its initial value.
13. When an accumulator must find a total inside an inner loop for each execution of the outer loop, the accumulator must be reset to zero between the FOR statements of the two loops.
14. A program may contain several levels of loops.
15. A program may contain several inner loops nested inside one outer loop.
16. A loop may not cross over (overlap) another loop.
17. Generally, a FOR/NEXT loop structure should be used when the loop must be executed a specific number of times. The WHILE/WEND loop structure should be used when the loop must be executed as long as a certain condition is met.
18. A RESTORE statement is used when a READ statement must read items from a data pool more than once.

Questions and Exercises

1. In the statement

```
2100 IF RESPONSE$ <> "y" AND RESPONSE$ <> "Y" AND RESPONSE$ <> "n" AND
        RESPONSE$ <> "N" THEN PRINT "Invalid response. Enter y or n." :
        GOTO 2090
```

why must the logical operator be AND and not OR?

2. Why is a FOR/NEXT loop called a counting loop?
3. Briefly state the purpose of each of the four parts of a FOR statement.
4. What is the purpose of the NEXT statement?
5. State the errors, if any, in the following FOR statements. Make the necessary corrections.

(a) `5010 FOR I = -3 TO 0 STEP -1`
(b) `5010 FOR J = -5 TO -25 STEP -3`
(c) `5010 FOR M/2 = 10 TO 50 STEP 10`
(d) `5010 FOR K = -30 TO 0`

6. Determine the outputs from the following program segments.

(a)
```
5010 FOR I = 1 TO 4
5020    PRINT I;
5030 NEXT I
5040 PRINT
5050 PRINT I
```
(b)
```
5010 TOTAL = 0
5020 FOR I = 10 TO 2 STEP -2
5030    TOTAL = TOTAL+I
5040    PRINT TOTAL;
5050 NEXT I
```
(c)
```
5010 TOTAL = 0
5020 FOR I = 1 TO 4
5030    FOR J = 1 TO 3
5040       TOTAL = TOTAL+J
5050       PRINT TOTAL;
5060    NEXT J
5070 NEXT I
```
(d)
```
5010 FOR I = 1 TO 4
5020    TOTAL = 0
5030    FOR J = 1 TO 3
5040       TOTAL = TOTAL+J
5050       PRINT TOTAL;
5060    NEXT J
5070 NEXT I
```

7. How many times will the loop be performed for each of the following FOR statements?

(a) `5010 FOR A = 0 TO 19 STEP 3`
(b) `5010 FOR A = 6 TO -2 STEP -2`
(c) `5010 FOR A = 0.5 TO 2.0 STEP 0.5`
(d) `5010 FOR A = -9 TO 9 STEP 4`

8. Identify the errors, if any, in the program segments shown below. Make the necessary corrections.

(a)
```
5010 FOR I = 1 TO 10
5020    FOR J = 2 TO 16 STEP 2
5030       K = I*J
5040       IF K > 20 THEN PRINT K; :
           GO TO 5060
5050    NEXT J
5060 NEXT I
```
(b)
```
5010 FOR J = 5 TO 14 STEP 3
5020    FOR K = J TO 20 STEP 1
5030       PRINT K;
5040    NEXT K
5050 NEXT J
```
(c)
```
5010 FOR I = 1 TO 3
5020    FOR J = 1 TO 4
5030       K = I+J
5040       J = 1
5050       PRINT K;
5060    NEXT J
5070 NEXT I
```
(d)
```
5010 FOR I = 0 TO -16 STEP 4
5020    FOR J = 10 TO 40 STEP 4
5030       PRINT J;
5040    NEXT J
5050 NEXT I
```

9. What is meant by a nested FOR/NEXT loop?
10. What is the output of each of the following programs?

(a)
```
5010 FOR I = 1 TO 2
5020    FOR J = 1 TO 3
5030       FOR K = 1 TO 4
5040          RESULT = I+J+K
5050          PRINT RESULT;
5060          NEXT K
5070    NEXT J
5080 NEXT I
5090 END
```
(b)
```
5010 PRINT
5020 N = 1
5030 FOR I = N TO 12
5040    FOR J = N TO I
5050       PRINT "*";
5060    NEXT J
5070    PRINT
5080 NEXT I
5090 END
```

Programming Problems

Write programs for the following problems. Other than the program for Problem 5, each program must allow a user to produce results as many times as desired. Centre all output as explained in Chapter Eight. In the programs for problems 1 and 7, verify data by the screenful.

1. A retailer, purchasing additional items of a line of goods, already knows the price at which the goods will be sold. What must be determined is the maximum purchase price the retailer can afford to pay in order to cover expenses and realize a profit. Suppose the retailer wishes to mark up the items by 40% based on the cost price. To produce a markup table, all the retailer must do is key in the rate of markup and the lowest and highest retail prices of a desired range.

   Generate the retail prices in a FOR/NEXT loop. Use the variables to which the lowest and highest retail prices have been assigned as the initial and test values in your FOR statement. Your program must be able to accept a price range of $1.00 to $999.99. Your control variable must be a retail price.

   Formulas:

   $$\text{Cost Price} = \frac{\text{Retail Price}}{(100 + \text{Rate of Markup})/100}$$

   Markup = Retail Price − Cost Price

```
                                                              (cleared screen)
                     Rate of markup? [40]

  Lowest retail price, highest price ($1.00 to $999.99)? [600.00,605.00]

 The rate of markup is 40%
 Is the rate correct (y/n)? [y]

 The lowest and highest retail prices are $600.00 and $605.00
 Are the prices correct (y/n)? [y]
                                                              (cleared screen)
            MARKUP TABLE

            Rate: 40%
            ========================================
            RETAIL PRICE      MARKUP      COST PRICE
            ========================================
            $600.00           $171.43     $428.57
            $601.00           $171.71     $429.29
            $602.00           $172.00     $430.00
            $603.00           $172.29     $430.71
            $604.00           $172.57     $431.43
            $605.00           $172.86     $432.14
 Do you wish to produce another table (y/n)?
```

2. Write a program that finds the value of a sample basket of goods if each year in the past five years inflation has increased its value. Allow the user to key in a base value of his/her choice (maximum of $500). Your program must produce an inflation table and a summary as shown in the rough layout.

   Following the INPUT statement that enters the base value, copy the value into another variable. This latter variable will be used to calculate the current value of the basket of goods for each of the five years. The value keyed in will be used to calculate the total amount of increase.

   Use the following rates of inflation to calculate the amount of inflation and the increased value for each of the five years:

   6.8%, 6.3%, 6.1%, 5.7%, 5.4%

To find an amount of inflation, multiply the current value by the appropriate rate. To find the new value, add the amount of inflation to the current value. Note that this is similar to an accumulator. The amount of inflation for the first year based on $500 would be $500 × 6.8 ÷ 100 = $34.00. The current value is now $500 + $34.00 = $534.00. The amount of inflation for the second year would be $534.00 × 6.3 ÷ 100 = $33.64. The current value is now $534.00 + $33.64 = $567.64. Find the values for the remaining years in a similar manner. Use the following formulas.

Formulas:

Amount of Inflation = Current Value × Rate of Inflation/100
Current Value = Current Value + Amount of Inflation

In a separate subroutine, enter the rates of inflation by means of the READ and DATA statements, calculate the amount of inflation and the current value, then print a detail line. Read, calculate, and print within a FOR/NEXT loop. Remember to code a RESTORE statement following the loop. The RESTORE is needed in case a user wishes to produce more than one table. Subroutine PRODUCE SUMMARY must find the increase and the rate of increase over the five years.

Formulas:

Increase = Current Value − Base Value

$$\text{Rate of Increase} = \frac{\text{Increase}}{\text{Base Value}} \times 100$$

```
                                                              (cleared screen)
     Base value of basket of goods (0.00 to 500.00)? [500]

Is the base value correct (y/n)? [y]

                                                              (cleared screen)
                INFLATION TABLE

                Based on $500.00
                =================================
                RATE        INFLATION      VALUE
                =================================
                6.8% ...... $34.00 ...... $534.00
                6.3% ...... $33.64 ...... $567.64
                6.1% ...... $34.63 ...... $602.27
                5.7% ...... $34.33 ...... $636.60
                5.4% ...... $34.38 ...... $670.97

                Increase                  $170.97
                Rate of increase           34.19%

Do you wish to produce another table (y/n)?
```

3. A new piece of equipment has just been installed in the repair shop of a garage. The life expectancy of the equipment is ten years. The owner of the garage would like to compare two methods of depreciation: straight line and fixed rate. Write a program that lists the amount of depreciation and the value of the equipment for each method for each of the ten years. The rate of depreciation for the fixed rate method is 25%.

Store the number of years and the fixed rate in a data file. Suggested filename: DEPREC.DAT. Before the WHILE/WEND loop begins in the main routine, call a subroutine to read the data file. In Subroutine INPUT DATA, allow the user to key in an original value. This original value will be the initial value for both the straight line method and the fixed rate method. Thus, you must copy the value into another variable. Perform the following tasks in Subroutine PERFORM CALCULATIONS using the formulas given.

(a) Find the straight line depreciation. This will be a fixed amount for each year.

Straight Line Depreciation = Straight Line Value/Number of Years

(b) In a FOR/NEXT loop, find the following and print a detail line.
— The straight line value.
— The fixed rate depreciation.
— The fixed rate value.

Straight Line Value = Straight Line Value − Straight Line Depreciation
Fixed Rate Depreciation = Fixed Rate Value × Rate/100
Fixed Rate Value = Fixed Rate Value − Fixed Rate Depreciation

```
                                                              (cleared screen)
                      Original value? [4000]

Is the original value correct (y/n)? [y]
                                                              (cleared screen)
          DEPRECIATION TABLE

          Original value: $4,000.00
          ===================================================
          STRAIGHT        STRAIGHT        FIXED           FIXED
          LINE DEPR.      LINE VALUE      RATE DEPR.      RATE VALUE
          ===================================================
          $400.00         $3,600.00       $1,000.00       $3,000.00
          $400.00         $3,200.00       $   750.00      $2,250.00
          $400.00         $2,800.00       $   562.50      $1,687.50
          $400.00         $2,400.00       $   421.88      $1,265.63
          $400.00         $2,000.00       $   316.41      $   949.22
          $400.00         $1,600.00       $   237.30      $   711.91
          $400.00         $1,200.00       $   177.98      $   533.94
          $400.00         $   800.00      $   133.48      $   400.45
          $400.00         $   400.00      $   100.11      $   300.34
          $400.00         $     0.00      $    75.08      $   225.25

Do you wish to produce another table (y/n)?
```

4. Amortization of a loan refers to the gradual reduction of the loan by regular payments that wipe out the debt in a specific period of time. A portion of each payment is applied to the interest and a portion is applied to the outstanding principal.

Suppose you wish to apply for a 20-year, $60,000 mortgage to purchase a new home. The current interest rate is 9 3/4%. Your monthly payment is $569.11. Write a program that allows you to INPUT the principal, the monthly payment, and the rate of interest. For each month of the first year, calculate the portion of the payment applied to the monthly interest, the portion applied to the principal, and the outstanding principal. Find the total amount of interest paid and the total amount applied to the principal for the twelve months. Perform all calculations and accumulations in Subroutine PERFORM CALCULATIONS. Hint: Initialize your accumulators to zero before the FOR/NEXT loop so that the totals from one table are not accumulated with the totals of the next table when more than one table is produced.

Produce a summary that displays the totals. Note: If you allow the program to process the calculations for the entire 20 years, the last amount applied to the principal and the totals will be out by a few cents due to rounding off errors. Ignore these minor errors.

Formulas:

$$\text{Interest} = \text{Principal} \times \frac{\text{Rate}}{(100 \times 12)}$$

Amount Applied to Principal = Payment − Interest
Principal = Principal − Amount Applied to Principal

```
                                                                    (cleared screen)
     Principal, monthly payment, interest rate? [60000,569.11,9.75]

Are the entries correct (y/n)? [y]

                                                                    (cleared screen)
          AMORTIZATION TABLE

          Principal        $60,000.00
          Monthly Payment  $569.11
          Interest Rate    9.75%
          ================================================
                                PAYMENT ON
          MONTH     INTEREST    PRINCIPAL       PRINCIPAL
          ================================================
          1         $487.50     $ 81.61         $59,918.39
          2         $486.84     $ 82.27         $59,836.12
          3         $486.17     $ 82.94         $59,753.18
          4         $485.49     $ 83.62         $59,669.56
          5         $484.82     $ 84.29         $59,585.27
          6         $484.13     $ 84.98         $59,500.29
          7         $483.44     $ 85.67         $59,414.62
          8         $482.74     $ 86.37         $59,328.25
          9         $482.04     $ 87.07         $59,241.18
          10        $481.33     $ 87.78         $59,153.41
          11        $480.62     $ 88.49         $59,064.92
          12        $479.90     $ 89.21         $58,975.71

          Interest paid the first year                      $ 5,805.03
          Amount paid on the principal the first year       $ 1,024.29

Do you wish to produce another table (y/n)?
```

5. At the end of every fourth week, a department store prepares a sales report similar to the one shown below. Assume there are three departments (in reality there are many more) and that the weekly sales amounts for each department are stored on disk under the filename STORSALE.DAT. Allow the user of your program to key in the date. Your program must find each department's total sales and find the total sales for the store. There is no need to produce more than one report since the data remains the same.

Use nested FOR/NEXT loops in the subroutine that reads the data file, accumulates the weekly sales of each department, finds the total sales for the store, and prints the detail lines. The outer loop keeps track of the departments, the inner loop keeps track of the weeks. To obtain the store's total sales, accumulate the total sales of the departments between the two NEXT statements. Refer to the program on page 244 if you need any help.

Use PRINT USING statements to print the report. You will need three images. One image edits a department name, another edits its weekly sales, and the third edits a department's total sales. Examples of images are given below.

```
4040 F1$ = "\_____________\" — Department name
4050 F2$ = "___$#####,.##"   — Department's weekly sales
4060 F3$ = "____$#####,.##"  — Department's total sales
```

Do not centre the entire report, however, centre the headings over the body of the report. As a summary, print the store's total sales.

STORSALE.DAT
Housewares — Department name
5423.18,4982.17,5125.42,5319.31
Furnishings
9436.15,10245.89,10467.21,10893.58 — Weekly sales
Appliances
12539.28,12984.98,13085.26,13562.67

```
                                                                  (cleared screen)
                 Enter month, day and year (e.g. September 30, 19XX)
                 Date? September 28, 19XX

Is the date correct (y/n)? y
                                                                  (cleared screen)
                              SALES REPORT

                 For the Four Weeks Ending September 28, 19XX
==========================================================================
                             SALES                         TOTAL DEPT. SALES
==========================================================================
Housewares
  $ 5,423.18    $ 4,982.17    $ 5,125.42    $ 5,319.31       $20,850.08

Furnishings
  $ 9,436.15    $10,245.89    $10,467.21    $10,893.58       $41,042.83

Appliances
  $12,539.28    $12,984.98    $13,085.26    $13,562.67       $52,172.20

                    Total store sales      $114,065.10
```

6. Write a program that produces a multiplication table for any five consecutive numbers from 1 through 12, such as numbers 1 through 5 or numbers 8 through 12. Allow the user to key in the lowest and highest numbers in the range.
   In the subroutine that calculates and prints the products, use nested FOR/NEXT loops. Each FOR statement must use, as its initial and test values, the numbers keyed in by the user. Between the FOR statements, print the value of the outer control variable to produce the marginal numbers. In the inner loop, simply multiply the control variables of the two loops and print the product. To produce the output shown below, you need three images:
   (a) One image edits the row of numbers at the top of the table. The image should begin with a desired number of spaces, followed by five numeric edit fields appropriately spaced. Print the row of numbers in Subroutine FORMAT TABLE AND PRINT HEADINGS. In the PRINT USING statement, print the value of the lowest keyed-in number, the value of the lowest keyed-in number+1, the value of the lowest keyed-in number+2, etc. Print five values.
   (b) The second image places a number in the left margin of the table. Begin the image with an appropriate number of spaces, followed by one numeric edit field. As mentioned above, print the value of the outer loop's control variable to obtain these numbers. Place the PRINT USING statement between the FOR statements and remember to end the statement with a semicolon.
   (c) The third image edits the products in the table. The image should begin with several spaces, followed by one numeric edit field. Place the PRINT USING statement within the inner loop and end the statement with a semicolon. Remember to code a blank PRINT between the two NEXT statements in order to display the next five products on a new line.

```
                                                        (cleared screen)
            Lowest number, highest number? [8,12]

Are the numbers correct (y/n)? [y]
                                                        (cleared screen)
                       MULTIPLICATION TABLE

                          Numbers 8 to 12
               ====================================
                 8       9       10       11       12
               ====================================
      8         64      72       80       88       96
      9         72      81       90       99      108
     10         80      90      100      110      120
     11         88      99      110      121      132
     12         96     108      120      132      144

Do you wish to produce another table (y/n)?
```

7. Recall that interest calculated on a principal to which the interest of a previous period has been added is called compound interest. The final principal is called the compound amount. Write a program that produces a table of compound amounts based on a principal keyed in by the user. The program must calculate the compound amounts for each of four years using three consecutive interest rates, such as 8%, 9%, 10%. Allow the user to key in the minimum rate of interest and the maximum rate of interest, in addition to the principal. Your program should be similar to the program that produced the multiplication table in Problem 6.

Use nested FOR/NEXT loops in the subroutine that calculates the compound amounts and prints the detail lines. The outer loop keeps track of the years, the inner loop generates the interest rates. To display a year number, print the value of the outer loop's control variable between the FOR statements. Use the interest rates keyed in by the user as the initial value and test value in the FOR statement of the inner loop. Within this loop calculate and print a compound amount. Use the following formula.

$$\text{Compound Amount} = \text{Principal}(1+\text{Rate}/100)^{\text{Year}}$$

```
                                                        (cleared screen)
             Principal? [4000.00]

             Minimum rate, maximum rate? [8,10]

The principal is $4,000.00
Is the principal correct (y/n)? [y]

The minimum and maximum rates are  8% and 10%
Are the rates correct (y/n)? [y]
                                                        (cleared screen)
        COMPOUND INTEREST TABLE

        Principal: $ 4,000.00
        ==============================================
        YEAR     8%              9%               10%
        ==============================================
        1     $ 4,320.00     $ 4,360.00       $ 4,400.00
        2     $ 4,665.60     $ 4,752.40       $ 4,840.00
        3     $ 5,038.85     $ 5,180.12       $ 5,324.00
        4     $ 5,441.96     $ 5,646.33       $ 5,856.40

Do you wish to produce another table (y/n)?
```

Solutions for Exercises

10.1 The WHILE/WEND Loop

1. `5020 WHILE RESPONSE$ <> "true"`
2. `5030 WHILE CODE <= 7`
3. `5040 WHILE RESPONSE$ <> "yes" AND RESPONSE$ <> "YES"`
4. `5050 WHILE NUMBER > 100 OR NUMBER < 200`

10.2 The FOR/NEXT Loop

1. (a) Nothing is wrong.

   (b) The step value must be negative.

   ```
   5010 FOR I = 25 TO 5 STEP -5
   ```

   (c) The step value must be positive.

   ```
   5010 FOR I = 0.5 TO 4.5 STEP 0.5
   ```

   (d) Nothing is wrong.

   (e) The step value must be negative.

   ```
   5010 FOR I = Ø TO -42 STEP -7
   ```

2. (a) 35,38,41,44,47
   (b) 0.5,1.0,1.5,2.0,2.5,3.0
   (c) 14,12,10,8,6,4,2,Ø
   (d) −8,−5,−2,1,4,7
   (e) 7,13,19,25,31,37

3. (a) 6 (b) 4 (c) 4

4. (a)

   ```
   RUN
    2              6
    5             11
    8             19
   11             30
   ```

   (b)

   ```
   RUN
   36  16  4  Ø  4  16  36
   ```

10.4 Nested FOR/NEXT Loops

1. (a) The step value in line 5020 must be negative.

   ```
   5020 FOR J = 4 TO 1 STEP -1
   ```

   (b) Nothing is wrong.

   (c) Nothing is wrong.

   (d) NEXT I and NEXT J must be interchanged.

   ```
   5040 NEXT J
   5050 NEXT I
   ```

2. The value of TOTAL.HOURS will be 113.

   TOTAL.HOURS must be initialized to zero between the two FOR statements. Change the line number for TOTAL.HOURS = Ø to 5035, then delete line 5010.

   ```
   5035 TOTAL.HOURS = Ø
   ```

3. (a) RUN

```
I = 1
J = 1          J = 3          J = 5

I = 2
J = 1          J = 3          J = 5

I = 3
J = 1          J = 3          J = 5
```

(b) RUN

```
************
***********
**********
*********
********
*******
******
*****
****
***
**
*
```

10.6 The RESTORE Statement

1. RUN

```
A = 3          B = 6
P = 9          Q = 12         R = 15
```

2. RUN

```
A = 3          B = 6
P = 3          Q = 6          R = 9
```

11

STRINGS

Objectives

Our use of strings so far has been very limited. We have coded strings in PRINT, INPUT, and LINE INPUT statements to print messages and prompts, compared strings in IF statements, and used a string in a WHILE statement to control a WHILE/WEND loop. There is much more that can be done with strings. For instance, addresses can be broken up into parts then the parts used to print an address label. Typed material, called text, can be edited by replacing and deleting portions of the text and by inserting new material into the text. Numbers stored as part of a string can be extracted from the string, then used in arithmetic calculations.

In this chapter, you will learn many of the functions that process strings. You will use these functions in a number of applications, including the ones mentioned above.

Contents

11.1 Storing Information in the Computer

The ASCII Codes

Before we learn how strings can be manipulated, let us first find out how the computer stores information. Every character (digit, letter, or other symbol) is stored as a series of electronic impulses. Each electronic impulse is referred to as a **bit** (**b**inary dig**it**). Each bit is either on or off. On paper, we use the digit 1 to represent an "on" bit and the digit Ø to represent an "off" bit. The series of bits for each character is called a byte.

The coding system used in most microcomputers is ASCII (**A**merican **S**tandard **C**ode for **I**nformation **I**nterchange). An ASCII code consists of seven binary digits. The binary numbers range from ØØØØØØØ to 1111111 creating a total of 128 codes whose decimal equivalents are Ø to 127 inclusive. The binary numbering system assigns a place value to each of the bits, based on the power of 2. These place values are 1, 2, 4, 8, 16, 32, and 64 moving from right to left on the binary number. The two examples below illustrate how the ASCII bit combination for the number 1 has a decimal code of 49 and how the ASCII bit combination for the letter A has a decimal code of 65. Each "1" digit signifies that a circuit is on. Adding the place values for all the "1" digits gives the decimal code for the character.

The number 1:

Ø	1	1	Ø	Ø	Ø	1	ASCII bit combination
64	**32**	**16**	8	4	2	**1**	32 + 16 + 1 = 49 (decimal code)

The letter A:

1	Ø	Ø	Ø	Ø	Ø	1	ASCII bit combination
64	32	16	8	4	2	**1**	64 + 1 = 65 (decimal code)

The following table lists some of the ASCII codes in decimal notation along with their character equivalents. A complete list is given in Appendix A.

ASCII Code	*Character*
32	space
36	$
48	Ø
57	9
62	>
65	A
90	Z
94	^
97	a
122	z

A number of ASCII codes are control codes that control such functions as form feed (ASCII code 12) and carriage return (ASCII code 13). They have no character equivalents as do the codes listed above. The remaining ASCII codes are more familiar to us. Many of their character equivalents can be displayed on the screen or printed on the printer. These codes represent digits; letters of the alphabet; and special characters, such as the comma, period, question mark, and arithmetic and relational operators.

It was mentioned that an ASCII code consists of seven binary digits. The IBM microcomputers use an eighth bit thus increasing the number of characters. These additional codes range from 128 to 255 inclusive and represent such characters as Greek letters and special mathematical symbols, such as the summation symbol (Σ).

The Difference in Storage Between Numeric Data and String Data

In Chapter Three, we learned that BASIC classifies numbers as integers, single-precision numbers and double-precision numbers. An integer requires two bytes of memory, a single-precision number requires four bytes of memory, and a double-precision number requires eight bytes of memory. A string requires one byte for each character in the string. Therefore, if a number is assigned to a string variable, each digit (and a possible negative sign and decimal point) requires one byte. Consider the following program segments.

(a)
```
5010 INPUT "Balance";BALANCE
5020 PRINT BALANCE
RUN
Balance? 1267.58
 1267.58
```

(b)
```
5010 INPUT "Balance";BALANCE$
5020 PRINT BALANCE$
RUN
Balance? 1267.58
1267.58
```

In (a), BASIC stores the number as a single-precision number requiring four bytes of memory. In (b), BASIC stores the number as a string requiring seven bytes of memory. The keyed-in number in (b) need not be enclosed in quotation marks. Only in the assignment statement must a number be enclosed in quotation marks when the number is assigned to a string variable.

A number assigned to a numeric variable, as in (a), can be used in arithmetic computations. A number assigned to a string variable, as in (b), cannot be used in arithmetic computations. Furthermore, since a number and a string are stored differently, they cannot be compared. Note that the number printed in (a) is preceded by a space (for the assumed plus sign), while the string printed in (b) has no preceding space.

Normally, we assign numbers to numeric variables. Strings must be assigned to string variables; we have no choice. However, occasions may arise when we must convert numbers to strings, or convert numbers stored as strings to numeric format. The library functions that perform these operations are discussed in Section 11-6.

Exercises

1. What is the decimal code for each of the following ASCII bit combinations? What character does each combination represent?

   (a) 0110110 (d) 0100000
   (b) 0101100 (e) 1011010
   (c) 1010010 (f) 1111010

2. Decipher the following ASCII codes.

   83 116 114 105 110 103 32 72 97 110 100 108 105 110 103

3. Convert the following characters to ASCII codes in decimal notation.

   ```
   4020 ENAME$ = "John"
   ```

11.2 Processing Strings

In our previous chapters, we learned how to compare two strings. The hierarchical ordering of the ASCII codes makes this possible. We used such statements as 2040 WHILE ENAME$ <> "End of file" to control a loop and 6010 IF STATUS$ = "S" THEN RATE = RATE1 ELSE RATE = RATE2 to make a decision. Examine the following programs. The first program reviews string comparison, the remaining programs introduce new concepts in string handling.

1. The program below uses the IF statement to compare two names, then prints the names in alphabetical order.

```
5010 NAME1$ = "Aiken"
5020 NAME2$ = "Aitken"
5030 PRINT
5040 IF NAME1$ <= NAME2$
        THEN PRINT NAME1$;" ";NAME2$
        ELSE PRINT NAME2$;" ";NAME1$
5050 END
RUN
```

```
Aiken Aitken
```

BASIC compares the two strings by comparing one character of Aiken with one character of Aitken moving in a left-to-right direction on both strings until a difference is found. In each PRINT statement, notice that a space must be coded between the string variables; otherwise, the names will be printed with no space between them.

2. As with numbers, strings can be transferred or copied from one storage location to another without altering the contents of the former location.

```
5010 DAY1$ = "Saturday"
5020 DAY2$ = "Sunday"
5030 DAY2$ = DAY1$
5040 PRINT
5050 PRINT DAY1$,DAY2$
5060 END
RUN
```

```
Saturday      Saturday
```

Line 5030 replaces the string Sunday stored in DAY2$ with the string Saturday. Saturday is now stored in two locations, DAY1$ and DAY2$.

3. Two strings can be combined, a process referred to as *concatenation.*

```
5010 A$ = "111"
5020 B$ = "222"
5030 C$ = A$+B$
5040 PRINT
5050 PRINT C$
5060 END
RUN
```

```
111222
```

The program attaches 222 to the tail end of 111 to produce 111222. Note that we use the plus (+) operator to concatenate strings. Care must be taken when concatenating strings since BASIC leaves no space between the strings. Examine the following program.

```
5010 B$ = "BASIC"
5020 P$ = "PASCAL"
5030 S$ = B$+" "+P$
5040 PRINT
5050 PRINT S$
5060 END
RUN
```

```
BASIC PASCAL
```

Line 5030 concatenates three strings: the string stored in B$, a space, and the string stored in P$.

4. Strings can be accumulated. The program shown below accumulates the five letters B, A, S, I, and C in the string variable WORD$.

```
5010 WORD$ = ""
5020 FOR I = 1 TO 5
5030    READ LETTER$
5040    WORD$ = WORD$+LETTER$
5050 NEXT I
5060 DATA "B","A","S","I","C"
5070 PRINT
5080 PRINT WORD$
5090 END
RUN

BASIC
```

Line 5010 initializes WORD$ to the null string. This means that nothing is stored in WORD$. The first time BASIC passes through the loop, the letter B is stored in WORD$. In each subsequent pass through the loop, BASIC concatenates a letter to the letters already accumulated in WORD$.

Exercises

1. Indicate the errors in the program segments shown below. Note: There may be more than one error in a program segment.

(a)
```
5010 PRINT
5020 NAME1$ = Richard
5030 IF NAME1$ = Richard THEN PRINT NAME1$
```

(b)
```
5010 COUNT.B = 0
5020 FOR I = 1 TO 7
5030    READ LETTER
5040    IF LETTER = "B" THEN COUNT.B = COUNT.B+1
5050 NEXT I
5060 PRINT
5070 PRINT "B appears";COUNT.B;times
5080 DATA "A","B","D","B","B","C","A"
```

(c)
```
5010 FIRST$ = "Leonard"
5020 SECOND$ = "Black"
5030 NAME1$ = FIRST$+SECOND$
5040 PRINT
5050 PRINT NAME1$
```

(d)
```
5010 INPUT "Is the answer true or false (T/F)";ANSWER$
5020 IF ANSWER$ <> T OR ANSWER$ <> F
     THEN PRINT "Invalid response. Enter T or F." : GOTO 5010
```

2. Fill in the incomplete lines.

(a)
```
5010 NAME1$ = "Andersen"
5020 NAME2$ = "Anderson"
5030 PRINT
5040 IF ______________________________
     THEN PRINT NAME2$;"   ";NAME1$
     ELSE PRINT NAME1$;"   ";NAME2$
5050 END
RUN

Andersen   Anderson
```

(b)
```
5010 PRINT
5020 FOR I = 1 TO 4
5030    READ MONTH$
5040    IF ________________________________
5050 NEXT I
5060 DATA "January","April","July","October"
```

```
5070 END
RUN
```

```
The report is due in July
```

3. Suppose your social insurance number has been broken up into three parts: 414, 237, and 815, with each part assigned to a string variable. Write a program that concatenates these parts and inserts a hyphen between each one.

```
RUN
```

```
414-237-815
```

11.3 Breaking Up a String

Until now, we have been working with a string in its entirety. Occasions often arise when we must access a portion of a string. Suppose each string consists of a person's last name, first name, and telephone number. We may want to extract just the last name from each string or we may want to extract just the telephone number. The piece of string that we extract is called a substring. BASIC offers three string-handling functions that enable us to extract substrings. These are LEFT$, RIGHT$, and MID$. In addition, the IBM microcomputers support another function that eases the task of breaking up a string. This is the INSTR function.

The four functions are explained below along with programs to illustrate how they can be used. The functions may be coded in most BASIC statements. In our examples, we will use **Dixon,Gary,123-4567** as the original string. It is important to note that the functions do not change the initial string.

The LEFT$ Function

The LEFT$ function extracts a desired number of left-most characters from a string. In the following program, five left-most characters are extracted from our original string and assigned to L$.

```
5010 S$ = "Dixon,Gary,123-4567"
5020 L$ = LEFT$(S$,5)
5030 PRINT
5040 PRINT L$
5050 END
RUN
```

```
Dixon
```

The first argument of the LEFT$ function is the string variable to which the string is assigned. The second argument specifies the number of characters we wish to extract.

The RIGHT$ Function

The RIGHT$ function extracts a desired number of right-most characters from a string. In the program below, eight right-most characters are extracted from our string. This time, the string handling function is coded in a PRINT statement. Furthermore, we have used the actual string as the first argument of the function. As with the LEFT$ function, the second argument specifies the number of characters to extract.

```
5010 PRINT
5020 PRINT RIGHT$("Dixon,Gary,123-4567",8)
5030 END
RUN
```

```
123-4567
```

The MID$ Function

The MID$ function extracts a desired number of characters from within a string. The following program extracts a substring of four characters, starting at the seventh character of our string. The function is coded in both an IF statement and a PRINT statement.

```
5010 S$ = "Dixon,Gary,123-4567"
5020 PRINT
5030 IF MID$(S$,7,4) = "Gary" THEN PRINT MID$(S$,7,4)
5040 END
RUN
```

```
Gary
```

The first argument of the MID$ function represents the string upon which the function will operate. The second argument indicates where the extraction must begin, the third argument specifies the number of characters to extract.

The MID$ function can also be used without the third argument. This version is particularly helpful when we wish to extract right-most characters and we do not know the number of characters to extract. However, we must know the starting position of the extraction. Suppose we wish to extract the first name and the telephone number from our string. The MID$ function in the following statement performs this operation.

```
5030 M$ = MID$(S$,7)
```

The function extracts all characters from position 7 to the end of the string. Thus, substring Gary,123-4567 is assigned to M$.

The INSTR Function

The INSTR function searches for a substring within a string and returns the substring's starting position. The following program finds the starting position of the string Gary.

```
5010 S$ = "Dixon,Gary,123-4567"
5020 WORD$ = "Gary"
5030 P = INSTR(1,S$,WORD$)
5040 PRINT
5050 PRINT "'";WORD$;"'";" starts at position";P
5060 END
RUN
```

```
'Gary' starts at position 7
```

The first argument of the INSTR function is the starting point of the search, the second argument is the string to be searched, the third argument is the substring to be found. The first argument is optional. If we do not specify a starting point, the search begins at the first character of the initial string. INSTR returns a zero when a substring is not found.

In the following example, we use a numeric variable as the first argument and strings as the second and third arguments.

```
5010 N = 4
5020 P = INSTR(N,"Brenda Clarke"," ")
```

The search for a space starts at the fourth character of the string Brenda Clarke. The space is found in position 7.

Here are a few more examples. Assume that the string "STRUCTURED PROGRAMMING" has been assigned to S$.

	Function	*Returned Value*
(a)	`5010 P1 = INSTR(1,S$,"R")`	3
(b)	`5020 P2 = INSTR(4,S$,"R")`	8
(c)	`5030 P3 = INSTR(14,S$,"R")`	16

```
(d) 5040 P4 = INSTR(3,S$,"RU")    3
(e) 5050 P5 = INSTR(7,S$,"RU")    0
```

A Sample Program

The program below finds the number of a's in the name Barbara.

```
5010 COUNT.A = 0
5020 NAME1$ = "Barbara"
5030 FOR I = 1 TO 7
5040   IF MID$(NAME1$,I,1) = "a" THEN COUNT.A = COUNT.A+1
5050 NEXT I
5060 PRINT
5070 PRINT "The number of a's in Barbara is:";COUNT.A
5080 END
RUN
```

```
The number of a's in Barbara is: 3
```

Extraction is performed in the IF/THEN statement by the MID$ function whose arguments are as follows:

(a) A string variable in which the name is stored.

(b) The control variable of the FOR statement. The variable represents the starting point of each extraction.

When I is 1, the extraction starts at B;
When I is 2, the extraction starts at a;
When I is 3, the extraction starts at r;
etc.

(c) The number 1 which specifies the length of the substring. In this case, the function extracts one letter at a time.

The IF statement compares each extracted letter with the string "a". If the extracted letter is an **a**, a counter is increased. If it is not, the next letter is extracted and tested. After extracting and testing all the letters in Barbara, the computer prints the message shown in the output.

Exercises

1. Evaluate the following given that N1$ equals "Hewitt, Laureen Carol" and N2$ equals "Garry W. Marshall".

```
(a) 5030 S1$ = MID$(N1$,9,7) + " " + LEFT$(N1$,6)
(b) 5040 S2$ = RIGHT$(N1$,13) + " " + LEFT$(N1$,6)
(c) 5050 S3$ = MID$(N1$,9,9) + ". " + LEFT$(N1$,6)
(d) 5060 S4$ = LEFT$(N2$,5) + " " + RIGHT$(N2$,8)
(e) 5070 S5$ = MID$(N2$,10) + ", " + LEFT$(N2$,8)
```

2. Find the value of P in each of the statements (a) to (f) inclusive.

```
5010 S$ = "Concatenation"

(a) 5020 P = INSTR(1,S$,"t")      (d) 5050 P = INSTR(1,S$,"on")
(b) 5030 P = INSTR(6,S$,"t")      (e) 5060 P = INSTR(7,S$,"on")
(c) 5040 P = INSTR(9,S$,"t")      (f) 5070 P = INSTR(8,S$,"en")
```

3. Show the results of the following programs.

(a)
```
5010 S$ = "Programming in BASIC"
5020 P = INSTR(1,S$," ")
5030 L$ = LEFT$(S$,P-1)
5040 PRINT
5050 PRINT L$
5060 END
```

(b)
```
5010 S$ = "Curious"
5020 N = 6
5030 PRINT
5040 PRINT S$
5050 FOR I = N TO 2 STEP -1
5060   PRINT TAB(I); MID$(S$,I,1)
5070 NEXT I
5080 PRINT S$
5090 END
```

4. Complete line 5050 with an IF/THEN statement that determines whether or not the last name is Smith. If it is, print the name and a running counter alongside the name.

```
5000 'SUBROUTINE ENTER AND PROCESS DATA
5010    COUNT.SMITH = 0
5020    PRINT
5030    FOR MEMBER = 1 TO 6
5040      READ CNAME$
5050      IF ________________________________________
5060    NEXT MEMBER
5070    DATA "Allan Smith","Laureen Hewitt","Sandra Smith"
5080    DATA "Peter Campbell","Jeffrey Smith","Mary Williams"
5090    RETURN
RUN

1            Allan Smith
2            Sandra Smith
3            Jeffrey Smith
```

11.4 Standardized Subroutines

Standardizing a Subroutine

As mentioned previously, often-called routines should be saved on disk in ASCII format. Saved in this manner, we can merge the routines with a resident program. At this point, we have two subroutines saved in ASCII format. The subroutines have been stored under filenames VERIFY.ASC and FREEZE.ASC. As we write more programs, we will be calling other frequently used routines. These routines should be standardized in such a way that they require little or no modification when merged with a program. Here are a few ways by which we can standardize a subroutine.

1. The line numbers of a standardized subroutine must be different than the line numbers of any other module. This includes the modules already stored on disk and the modules of any prospective program with which the subroutine may be merged.

2. Recall that, with one exception, all variables in a BASIC program are global which means that variables may be referenced by any module. A variable that can be accessed by only one module is referred to as a local variable. Several languages offer this feature. In BASIC, we can simulate a local variable by designating a specific variable, say IN1$, for use in a module.

3. Before calling the subroutine, we copy the value upon which the subroutine must operate into IN1$, our local variable. The subroutine performs the processing on IN1$ and assigns the result to another local variable, say OUT1$. When BASIC returns to the calling module, the result in OUT1$ is copied into a variable used in the calling module. We will call this latter variable our program variable.

4. A result should not be printed in a standardized subroutine. We must send the result back to the calling module for further processing or for printing.

A Sample Program

The following program includes a standardized subroutine and shows the interactions between a resident program and the merged, standardized subroutine. The program separates an address into three parts:

1. The number and the street.
2. The city and the province.
3. The postal code.

Sample Output:

(cleared screen)

```
         10        20        30        40        50        60        70        80
12345678901234567890123456789012345678901234567890123456789012345678901234567890
          Enter street address, city and province, and postal code
          separated by slashes (e.g. 123 Main St./Anycity  ZZ/M3L 6S7

          Address? 697 Main St./Anycity  ZZ/M3L 2W9

Is the address correct (y/n)? y
```

(cleared screen)

```
                                697 Main St.
                                Anycity  ZZ
                                M3L 2W9
```

```
1000 'SEPARATE AN ADDRESS                    M. MCRITCHIE                    SEPT 6
1002 '*************************************************************************
1004 '             THIS PROGRAM SEPARATES AN ADDRESS INTO THREE PARTS:
1006 '             NUMBER AND STREET, CITY AND PROVINCE, POSTAL CODE
1008 '*************************************************************************
1010 'ADDRESS$         - ADDRESS (STREET ADDRESS, CITY AND PROVINCE, POSTAL CODE)
1020 'RESPONSE$        - USER'S RESPONSE (y/n)
1030 'IN1$             - LOCAL VARIABLE. STORES AN ADDRESS.
1040 'P1,P2            - POSITIONS OF THE SLASHES IN THE INITIAL ADDRESS
1050 'OUT1$,OUT2$,OUT3$ - LOCAL VARIABLES STORING NUMBER AND STREET, CITY
1060 '                   AND PROVINCE, POSTAL CODE
1070 'STREET$          - NUMBER AND STREET
1080 'CITY.PROVINCE$ - CITY AND PROVINCE
1090 'POSTAL$          - POSTAL CODE
2000 '*************************************************************************
2002 '                              MAIN ROUTINE
2004 '*************************************************************************
2010   GOSUB 3000                        'INPUT and print address
2020   END
3000 '*************************************************************************
3002 '                         INPUT AND PRINT ADDRESS
3004 '*************************************************************************
3010   CLS
3020   LOCATE 9
3030   PRINT TAB(11) "Enter street address, city and province, and postal code"
3040   PRINT TAB(11) "separated by slashes (e.g. 123 Main St./Anycity  ZZ/";
3050   PRINT "M3L 6S7"
3060   PRINT
3070   INPUT "__________Address";ADDRESS$
3080   PRINT
3090   INPUT "Is the address correct (y/n)";RESPONSE$
3100   IF RESPONSE$ <> "y" AND RESPONSE$ <> "Y"
          THEN INPUT "Re-enter the address--",ADDRESS$ : GOTO 3090
3110   IN1$ = ADDRESS$
3120   GOSUB 12000                       'Separate data (address)
```

```
3130   STREET$ = OUT1$
3140   CITY.PROVINCE$ = OUT2$
3150   POSTAL$ = OUT3$
3160   CLS
3170   LOCATE 12
3180   PRINT TAB(35) STREET$
3190   PRINT TAB(35) CITY.PROVINCE$
3200   PRINT TAB(35) POSTAL$
3210   RETURN
12000 '*******************************************************************
12002 '                       SEPARATE DATA (ADDRESS)
12004 '*******************************************************************
12010  P1 = INSTR(1,IN1$,"/")
12020  P2 = INSTR(P1+1,IN1$,"/")
12030  OUT1$ = LEFT$(IN1$,P1-1)
12040  OUT2$ = MID$(IN1$,P1+1,(P2-P1)-1)
12050  OUT3$ = MID$(IN1$,P2+1)
12060  RETURN
65529 'End of program listing
```

Save Subroutine SEPARATE DATA on disk in ASCII format as the subroutine will be used with only slight modifications in subsequent programs. Suggested filename: SEPARATE.ASC

Note the interaction between Subroutine 3000 and Subroutine 12000. Line 3110 copies the address into local variable IN1$. Subroutine 12000 operates on variable IN1$, then stores the three parts of the address in variables OUT1$, OUT2$, and OUT3$. When BASIC returns from the subroutine, the values of OUT1$, OUT2$, and OUT3$ are copied into variables STREET$, CITY.PROVINCE$, and POSTAL$, then printed from these program variables.

Here is how the address is separated.

To extract 697 Main St., we must find the position of the first slash and extract the characters to the left of the slash.

```
                                         P1
                                         ↓
6 9 7   M a i n   S t . /
1 2 3 4 5 6 7 8 9 10 11 12 13
```

The INSTR function in line 12010 finds the first slash in position 13. The position is assigned to P1. In line 12030, we extract the required number of left-most characters from IN1$. The number of characters extracted is P1-1 since the slash must not be extracted. 697 Main St. is assigned to OUT1$.

To extract Anycity ZZ, we must find the position of the second slash, then extract the characters between the two slashes.

```
P1                                          P2
↓                                           ↓
/  A  n  y  c  i  t  y        Z  Z  /
13 14 15 16 17 18 19 20 21 22 23 24 25
```

The INSTR function in line 12020 finds the position of the second slash. The search starts at the fourteenth character of IN1$ (P1+1 = 13+1 = 14). The second slash is found in position 25. We assign this position to P2. The MID$ function in line 12040 extracts Anycity ZZ from IN1$. The extraction begins with the 14th character (P1+1). The function extracts the characters between P2 and P1; that is, the characters between the two slashes. Note that we must subtract 1 from the number of characters since the second slash must not be included in the extraction. Anycity ZZ is assigned to OUT2$.

To extract M3L 2W9, we must find the substring's starting position and then extract all characters from this position to the end of the initial string. The starting position of M3L 2W9 is found by adding 1 to the position of the second slash. The substring starts at position 26 (P2+1 = 25+1 = 26).

```
P2
↓
/  M  3  L     2  W  9
25 26 27 28 29 30 31 32
```

The MID$ function in line 12050 extracts all characters starting at position 26. The postal code M3L 2W9 is assigned to OUT3$.

Exercise

Write a program that separates a name into three parts: title, first name, and last name. Allow a user of your program to key in a name and inform the user that the title, first name, and last name must be separated from each other by a space. Merge the subroutine that separates data with your program and customize the subroutine. This time, find the position of a space rather than a slash (/).

Sample Output:

(cleared screen)

```
         10        20        30        40        50        60        70        80
12345678901234567890123456789012345678901234567890123456789012345678901234567890

                Enter title, first name, last name separated
                from each other by a space (e.g. Mr. John Smith)

                Name? Mr. Andrew Jones

Is the name correct (y/n)? y
```

(cleared screen)

```
                                   Mr.
                                   Andrew
                                   Jones
```

11.5 The MID$ Statement

A variation of the MID$ function is the MID$ statement. Its purpose is to replace specific characters of a string. Here are two examples.

(a)

```
5010 NAME1$ = "Harold Peters"
5020 MID$(NAME1$,4) = "vey"
5030 PRINT
5040 PRINT NAME1$
5050 END
RUN

Harvey Peters
```

(b)

```
5010 NAME1$ = "Harold Peters"
5020 MID$(NAME1$,8) = "Sigurdson"
5030 PRINT
5040 PRINT NAME1$
5050 END
RUN

Harold Sigurd
```

The MID$ instruction is placed in an assignment statement on the left side of the assignment operator. The second argument of MID$ is the position where replacement begins. The statement performs a one-for-one replacement. In Program (a), replacement starts at position 4 of Harold Peters. The letters "vey" replace the letters "old". In Program (b), replacement starts at position 8. The letters "Sigurd" replace the letters "Peters". Note that the length of the string does not change. In Program (b), the new string contains 13 characters as did the original string.

Exercise

What will be the value of ADDRESS$ after execution of the following program?

```
5010 ADDRESS$ = "394 Broadway Street"
5020 MID$(ADDRESS$,1) = "123"
5030 MID$(ADDRESS$,14) = "Avenue"
5040 MID$(ADDRESS$,5) = "Grand"
5050 PRINT
5060 PRINT ADDRESS$
5070 END
```

11.6 Other String-Handling Functions

Strings can be manipulated in a number of other ways. The various string-handling functions are explained below. For most of the functions, a program is listed to illustrate the function's use.

The LEN Function

The LEN function counts the number of characters in a string. The program below finds and prints the number of characters in the string Maureen.

```
5010 READ NAME1$
5020 LENGTH = LEN(NAME1$)
5030 PRINT
5040 PRINT "The number of characters"
5050 PRINT "in ";NAME1$;" is";LENGTH
5060 DATA "Maureen"
5070 END
RUN
```

```
The number of characters
in Maureen is 7
```

The LEN function is often used as the test value in a FOR statement as illustrated below.

```
5010 FOR I = 1 TO LEN(S$)
```

The VAL Function

VAL(S$) VAL("24.68")

The VAL function converts a string consisting of digits (and a possible minus sign and decimal point) to its numeric value. For example, the function converts the string "24.68" to the number 24.68. A space is displayed before the converted number when the number is positive and printed. If the first character in the string is not numeric, VAL returns a zero.

```
5010 S$ = "Darryl Brown,38,9.54"
5020 NAME1$ = LEFT$(S$,12)
5030 HOURS$ = MID$(S$,14,2)
5040 RATE$ = MID$(S$,17)
5050 HOURS = VAL(HOURS$)
5060 RATE = VAL(RATE$)
5070 GROSS.PAY = HOURS*RATE
5080 PRINT
5090 PRINT "Name: ";NAME1$
5100 PRINT "Hours:";HOURS,"Rate:";RATE
5110 PRINT "Gross pay:";GROSS.PAY
5120 END
RUN
```

```
Name: Darryl Brown
Hours: 38      Rate: 9.54
Gross pay: 362.52
```

In line 5010, we assign a string that consists of a name, hours of work, and rate of pay to S$. Lines 5020, 5030, and 5040 extract the name, hours, and rate from the string. Note that the hours and rate must be assigned to string variables. Since line 5070 uses the hours and rate in an arithmetic expression, we must convert the values of these two string variables to numeric values. The VAL function in each of lines 5050 and 5060 performs a conversion. We now use the numeric variables in the expression in line 5070.

The STR$ Function

STR$(NUMBER) STR$(2468) STR$(16+85)

STR$ is the opposite of VAL. It converts a number to its string equivalent. If the argument is an expression, BASIC first evaluates the expression. Recall that a space is left before a positive number. Since the space is considered part of the number, the space becomes part of the string when STR$ converts the number to its string equivalent. For example, the number 2468 would be converted to b̸2468 where b̸ represents a space.

```
5010 DATE1 = 102799
5020 S$ = STR$(DATE1)
5030 MONTH$ = MID$(S$,2,2)
5040 DAY$ = MID$(S$,4,2)
5050 YEAR$ = MID$(S$,6)
5060 DATE1$ = MONTH$ + "/" + DAY$ + "/" + YEAR$
5070 PRINT
5080 PRINT DATE1$
5090 END
RUN

10/27/99
```

The above program changes a six-digit number in such a way that it represents a date. In line 5010, we assign the number 102799 to numeric variable DATE1. (DATE$ is a reserved word, therefore, we cannot use DATE as a variable.) The STR$ function in line 5020 converts the number to its string equivalent. Each of lines 5030, 5040, and 5050 extracts two digits from the newly formed string. In line 5060, we concatenate the substrings and insert slashes between the substrings.

Since the first character of a positive number is a space, we must use the MID$ function instead of the LEFT$ function to extract the first two digits. We must include the space in our count when determining the starting position of each substring. The starting position of 10 is 2, of 27 it is 4, of 99 it is 6.

The CHR$ Function

CHR$(NUMBER) CHR$(65) CHR$(64+1.5)

This function converts a number to its ASCII character equivalent. The number must be an ASCII code; otherwise, the computer prints **Illegal function call in xxxx** where xxxx is the number of the statement that contains the function. When the argument is an expression, BASIC first evaluates the expression; when the argument is a decimal number, BASIC rounds off the number to an integer.

No character can be printed when the code represents a control command, as no such character exists. However, we can place the command in a statement by using either the CHR$ function or a variable to which the command has been assigned. For example, the number 13 is the ASCII code for a carriage return. In Program (a) below, we assign the command to a variable and use the variable in the PRINT statement. In Program (b), we use the CHR$ function in the PRINT statement.

(a)

```
5010 C$ = CHR$(13)
5020 PRINT
5030 PRINT "First";C$;"Second"
5040 END
RUN

First
Second
```

(b)

```
5010 PRINT
5020 PRINT "First";CHR$(13);"Second"
5030 END
RUN

First
Second
```

In both programs, the cursor drops down to the next screen line before BASIC prints Second.

The CHR$ function is often used to obtain quotation marks in an output line. Recall that quotation marks delimit a string; therefore, we may not use quotation marks as part of a string in a PRINT statement. The quotation marks identified by the arrows below are invalid.

```
                                ↓                   ↓
5030 PRINT "Susan replied, "We should meet tomorrow"."
```

The CHR$ function in the following program solves this problem. ASCII code 34 represents a quotation mark.

```
5010 QUOTE$ = CHR$(34)
5020 PRINT
5030 PRINT "Susan replied, ";QUOTE$;"We should meet tomorrow.";QUOTE$
```

```
5040 END
RUN
```

```
Susan replied, "We should meet tomorrow."
```

We divide the string into two parts: **Susan replied,ƀ** and **We should meet tomorrow**. (ƀ represents a space.) Each of these strings must be enclosed in quotation marks. The computer does not print these quotation marks because the quotation marks are delimiters.

To obtain the quotation marks in the output, we use the CHR$ function to convert ASCII code 34 to its character equivalent. We assign the character to a string variable (to QUOTE$ in the above program) and use this string variable wherever we want a quotation mark in the output. In the PRINT statement, QUOTE$ is placed before and after "We should meet tomorrow.". Each quotation mark printed in the output is the value of QUOTE$. As mentioned earlier, an alternative is to place the CHR$ function directly in the PRINT statement.

```
5030 PRINT "Susan replied, ";CHR$(34);"We should meet tomorrow.";CHR$(34)
```

The ASC Function

ASC(C$) ASC("A")

ASC is the opposite of CHR$. It gives the ASCII code of a character. If the argument consists of a series of characters, the function returns the ASCII code for just the first character. The following program converts an A to its ASCII code.

```
5010 LETTER$ = "A"
5020 CODE = ASC(LETTER$)
5030 PRINT
5040 PRINT LETTER$,CODE
5050 END
RUN
```

```
A             65
```

We will be using the ASC function mainly to convert letters to upper case or lower case. These routines are given in Section 11.7.

The STRING$ Function

STRING$(9,".") STRING$(9,A$) STRING$(9,46) (46 = ASCII code)

Although we have been using the STRING$ function to generate a series of characters, we should be aware of some of its other features. The number of characters we desire must be in the range Ø to 255. If the second argument is a series of characters, such as "-+-+-+", the function repeats only the first character. And, if the second argument is an ASCII code, the function converts the ASCII code to its character equivalent. In the third example above, the function returns nine periods.

The SPACE$ Function

SPACE$(9) SPACE$(N)

The SPACE$ function returns a string of spaces. The argument, which must be in the range Ø to 255, specifies the number of spaces. Rather than use the TAB function, we can use the SPACE$ function to centre column headings. For example, we can use

```
4080 PRINT SPACE$(14); "QUANTITY"; SPACE$(8); "ITEM"; SPACE$(8) "UNIT PRICE";
     SPACE$(7) "COST"
```

to produce the output below.

```
12345678901234567890123456789012345678901234567890123456789012345678901234567890123
              QUANTITY          ITEM          UNIT PRICE          COST
```

Nested Functions

A function can be used as the argument of another function. For example, statements 5050 and 5060 in the program on page 275 could have used the MID$ function as the argument of the VAL function. The program is rewritten below.

```
5010 S$ = "Darryl Brown,38,9.54"
5020 NAME1$ = LEFT$(S$,12)
5030 HOURS = VAL(MID$(S$,14,2))
5040 RATE = VAL(MID$(S$,17))
5050 GROSS.PAY = HOURS*RATE
5060 PRINT
5070 PRINT "Name: ";NAME1$
5080 PRINT "Hours:";HOURS,"Rate:";RATE
5090 PRINT "Gross pay:";GROSS.PAY
5100 END
```

In line 5030, the MID$ function extracts substring 38, the VAL function converts the substring to a numeric value. Line 5040 performs the same operations on substring 9.54.

Exercises

1. What is the output of each of the following programs?

(a)
```
5010 S$ = "5789"
5020 PRINT
5030 PRINT VAL(S$)
5040 PRINT S$
5050 END
```

(b)
```
5010 N = 3456
5020 PRINT
5030 PRINT STR$(N)
5040 PRINT N
5050 END
```

(c)
```
5010 READ N
5020 PRINT
5030 PRINT N,CHR$(N)
5040 DATA 67
5050 END
```

(d)
```
5010 READ S$
5020 PRINT
5030 PRINT S$,ASC(S$)
5040 DATA "T"
5050 END
```

(e)
```
5010 R$ = "Ribbons"
5020 N = 2
5030 S$ = STRING$(6,46)
5040 PRINT
5050 PRINT R$;" ";S$;N
5060 END
```

(f)
```
5010 P$ = "Printer"
5020 R$ = "Ribbons"
5030 S$ = P$ + SPACE$(4) + R$
5040 PRINT
5050 PRINT S$
5060 END
```

2. What output will each of the following programs produce?

(a)
```
5010 READ S$
5020 WORD$ = ""
5030 FOR N = 1 TO LEN(S$)
5040    CODE = ASC(MID$(S$,N,1))-1
5050    IF CODE = 96 THEN CODE = 122
5060    WORD$ = WORD$+CHR$(CODE)
5070 NEXT N
5080 PRINT
5090 PRINT WORD$
5100 DATA "vosfdphojabcmf"
5110 END
```

(b)
```
5010 S$ = "String handling"
5020 P = INSTR(1,S$," ")
5030 M$ = MID$(S$,P+1)
5040 L = LEN(M$)
5050 PRINT
5060 FOR I = 1 TO L
5070    T$ = MID$(S$,I,L)
5080    PRINT T$
5090 NEXT I
5100 END
```

Code subroutines for the following problems. To test a subroutine, write a routine that calls the subroutine. Do not use the INSTR function to find positions of substrings.

3. Extract the name and each score from the following string, then find the average score.

"Nancy Johnson 86 82 87"

```
RUN
```

```
Enter the name and scores separated by spaces
(e.g. John Smith 94 89 93)

Name and scores? Nancy Johnson 86 82 87
Average score: 85
```

(a) Extract the name.
(b) In one statement extract a score, convert the score to a numeric value and assign the value to a numeric variable. Refer to the "nested functions" program on page 278 if you need help. Since there are three scores, you will need three such statements.
(c) Find the average score.

4. Assign the number 1004238 to a numeric variable and convert the number to **100: 4/238**. The first three digits of the number represent a course number, the fourth digit represents the period during which the course is offered, and the last three digits represent the room in which the course is taught.

```
RUN
```

```
100: 4/238
```

(a) Convert the number to its string equivalent.
(b) Extract substrings 100, 4, and 238.
(c) Concatenate the substrings and insert a colon, a space, and a slash character as shown in the output. Note that no space precedes the result.

11.7 Often-Used Routines

Several functions discussed in the previous section will be incorporated in the routines given below.

Converting a Letter to Upper Case or Lower Case

The ASCII table in Appendix A shows that the difference between an uppercase letter and its lowercase counterpart is 32. The code for "Y" is 89, the code for "y" is 121. We can use this concept to convert a letter to upper case or lower case. The following routine converts an uppercase letter to a lowercase letter.

```
3000 PRINT
3010 INPUT "Enter a letter--",LETTER$
3020 CODE = ASC(LETTER$)
3030 IF CODE >= 65 AND CODE <= 90 THEN LETTER$ = CHR$(CODE+32)
3040 PRINT LETTER$
RUN                          or          RUN
```

```
Enter a letter--Y
y
```

```
Enter a letter--y
y
```

First, a keyed-in letter is converted to its ASCII code (line 3020). The IF statement in line 3030 checks the code. If the code lies between 65 and 90 inclusive, the letter is in upper case. We add 32 to the code which gives us the code of a lowercase letter, convert the new code to its character equivalent, and assign the lowercase letter to LETTER$. If the letter is already in lower case, no change is made to the value of LETTER$.

To convert a lowercase letter to an uppercase letter, the IF statement should be changed as follows:

```
3030 IF CODE >= 97 AND CODE <= 122 THEN LETTER$ = CHR$(CODE-32)
```

If the code lies between 97 and 122 inclusive, the letter is a lowercase letter. We subtract 32 from its code, convert the new code to its character equivalent, and assign the uppercase letter to LETTER$.

Automatic Centring of a Heading

So far, we have been centring headings by counting the number of characters in a heading, subtracting this number from 80 and dividing the difference by two. The result gives us the number of spaces to the left of the heading. Now that we are familiar with the LEN function, we can ask the computer to centre headings for us. Here is how we combine the TAB function with the LEN function in a PRINT statement to centre a heading. The statement below centres PROGRESS REPORT.

```
3010 HEADING$ = "PROGRESS REPORT"
3020 PRINT TAB((80-LEN(HEADING$))/2+.5); HEADING$
```

Working from the middle of the expression in line 3020 outward, the argument of the TAB function is calculated as follows:

Expression	*Result*
LEN(HEADING$)	15
80-LEN(HEADING$)	80-15 = 65
(80-LEN(HEADING$))/2+.5	(80-15)/2+.5 = 33

Thus, the printing of PROGRESS REPORT starts in column 33.

```
12345678901234567890123456789012345678901234567890123456789012345678901234567890
                                PROGRESS REPORT
```

Notice how the parentheses are paired.

```
TAB((80-LEN(HEADING$))/2+.5); HEADING$
```

Exercise

Write a subroutine that allows a user to key a first name into the computer, then prints the name with the first letter in upper case and the remaining letters in lower case. The first letter of the name may be typed in either upper case or lower case, the remaining letters must be typed in lower case. The conversion of all letters is left as a programming problem at the end of this chapter. Test your subroutine by calling the module from a skeleton main routine.

```
RUN

First name? john
John
```

Extract the first letter from the keyed-in name. Use the MID$ function to extract the remaining letters from the name (do not use a third argument). Convert the first letter to upper case (if necessary). Refer to the routine given on page 279. Concatenate the first letter with the remaining letters in the name and print the name.

11.8 Program Design

A text editor is a sophisticated program comprised of several subroutines, each performing one of the many types of text alterations. A common alteration is the replacement of a text's substring with another substring. We will design just this routine. The subroutine will be kept simple. Most text editors contain more complex routines that are beyond the scope of this book.

The subroutine uses several of the string-handling functions introduced in this chapter. We will be replacing YEAR with MONTH in the string THIS YEAR AND NEXT YEAR THE RATE WILL BE THE SAME. Save the subroutine in ASCII format as it is needed for two programming problems at the end of the chapter. Suggested filename: REPLACE.ASC. Before we design the subroutine, let us key in a simple main routine and Subroutine INPUT TEXT AND PRINT RESULT.

```
1000 'REPLACE TEXT                    M. MCRITCHIE                      SEPT 13
1002 '*********************************************************************
1004 '          THIS PROGRAM REPLACES A SUBSTRING IN A STRING
1006 '*********************************************************************
1010 'S$ - ORIGINAL AND MODIFIED STRING
2000 '*********************************************************************
2002 '                                 MAIN ROUTINE
2004 '*********************************************************************
2010  GOSUB 3000                      'INPUT text and print result
2020  END
3000 '*********************************************************************
3002 '                    INPUT TEXT AND PRINT RESULT
3004 '*********************************************************************
3010  PRINT
3020  PRINT "Original string:"
3030  PRINT
3040  S$ = "THIS YEAR AND NEXT YEAR THE RATE WILL BE THE SAME"
3050  PRINT S$
3060  GOSUB 13000                     'Replace text
3070  PRINT
3080  PRINT S$
3090  RETURN
```

After completing the design, the output should be as follows:

```
Original string:

THIS YEAR AND NEXT YEAR THE RATE WILL BE THE SAME

Text to replace? YEAR
New text? MONTH

THIS MONTH AND NEXT MONTH THE RATE WILL BE THE SAME
```

Because of the complexity of the statement that creates new text, we will break up this statement into three parts. The statement is broken up under the heading "Create new text" in both designs.

FIGURE 11-1 STRUCTURE CHART

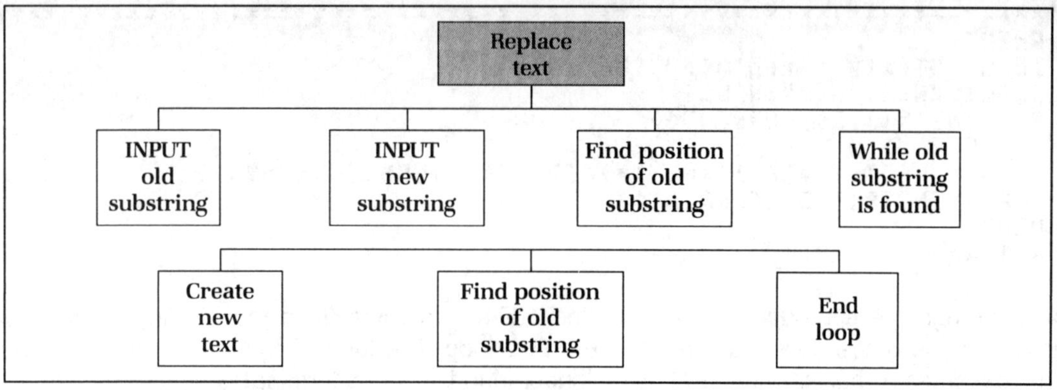

Figure 11-1 Continued

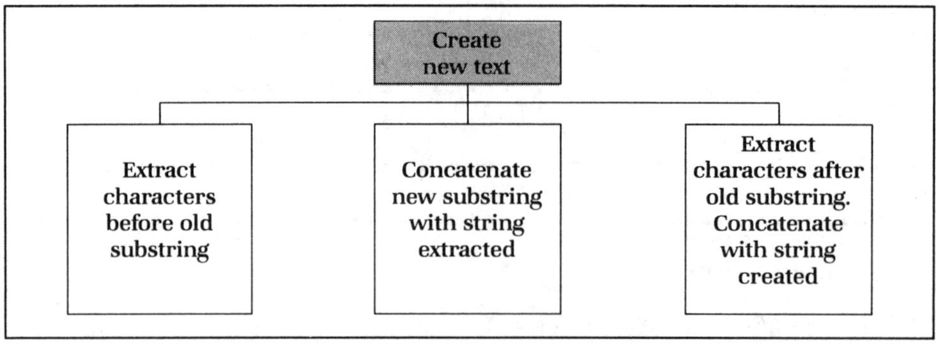

FIGURE 11-2 PSEUDOCODE

REPLACE TEXT	
INPUT old substring	CURRENT$
INPUT new substring	NEW1$
Find position of old substring	P
While old substring is found	
Create new text	(refined further)
Find position of old substring	
End loop	

Create New Text (one statement)
Extract characters before old substring
Concatenate new substring with string extracted
Extract characters after old substring.
Concatenate with string created.

```
1020 'CURRENT$ - OLD SUBSTRING
1030 'NEW1$    - NEW SUBSTRING
1040 'P        - POSITION OF OLD SUBSTRING
13000 '*******************************************************************
13002 '                              REPLACE TEXT
13004 '*******************************************************************
13010  PRINT
13020  INPUT "Text to replace";CURRENT$
13030  INPUT "New text";NEW1$
13040  P = INSTR(1,S$,CURRENT$)
13050  WHILE P <> 0
13060    S$ = LEFT$(S$,P-1)+NEW1$+MID$(S$,P+LEN(CURRENT$))
13070    P = INSTR(1,S$,CURRENT$)
13080  WEND
13090  RETURN
```

Let us trace through the subroutine starting at line 13040. This line finds the starting position of the first YEAR. The position is 6. We now enter the WHILE/WEND loop. The loop continues as long as P is not equal to Ø. When P becomes Ø; that is, when YEAR is no longer found, the loop terminates.

The first time through the loop:

Line 13060 creates new text by replacing the first YEAR found in the initial text with MONTH in the following manner:

LEFT$(S$,P−1) extracts the five left-most characters from the initial text. Recall that the value of P is 6.

```
T H I S
1 2 3 4 5
```

\+ NEW1$ concatenates MONTH with the above substring.

```
T H I S   M O N T H
1 2 3 4 5 6 7 8 9 10
```

MID$(S$,P+LEN(CURRENT$)) extracts characters from the initial text from the tenth character to the end of the string. P+LEN(CURRENT$) = 6+LEN(YEAR) = 6+4 = 10.

```
THIS YEAR AND NEXT YEAR THE RATE WILL BE THE SAME
         ↑
         10
```

The extracted characters are concatenated with THIS MONTH.

```
THIS MONTH AND NEXT YEAR THE RATE WILL BE THE SAME
```

The above text is now considered the initial text. Line 13070 finds the position of YEAR in this text. YEAR is found in position 21. The position is assigned to P.

```
T H I S   M O N T H   A  N  D     N  E  X  T     Y E A R
1 2 3 4 5 6 7 8 9 10 11 12 13 14 15 16 17 18 19 20 21
```

Since P is not equal to zero, the loop is executed again.

The second time through the loop:
Line 13060 creates new text by replacing YEAR in the initial text with MONTH. The new text is created in the following manner:

LEFT$(S$,P−1) extracts 20 left-most characters from the initial text. Recall that the value of P is 21.

```
T H I S   M O N T H   A  N  D     N  E  X  T
1 2 3 4 5 6 7 8 9 10 11 12 13 14 15 16 17 18 19 20
```

+ NEW1$ concatenates MONTH with the above substring.

```
T H I S   M O N T H   A  N  D     N  E  X  T     M  O  N  T  H
1 2 3 4 5 6 7 8 9 10 11 12 13 14 15 16 17 18 19 20 21 22 23 24 25
```

MID$(S$,P+LEN(CURRENT$)) extracts characters from the initial text from the 25th character to the end of the string. P+LEN(CURRENT$) = 21+LEN(YEAR) = 21+4 = 25.

```
THIS MONTH AND NEXT YEAR THE RATE WILL BE THE SAME
                        ↑
                        25
```

The extracted characters are concatenated with the substring created so far.

```
THIS MONTH AND NEXT MONTH THE RATE WILL BE THE SAME
```

In line 13070, P becomes zero since the INSTR function cannot find another YEAR. The loop terminates.

The modified text is printed in Subroutine INPUT TEXT AND PRINT RESULT in line 3080. If the substring stored in CURRENT$ cannot be found in the original text, our subroutine makes no changes and the calling module prints the original text. Suppose the value assigned to CURRENT$ is DAY. Since DAY cannot be found in the original text, Subroutine 13000 makes no changes and line 3080 prints the original text.

Summary of BASIC Statements

MID$(S$,n) = T$ — Replaces characters in the string S$ with characters from the string T$, starting at position n in S$.

```
5030 MID$(NAME1$,4)= "vey"
```

Summary of BASIC Functions

ASC(C$) Converts the first character in the string C$ to its ASCII code.

```
5030 CODE = ASC(RESPONSE$)
```

CHR$(CODE) Changes an ASCII code to its ASCII character.

```
5030 QUOTE$ = CHR$(34)
```

INSTR(n,S$,T$) Returns the position of the string T$ (its first occurrence) in the string S$. The search starts at position n. Returns a Ø if string T$ is not found.

```
5030 P = INSTR(1,S$,WORD$)
```

LEFT$(S$,n) Returns the left-most n characters from the string S$.

```
5030 L$ = LEFT$(S$,3)
```

LEN(S$) Returns the length of the string S$.

```
5030 LENGTH = LEN(NAME1$)
```

MID$(S$,m,n) Returns n characters from the string S$ beginning at position m.

```
5030 M$ = MID$(S$,2,7)
```

MID$(S$,m) Returns all characters from position m of the string S$ to the end of the string.

```
5030 M$ = MID$(S$,8)
```

RIGHT$(S$,n) Returns the right-most n characters from the string S$.

```
5030 R$ = RIGHT$(S$,6)
```

SPACE$(n) Returns a series of n spaces.

```
5030 PRINT "QUANTITY"; SPACE$(10) "ITEM"; SPACE$(10); "PRICE"
```

STR$(N) Converts a number to its string equivalent.

```
5030 S$ = STR$(NUMBER)
```

VAL(S$) Converts a numeric quantity stored as a string to its numeric value.

```
5030 HOURS = VAL(HOURS$)
```

Summary of Library Files

REPLACE.ASC Replaces strings in text.

SEPARATE.ASC Separates a string into three parts.

Chapter Summary

1. The computer stores every character (digit, letter, or other symbol) as a series of electronic impulses referred to as bits. Each bit (**b**inary dig**it**) is either on or off.
2. On paper, we use the digit 1 to represent an "on" bit and the digit Ø to represent an "off" bit.
3. The ASCII code (**A**merican **S**tandard **C**ode for **I**nformation **I**nterchange) consists of seven binary digits ranging from ØØØØØØØ to 1111111 thus creating a total of 128 codes. The order of the bits produces the decimal equivalent of a character.
4. The IBM microcomputers use an eighth bit thus increasing the number of characters to 255. Some of the additional characters are Greek letters and special mathematical symbols.
5. Numbers are stored differently than strings. A number may require 2, 4, or 8 bytes of storage depending on whether the number is an integer, a single-precision number, or a double-precision number. A string requires one byte of storage for each character in the string.
6. The hierarchical ordering of the ASCII codes makes it possible to compare strings.
7. BASIC compares two strings by comparing two characters at a time, one from each string, moving in a left-to-right direction on each string until a difference is found.
8. Strings can be copied from one storage location to another without altering the contents of the former location.
9. Concatenation is the process of attaching one string to the tail end of another. The "+" operator concatenates two strings.
10. It is possible to accumulate strings in a string variable. The strings are concatenated one at a time in a loop. Sample statement: 5030 WORD$ = WORD$+LETTER$.
11. A portion of a string can be extracted from another string by means of the LEFT$, RIGHT$, or MID$ functions. The portion of string extracted is called a substring.
12. A local variable is a variable that can be referenced by only one module. This can be simulated in BASIC by designating a specific variable for use in a module.
13. Frequently called subroutines should be written in such a way that they can be used with few or no modifications. They should be saved on disk in ASCII format.
14. The maximum number of characters that can be returned by the STRING$ function is 255. The maximum number of spaces that can be returned by the SPACE$ function is 255.
15. A function can be used as the argument of another function. Sample statement: 5030 HOURS = VAL(MID$(S$,14,2)). Here, BASIC executes the MID$ function, then executes the VAL function using the result of the MID$ function as the argument.
16. The difference between the ASCII code of an uppercase letter and that of its lowercase counterpart is 32. This concept is used to convert uppercase letters to lowercase letters and vice versa.
17. Headings can be centred automatically by combining the TAB and LEN functions in a PRINT statement in the following manner: 3020 PRINT TAB((80-LEN(HEADING$))/2+.5); HEADING$ where HEADING$ stores the heading to be centred.

Questions and Exercises

1. (a) Explain how a character (digit, letter of the alphabet, or other symbol) is stored in a computer.
   (b) What does ASCII represent?
   (c) How many binary digits make up an ASCII binary code? How many ASCII decimal codes are available?
   (d) The IBM microcomputers use an extra bit in their binary codes. What is the range of the additional decimal codes? Name two types of characters (among others) represented by the additional codes.

2. (a) How are numbers stored in a computer?
   (b) How are strings stored in a computer?

3. State whether the following relational expressions are true or false. Write the decimal notation beneath each character until a difference is found.

   (a) `Johnston <= Johnson`
   (b) `#12345 > 12345#`
   (c) `AB3 DEF <= AB3DEF`
   (d) `TRUE < true`
   (e) `Yes > YES`
   (f) `M3L 2T6 >= M3L 3T6`

4. Indicate the errors in the programs shown below. Note: There may be more than one error in a program.

   (a)
```
5010 NAME1$ = "Hanson"
5020 NAME2$ = "Hansen"
5030 PRINT
5040 IF NAME2$ >= NAME1$
       THEN PRINT NAME2$,NAME1$
       ELSE PRINT NAME2$,NAME1$
5050 END
RUN

Hansen         Hanson
```

   (b)
```
5010 NAME1$ = ""
5020 FOR I = 1 TO 3
5030   READ N$
5040   NAME1$ = NAME1$+N$
5050 NEXT I
5060 PRINT
5070 PRINT NAME1$
5080 DATA "Mr.","Jim","Dawes"
5090 END
```

   (c)
```
5010 WORD$ = ""
5020 FOR I = 1 TO 5
5030   INPUT "Enter a letter";L$
5040   IF L$ <> Z THEN WORD = WORD+L$
5050 NEXT I
5060 PRINT
5070 PRINT WORD
5080 END
```

5. Evaluate the following given that:
   D$ equals "Thursday, Day 4, Period 2" and N$ equals "Edward Martin, Vice-president".

```
(a) 5030 S1$ = LEFT$(D$,9) + " " + RIGHT$(D$,8) + ", " + MID$(D$,11,5)
(b) 5040 S2$ = RIGHT$(D$,8) + ", " + LEFT$(D$,15)
(c) 5050 S3$ = MID$(D$,11,6) + " " + LEFT$(D$,10) + MID$(D$,18)
(d) 5060 S4$ = RIGHT$(N$,14) + ": " + LEFT$(N$,13)
(e) 5070 S5$ = MID$(N$,16) + ": " + MID$(N$,8,8) + LEFT$(N$,6)
(f) 5080 MID$(N$,12) = "e"
```

6. Find the value of P in each of the statements (a) to (f) inclusive.

```
5010 S$ = "QUESTIONS AND EXERCISES"

(a) 5020 P = INSTR(3,S$,"S")
(b) 5030 P = INSTR(4,S$,"S")
(c) 5040 P = INSTR(6,S$," ")
(d) 5050 P = INSTR(4,S$,"ES")
(e) 5060 P = INSTR(3,S$,"es")
(f) 5070 P = INSTR(5,S$,"ST")
```

7. What will each of the following programs produce?

   (a)
```
5010 S1$ = "Extraction of Substrings"
5020 P = INSTR(12,S1$," ")
5030 M$ = MID$(S1$,P+1,9)
5040 L$ = LEFT$(S1$,10)
5050 S2$ = M$ + " " + L$
5060 PRINT
5070 PRINT S1$
5080 PRINT S2$
5090 END
```

   (b)
```
5010 A1$ = "493 Oakview Crescent"
5020 P1 = INSTR(1,A1$," ")
5030 P2 = INSTR(5,A1$," ")
5040 A2$ = MID$(A1$,P1+1,8) + MID$(A1$,P2+1,2) + "."
```

```
5050 PRINT
5060 PRINT A1$
5070 PRINT A2$
5080 END
```

(c)

```
5010 S$ = "Strings"
5020 L = LEN(S$)
5030 PRINT
5040 FOR I = L TO 1 STEP -1
5050   S$ = LEFT$(S$,I)
5060   PRINT S$
5070 NEXT I
5080 END
```

(d)

```
5010 S$ = "EAGER"
5020 L = LEN(S$)
5030 PRINT
5040 PRINT S$
5050 FOR I = 1 TO L
5060   PRINT TAB((L-I)+1);MID$(S$,I,1)
5070 NEXT I
5080 PRINT S$
5090 END
```

8. What is wrong with each of the following programs? Make the necessary corrections.

(a)

```
5010 S$ = "Something wrong"
5020 L = LEN$(S$)
5030 PRINT
5040 PRINT L
5050 END
```

(b)

```
5010 N = 1234
5020 PRINT
5030 PRINT VAL(N)
5040 END
```

(c)

```
5010 S$ = "90"
5020 PRINT
5030 PRINT CHR$(S$)
5040 END
```

(d)

```
5010 READ N
5020 DATA 5678
5030 PRINT
5040 PRINT STR(N)
5050 END
```

(e)

```
5010 ITEM$ = "Paper"
5020 PRICE = 60
5030 S$ = STRING(10,".")
5040 PRINT
5050 PRINT ITEM$;" ";S$;PRICE
5060 END
```

Write programs for the following problems. Do not verify INPUTed data. In each of Problems 9 and 11, standardize the subroutine that processes the data.

9. Use the INPUT statement within a FOR/NEXT loop to allow a user to enter names into the computer. Instruct the user to enter the first name, leave a space, then enter the last name. Your program must print the name in the following manner: Last name,First name. Refer to the sample program on page 272 if you need help in transferring values to and from your standardized subroutine.

Partial Output:

```
Enter first name, a space, last name

Name? Ellen Miller
Miller,Ellen

Name? Steven Taylor
Taylor,Steven

Name?
```

In the subroutine that extracts the first and last names, find the position of the space, then extract the names. Use an expression as the second argument of the LEFT$ and MID$ functions. The expression either increases or decreases the position by 1. In a PRINT statement of the calling module, concatenate the two substrings and insert a comma between them.

10. The string shown below supplies an employee's name, the rate of pay, and the number of working hours for each day of a particular week. Extract each of the seven substrings, then find the wages for the week.

```
"Paul Reid,10.24,8,8,7,7,8"
```

Wages = Total Number of Hours × Rate of Pay

RUN

```
Name: Paul Reid
Total hours: 38
Wages: 389.12
```

(a) Extract the employee's name.
(b) In one statement, extract the rate of pay, convert the rate to a numeric value and assign the value to a numeric variable.
(c) Set up a FOR/NEXT loop. The parameters in the FOR statement should be as follows:
   (i) Initial value — the position of the first number of hours.
   (ii) Test value — the position of the last number of hours.
   (iii) Step value — the number 2.
   Determine each position by merely examining the string. Do not use the INSTR function to find a position. Perform the following within the loop:
   (i) In one statement, extract one of the hours, convert the hours to a numeric value and assign the value to a numeric variable. Use the control variable as the second argument of the MID$ function.
   (ii) Accumulate the hours.
(d) Find the wages.

11. Assign a six-digit number to a numeric variable, then convert the number to a date, such as 10/27/99. Just before calling the subroutine that converts the number, assign the number, in string form, to a local string variable.

RUN

```
Number? 102799
Date: 10/27/99
```

In the subroutine that converts the number to a date, perform the following:

(a) Extract substrings 10, 27, and 99 from the string.
(b) Concatenate the substrings and insert slash characters to produce the date as shown above.

In the calling module, transfer the date from your local "out" variable to a program variable and print the date.

12. Print the output shown below. Use CHR$(34) to obtain the quotation marks.

RUN

```
Nancy stated, "I obtained 85 percent.".
```

Programming Problems

Design and code programs for the following problems. Standardize subroutines where instructed. You may decide to standardize a number of other subroutines.

1. Suppose your computer does not support the PRINT USING statement. Write a program that uses the READ and DATA statements to enter the following decimal numbers into the computer, then prints the numbers aligned at their decimal points.

   9.67, −3125.49, .26, 89.17, −123.45, 14.21

```
RUN
12345678

    9.67
-3125.49
     .26
   89.17
 -123.45
   14.21
```

   Convert a number just read to its string equivalent. Find the position of the decimal point and assign the position to a variable, say P. Use a PRINT statement with the TAB function to print the numeric value of the number (not its string equivalent). To align the decimal points, the argument of the TAB function should be an appropriate number of print positions for the integer part of the number minus P.

   Suppose you wish to print each decimal point in column 6. The argument of the TAB function would be 7−P. The number 7 is obtained by adding 1 to the column number designated for the aligned decimal points, in this case column 6. If you wish to align all decimal points in column 9, the argument would be 10−P.

2. In an exercise in Chapter Eight, a program printed address labels on the screen as well as to the printer. Names and addresses were entered into the computer by the READ and DATA statements. For this program, store at least five names and addresses in a data file in the manner shown below. Suggested filename: ADDRESS.DAT. The data file will also be used in a programming problem in Chapter 12.

   Mr. John Smith,123 Main Street/Anycity ZZ/M3L 6S7 — Name, address

   Your program must read the names and addresses from the data file, then print the labels one under the other with two blank lines between labels. Print the labels to the printer as well as on the screen. Use the standardized subroutine listed on page 273 to separate an address.

Sample Output:

(cleared screen)

```
         10        20        30        40        50        60        70        80
12345678901234567890123456789012345678901234567890123456789012345678901234567890
                               Mr. John Smith
                               123 Main Street
                               Anycity  ZZ
                               M3L 6S7


                               Mrs. Doris Moore
                               1394 Harcourt Street
                               Anycity  ZZ
                               M3L 1R4
```

3. Write a program that produces a multiple-choice test. For each question, display four possible answers from which the user must choose one. Your program must also count the number of correct answers chosen by the user and calculate the percentage of correct answers. Test your program on data stored in a data file. Sample data is given below. Each record contains one question, the four optional answers, and the correct answer.

TEST.DAT
The symbol > means:,A. Less than.,B. Greater than.,C. Equal to.,D. Not equal to.,B
The symbol < means:,A. Less than.,B. Greater than.,C. Equal to.,D. Not equal to.,A
The symbol <> means:,A. Less than.,B. Greater than.,C. Not equal to.,D. The symbols are invalid.,C

Your program should produce the following output.

(cleared screen)

```
         10        20        30        40        50        60        70        80
12345678901234567890123456789012345678901234567890123456789012345678901234567890
********************************************************************************
*                            MULTIPLE-CHOICE TEST                              *
********************************************************************************
Choose A, B, C, or D.

The symbol > means:
     A. Less than.
     B. Greater than.
     C. Equal to.
     D. Not equal to.
Enter your answer--B

The symbol < means:
     A. Less than.
     B. Greater than.
     C. Equal to.
     D. Not equal to.
Enter your answer--A

The symbol <> means:
     A. Less than.
     B. Greater than.
     C. Not equal to.
     D. The symbols are invalid.
Enter your answer--D

                        You chose 2 correct answer(s)
                        out of 3 questions.
                        Your percentage is  67%.
```

(cleared screen)

Code the heading and the one-line instruction in a separate subroutine. In the subroutine that reads the data file, count the number of questions read from the file and display the question and the four options. Allow the user to key in an answer (A, B, C, or D) and compare the answer with the answer read from the data file. Note that the answer in the data file is stored in upper case. In the event that the user types the answer in lower case, your IF statement must contain two conditions combined by the OR operator. The first condition compares the user's answer (in upper case) with the answer on disk. The second condition converts the user's answer to ASCII code and changes the code to that of an uppercase letter, then compares the converted code with the ASCII code of the answer on disk. Refer to page 279 where the conversion of a letter from lower case to upper case was discussed. If the user's answer is correct, increase a counter that counts the number of correct answers.

In another subroutine, calculate the percentage by dividing the number of correct answers by the number of questions and multiplying the result by 100. Use the PRINT USING statement to display the percentage.

4. The subroutine designed on pages 280 to 283 altered text by replacing strings. Write a program that deletes and inserts text (strings) as well as replaces text. Place each routine in a separate module. Your program must perform the following operations on the original text which is given in the output below.

   Replace: MATERIAL with TEXT
   Delete: TOGETHER
   Insert: YOUR between ALTERING and MATERIAL in the first sentence.

   (a) Type the original text in upper case.
   (b) Use CURRENT$ in all subroutines to store a substring of the original text. In subroutine REPLACE, the substring is MATERIAL; in subroutine DELETE, the substring is TOGETHER; and in subroutine INSERT, the substring is ALTERING.
   (c) Use NEW1$ to store a new word. In subroutine REPLACE, the new word is TEXT; in subroutine INSERT, the new word is YOUR.
   (d) Save the program as it will be modified in Problem 6.

Sample Output:

(cleared screen)

```
        10        20        30        40        50        60        70        80
12345678901234567890123456789012345678901234567890123456789012345678901234567890
Original text:

THE PROCESS OF ALTERING MATERIAL IS ACCOMPLISHED BY SEVERAL ROUTINES WHICH TOGET
HER FORM A TEXT EDITOR.  THREE COMMON ALTERATIONS ARE THE REPLACEMENT OF MATERIA
L, THE DELETION OF MATERIAL, AND THE INSERTION OF MATERIAL.

Enter R for replace, D for delete, I for insert, Q for quit R

Text to replace? MATERIAL
New text? TEXT

Enter R for replace, D for delete, I for insert, Q for quit--D

Text to delete? TOGETHER

Enter R for replace, D for delete, I for insert, Q for quit--I

Text to insert? YOUR
Previous word? ALTERING

Enter R for replace, D for delete, I for insert, Q for quit--Q

                                                               (cleared screen)
THE PROCESS OF ALTERING YOUR TEXT IS ACCOMPLISHED BY SEVERAL ROUTINES WHICH FORM
 A TEXT EDITOR.  THREE COMMON ALTERATIONS ARE THE REPLACEMENT OF TEXT, THE DELET
ION OF TEXT, AND THE INSERTION OF TEXT.
```

The Main Routine

Use the assignment statement to assign the original text to a variable, say S$. When keying in the text, do not insert spaces at the end of a screen line. Simply allow the cursor to drop to the next line and continue typing the material. Print the original text on a cleared screen.

Set up a WHILE/WEND loop that continues as long as a variable, say RESPONSE$, is not equal to Q (Quit). Inside the loop, use an INPUT statement to allow a user to enter R for Replace, D for Delete, I for Insert, or Q for Quit. Display an appropriate prompt. Do not check the response for validity.

Use multiple IF/THEN statements to determine which letter was entered. In each IF/THEN statement, call an appropriate subroutine. Example:

```
2110 IF RESPONSE$ = "R" THEN GOSUB 13000        'Replace text
```

Following the WHILE/WEND loop, print the modified text on a cleared screen.

Subroutine REPLACE TEXT

Merge the subroutine listed on page 282 with your main routine.

Subroutine DELETE TEXT

Use the INPUT statement to assign the word to be deleted (TOGETHER) to CURRENT$. Find the position of TOGETHER and store the position in a numeric variable, say P. In one statement, create new text as follows:

(a) Extract all text up to and including the word immediately before TOGETHER (WHICH). The second argument of the LEFT$ function should be the value of P less two characters.
(b) Extract all text starting at the space immediately after TOGETHER. The arguments of the MID$ function should be the same as those of the MID$ function in Subroutine REPLACE TEXT.

```
WHICH TOGETHER FORM
      ↑
  Value of P
```

(c) Concatenate these two substrings. Assign the newly created text to S$.

Subroutine INSERT TEXT

Use an INPUT statement to assign to NEW1$ the word to be inserted (YOUR) and a second INPUT statement to assign to CURRENT$ the word that will precede the inserted word. (The preceding word is ALTERING.) Find the position of ALTERING and store the position in a numeric variable, say P. In one statement, create new text as follows:

(a) Extract all text up to and including the space after ALTERING. The second argument of the LEFT$ function should be the value of P plus the length of ALTERING.
(b) Concatenate YOUR with the above substring.
(c) Extract all text starting at the space after ALTERING. The arguments of the MID$ function should be the same as those of the MID$ function in the two previous subroutines.
(d) Concatenate the substring obtained in (c) with the text created in (b). Assign the newly created text to S$.

```
ALTERING MATERIAL
↑        ↑
Value of P    P + LEN(ALTERING)
```

5. Write a program that converts all letters in a word (or words) to upper case. The subroutine that converts letters should be standardized and saved in ASCII format as it is needed in the next problem to modify the text editor. Suggested filename: CONVERT.ASC. Use a block of line numbers in the 14 000 range for the subroutine.

Output Samples:

```
Current text? material
MATERIAL
```

```
Current text? Your Material
YOUR MATERIAL
```

Allow the user to key in a string and store the string in variable CURRENT$. Copy the string into a local variable, say IN1$, then call the subroutine that converts letters to upper case.

Set up a FOR/NEXT loop in the subroutine that converts the letters. The test value of the FOR statement must be the length of the INPUTed string (stored in IN1$). Perform the following operations inside the loop:

(a) Extract a letter, convert the letter to its ASCII code, and assign the code to CODE. The arguments of the MID$ function should be IN1$, your control variable, and 1.

(b) In an IF statement, check the letter's ASCII code to determine if the letter is in lower case. If it is, convert its code to that of an uppercase letter by subtracting 32 from its code. Concatenate the character equivalent of this converted code with OUT1$. The THEN alternative should look as follows:

```
THEN OUT1$ = OUT1$+CHR$(CODE-32)
```

If the letter is already in upper case, simply concatenate the character equivalent of its code with OUT1$.

Remember to initialize OUT1$ to the null string before the loop begins. In the calling module, copy the string from OUT1$ into CURRENT$ and print the value of CURRENT$.

6. Modify your text editor written for Problem 4 so that a user may key in a lowercase r, d, i, or q and a lowercase word (or words) for text editing.

Immediately after the INPUT statement that allows a user to key in an R, D, I, or Q; convert the letter to its ASCII code. If the code is that of a lowercase letter, convert the code to that of an uppercase letter and assign the character equivalent of this converted code to your variable that stores an R, D, I, or Q. In another IF statement, check the uppercase letter. If the letter is not R, D, I, or Q, give the user the opportunity to key in another response. Display a prompt such as the following:

```
Invalid response. Enter R, D, I, or Q
```

Each subroutine of your text editor uses an INPUT statement to assign a word currently in the text to variable CURRENT$. Note that the original text is in upper case. If the word is entered in lower case, the functions using CURRENT$ will produce unexpected results. A subroutine for Problem 5 converts a lowercase string to upper case. Merge this subroutine with your program and call the subroutine after each INPUT statement that assigns a string to CURRENT$. Remember to copy the value of CURRENT$ into local variable IN1$ before calling the subroutine, and to assign the converted string to CURRENT$ after the subroutine has been called.

7. The program for the exercise on page 274 called a subroutine that separated a name into three parts: title, first name, and last name. No consideration was given to the manner in which the name was keyed in. Rewrite the program. In addition to extracting the substrings, print each substring with the first letter in upper case and the remaining letters in lower case regardless of the way the name was originally entered. Conversion should take place in a separate subroutine. Save both subroutines as one file in ASCII format (the subroutine that separates and the one that converts). Suggested filename: SEP-NAME.ASC. The file will be needed in a subsequent chapter. Use a block of line numbers in the 15 000 range for the subroutine that separates a name and a block of line numbers in the 16 000 range for the subroutine that converts letters.

Sample Output:

```
                                                                                (cleared screen)
         10        20        30        40        50        60        70        80
12345678901234567890123456789012345678901234567890123456789012345678901234567890
                Enter title, first name, last name in uppercase
                or lowercase letters. Separate parts by a space.
                Example: mr. john smith

                Name? [mr. andrew jones]

Is the name correct (y/n)? [y]
                                                                                (cleared screen)
                                Mr.
                                Andrew
                                Jones
```

Subroutine SEPARATE A NAME

Suppose the keyed-in name is assigned to NAME1$. In the subroutine that separates the name, use NAME1$ as the argument upon which each function operates. Find the positions of the two spaces. Extract the title, copy the title into local variable IN1$ and call the subroutine that converts letters. This called subroutine will send the converted title back through a local variable, say OUT1$. After calling the subroutine, concatenate a period to OUT1$ and assign the concatenated string to TITLE$.

```
xxxx TITLE$ = OUT1$+"."
```

Extract the first name, copy the first name into IN1$ and call the subroutine that converts letters. Following the GOSUB statement that called this subroutine, copy the value of OUT1$ into FIRST$. Perform a similar routine for the last name.

Subroutine CONVERT LETTERS

Initialize OUT1$ to the null string. The variable must accumulate the letters of each part of a name, not the letters of the entire name. Convert the first letter of IN1$ to its ASCII code and assign the code to CODE. In an IF statement, check the letter's ASCII code to determine if the letter is in lower case. If it is, convert its code to that of an uppercase letter by subtracting 32 from its code. Assign the character equivalent of this converted code to OUT1$. If the letter is already in upper case, merely assign the character equivalent of its code to OUT1$. Your IF statement should look as follows:

```
xxxx IF CODE >= 97 AND CODE <= 122
       THEN OUT1$ = CHR$(CODE-32)
       ELSE OUT1$ = CHR$(CODE)
```

Assign 2 to a variable, say N. You must now examine the remaining letters in the substring, starting with the second letter. Perform the operations in a WHILE/WEND loop. Use N as the counter that controls the loop and use the following WHILE statement to test two conditions:

```
xxxx WHILE N <= LEN(IN1$) AND MID$(IN1$,N,1) <> "."
```

Inside the loop, perform operations similar to those in the FOR/NEXT loop of the program for Problem 5. The major difference here is that you must convert a letter to lower case where in the former program you converted a letter to upper case. Remember to increase N just before the WEND statement.

Solutions for Exercises

11.1 Storing Information in the Computer

1. (a) Code: 54 Character: 6
   (b) Code: 44 Character: ,
   (c) Code: 82 Character: R
   (d) Code: 32 Character: a space
   (e) Code: 90 Character: Z
   (f) Code: 122 Character: z

2. String Handling

3. 52 48 50 48 32 69 78 65 77 69 36 32 61 32 34 74 111 104 110 34

11.2 Processing Strings

1. (a) In lines 5020 and 5030, Richard must be enclosed in quotation marks.
   (b) Lines 5030 and 5040 — LETTER must be a string variable.
   Line 5070 — The string **times** must be enclosed in quotation marks.
   (c) Line 5030 — A space must be concatenated between the two string variables, otherwise the names Leonard and Black are attached with no space between them.
   ```
   5030 NAME1$ = FIRST$ + " " + SECOND$
   ```
   (d) Line 5020 — T and F must each be enclosed in quotation marks.
   The logical operator must be AND.

2. (a)
   ```
   5040 IF NAME2$ <= NAME1$
        THEN PRINT NAME2$;"    ";NAME1$
        ELSE PRINT NAME1$;"    ";NAME2$
   ```
   (b)
   ```
   5040 IF MONTH$ = "July" THEN PRINT "The report is due in ";MONTH$
   ```

3.
```
5010 READ N1$,N2$,N3$
5020 SOCIAL$ = N1$ + "-" + N2$ + "-" + N3$
5030 PRINT
5040 PRINT SOCIAL$
5050 DATA "414","237","815"
5060 END
```

11.3 Breaking Up a String

1. (a) Laureen Hewitt
   (b) Laureen Carol Hewitt
   (c) Laureen C. Hewitt
   (d) Garry Marshall
   (e) Marshall, Garry W.

2. (a) 6
   (b) 6
   (c) 10
   (d) 2
   (e) 12
   (f) Ø

3. (a)
   ```
   RUN
   Programming
   ```
   (b)
   ```
   RUN
   Curious
         u
        o
       i
     r
    u
   Curious
   ```

4.
```
5050 IF RIGHT$(CNAME$,5) = "Smith" THEN COUNT.SMITH = COUNT.SMITH+1 :
     PRINT COUNT.SMITH,CNAME$
```

11.4 Standardized Subroutines

```
1000 'SEPARATE A NAME                    M. MCRITCHIE                    SEPT 6
1002 '*********************************************************************
1004 '    THIS PROGRAM SEPARATES A NAME INTO TITLE, FIRST NAME, LAST NAME
1006 '*********************************************************************
1010 'NAME1$                 - NAME
1020 'RESPONSE$              - USER'S RESPONSE (y/n)
1030 'IN1$                   - LOCAL VARIABLE. STORES THE NAME.
1040 'P1,P2                  - POSITIONS OF THE SPACES IN THE NAME
1050 'OUT1$,OUT2$,OUT3$      - LOCAL VARIABLES STORING TITLE, FIRST NAME,
1060 '                         LAST NAME
1070 'TITLE$,FIRST$,LAST$ - TITLE, FIRST NAME, LAST NAME
2000 '*********************************************************************
2002 '                               MAIN ROUTINE
2004 '*********************************************************************
2010  GOSUB 3000                     'INPUT and print name
2020  END
3000 '*********************************************************************
3002 '                            INPUT AND PRINT NAME
3004 '*********************************************************************
3010  CLS
3020  LOCATE 9
3030  PRINT TAB(17) "Enter title, first name, last name separated"
3040  PRINT TAB(17) "from each other by a space (e.g. Mr. John Smith)"
3050  PRINT
3060  INPUT "________________Name";NAME1$
3070  PRINT
3080  INPUT "Is the name correct (y/n)";RESPONSE$
3090  IF RESPONSE$ <> "y" AND RESPONSE$ <> "Y"
         THEN INPUT "Re-enter the name--",NAME1$ : GOTO 3080
3100  IN1$ = NAME1$
3110  GOSUB 12000                       'Separate data (name)
3120  TITLE$ = OUT1$
3130  FIRST$ = OUT2$
3140  LAST$ = OUT3$
3150  CLS
3160  LOCATE 12
3170  PRINT TAB(38) TITLE$
3180  PRINT TAB(38) FIRST$
3190  PRINT TAB(38) LAST$
3200  RETURN
12000 '********************************************************************
12002 '                          SEPARATE DATA (NAME)
12004 '********************************************************************
12010  P1 = INSTR(1,IN1$," ")
12020  P2 = INSTR(P1+1,IN1$," ")
12030  OUT1$ = LEFT$(IN1$,P1-1)
12040  OUT2$ = MID$(IN1$,P1+1,(P2-P1)-1)
12050  OUT3$ = MID$(IN1$,P2+1)
12060  RETURN
65529 'End of program listing
```

11.5 The MID$ Statement

The value of ADDRESS$ will be 123 Grandway Avenue.

11.6 Other String-Handling Functions

1. (a)
```
RUN
  5789
 5789
```

(c)
```
RUN
 67          C
```

(e)
```
RUN
Ribbons ...... 2
```

(b)
```
RUN

 3456
 3456
```

(d)
```
RUN

T               84
```

(f)
```
RUN

Printer    Ribbons
```

2. (a)
```
RUN

unrecognizable
```

(b)
```
RUN

String h
tring ha
ring han
ing hand
ng handl
g handli
 handlin
handling
```

3.
```
1000 'EXTRACT NAME AND SCORES
2000 'MAIN ROUTINE
2010   GOSUB 3000                 'INPUT name and scores
2020   END
3000 'SUBROUTINE INPUT NAME AND SCORES
3010   PRINT
3020   PRINT "Enter the name and scores separated by spaces"
3030   PRINT "(e.g. John Smith 94 89 93)
3040   PRINT
3050   INPUT "Name and scores";S$
3060   GOSUB 4000              'Calculate average
3070   PRINT "Average score:";AVERAGE.SCORE
3080   RETURN
4000 'SUBROUTINE CALCULATE AVERAGE
4010   SNAME$ = LEFT$(S$,13)
4020   SCORE1 = VAL(MID$(S$,15,2))
4030   SCORE2 = VAL(MID$(S$,18,2))
4040   SCORE3 = VAL(MID$(S$,21))
4050   TOTAL.SCORE = SCORE1+SCORE2+SCORE3
4060   AVERAGE.SCORE = TOTAL.SCORE/3
4070   RETURN
65529 'End of program listing
```

4.
```
1000 'CONVERT NUMBER TO COURSE NAME
2000 'MAIN ROUTINE
2010   GOSUB 3000              'Enter number, extract and print
2020   END
3000 'SUBROUTINE ENTER NUMBER, EXTRACT AND PRINT
3010   COURSE# = 1004238
3020   S$ = STR$(COURSE#)
3030   NUMBER$ = MID$(S$,2,3)
3040   PERIOD$ = MID$(S$,5,1)
3050   ROOM$ = MID$(S$,6)
3060   COURSE$ = NUMBER$ + ": " + PERIOD$ + "/" + ROOM$
3070   PRINT
3080   PRINT COURSE$
3090   RETURN
65529 'End of program listing
```

11.7 Often-Used Routines

```
1000 'CONVERT FIRST LETTER TO UPPER CASE
2000 'MAIN ROUTINE
2010   GOSUB 3000         'INPUT name and convert first letter
2020   END
3000 'SUBROUTINE INPUT NAME AND CONVERT FIRST LETTER
3010   PRINT
3020   INPUT "First name";NAME1$
3030   FIRST$ = LEFT$(NAME1$,1)
3040   REM.LETTERS$ = MID$(NAME1$,2)
3050   CODE = ASC(FIRST$)
3060   IF CODE >= 97 AND CODE <= 122 THEN FIRST$ = CHR$(CODE-32)
3070   NAME1$ = FIRST$ + REM.LETTERS$
3080   PRINT NAME1$
3090   RETURN
65529 'End of program listing
```

12

ONE-DIMENSIONAL ARRAYS

Objectives

Occasions arise when we must store and manipulate large amounts of data that must be held in memory for processing more than once. Assigning each data item to a different variable would be an extremely tedious exercise. The storage of large quantities of data items in memory and the reprocessing of the items is made possible through the use of arrays. An array is a collection of related items. In this chapter, you will learn how to:

- Store data items in an array.
- Access the data items stored in an array.
- Process the data stored in an array.
- Search an array for a particular value.
- Sort the contents of an array.
- Update records using arrays.
- Write updated records to the same data file.

Contents

12.1 Creating Arrays

Basic Concepts of an Array

Until now, most of our programs read a data record from a data file, performed calculations on the values, printed the results, then read the next data record. Each time a record was read, the former record in memory was lost.

The above principle of data entry cannot be used in situations where we must keep all data items in memory for subsequent reprocessing. Suppose we wish to find the average score of a set of test scores, then print those scores that are higher than the average. Obviously, each score must be reaccessed after the average is found so that we can compare each score with the average.

As mentioned, we can store the data items in an array. Our test scores could be considered an array with each score an element of the array. Let us use "s" as the name of the array. In mathematics, we denote the elements of an array by using subscripts. The elements of array "s" would be as follows: s_1, s_2, s_3, s_4, . . . ,etc.

The fundamental structure of an array in computer programming is similar to the structure of an array used in mathematics. The array consists of a collection of related items which are identified by means of subscripts. To set up an array within the computer, a sufficient number of memory locations must be set aside to store the data. These locations are adjacent to one another in a block of storage considered an array. The array must be named. Each storage location within the block is referred to as an element of the array and each is capable of storing one value. Each element must have an address that is unique. The address must consist of the name of the array and the location of the element within the array. In this way, BASIC will know which array and which element in the array it must reference.

Subscripted Variables

Suppose we wish to store six test scores in an array. Let us call our array SCORE. As mentioned above, a value stored in an array must be accessed by referencing the name of the array in which the value is stored and its location within the array. If the scores are stored in elements 1 through 6 of array SCORE, we must use the following notations to gain access to the scores: SCORE(1), SCORE(2), SCORE(3), SCORE(4), SCORE(5), SCORE(6). The number within parentheses is called a subscript. SCORE(1), SCORE(2) etc. are called subscripted variables. (We refer to these variables as SCORE sub 1, SCORE sub 2, etc.)

To name an array, we must apply the same rules used for naming variables. As with variable names, it is a good idea to use a name that indicates what is stored in the array. A subscripted variable and a simple variable may have the same name. For example, X(1) and X are two distinct variables. If the array name is numeric, such as SCORE, the array can store only numeric data. If the array name is type string, such as SNAME$, the array can store only strings. Strings stored in an array need not all be the same length. The lengths may vary from the null string (no characters) to 255 characters.

We reference each element of array SCORE by an appropriate subscripted variable. SCORE(1) references the first element of array SCORE, SCORE(2) references the second element of array SCORE. The subscript of a subscripted variable may be expressed as a number, a numeric variable, or a numeric expression. For instance, if N=1, SCORE(N) references the first element of array SCORE; if N=5, SCORE(N-3) references the second element of array SCORE. Subscripts should be integers. If we use a decimal number as a subscript, BASIC rounds off the number to the nearest integer. SCORE(2.4) references the second element of the array; SCORE(2.5) references the third element of the array.

Dimensioning an Array

An array is created by means of a DIM statement. DIM is the abbreviation for DIMENSION. Two examples of DIM statements are given below.

(a) `2010 DIM SNAME$(25)` (b) `2010 DIM SCORE(10)`

Each statement contains the key word DIM followed by the array name and the dimension within parentheses. The DIM statement performs the following functions:

1. It names an array. The name, in turn, declares the array's type. In example (a), the array is a string array named SNAME$; in example (b), the array is a numeric array named SCORE.
2. It allocates storage locations to the array. Actually, 26 elements are created in example (a) and 11 in example (b). This is because BASIC creates an element Ø. Thus, elements range from Ø to 25 in example (a) and from Ø to 10 in example (b). Since counting from 1 is simpler than counting from Ø, our programs will not be using element Ø.

We must be aware of a number of additional features concerning the DIM statement.

1. More than one array may be dimensioned in a DIM statement. The arrays must be separated by commas.

```
2010 DIM STUDENT.NO(25),SNAME$(25),SCORE(6)
```

2. A DIM statement must be placed before any statement that references an array. In our programs, we will place the DIM statement in the main routine.
3. An array may not be dimensioned more than once.
4. When an array with 11 or fewer elements is required, the array need not be dimensioned. For any undimensioned array, BASIC automatically allocates 11 elements to the array (elements Ø through 10). However, it is best to dimension all arrays regardless of their sizes.
5. We may allocate more locations than we need in an array but not less. When we attempt to reference an element out of the dimensioned range, BASIC displays **Subscript out of range in xxxx** where xxxx is the line number of the statement referencing the element. When we allocate more locations than we need, the elements not filled by our program will contain zeros or null strings depending on the type of array. As with simple variables, BASIC places zeros or null strings in subscripted variables (and thus in elements) before a program is executed.
6. In the DIM statement, the array's dimension may be expressed as a number, a numeric variable, or a numeric expression.

Exercises

1. Code DIM statements to dimension the following. Use one DIM statement for each exercise. Ignore element zero.

   (a) A numeric array with 30 elements.
   (b) A string array with 15 elements.
   (c) A numeric array and a string array each with 20 elements.
   (d) Two numeric arrays, one with 20 elements and the other with 25 elements; two string arrays, one with 15 elements and the other with 18 elements.

2. Indicate the errors, if any, in the following statements. Make the necessary corrections.

   (a) `2010 DIM MARK`
   (b) `2010 N = 12`
   `2020 DIM MONTH(N-2)`
   (d) `2010 DIM A(14);B(14);C(14)`
   (e) `2010 DIM SNAME$(23),SALES(23)`

(c)
```
2010 A$ = "14"
2020 DIM ADDRESS$(A$)
```

(f)
```
2010 DIM TELEPHONE$(N)
2020 N = 40
```

12.2 Data Entry and Data Output Using Arrays

Loading an Array

Data items are stored in an array by assigning a value to each subscripted variable of the array. Any of the four methods that we used to assign values to simple variables may be used to assign values to subscripted variables. We can use one of the following statements to assign 69 to subscripted variable SCORE(1).

```
3020 SCORE(1) = 69
3020 INPUT SCORE(1)
3020 INPUT #1, SCORE(1)
3020 READ SCORE(1)
3030 DATA 69
```

To store six scores in array SCORE by means of the INPUT statement, the sequence of statements would be as follows:

```
3020 INPUT SCORE(1)
3030 INPUT SCORE(2)
3040 INPUT SCORE(3)
3050 INPUT SCORE(4)
3060 INPUT SCORE(5)
3070 INPUT SCORE(6)
```

This approach to entering values in an array leaves much to be desired, particularly when the number of values is large. A great advantage in using subscripted variables is the fact that we can use a variable as a subscript. Combining this feature with the features of a FOR/NEXT loop produces a much superior method of filling an array. By changing the value of NO.STUDENTS in the FOR statement below, we can store any number of values in array SCORE. Let us store the six scores 69,93,85,71,67,82 in the array.

```
3030 INPUT "-------------------------------Number of students";NO.STUDENTS
3040 PRINT
3050 FOR STUDENT = 1 TO NO.STUDENTS
3060   INPUT "------------------------------------Score";SCORE(STUDENT)
3070 NEXT STUDENT
```

The first time BASIC passes through the loop, STUDENT = 1. When a user keys in 69 in response to the INPUT statement, BASIC assigns 69 to SCORE(1).

SCORE(1) 69

The second time BASIC passes through the loop, STUDENT = 2. When a user keys in 93, BASIC assigns 93 to SCORE(2).

SCORE(1) 69
SCORE(2) 93

This continues until the loop terminates. At that time, our array will contain the following values:

SCORE(1) 69
SCORE(2) 93
SCORE(3) 85
SCORE(4) 71
SCORE(5) 67
SCORE(6) 82

The FOR/NEXT loop below loads two arrays: one array stores the student numbers 4931, 2867, 5263, 1942, 6429, 3917; the other array stores the scores.

```
3050 FOR STUDENT = 1 TO NO.STUDENTS
3060    INPUT "_____Student number, score";STUDENT.NO(STUDENT),SCORE(STUDENT)
3070 NEXT STUDENT
```

The arrays will contain the following values:

STUDENT.NO(1)	4931	SCORE(1)	69
STUDENT.NO(2)	2867	SCORE(2)	93
STUDENT.NO(3)	5263	SCORE(3)	85
STUDENT.NO(4)	1942	SCORE(4)	71
STUDENT.NO(5)	6429	SCORE(5)	67
STUDENT.NO(6)	3917	SCORE(6)	82

Printing from an Array

Printing values from an array is very similar to loading an array. We use a FOR/NEXT loop to reference each element of the array.

```
4060 FOR STUDENT = 1 TO NO.STUDENTS
4070    PRINT SCORE(STUDENT);
4080 NEXT STUDENT
RUN

 69  93  85  71  67  82
```

As the control variable changes from 1 to 6, the subscript of variable SCORE also changes from 1 to 6. Each time BASIC passes through the loop, a value is printed from one of the subscripted variables; first from SCORE(1), then from SCORE(2), etc. The above routine prints the output on one line because of the trailing semicolon in the PRINT statement.

Exercises

1. Use the READ and DATA statements to load the data given below into three arrays. Print the contents of the arrays in a separate subroutine. Use a PRINT USING statement that includes an image. Call the subroutines from a skeleton main routine. The items in the second column are amounts purchased, the items in the third column are payments made.

```
RUN
         10        20        30        40        50        60        70        80
12345678901234567890123456789012345678901234567890123456789012345678901234567890

                    ABC Fashions              $1,567.32      $694.82
                    New Clothiers             $   984.57     $463.48
                    Rite-Shoes                $   862.43     $426.43
                    Modern Sportswear         $1,942.31      $854.67
```

2. Modify the program for Exercise 1 by loading the arrays and printing their contents in one subroutine.

12.3 Processing Data Stored in an Array

A Sample Program

The program on the following page stores our six scores in an array, prints the scores, calculates the average score, then determines which scores are higher than the average. These higher scores are subsequently printed. For this program, we will omit the verification of data.

```
1000 'AVERAGE SCORE                         M. MCRITCHIE                    OCT 2
1002 '*********************************************************************
1004 '        THIS PROGRAM CALCULATES AN AVERAGE SCORE AND DETERMINES
1006 '                WHICH SCORES ARE HIGHER THAN THE AVERAGE
1008 '*********************************************************************
1010 'TOTAL.SCORE - TOTAL STUDENT SCORES
1020 'NO.STUDENTS - NUMBER OF STUDENTS
1030 'STUDENT     - CONTROL VARIABLE AND SUBSCRIPT OF SUBSCRIPTED VARIABLES
1040 'SCORE()     - ARRAY THAT STORES THE STUDENTS' SCORES
1050 'HEADING1$   - FIRST HEADING
1060 'AVERAGE     - AVERAGE SCORE
1070 'HEADING2$   - SECOND HEADING
2000 '*********************************************************************
2002 '                              MAIN ROUTINE
2004 '*********************************************************************
2010  DIM SCORE(30)
2020  GOSUB 3000                'Load array, accumulate scores
2030  GOSUB 4000                'Print scores
2040  GOSUB 5000                'Process data
2050  END
3000 '*********************************************************************
3002 '                       LOAD ARRAY, ACCUMULATE SCORES
3004 '*********************************************************************
3010  TOTAL.SCORE = 0
3020  CLS
3030  LOCATE 9
3040  INPUT "______________________________Number of students";NO.STUDENTS
3050  PRINT
3060  FOR STUDENT = 1 TO NO.STUDENTS
3070    INPUT "___________________________________Score";SCORE(STUDENT)
3080    TOTAL.SCORE = TOTAL.SCORE+SCORE(STUDENT)
3090  NEXT STUDENT
3100  RETURN
4000 '*********************************************************************
4002 '                              PRINT SCORES
4004 '*********************************************************************
4010  CLS
4020  LOCATE 5
4030  HEADING1$ = "SCORES"
4040  PRINT TAB((80-LEN(HEADING1$))/2+.5); HEADING1$
4050  PRINT
4060  FOR STUDENT = 1 TO NO.STUDENTS
4070    PRINT TAB(39) SCORE(STUDENT)
4080  NEXT STUDENT
4090  RETURN
5000 '*********************************************************************
5002 '                              PROCESS DATA
5004 '*********************************************************************
5010  AVERAGE = TOTAL.SCORE/NO.STUDENTS
5020  PRINT
5030  PRINT TAB(31) USING "Average score:_##.##";AVERAGE
5040  PRINT
5050  HEADING2$ = "SCORES HIGHER THAN THE AVERAGE SCORE"
5060  PRINT TAB((80-LEN(HEADING2$))/2+.5); HEADING2$
5070  PRINT
5080  FOR STUDENT = 1 TO NO.STUDENTS
5090    IF SCORE(STUDENT) > AVERAGE THEN PRINT TAB(39) SCORE(STUDENT)
5100  NEXT STUDENT
5110  RETURN
65529 'End of program listing
RUN
```

(cleared screen)

```
         10        20        30        40        50        60        70        80
12345678901234567890123456789012345678901234567890123456789012345678901234567890
                        Number of students? 6

                             Score? 69
                             Score? 93
                             Score? 85
                             Score? 71
                             Score? 67
                             Score? 82

                               SCORES

                                 69
                                 93
                                 85
                                 71
                                 67
                                 82

                        Average score: 77.83

                SCORES HIGHER THAN THE AVERAGE SCORE

                                 93
                                 85
                                 82
```

(cleared screen)

The scores are accumulated in the subroutine that loads the array. Subscripted variable SCORE(STUDENT) is used to access each score in the statement that accumulates. In Subroutine 5000, we find and print the average score. After the average is printed, each score must be reaccessed so that we can compare each score with the average. Therefore, it was necessary, in Subroutine 3000, to store the scores in an array. In this way, the scores remain in memory ready to be referenced anytime they are needed.

Finding scores higher than the average takes place in the FOR/NEXT loop in line 5090. If a score is higher than the average, the IF statement prints the score. Note that the headings SCORES and SCORES HIGHER THAN THE AVERAGE SCORE are automatically centred. This concept was discussed in Chapter Eleven.

Our array SCORE is only partially filled with scores. To keep the output short, we entered only six scores in an array that has been dimensioned DIM SCORE(30). The scores are stored in variables SCORE(1) through SCORE(6). SCORE(Ø), and SCORE(7) through SCORE(30) are filled with zeros, placed there by BASIC before the program was executed.

Programs that use the INPUT statement to enter data and that subsequently print the data, as does the above program, must store the values in an array. In this way, the prompts and the keyed-in values are not interspersed with the printed data since the data can be printed after all values have been INPUTed.

Exercises

1. What would be the output from the following program segment? Why does the segment produce the output that it does?

```
2000 '*********************************************************************
2002 '                          MAIN ROUTINE
2004 '*********************************************************************
2010  DIM ENAME$(10),SALES(10)
2020  GOSUB 3000              'Load array, process data
2030  GOSUB 4000              'Print detail lines
2040  END
```

```
3000 '***************************************************************
3002 '                        LOAD ARRAY, PROCESS DATA
3004 '***************************************************************
3010  RATE = 10
3020  FOR EMPLOYEE = 1 TO 3
3030    READ ENAME$(EMPLOYEE),SALES(EMPLOYEE)
3040    COMMISSION = SALES(EMPLOYEE)*RATE/100
3050  NEXT EMPLOYEE
3060  DATA "Adrian Johnson"   ,3000
3070  DATA "Larry Cook"       ,4000
3080  DATA "Patricia Forrest",5000
3090  RETURN
4000 '***************************************************************
4002 '                           PRINT DETAIL LINES
4004 '***************************************************************
4010  FOR EMPLOYEE = 1 TO 3
4020    PRINT TAB(20) USING "\______________\_____$####,.##_____$###.##";
        ENAME$(EMPLOYEE),SALES(EMPLOYEE),COMMISSION
4030  NEXT EMPLOYEE
4040  RETURN
```

2. To determine the financial security of a company, one can divide the current assets by the current liabilities. The result is the working capital ratio. A ratio greater than one indicates that assets are greater than liabilities, a ratio less than one indicates that liabilities are greater than assets.

   Write a program that calculates the ratio for each of three years. Allow a user to key in the year, the assets, and the liabilities for each year. Do not centre the output. Use the PRINT USING statement that includes the image to print the assets, liabilities, and ratio. Call your subroutines from a skeleton main routine.

   Sample Output:

   (cleared screen)

```
Year, assets, liabilities? 19XX,100000,85000
Year, assets, liabilities? 19XX,150000,159000
Year, Assets, liabilities? 19XX,200000,200000

Year: 19XX
Assets: $100,000.00   Liabilities: $ 85,000.00   Ratio: 1.176

Year: 19XX
Assets: $150,000.00   Liabilities: $159,000.00   Ratio: 0.943

Year: 19XX
Assets: $200,000.00   Liabilities: $200,000.00   Ratio: 1.000
```

12.4 Searching an Array

Introduction to an Array Search

Searching an array for a particular item is an important activity in data processing. The value to be found is called the key. To find the key, the contents of each subscripted variable of the array must be examined. If the key is found, the record containing the "found" key can be processed; if the key is not found, an appropriate message should be displayed.

Our program requires the two data files given below. Each record in the master file consists of a student's number, name, address, and telephone number. Records are stored in order by student number in the master file but not in the scores file.

Although the program will be reading fields from MASTER.DAT into arrays, the data file can be created in the usual manner. That is, we INPUT the student's number, name, address, and telephone number into simple variables, then write the values of these variables to MASTER.DAT. Arrays are not needed in the program that creates the file, since we write a record to the file immediately after we INPUT the record. Just remember to place the name in quotation marks as the name includes a comma and, as in the addresses of our Accounts Receivable file, leave two spaces between the street address and the city, between the city and the province, and between the province and the postal code.

MASTER.DAT
1942,"Lindsay,Donna",637 North Avenue Anycity ZZ M3L 4T8,593-2184
2593,"Meyer,Tom",485 First Avenue Anycity ZZ M3L 3W7,334-9815
2867,"Saunders,Bryan",942 South Avenue Anycity ZZ M3L 6V4,243-1825
3917,"Kent,Sherri",153 East Street Anycity ZZ M3L 2Y5,413-9426
4931,"Hughes,James",984 West Street Anycity ZZ M3L 1X6,458-6218
6429,"Walker,Anna",325 Third Street Anycity ZZ M3L 8S5,334-1628

SCORES2.DAT
4931,69
2867,93
5263,85 — Student number and score
1942,71
6429,67
3917,82

Note that one student number in the scores file does not appear in the master file and vice versa. What our program must do is match the scores in the scores file with the students in the master file. One field common to both files is the student number. To match scores with students, each student number in the scores file will be used as the key to find the corresponding student number in the master file. When a match occurs, the program prints the "found" record from the master file and the score from the scores file.

The Program

```
1000 'ARRAY SEARCH                        M. MCRITCHIE                   OCT 6
1002 '*********************************************************************
1004 '          THIS PROGRAM SEARCHES A MASTER FILE FOR A STUDENT NUMBER
1006 '              AND MATCHES A TEST SCORE WITH THE "FOUND" RECORD
1008 '*********************************************************************
1010 'I              - COUNTER AND SUBSCRIPT OF SUBSCRIPTED VARIABLES
1020 'STUDENT.NO() - ARRAY THAT STORES STUDENT NUMBERS FROM THE MASTER FILE
1030 'SNAME$()      - ARRAY THAT STORES STUDENT NAMES
1040 'ADDRESS$()    - ARRAY THAT STORES STUDENT ADDRESSES
1050 'TELEPHONE$() - ARRAY THAT STORES STUDENT TELEPHONE NUMBERS
1060 'IN1$()        - LOCAL ARRAY. STORES STUDENT NUMBERS FROM MASTER FILE.
1070 'ARRAY.SIZE    - SIZE OF AN ARRAY
1080 'ST.NO         - STUDENT NUMBER FROM THE SCORES FILE
1090 'SCORE         - SCORE FROM THE SCORES FILE
1100 'IKEY$         - THE KEY. A STUDENT NUMBER FROM THE SCORES FILE.
1110 'FLAG          - A FLAG OF 1 INDICATES THAT THE KEY WAS FOUND. A FLAG
1120 '                OF 0 INDICATES THAT THE KEY WAS NOT FOUND.
1130 'W             - LOCAL CONTROL VARIABLE
1140 'OUT1          - LOCAL VARIABLE. HOLDS THE POSITION (ELEMENT NUMBER) OF
1150 '                THE FOUND KEY.
1160 'RECORD.NO     - POSITION OF THE FOUND KEY
2000 '*********************************************************************
2002 '                              MAIN ROUTINE
2004 '*********************************************************************
2010   CLS
2020   LOCATE 5
2030   OPEN "B:MASTER.DAT" FOR INPUT AS #1
2040   OPEN "B:SCORES2.DAT" FOR INPUT AS #2
2050   DIM STUDENT.NO(30),SNAME$(30),ADDRESS$(30),TELEPHONE$(30),IN1$(30)
2060   GOSUB 3000                        'Read master data file
2070   GOSUB 4000                        'Read scores data file
2080   CLOSE #1,#2
2090   END
```

```
3000 '**********************************************************************
3002 '                            READ MASTER DATA FILE
3004 '**********************************************************************
3010  I = 0
3020  WHILE NOT EOF(1)
3030    I = I+1
3040    INPUT #1, STUDENT.NO(I),SNAME$(I),ADDRESS$(I),TELEPHONE$(I)
3050    IN1$(I) = STR$(STUDENT.NO(I))
3060  WEND
3070  ARRAY.SIZE = I
3080  RETURN
4000 '**********************************************************************
4002 ' READ SCORES DATA FILE, CALL SUBROUTINE TO SEARCH FOR A STUDENT NUMBER
4004 '**********************************************************************
4010  WHILE NOT EOF(2)
4020    INPUT #2, ST.NO,SCORE
4030    IKEY$ = STR$(ST.NO)
4040    GOSUB 17000               'Search one-dimensional array
4050    RECORD.NO = OUT1
4060    IF FLAG = 1
           THEN GOSUB 5000
           ELSE PRINT "Student number";ST.NO;"not found" : PRINT
4065       'Subroutine 5000 prints the "found" student's record and score
4070  WEND
4080  RETURN
5000 '**********************************************************************
5002 '                       PRINT STUDENT'S RECORD AND SCORE
5004 '**********************************************************************
5010  PRINT USING "####___\____________\___\__________________________________
_\____\______\";STUDENT.NO(RECORD.NO),SNAME$(RECORD.NO),ADDRESS$(RECORD.NO),
             TELEPHONE$(RECORD.NO)
5020  PRINT "Score:";SCORE
5030  PRINT
5040  RETURN
17000 '*********************************************************************
17002 '                          SEARCH ONE-DIMENSIONAL ARRAY
17004 '*********************************************************************
17010  FLAG = 0
17020  W = 0
17030  WHILE W < ARRAY.SIZE AND FLAG = 0
17040    W = W+1
17050    IF IN1$(W) = IKEY$ THEN FLAG = 1
17060  WEND
17070  OUT1 = W
17080  RETURN
65529 'End of program listing
```

The output of matched scores and student records will be as follows:

```
4931   Hughes,James      984 West Street   Anycity  ZZ  M3L 1X6     458-6218
Score: 69

2867   Saunders,Bryan    942 South Avenue   Anycity  ZZ  M3L 6V4    243-1825
Score: 93

Student number 5263 not found

1942   Lindsay,Donna     637 North Avenue   Anycity  ZZ  M3L 4T8    593-2184
Score: 71

6429   Walker,Anna       325 Third Street   Anycity  ZZ  M3L 8S5    334-1628
Score: 67

3917   Kent,Sherri       153 East Street   Anycity  ZZ  M3L 2Y5     413-9426
Score: 82
```

As mentioned on page 307, we will be searching for a student number in the master file. Note that the student numbers from the master file are stored in a numeric array (line 3040) and that a student number from the scores file is stored in a numeric variable (line 4020). To standardize the subroutine that searches for an item, we will conduct the search on strings. This means that if we are searching for a number, the number must be converted to string form and the string stored in a string variable. Furthermore, the numbers to be searched must also be converted to string form but stored in a string array. These conversions must be performed before the subroutine is called. If we are searching for a string, for example a name, no conversion is necessary. Thus, regardless of the type of value to be found, our "search" subroutine needs no modification.*

The main routine opens the two files. The master file is numbered #1 and the scores file is numbered #2. Two subroutines are called to read the files. Subroutine 3000 reads the master file. The values are stored in four arrays: STUDENT.NO, SNAME$, ADDRESS$, and TELEPHONE$. After a value has been placed in each of the arrays, the student number is converted to type string and stored in local array IN1$ (line 3050). The STR$ function converts a numeric value to a string. Array IN1$ will be searched for a student number in Subroutine SEARCH ONE-DIMENSIONAL ARRAY.

Note how we make use of variable I. It serves as the subscript for the subscripted variables and as a counter which determines the size of each array listed in lines 3040 and 3050. The size is copied into variable ARRAY.SIZE for use in Subroutine SEARCH ONE-DIMENSIONAL ARRAY.

Subroutine 4000 reads the scores file. The fields need not be stored in arrays since we will not be referencing the records again after they have been processed. As each record is read, the student number is converted to type string and stored in local variable IKEY$ (line 4030). Again, we use the STR$ function to convert a student number to a string. The student number in IKEY$ is our key. Subroutine SEARCH ONE-DIMENSIONAL ARRAY is called to search for the key.

Subroutine 17000 searches array IN1$ for the key. Recall that array IN1$ contains the student numbers from our master file and IKEY$ contains a student number (the key) from our scores file. All these values have been converted to string form. We first set a variable, named FLAG, to zero. Its value will change to one if the key is found, otherwise, its value will remain zero. We also initialize a control variable, W, to zero.

The WHILE/WEND loop continues as long as two conditions are true: as long as control variable W is less than the size of array IN1$ and as long as the value of FLAG remains zero. In the first condition, the loop terminates when the value of W is equal to the size of the array; that is, when the entire array has been searched. In this case, the key has not been found and the value of FLAG remains zero. In the second condition, the loop terminates when FLAG becomes one, an indication that the key has been found.

Statement 17050 examines each element of array IN1$. Suppose we are searching for student number 3917.

Variable IKEY$	*Array IN1$*
3917	IN1$(1) 1942
	IN1$(2) 2593
	IN1$(3) 2867
	IN1$(4) 3917
	IN1$(5) 4931
	IN1$(6) 6429

The key is found in element 4 of array IN1$. This means we will be printing the fourth record from our master file. Because the key has been found, FLAG is set to 1. At this point, the value of W is 4, the position of the element where the key was found. This position is sent to Subroutine 4000 through local variable OUT1.

Note that we use a WHILE/WEND loop in our search for the key. If we used a FOR/NEXT loop, we would be breaking out of the loop when the key was found, thus violating the structured programming rule "exit at end of structure".

When control returns from the search subroutine, the value of OUT1 is copied into RECORD.NO. This is performed in line 4050, the statement immediately after the GOSUB that called Subroutine SEARCH ONE-DIMENSIONAL ARRAY. The flag is now checked for a 1. If the value of FLAG is 1, the student number has been found. We call Subroutine 5000 to print the student's record from the master file and the student's score from the scores file.

To print the student's number, name, address, and telephone number, we print a value from each of the arrays. To print the record that corresponds with the key, we use RECORD.NO as the subscript of subscripted variables. Note that the records and the "not found" message are printed in the order of the student numbers in the scores file. This is because a search is performed and lines are printed after a student number has been read from the scores file.

---

* An alternative would be to store numbers in string format. However, if a "found" number, such as a rate, must be used in a calculation, the number would have to be converted to numeric format before the calculation.

On page 309, we illustrated how student number 3917 was found in element 4 of array IN1$. The number 4 is assigned to RECORD.NO in line 4050 after being copied from W to OUT1 and now to RECORD.NO. Since we use RECORD.NO as the subscript for each subscripted variable in our PRINT USING statement (line 5010), the statement prints the contents of element 4 from each array. Thus, the fourth record in our master file will be printed.

IKEY$	RECORD.NO	IN1$(4)
3917	4	3917

STUDENT.NO(4)	SNAME$(4)	ADDRESS$(4)	TELEPHONE$(4)
3917	Kent,Sherri	153 East Street Anycity ZZ M3L 2Y5	413-9426

The student score is printed by printing the value of SCORE. This value was stored in SCORE when a record was read from the scores file in line 4020. If the value of FLAG is not 1, we display a message that the student number has not been found.

It is important to understand the reason for storing the master data in arrays. Each time a student number is read from the scores file, the student numbers in the master file must be searched for the student number just read. Since the scores file contains six student numbers, the student numbers in the master file must be searched six times. The best way to accomplish this is by transferring the student numbers from the master file to memory so the numbers can be examined and re-examined internally. We keep the numbers in memory by placing them in an array.

The remaining fields of the master file, that is, the names, addresses, and telephone numbers should also be stored in arrays. To print the name, address, and telephone number corresponding to the "found" student number, we must reference the appropriate record. If we did not place the fields of all records in arrays, we must retrieve, from disk, all records preceding the one to be printed. This operation would be required for each student number found in the student number array. When we store all records in memory, BASIC can go directly to the appropriate element in each array and print its contents. The constant retrieval of records is not necessary.

To print the student number in our "not found" message, we use ST.NO, the variable that stores the student number to be found. We do not print the value of IKEY$ since this is a local variable created to send a value to a standardized subroutine and then used in this subroutine. The variable should not be used for any other purpose.

It would be wise to save Subroutine SEARCH ONE-DIMENSIONAL ARRAY in ASCII format as the subroutine will be used frequently in this chapter and in subsequent chapters. Suggested filename: SEARCH1.ASC

Exercises

1. In Subroutine 3000 of the program on page 307, what would happen if we initialized I to 1 and placed the statement xxxx I = I+1 just before the WEND statement?
2. Why is it not necessary to store the data from data file SCORES2.DAT in two arrays?
3. What is the purpose of the variable FLAG in Subroutine SEARCH ONE-DIMENSIONAL ARRAY?

12.5 Sorting the Contents of an Array

Introduction to the Selection Sort

Another function essential in data processing is the sorting of data. A telephone company sorts names alphabetically, insurance companies sort policies by policy number, and airline companies sort incoming and outgoing flights by time. Because the need to sort is so universal, many sorting algorithms have come into existence, some more efficient than others. We will discuss one of these sorts, the selection sort.

Let us sort, in ascending order, the student numbers stored in our data file SCORES2.DAT. The selection sort selects, during its first pass, the smallest number in the list and places this selected number at the beginning of the list. In the second pass, the sort starts with the second number, selects the smallest number from the second number on and places this selected number in the second position of the list. In the third pass, the sort starts with the third number, selects the smallest number from the third number on and places this selected number in the third position of the list. The process continues for the remaining numbers.

The Program

```
1000 'SORT STUDENT NUMBERS                    M. MCRITCHIE                OCT 10
1002 '************************************************************************
1004 '          THIS PROGRAM SORTS STUDENT NUMBERS IN ASCENDING ORDER
1006 '************************************************************************
1010 'I          - COUNTER AND SUBSCRIPT OF SUBSCRIPTED VARIABLES
1020 'ST.NO()    - ARRAY THAT STORES STUDENT NUMBERS
1030 'SCORE()    - ARRAY THAT STORES TEST SCORES
1040 'IN1$()     - LOCAL ARRAY. INITIALLY STORES UNSORTED STUDENT NUMBERS.
1050 'ARRAY.SIZE - SIZE OF AN ARRAY
1060 'W          - LOCAL CONTROL VARIABLE (OUTER LOOP)
1070 'X          - LOCAL CONTROL VARIABLE (INNER LOOP)
1080 'OUT1$()    - LOCAL ARRAY. STORES SORTED STUDENT NUMBERS.
2000 '************************************************************************
2002 '                           MAIN ROUTINE
2004 '************************************************************************
2010  OPEN "B:SCORES2.DAT" FOR INPUT AS #1
2020  DIM ST.NO(30),SCORE(30),IN1$(30),OUT1$(30)
2030  GOSUB 3000                    'Read data file
2040  GOSUB 4000                    'Print sorted numbers
2050  CLOSE #1
2060  END
3000 '************************************************************************
3002 '                            READ DATA FILE
3004 '************************************************************************
3010  I = 0
3020  WHILE NOT EOF(1)
3030    I = I+1
3040    INPUT #1, ST.NO(I),SCORE(I)
3050    IN1$(I) = STR$(ST.NO(I))
3060  WEND
3070  ARRAY.SIZE = I
3080  GOSUB 18000                   'Selection sort
3090  RETURN
4000 '************************************************************************
4002 '                         PRINT SORTED NUMBERS
4004 '************************************************************************
4010  PRINT
4020  FOR I = 1 TO ARRAY.SIZE
4030    ST.NO(I) = VAL(OUT1$(I))
4040    PRINT ST.NO(I);
4050  NEXT I
4060  RETURN
18000 '***********************************************************************
18002 '                           SELECTION SORT
18004 '***********************************************************************
18010  FOR W = 2 TO ARRAY.SIZE
18020    FOR X = W TO ARRAY.SIZE
18030      IF IN1$(W-1) > IN1$(X) THEN SWAP IN1$(W-1),IN1$(X)
18040    NEXT X
18050  NEXT W
18060  FOR W = 1 TO ARRAY.SIZE
18070    OUT1$(W) = IN1$(W)
18080  NEXT W
18090  RETURN
65529 'End of program listing
RUN
```

```
 1942  2867  3917  4931  5263  6429
```

In order to maintain a standardized subroutine, our sort subroutine will work on strings. This is similar to the subroutine that searches for a value. Thus, if we wish to sort numbers, all numbers will be converted to strings and stored in a string array before the sort subroutine is called. The procedure is explained below.

In Subroutine 3000, the unsorted numbers are read from the data file and stored in array ST.NO. Each time a student number is read, the number is converted to a string and the string is stored in our local string array IN1$. As in our previous program, we use the STR$ function to convert the number to a string. Line 3070 assigns the array size (the three arrays are all the same size) to ARRAY. SIZE. We call Subroutine SELECTION SORT to sort the numbers which are now in string form. Note that the subroutine must be called after all the student numbers have been stored in local array IN1$ as the subroutine needs all the numbers in order to sort them.

The sort makes use of a SWAP statement to exchange two numbers. For example, 5020 SWAP A,B exchanges the values of A and B. The dialogue below explains how the selection sort sorts the numbers. The value of X, which is the control variable of the inner loop, is displayed as a heading over each comparison. The list of numbers under the heading "Result" gives the result of a pass through the outer loop.

The first time BASIC passes through the outer loop, W = 2 and X = W = 2. In line 18030, the first number, which is stored in element 1 of array IN1$ (W−1 = 2−1 = 1), is compared with the second number stored in IN1$. Remember, X = 2. The numbers are exchanged since 4931 is greater than 2867. X becomes 3. In line 18030, the first number is now compared with the third. No exchange takes place since 2867 is less than 5263. X becomes 4. The first number is compared with the fourth. The numbers are exchanged since 2867 is greater than 1942. When X is 5, the first number is compared with the fifth; when X is 6, the first number is compared with the sixth. No exchanges take place.

X=2	X=3	X=4	X=5	X=6	Result
4931	2867	2867	1942	1942	**1942**
2867	4931	4931	4931	4931	4931
5263	5263	5263	5263	5263	5263
1942	1942	1942	2867	2867	2867
6429	6429	6429	6429	6429	6429
3917	3917	3917	3917	3917	3917

The smallest number, 1942, has been sifted to the top of the list and will no longer be compared with the other numbers. The number is shown in bold face. We ignore this number and concentrate only on the remaining numbers in the list. The exchanges in the second pass through the outer loop are given below. W = 3.

X=3	X=4	X=5	X=6	Result
1942	**1942**	**1942**	**1942**	**1942**
4931	4931	2867	2867	**2867**
5263	5263	5263	5263	5263
2867	2867	4931	4931	4931
6429	6429	6429	6429	6429
3917	3917	3917	3917	3917

Ignoring 1942 and 2867, which are now in their proper positions, we concentrate on the remaining numbers. Exchanges in the third pass through the outer loop are as follows. W = 4.

X=4	X=5	X=6	Result
1942	**1942**	**1942**	**1942**
2867	**2867**	**2867**	**2867**
5263	4931	4931	**3917**
4931	5263	5263	5263
6429	6429	6429	6429
3917	3917	3917	4931

Ignoring 1942, 2867, and 3917, which are now in their proper positions, the following exchanges take place. W = 5.

X=5	X=6	Result
1942	**1942**	**1942**
2867	**2867**	**2867**
3917	**3917**	**3917**
5263	5263	**4931**
6429	6429	6429
4931	4931	5263

Finally, the last two numbers are compared. W = 6.

X=6	Result
1942	**1942**
2867	**2867**
3917	**3917**
4931	**4931**
6429	**5263**
5263	**6429**

The last routine in Subroutine SELECTION SORT copies the sorted numbers into array OUT1$. This is performed in a FOR/NEXT loop. Control returns to the main routine where Subroutine PRINT SORTED NUMBERS is called. In a FOR/NEXT loop (lines 4020 to 4050), the sorted numbers are converted back to numeric form by the VAL function which is used on each number in the string array OUT1$. Each converted number is stored in our original, numeric array ST.NO. Following a conversion, a student number from array ST.NO is printed. As with Subroutine SEARCH ONE-DIMENSIONAL ARRAY, it would be wise to save Subroutine SELECTION SORT in ASCII format. Suggested filename: SEL-SORT.ASC

Exercise

The selection sort in the previous program sorted numbers in ascending order. Modify the subroutine so that it sorts numbers in descending order (from largest to smallest).

12.6 Updating an Account

A programming problem in each of Chapters 7 and 8 involved updating Accounts Receivable accounts. Entries were made into every account stored in the data file. In an actual business environment, entries are made into only those accounts for which transactions occur. A transaction can be a sale, a payment, or both. Furthermore, the accounting clerk should be able to enter more than one transaction into an account.

We will be entering transactions into one of the Accounts Receivable accounts created for Problem 8 in Chapter Eight. The subroutines that update an account are given on page 315. Other routines, such as opening and closing the data file, printing the initial account, and calculating and printing the current balance are performed in other modules which will be written later on.

Codes are used to differentiate between a sale and a payment received. A code of 1 denotes a sale, a code of 2 denotes a payment. A user must key in the number of the account for which transactions are to be entered; the date, the code, and the amount of a transaction.

Since only specific accounts will be updated, the program must search for these accounts. All accounts are stored in the data file as records. Recall that a record consists of an account number; the customer's name, address, and telephone number; the credit limit; the date of the last transaction; and the balance due. Subroutine SEARCH ONE-DIMENSIONAL ARRAY will search for a keyed-in account number.

The program must first read all records from the data file and store the fields in arrays. The keyed-in account number is converted to string form and the string is stored in a local string array. The program searches for this account number then updates the "found" record by changing one or several of its fields. After the required records have been updated, all records must be written back to the same data file or written to a new file.

The entire program will be written for a programming problem at the end of the chapter. The output below illustrates how account number 31001 has been updated.

Sample Output

The first display of account number 31001 on page 314 gives the account number; the customer's name, address, and telephone number; the date of the last transaction and the balance due.

(cleared screen)

```
         10        20        30        40        50        60        70        80
12345678901234567890123456789012345678901234567890123456789012345678901234567890

        Account number 31001
        ****************************************************************
        * NAME: Diane Fraser                                  TELEPHONE *
        * ADDRESS: 367 River Road  Anycity  ZZ  M3L 4S8       339-8542  *
        *-----------------------------------------------------------------*
        * DATE             ITEM             DEBIT      CREDIT     BALANCE *
        *-----------------------------------------------------------------*
        * Nov. 12          Balance                              $  342.16 *
        *                                                                 *
        *                                                                 *
        *                                                                 *
        *                                                                 *
        *                                                                 *
        *                                                                 *
        *                                                                 *
        ****************************************************************
Date, code, amount? [Nov. 14,1,59.31]
Are the entries correct (y/n)? [n]
Re-enter the date, code, amount--[Nov. 14,1,59.21]
Are the entries correct (y/n)? [y]
```

The user keys in the transaction beneath the account. After the transaction data has been keyed in; the date, the amount of the transaction, and the new balance appear on the account as shown below. Since the transaction is a sale, the account is debited and the balance is increased by the amount of the sale.

(cleared screen)

```
        Account number 31001
        ****************************************************************
        * NAME: Diane Fraser                                  TELEPHONE *
        * ADDRESS: 367 River Road  Anycity  ZZ  M3L 4S8       339-8542  *
        *-----------------------------------------------------------------*
        * DATE             ITEM             DEBIT      CREDIT     BALANCE *
        *-----------------------------------------------------------------*
        * Nov. 12          Balance                              $  342.16 *
        * Nov. 14                         $ 59.21               $  401.37 *
        *                                                                 *
        *                                                                 *
        *                                                                 *
        *                                                                 *
        *                                                                 *
        *                                                                 *
        ****************************************************************
Another transaction for account number 31001 (y/n)? [y]
Date, code, amount? [Nov. 19,2,100.00]
Are the entries correct (y/n)? [y]
```

The amount of 100.00 keyed in for Nov. 19 is a payment and would be credited to the account. This transaction decreases the balance by $100.00, causing a new balance of $301.37. The date, the amount of the transaction, and the balance of $301.37 would be displayed on the next line of the account.

The Subroutines

Let us now examine the subroutines that update an account. Although the account number can be corrected as often as necessary, the transaction data can be corrected just once. Further corrections affect the spacing between the latter transactions displayed on the account. This problem would be rectified in a more sophisticated program.

```
5000 '************************************************************************
5002 '                        INPUT KEY (ACCOUNT NUMBER)
5004 '************************************************************************
5010  CLS
5020  LOCATE 9
5030  INPUT "______________________________Account number";ACCOUNT.NO
5040  PRINT
5050  INPUT "Is the account number correct (y/n)";RESPONSE$
5060  IF RESPONSE$ <> "y" AND RESPONSE$ <> "Y"
         THEN INPUT "Re-enter the account number--",ACCOUNT.NO : GOTO 5050
5070  IKEY$ = STR$(ACCOUNT.NO)
5080  GOSUB 17000                    'Search one-dimensional array
5090  RECORD.NO = OUT1
5100  IF FLAG = 1 THEN GOSUB 6000
         ELSE PRINT : PRINT TAB(27) USING "Account number ##### not found";
         ACCOUNT.NO
5105     'Subroutine 6000 updates the found account
5110  RETURN
6000 '************************************************************************
6002 '                              UPDATE ACCOUNT
6004 '************************************************************************
6010  GOSUB 7000                     'Print initial account
6020  ROW = 9
6030  RESPONSE$ = "y"
6040  WHILE RESPONSE$ = "y" OR RESPONSE$ = "Y"
6050    INPUT "Date, code, amount";DATE1$(RECORD.NO),CODE,AMOUNT
6060    INPUT "Are the entries correct (y/n)";RESPONSE$
6070    IF RESPONSE$ <> "y" AND RESPONSE$ <> "Y"
           THEN INPUT "Re-enter the date, code, amount--",DATE1$(RECORD.NO),
           CODE,AMOUNT : GOTO 6060
6080    GOSUB 8000                   'Perform calculations
6090    LOCATE 18
6100    PRINT "                                                              "
6110    PRINT "                                                              "
6120    PRINT "                                                              "
6130    PRINT "                                                              "
6140    PRINT "                                                              "
6150    PRINT "                                                              "
6160    LOCATE 18
6170    PRINT USING "Another transaction for account number ##### ";ACCOUNT.NO;
6180    INPUT "(y/n)";RESPONSE$
6190    IF RESPONSE$ <> "y" AND RESPONSE$ <> "Y" AND RESPONSE$ <> "n" AND
           RESPONSE$ <> "N" THEN PRINT "Invalid response. Enter y or n." :
           GOTO 6170
6200  WEND
6210  RETURN
```

Line 5030 allows the user to key in the number of an account. In line 5070, this number is converted to a string and the string is assigned to our local string variable IKEY$. The number (in string form) serves as the key in the search for the desired account. We now call Subroutine SEARCH ONE-DIMENSIONAL ARRAY. When control returns from the search routine, the position of the "found" record is copied into variable RECORD.NO and the value of the flag is checked. If FLAG is equal to 1, we call Subroutine 6000 to update the account. If FLAG is not equal to 1, we display a message announcing that the account number was not found.

The first statement in Subroutine 6000 calls a subroutine to format the account and to print basic information concerning the account just found. The items printed will be the account number; the customer's name, address, and telephone number; the date of the last transaction; and the balance due. When BASIC returns to Subroutine 6000, line 6020 assigns the number 9 to variable ROW. Row 9 is the row on which the balance due has just been printed. The subroutine that prints a detail line will contain the statement ROW = ROW+1 which causes printing to occur on a new row each time a transaction is entered.

The WHILE statement in line 6040 checks the status of RESPONSE$ (we assume the user wishes to enter at least one transaction). As long as RESPONSE$ equals "y" or "Y", transactions can be entered into the account. The INPUT statement in line 6050 allows the user to enter the date of the transaction, the code, and the amount. Since this INPUT statement follows the PRINT statements that print the account, the prompt will be placed beneath the account. Note that we assign the date to a subscripted variable of array DATE1$. We use subscript RECORD.NO, the position of the "found" account number.

Subroutine 8000 is called to calculate the new balance and to display the date, the amount of the transaction, and the new balance within the account. The date and balance fields of this record now contain a new date and a new balance. The data file will be updated when the records are sent to disk.

After Subroutine 8000 is executed, we locate the row immediately below the account. The PRINT statements in lines 6100 to 6150 inclusive clear out all previous prompts beneath the account. Line 6160 brings the cursor back to the row immediately below the account where a new prompt is displayed by the statement in line 6170. Note the trailing semicolon in this line. Line 6180 allows the user to respond to the prompt displayed by line 6170. In line 6200, we end the WHILE/WEND loop.

Exercises

1. What would happen if we changed the subscripted variable DATE1$(RECORD.NO) in lines 6050 and 6070 to a simple variable?
2. What would happen if we deleted PRINT statements 6100 to 6150 inclusive?

12.7 Writing Updated Records to the Original Data File

In Chapter Seven, we illustrated how updated records can be written to a new file. The original file was opened for an INPUT and the new file was opened for an OUTPUT. Suppose we wish to write updated records to the original file. This means we must read the records from the original file, update the records, then write the records to the same file. Thus, the file must first be opened for an INPUT, closed, then reopened for an OUTPUT. A sample main routine is given below.

```
2010 OPEN "B:NAMES.DAT" FOR INPUT AS #1
2020 GOSUB 3000                        'Read data file and update records
2030 CLOSE #1
2040 OPEN "B:NAMES.DAT" FOR OUTPUT AS #1
2050 GOSUB 4000                        'Write updated records to the same file
2060 CLOSE #1
```

The subroutine that writes the updated records to the same file may look like this:

```
4000 'SUBROUTINE WRITE UPDATED RECORDS TO THE SAME FILE
4010   FOR I = 1 TO ARRAY.SIZE
4020     WRITE #1, ENAME$(I)
4030   NEXT I
4040   RETURN
```

You will be writing updated records to the original data file for the Accounts Receivable problem and for the project at the end of this chapter.

12.8 Program Design

The records in our data file MASTER.DAT (given on page 307) were stored in numeric order by student number. The contents of the file are shown below.

MASTER.DAT
1942,"Lindsay,Donna",637 North Avenue Anycity ZZ M3L 4T8,593-2184
2593,"Meyer,Tom",485 First Avenue Anycity ZZ M3L 3W7,334-9815
2867,"Saunders,Bryan",942 South Avenue Anycity ZZ M3L 6V4,243-1825
3917,"Kent,Sherri",153 East Street Anycity ZZ M3L 2Y5,413-9426
4931,"Hughes,James",984 West Street Anycity ZZ M3L 1X6,458-6218
6429,"Walker,Anna",325 Third Street Anycity ZZ M3L 8S5,334-1628

Suppose the information stored in the above file must be printed in alphabetic order by student name. It now becomes necessary to sort the names. However, when we sort the names, the other fields in each record (student number, address, and telephone number) no longer correspond with a name. To obtain corresponding fields, we must first store the fields of all the records in arrays. We then use a pointer that will point to the appropriate element in the student number, address, and telephone number arrays so we can match a name with its corresponding fields. The sorted records will be written to a new file. Dialogue following the program listing explains the use of pointers.

Size of each Field:

Number field	— 4 digits
Name field	— 15 characters
Address field	— 38 characters
Telephone field	— 8 characters

Rough Layout of the Report:

```
MASTER STUDENT FILE
==============================================================================
NUMBER        NAME                     ADDRESS                      TELEPHONE
==============================================================================
4931      Hughes,James         984 West Street  Anycity  ZZ  M3L 1X6   458-6218
3917      Kent,Sherri          153 East Street  Anycity  ZZ  M3L 2Y5   413-9426
1942      Lindsay,Donna        637 North Avenue  Anycity  ZZ  M3L 4T8  593-2184
2593      Meyer,Tom            485 First Avenue  Anycity  ZZ  M3L 3W7  334-9815
2867      Saunders,Bryan       942 South Avenue  Anycity  ZZ  M3L 6V4  243-1825
6429      Walker,Anna          325 Third Street  Anycity  ZZ  M3L 8S5  334-1628
```

FIGURE 12-1 LAYOUT CHART

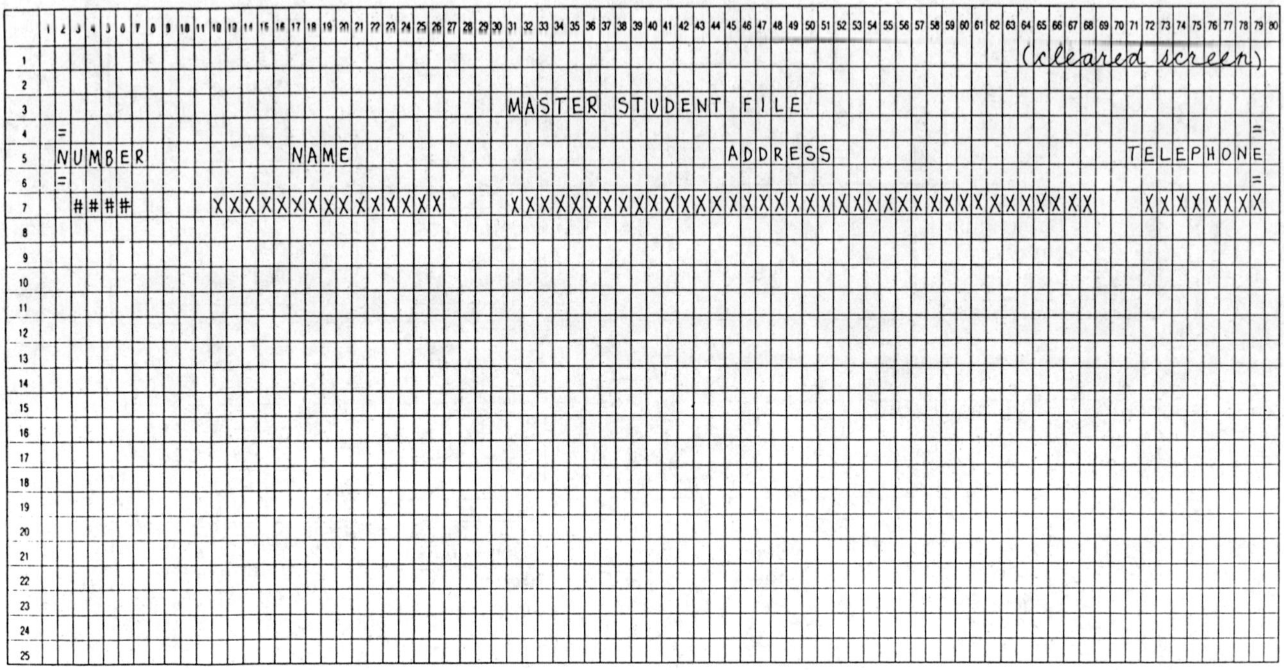

FIGURE 12-2 STRUCTURE CHART

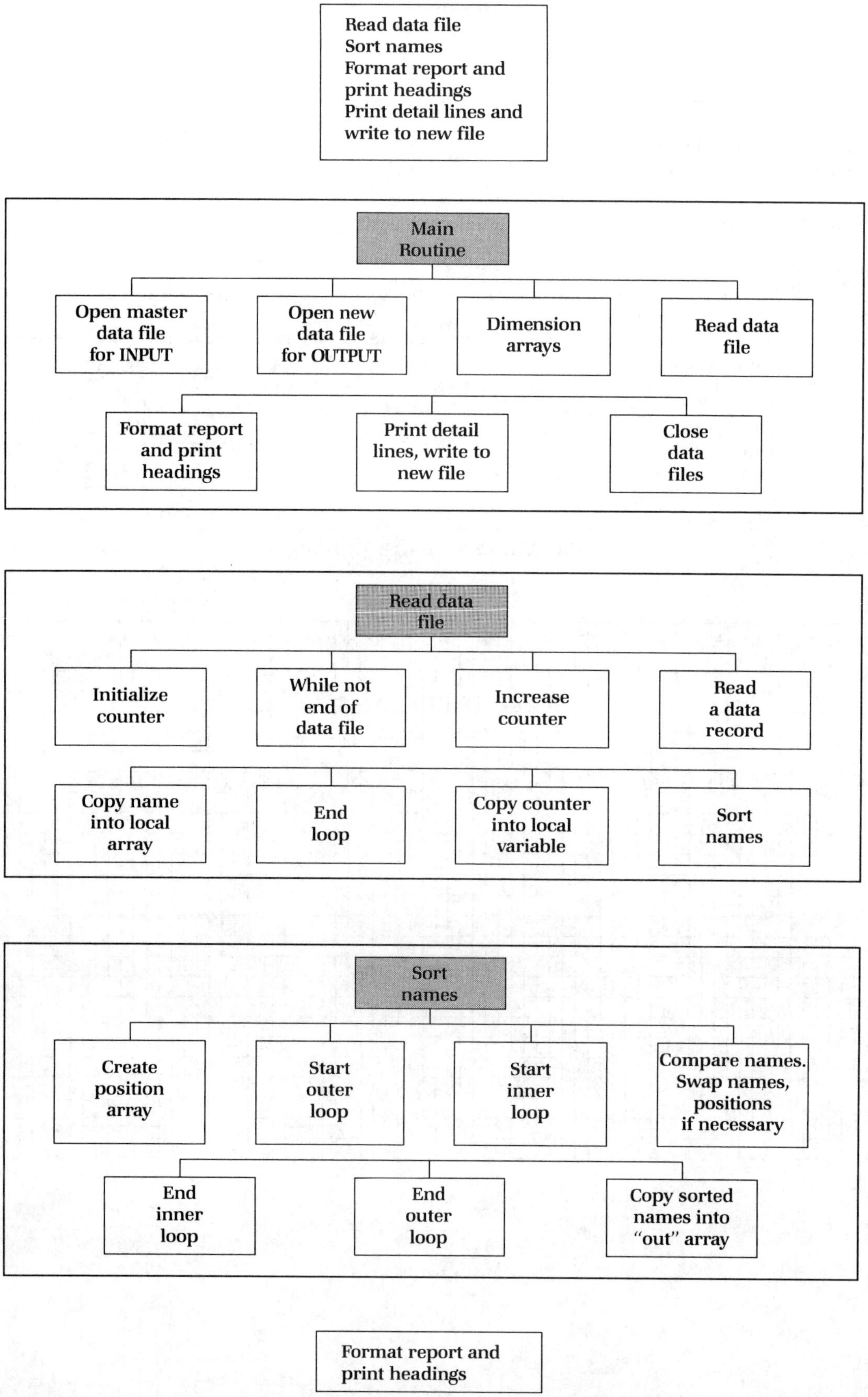

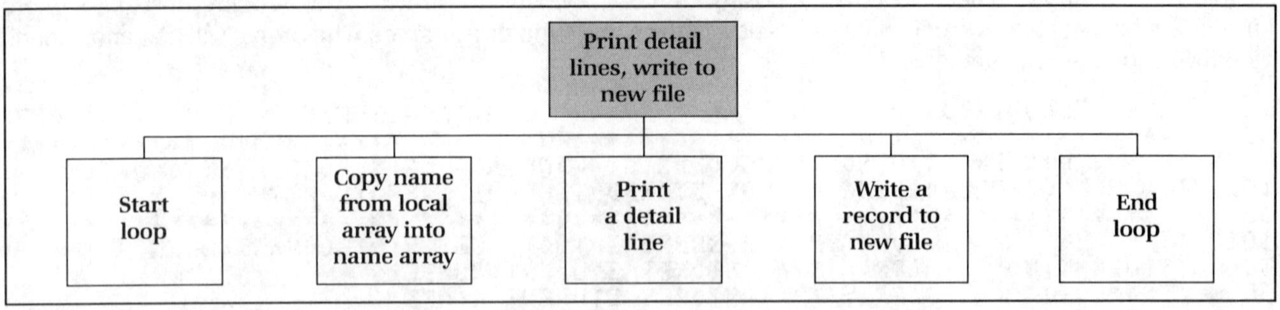

FIGURE 12-3 PSEUDOCODE

MAJOR TASKS
Read data file
Sort names
Format report and print headings
Print detail lines and write to new file

MAIN ROUTINE	
Open master data file for INPUT	
Open new data file for OUTPUT	
Dimension arrays	
Read data file	(subroutine)
Format report and print headings	(subroutine)
Print detail lines and write to new file	(subroutine)
Close data files	

READ DATA FILE	
Initialize counter	I
While not end of data file	
Increase counter	
Read a data record	STUDENT.NO( ),SNAME$( ),
	ADDRESS$( ),TELEPHONE$( )
Copy name into local array	IN1$( )
End loop	
Copy counter into local variable	ARRAY.SIZE
Sort names	(merged subroutine)

SORT NAMES	
Create position array	Z, P( )
Start outer loop (parameters: 2 to ARRAY.SIZE)	W
Start inner loop (parameters: W to ARRAY.SIZE)	X
Compare names. If name > following name	
swap names and positions	
End inner loop	
End outer loop	
Copy sorted names into "out" array	OUT1$( )

FORMAT REPORT AND PRINT HEADINGS

PRINT DETAIL LINES AND WRITE TO NEW FILE	
Start loop (parameters: 1 to ARRAY.SIZE)	J
Copy name from local "out" array into name array	
Print a detail line	
Write a record to new file	
End loop	

Note that no array names are listed opposite the task "Dimension arrays". At this point, no variables are known. It is not until after we complete the design that we know the array names. The arrays will be dimensioned when we code the program.

```
1000 'SORT RECORDS USING POINTERS              M. MCRITCHIE                   OCT 15
1002 '***********************************************************************
1004 '      THIS PROGRAM SORTS RECORDS BY NAME AND USES POINTERS TO MATCH
1006 '        CORRESPONDING FIELDS STORED IN OTHER ARRAYS WITH THE NAME
1008 '***********************************************************************
1010 'I              - COUNTER AND SUBSCRIPT OF SUBSCRIPTED VARIABLES
1020 'STUDENT.NO() - ARRAY THAT STORES STUDENT NUMBERS
1030 'SNAME$()       - ARRAY THAT STORES STUDENT NAMES
1040 'ADDRESS$()     - ARRAY THAT STORES ADDRESSES
1050 'TELEPHONE$() - ARRAY THAT STORES TELEPHONE NUMBERS
1060 'IN1$()         - LOCAL ARRAY. INITIALLY STORES UNSORTED STUDENT NAMES.
1070 'ARRAY.SIZE     - SIZE OF AN ARRAY
1080 'Z              - LOCAL CONTROL VARIABLE, SUBSCRIPT OF SUBSCRIPTED VARIABLES
1090 'P()            - POSITION ARRAY
1100 'W              - LOCAL CONTROL VARIABLE (OUTER LOOP)
1110 'X              - LOCAL CONTROL VARIABLE (INNER LOOP)
1120 'OUT1$()        - LOCAL ARRAY. STORES THE SORTED NAMES.
1130 'S$             - EQUAL SIGNS
1140 'F$             - IMAGE OF A DETAIL LINE
1150 'HEADING$       - HEADING
1160 'J              - CONTROL VARIABLE AND SUBSCRIPT OF SUBSCRIPTED VARIABLES
2000 '***********************************************************************
2002 '                                  MAIN ROUTINE
2004 '***********************************************************************
2010  OPEN "B:MASTER.DAT" FOR INPUT AS #1
2020  OPEN "B:SORTED.DAT" FOR OUTPUT AS #2
2030  DIM STUDENT.NO(30),SNAME$(30),ADDRESS$(30),TELEPHONE$(30),IN1$(30),P(30),
      OUT1$(30)
2040  GOSUB 3000                        'Read data file
2050  GOSUB 4000                        'Format report and print headings
2060  GOSUB 5000                        'Print detail lines and write to new file
2070  CLOSE #1,#2
2080  END
3000 '***********************************************************************
3002 '                                  READ DATA FILE
3004 '***********************************************************************
3010  I = 0
3020  WHILE NOT EOF(1)
3030    I = I+1
3040    INPUT #1, STUDENT.NO(I),SNAME$(I),ADDRESS$(I),TELEPHONE$(I)
3050    IN1$(I) = SNAME$(I)
3060  WEND
3070  ARRAY.SIZE = I
3080  GOSUB 19000                       'Selection sort with pointers
3090  RETURN
4000 '***********************************************************************
4002 '                         FORMAT REPORT AND PRINT HEADINGS
4004 '***********************************************************************
4010  CLS
4020  LOCATE 8
4030  S$ = STRING$(78,"=")
4040  F$ = "__####_____\______________\____\_____________________________________\
___\______\"
4050  HEADING$ = "MASTER STUDENT FILE"
4060  PRINT TAB((80-LEN(HEADING$))/2+.5); HEADING$
4070  PRINT TAB(2) S$
4080  PRINT TAB(2) "NUMBER"; TAB(17) "NAME"; TAB(45) "ADDRESS";
      TAB(71) "TELEPHONE"
4090  PRINT TAB(2) S$
4100  RETURN
```

```
5000 '***********************************************************************
5002 '                   PRINT DETAIL LINES AND WRITE TO NEW FILE
5004 '***********************************************************************
5010  FOR J = 1 TO ARRAY.SIZE
5020    SNAME$(J) = OUT1$(J)
5030    PRINT USING F$; STUDENT.NO(P(J)),SNAME$(J),ADDRESS$(P(J)),
        TELEPHONE$(P(J))
5040    WRITE #2, STUDENT.NO(P(J)),SNAME$(J),ADDRESS$(P(J)),TELEPHONE$(P(J))
5050  NEXT J
5060  RETURN
19000 '**********************************************************************
19002 '                        SELECTION SORT WITH POINTERS
19004 '**********************************************************************
19010  FOR Z = 1 TO ARRAY.SIZE
19020    P(Z) = Z
19030  NEXT Z
19040  FOR W = 2 TO ARRAY.SIZE
19050    FOR X = W TO ARRAY.SIZE
19060      IF IN1$(W-1) > IN1$(X)
              THEN SWAP IN1$(W-1),IN1$(X) : SWAP P(W-1),P(X)
19070    NEXT X
19080  NEXT W
19090  FOR W = 1 TO ARRAY.SIZE
19100    OUT1$(W) = IN1$(W)
19110  NEXT W
19120  RETURN
65529 'End of program listing
```

The Output:

(cleared screen)

```
         10        20        30        40        50        60        70        80
12345678901234567890123456789012345678901234567890123456789012345678901234567890

                             MASTER STUDENT FILE
===============================================================================
NUMBER           NAME                        ADDRESS                   TELEPHONE
===============================================================================
 4931       Hughes,James        984 West Street   Anycity  ZZ  M3L 1X6   458-6218
 3917       Kent,Sherri         153 East Street   Anycity  ZZ  M3L 2Y5   413-9426
 1942       Lindsay,Donna       637 North Avenue   Anycity  ZZ  M3L 4T8   593-2184
 2593       Meyer,Tom           485 First Avenue   Anycity  ZZ  M3L 3W7   334-9815
 2867       Saunders,Bryan      942 South Avenue   Anycity  ZZ  M3L 6V4   243-1825
 6429       Walker,Anna         325 Third Street   Anycity  ZZ  M3L 8S5   334-1628
```

In Subroutine READ DATA FILE, no conversion of data is necessary for the sort subroutine as the names are already in string form when they are read from the data file. However, Subroutine SELECTION SORT must be modified so that it saves the positions of the unsorted names. A position is used to access the student number, the address, and the telephone number corresponding to a name. You should save, in ASCII format, the modified version of the subroutine as it will be used for a problem at the end of this chapter. Suggested filename: SORT-P.ASC

The student number array, the name array, the position array, and the address array (only partially shown below) look as follows before the sort. A telephone number array would also be created.

STUDENT.NO(1) 1942	SNAME$(1) Lindsay,Donna	P(1) 1	ADDRESS$(1) 637 North Avenue
STUDENT.NO(2) 2593	SNAME$(2) Meyer,Tom	P(2) 2	ADDRESS$(2) 485 First Avenue
STUDENT.NO(3) 2867	SNAME$(3) Saunders,Bryan	P(3) 3	ADDRESS$(3) 942 South Avenue
STUDENT.NO(4) 3917	SNAME$(4) Kent,Sherri	P(4) 4	ADDRESS$(4) 153 East Street
STUDENT.NO(5) 4931	SNAME$(5) Hughes,James	P(5) 5	ADDRESS$(5) 984 West Street
STUDENT.NO(6) 6429	SNAME$(6) Walker,Anna	P(6) 6	ADDRESS$(6) 325 Third Street

The position array is created by the FOR/NEXT loop in lines 19010 to 19030. Each time BASIC passes through the loop, a value of Z is stored in array P: first 1, then 2, 3, 4, 5, and 6. After the sort, the position and name arrays are changed as follows:

STUDENT.NO(1) **1942**	SNAME$(1) Hughes,James	P(1) 5	ADDRESS$(1) **637 North Avenue**
STUDENT.NO(2) 2593	SNAME$(2) Kent,Sherri	P(2) 4	ADDRESS$(2) 485 First Avenue
STUDENT.NO(3) 2867	SNAME$(3) **Lindsay,Donna**	P(3) 1	ADDRESS$(3) 942 South Avenue
STUDENT.NO(4) 3917	SNAME$(4) Meyer,Tom	P(4) 2	ADDRESS$(4) 153 East Street
STUDENT.NO(5) 4931	SNAME$(5) Saunders,Bryan	P(5) 3	ADDRESS$(5) 984 West Street
STUDENT.NO(6) 6429	SNAME$(6) Walker,Anna	P(6) 6	ADDRESS$(6) 325 Third Street

Each time two names are swapped in line 19060, the positions of these names are swapped. After the names are sorted, array P stores the former positions of the names. Hughes was formerly in position 5, P(1) stores the number 5. Kent was formerly in position 4, P(2) stores the number 4. Lindsay was formerly in position 1, P(3) stores the number 1. The same principle applies to the remaining names.

Just before control returns to the calling module from the sort subroutine, the sorted names are copied into array OUT1$ (lines 19090 to 19110). In the FOR/NEXT loop in Subroutine 5000, the names stored in array OUT1$ are copied into our original name array, SNAME$.

Let us find out how the record for Lindsay,Donna can be accessed. After the swap, the name is stored in element 3 of OUT1$ and the name's former position, 1, is stored in element 3 of P. Thus OUT1$(3) contains Lindsay,Donna and P(3) contains 1. In the FOR/NEXT loop that copies the names from array OUT1$ into array SNAME$, Lindsay,Donna will be copied into array SNAME$ when J, the control variable, is 3. Thus, the name will be stored in SNAME$(3). The student number, address, and telephone number remain in element 1 of the other arrays. The number 1 stored in P(3) will be used as a pointer to access element 1 of arrays STUDENT.NO, ADDRESS$, and TELEPHONE$.

To display Lindsay's name, we simply ask BASIC to print the contents of SNAME$(J). The name will be displayed when J is equal to 3. To display the student number, address, and telephone number, we use the value of P(J) which will be 1 when J is equal to 3, to point to element 1 of each of the student number, address, and telephone number arrays.

STUDENT.NO(P(J)) = STUDENT.NO(P(3)). As mentioned above, P(3) = 1. Thus, STUDENT.NO(P(3)) = STUDENT.NO(1) = 1942 as shown above.

Lindsay's address is referenced as follows:

ADDRESS$(P(J)) = ADDRESS$(P(3)) = ADDRESS$(1) = 637 North Avenue   Anycity   ZZ   M3L 4T8

The telephone number would be referenced in a similar manner.

The sorted records are displayed on the screen and written to the new file SORTED.DAT by the statements in lines 5030 and 5040.

Summary of BASIC Statements

DIM — Declares the maximum values for the subscripts of subscripted variables and allocates space for each element of the arrays.

```
2020 DIM SNAME$(25),SCORE(4)
```

SWAP — Interchanges the values of two variables.

```
5070 SWAP A,B
```

Summary of Library Files

SEARCH1.ASC — Searches a one-dimensional array.

SEL-SORT.ASC — A selection sort that sorts items in a one-dimensional array.

SORT-P.ASC — A selection sort with pointers.

Chapter Summary

1. An array is a collection of related items. When the term is applied to information stored in a computer, an array is a block of adjacent memory locations storing related items. Each location within the block is referred to as an element of the array. An element can store only one value.
2. An array is used when a program must examine values more than once. Each value stored in the array can be accessed any time and as often as necessary.
3. The same rules used for naming variables apply to naming arrays. A subscripted variable and a simple variable may have the same name.
4. If the array name is numeric it can store only numeric data. If the array name is type string, it can store only string data. The strings stored in a string array may vary in length.
5. To reference an element of an array, we must specify the name of the array of which the element is a member and its position in the array. For example, A(6) references the sixth element of array A. The number in parentheses is called the subscript. A(6) is referred to as a subscripted variable.
6. The subscript of a subscripted variable may be expressed as a number, a numeric variable, or a numeric expression. Subscripts should be integers. BASIC rounds off a decimal subscript to its nearest integer.
7. More than one array may be dimensioned in a DIM statement. The arrays must be separated by commas.
8. A DIM statement must be placed before any statement that references an array.
9. An array may not be dimensioned more than once.
10. When an array of 11 or fewer elements is required, the array need not be dimensioned. For any undimensioned array, BASIC automatically allocates 11 elements to the array (elements Ø through 10).
11. More locations may be allocated to an array than are needed, but not less.
12. When more locations are allocated than are required, the elements not filled by a program are filled with zeros or null strings placed there by BASIC before the program is executed.
13. When an insufficient number of locations is allocated, an attempt to reference an element out of the dimensioned range results in the error message **Subscript out of range in xxxx** where xxxx is the line number of the statement referencing the element.
14. Data items are stored in an array by assigning a value to each subscripted variable of the array. This is usually performed inside a FOR/NEXT loop. The control variable of the FOR statement serves as the subscript.
15. It is possible to search an array for a specific item of data. The item to be found is called a key. The search is conducted by examining each element of the array until all elements are examined or until the key is found.
16. When items are read from a data file into an array, a variable must be initialized to Ø before the WHILE/WEND loop begins, then increased by 1 inside the loop. The variable serves as a subscript of the subscripted variables and as a counter which determines the size of the array.
17. Data stored in an array may be sorted in ascending order (from smallest to largest) or in descending order (from largest to smallest).
18. The selection sort selects, during its first pass, the smallest number in a list and places the selected number at the beginning of the list. In the second pass, the sort starts with the second number, selects the smallest number from the second number on and places this selected number in the second position of the list. The process continues until all passes are performed.
19. A data file can be updated by reading the fields of all records into arrays, changing the contents of specific elements of the arrays, then writing the contents of the arrays to the same file or to a new file.
20. When updated records are written to the same file from which the original records were read, the file must be opened for an INPUT, closed after the records have been read and updated, opened for an OUTPUT to write the updated records to the file, and closed once more.

21. Pointers can be used to access corresponding elements of several arrays when the contents of one of the arrays have been sorted. Suppose a student's number, name, address, and telephone number must be printed from four arrays after the names have been sorted. First, a position array must be created to store the positions of the names before the sort. As the names are sorted, the positions must be sorted in the same order as the names. A stored position can now be used as a pointer (since its value is a former position) to point to a corresponding element of another array.

Questions and Exercises

1. Define the following terms.
   (a) An element of an array.
   (b) A subscripted variable.
2. Can variables A and A(1) be used in the same program to store different values? Explain.
3. (a) How may the subscript of a subscripted variable be expressed? State three ways.
   (b) What happens when the subscript is a decimal number?
   (c) What lowest value can be used as the subscript of a subscripted variable?
4. State two functions performed by the DIM statement.
5. (a) When must an array be dimensioned?
   (b) What happens when an insufficient number of locations is allocated to an array?
   (c) What values does BASIC store in subscripted variables when a program assigns no values to the variables? When does BASIC place these values in the variables? Refer to both numeric and string variables in your answer.
6. How many memory locations are allocated by each of the following?
   (a) `2020 DIM A(30)`
   (b) An array that has not been dimensioned.
7. Indicate the errors, if any, in the following statements. Make the necessary corrections.
   (a) `2020 DIM EMPLOYEE$(15);PHONE(15)`
   (b)
   ```
   2010 N = 25
   2020 DIM NUMBER(N)
   ```
   (c) `2020 DIM NAME$(25)`
   (d)
   ```
   2010 C$ = "14"
   2020 DIM CITY$(C$)
   ```
8. Code two routines each of which stores eleven data items (numbers 10 to 20 inclusive) in array A. In each routine, use a FOR/NEXT loop.
   (a) In one routine, use the READ and DATA statements to load the array.
   (b) In the second routine, use the INPUT statement to load the array.
9. Code a routine that reads the following data into arrays A and B. Use one READ statement in the FOR/NEXT loop.

Array A	*Array B*
4	16
7	49
2	4
5	25

10. Is there anything wrong with each of the following subroutines? If there is an error, make the necessary correction. Assume that the main routine calls a subroutine. The DIM statement in line 2020 would be coded in the main routine.
   (a)
   ```
   2020 DIM C(15)

   3000 'SUBROUTINE ENTER DATA
   3010    FOR I = 1 TO 15
   3020       READ C(I)
   ```
   (c)
   ```
   2020 DIM A(25),B(25)

   3000 'SUBROUTINE READ DATA FILE
   3010    I = 1
   3020    WHILE NOT EOF(1)
   ```

```
3030   NEXT I
3040   DATA -,-,...(15 data items)
3050   RETURN
4000 'SUBROUTINE PRINT
4010   FOR I = 1 TO 20
4020     PRINT C(I);
4030   NEXT I
4040   RETURN
```

```
3030       INPUT #1, A(I),B(I)
3040       PRINT A(I),B(I)
3050       I = I+1
3060     WEND
3070     ARRAY.SIZE = I
3080     RETURN
```

(b)
```
2020 DIM A(25),B(25)

3000 'SUBROUTINE ENTER DATA
3010   FOR I = 1 TO 25
3020     INPUT "Enter two numbers--",A(I),B(I)
3030   NEXT I
3040   RETURN
4000 'SUBROUTINE PRINT
4010   DIM A(20),B(20)
4020   FOR I = 1 TO 20
4030     PRINT A(I),B(I)
4040   NEXT I
4050   RETURN
```

11. Write a program that calculates simple interest for three investments. Allow a user to key in the principal, the rate of interest, and the period of time in years. Store the data in three arrays. Use PRINT USING statements each of which contains an image to produce the output. The formula for finding simple interest is as follows:

$$\text{Interest} = \text{Principal} \times \text{Rate of Interest}/100 \times \text{Time (in years)}$$

Sample Output:

```
Principal,rate,years? 1000,8,1
Principal,rate,years? 2000,9,2
Principal,rate,years? 3000,10,3

Principal: $1,000.00    Rate:  8%    Years: 1
Interest: $ 80.00

Principal: $2,000.00    Rate:  9%    Years: 2
Interest: $360.00

Principal: $3,000.00    Rate: 10%    Years: 3
Interest: $900.00
```

12. Write a program that searches for a name stored in the data file given below. Allow the user to type in the name to be found (the key). Use separate subroutines to (a) read the data file (b) INPUT the key and print the result. Merge Subroutine SEARCH ONE-DIMENSIONAL ARRAY with your program. Since the result of the search consists of just one line, print the output line in your IF statement.

NAMES1.DAT
Hodge,Earl
Elliott,Sharon
Logan,Tom
Janzen,Cheryl
Taylor,Barbara
Gill,Norman

```
RUN

Type in last name, a comma, first name
(e.g. Smith,John)

Name to search? Janzen,Cheryl

Janzen,Cheryl
```

or

```
Salesperson Smith,John not found
```

13. Write a program that sorts the names in the data file on page 325 in alphabetic order. Use the program on page 311 as a guide.

```
RUN

Elliott,Sharon
Gill,Norman
Hodge,Earl
Janzen,Cheryl
Logan,Tom
Taylor,Barbara
```

Programming Problems

Write programs for the following problems. Centre headings automatically as shown in the program on page 304. In programs that use the search or sort subroutine, remember to send string values to the subroutine.

1. A local community club would like to honour those members who belong to two committees. Write a program that reads names from two data files into two arrays, then searches for a name that is common to both arrays. Do not assume that the committees have the same number of members. Use the data file created for Exercise 12 as one of your files and create NAMES2.DAT as a second file.

   Compare each name in the first array with all the names in the second array. You will need nested FOR/NEXT loops. The test value of a FOR statement must be the size of an array. If a name common to both arrays is found, print the name.

   Sample Output:

(cleared screen)

```
THE FOLLOWING ARE MEMBERS OF BOTH COMMITTEES

                     Elliott,Sharon
                     Logan,Tom
```

2. The program for Problem 2 in Chapter 11 read names and addresses from a data file, then printed address labels on the screen and to the printer; one label under the other. The names and addresses were stored under filename ADDRESS.DAT. Modify the program so that it prints three labels side by side as shown below. The message "End of processing" should appear only on the screen.

```
         10        20        30        40        50        60        70        80
12345678901234567890123456789012345678901234567890123456789012345678901234567890

Mr. John Smith            Mrs. Doris Moore          Mr. Russell Knight
123 Main Street           1394 Harcourt Street      498 Ashberry Drive
Anycity  ZZ               Anycity  ZZ               Mytown  XX
M3L 6S7                   M3L 1R4                   N6Y 3A2


Ms. A. Granger            Mr. Fred Harrington
584 Knightbridge Road     667 West Lakeview Bay
Mytown  XX                Mytown  XX
N6Y 5B7                   N6Y 4A9

End of processing
```

In the subroutine that reads the data file, read a name into an array but read an address into a simple variable. Assign the address to local variable IN1$, then call Subroutine SEPARATE DATA to separate the address. After calling the subroutine, copy the street address, the city and province, and the postal code from local "out" variables into subscripted program variables.

Your PRINT and LPRINT statements must be placed within a FOR/NEXT loop. To print the labels side by side, use your control variable, say I, as the subscript of the variables for the left-most label, I+1 as the subscript of the variables for the centre label, and I+2 as the subscript of the variables for the right-most label. The step value in the FOR statement must be 3 since three labels are printed during each pass through the loop. (An exception may be the last pass.)

Merge Subroutine SEPARATE DATA with your program. When your program is error-free, save the program and produce a hard copy as the listing will be useful for a problem in Chapter 14.

3. Write a program that produces the September safety record for five drivers. Allow a user of your program to key in the month and year. Display an appropriate prompt. After reading the data from a data file, sort the names then print the names, the license numbers, and the merit points as a report. Use pointers to access the license numbers and the merit points. Store the sorted records in a new data file. Use the program designed on pages 316 to 322 as a guide. Data is provided below.

```
DRIVERS1.DAT
"Walker,Dennis",168B23,2
"Johnson,Shirley",284A61,1
"Parker,Dorothy",159B37,3      — Name, license number, merit points
"Morrison,Fred",241A63,Ø
"Pearson,Wade",185A27,2
```

Rough Layout of the Report:

```
RECORD OF MERIT POINTS FOR SAFE DRIVING

September, 19XX
=======================================
NAME                LICENSE      POINTS
=======================================
Johnson,Shirley     284A61          1
Morrison,Fred       241A63          Ø
Parker,Dorothy      159B37          3
Pearson,Wade        185A27          2
Walker,Dennis       168B23          2
```

4. The accounting department of a store has created a data file in which each record consists of the number of a department, the name of the department, and the rate of markup used by the department. The data file is given below.

```
DEPART.DAT
37,Appliances,50
40,Housewares,33      — Department number, department name, rate of markup
41,China,40
43,Furniture,50
```

Your program must read the data into three arrays and allow an accounting clerk to key in the total number of purchases made by the store, a department number, and the value of merchandise purchased by that department. The number of purchases made should be the test value of a FOR statement, the department number and purchase value should be INPUTed inside the loop. Use the department number typed in by the user as the key to find a record. Your program must calculate the retail value of the purchase made by that department.

Subroutine SEARCH ONE-DIMENSIONAL ARRAY must search the department number array for the key. When a department number is found, use its position in the array as the subscript of a subscripted variable to access the department's rate of markup stored in the "rate" array. Use the rate to calculate the amount of markup, then find the retail value. The position must also be used as a subscript to access a department name. Your program must consider a department number that is not found.

Use the program listed on page 307 as a guide. Most routines need only minor modifications. However, there is one major difference between the two programs. In the current program, the number of purchases made, the department number, and the purchase value must be INPUTed. This is unlike Subroutine 4000 on page 308 where data is read from a second data file.

Output for each department must be displayed on a cleared screen. Display an appropriate message for a department number not found. You need to call Subroutine FREEZE DISPLAY to freeze a report on the screen and to freeze the "not found" message. End the entire output with the message "End of processing".

Formulas:

Markup = Purchase Value × Rate of Markup/100
Retail Value = Purchase Value + Markup

Partial Output:

```
                                                                    (cleared screen)
                         Number of purchases? [6]

Is the number correct (y/n)? [y]
                                                                    (cleared screen)
                   Department number, purchase? [40,10000.00]

Are the entries correct (y/n)? [y]
                                                                    (cleared screen)
          =========================================================
          DEPT. NO      DEPT. NAME          PURCHASE        RETAIL
          =========================================================
             40         Housewares        $10,000.00    $13,300.00

Press any key to continue
```

5. The program on page 307 searched a students' master file for a student number. The key was a student number from a scores file. If the number was found, the student's record from the master file and the student's score from the scores file were printed. If the number was not found, a message was displayed stating that the student number was not found.

   Modify the program. Rather than printing the student's number, name, address, telephone number, and score; print a report card. A sample report card is given on page 330. Furthermore, your program must check for students whose scores have not been submitted. Thus, the program must contain two search subroutines. One subroutine examines the student numbers stored in the master file. If a student number is found, a report card is printed; if the number is not found, a message; such as, **Student xxxx not on register** is displayed. The other subroutine examines the student numbers stored in the scores file. If a student number is not found, a message; such as, **Scores for student xxxx not submitted** must be displayed.

   To illustrate, let us use the student numbers from our two files MASTER.DAT and SCORES2.DAT. (Each record contains other information in addition to a student number.)

Student number array	*Student number array*
Master File	*Scores File*
1942	4931
2593*	2867
2867	5263*
3917	1942
4931	6429
6429	3917

*2593 is not found in the scores file. Therefore, the scores were not submitted.

*5263 is not found in the master file. Therefore, the student is not on the register.

Store all data read from both files in arrays. Do not assume that the number of records in the master file is the same as the number of records in the scores file. Thus, it is necessary to find the size of each file as records are being read. In addition to counting the records in both files, create local string arrays that store the student numbers read from the files.

In a separate subroutine, perform the tasks listed below within two FOR/NEXT loops. We will call the subroutine CREATE KEYS AND CALL SEARCH SUBROUTINES. In the dialogue, a reference to a file is actually a reference to an array. The first loop must:

(a) Assign a student number from the master file to IKEY1$. The student number will be the key in a search for a student number in the scores file.
(b) Call Subroutine SEARCH SCORES FILE.
(c) Determine whether or not a student number has been found. If the student number was not found (FLAG = Ø), the scores for this student have not been submitted. Display an appropriate message.

In the second FOR/NEXT loop, code statements similar to the ones for tasks (a) and (b) above. This time, assign a student number from the scores file to IKEY2$. The student number will be the key in a search for a student number in the master file. Call Subroutine SEARCH MASTER FILE. After calling the subroutine, copy the position of the "found" student number into a program variable, such as RECORD.NO. If the student number was found, call a subroutine to print the report card. If the number was not found, the student is not on the register. Display an appropriate message.

Code the subroutine that prints the report card. Use the position sent from the search subroutine (it was suggested that the position be stored in RECORD.NO) as a subscript to print the student's name and number. Use the control variable of the FOR statement in Subroutine CREATE KEYS AND CALL SEARCH SUBROUTINES as a subscript to print the course and the score. Each report card and each "not found" message must be displayed on a cleared screen. Remember to call Subroutine FREEZE DISPLAY.

The contents of the two data files and a partial output are given below. Data file MASTER.DAT is the one given on page 307, data file SCORES3.DAT is new.

```
MASTER.DAT
1942,"Lindsay,Donna",637 North Avenue    Anycity   ZZ   M3L 4T8,593-2184
2593,"Meyer,Tom",485 First Avenue    Anycity   ZZ   M3L 3W7,334-9815
2867,"Saunders,Bryan",942 South Avenue    Anycity   ZZ   M3L 6V4,243-1825
3917,"Kent,Sherri",153 East Street    Anycity   ZZ   M3L 2Y5,413-9426
4931,"Hughes,James",984 West Street    Anycity   ZZ   M3L 1X6,458-6218
6429,"Walker,Anna",325 Third Street    Anycity   ZZ   M3L 8S5,334-1628

SCORES3.DAT
4931,101 Geography,69,101 English,74,101 Science,82
2867,200 Physics,93,200 English,85,200 Mathematics,94
5263,200 History,85,200 Chemistry,71,202 Data Processing,82
1942,301 English,71,302 Business Law,86,301 Mathematics,84
6429,101 Geography,67,101 Science,82,101 English,84
3917,300 Chemistry,82,302 Data Processing,78,300 English,93
```

Partial Output:

(cleared screen)

```
         10        20        30        40        50        60        70        80
12345678901234567890123456789012345678901234567890123456789012345678901234567890
                      Scores for student 2593 not submitted

Press any key to continue
```

(cleared screen)

```
    *********************************************************************
    * Anycity College  985 First Street                Telephone: 123-4567 *
    *                  Anycity  ZZ  M3L 1V2                                *
    *-------------------------------------------------------------------*
    * STUDENT NAME: Hughes,James                       STUDENT NUMBER 4931 *
    *-------------------------------------------------------------------*
    * Course: 101 Geography             Score: 69                          *
    * Course: 101 English               Score: 74                          *
    * Course: 101 Science               Score: 82                          *
    *                                                                      *
    *                                                                      *
    *                                                                      *
    *                                                                      *
    *                                                                      *
    *                                                                      *
    *********************************************************************

Press any key to continue
```

(cleared screen)

```
                          Student 5263 not on register

Press any key to continue
```

6. Use the subroutines given on page 315 to update specific accounts in your Accounts Receivable file, AR2.DAT. Write the records (some of which will be updated) to the same file from which they were read. However, it is wise to write the records first to a new file, say AR3.DAT. When your program is error-free, write the records to the original file by changing, in your program, the name of the new file to that of the original file and then rerunning the program. Or, rename the new file to that of the original by using the BASIC command NAME or the DOS command RENAME. Refer to Appendix D or Appendix E for instructions in renaming a file. **Remember to save your program before using the DOS command RENAME.**

   Recall that codes are used to denote a sale and a payment (a code of 1 means a sale, a code of 2 means a payment). In your main routine, open file AR2.DAT and call subroutines that (a) display the instructions concerning the codes, (b) read the data file, and (c) freeze a display. Set up a WHILE/WEND loop where the WHILE statement checks for a "q" entered by the user in Subroutine FREEZE DISPLAY. Inside the loop, call the subroutine that INPUTs the key (an account number) and call Subroutine FREEZE DISPLAY. Following the loop, close the data file and open a file for an OUTPUT (preferably a new file while you are testing your program). Call the subroutine that writes the records to the file just opened, close the file, then print the message "End of Processing".

   Read all the data into arrays and create a local string array that stores the account numbers. Remember to find the size of each array by counting the records as they are read. Subroutine SEARCH ONE-DIMENSIONAL ARRAY will search the account number array for the keyed-in account number.

   In the subroutine that calculates a new balance, check whether the code entered is 1 or 2. If the code is "1", call another module within this subroutine to (a) increase the previous balance by the amount of the transaction, (b) increase the row number by 1, (c) LOCATE this row, and (d) print a detail line (debit the account). If the code is "2", call a different module whose statements will be similar to those mentioned above. However, here you must decrease the previous balance by the amount of the transaction and credit the account.

Refer to the account displayed on page 314 to format your output. Print the heading **Account number xxxxx** on row 2 (xxxxx represents an account number). After the row of hyphens under the column headings is printed, the date and the initial balance will be printed on row 9. For subscripted variables, use RECORD.NO as the subscript. RECORD.NO is the position of the found account.

You will need three images for your PRINT USING statements. One image edits the line that displays the initial balance, another edits a debited transaction, and the third edits a credited transaction. Write a subroutine similar to the one shown on page 316 to write the records to your output file.

An account for which no further transactions are to be entered must be followed by the messages shown below. (xxxxx denotes an account number.)

```
         *                                                                    *
         *                                                                    *
         **********************************************************************
Another transaction for account number xxxxx (y/n)? n

Press any key to continue, press 'q' to quit
```

The message "Press any key to continue, press 'q' to quit" is displayed by a PRINT statement in Subroutine FREEZE DISPLAY. Refer to Chapter 10, page 237 for a listing of this subroutine. If a user presses any key, another account can be updated; if the user presses a "q", processing ends. Note: You will need two versions of Subroutine FREEZE DISPLAY. One includes the "quit" message, the other does not.

Make a hard copy of your program as it will be useful for solving a problem in Chapter 15.

7. Modify the program for Problem 6 by sending an account number, name, address, telephone number, date, initial balance, and transactions to the printer. Assume you will be printing on preprinted forms similar to the accounts prepared for Problem 6. Remember to blank out the asterisks, the column headings, and the two rows of hyphens with LPRINT statements. In addition to deleting the strings Account number, NAME, ADDRESS, and TELEPHONE, delete the word "Balance" in the line that displays the initial balance. Output directed to the printer is shown below in bold face.

```
         10        20        30        40        50        60        70        80
12345678901234567890123456789012345678901234567890123456789012345678901234567890

      Account number 31001
      **********************************************************************
      * NAME: Diane Fraser                                        TELEPHONE *
      * ADDRESS: 367 River Road  Anycity  ZZ  M3L 4S8             339-8542  *
      *---------------------------------------------------------------------*
      * DATE           ITEM               DEBIT       CREDIT       BALANCE  *
      *---------------------------------------------------------------------*
      * Nov. 12        Balance                                   $  342.16  *
      * Nov. 14                          $ 59.21                 $  401.37  *
      * Nov. 17                                      $100.00     $  301.37  *
      *                                                                     *
      *                                                                     *
      *                                                                     *
      *                                                                     *
      *                                                                     *
      **********************************************************************
```

Project

A separate program for the project in Chapter Nine listed, by department, those accounts with balances less than the minimum. Suppose stock has been replenished. The accounts must now be updated. Write a program that uses the update module given on page 315 to update accounts in INVENT2.DAT. Do not INPUT a stock number. Your program must check the balances of all accounts. If a balance is below the minimum, display and update the account. Note that there is no need to call Subroutine SEARCH ONE-DIMENSIONAL ARRAY.

Use codes to denote an order and a sale (there may have been other sales before an order is recorded). A "1" means an order has been filled, a "2" means a sale has been made. As in Subroutine UPDATE ACCOUNT on page 315, display prompts asking a user to key in the date, the code, and the amount of the transaction. Your program must calculate the new balance.

After the required accounts have been updated and all records have been written to disk, group print all stock by department as in the project for Chapter Nine (use the subroutines from this project). Also display a summary which gives the total number of accounts whose balances are below their minimums.

As with the Accounts Receivable program, write all records first to a new file. When your program is error-free, rename the new file INVENT2.DAT which is the name of the original file. Do this within your program, then rerun the program. Or, use the BASIC command NAME or the DOS command RENAME to rename the new file. **Remember, save your program before using the DOS command RENAME.** Furthermore, the program is needed for the project in Chapter 14.

To update accounts, you will need subroutines to:

1. Read the original data file.
2. Compare the balance in an account with the minimum allowed and call the subroutine that updates an account if the balance is less than the minimum.
3. Update an account. This subroutine is similar to the one given on page 315. The subroutine calls two other subroutines. One prints the initial account, the other performs the calculations.
4. Print the initial account. A sample account is given below.

(cleared screen)

```
         10        20        30        40        50        60        70        80
12345678901234567890123456789012345678901234567890123456789012345678901234567890
          Stock number F001
          ****************************************************************
          * DEPARTMENT: Furnishings                                      *
          * ITEM: Sofa (contemporary)                       Minimum: 3   *
          *--------------------------------------------------------------*
          * DATE                          ORDERED     SOLD     BALANCE   *
          *--------------------------------------------------------------*
          * Jan. 8                                                2      *
          *                                                              *
          *                                                              *
          *                                                              *
          *                                                              *
          *                                                              *
          *                                                              *
          *                                                              *
          ****************************************************************
Date, code, quantity? Jan. 10,1,3
Are the entries correct (y/n)? y
```

5. Perform the calculations. As in the Accounts Receivable program, submodules are needed in this subroutine. One submodule increases the balance by the amount ordered, the other decreases the balance by the amount sold. Each submodule prints a detail line. From the transaction data keyed in above, account F001 would now look as follows:

```
          Stock number F001
          ****************************************************************
          * DEPARTMENT: Furnishings                                      *
          * ITEM: Sofa (contemporary)                       Minimum: 3   *
          *--------------------------------------------------------------*
          * DATE                          ORDERED     SOLD     BALANCE   *
          *--------------------------------------------------------------*
          * Jan. 8                                                2      *
          * Jan. 10                          3                    5      *
```

```
*                                                                   *
*                                                                   *
*                                                                   *
*                                                                   *
*                                                                   *
*                                                                   *
*********************************************************************
Another transaction for stock number F001 (y/n)?
```

6. Write all accounts to a data file.

To group print by department, you will need subroutines to:

1. Format the report.
2. Print the headings.
3. Read the updated file and process the data. The subroutine must determine when data for another department must be processed and when a page is full. It must print a detail line and check the balance of an account for the minimum. A counter must be increased by 1 if the balance is less than the minimum.
4. Print the group counter (the total number of accounts with balances below the minimum for that department) and accumulate these group counters. The subroutine must cause the printer to skip to a new page to print the inventory report for the next department. A sample report is shown below.

```
          Department: Furnishings          01-15-19XX          Page  2

                                  INVENTORY REPORT
          ============================================================
          STOCK NO.              ITEM                MINIMUM   BALANCE
          ============================================================
            F001       Sofa (contemporary)              3          5
            F002       Sofa (French)                    2          4
            F003       Sofa (Italian)                   2          3

          Number of accounts under the minimum          0

  Press any key to continue
```

5. On a new page, produce a summary that gives the total number of accounts with balances under the minimums. Your summary page could look as follows:

```
                       NUMBER OF ACCOUNTS UNDER THE MINIMUM    Page  4
                                    01-15-19XX

                  Total number of accounts under the minimum  3

End of processing
```

Solutions for Exercises

12.1 Creating Arrays

1. (a) `2010 DIM NUM1(30)`
   (b) `2010 DIM NAME1$(15)`
   (c) `2010 DIM NUM1(20),NAME1$(20)`
   (d) `2010 DIM NUM1(20),NUM2(25),NAME1$(15),NAME2$(18)`

2. (a) Array MARK must have a dimension.
   `2010 DIM MARK(30)`
   (b) If array MONTH stores the names of the months, the array must be type string. If the array stores the numbers of the months, nothing is wrong.
   `2020 DIM MONTH$(N-2)` or `2020 DIM MONTH(N-2)`
   (c) Variable A$ and its contents must be numeric.
   ```
   2010 A = 14
   2020 DIM ADDRESS$(A)
   ```
   (d) The arrays must be separated by commas.
   `2010 DIM A(14),B(14),C(14)`
   (e) Nothing is wrong.
   (f) N must be assigned a value before the array is dimensioned.
   ```
   2010 N = 40
   2020 DIM TELEPHONE$(N)
   ```

12.2 Data Entry and Data Output Using Arrays

Exercise 1.

```
1000 'PURCHASES
2000 'MAIN ROUTINE
2010   DIM CREDITOR$(10),PURCHASE(10),PAYMENT(10)
2020   GOSUB 3000                     'Enter data
2030   GOSUB 4000                     'Print data
2040   END
3000 'SUBROUTINE ENTER DATA
3010   FOR P = 1 TO 4
3020     READ CREDITOR$(P),PURCHASE(P),PAYMENT(P)
3030   NEXT P
3040   DATA "ABC Fashions"      ,1567.32,694.82
3050   DATA "New Clothiers"     ,984.57 ,463.48
3060   DATA "Rite-Shoes"        ,862.43 ,426.43
3070   DATA "Modern Sportswear",1942.31,854.67
3080   RETURN
4000 'SUBROUTINE PRINT DATA
4010   CLS
4020   LOCATE 11
4030   FOR P = 1 TO 4
4040     PRINT TAB(19) USING "\______________\_____$####,.##_____$###.##";
         CREDITOR$(P),PURCHASE(P),PAYMENT(P)
4050   NEXT P
4060   RETURN
65529 'End of program listing
```

Exercise 2.

```
1000 'PURCHASES
2000 'MAIN ROUTINE
2010   DIM CREDITOR$(10),PURCHASE(10),PAYMENT(10)
2020   GOSUB 3000                     'Enter and print data
2030   END
```

```
3000 'SUBROUTINE ENTER AND PRINT DATA
3010   CLS
3020   LOCATE 11
3030   FOR P = 1 TO 4
3040     READ CREDITOR$(P),PURCHASE(P),PAYMENT(P)
3050     PRINT TAB(19) USING "\_______________\_____$####,.##_____$###.##";
         CREDITOR$(P),PURCHASE(P),PAYMENT(P)
3060   NEXT P
3070   DATA "ABC Fashions"        ,1567.32,694.82
3080   DATA "New Clothiers"       ,984.57 ,463.48
3090   DATA "Rite-Shoes"          ,862.43 ,426.43
3100   DATA "Modern Sportswear",1942.31,854.67
3110   RETURN
65529 'End of program listing
```

12.3 Processing Data Stored in an Array

1.

```
Adrian Johnson        $3,000.00      $500.00
Larry Cook            $4,000.00      $500.00
Patricia Forrest      $5,000.00      $500.00
```

The program segment produces the same commission for each employee. This is because the commissions were not stored in an array and printing occurs after all the commissions were calculated. Each commission, except the last one, was replaced by the one currently being stored.

Exercise 2.

```
1000 'CURRENT RATIO
2000 'MAIN ROUTINE
2010   DIM YEAR(5),ASSETS(5),LIABILITIES(5)
2020   GOSUB 3000                    'INPUT data
2030   GOSUB 4000                    'Process data
2040   END
3000 'SUBROUTINE INPUT DATA
3010   CLS
3020   LOCATE 7
3030   FOR Y = 1 TO 3
3040     INPUT "Year, assets, liabilities";YEAR(Y),ASSETS(Y),LIABILITIES(Y)
3050   NEXT Y
3060   RETURN
4000 'SUBROUTINE PROCESS DATA
4010   FOR Y = 1 TO 3
4020     RATIO = ASSETS(Y)/LIABILITIES(Y)
4030     PRINT
4040     PRINT "Year:";YEAR(Y)
4050     PRINT USING "Assets:_$######,.##___Liabilities:_$######,.##___Ratio:_#.
###";ASSETS(Y),LIABILITIES(Y),RATIO
4060   NEXT Y
4070   RETURN
65529 'End of program listing
```

12.4 Searching an Array

1. The value of variable ARRAY.SIZE would be higher than the number of records in the data file by one. Suppose the DIM statement reserved the exact number of elements needed for each array. When ARRAY.SIZE is used as the test value of a FOR/NEXT loop which references an array, BASIC will print a **Subscript out of range** error.

2. A record is read from file SCORES2.DAT, processed immediately, then another record is read and processed. The fields in each record are not needed for reprocessing. Therefore, there is no need to place the data items in arrays.

3. FLAG signals whether or not the key is found. The variable terminates the WHILE/WEND loop when BASIC finds the key.

12.5 Sorting the Contents of an Array

Statement 18030 must be changed as follows:

```
18030 IF IN1$(W-1) <= IN1$(X) THEN SWAP IN1$(W-1),IN1$(X)
```

12.6 Updating an Account

1. The latest date entered for an account transaction would be displayed as the date of the initial balance in the next account retrieved and printed.
2. Prompts displayed beneath the account would not be erased before new prompts are displayed. Thus, some of the previous prompts may remain on the screen.

13

TWO-DIMENSIONAL ARRAYS

Objectives

A one-dimensional array is suitable for handling a list of data items, such as a list of numbers or a list of names. However, when data is in tabular form, the items are more conveniently handled by a two-dimensional array. An example of data in tabular form is an income tax table where data is presented in several rows and several columns. Although three- and higher-dimensional arrays are also available, we shall restrict our discussions mainly to two-dimensional arrays.

In this chapter, you will learn how to:

- Store data in a two-dimensional array.
- Access data stored in a two-dimensional array.
- Process the data stored in a two-dimensional array.
- Search a two-dimensional array for a particular value.

Contents

13.1 Creating a Multi-dimensional Array

Basic Concepts of a Two-dimensional Array

A two-dimensional array consists of two or more rows and two or more columns. Suppose a library stores books on long shelves with the shelves partitioned into sections. Although there are many more bookshelves in the library than the number used in this illustration, let us assume there are three shelves and that each shelf is partitioned into four sections, giving a total of twelve storage areas.

Each storage area holds a different type of book. Assume the top shelf,first section contains history books; the top shelf, second section contains science-fiction books; the top shelf, third section contains autobiographies; etc. The numbers of books in the library can be presented as a two-dimensional array in the following manner:

BOOKS

	Column 1	Column 2	Column 3	Column 4
Row 1	3	2	Ø	1
Row 2	1	Ø	2	3
Row 3	2	4	1	Ø

We have named our array BOOKS. The shelves are considered rows and the sections are considered columns. As with a one-dimensional array, we need a subscripted variable to gain access to a specific storage area. Each storage area is referred to as an element of the array and is capable of storing one value. The subscripted variable of a two-dimensional array requires two subscripts: one subscript to denote the number of the row, the other to denote the number of the column.

Suppose mystery books are stored on the third shelf (row 3) in the first section (column 1). This storage area is represented by the subscripted variable BOOKS(3,1) where BOOKS is the name of the array, 3 is the number of the row, and 1 is the number of the column.

```
BOOKS    (      3      ,      1     )←—— Subscripts enclosed
  ↑             ↑             ↑          in parentheses
Array name   Row number   Column number
```

It is important to note that the row must always be specified before the column. If we wish to gain access to the science-fiction books which are stored on the first shelf (row), second section (column), the subscripted variable will be BOOKS(1,2).

The name of a two-dimensional array may not be the same as that of a one-dimensional array. However, a subscripted variable of a two-dimensional array and a simple variable may have the same name. For example, X(1,2) and X are two distinct variables. A good idea is to give the array a name that represents the kind of data stored in the array, such as ENAME$ for employee names and SALES for sales amounts.

A two-dimensional array can store only one type of data: numeric or string. If the array name is numeric, the array can store only numbers; if the array name is type string, the array can store only strings. The strings need not all be the same length. It should be pointed out that the data items stored in a two-dimensional array are not actually organized in rows and columns in the computer. The items are stored as lists. We can, though, print them out in tabular form.

Dimensioning a Two-dimensional Array

A two-dimensional array must be dimensioned if one of its dimensions is greater than 10. We use the same DIM statement that we used to dimension a one-dimensional array. However, the name of the array must be followed by two values within parentheses. The values represent the number of rows and the number of columns in the array rather than a particular row and a particular column as with a subscripted variable. The following DIM statement dimensions a two-dimensional array named NUMBER.

```
2010 DIM NUMBER(12,14)
                 ↑  ↑
                 |  Number of columns in the array
                 |
           Number of rows in the array
```

A one-dimensional array and a two-dimensional array may be dimensioned in the same DIM statement as shown in the statement below.

```
2010 DIM NUMBER(12,14),ENAME$(16)
```

As previously explained, BASIC creates an element Ø for a one-dimensional array. BASIC also recognizes a row Ø and a column Ø. Thus, array NUMBER consists of 13 rows (Ø through 12) and 15 columns (Ø through 14) which produces 195 elements (13 × 15 = 195). Since counting from 1 is simpler than counting from Ø, our programs will not consider row Ø and column Ø.

General Concepts of a Three-dimensional Array

Although we will be discussing mainly two-dimensional arrays, let us briefly examine a three-dimensional array. To dimension such an array, the array name in the DIM statement must be followed by three dimensions enclosed in parentheses. The DIM statement could look as follows.

```
2010 DIM SALES(4,5,3)
```

The diagram below depicts a three-dimensional array. Each subscripted variable must have three subscripts. The first subscript represents the row, the second subscript represents the column, the third subscript represents the depth.

FIGURE 13-1 REPRESENTATION OF A THREE-DIMENSIONAL ARRAY

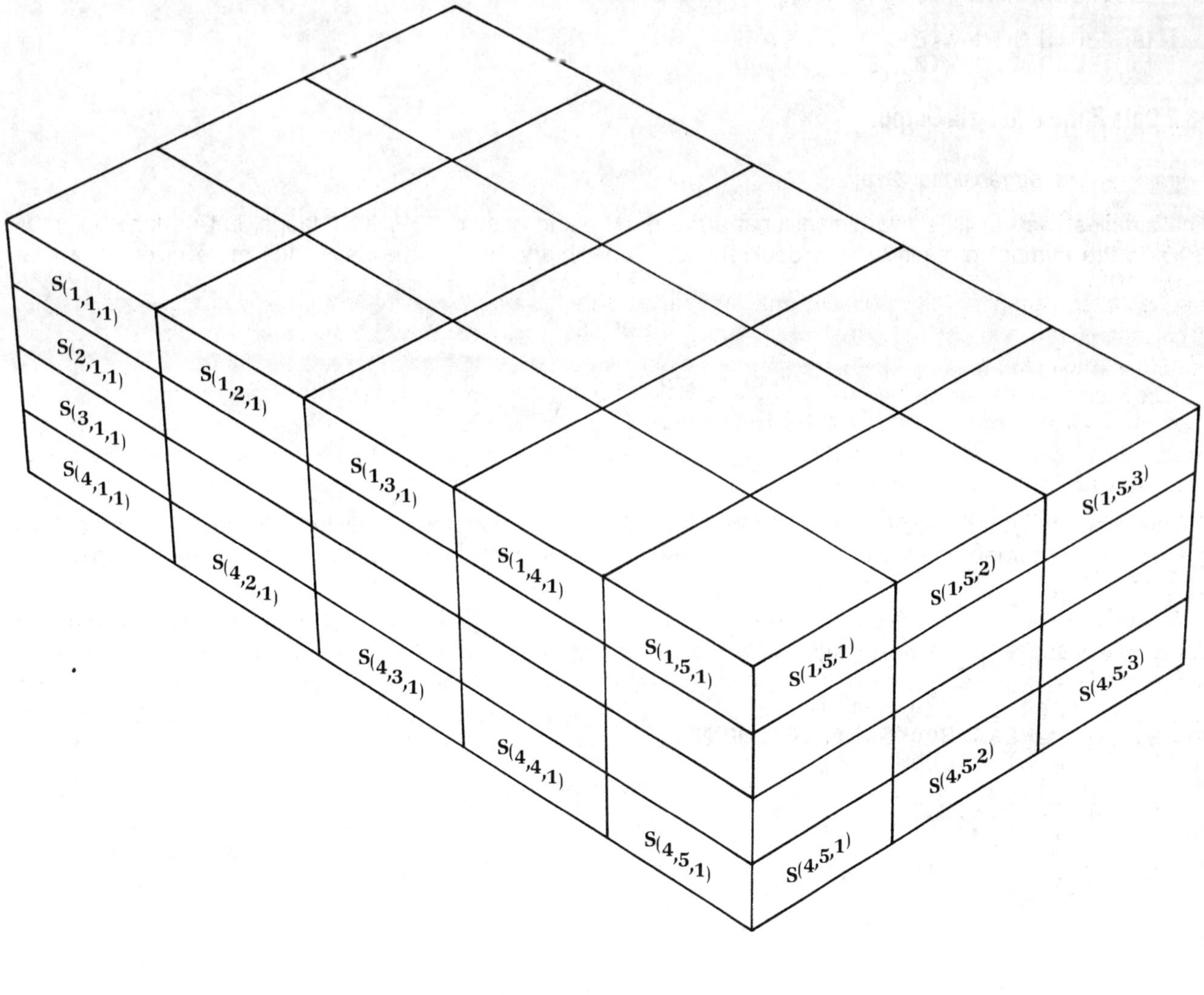

An application of a three-dimensional array would be the description of a person's sales by province, county, and district. To find the amount sold by a person working in a particular district, we must give the computer three items of information: the specific province in which the person works (the row), the specific county within the province (the column), and the specific district within the county (the depth). Subscripted variable SALES(3,4,2) directs the computer to the storage location storing the sales of a person working in the third province, in the fourth county within the third province, in the second district within the fourth county of the third province.

Exercises

1. Code DIM statements to dimension the following. Use one DIM statement for each exercise. Ignore row zero and column zero.
   (a) A two-dimensional numeric array with 4 rows and 4 columns.
   (b) A two-dimensional string array with 6 rows and 7 columns and a two-dimensional numeric array with 7 rows and 6 columns.
   (c) A one-dimensional string array with 8 elements, a two-dimensional string array and a two-dimensional numeric array each with 8 rows and 9 columns.
2. Indicate the errors, if any, in the following statements. Make the necessary corrections.
   (a) `2010 DIM NAME$(4,5)`
   (b) `2010 DIM TELEPHONE$(12,13)`
   (c) `2010 DIM ADDRESS$(A,B)`
   (d) `2010 DIM SUBJECT$(3);SCORES(15,6)`
3. Is there any difference between the following arrays?
   (a) `2010 DIM A(25)`
   (b) `2010 DIM A(0,25)`

13.2 Data Entry and Data Output

Loading a Two-dimensional Array

The simplest way to fill a two-dimensional array is by using nested FOR/NEXT loops. Let us load, in array BOOKS, the number of each type of book stored in our library. Here is the data once more given in tabular form.

BOOKS

3	2	Ø	1
1	Ø	2	3
2	4	1	Ø

The subroutine that loads the array is listed below. The outer loop of the nested FOR/NEXT loops controls the rows, the inner loop controls the columns. The DIM statement would normally be coded in the main routine.

```
2010 DIM BOOKS(3,4)

4000 'SUBROUTINE ENTER DATA
4010   FOR ROW = 1 TO 3
4020     FOR COLUMN = 1 TO 4
4030       READ BOOKS(ROW,COLUMN)
4040     NEXT COLUMN
4050   NEXT ROW
4060   DATA 3,2,0,1
4070   DATA 1,0,2,3
4080   DATA 2,4,1,0
4090   RETURN
```

Here is how the data is stored in the array.

The first time the loops are executed, ROW = 1 and COLUMN = 1. In line 4030, BOOKS(ROW,COLUMN) is actually BOOKS(1,1). The number 3 is stored in the first row, first column.

	Column 1	Column 2	Column 3	Column 4
Row 1	3			
Row 2				
Row 3				

The value of ROW now remains constant while the column loop goes through its cycles. The value of COLUMN changes.

The second time the column loop is executed, ROW = 1 and COLUMN = 2. In line 4030, BOOKS(ROW,COLUMN) is actually BOOKS(1,2). The number 2 is stored in the first row, second column.

	Column 1	Column 2	Column 3	Column 4
Row 1	3	2		
Row 2				
Row 3				

The third time the column loop is executed, ROW = 1 and COLUMN = 3. In line 4030, BOOKS(ROW,COLUMN) is actually BOOKS(1,3). The number Ø is stored in the first row, third column.

	Column 1	Column 2	Column 3	Column 4
Row 1	3	2	Ø	
Row 2				
Row 3				

The fourth time the column loop is executed, ROW = 1 and COLUMN = 4. In line 4030, BOOKS(ROW,COLUMN) is actually BOOKS(1,4). The number 1 is stored in the first row, fourth column.

	Column 1	Column 2	Column 3	Column 4
Row 1	3	2	Ø	1
Row 2				
Row 3				

The column loop is now complete and BASIC enters the row loop. The value of ROW changes to 2 and the value of COLUMN reverts to 1. All four columns of the second row will be filled as the column loop goes through its cycles. The process is repeated when ROW changes to 3; that is, the four columns of the third row will be filled as the column loop goes through its cycles.

Notice that the numbers are stored by rows. The first row is filled, then the second row, and finally the third row. This is because the row loop is the outer loop and the column loop is the inner loop.

```
4010    FOR ROW = 1 TO 3                  — Row loop on the outside.
4020      FOR COLUMN = 1 TO 4             — Column loop on the inside.
4030        READ BOOKS(ROW,COLUMN)
4040      NEXT COLUMN
4050    NEXT ROW
```

While the value of ROW remains one, the value of COLUMN changes, from 1 to 2, 3, and 4. Thus, the first row is filled. After the column loop is complete, the value of ROW changes to 2 and the value of COLUMN reverts to 1. The second row is filled as the column loop goes through its cycles once more. The third row is filled when ROW equals 3 and after the column loop has gone through all of its cycles. When ROW equals 4, looping terminates.

Care must be taken in listing the numbers in the DATA statements. Since the data is stored by rows, the numbers in the DATA statements must be listed by rows. The data may also be placed in one DATA statement.

Although not used as often, an alternative method is to load an array by columns. The first column is filled, then the second, the third, etc. Using this method, the column loop must be the outer loop and the row loop the inner loop. Furthermore, the data items must be listed by columns rather than by rows. A sample subroutine is shown on the following page.

```
2010 DIM BOOKS(3,4)

4000 'SUBROUTINE ENTER DATA
4010   FOR COLUMN = 1 TO 4
4020     FOR ROW = 1 TO 3
4030       READ BOOKS(ROW,COLUMN)
4040     NEXT ROW
4050   NEXT COLUMN
4060   DATA 3,1,2
4070   DATA 2,0,4
4080   DATA 0,2,1
4090   DATA 1,3,0
4100   RETURN
```

Here are two other examples of subroutines that load arrays. Although the amount of data is small, larger amounts (or even smaller amounts) can be stored simply by changing the dimensions of the arrays and by changing one or both of the test values in the FOR statements.

1. The following subroutine reads data into two arrays.

A			B		
1	2	3	9	8	7
4	5	6	6	5	4
7	8	9	3	2	1

```
2010 DIM A(3,3),B(3,3)

4000 'SUBROUTINE ENTER DATA
4010   FOR ROW = 1 TO 3
4020     FOR COLUMN = 1 TO 3
4030       READ A(ROW,COLUMN),B(ROW,COLUMN)
4040     NEXT COLUMN
4050   NEXT ROW
4060   DATA 1,9,2,8,3,7
4070   DATA 4,6,5,5,6,4
4080   DATA 7,3,8,2,9,1
4090   RETURN
```

The subroutine assigns the data items to variables in pairs. The first member of each pair is read into array A, the second member of each pair is read into array B. Thus, the items in the DATA statements must alternate between a value for array A and a value for array B.

```
4030 READ A(ROW,COLUMN),B(ROW,COLUMN)
               ↑                ↑
4060 DATA      1,               9,          2,8,3,7
```

2. The subroutine listed below stores the names of three employees and the number of parts produced each day by each employee.

Employee Name	*Monday*	*Tuesday*	*Wednesday*	*Thursday*	*Friday*
Mayer,John	43	41	40	42	40
Carr,Steve	41	42	40	43	41
Lang,Norman	40	39	41	42	43

The data cannot be stored in a two-dimensional array since it consists of strings and numbers. Instead, we consider the data as two parallel arrays. The names will be stored in a one-dimensional string array and the parts produced in a two-dimensional numeric array.

```
2010 DIM ENAME$(3),PARTS(3,5)

4000 'SUBROUTINE LOAD ARRAYS
4010   FOR EMPLOYEE = 1 TO 3
```

```
4020        READ ENAME$(EMPLOYEE)
4030      NEXT EMPLOYEE
4040      FOR EMPLOYEE = 1 TO 3
4050        FOR DAY = 1 TO 5
4060          READ PARTS(EMPLOYEE,DAY)
4070        NEXT DAY
4080      NEXT EMPLOYEE
4090      DATA "Mayer,John","Carr,Steve","Lang,Norman"
4100      DATA 43,41,40,42,40
4110      DATA 41,42,40,43,41
4120      DATA 40,39,41,42,43
4130      RETURN
```

A single FOR/NEXT loop stores the names in a one-dimensional array while nested FOR/NEXT loops store the numbers of parts in a two-dimensional array. Note that we list the names in a separate DATA statement. An employee name and the parts produced by that employee cannot be listed as a record in a DATA statement, since we must read all the names before we begin reading the numbers of parts.

Notice, also, the use of distinctive array names that identify the kinds of data stored in the arrays. Array ENAME$ stores the employee names while array PARTS stores the parts produced by each employee. The same principle applies to the control variables. EMPLOYEE keeps track of the employees while DAY keeps track of the days.

Printing from a Two-dimensional Array

Printing values from a two-dimensional array is very similar to loading the array. We use nested FOR/NEXT loops to reference each element of the array.

1. The subroutine below prints the number of each type of book in our library. The numbers are stored in the array BOOKS.

```
2010   DIM BOOKS(3,4)

5000 'SUBROUTINE PRINT DATA
5010      PRINT
5020      FOR ROW = 1 TO 3
5030        FOR COLUMN = 1 TO 4
5040          PRINT BOOKS(ROW,COLUMN);
5050        NEXT COLUMN
5060        PRINT
5070      NEXT ROW
5080      RETURN
RUN
```

This PRINT statement counteracts the semicolon in line 5040. The next item is printed on a new line.

```
 3  2  0  1
 1  0  2  3
 2  4  1  0
```

The output is produced in tabular form by the PRINT statement in line 5040 (which ends with a semicolon) and the "blank" PRINT in line 5060. The PRINT statement with the trailing semicolon prints numbers on one line closely spaced. The "blank" PRINT moves the cursor to the next output line before BASIC prints the next row of numbers.

2. It is also possible to print the data in the same subroutine that loads the array.

```
2010   DIM BOOKS(3,4)

4000 'SUBROUTINE ENTER AND PRINT DATA
4010      PRINT
4020      FOR ROW = 1 TO 3
4030        FOR COLUMN = 1 TO 4
4040          READ BOOKS(ROW,COLUMN)
4050          PRINT BOOKS(ROW,COLUMN);
4060        NEXT COLUMN
4070        PRINT
4080      NEXT ROW
4090      DATA 3,2,0,1
```

```
4100    DATA 1,0,2,3
4110    DATA 2,4,1,0
4120    RETURN
```

The output will be the same as that shown for Example 1. We could have assigned each item of data to a simple variable since each item is printed immediately after it is read. However, if the data items need to be processed several times, we must store the data in an array. In this way, all data items are saved and ready for use.

3. The following subroutine prints the numbers of books stored on the first shelf (row).

```
2010   DIM BOOKS(3,4)

5000 'SUBROUTINE PRINT VALUES IN FIRST ROW
5010    PRINT
5020    FOR COLUMN = 1 TO 4
5030      PRINT BOOKS(1,COLUMN);
5040    NEXT COLUMN
5050    RETURN
RUN
```

```
 3  2  0  1
```

There is no need to use a variable for the row subscript since the routine remains on row one throughout the printing. A variable is needed for the column subscript as the column number must change from 1 to 2, 3, and 4. Thus, the routine requires a loop for the columns only.

4. The subroutine on page 342 stored the names of three employees in a one-dimensional string array and the numbers of parts produced by each employee in a two-dimensional numeric array. The subroutine below prints the data.

```
2010   DIM ENAME$(3),PARTS(3,5)

5000 'SUBROUTINE PRINT DATA
5010    PRINT
5020    FOR EMPLOYEE = 1 TO 3
5030      PRINT USING F1$; ENAME$(EMPLOYEE);
5040      FOR DAY = 1 TO 5
5050        PRINT USING F2$; PARTS(EMPLOYEE,DAY);
5060      NEXT DAY
5070      PRINT
5080    NEXT EMPLOYEE
5090    RETURN
RUN
```

```
Mayer,John        43    41    40    42    40
Carr,Steve        41    42    40    43    41
Lang,Norman       40    39    41    42    43
```

The PRINT statement that prints an employee's name is placed between the two FOR statements. The DAY (inner) loop prints the number of parts produced each day by this employee. When the DAY loop is complete, BASIC enters the EMPLOYEE (outer) loop and another employee's name is printed. The DAY loop prints the numbers of parts produced by this second employee. The process of printing an employee's name and the number of parts produced each day by the employee is repeated until EMPLOYEE = 4 at which point looping terminates.

The semicolons at the end of both PRINT USING statements cause an employee's name and the numbers of parts produced by the employee to be printed on the same line. The "blank" PRINT in line 5070 moves the cursor from the current output line to the next output line where another employee's name and numbers of parts are printed.

Exercises

1. Identify the errors, if any, in the program segments shown below. Make the necessary corrections.

(a)
```
2010 DIM A(4,5)

4010 FOR ROW = 1 TO 5
4020   FOR COLUMN = 1 TO 4
4030     READ A(ROW,COLUMN)
4040   NEXT COLUMN
4050 NEXT ROW
4060 DATA -,-,-,......(20 data items)
```

(b)
```
2010 DIM A(3,2),B(3,2)

4010 FOR COLUMN = 1 TO 2
4020   FOR ROW = 1 TO 3
4030     READ A(ROW,COLUMN),B(ROW,COLUMN)
4040   NEXT ROW
4050 NEXT COLUMN
4060 DATA -,-,-,......(6 data items)
```

(c)
```
2010 DIM A(7,8),B(8,7)

4010 FOR COLUMN = 1 TO 7
4020   FOR ROW = 1 TO 7
4030     READ A(ROW,COLUMN),B(ROW,COLUMN)
4040   NEXT ROW
4050 NEXT COLUMN
4060 DATA -,-,-,......(98 data items)
```

(d)
```
2010 DIM A(4),B(3,4)

4010 FOR ROW = 1 TO 3
4020   FOR COLUMN = 1 TO 4
4030     READ A(ROW,COLUMN),B(ROW,COLUMN)
4040   NEXT COLUMN
4050 NEXT ROW
4060 DATA -,-,-,......(24 data items)
```

2. Answer the following questions for each program segment given below.

(i) How is the data read, by rows or by columns?

(ii) What will be stored in the array(s) after execution of each program segment? Show the contents in tabular form. For example, if there are two 2×3 arrays, display the contents in the following manner.

C			D		
1	2	3	10	20	30
4	5	6	40	50	60

(a)
```
2010 DIM A(3,4)

4010 FOR COLUMN = 1 TO 4
4020   FOR ROW = 1 TO 3
4030     READ A(ROW,COLUMN)
4040   NEXT ROW
4050 NEXT COLUMN
4060 DATA 10,12,14,16,18,20
4070 DATA 22,24,26,28,30,32
```

(c)
```
2010 DIM A(2,3),B(2,3)

4010 FOR ROW = 1 TO 2
4020   FOR COLUMN = 1 TO 3
4030     READ A(ROW,COLUMN),B(ROW,COLUMN)
4040   NEXT COLUMN
4050 NEXT ROW
4060 DATA 10,20,30,40,50,60
4070 DATA 15,25,35,45,55,65
```

(b)
```
2010 DIM A(2,3),B(2,3)

4010 FOR ROW = 1 TO 2
4020    FOR COLUMN = 1 TO 3
4030       READ A(ROW,COLUMN)
4040    NEXT COLUMN
4050 NEXT ROW
4060 FOR ROW = 1 TO 2
4070    FOR COLUMN = 1 TO 3
4080       READ B(ROW,COLUMN)
4090    NEXT COLUMN
4100 NEXT ROW
4110 DATA 10,20,30,40,50,60
4120 DATA 15,25,35,45,55,65
```

(d)
```
2010 DIM A(2,3),B(2,3)

4010 FOR COLUMN = 1 TO 3
4020    FOR ROW = 1 TO 2
4030       READ A(ROW,COLUMN),B(ROW,COLUMN)
4040    NEXT ROW
4050 NEXT COLUMN
4060 DATA 10,20,30,40,50,60
4070 DATA 15,25,35,45,55,65
```

3. As shown on page 338, the subscripts of a subscripted variable may be explicit numbers. For example, to access the value in row 2, column 3 of array BOOKS, we would use variable BOOKS(2,3). For several of the exercises below, use numbers as subscripts. Assume that the data has already been stored in a 4×4 array named A starting at element (1,1).

A

```
1 2 3 4
5 6 7 8
9 8 7 6
5 4 3 2
```

(a) Code a PRINT statement that prints the last value in the array.
(b) Code a PRINT statement that prints the first and last values in the array on one line widely spaced.
(c) Code a program segment that prints the values in the second row of the array on one line closely spaced.
(d) Code a program segment that prints the values in the second column of the array on one line closely spaced.
(e) Code a program segment that prints the values in the principal diagonal of the array on one line closely spaced. The diagonal is shown below.

A

```
1 2 3 4
5 6 7 8
9 8 7 6
5 4 3 2
```

Notice that the diagonal falls on those elements whose row numbers and column numbers are the same. Thus, if ROW = COLUMN, the value of the element must be printed. Use nested FOR/NEXT loops.

4. Is there anything wrong with each of the following program segments? The data, given below, must be printed in tabular form closely spaced.

A

```
1 2 3
4 5 6
```

B

```
9 8 7
6 5 4
```

(a)
```
2010 DIM A(2,3)

4010 PRINT
4020 FOR ROW = 1 TO 3
4030    FOR COLUMN = 1 TO 2
4040       READ A(ROW,COLUMN)
4050       PRINT A(ROW,COLUMN)
4060    NEXT COLUMN
4070    PRINT
```

(b)
```
2010 DIM A(2,3),B(2,3)

4010 PRINT
4020 FOR ROW = 1 TO 2
4030    FOR COLUMN = 1 TO 3
4040       READ A(ROW,COLUMN),B(ROW,COLUMN)
4050       PRINT B(ROW,COLUMN);
4060    NEXT COLUMN
4070 NEXT ROW
```

```
4080 NEXT ROW
4090 DATA 1,2,3
4100 DATA 4,5,6
```

```
4080 DATA 1,2,3,4,5,6
4090 DATA 9,8,7,6,5,4
```

5. From the rough layout below, code three subroutines to produce a centred report. Use the sample subroutines on pages 342 and 344 as guides.

   (a) The first subroutine formats the report and prints the headings.
   (b) The second subroutine loads the arrays. Store the names of the computer stores in a one-dimensional string array and the sales in a two-dimensional numeric array.
   (c) The third subroutine prints the detail lines. Print the report on a cleared screen. Centre the heading automatically as shown on page 280. Call your subroutines from a skeleton main routine.

Rough Layout of the Report:

```
SALES REPORT
===========================================================
STORE                  JAN              FEB           MAR
===========================================================
Micro Products     $37,628.50      $34,657.68    $40,985.57
Computer Services  $32,437.70      $33,978.42    $39,467.85
Data Systems       $42,469.71      $39,582.15    $41,523.13
Intermedia         $38,571.80      $37,961.32    $40,159.62
```

13.3 Processing Data Stored in a Two-dimensional Array

Sample Routines

Let us now process data that has been stored in a two-dimensional array. In the following examples, we will process the values stored in our array BOOKS.

BOOKS

	Column 1	Column 2	Column 3	Column 4
Row 1	3	2	Ø	1
Row 2	1	Ø	2	3
Row 3	2	4	1	Ø

1. The following subroutine finds the total number of books stored in our library.

```
2010   DIM BOOKS(3,4)

5000 'SUBROUTINE TOTAL BOOKS IN LIBRARY
5010    TOTAL.BOOKS = Ø
5020    PRINT
5030    FOR ROW = 1 TO 3
5040       FOR COLUMN = 1 TO 4
5050          TOTAL.BOOKS = TOTAL.BOOKS+BOOKS(ROW,COLUMN)
5060          PRINT TOTAL.BOOKS;
5070       NEXT COLUMN
5080    NEXT ROW
5090    RETURN
RUN
```

```
 3  5  5  6  7  7  9  12  14  18  19  19
```

TOTAL.BOOKS is the accumulator. Placing the statement PRINT TOTAL.BOOKS inside the inner loop displays subtotals. The first time BASIC passes through the outer loop, ROW = 1. During each pass through the inner loop, BASIC accumulates the numbers stored in the columns of the first row. When the inner loop is complete, ROW changes to 2 and the numbers in the second row are accumulated with the total obtained so far. The process is repeated for the third row. When ROW becomes 4, looping terminates.

2. To print just the total without subtotals, we place the statement that prints the total outside the nested loops.

```
2010   DIM BOOKS(3,4)

5000 'SUBROUTINE TOTAL BOOKS IN LIBRARY
5010    TOTAL.BOOKS = 0
5020    PRINT
5030    FOR ROW = 1 TO 3
5040       FOR COLUMN = 1 TO 4
5050          TOTAL.BOOKS = TOTAL.BOOKS+BOOKS(ROW,COLUMN)
5060       NEXT COLUMN
5070    NEXT ROW
5080    PRINT TOTAL.BOOKS
5090    RETURN
RUN
```

```

  19
```

3. The following subroutine finds the total number of books stored on the first shelf (row).

```
2010   DIM BOOKS(3,4)

5000 'SUBROUTINE TOTAL BOOKS ON FIRST SHELF
5010    SUM = 0
5020    PRINT
5030    FOR COLUMN = 1 TO 4
5040       SUM = SUM+BOOKS(1,COLUMN)
5050    NEXT COLUMN
5060    PRINT SUM
5070    RETURN
RUN
```

```

  6
```

As in Example 3 on page 344 where we printed the numbers stored in the first row, we use 1 as the row subscript since we are accumulating the numbers stored only in row one. A variable is needed for the ever changing column subscript.

4. The following subroutine prints the row number and the column number of each storage area that contains no books.

```
2010   DIM BOOKS(3,4)

5000 'SUBROUTINE STORAGE AREAS CONTAINING NO BOOKS
5010    PRINT
5020    FOR ROW = 1 TO 3
5030       FOR COLUMN = 1 TO 4
5040          IF BOOKS(ROW,COLUMN) = 0 THEN PRINT "Row:";ROW,"Column:";COLUMN
5050       NEXT COLUMN
5060    NEXT ROW
5070    RETURN
RUN
```

```

Row: 1         Column: 3
Row: 2         Column: 2
Row: 3         Column: 4
```

In line 5040, BASIC compares each value in the first row with zero as it executes the column loop. If it finds a zero, it prints the number of the row and the number of the column where the zero was found. When the column loop is complete, BASIC re-enters the row loop and compares each value in the second row with zero as it executes the column loop once more. The values in the third row are compared in a similar manner.

5. Suppose all the books have been signed out. The simplest way to assign zero to each subscripted variable is by using nested FOR/NEXT loops.

```
5020 FOR ROW = 1 TO 3
5030   FOR COLUMN = 1 TO 4
5040     BOOKS(ROW,COLUMN) = 0
5050   NEXT COLUMN
5060 NEXT ROW
```

6. The examples below use explicit numbers as subscripts to access values.

   (a) `5010 PRODUCT = BOOKS(1,3)*2`

   Multiplies the value in row 1, column 3 by 2 and stores the result in PRODUCT.

   (b) `5010 TOTAL = BOOKS(1,1) + BOOKS(1,2)`

   Adds the value in row 1, column 1 to the value in row 1, column 2 and stores the sum in TOTAL.

   (c) `5010 BOOKS(3,1) = BOOKS(2,4)`

   Copies the value in row 2, column 4 and places the value in row 3, column 1.

A Sample Program

The subroutines on pages 342 and 344 stored and printed the names of three employees along with the number of parts produced by each employee in each of five days. Let us find the total number of parts produced by each employee and the total number produced by all employees. The complete program is listed below.

```
1000 'PARTS PRODUCED                   M. MCRITCHIE                    NOV 6
1002 '*******************************************************************
1004 '                 THIS PROGRAM PRODUCES A PRODUCTION REPORT
1006 '*******************************************************************
1010 'S$              - EQUAL SIGNS
1020 'F1$             - IMAGE FOR AN EMPLOYEE NAME
1030 'F2$             - IMAGE FOR THE DAILY NUMBER OF PARTS PRODUCED BY
1040 '                  AN EMPLOYEE
1050 'F3$             - IMAGE FOR THE TOTAL NUMBER OF PARTS PRODUCED BY
1060 '                  AN EMPLOYEE
1070 'HEADING$        - HEADING
1080 'GRAND.TOTAL     - TOTAL NUMBER OF PARTS PRODUCED BY ALL EMPLOYEES
1090 'EMPLOYEE        - CONTROL VARIABLE, VARIABLE SUBSCRIPT FOR EMPLOYEE LOOP
1100 'ENAME$()        - A ONE-DIMENSIONAL ARRAY THAT STORES EMPLOYEE NAMES
1110 'TOTAL.PARTS()   - A ONE-DIMENSIONAL ARRAY THAT STORES THE TOTAL NUMBER
1120 '                  OF PARTS PRODUCED BY EACH EMPLOYEE
1130 'DAY             - CONTROL VARIABLE AND COLUMN SUBSCRIPT FOR THE DAY LOOP
1140 'PARTS()         - A TWO-DIMENSIONAL ARRAY THAT STORES THE DAILY NUMBER
1150 '                  OF PARTS PRODUCED BY EACH EMPLOYEE
2000 '*******************************************************************
2002 '                            MAIN ROUTINE
2004 '*******************************************************************
2010  DIM ENAME$(20),PARTS(20,5),TOTAL.PARTS(20)
2020  GOSUB 3000                   'Format report and print headings
2030  GOSUB 4000                   'Load arrays
2040  GOSUB 5000                   'Print report
2050  END
3000 '*******************************************************************
3002 '                   FORMAT REPORT AND PRINT HEADINGS
3004 '*******************************************************************
3010  CLS
3020  LOCATE 9
3030  S$ = STRING$(49,"=")
3040  F1$ = "_____________\____________\"
3050  F2$ = "___##"
3060  F3$ = "_____###"
3070  HEADING$ = "PRODUCTION REPORT"
3080  PRINT TAB((80-LEN(HEADING$))/2+.5); HEADING$
3090  PRINT TAB(16) S$
3100  PRINT TAB(21) "NAME"; TAB(38) "PARTS PRODUCED"; TAB(60) "TOTAL"
```

```
3110  PRINT TAB(16) S$
3120  RETURN
4000 '*********************************************************************
4002 '                              LOAD ARRAYS
4004 '*********************************************************************
4010  GRAND.TOTAL = 0
4020  FOR EMPLOYEE = 1 TO 3
4030    READ ENAME$(EMPLOYEE)
4040  NEXT EMPLOYEE
4050  FOR EMPLOYEE = 1 TO 3
4060    TOTAL.PARTS(EMPLOYEE) = 0
4070    FOR DAY = 1 TO 5
4080      READ PARTS(EMPLOYEE,DAY)
4090      TOTAL.PARTS(EMPLOYEE) = TOTAL.PARTS(EMPLOYEE)+PARTS(EMPLOYEE,DAY)
4100    NEXT DAY
4110    GRAND.TOTAL = GRAND.TOTAL+TOTAL.PARTS(EMPLOYEE)
4120  NEXT EMPLOYEE
4130  DATA "Mayer,John","Carr,Steve","Lang,Norman"
4140  DATA 43,41,40,42,40
4150  DATA 41,42,40,43,41
4160  DATA 40,39,41,42,43
4170  RETURN
5000 '*********************************************************************
5002 '                              PRINT REPORT
5004 '*********************************************************************
5010  FOR EMPLOYEE = 1 TO 3
5020    PRINT USING F1$; ENAME$(EMPLOYEE);
5030    FOR DAY = 1 TO 5
5040      PRINT USING F2$; PARTS(EMPLOYEE,DAY);
5050    NEXT DAY
5060    PRINT USING F3$; TOTAL.PARTS(EMPLOYEE)
5070  NEXT EMPLOYEE
5080  PRINT
5090  PRINT TAB(16) USING "Total parts produced__________________________###";
      GRAND.TOTAL
5100  RETURN
65529 'End of program listing
RUN
```

(cleared screen)

```
         10        20        30        40        50        60        70        80
12345678901234567890123456789012345678901234567890123456789012345678901234567890

                              PRODUCTION REPORT
               =================================================
                   NAME            PARTS PRODUCED          TOTAL
               =================================================
               Mayer,John       43    41    40    42    40    206
               Carr,Steve       41    42    40    43    41    207
               Lang,Norman      40    39    41    42    43    205

               Total parts produced                         618
```

As explained in a similar subroutine in Chapter Ten, the accumulator that finds the total number of parts produced by each employee must be initialized to zero between the two FOR statements in the subroutine that loads the arrays. In this way, the accumulator starts at zero before the numbers of parts for each employee are accumulated. The numbers are accumulated within the inner loop, immediately after a number is read into variable PARTS(EMPLOYEE,DAY). Note that the totals are stored in a one-dimensional array. Each subscripted variable stores a total for one of the employees.

After finding the total number of parts produced by an employee, we accumulate these totals to find the total number produced by all employees. The totals are accumulated immediately after the inner loop has found the total number of parts for one employee but before BASIC drops into the outer loop to process the data for the next employee. Thus, we place the statement that finds the grand total between the two NEXT statements. The accumulator should be a simple variable since the result is just one value.

In Subroutine PRINT REPORT, we place the PRINT statement that prints the total number of parts produced by one employee between the two NEXT statements. The total is printed just before BASIC enters the outer loop to print another employee name. The total number of parts produced by all employees is printed outside the loop structure.

Exercises

1. Code one or more statements to perform each of the operations listed below on a 4×4 array named A. Assume that the data has already been stored in the array starting at element (1,1).

A

10	14	12	18
12	20	16	24
22	12	26	34
28	36	30	12

(a) Print the row number and the column number of each storage location that contains the number 12.
(b) Replace the value in row 2, column 4 by 42.
(c) Copy the value in row 3, column 1 by storing the value in row 4, column 1.
(d) Subtract the value in row 1, column 3 from the value in row 4, column 2. Store the difference in row 3, column 4.
(e) Increase the value in row 1, column 1 by 10.
(f) Find the sum of the values in the third row. Use one FOR/NEXT loop. Store the sum in a simple variable.
(g) Find the sum of the values in the third column. Use one FOR/NEXT loop. Store the sum in a simple variable.
(h) Multiply each value in the array by 4 and store the products in a two-dimensional array named P.
(i) Initialize all 16 variables of the array to zero.

2. (a) Code a subroutine that stores the daily working hours given below in a two-dimensional array. Use this subroutine in exercises (b), (c), and (d). Call all subroutines from a skeleton main routine.

HOURS

	M	T	W	T	F
Employee 1	8	7	9	9	7
Employee 2	9	8	9	7	8
Employee 3	7	9	8	8	8

(b) Code a subroutine that finds and prints the total number of hours for each employee.

```
RUN

Employee: 1     Total hours: 40
Employee: 2     Total hours: 41
Employee: 3     Total hours: 40
```

(c) Code a subroutine that finds and prints the total number of hours for each day of the week. Hint: Consider carefully which loop should be placed on the outside.

```
RUN

Day: 1          Total hours: 24
Day: 2          Total hours: 24
Day: 3          Total hours: 26
Day: 4          Total hours: 24
Day: 5          Total hours: 23
```

(d) A regular working day consists of eight hours of work. Any employee who works more than eight hours in a day receives overtime pay. Code a subroutine that finds and prints the number of daily hours that include overtime.

```
RUN

Number of daily hours that include overtime: 5
```

3. The following subroutine must find the total number of working hours for each of the three employees mentioned in Problem 2. It must then multiply each total by $9.46 to find each employee's wages. The subroutine has a number of errors. Make the necessary corrections so that it produces the output shown.

```
4000 'SUBROUTINE READ AND PROCESS DATA
4010   PRINT
4020   PRINT "TOTAL NUMBER OF HOURS AND WAGES FOR EACH EMPLOYEE"
4030   PRINT
4040   FOR EMPLOYEE = 1 TO 3
4050     TOTAL.HOURS = 0
4060     FOR DAY = 1 TO 5
4070       READ HOURS(EMPLOYEE)
4080       TOTAL.HOURS(EMPLOYEE) = TOTAL.HOURS(EMPLOYEE)+HOURS(EMPLOYEE)
4090       WAGES(EMPLOYEE) = TOTAL.HOURS(EMPLOYEE)*RATE
4100       PRINT USING "___________Employee_#:___##____$###.##";
           EMPLOYEE,TOTAL.HOURS(EMPLOYEE),WAGES(EMPLOYEE)
4110     NEXT DAY
4120   NEXT EMPLOYEE
4130   DATA 8,7,9,9,7
4140   DATA 9,8,9,7,8
4150   DATA 7,9,8,8,8
4160   RETURN
RUN

TOTAL NUMBER OF HOURS AND WAGES FOR EACH EMPLOYEE

           Employee 1:    40     $378.40
           Employee 2:    41     $387.86
           Employee 3:    40     $378.40
```

4. Suppose the data given below is stored in array A.

	A	
18	23	17
32	26	15
13	39	14

What would be the output from the following subroutine?

```
2010 DIM A(3,3)

5000 'SUBROUTINE PROCESS DATA
5010   L = -1
5020   FOR ROW = 1 TO 3
5030     FOR COLUMN = 1 TO 3
5040       IF A(ROW,COLUMN) > L THEN L = A(ROW,COLUMN)
5050     NEXT COLUMN
5060   NEXT ROW
5070   PRINT
5080   PRINT L
5090   RETURN
```

13.4 Searching a Two-dimensional Array

Sample Subroutine 4 on page 348 searches a two-dimensional array for zeros. When it finds a zero, the zero's location (row number and column number) is printed. The subroutine works well in this particular situation since all the zeros in the array are to be found. However, if we wish to end a search as soon as a desired value is found, the subroutine is inefficient, since the search continues even after the value is found. The following program rectifies this problem. The program searches for a number stored in the two-dimensional array given below, then ends the search when it finds the number.

To simplify the program, we will search for just one value. Save the "search" subroutine in ASCII format as it is needed in Problem 2 at the end of the chapter. Suggested filename: SEARCH2.ASC

NUMBER

	Column 1	Column 2	Column 3	Column 4
Row 1	126	185	167	194
Row 2	131	118	157	195
Row 3	123	187	199	201

```
1000 'NUMERIC SEARCH                    M. MCRITCHIE                    NOV 8
1002 '*******************************************************************
1004 '     THIS PROGRAM SEARCHES FOR A VALUE IN A TWO-DIMENSIONAL ARRAY
1006 '*******************************************************************
1010 'ROW.NO      - CONTROL VARIABLE OF OUTER LOOP
1020 'COLUMN.NO   - CONTROL VARIABLE OF INNER LOOP
1030 'NUMBER()    - A TWO-DIMENSIONAL ARRAY THAT STORES NUMBERS
1040 'IN1$()      - A LOCAL TWO-DIMENSIONAL ARRAY THAT STORES NUMBERS
1050 'R           - NUMBER OF ROWS
1060 'C           - NUMBER OF COLUMNS
1070 'NUMBER      - THE NUMBER TO BE FOUND
1080 'RESPONSE$   - USER'S RESPONSE (y/n)
1090 'IKEY$       - THE KEY (THE NUMBER TO BE FOUND)
1100 'ROW         - LOCAL VARIABLE FOR ROW NUMBER
1110 'FLAG        - A FLAG OF 1 INDICATES THAT THE KEY WAS FOUND. A FLAG
1120 '              OF 0 INDICATES THAT THE KEY WAS NOT FOUND.
1130 'COLUMN      - LOCAL VARIABLE FOR COLUMN NUMBER
1140 'OUT1        - LOCAL VARIABLE. ROW NUMBER WHERE THE KEY WAS FOUND.
1150 'OUT2        - LOCAL VARIABLE. COLUMN NUMBER WHERE THE KEY WAS FOUND.
2000 '*******************************************************************
2002 '                          MAIN ROUTINE
2004 '*******************************************************************
2010  DIM NUMBER(10,15),IN1$(10,15)
2020  GOSUB 3000                        'Load array
2030  GOSUB 4000                        'INPUT number to be found
2040  GOSUB 5000                        'Print result
2050  END
3000 '*******************************************************************
3002 '                           LOAD ARRAY
3004 '*******************************************************************
3010  FOR ROW.NO = 1 TO 3
3020    FOR COLUMN.NO = 1 TO 4
3030      READ NUMBER(ROW.NO,COLUMN.NO)
3040      IN1$(ROW.NO,COLUMN.NO) = STR$(NUMBER(ROW.NO,COLUMN.NO))
3050    NEXT COLUMN.NO
3060  NEXT ROW.NO
3070  R = ROW.NO-1
3080  C = COLUMN.NO-1
3090  DATA 126,185,167,194
3100  DATA 131,118,157,195
3110  DATA 123,187,199,201
3120  RETURN
4000 '*******************************************************************
4002 '                    INPUT NUMBER TO BE FOUND
4004 '*******************************************************************
4010  CLS
4020  LOCATE 11
```

```
4030   INPUT "-----------------------------Number to be found";NUMBER
4040   PRINT
4050   INPUT "Is the number correct (y/n)";RESPONSE$
4060   IF RESPONSE$ <> "y" AND RESPONSE$ <> "Y"
           THEN INPUT "Re-enter the number--",NUMBER : GOTO 4050
4070   IKEY$ = STR$(NUMBER)
4080   GOSUB 20000                       'Search two-dimensional array
4090   RETURN
5000 '*********************************************************************
5002 '                                   PRINT RESULT
5004 '*********************************************************************
5010   ROW.NO = OUT1
5020   COLUMN.NO = OUT2
5030   CLS
5040   LOCATE 12
5050   IF FLAG = 1
           THEN PRINT TAB(33) "Number";NUMBER(ROW.NO,COLUMN.NO);"found"
           ELSE PRINT TAB(31) "Number";NUMBER;"not found"
5060   RETURN
20000 '********************************************************************
20002 '                        SEARCH TWO-DIMENSIONAL ARRAY
20004 '********************************************************************
20010   ROW = 0
20020   FLAG = 0
20030   WHILE ROW < R AND FLAG = 0
20040     ROW = ROW+1
20050     COLUMN = 0
20060     WHILE COLUMN < C AND FLAG = 0
20070       COLUMN = COLUMN+1
20080       IF IN1$(ROW,COLUMN) = IKEY$ THEN FLAG = 1
20090     WEND
20100   WEND
20110   OUT1 = ROW
20120   OUT2 = COLUMN
20130   RETURN
65529 'End of program listing
RUN
```

```
                                                                  (cleared screen)
         10        20        30        40        50        60        70        80
12345678901234567890123456789012345678901234567890123456789012345678901234567890
                                Number to be found? 157

Is the number correct (y/n)? y
                                                                  (cleared screen)
                                   Number 157 found
```

If the number is not found, the message **Number xxx not found** will be displayed where xxx is the number to be found.

After a number is read into array NUMBER in line 3030, the value is converted to string format and stored in local array IN1$. Array IN1$ will be searched for a number in Subroutine SEARCH TWO-DIMENSIONAL ARRAY. In lines 3070 and 3080, we pass the size of our array; that is, the number of rows and the number of columns in the array, to the "search" subroutine. We do this by subtracting one from each of the control variables used in Subroutine LOAD ARRAY and assigning the results to local variables R and C. Recall that upon completion of a FOR/NEXT loop, the control variable is greater than the test value. In our program, the control variables are greater than the test values by one. When we assign the values to R and C and use R and C in our "search" subroutine, we standardize the subroutine.

Subroutine 4000 allows a user to type in the number to be found. We convert this number to string form and assign the string to local variable IKEY$. The subroutine that searches for this number (the key) is now called.

Subroutine SEARCH TWO-DIMENSIONAL ARRAY compares the content of each element of the array with the key until either the key is found or the entire array is searched. The comparison is performed in line 20080. We use nested WHILE/WEND loops rather than nested FOR/NEXT loops since we can exit from the search at the end of the structure when the key is found. In a FOR/NEXT loop structure, we would exit from within the structure when the key is found, thus violating the "exit at end of structure" rule applied to structured programming.

Note that ROW and COLUMN are each initialized to zero before a respective loop begins. The variable is increased by one immediately after BASIC enters the loop. The loops are executed as long as the value of ROW is less than the number of rows in the array and as long as FLAG equals Ø. When ROW equals the number of rows, the loops terminate. In this case, BASIC has searched the entire array and has not found the key. Or, the loops terminate when FLAG becomes one, an indication that the key has been found. Just before BASIC returns to the calling module, we save, in variables OUT1 and OUT2, the number of the row and the number of the column where the key was found.

In Subroutine PRINT RESULT, we assign the values of OUT1 and OUT2 to our control variables ROW.NO and COLUMN.NO. If FLAG is equal to 1, the number has been found. We print the "found" number by using ROW.NO and COLUMN.NO as subscripts of variable NUMBER in our PRINT statement. If the number was not found, we print the number along with an appropriate message.

13.5 Program Design

The program in Section 13.4 searched for a single value in a two-dimensional array. Suppose we wish to find a record whose first field, an employee's name, is stored in a one-dimensional array and whose remaining fields, the numbers of parts produced by the employee, are stored in a two-dimensional array. A program on page 349 stored the records in this manner. Here is the data once more.

Name	*Parts Produced*				
Mayer,John	43	41	40	42	40
Carr,Steve	41	42	40	43	41
Lang,Norman	40	39	41	42	43

Rough Layout of an Output Line:

```
Carr,Steve          41    42    40    43    41
```

or

```
Smith,John        not found
```

FIGURE 13-2 LAYOUT CHART

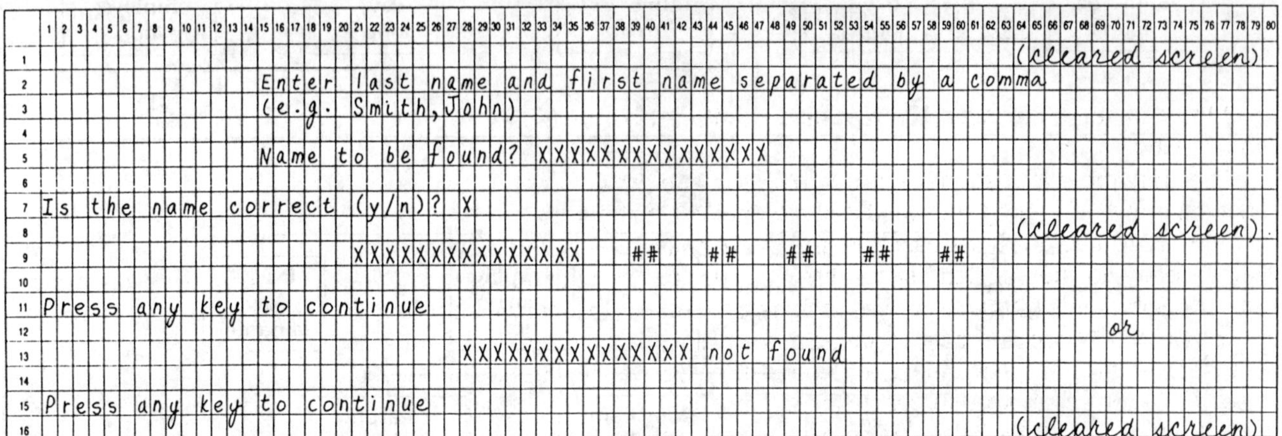

FIGURE 13-3 STRUCTURE CHART

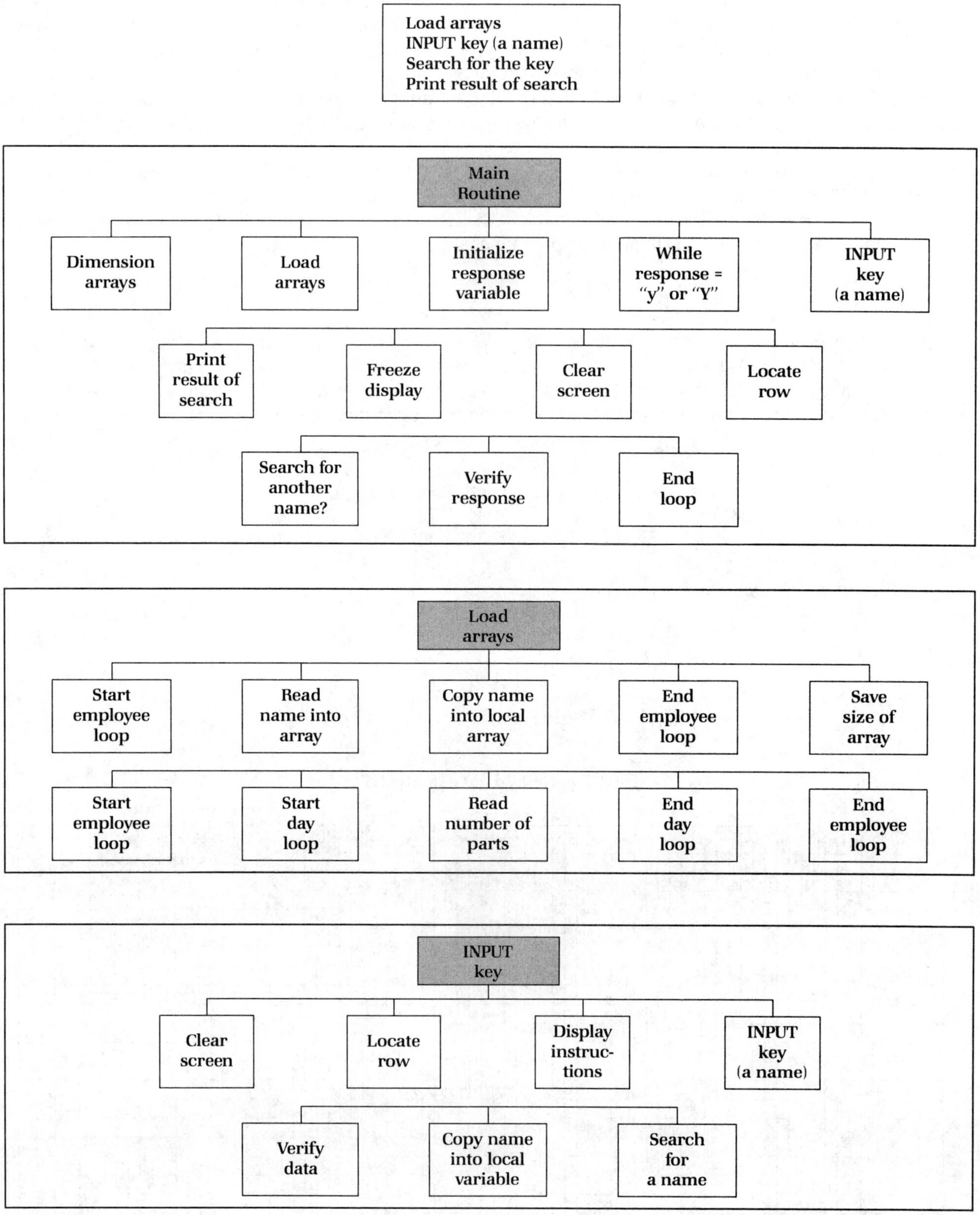

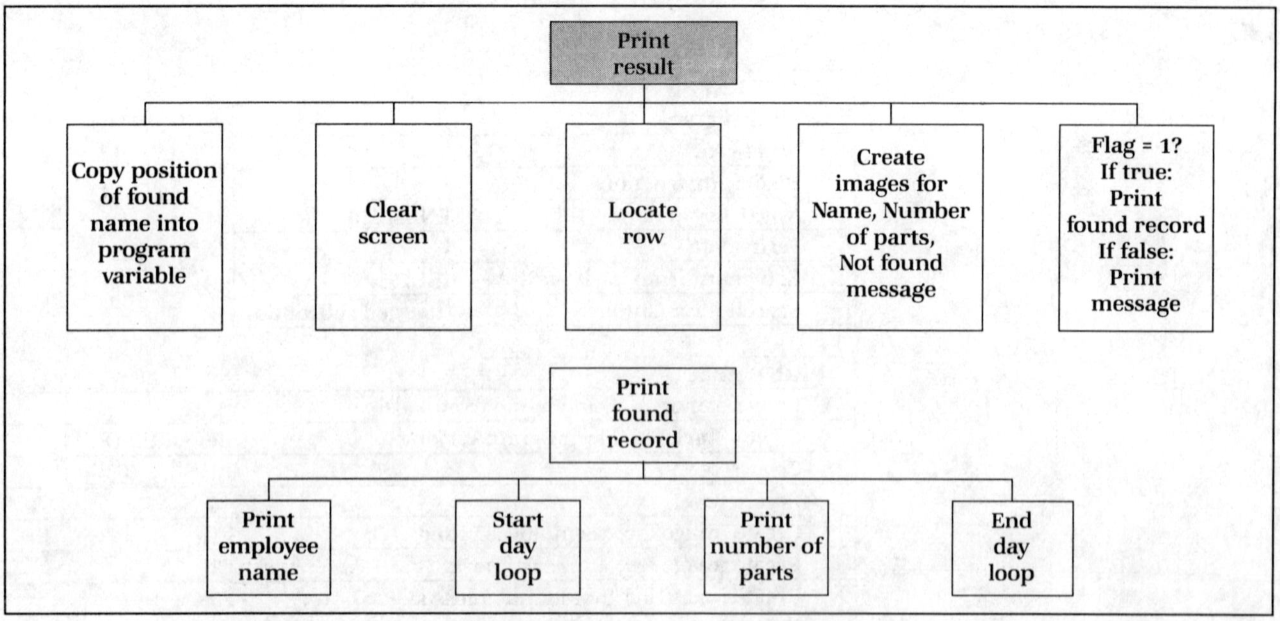

FIGURE 13-4 PSEUDOCODE

MAJOR TASKS
Load arrays
INPUT key (a name)
Search for the key
Print result of search

MAIN ROUTINE	
Dimension arrays	
Load arrays	(subroutine)
Initialize "response" variable	RESPONSE$
While response is "y" or "Y"	
INPUT key (a name)	(subroutine)
Print result of search	(subroutine)
Freeze display	(merged subroutine)
Clear screen	
Locate row	
Search for another name (y/n)?	
Verify response	
End loop	

LOAD ARRAYS	
Start employee loop (parameters: 1 to 3)	EMPLOYEE
Read name into array	ENAME$( )
Copy name into local array	IN1$( )
End employee loop	
Save size of array	ARRAY.SIZE
Start employee loop (parameters: 1 to 3)	EMPLOYEE
Start day loop (parameters: 1 to 5)	DAY
Read number of parts into array	PARTS( )
End day loop	
End employee loop	
Data records	

Figure 13-4 Continued

INPUT KEY	
Clear screen	
Locate row	
Display instructions	
INPUT key (a name)	ENAME$
Verify data	
Copy name into local variable	IKEY$
Search for a name	(merged subroutine)

PRINT RESULT	
Copy position of found name from local "out" variable into program variable	RECORD.NO
Clear screen	
Locate row	
Create image for an employee name	F1$
Create image for number of parts	F2$
Create image for "not found" message	F3$
FLAG = 1?	FLAG
If true, print found record	(subroutine)
If false, print "not found" message	

Print found record
Print employee name
Start day loop (parameters: 1 to 5)
Print number of parts
End day loop

Although subroutines SEARCH ONE-DIMENSIONAL ARRAY and FREEZE DISPLAY form part of the program, we do not include the modules in our designs as these are ASCII files stored on our BASIC diskette and with which we are already familiar. Nor do we normally include, in our listings, modules merged with our programs. However, we make an exception in the program below where we include the search subroutine so you can see the link between the program and the subroutine. Note that module "Print found record" is part of module PRINT RESULT OF SEARCH.

```
1000 'RECORD SEARCH                    M. MCRITCHIE                    NOV 16
1002 '***********************************************************************
1004 '     THIS PROGRAM SEARCHES FOR A RECORD. THE NAMES ARE STORED IN A
1006 '     ONE-DIMENSIONAL ARRAY, THE NUMBERS OF PARTS PRODUCED ARE STORED
1008 '     IN A TWO-DIMENSIONAL ARRAY.
1009 '***********************************************************************
1010 'EMPLOYEE    - CONTROL VARIABLE FOR EMPLOYEE LOOP
1020 'ENAME$()    - A ONE-DIMENSIONAL ARRAY THAT STORES EMPLOYEE NAMES
1030 'IN1$()      - A LOCAL ONE-DIMENSIONAL ARRAY THAT STORES EMPLOYEE NAMES
1040 'ARRAY.SIZE - SIZE OF THE ONE-DIMENSIONAL ARRAY
1050 'DAY         - CONTROL VARIABLE AND COLUMN SUBSCRIPT FOR THE DAY LOOP
1060 'PARTS()     - A TWO-DIMENSIONAL ARRAY THAT STORES NUMBERS OF PARTS PRODUCED
1070 'ENAME$      - NAME TO BE FOUND
1080 'RESPONSE$   - USER'S RESPONSE (y/n)
1090 'IKEY$       - THE KEY (AN EMPLOYEE NAME)
1100 'FLAG        - A FLAG OF 1 INDICATES THAT THE KEY WAS FOUND. A FLAG
1110 '              OF 0 INDICATES THAT THE KEY WAS NOT FOUND.
1120 'W           - LOCAL CONTROL VARIABLE
1130 'OUT1        - LOCAL VARIABLE. HOLDS THE POSITION (ELEMENT NUMBER) OF
1140 '              THE FOUND KEY.
1150 'RECORD.NO   - POSITION OF THE FOUND KEY.
1160 'F1$         - IMAGE FOR AN EMPLOYEE NAME
1170 'F2$         - IMAGE FOR THE NUMBER OF PARTS PRODUCED
1180 'F3$         - IMAGE FOR THE "NOT FOUND" MESSAGE
```

```
2000 '*********************************************************************
2002 '                                 MAIN ROUTINE
2004 '*********************************************************************
2010  DIM ENAME$(20),PARTS(20,5),IN1$(20)
2020  GOSUB 3000                      'Load arrays
2030  RESPONSE$ = "y"
2040  WHILE RESPONSE$ = "y" OR RESPONSE$ = "Y"
2050    GOSUB 4000                         'INPUT key
2060    GOSUB 5000                         'Print result of search
2070    GOSUB 11000                        'Freeze display
2080    CLS
2090    LOCATE 12
2100    INPUT "____________Do you wish to search for another employee name (y/n)
";RESPONSE$
2110    IF RESPONSE$ <> "y" AND RESPONSE$ <> "Y" AND RESPONSE$ <> "n" AND
           RESPONSE$ <> "N" THEN PRINT "Invalid response. Enter y or n." :
           GOTO 2100
2120  WEND
2130  END
3000 '*********************************************************************
3002 '                                 LOAD ARRAYS
3004 '*********************************************************************
3010  FOR EMPLOYEE = 1 TO 3
3020    READ ENAME$(EMPLOYEE)
3030    IN1$(EMPLOYEE) = ENAME$(EMPLOYEE)
3040  NEXT EMPLOYEE
3050  ARRAY.SIZE = EMPLOYEE-1
3060  FOR EMPLOYEE = 1 TO 3
3070    FOR DAY = 1 TO 5
3080      READ PARTS(EMPLOYEE,DAY)
3090    NEXT DAY
3100  NEXT EMPLOYEE
3110  DATA "Mayer,John","Carr,Steve","Lang,Norman"
3120  DATA 43,41,40,42,40
3130  DATA 41,42,40,43,41
3140  DATA 40,39,41,42,43
3150  RETURN
4000 '*********************************************************************
4002 '                              INPUT KEY (A NAME)
4004 '*********************************************************************
4010  CLS
4020  LOCATE 9
4030  PRINT TAB(15) "Enter last name and first name separated by a comma"
4040  PRINT TAB(15) "(e.g. Smith,John)"
4050  PRINT
4060  LINE INPUT "______________Name to be found?_";ENAME$
4070  PRINT
4080  INPUT "Is the name correct (y/n)";RESPONSE$
4090  IF RESPONSE$ <> "y" AND RESPONSE$ <> "Y"
         THEN LINE INPUT "Re-enter the name--";ENAME$ : GOTO 4080
4100  IKEY$ = ENAME$
4110  GOSUB 17000                      'Search one-dimensional array
4120  RETURN
5000 '*********************************************************************
5002 '                           PRINT RESULT OF SEARCH
5004 '*********************************************************************
5010  RECORD.NO = OUT1
5020  CLS
5030  LOCATE 12
5040  F1$ = "____________________\_____________\"
5050  F2$ = "___##"
5060  F3$ = "____________________________\_____________\_not found"
5070  IF FLAG = 1 THEN GOSUB 5500 ELSE PRINT USING F3$; ENAME$
5080  RETURN
```

```
5500 'SUBROUTINE PRINT FOUND RECORD
5510   PRINT USING F1$; ENAME$(RECORD.NO);
5520   FOR DAY = 1 TO 5
5530     PRINT USING F2$; PARTS(RECORD.NO,DAY);
5540   NEXT DAY
5550   PRINT
5560   RETURN
17000 '*********************************************************************
17002 '                      SEARCH ONE-DIMENSIONAL ARRAY
17004 '*********************************************************************
17010  FLAG = 0
17020  W = 0
17030  WHILE W < ARRAY.SIZE AND FLAG = 0
17040    W = W+1
17050    IF IN1$(W) = IKEY$ THEN FLAG = 1
17060  WEND
17070  OUT1 = W
17080  RETURN
65529 'End of program listing
```

Partial Output:

```
                                                                      (cleared screen)
         10        20        30        40        50        60        70        80
12345678901234567890123456789012345678901234567890123456789012345678901234567890
              Enter last name and first name separated by a comma
              (e.g. Smith,John)

              Name to be found? Carr,Steve

Is the name correct (y/n)? y

                                                                      (cleared screen)
                   Carr,Steve         41    42    40    43    41

Press any key to continue

                                                                      (cleared screen)
            Do you wish to search for another employee name (y/n)?
```

If a name; for example, Smith,John is not found, the program displays:

```
Smith,John      not found
```

In Subroutine PRINT RESULT OF SEARCH, variable RECORD.NO stores the position of the "found" name and is, therefore, used as a subscript for variables ENAME$ and PARTS in lines 5510 and 5530.

Summary of Library Files

SEARCH2.ASC Searches a two-dimensional array.

Chapter Summary

1. A two-dimensional array is used to store data presented in tabular form, such as data in income tax tables. The array consists of two or more rows and two or more columns. A DIM statement must specify the number of rows and the number of columns in the array.
2. To access an element in a two-dimensional array, two subscripts are needed by the subscripted variable. The first subscript represents the number of the row, the second subscript represents the number of the column. Example: BOOKS(3,1)
3. The name of a two-dimensional array may not be the same as that of a one-dimensional array. However, a subscripted variable of a two-dimensional array and a simple variable may have the same name.
4. A two-dimensional array must be dimensioned when one of its dimensions is greater than 10.
5. BASIC recognizes a row Ø and a column Ø. The programs in this book do not consider these subscripts.
6. A variable of a three-dimensional array needs three subscripts. The first subscript represents the row, the second subscript represents the column, the third subscript represents the depth.
7. The simplest way to load a two-dimensional array is by using nested FOR/NEXT loops; one loop for the rows, the other loop for the columns.
8. Data may be loaded into a two-dimensional array by rows or by columns. To load data into the array by rows, the row loop must be the outer loop and the data in the DATA statement must be listed by rows.
9. The number of data items loaded into a two-dimensional array depends on the dimensions of the array and on the test value in each FOR statement.
10. Records that consist of strings and numbers cannot be stored in a two-dimensional array since an array may hold only one type of data: string or numeric. If the data consists of one column of strings and several columns of numbers, the items can be stored in two parallel arrays. The strings can be stored in a one-dimensional string array, the numbers can be stored in a two-dimensional numeric array.
11. The process of accessing values stored in a two-dimensional array is usually performed in nested FOR/NEXT loops.
12. We can display the data stored in a two-dimensional array in tabular form by placing a semicolon at the end of the PRINT statement that prints the values and placing a "blank" PRINT between the two NEXT statements of the nested FOR/NEXT loops.
13. It is possible to print a string from a one-dimensional array and several numbers from a two-dimensional array as a record on one output line. Nested FOR/NEXT loops must be used. We place the PRINT statement that prints the string between the FOR statements and end the PRINT statement with a semicolon. We place the PRINT statement that prints the numbers within the inner loop and end this PRINT statement with a semicolon. A "blank" PRINT must be coded between the two NEXT statements.
14. We can reference a specific element in a two-dimensional array by using explicit numbers as subscripts. Example: 4020 PRINT BOOKS(3,1)
15. We can total numbers stored in a two-dimensional array by placing the accumulator in the inner loop of nested FOR/NEXT loops.
16. To total numbers in a particular row, we use an explicit number as the row subscript of the subscripted variable and a variable as the column subscript. The accumulation of numbers must be performed in a FOR/NEXT loop. To total numbers in a particular column, we use a variable as the row subscript and an explicit number as the column subscript.
17. It is possible to search for a specific value in a two-dimensional array. The contents of each element of the array is compared with the desired value. This is performed within the inner loop of nested WHILE/WEND loops. When the value is found, a flag is reset which causes the outer WHILE statement to transfer control out of the loop structure. Thus, exit occurs at the end of the structure.

18. To find a record whose string is stored in a one-dimensional array and whose numbers are stored in a two-dimensional array, we must first find the position of the string in the one-dimensional array. We access the string by using its position as the subscript of a subscripted variable. We access the corresponding numbers in the two-dimensional array by using the position of the string as the row subscript of the subscripted variable and the control variable of the FOR statement as the column subscript.

Questions and Exercises

1. (a) How does a two-dimensional array differ from a one-dimensional array?

   (b) How does a subscripted variable of a two-dimensional array differ from that of a one-dimensional array?

2. Identify the errors, if any, in the program segments shown below. There may be more than one error in each segment. Make the necessary corrections.

   (a)
```
2010 DIM A(4,3)

4010 FOR ROW = 1 TO 3
4020   FOR COLUMN = 1 TO 4
4030     READ A(ROW,COLUMN)
4040   NEXT ROW
4050 NEXT COLUMN
4060 DATA -,-,-,......(12 data items)
```

   (b)
```
2010 DIM A(5,4),B(6,3)

4010 FOR COLUMN = 1 TO 3
4020   FOR ROW = 1 TO 5
4030     READ A(ROW,COLUMN),B(ROW,COLUMN)
4040   NEXT ROW
4050 NEXT COLUMN
4060 DATA -,-,-,......(30 data items)
```

   (c)
```
2010 DIM NAMES$(10),SALES(10,6)

4010 FOR ROW = 1 TO 10
4020   FOR COLUMN = 1 TO 6
4030     READ NAMES$(ROW,COLUMN),SALES(ROW,COLUMN)
4040   NEXT COLUMN
4050 NEXT ROW
4060 DATA "Stevens,Glen"      ,6023,5798,5942,6189,6257
4070 DATA "Bates,Angela"      ,5893,6437,5931,6243,6367
4080 DATA "Anderson,Harvey",6241,6085,5994,6121,6084
.... (7 additional DATA statements)
```

3. Using the data given below, code a program that stores the data in two two-dimensional arrays, then prints the contents of both arrays in tabular form, one array under the other. Print a heading above each array. Example: ARRAY A.

A

15	20	25	30
35	40	45	50
55	60	65	70

B

100	110	120	130
140	150	160	170
180	190	200	210

4. Array SALES given at the top of page 363, stores the amounts sold by four employees during the first three months of the current year. Code a subroutine that stores the data in a two-dimensional array, then code subroutines for exercises (a), (b), and (c). Call each subroutine from a skeleton main routine.

SALES

	Month 1	Month 2	Month 3
Employee 1	650	894	699
Employee 2	742	831	648
Employee 3	659	724	819
Employee 4	826	718	657

(a) Code a subroutine that finds the total amount of sales for each of the three months.

RUN

```
Month: 1       Sales: 2877
Month: 2       Sales: 3167
Month: 3       Sales: 2823
```

(b) Code a subroutine that finds the total amount of sales for each employee.

RUN

```
Employee: 1    Sales: 2243
Employee: 2    Sales: 2221
Employee: 3    Sales: 2202
Employee: 4    Sales: 2201
```

(c) Code a subroutine that prints the number of the employee who sold more than $850 in any one month. Include the number of the month in the output line.

RUN

```
Employee: 1    Month: 2
```

5. A courier service delivers packages up to a radius of 2000 miles. From the information shown in the rough layout below, code three subroutines:

(a) The first subroutine formats the report and prints the headings.
(b) The second subroutine loads the arrays. Store the distances in a one-dimensional string array and the costs in a two-dimensional numeric array.
(c) The third subroutine prints the detail lines.

Print the report on a cleared screen. Call your subroutines from a skeleton main routine. Save your program as you will need it for the next exercise.

Rough Layout of the Report:

```
COURIER SERVICE
====================================================
DISTANCE              01-32 OZ.    33-80 OZ.    81-99 OZ.
====================================================
Local                 $ 4.25       $ 6.50       $ 8.95
1000 Mile Radius      $ 8.95       $10.45       $12.50
2000 Mile Radius      $10.25       $12.15       $14.95
```

6. To the program written for Problem 5, add a subroutine that:

(a) Finds the charge for sending four local packages, each package weighing between 01 and 32 ounces inclusive.
(b) Finds the charge for sending two packages within a 1000 mile radius, each package weighing between 81 and 99 ounces inclusive.

(c) Finds the charge for sending three packages within a 2000 mile radius, each package weighing between 33 and 80 ounces inclusive.
(d) Finds the total charge for sending all the above packages.
Use explicit numbers as subscripts to access a cost in the two-dimensional array. For example, to calculate the charge for sending the packages described in (b) above, use a statement similar to the following:

```
xxxx RADIUS.1000 = COST(2,3)*2
```

Use the PRINT USING statement to print the charge and the appropriate radius in the summary. Use an explicit number as the subscript to access a radius. To print the charge calculated above, your statement could look as follows:

```
xxxx PRINT TAB(27) USING "\______________\_____$###.##";MILES$(2),RADIUS.1000
```

where MILES$ is the array storing the radii.

Rough Layout of the Report:

```
COURIER SERVICE
=========================================================
DISTANCE                01-32 OZ.     33-80 OZ.     81-99 OZ.
=========================================================
Local                   $ 4.25        $ 6.50        $ 8.95
1000 Mile Radius        $ 8.95        $10.45        $12.50
2000 Mile Radius        $10.25        $12.15        $14.95

             Local                    $ 17.00
             1000 Mile Radius         $ 25.00
             2000 Mile Radius         $ 36.45

             Total cost               $ 78.45
```

Programming Problems

Write programs for the following problems. Remember to centre headings automatically. Other than the program for Problem Six, use the READ and DATA statements to load arrays.

1. In an exercise on page 347, you were to write a program that displayed the January, February, and March sales for each of four computer stores. The owner of the four stores would like the January sales broken down in the following manner:

   (a) The total number of units sold and the total sales (dollar amount) for each store.
   (b) The total number of units sold and the total sales (dollar amount) for each model of computer.

   The names of the stores and the numbers of units sold are given in the report on page 365. The unit price for each model is as follows:

Model 1	$ 849.50
Model 2	$1,495.95
Model 3	$1,995.85

Rough Layout of the Output:

```
                                                              (cleared screen)
                    Date? [JANUARY, 19XX]

Is the date correct (y/n)? [y]

                                                              (cleared screen)
           UNIT SALES FOR JANUARY, 19XX
           =================================================
            STORE                  MODEL 1    MODEL 2    MODEL 3
           =================================================
           Micro Products            12          9          7
           Computer Services         10          8          6
           Data Systems              13          9          9
           Intermedia                 9         10          8

SALES PER STORE

Micro Products           28 units      Total sales     $37,628.50
Computer Services        24 units      Total sales     $32,437.70
Data Systems             31 units      Total sales     $42,469.71
Intermedia               27 units      Total sales     $38,571.80

SALES PER MODEL

Model 1                  44 units      Total sales     $37,378.00
Model 2                  36 units      Total sales     $53,854.20
Model 3                  30 units      Total sales     $59,875.50
```

Due to internal round off errors, there is a difference of $.01 between the total sales for all stores and the total sales for all models. Ignore this error. Store the unit prices in a one-dimensional numeric array, the names of the stores in a one-dimensional string array, and the units sold in a two-dimensional numeric array.

In the subroutine that calculates the sales per store, perform the following.

(a) Accumulate the number of units sold by each store. Remember to initialize the accumulator to zero between the FOR statements.
(b) Multiply the units sold of each model by its price.
(c) Accumulate the results obtained in (b). This accumulator must also be initialized to zero between the FOR statements.

In the subroutine that calculates the sales per model, perform the following. Caution: Consider carefully which loop should be the outer loop.

(a) Accumulate the number of units sold of each model.
(b) Multiply the total units of each model by its price.

Hint: To line up the number of units under each column heading in the report, code one or more extra spaces after the numeric field in the image for the number sold. For example, the images that format the name of a store and the number of units sold could be as follows:

```
xxxx F1$ = "_______________\_______________\"
xxxx F2$ = "________##__"
```

2. Write a program that stores, in a two-dimensional string array, the names, the addresses, and the telephone numbers of subscribers to a local newspaper. Your program must allow the publisher to extract the name, the address, and the telephone number (the record) of any subscriber from the array and display the record on a cleared screen. Use the name as the key. Use the data on page 366.

Name	*Address*	*Telephone*
Davis,Robyn	842 West Street	642-8521
Fraser,Martin	384 South Street	426-1527
Hayden,Ken	581 Main Street	394-2617
Jones,Tammy	469 North Street	597-6415
Peters,Brian	694 East Street	243-6925
Wiebe,Joan	249 Oak Street	851-9413

Rough Layout of the Output:

```
                                                    (cleared screen)
          Enter last name and first name separated by a comma
          (e.g. Smith,John)

          Subscriber's name? [Davis,Robyn]

Is the name correct (y/n)? [y]
                                                    (cleared screen)
Davis,Robyn      842 West Street   642-8521

Press any key to continue
                                                    (cleared screen)
          Do you wish to search for another subscriber (y/n)?
```

If a name is not found, your program should display an appropriate message. Allow a user to search for more than one record. (Call all subroutines, except the one that loads the array, from within a WHILE/WEND loop.) Use the program on page 353 as a guide to code the subroutine that loads the array. Make a copy of the array and save its dimensions; that is, save the number of rows and the number of columns in the array. The duplicate array and the dimensions are needed in the subroutine that searches for a name. In a separate subroutine, code the statement that INPUTs a name (the key) and copy the name into a local string variable. Merge Subroutine SEARCH TWO-DIMENSIONAL ARRAY with your program.

In the subroutine that prints, copy only the value of local variable OUT1 (sent from the search subroutine) into a variable, say RECORD.NO. The value of OUT2 is not needed. If FLAG is equal to 1, call a subroutine to print the three fields of the record whose name field was just found; otherwise, print a "not found" message. The subroutine that prints the "found" record should use a single FOR/NEXT loop whose test value is 3, the number of columns in the array. Use RECORD.NO as the row subscript of your subscripted variable and the control variable of your FOR statement as the column subscript.

You will need two images: one to edit each of the fields of the "found" record, the other to edit the "not found" message. The image for the "found" record should consist of just one field. This image will be referenced three times: first for the name, then for the address, and finally for the telephone number. Make certain that the field is large enough for an address.

3. Write a program that produces the mileage chart shown below. Your program must allow a user to key in the names of two cities, then print the distance (in miles and kilometres) between the cities.

Rough Layout of the Output:

```
                                                    (cleared screen)
                              Origin? [Toronto]
                              Destination? [New York]

The origin is Toronto
Is the origin correct (y/n)? [y]
```

```
The destination is New York
Is the destination correct (y/n)? [y]
```

(cleared screen)

MILEAGE CHART

	Dallas	New York	Seattle	Toronto	Vancouver	Winnipeg
Dallas	0	1583	2140	1366	2233	1291
New York	1583	0	2985	478	2970	1645
Seattle	2140	2985	0	2745	145	1435
Toronto	1366	478	2745	0	2800	1310
Vancouver	2233	2970	145	2800	0	1490
Winnipeg	1291	1645	1435	1310	1490	0

```
The distance from Toronto to New York is 478 miles
which is  769 kilometres

Press any key to continue
```

(cleared screen)

```
Do you wish to find another distance (y/n)?
```

If a keyed-in city name is not on the mileage chart, a message such as **Anycity not found** should be displayed beneath the chart.

Load the city names into a one-dimensional array and make a duplicate copy of the array. The copy will be used in two search subroutines. Save the size of the array in ARRAY.SIZE. Load the mileages into a two-dimensional array.

In a separate subroutine, code the statements that input the city of origin and the destination. Copy the city names into local string variables and call two versions of Subroutine SEARCH ONE-DIMENSIONAL ARRAY. One version searches for the city of origin, the other version searches for the destination. Use different flags in the subroutines and different local "out" variables, such as OUT1 and OUT2.

In the subroutine that formats the mileage chart, perform the following:

(a) Assign the symbol "I" to a string variable, say VERTICAL$.
(b) Assign hyphens to S1$ and S2$ by means of the STRING$ function. The hyphens in S1$ will be used to underscore the main heading of the chart, the hyphens in S2$ will separate the detail lines.
(c) Code three images. One image positions the city names over the columns, the second image positions the city names to the left of the rows, and the third image positions the mileages. The first image may require spaces following the string field, each of the second and third images must end with a few spaces and an exclamation mark (!). The exclamation mark reserves a position for the value stored in VERTICAL$.
(d) Clear the screen, locate the row, and print the main heading underscored.

To print the mileage chart, perform the following:

(a) Print spaces over the column of city names.
(b) In a FOR/NEXT loop, print the six city names as column headings.
(c) Print the hyphens stored in S2$.
(d) Print the name of a city and the corresponding mileages using nested FOR/NEXT loops. Your two PRINT USING statements must also print the value of VERTICAL$ and end with a semicolon. Remember to place the PRINT that prints a city name between the two FOR statements.
(e) Place the PRINT statement that prints the hyphens stored in S2$ between the NEXT statements.

Use a separate module to print, under the chart, the distance between the city of origin and the destination. Copy the values of OUT1 and OUT2 into the control variables used to represent the rows and columns in your nested loops. These local variables store the positions where the names of the desired cities were found in the "city name" array. Determine whether or not both flags are equal to 1. If they are, call a subroutine within this module to print the number of miles between the two cities. Use the control variables just mentioned as subscripts of your mileage variable. Convert the miles to kilometres and print the kilometres. To convert miles to kilometres, multiply the miles by 1.609. Incorporate this expression in a PRINT USING statement which may look as follows:

```
xxxx PRINT USING "which is #### kilometres";MILES(ROW.NO,COLUMN.NO)*1.609
```

MILES is the array that stores the mileages, ROW.NO stores the value of OUT1 and COLUMN.NO stores the value of OUT2.

If either of the city names is not found, print the "not found" message. Your main routine must call the following subroutines:

(a) Load arrays
(b) INPUT data (names of cities)
(c) Format chart and print headings
(d) Print mileage chart
(e) Print distance
(f) Freeze display

4. Write a program that loads the records shown in the rough layout below into a two-dimensional array, then extracts all the items from either column 1 or column 2. Allow a user to choose the column. Store the extracted items in a one-dimensional array. Sort the extracted items using the SELECTION sort, then print the sorted items.

Rough Layout of the Output:

```
                                                          (cleared screen)
          DRIVERS' LICENSES
          ============================================
            NAME                LICENSE NO.    BIRTH DATE
          ============================================
          Wright,Erin           168B23         10/21/42
          Johnson,Brent         284A61         06/15/48
          Palmer,Alyson         159B37         12/09/37
          Morrison,Shelley      241A63         04/23/53
          Pearson,Shaun         185A27         01/19/61

          Column number? [1]

 Is the column number correct (y/n)? [y]
                                                          (cleared screen)
                         LICENSED DRIVERS

                         Johnson,Brent
                         Morrison,Shelley
                         Palmer,Alyson
                         Pearson,Shaun
                         Wright,Erin
```

If the user chooses column 2, the output should be:

```
                         LICENSE NUMBERS

                          159B37
                          168B23
                          185A27
                          241A63
                          284A61
```

Use nested FOR/NEXT loops to read the records into a two-dimensional array and to print the records. To print the three fields of a record, use three subscripted variables and place your PRINT USING statement between the NEXT statements. Sample statement:

```
xxxx PRINT USING F$; INFO$(RECORD,1),INFO$(RECORD,2),INFO$(RECORD,3)
```

RECORD is the outer control variable and INFO$ is the name of the array. Do not place the PRINT USING statement within the inner loop. There, the statement would need only one subscripted variable and reference an image of one field. Since each field in the record is a different size, the one-field image would not place the three items of a detail line in their proper positions.

Allow the user to choose the column whose items are to be extracted and sorted. In a separate subroutine, transfer the items from the chosen column to a one-dimensional array. Place the statement that performs this in a FOR/NEXT loop. Use your control variable as the row subscript and the keyed-in column number as the column subscript. Sample statement:

```
xxxx EXTRACTED.COLUMN$(RECORD) = INFO$(RECORD,COLUMN.NUM)
```

Make a copy of the one-dimensional array for use in the sort subroutine. Following the loop, call Subroutine SELECTION SORT.

In another module named, perhaps, PRINT SORTED COLUMN, use a FOR/NEXT loop to copy the sorted items from local array OUT1$ into your one-dimensional array. These items will be either sorted names or sorted license numbers depending on the column number chosen. Following the loop, check the keyed-in column number. If the number is 1, call a subroutine to print the sorted *names* from your one-dimensional array; otherwise, call a subroutine to print the sorted *license numbers* from the array. Print a heading before the list as shown in the rough layout. Both subroutines should be coded within the module PRINT SORTED COLUMN.

Merge Subroutine SELECTION SORT with your resident program. Your main routine must call the following subroutines:

(a) Format report and print headings
(b) Load array and print records
(c) INPUT data (column number)
(d) Extract a column
(e) Print sorted column

5. Four intersections are being monitored for traffic flow to determine whether or not stop signs should be installed. A stop sign is installed when one of the following conditions occurs in any one day:

(a) The number of cars exceeds 100.
(b) The number of trucks exceeds 50.
(c) The number of semitrailers exceeds 30.
(d) The total number of vehicles exceeds 150.

Rough Layout of the Report:

```
TRAFFIC FREQUENCY
================================================
INTERSECTION          CARS        TRUCKS    SEMI'S
================================================
1                      150          42        34
2                      225          96        58
3                       99          49        29
4                       89          41        19

        TOTAL TRAFFIC AT EACH INTERSECTION

           Intersection 1:     226
           Intersection 2:     379
           Intersection 3:     177
           Intersection 4:     149

     Stop sign required at intersection 1
     Stop sign required at intersection 2
     Stop sign required at intersection 3
     No stop sign required at intersection 4
```

Load, into a two-dimensional array, the numbers of cars, trucks, and semitrailers crossing each intersection. The numbers are given in the rough layout on page 369. Use nested FOR/NEXT loops and READ and DATA statements. Place the PRINT statement that prints a detail line between the NEXT statements. Your PRINT USING statement could look as follows:

```
xxxx PRINT USING F$; I,TRAF(I,1),TRAF(I,2),TRAF(I,3)
```

I (for Intersection) is the outer control variable and TRAF is the name of the array.

In a separate subroutine, accumulate the amount of traffic at each intersection. Use nested FOR/NEXT loops. Store the totals in a one-dimensional array and place the PRINT that prints a total between the NEXT statements. Remember to initialize each subscripted variable of this one-dimensional array to zero between the FOR statements.

In another subroutine, initialize a variable, say V for vehicle, to 1. Set up a FOR/NEXT loop for the four intersections. Inside the loop, use an IF statement to determine whether or not one of the conditions mentioned on page 369 has been met. A partial statement is given below. (The underscores must be replaced with PRINT statements.)

```
xxxx IF TRAF(I,V) > 100 OR TRAF(I,V+1) > 50 OR TRAF(I,V+2) > 30 OR
        TOTAL.TRAF(I) > 150 THEN ___ ELSE ___
```

I (for intersection) is the control variable of the FOR/NEXT loop. V, V+1, V+2, represent the types of vehicles.

6. On a true/false test, students must pencil in their ID's and their answers for ten questions. A digit 1 denotes true, a digit Ø denotes false. The students' names and the key (the answers to the questions) are stored in the following two data files.

STUDENT1.DAT	KEY1.DAT	
"Burton,Anna"	1	
"Gillies,Richard"	1	
"Kendall,Paul"	Ø	
"Mills,Gayle"	1	
"Stewart,John"	Ø	— Answers to questions
	Ø	
	1	
	Ø	
	1	
	1	

Write a program that performs the following:

(a) Reads the two data files.

(b) Allows a user of your program to type in the date and each student's ID and answers which are given below. The first digit in each record represents a student's ID.

3,1,1,Ø,1,Ø,Ø,1,Ø,1,1
1,Ø,Ø,1,1,1,Ø,1,1,Ø,1
5,Ø,1,1,1,Ø,1,1,1,1,1
4,1,Ø,1,Ø,1,1,1,Ø,1,1
2,1,1,Ø,Ø,1,Ø,1,1,1,1

(c) Matches a student's name with his/her answers.

(d) Marks each student's answers, counts the number of correct answers for each student and converts the count to a percent.

(e) Prints the report.

Rough Layout of the Report:

```
TEST RESULTS

September, 19XX
================================================================
ID          NAME                      NO. CORRECT        PERCENT
================================================================
3           Kendall,Paul              10                 100%
1           Burton,Anna               4                  40%
5           Stewart,John              6                  60%
4           Mills,Gayle               5                  50%
2           Gillies,Richard           7                  70%
```

Instructions for writing the more difficult modules are given below.

Subroutine READ DATA FILES

Use two WHILE/WEND loops to read the files into two one-dimensional arrays. One loop reads the student names, the other loop reads the key. Remember to use a counter to find the size of each array. At the end of each loop, store the array size in a numeric variable, say, NO.STUDENTS for the number of students in the student name file and NO.QUESTIONS for the number of answers in the key file.

Subroutine INPUT DATE, STUDENTS' IDs AND ANSWERS

Code the statement that INPUTs the date. Use nested FOR/NEXT loops to INPUT a student's ID and answers. INPUT a student's ID between the FOR statements and a student's answers inside the inner loop. A partial output from this module could be:

```
ID? [3]
Student's answer? [1]
Student's answer? [1]
Student's answer? [0]
etc. for 10 answers

ID? [1]
```

Subroutine MATCH

Use nested FOR/NEXT loops. Determine whether or not the control variable of the inner loop is equal to a student's ID. If it is, call a subroutine to mark the student's answers. Sample statement:

```
6030 IF STUDENT = ID(RECORD) THEN GOSUB 7000
```

STUDENT is the control variable of the inner loop and RECORD is the control variable of the outer loop. STUDENT keeps track of the students, RECORD keeps track of the student records. Remember, each record consists of a student's ID and ten answers. Both control variables range from 1 to NO.STUDENTS. Suppose RECORD = 1. The ID from the first record is examined. The ID on this record is 3. When control variable STUDENT becomes 3, BASIC will mark the third student's answers. The student's name is Kendall,Paul since this is the third name read from the name file.

Subroutine MARK TESTS AND PRODUCE REPORT

In a FOR/NEXT loop, compare a student's answer with the answer in the key array. The control variable of the FOR statement must range from 1 to NO.QUESTIONS. Store the number of correct answers obtained by each student in a subscripted variable of a one-dimensional array. Thus, each subscripted variable represents a counter that counts the number of correct answers obtained by a student. If the answer is correct, increase the student's counter by 1. Sample statement:

```
7030 IF ANSWER(RECORD,QUESTION) = KEYS(QUESTION)
          THEN NO.CORRECT(STUDENT) = NO.CORRECT(STUDENT)+1
```

ANSWER is the array that stores the INPUTted students' answers while KEYS is the array that stores the answers read from data file KEY1.DAT. RECORD keeps track of the records, QUESTION keeps track of the questions, and STUDENT keeps track of the students. Suppose RECORD = 1. As shown in Subroutine MATCH, this is the record for student number three. And, suppose QUESTION = 1. If the first answer on the first record is the same as the first answer in the key array, the counter for the third student is increased by one.

Following the loop, calculate a student's percentage by dividing the student's counter by NO.QUESTIONS and multiplying the result by 100. Print the student's ID, name, number of correct answers, and percentage. Sample statement:

```
7060 PRINT USING F$; ID(RECORD),SNAME$(STUDENT),NO.CORRECT(STUDENT),
     PERCENT(STUDENT)
```

If RECORD = 1, then STUDENT = 3. The above statement will print the following detail line. Spacing between the items will be different.

3	Kendall,Paul	10	100%
↑	↑	↑	↑
ID from first record	Name of third student	Number of correct answers obtained by third student	Percent obtained by third student

Solutions for Exercises

13.1 Creating a Multi-dimensional Array

1. (a) `2010 DIM NUMBER(4,4)`
   (b) `2010 DIM ENAME$(6,7),NUMBER(7,6)`
   (c) `2010 DIM ENAME$(8),ADDRESS$(8,9),CODE(8,9)`

2. (a) NAME is a reserved word, therefore, NAME$ cannot be used as an array name.

```
2010 DIM ENAME$(4,5)
```

   (b) Nothing is wrong.
   (c) Nothing is wrong, assuming that A and B have previously been assigned values.
   (d) The arrays must be separated by a comma, not a semicolon.

```
2010 DIM SUBJECT$(3),SCORES(15,6)
```

3. Both arrays have the same dimensions. Statement (a) dimensions A as a one-dimensional array with 26 elements. Statement (b) dimensions A as a two-dimensional array. The array also contains 26 elements since it consists of one row and 26 columns.

13.2 Data Entry and Data Output

1. (a) If all the data is read, the test value in statement 4010 must be 4, the test value in statement 4020 must be 5.

```
4010 FOR ROW = 1 TO 4
4020    FOR COLUMN = 1 TO 5
```

   (b) The number of data items indicated must be 12, not 6.

```
4060 DATA -,-,-,......(12 data items)
```

   (c) Nothing is wrong.
   (d) Array A must be dimensioned as a 3×4 two-dimensional array.

```
2010 DIM A(3,4),B(3,4)
```

2. (a) The data is read by columns.

A

10	16	22	28
12	18	24	30
14	20	26	32

   (b) The data is read by rows.

A			B		
10	20	30	15	25	35
40	50	60	45	55	65

   (c) The data is read by rows.

A			B		
10	30	50	20	40	60
15	35	55	25	45	65

   (d) The data is read by columns.

A			B		
10	50	35	20	60	45
30	15	55	40	25	65

3. (a) `5040 PRINT A(4,4)`
   (b) `5040 PRINT A(1,1),A(4,4)`
   (c)

```
5020 FOR COLUMN = 1 TO 4
5030    PRINT A(2,COLUMN);
5040 NEXT COLUMN
```

   (d)

```
5020 FOR ROW = 1 TO 4
5030    PRINT A(ROW,2);
5040 NEXT ROW
```

   (e)

```
5020 FOR ROW = 1 TO 4
5030    FOR COLUMN = 1 TO 4
5040       IF ROW = COLUMN THEN PRINT A(ROW,COLUMN);
5050    NEXT COLUMN
5060 NEXT ROW
```

4. (a) The test value in statement 4020 must be 2, the test value in statement 4030 must be 3. The PRINT statement in line 4050 must end with a semicolon.

```
4020 FOR ROW = 1 TO 2
4030   FOR COLUMN = 1 TO 3
4050     PRINT A(ROW,COLUMN);
```

(b) The data items in the DATA statements must alternate between a value for array A and a value for array B. A "blank" PRINT must be coded between the NEXT statements.

```
4065 PRINT
4080 DATA 1,9,2,8,3,7
4090 DATA 4,6,5,5,6,4
```

Exercise 5.

```
2000 'MAIN ROUTINE
2010   DIM STORE.NAME$(13),SALES(13,3)
2020   GOSUB 3000                     'Format report and print headings
2030   GOSUB 4000                     'Load arrays
2040   GOSUB 5000                     'Print detail lines
2050   END
3000 'SUBROUTINE FORMAT REPORT AND PRINT HEADINGS
3010   CLS
3020   LOCATE 9
3030   S$ = STRING$(59,"=")
3040   F1$ = "__________\_______________\"
3050   F2$ = "____$#####,.##"
3060   HEADING$ = "SALES REPORT"
3070   PRINT TAB((80-LEN(HEADING$))/2+.5); HEADING$
3080   PRINT TAB(11) S$
3090   PRINT TAB(17) "STORE"; TAB(36) "JAN"; TAB(50) "FEB"; TAB(64) "MAR"
3100   PRINT TAB(11) S$
3110   RETURN
4000 'SUBROUTINE LOAD ARRAYS
4010   FOR STORE = 1 TO 4
4020     READ STORE.NAME$(STORE)
4030   NEXT STORE
4040   FOR STORE = 1 TO 4
4050     FOR MONTH = 1 TO 3
4060       READ SALES(STORE,MONTH)
4070     NEXT MONTH
4080   NEXT STORE
4090   DATA "Micro Products","Computer Services","Data Systems","Intermedia"
4100   DATA 37628.50,34657.68,40985.57
4110   DATA 32437.70,33978.42,39467.85
4120   DATA 42469.71,39582.15,41523.13
4130   DATA 38571.80,37961.32,40159.62
4140   RETURN
5000 'SUBROUTINE PRINT DETAIL LINES
5010   FOR STORE = 1 TO 4
5020     PRINT USING F1$; STORE.NAME$(STORE);
5030     FOR MONTH = 1 TO 3
5040       PRINT USING F2$; SALES(STORE,MONTH);
5050     NEXT MONTH
5060     PRINT
5070   NEXT STORE
5080   RETURN
65529 'End of program listing
```

13.3 Processing Data Stored in a Two-Dimensional Array

1. (a)
```
5020 FOR ROW = 1 TO 4
5030   FOR COLUMN = 1 TO 4
5040     IF A(ROW,COLUMN) = 12 THEN PRINT "Row:";ROW,"Column:";COLUMN
5050   NEXT COLUMN
5060 NEXT ROW
```

(b)
```
5030 A(2,4) = 42
```

(c)
```
5030 A(4,1) = A(3,1)
```

(d)
```
5030 A(3,4) = A(4,2)-A(1,3)
```

(e)
```
5030 A(1,1) = A(1,1)+10
```

(f)
```
5020 FOR COLUMN = 1 TO 4
5030   SUM = SUM+A(3,COLUMN)
5040 NEXT COLUMN
```

(g)
```
5020 FOR ROW = 1 TO 4
5030   SUM = SUM+A(ROW,3)
5040 NEXT ROW
```

(h)
```
5020 FOR ROW = 1 TO 4
5030   FOR COLUMN = 1 TO 4
5040     P(ROW,COLUMN) = A(ROW,COLUMN)*4
5050   NEXT COLUMN
5060 NEXT ROW
```

(i)
```
5020 FOR ROW = 1 TO 4
5030   FOR COLUMN = 1 TO 4
5040     A(ROW,COLUMN) = 0
5050   NEXT COLUMN
5060 NEXT ROW
```

Exercise 2.

(a)
```
2000 'MAIN ROUTINE
2010   DIM HOURS(10,5)
2020   GOSUB 3000              'Load array
2030   END
3000 'SUBROUTINE LOAD ARRAY
3010   FOR EMPLOYEE = 1 TO 3
3020     FOR DAY = 1 TO 5
3030       READ HOURS(EMPLOYEE,DAY)
3040     NEXT DAY
3050   NEXT EMPLOYEE
3060   DATA 8,7,9,9,7
3070   DATA 9,8,9,7,8
3080   DATA 7,9,8,8,8
3090   RETURN
```

(b)
```
4000 'SUBROUTINE CALCULATE TOTAL EMPLOYEE HOURS
4010   PRINT
4020   FOR EMPLOYEE = 1 TO 3
4030     TOTAL.HOURS = 0
4040     FOR DAY = 1 TO 5
4050       TOTAL.HOURS = TOTAL.HOURS+HOURS(EMPLOYEE,DAY)
4060     NEXT DAY
4070     PRINT "Employee:";EMPLOYEE; TAB(16) "Total hours:";TOTAL.HOURS
4080   NEXT EMPLOYEE
4090   RETURN
```

(c)
```
5000 'SUBROUTINE CALCULATE TOTAL DAILY HOURS
5010   PRINT
5020   FOR DAY = 1 TO 5
5030     TOTAL.HOURS = 0
5040     FOR EMPLOYEE = 1 TO 3
5050       TOTAL.HOURS = TOTAL.HOURS+HOURS(EMPLOYEE,DAY)
5060     NEXT EMPLOYEE
5070     PRINT "Day:";DAY; TAB(16) "Total hours:";TOTAL.HOURS
5080   NEXT DAY
5090   RETURN
```

(d)
```
6000 'SUBROUTINE FIND NUMBER OF HOURS WITH OVERTIME
6010   FOR EMPLOYEE = 1 TO 3
6020     FOR DAY = 1 TO 5
6030       IF HOURS(EMPLOYEE,DAY) > 8 THEN COUNT.HOURS = COUNT.HOURS+1
6040     NEXT DAY
6050   NEXT EMPLOYEE
6060   PRINT
6070   PRINT "Number of daily hours that include overtime:";COUNT.HOURS
6080 RETURN
```

3.
```
4000 'SUBROUTINE READ AND PROCESS DATA
4010   PRINT
4020   PRINT "TOTAL NUMBER OF HOURS AND WAGES FOR EACH EMPLOYEE"
4030   PRINT
4040   FOR EMPLOYEE = 1 TO 3
4050     TOTAL.HOURS(EMPLOYEE) = 0
4060     FOR DAY = 1 TO 5
4070       READ HOURS(EMPLOYEE,DAY)
4080       TOTAL.HOURS(EMPLOYEE) = TOTAL.HOURS(EMPLOYEE)+HOURS(EMPLOYEE,DAY)
4090     NEXT DAY
4100     WAGES(EMPLOYEE) = TOTAL.HOURS(EMPLOYEE)*RATE
4110     PRINT USING "___________Employee_#:___##____$###.##";
         EMPLOYEE,TOTAL.HOURS(EMPLOYEE),WAGES(EMPLOYEE)
4120   NEXT EMPLOYEE
4130   DATA 8,7,9,9,7
4140   DATA 9,8,9,7,8
4150   DATA 7,9,8,8,8
4160   RETURN
```

In line 4050, the variable accumulating the hours for each employee must be a subscripted variable. TOTAL.HOURS(EMPLOYEE)

In lines 4070 and 4080, variable HOURS must have two subscripts: EMPLOYEE and DAY. HOURS(EMPLOYEE,DAY)

The statement that finds the wages for each employee and the one that prints a detail line must be coded between the two NEXT statements.

4.
```
RUN
```

39

14

OTHER TOPICS

Objectives

In this chapter, you will learn four major concepts:

- The random number generator often used in drill and practice programs.
- The user-defined function; a function written by a programmer, coded within a program, and called by a statement in the same program.
- The ON . . . GOSUB statement which transfers control to one of several line numbers listed in the statement. The line number chosen depends on a value (called the case selector) placed between ON and GOSUB.
- A menu-driven program which allows a user to select a routine from a list of options. The list is referred to as a menu.

You will also become familiar with:

- The INT function which discards the decimal portion of a decimal number and returns just the integer portion.
- A verification routine that checks the case selector of an ON . . . GOSUB statement.
- The early exit from a program.
- External documentation of a program.

Contents

Summary of BASIC Functions

Chapter Summary

Questions and Exercises

Programming Problems

Project

14.1 Rounding Off Numbers

Until now, we have rounded off a number by using the PRINT USING statement. The rounded number, however, is not stored in memory. To round off a number and store the result in memory, we include the INT function in an expression and assign the rounded result to a variable. The INT function discards the decimal portion of a decimal number and returns just the integer part. Statement 3010 below rounds off 164.527 to two decimal places.

```
3000 NUMBER = 164.527
3010 ROUNDED = INT(NUMBER*100+.5)/100
3020 PRINT NUMBER,ROUNDED
3030 END
RUN
```

```
 164.527         164.53
```

Line 3010 rounds off 164.527 to two decimal places in the following manner.

```
ROUNDED = INT(NUMBER*100+.5)/100
        = INT(164.527*100+.5)/100
        = INT(16452.7+.5)/100
        = INT(16453.2)/100
        = 16453/100
        = 164.53
```

BASIC first multiplies 164.527 by 100 which produces 16452.7. When .5 is added to this number, the result is 16453.2. The INT function discards the decimal portion of 16453.2 to produce the integer number 16453. This latter number is now divided by 100 which gives us 164.53.

To round off a number to one decimal place, we simply multiply and divide by 10 rather than by 100. For three decimal places, we use 1000; for four decimal places, we use 10000; etc. To round off a decimal number to a whole number, we just add .5 to the number. No multiplication or division is necessary.

When a decimal number is stored, small inaccuracies may occur in one or several of the low-order digits of the decimal. This can happen to both single- and double-precision numbers. Here are two examples.

Single-precision numbers

```
3000 A = 13.2
3010 B = 13
3020 C = (A-B)*100
3030 PRINT
3040 PRINT C
3050 END
RUN
```

```
 19.99998
```

Double-precision numbers

```
3000 A# = 10013.2#
3010 B# = 10013#
3020 C# = (A#-B#)*100
3030 PRINT
3040 PRINT C#
3050 END
RUN
```

```
 20.00000000000455
```

In the example that uses single-precision numbers, the calculations should produce 20, yet BASIC prints out 19.99998. To rectify this error, we can increase 19.99998 by a small amount, say .001, then INT the result.

The entire operations can be performed in one statement as follows:

```
3020 C = INT((A-B)*100+.001)
```

When we incorporate the modified statement in our program, the difference of 20 is obtained.

In the example that uses double-precision numbers, BASIC prints out 20.0000000000455 instead of 20. Here, we can simply INT the result. In cases where BASIC produces a value smaller than what we expect, we must add a small amount to the value, then INT this result.

Exercises

1. Write statements that round off the following numbers as indicated. In each exercise, assign the original number to a variable. Use the INT function in each statement.

   (a) The number 45.16 to one decimal place.
   (b) The number 45.164 to two decimal places.
   (c) The number 45.6879 to three decimal places.
   (d) The number 24.68 to the nearest whole number.

2. Evaluate the following expressions by hand. Do one step at a time.

   (a) INT(42.15*10+.5)/10
   (b) INT(3.1578*100+.5)/100
   (c) INT(26.3941*1000+.5)/1000
   (d) INT(823.694+.5)

14.2 Generating a Random Number

Occasions may arise when we must use random numbers in our programs. For example, a drill and practice program in mathematics should generate the numbers that make up the questions. To generate a random number, we must call upon the RND function. Listed below are a number of programs that use this function.

1. The RND function generates a random number between Ø and 1. If the number is very small (that is, too close to zero), it is expressed in exponential form. The following program generates three random numbers.

```
3000 PRINT
3010 FOR I = 1 TO 3
3020    R = RND(1)
3030    PRINT R
3040 NEXT I
3050 END
RUN
```

```
.1213501
1.531542E-02
.8688612
```

The random number generated by RND(1) is assigned to R in line 3020, then printed in the next statement. The argument of the RND need not always be 1. It should, however, be positive. When the argument in the above program is replaced by a negative number, the RND function generates a series of numbers in which all the numbers are the same. This also applies to an argument of zero.

2. The above program does not give truly random numbers. Each time the program is executed, it produces the same series of numbers. To produce a different series of numbers, we make use of the computer's internal clock and the RANDOMIZE statement. First, we set the date and time after loading up DOS, then load up BASICA. Two methods of producing random numbers are given below. The method used depends on the version of DOS loaded into the system.

(a)

```
3000 SECONDS$ = RIGHT$(TIME$,2)
3010 RANDOMIZE VAL(SECONDS$)
3020 PRINT
3030 FOR I = 1 TO 3
3040    R = RND(1)
```

(b)

```
3000 RANDOMIZE TIMER
3010 PRINT
3020 FOR I = 1 TO 3
3030    R = RND(1)
3040    PRINT R
```

```
3050    PRINT R
3060 NEXT I
3070 END
RUN
```

```
7.039433E-02
.3202925
.5082812
```

```
3050 NEXT I
3060 END
RUN
```

```
.7877558
.1174269
4.048706E-02
```

In method (a) TIME$ is a function that retrieves the time in the form hh:mm:ss where hh are the hours ranging from ØØ to 23, mm are the minutes ranging from ØØ to 59, and ss are the seconds ranging from ØØ to 59. The time retrieved by TIME$ is in string form. The time, first set by the user when DOS is loaded, is continually updated by DOS. Thus, TIME$ retrieves a different value each time the function is executed.

Line 3000 extracts the last two digits of TIME$ and stores the digits as a string in SECONDS$. The VAL function in line 3010 converts the two-digit string to its numeric value. This numeric value is used in the RANDOMIZE statement which seeds the random number generator. Each time we execute the program, a different value (the seconds obtained by the TIME$ function) is used as the seed in the RANDOMIZE statement. Thus, a different series of random numbers is generated each time the program is executed.

In method (b) TIMER returns, in numeric form, the seconds generated by DOS. Recall that the seconds, first set by the user, are constantly updated by DOS. When we use TIMER in the RANDOMIZE statement, the random number generator is seeded with a different number each time we execute the program. This produces a different series of random numbers with each RUN. In our programs, we will use TIMER to obtain the seed for the RANDOMIZE statement.

3. The numbers generated by the above programs lie between Ø and 1, a form of number not normally used in programs. Whole numbers would be more useful. Here is a program that generates whole numbers between 1 and 9 inclusive.

```
3000 RANDOMIZE TIMER
3010 PRINT
3020 FOR I = 1 TO 10
3030   R = INT(9*RND(1)+1)
3040   PRINT R;
3050 NEXT I
3060 END
RUN
```

```
 5  7  8  7  1  2  3  9  4  4
```

Note the use of the INT function in line 3030. First, we multiply the number generated by RND(1) by 9, the highest number in the desired range. To the product we add 1, the lowest number in the range. The INT function discards the decimal fraction of this result and the whole number is assigned to R. To generate a number ranging between 1 and 6 inclusive, the statement would be: 3030 R = INT(6*RND(1)+1).

4. When the first number in the range is a number other than 1, we can use the following formula:

R = INT(N*RND(1)+LOW)

N is the "number" of numbers in the range, LOW is the lowest number desired. To find the "number" of numbers in any range, we use the formula

N = (HIGH-LOW) + 1

where HIGH is the highest number in the range and LOW is the lowest number. The program listed at the top of page 381 generates numbers between 3 and 12 inclusive.

```
3000 RANDOMIZE TIMER
3010 LOW = 3
3020 HIGH = 12
3030 N = (HIGH-LOW)+1
3040 PRINT
3050 FOR I = 1 TO 10
3060   R = INT(N*RND(1)+LOW)
3070   PRINT R;
3080 NEXT I
3090 END
RUN
```

```
 7  3  6  10  12  8  11  4  5  9
```

Exercises

1. For each of the following, write a program that generates a random number. Use the seconds retrieved by TIME$ or TIMER as the seed in the RANDOMIZE statement.
   (a) A decimal number between Ø and 1.
   (b) A whole number between 1 and 10 inclusive.
   (c) A whole number between 20 and 36 inclusive.

2. Write a program that simulates the roll of a pair of dice. Print the number rolled on the first die, the number rolled on the second die, and the total rolled on both dice. The pair of dice are rolled three times. Hint: Use the random number generator to simulate the roll of each die. A generated number must lie in the range 1 through 6.

   Sample Output:

```
Die 1: 1        Die 2: 2
Total: 3

Die 1: 5        Die 2: 2
Total: 7

Die 1: 2        Die 2: 6
Total: 8
```

3. Random numbers can be used to simulate the tossing of a coin. Since there are only two possibilities (heads or tails), use random number 1 to represent heads and random number 2 to represent tails. Thus, the range of random numbers is 1 to 2 inclusive. Write a program that counts the number of heads and the number of tails flipped out of ten tosses. If the random number is 1, increase the number of heads by one. If the random number is 2, increase the number of tails by one.

   Sample Output:

```
Heads: 6
Tails: 4
```

14.3 User-defined Functions

In many of our programs, we used a number of prewritten routines provided by BASIC. These are known as built-in functions. Some of the functions we used were INT, TAB, and EOF as well as a number of string-handling functions such as LEFT$, CHR$, and STRING$.

BASIC allows us to write our own functions. These are called user-defined functions. A user-defined function can be referenced from several places in a program to perform a particular operation. The two programs listed below illustrate how a user-defined function can be created and referenced.

A User-defined Function with One Argument

```
2000 'MAIN ROUTINE
2010   DEF FNTAX(RETAIL) = RETAIL*6/100
2020   GOSUB 3000                    'Enter data and print result
2030   END
3000 'SUBROUTINE ENTER DATA AND PRINT RESULT
3010   RETAIL.PRICE = 64.15
3020   SALES.TAX = FNTAX(RETAIL.PRICE)
3030   PRINT
3040   PRINT RETAIL.PRICE,SALES.TAX
3050   RETURN
65529 'End of program listing
RUN
```

```
 64.15          3.849
```

Line 2010 contains our user-defined function. The function must be named and defined in a DEF statement. If there is more than one user-defined function in a program, each function must be defined in its own DEF statement. The function must be defined before it is called. Thus, it is wise to place all DEF statements at the beginning of a program. The function may be called from anywhere in the program after it is defined. Furthermore, it may be called more than once. The DEF statement is explained in detail below.

2010	DEF	FNTAX	(RETAIL)	=	RETAIL*6/100
↑	↑	↑	↑		↑
Statement number	Reserved word meaning "defined"	Name of the function	Dummy argument which takes on the actual value when the function is called		Function written by the user

The function name may be any valid variable name, however, it must be preceded by FN. The name may be either numeric or string, such as FNTAX or FNTEXT$. A numeric function must be comprised of numeric values, a string function must be comprised of string values.

The variable within the parentheses is called the function's argument. The argument must be a simple variable, it cannot be a subscripted variable. Nor can it be an expression. The argument appears in the function which must be coded on the right-hand side of the assignment operator. The argument is referred to as the dummy argument. It plays no significant role, other than to act as a placeholder for the value passed to the function when the function is called. The variable representing the dummy argument is a local variable as its value is known only in the DEF statement. This means we may use RETAIL elsewhere in the program and the variable will be considered separate and unique. For program readability, it is wise to use different variable names.

The function on the right-hand side of the assignment operator is the one written by the programmer. Its type (either numeric or string) must be the same as that of the function name.

2010 DEF	FNTAX	(RETAIL) =	RETAIL*6/100
	↑		↑
	Numeric function name		Numeric function

Besides the dummy argument, the function may contain constants, library functions, other previously defined functions, simple variables, and subscripted variables.

A user-defined function may be called from most BASIC statements. It is not evaluated until it is called.

The following examples illustrate how the function FNTAX may be called from an assignment statement and from a PRINT statement.

```
3020 SALES.TAX = FNTAX(RETAIL.PRICE)          3020 PRINT FNTAX(RETAIL.PRICE)
                 Function reference                        Actual argument
```

FNTAX(RETAIL.PRICE), referred to as the function reference, calls the function named FNTAX. Its argument, RETAIL.PRICE, is called the actual argument. Although the same variable may be used as the actual argument and as the dummy argument, the dummy argument remains a local variable. The actual argument is a global variable; that is, its value can be accessed by all modules. In our programs, we will use different variables for the arguments.

The value of the actual argument is passed to the dummy argument, then used in the function if the dummy argument appears there. Upon evaluation of the function, the result is passed back to the function reference by means of the function's name.

A User-defined Function with More Than One Argument

```
2000 'MAIN ROUTINE
2010    DEF FNTAX(RETAIL,RATE) = RETAIL*RATE/100
2020    GOSUB 3000                  'Enter data and print result
2030    END
3000 'SUBROUTINE ENTER DATA AND PRINT RESULT
3010    RETAIL.PRICE = 64.15
3020    TAX.RATE = 6
3030    PRINT
3040    PRINT TAB(4) USING "Retail price:_$##.##_____Sales tax:_$#.##";
        RETAIL.PRICE,FNTAX(RETAIL.PRICE,TAX.RATE)
3050    RETURN
65529 'End of program listing
RUN

   Retail price: $64.15      Sales tax: $3.85
```

The function reference passes the value of RETAIL.PRICE to RETAIL and the value of TAX.RATE to RATE. RETAIL.PRICE and TAX.RATE are the actual arguments, RETAIL and RATE are the dummy arguments. The actual arguments must correspond with the dummy arguments in number, order, and type.

Note that the function is called from a PRINT USING statement. When the result returns to the function reference, it is formatted and printed.

Exercises

1. Using the following DEF statement, identify the terms listed below:

   ```
   2010 DEF FNINTEREST(PRINCIPAL,RATE) = PRINCIPAL*TIME*RATE/100
   ```

   (a) The function.
   (b) The function name.
   (c) The dummy argument(s).
   (d) The local variable(s).
   (e) The global variable(s).

2. Write user-defined functions and function references for the following problems. For exercise (a), code the function reference in an assignment statement. For exercises (b) and (c), code the function references in PRINT USING statements.

   (a) Convert miles to kilometres. Kilometres = Miles × 1.609.
   (b) Find the amount of commission received by a salesperson. Use two arguments: the amount of sales and the rate of commission. Round off the commission to the nearest cent. Commission = Sales × Rate/100

(c) Find the average of four test scores. Use two arguments: the total score and the number of tests. Round off the average to the nearest whole number. Average = Total Score/Number of Tests

3. Write a skeleton main routine and Subroutine READ DATA AND PRINT RESULT to find the weekly wages for an employee who worked overtime. The regular hours are 40. The employee worked 44 hours, the regular pay was $9.15 per hour, and the total deductions were $63.85. Use a user-defined function whose arguments are the hours of work, the rate of pay, and the total deductions. Round off the wages to the nearest cent. Use the following formula which includes overtime based on time and a half.

$$\text{Wages} = \text{Rate} \times 40 + (\text{Hours}-40) \times \text{Rate} \times 1.5 - \text{Deductions}$$

```
RUN
```

```
Hours: 44      Weekly wages: $357.05
```

14.4 Multiple Alternatives—The Case Structure

A Short Review of the Multiple IF Statement and Multiple IF/THEN's

In Chapter Six, we learned two ways to write a decision structure that offers several alternatives. Examples of these decision structures are given below.

The Multiple IF Statement:

```
3040 IF YEARS <= 5 THEN RATE = 6.5 ELSE IF YEARS = 6 THEN RATE = 8 ELSE IF
        YEARS = 7 THEN RATE = 9.5 ELSE IF YEARS = 8 THEN RATE = 10.5
```

Multiple IF/THEN's:

```
6010 IF HOURS.WORK <= 39 THEN REGULAR.PAY = HOURS.WORK*RATE :
        OVERTIME.HALF = 0 :
        OVERTIME.DOUBLE = 0
6020 IF HOURS.WORK>39 AND HOURS.WORK<=45 THEN REGULAR.PAY=REGULAR.HOURS*RATE :
        OVERTIME.HALF = (HOURS.WORK-REGULAR.HOURS)*RATE*1.5 :
        OVERTIME.DOUBLE = 0
6030 IF HOURS.WORK > 45 THEN REGULAR.PAY = REGULAR.HOURS*RATE :
        OVERTIME.HALF = (BASE.DOUBLE-REGULAR.HOURS)*RATE*1.5 :
        OVERTIME.DOUBLE = (HOURS.WORK-BASE.DOUBLE)*RATE*2
```

The Case Structure

Another decision structure that offers multiple alternatives is the case structure. In this structure, an ON . . . GOSUB statement allows a transfer to any one of a number of subroutines. Here is an example of an ON . . . GOSUB statement (also referred to as a case statement).

```
4040 ON CODE GOSUB 5000,6000,7000,8000
```

↑ Variable or expression (CODE) ↑ List of line numbers (5000,6000,7000,8000)

The variable or expression in the ON . . . GOSUB statement is called the case selector. BASIC uses the case selector to select one of the line numbers listed in the statement. It then transfers to that line number. When the case selector is an expression, BASIC evaluates the expression, then uses the result to select a line number.

A partial case structure using the above case statement is shown below. The periods indicate additional statements.

```
4040 ON CODE GOSUB 5000,6000,7000,8000
5000 'SUBROUTINE CASE 1
.... ....
5050   RETURN
6000 'SUBROUTINE CASE 2
.... ....
6080   RETURN
7000 'SUBROUTINE CASE 3
```

```
....  ....
7070   RETURN
8000 'SUBROUTINE CASE 4
....  ....
8090   RETURN
```

The line number selected by the case selector is actually the first statement of a subroutine. We refer to the subroutine as a case block. In the ON . . . GOSUB statement above, if the value of the case selector is 1, BASIC transfers to line number 5000, the first line number in the ON . . . GOSUB statement. Line number 5000 is the first statement of a case block. If the value of the case selector is 2, BASIC transfers to line number 6000, the second line number in the ON . . . GOSUB statement. Line number 6000 is the first statement of another case block. The remaining case blocks are referenced in a similar manner.

The alternatives given in the multiple IF statement on page 384 are offered in the following ON . . . GOSUB statement.

```
3040 ON YEARS GOSUB 4000,4000,4000,4000,4000,5000,6000,7000
```

Here, YEARS is our case selector. Note that line number 4000 appears five times in the ON . . . GOSUB statement. This is to accommodate years 1, 2, 3, 4, and 5. A skeleton case structure that uses the above ON . . . GOSUB statement is given below.

```
3000 'SUBROUTINE INTEREST
3010   FOR INVESTMENT = 1 TO 10
3020     PRINT
3030     INPUT "Years";YEARS
3040     ON YEARS GOSUB 4000,4000,4000,4000,4000,5000,6000,7000
3050   NEXT INVESTMENT
3060   RETURN
4000 'SUBROUTINE CASE 1           'Number of years <= 5
4010   RATE = 6.5
....   ....
4060   RETURN
5000 'SUBROUTINE CASE 2           'Number of years = 6
5010   RATE = 8
....   ....
5060   RETURN
6000 'SUBROUTINE CASE 3           'Number of years = 7
6010   RATE = 9.5
....   ....
6060   RETURN
7000 'SUBROUTINE CASE 4           'Number of years = 8
7010   RATE = 10.5
....   ....
7060   RETURN
```

If a user keys in 1, 2, 3, 4, or 5 in response to the prompt **Years**?, BASIC transfers to case block 4000. If the user keys in a 6, BASIC transfers to case block 5000. If the user keys in an 8, BASIC transfers to case block 7000. Note that the user need not key in the number of years in order. The number keyed in, however, must lie within the range 1 through 8.

When should a case structure be used rather than a multiple IF statement? We should use a case structure when each alternative consists of several statements or when the multiple IF statement contains more than 255 characters.

Verifying a Case Selector

The value of a case selector cannot be less than one (negative or zero) nor can it exceed the number of line numbers listed in the ON . . . GOSUB statement. Thus, we should verify a case selector. Let us modify Subroutine INTEREST shown above by adding a "range test" immediately after the INPUT statement that INPUTs a year.

```
3000 'SUBROUTINE INTEREST
3010   FOR INVESTMENT = 1 TO 10
3020     PRINT
3030     INPUT "Years";YEARS
```

```
3035      IF YEARS < 1 OR YEARS > 8
             THEN PRINT "The number of years must be between 1 and 8 inclusive"
             : GOTO 3030
3040      ON YEARS GOSUB 4000,4000,4000,4000,4000,5000,6000,7000
3050    NEXT INVESTMENT
3060    RETURN
```

When the value of the case selector is within the required range, no message is displayed. When the value of the case selector is not within the range, the routine produces the following:

```
Years? [Ø]
The number of years must be between 1 and 8 inclusive
Years? [6]
```

The "range test" produces a tidy output since a message is displayed only when the value of the case selector is outside the range. No messages are displayed for values inside the range. Unfortunately, if the user types in an incorrect case selector and its value lies within the required range, the above routine will not allow the user to correct the case selector.

To verify a case selector, we must use the verification routine we have been using all along. Although the output will not be as neat as the one above (since a prompt is displayed after each case selector is keyed in) the user does have the opportunity to correct a case selector. The verification routine for the keyed-in years will be as follows:

```
3030      INPUT "Years";YEARS
3035      INPUT "Are the years correct (y/n)";RESPONSE$
3037      IF RESPONSE$ <> "y" AND RESPONSE$ <> "Y"
             THEN INPUT "Re-enter the years (1 to 8 inclusive)--",YEARS :
             GOTO 3035
```

Sample Output:

```
Years? [Ø]
Are the years correct (y/n)? [n]
Re-enter the years (1 to 8 inclusive)--[5]
Are the years correct (y/n)? [y]
```

Sample Output:

```
Years? [5]
Are the years correct (y/n)? [y]
```

Other Features of the Case Structure

The above examples illustrate several features of the case structure. However, a number of other items should be pointed out.

1. There must be a case block for each line number referenced by the case selector.
2. BASIC rounds off the value of the case selector to the nearest integer. For instance, 1.4 is rounded off to 1 while 1.5 is rounded off to 2. The values between .1 and .4 inclusive are raised to 1.
3. If the value of the case selector is negative, BASIC prints **Illegal function call in xxxx** where xxxx is the line number of the ON . . . GOSUB statement. Furthermore, if the value of the case selector is either Ø or larger than the number of line numbers listed in the ON . . . GOSUB statement, the statement is not executed. Instead, BASIC drops through to the statement following the ON . . . GOSUB statement.

Exercises

1. Identify the errors, if any, in the ON . . . GOSUB statements shown below. How does BASIC respond to the statements in (a), (d), and (e)?

   (a)
   ```
   3010 K = 3
   3020 ON K-4 GOSUB 4000,5000,6000,7000
   ```
   (b)
   ```
   3010 K = 12
   3020 ON K/6 GOSUB 4000,5000,6000,7000
   ```

(c)
```
3010 K = 10
3020 ON K/4 GOSUB 4000,5000,6000,7000
```

(d)
```
3010 K = 3
3020 ON K*2 GOSUB 4000,5000,6000,7000
```

(e)
```
3010 K = 4
3020 ON K-4 GOSUB 4000,5000,6000,7000
```

2. Write a program that allows a user to key in ten scores, then converts the scores to grades and prints the grades along with comments. Place the INPUT statement and the ON . . . GOSUB statement within a FOR/NEXT loop. Use the following scale to apply grades:

Score	*Grade*
Score >= ØØ and score <= 49	F
Score >= 50 and score <= 59	D
Score >= 60 and score <= 69	C
Score >= 70 and score <= 79	B
Score >= 80 and score <= 89	A
Score >= 90 and score <= 100	A+

In each case block, assign a grade to a variable then print the grade and an appropriate comment. To reference a case block, your case selector should consist of the score divided by 10 plus 1. Since BASIC raises a selector that has a decimal fraction greater than .4, the value of the case selector for scores such as 49 and 50 will be the same.

Score of 49: 49/10 + 1 = 4.9 + 1 = 5.9 = 6
Score of 50: 50/10 + 1 = 5.0 + 1 = 6.0 = 6

To obtain different values use the INT function.

Score of 49: INT(49/10+1) = INT(4.9+1) = INT(5.9) = 5
Score of 50: INT(50/10+1) = INT(5.0+1) = INT(6.0) = 6

Your ON . . . GOSUB statement should look as follows. (xxxx represents a line number.)

```
xxxx ON INT(SCORE/10+1) GOSUB xxxx,xxxx,xxxx, etc.
```

The list of line numbers in the ON . . . GOSUB statement must include the same line number five times so that you can obtain an F for each of the following five ranges: Ø to 9 inclusive, 10 to 19 inclusive, 20 to 29 inclusive, 30 to 39 inclusive, and 40 to 49 inclusive. You also need two identical line numbers to obtain A+: one for the range 90 to 99 inclusive and the other for a score of 100.

Score of 99: INT(99/10+1) = INT(9.9+1) = INT(10.9) = 10
Score of 100: INT(100/10+1) = INT(10.0+1) = INT(11.0) = 11

Thus, case selector values 10 and 11 must both reference the line number of the "A+" block.

Partial Output:

```
Score? 58
Grade: D        More work required

Score? 85
Grade: A        Excellent

Score? 60
Grade: C        Doing average work
```

14.5 Storing Text on Disk

The following program stores text, such as a letter, on disk. Our text consists of instructions on how each line should be typed. For this program, we have omitted the verification of the keyed-in lines. Note that the text includes quotation marks.

```
1000 OPEN "B:TEXT.DAT" FOR OUTPUT AS #1
1010 PRINT
1020 LINES$ = ""
1030 WHILE LINES$ <> "q"
1040   PRINT #1, LINES$
1050   LINE INPUT "LINE:";LINES$
1060 WEND
1070 CLOSE #1
1080 END
RUN
```

```
LINE:       We indent each line of the text by seven spaces in order to
LINE:       obtain a one-inch left margin when the text is printed. We
LINE:       continue typing until the end of a screen line is reached, then
LINE:       we press Enter. The prompt LINE: appears on the next screen line
LINE:       where we type the next line of our text. To terminate our
LINE:       program, we must press "q" for "quit".
LINE:q
```

Note that we use the PRINT # statement rather than the WRITE # statement to write a line to the file. The PRINT # statement does not enclose a string in quotation marks as does the WRITE # statement. Thus, a line read from the file by the LINE INPUT # statement (shown below) will not be enclosed in quotation marks when the line is displayed on the screen or when it is directed to the printer.

We place the PRINT # and LINE INPUT statements within a WHILE/WEND loop. The null string assigned to LINES$ in statement 1020 is stored as a blank line in the file and will be read as a blank line when the text is read. To read the text from the file, we use LINE INPUT # rather than INPUT #. LINE INPUT reads the entire contents of a string including commas and quotation marks. The following routine reads and prints the text we have stored in data file TEXT.DAT.

```
7150 WHILE NOT EOF(1)
7160   LINE INPUT #1, LINES$
7170   PRINT LINES$
7180   LPRINT LINES$
7190 WEND
```

The first line printed will be a blank line, the text follows.

14.6 Early Exit from a Program

Until now, we assumed that a user would execute a program at least once. Suppose the user loads the wrong program into the computer and has started its execution. The user should be able to exit from the program immediately upon entry. To allow for an early exit, place statements similar to the ones given below at the beginning of the main routine. We will call these statements our preliminary prompts.

```
2000 'MAIN ROUTINE
2010   CLS
2020   LOCATE 10
2030   PRINT TAB(23) "This program produces address labels"
2040   INPUT "______________________Do you wish to continue (y/n)";RESPONSE$
2050   IF RESPONSE$ <> "y" AND RESPONSE$ <> "Y" AND RESPONSE$ <> "n" AND
          RESPONSE$ <> "N" THEN PRINT : PRINT "Invalid response. Enter y or n."
          : PRINT : GOTO 2040
2060   IF RESPONSE$ = "n" OR RESPONSE$ = "N" THEN END
```

Line 2030 displays the purpose of the program. The user must respond to line 2040 with a lowercase "y" or "n" or an uppercase "y" or "n". If the response is "n" or "N", the program ends.

14.7 External Documentation

In our discussion on program development in Chapter Three, we mentioned that programs should be documented externally with support material. Listed below are some of the items that may be included. You may wish to add others for your particular program.

NAME(S) OF THE AUTHOR(S)	The name(s) of the programmer(s).
NAME OF THE PROGRAM	A name that identifies the program. The name is often used as a filename when saving the program on disk.
DATES	The date the program was started and the date it was completed.
DESCRIPTION OF THE PROGRAM	The purpose of the program, the type of data the program uses, a general overview of the calculations it performs, and a brief description of the output it produces.
APPLICATIONS	The field in which the program can be used such as engineering, school administration, electronics, computer assisted instruction, etc.
LANGUAGE USED	The language in which the program is written.
COMPUTER SYSTEM	The make and model of computer and the peripherals used to develop the program.
APPROXIMATE MEMORY AND RUNNING TIME	The approximate amount of memory required by the program and the approximate amount of time it takes to execute the program.
OPERATING INSTRUCTIONS	Any operations unique to the program in order to produce the desired output.
RESTRICTIONS	Any restrictions such as the maximum number of data items or the highest value of a data item.
FEATURES OF THE PROGRAM	A brief description of each module. Any other features not already mentioned.
FIELD TESTING	State whether or not the program has been tested. Field testing should be performed by someone from the intended audience.
PROGRAM LISTING AND OUTPUT	The external documentation should accompany a listing of the program and its output.

14.8 Program Design

Now that we have learned how to write programs in modular form, it is a simple matter to extend this concept to the writing of menu-driven programs. A menu-driven program displays a list of its major tasks, which are numbered. These tasks are coded as subroutines. The list is referred to as a menu. The user selects a desired task from the menu by keying in the number of the task. This number becomes the case selector of an ON . . . GOSUB statement.

We will design the main routine and one subroutine of a program that retrieves and prints a collection letter stored on disk. The subroutine displays a menu from which the user can select a task. The remaining subroutines will be assigned as a programming problem at the end of the chapter.

The output produced by the modules designed here is as follows:

(cleared screen)

```
         10        20        30        40        50        60        70        80
12345678901234567890123456789012345678901234567890123456789012345678901234567890
                  This program prints a collection letter stored on disk
                  Do you wish to continue (y/n)? [y]
```

(cleared screen)

```
                 Select one of the options shown below, then press ENTER

                                  1.  Display instructions
                                  2.  Enter title and name
                                  3.  Enter address and date
                                  4.  Print the letter
                                  5.  Print the label
                                  6.  End the program

                 Enter an option: 1,2,3,4,5, or 6--
```

FIGURE 14-1 STRUCTURE CHART

Display menu
Display program instructions
INPUT title and name
INPUT address and date
Read and print letter
Print label
End the program

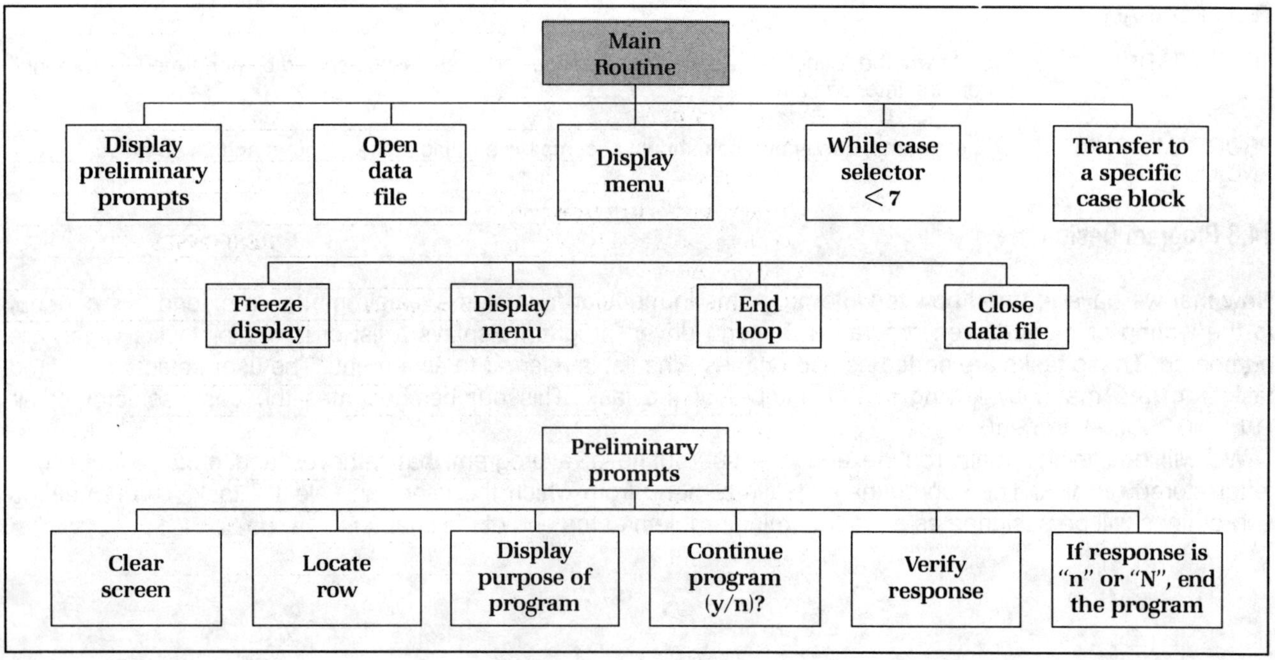

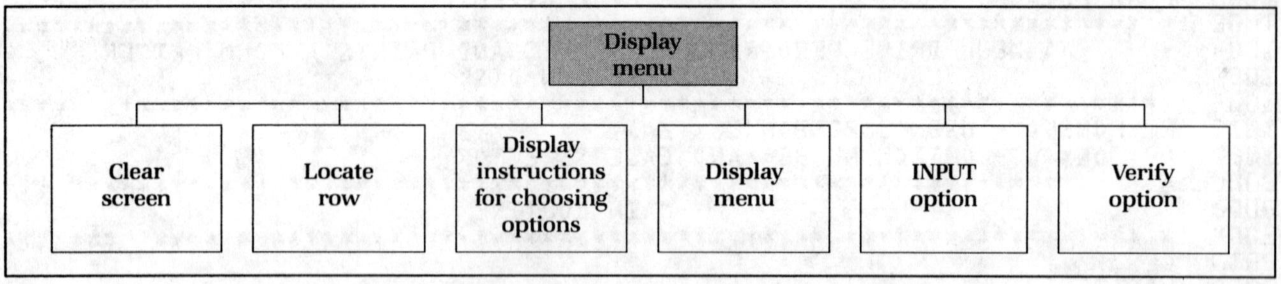

FIGURE 14-2 PSEUDOCODE

MAJOR TASKS
Display menu
Display program instructions
INPUT title and name
INPUT address and date
Read and print letter
Print label
End the program

MAIN ROUTINE	
Display preliminary prompts	(refined further)
Open data file	
Display menu	(subroutine)
While case selector < 7	OPTION1
Transfer to a specific case block	(one subroutine out of 6)
Freeze display	(merged subroutine)
Display menu	(subroutine)
End loop	
Close data file	

Preliminary prompts	
Clear screen	
Locate row	
Display purpose of program	
Continue program (y/n)?	RESPONSE$
Verify response	
If response is "n" or "N", end the program	

DISPLAY MENU	
Clear screen	
Locate row	
Display instructions for choosing options	
Display menu	
INPUT option	OPTION1
Verify option	

```
1000 'FORM LETTER                          M. MCRITCHIE                         DEC 16
1002 '*********************************************************************************
1004 '        A MENU-DRIVEN PROGRAM. RETRIEVES AND PRINTS A FORM LETTER
1006 '                             STORED ON DISK
1008 '*********************************************************************************
1010 'RESPONSE$ - USER'S RESPONSE (y/n)
1020 'OPTION1   - OPTION NUMBER AND CASE SELECTOR
2000 '*********************************************************************************
2002 '                              MAIN ROUTINE
2004 '*********************************************************************************
2010  CLS
2020  LOCATE 12
2030  PRINT TAB(14) "This program prints a collection letter stored on disk"
2040  INPUT "_____________Do you wish to continue (y/n)";RESPONSE$
2050  IF RESPONSE$ <> "y" AND RESPONSE$ <> "Y" AND RESPONSE$ <> "n" AND
         RESPONSE$ <> "N" THEN PRINT : PRINT "Invalid response. Enter y or n."
         : PRINT : GOTO 2040
2060  IF RESPONSE$ = "n" OR RESPONSE$ = "N" THEN END
2070  OPEN "B:LETTER.DAT" FOR INPUT AS #1
2080  GOSUB 3000                  'Display menu
2090  WHILE OPTION1 < 7
2100    ON OPTION1 GOSUB 4000,5000,6000,7000,8000,9000
2110    GOSUB 11000               'Freeze display
2120    GOSUB 3000                'Display menu
2130  WEND
2140  CLOSE #1
2150  END
3000 '*********************************************************************************
3002 '                              DISPLAY MENU
3004 '*********************************************************************************
3010  CLS
3020  LOCATE 7
3030  PRINT TAB(13) "Select one of the options shown below, then press ENTER"
3040  PRINT
3050  PRINT TAB(28) "1.  Display instructions"
3060  PRINT TAB(28) "2.  Enter title and name"
3070  PRINT TAB(28) "3.  Enter address and date"
3080  PRINT TAB(28) "4.  Print the letter"
3090  PRINT TAB(28) "5.  Print the label"
3100  PRINT TAB(28) "6.  End the program"
3110  PRINT
3120  INPUT "____________Enter an option: 1,2,3,4,5, or 6--",OPTION1
3130  PRINT
3140  INPUT "Is the option number correct (y/n)";RESPONSE$
3150  IF RESPONSE$ <> "y" AND RESPONSE$ <> "Y"
         THEN INPUT "Re-enter the option number--",OPTION1 : GOTO 3140
3160  RETURN
65529 'End of program listing
```

Subroutine DISPLAY MENU is called first before the WHILE/WEND loop, then from within the loop. In this way, the menu will be displayed each time an option must be chosen.

Summary of BASIC Statements

DEF — Defines a function written by a programmer.

```
2010 DEF FNTAX(RETAIL) = RETAIL*6/100
```

On n GOSUB — Transfers control to one of several line numbers listed in the statement. The line number chosen depends on the value of n, the case selector.

```
4040 ON CODE GOSUB 5000,6000,7000,8000
```

RANDOMIZE n — Reseeds the random number generator using n as the seed.

```
3010 RANDOMIZE TIMER
```

Summary of BASIC Functions

INT(n) — Returns the integer portion of a decimal number.

```
3010 WHOLE = INT(12.85)
```

RND(n) — Generates a random number between Ø and 1. The symbol n represents a numeric value.

```
3020 RANDOM.NUMBER = RND(1)
```

TIMER — Retrieves the seconds generated by DOS. The seconds are in numeric form.

```
3010 RANDOMIZE TIMER
```

Chapter Summary

1. The INT function is used in an expression to round off a number to a desired number of decimal places. For example, INT(125.678*100+.5)/100 rounds off 125.678 to 125.68.
2. To produce a truly random number, we can use the time in seconds, generated by DOS, as the seed in the RANDOMIZE statement. These seconds can be obtained by extracting the seconds from TIME$ and converting the seconds to numeric notation or by using the function TIMER which returns the seconds in numeric form.
3. To produce a random whole number, we use the formula INT(N*RND(1)+LOW) where N is the number of numbers in the desired range and LOW is the smallest number in the range.
4. A user-defined function is a function written by a programmer and incorporated in a program. The function must be named and defined in a DEF statement before it is called. Sample DEF statement:

```
2010 DEF FNTAX(RETAIL) = RETAIL*6/100
```

5. The name of a user-defined function may be any valid variable name, however, it must be preceded by FN.
6. The function name must be followed by one or several arguments in parentheses. Each argument must be a simple variable which normally appears in the function.
7. An argument in the DEF statement is referred to as the dummy argument. It plays no significant role, other than to act as a place-holder for a value passed to the function.
8. The function is called by means of a function reference which may be placed in most BASIC statements. A function reference consists of the function name followed by one or several arguments. Sample statement that contains a function reference:

```
5030 SALES.TAX = FNTAX(RETAIL.PRICE)
```

   FNTAX(RETAIL.PRICE) is the function reference, RETAIL.PRICE is called the actual argument.
9. The dummy argument is local to the DEF statement, the actual argument is global.
10. The value of the actual argument is passed from the function reference to the dummy argument in the DEF statement. The value is used in the function if the dummy argument appears there. The result of the function is passed back to the function reference by means of the function's name.
11. When more than one value is passed to the function, the actual arguments must correspond with the dummy arguments in number, order, and type.
12. Besides a multiple IF statement and multiple IF/THEN's, BASIC supports another decision structure that offers multiple alternatives. This is the case structure.
13. The case structure consists of an ON . . . GOSUB statement and several subroutines each referred to as a case block. Control transfers from the ON . . . GOSUB statement to one of the case blocks. The case block executed depends on the value of the case selector in the ON . . . GOSUB.
14. The case selector of an ON . . . GOSUB statement should be verified before it is used in the statement.
15. A user should be given the opportunity to exit from a program immediately upon entry.
16. A program should be documented externally with support material that fully describes the program, its applications, the computer system and the language used. The external documentation should accompany the program listing and the output.
17. A menu-driven program displays a list of its major tasks which are numbered. These tasks are coded as subroutines. The list is referred to as a menu. The user selects a desired task from the menu by keying in its number. This number becomes the case selector of an ON . . . GOSUB statement.

Questions and Exercises

1. Evaluate the following expressions by hand. Do one step at a time.

   (a) INT(8.46*10+.5)/10
   (b) INT(17.2548*100+.5)/100
   (c) INT(94.8216*1000+.5)/1000
   (d) INT(358.987+.5)

2. Write a program that reads six whole numbers and determines which numbers are odd and which are even. To determine whether a number is odd or even use the expression:

   INT(NUMBER/2)*2

   where NUMBER stores the number to be tested. If the result of the expression equals NUMBER, then the number is even.

   Sample Output:

```
21   (odd)
34   (even)
19   (odd)
17   (odd)
42   (even)
54   (even)
```

3. For each of the following, code a program that generates four random numbers. Use the seconds retrieved by TIME$ or TIMER as the seed in the RANDOMIZE statement. Use a FOR/NEXT loop in each program.

   (a) Decimal numbers between Ø and 1.
   (b) Whole numbers between 1 and 6 inclusive.
   (c) Whole numbers between Ø and 30 inclusive.
   (d) Whole numbers between 5 and 25 inclusive.

4. Suppose two players are playing a game in which each player moves his/her chip a certain number of times depending on where the dial stops on a spinner. The dial may stop at any number from 1 to 9 inclusive. Write a program that simulates this game. Determine which player made the greater number of moves after each player has had 10 plays.

   In a FOR/NEXT loop, use the random number generator to simulate the spinning of the dial. You will need two random number generators, one for each player. After obtaining a random number for one of the players, accumulate the number of moves for the player. Do the same for the second player. Outside the loop, compare the accumulators to determine the winner.

   Sample Output:

```
Player 1 is the winner with a total of 58 moves
```

   Sample Output:

```
Player 2 is the winner with a total of 51 moves
```

   Sample Output:

```
Both players obtained the same number of moves
```

5. Write user-defined functions and function references for the following. Code each function reference in a PRINT USING statement. In the user-defined function, use the formulas given. Use three arguments in each exercise.

   (a) Calculate an appliance dealer's yearly net profit. Round off the net profit to the nearest cent.
   Net Profit = Sales − (Cost of Goods + Operating Expenses)

   (b) Calculate the rate of return on one share of stock. Round off the rate to one decimal place.

$$\text{Rate of Return} = \frac{(\text{Current Price} - \text{Initial Price}) + \text{Dividends}}{\text{Initial Price}}$$

6. Code a skeleton main routine and Subroutine ENTER DATA AND PRINT RESULT to find the compound amount of a $10,000 investment. The interest rate is 9 1/4% and the period of time is 5 years. Use the following formula in a user-defined function to calculate the compound amount.

$$\text{Compound Amount} = \text{Principal}(1 + \text{Rate of Interest}/100)^{\text{Period of Time}}$$

Principal is the amount invested. Use arguments for the principal, the rate of interest, and the period of time. Round off the compound amount to the nearest cent.

The Output:

```
Initial investment: $10,000.00      Compound amount: $15,563.50
```

Programming Problems

1. Complete the program whose design was started on page 389. This is a menu-driven program that must read a letter stored on disk, then print the letter and an address label. A date, a name, and an address must be keyed in by the user. Use the program on page 388 to store on disk the sample letter given below. Suggested filename: LETTER.DAT

```
Please be advised that the balance in your account has now exceeded
the credit limit allowed on your charge account. We assume this is
an oversight on your part and that you will remit the amount shown
on the enclosed invoice within the next few days. However, if we
do not receive payment within the date specified on the invoice,
interest at the rate of 1.5% per month will be charged.

Kindly look after this matter as soon as possible in order to
maintain your excellent credit rating.

Yours truly,

HOWARD ELECTRONICS LTD.


Mr. Kenneth Davies, Accountant
Enclosure: 1
```

In the main routine given on page 392, the ON . . . GOSUB statement lists line numbers for six subroutines. A rough layout for the output from each of the subroutines is given below. Subroutine FREEZE DISPLAY, called from the main routine, displays the message **Press any key to continue** beneath each output. (The message is not shown in the outputs below.) Within each subroutine, you should clear the screen and locate the row.

Subroutine DISPLAY INSTRUCTIONS

Option 1 displays instructions.

```
This program allows you to print a personalized form
letter. Specific instructions for entering a name and
an address are given when you choose options 2 and 3.
Option 4 prints the letter and option 5 prints the
label for the envelope. Rechoose options 2,3,4 and 5
if you wish to send the letter to another recipient.
Choose option 6 after all the required letters and
labels have been printed.
```

Subroutine INPUT TITLE AND NAME

Option 2 allows a user to key in a title and a name.

```
          Enter the title, first name, and last name separated by
          spaces. You may type the name in upper case, lower case
          or both. (e.g. Mr. John Smith)

          Name? mr. john smith

Is the name correct (y/n)? y
```

Call the subroutine that separates a name. This subroutine, in turn, calls the subroutine that converts letters to upper case or lower case. These two subroutines, written for Problem 7 in Chapter 11, should be stored on your BASIC diskette under filename SEP-NAME.ASC.

Subroutine INPUT ADDRESS AND DATE

Option 3 allows a user to key in an address and a date.

```
          Enter street address, city-province, and postal code separated
          by slashes. (e.g. 123 Main Street/Anycity  ZZ/M3L 6S7)
          Enter the date in the normal manner. (e.g. June 7, 19XX)

          Address? 123 Main Street/Anycity  ZZ/M3L 6S7

          Date? November 18, 19XX

The address is 123 Main Street/Anycity  ZZ/M3L 6S7
Is the address correct (y/n)? y

The date is November 18, 19XX
Is the date correct (y/n)? y
```

Copy the address into local variable IN1$, and call the subroutine that separates data. This subroutine should be stored on your BASIC diskette under filename SEPARATE.ASC. After the subroutine has separated the address and assigned the street, city/province, and postal code to local variables OUT1$, OUT2$, and OUT3$; copy the values of these variables into program variables.

Subroutine READ AND PRINT LETTER

Option 4 reads the letter from the data file and prints the letter on the printer. The keyed-in name, address, and date must be incorporated into the letter. Remind the user to turn on the printer.

Screen output:

```
Please turn on the printer
```

Directed to the printer:

```
November 18, 19XX


Mr. John Smith
123 Main Street
Anycity  ZZ
M3L 6S7

Dear Mr. Smith:

    (The letter read from the data file will be printed here.)
```

Following the reminder, call subroutine FREEZE DISPLAY to give the user time to turn on the printer. Print the date, the name, and the address on the printer as shown above. To print the name, print the title, the first name, and the last name stored in the three variables TITLE$, FIRST$, LAST$ by your ASCII file SEP-NAME.ASC. To print the address, print the values returned from ASCII file SEPARATE.ASC through OUT1$, OUT2$, and OUT3$. These were copied into three program variables as mentioned earlier. Print the salutation.

In a WHILE/WEND loop, read each line of the letter from the data file and send each line to the printer. Use the LINE INPUT # statement to read a line. Refer to page 388 for the routine that reads text from a data file.

Subroutine PRINT LABEL

Option 5 prints an address label.

Inform the user to leave the printer on, then call Subroutine FREEZE DISPLAY. Direct the title, the first name, and the last name to the printer. Direct each part of the address to the printer.

Screen output:

```
Please leave the printer on
```

Directed to the printer:

```
Mr. John Smith
123 Main Street
Anycity  ZZ
M3L 6S7
```

Subroutine END PROGRAM

Option 6 ends the program.

Screen output:

```
End of the program
```

Merge and customize the subroutines needed by your program.

2. Design and code a menu-driven program that performs the following:

   (a) Displays a menu.
   (b) Displays instructions.
   (c) Produces a table of earnings based on hourly wages.
   (d) Produces a table of commissions based on sales.
   (e) Produces a table of graduated commissions based on sales.
   (f) Ends the program.

Sample Menu:

```
Select one of the options shown below, then press ENTER

        1.  Display instructions
        2.  Produce a table of hourly wages
        3.  Produce a table of commissions
        4.  Produce a table of graduated commissions
        5.  End the program

Enter an option: 1,2,3,4, or 5--
```

Partial outputs for options 2, 3, and 4 are shown below. The periods represent additional detail lines.

Option 2:

```
                 HOURLY WAGES

         Hourly Rate of Pay? 10.00
Minimum and Maximum Number of Hours? 35,45
     ================================
     HOURS      OVERTIME       WAGES
     ================================
      35        $ 0.00       $350.00
      36        $ 0.00       $360.00
      ..        ......       .......
      44        $60.00       $460.00
      45        $75.00       $475.00
```

Option 3:

```
              COMMISSIONS

        Rate of Commission? 10
Minimum and Maximum Sales? 3000,4000
     ============================
      SALES           COMMISSION
     ============================
     $3,000.00         $300.00
     $3,100.00         $310.00
     .........         .......
     $3,900.00         $390.00
     $4,000.00         $400.00
```

Option 4:

```
                 GRADUATED COMMISSIONS

                 Quota? [3600]
                 Rate of Commission? [10]
                 Rate on Excess? [13]
           Minimum and Maximum Sales? [3000,4000]
=================================================
  SALES          COMM. ON EXCESS       COMMISSION
=================================================
$3,000.00           $ 0.00               $300.00
$3,100.00           $ 0.00               $310.00
.........           ......               .......
$3,900.00           $39.00               $399.00
$4,000.00           $52.00               $412.00
```

On a cleared screen, give instructions stating what must be entered for each of options 2, 3, and 4 and state what each option displays. For example, the following could be given concerning Option 2: "For Option 2, enter the hourly rate of pay and the minimum and maximum hours of work for a desired range. The table displays the wages for the hours specified."

Display each table on a cleared screen. In each subroutine that produces a table, format the table, INPUT the data for the table, perform the calculations, and print the detail lines.

Subroutine HOURLY WAGES

Allow the user to key in the hourly rate of pay and the minimum and maximum hours of work for a desired range. Set up a FOR/NEXT loop using the minimum and maximum hours as the parameters of the FOR. Consider 40 hours as the regular hours. If there is no overtime, assign zero to the variable that represents overtime pay and use the formula **Wages = Rate × Hours** to find the wages. If there is overtime, find the overtime pay and the wages as follows:

Overtime pay = (Hours-40) × (Rate × 1.5)
Wages = 40 × Rate + Overtime pay

Subroutine COMMISSIONS

Allow the user to key in the rate of commission and the minimum and maximum sales for a desired range. Set up a FOR/NEXT loop using the minimum and maximum sales as the parameters of the FOR. To find the commission, use the formula **Commission = Sale × Rate/100.**

Subroutine GRADUATED COMMISSIONS

In addition to the values keyed in for the above table, allow the user to type in a quota (an amount that should be sold) and the rate of commission on excess sales which is the difference between a sale and the quota. Set up a FOR/NEXT loop similar to the one mentioned above. For any sale greater than the quota, the salesperson receives a higher rate of commission on the excess. Use the following formulas:

If Sale <= Quota:
Commission on Excess = Ø
Commission = Sale × Regular Rate/100

If Sale > Quota:
Regular Commission = Quota × Regular Rate/100
Excess = Sale−Quota
Commission on Excess = Excess × Rate on Excess/100
Commission = Regular Commission + Commission on Excess

3. Computer Assisted Instruction (CAI) programs are often used to provide drill and practice in specific subjects. Write a Mathematics CAI program that gives a student practice in addition. Use the random number generator to generate the numbers to be added and to select a comment on the student's answer. Sample output is given below.

```
                                                        (cleared screen)
   This program gives you practice in addition.
   Do you wish to continue? Type y or n, then press ENTER--[y]
                                                        (cleared screen)
      Type your first name when the computer asks for your
      name. Press the ENTER key after typing the answer to
      any question.

      What is your name? [Susan]
      Please answer the following questions, Susan

      How many addition questions would you like? [6]
      What smallest number would you like to use? [1]
      What largest number would you like to use? [10]
                                                        (cleared screen)
                           QUESTION: 1

                           3 + 2 = [5]

                           You got it!

Press any key to continue
                                                        (cleared screen)
                           QUESTION: 2

                           5 + 2 = [6]
   That's not the right answer, Susan. Please try once more.

                           5 + 2 = [9]
         Your answer is wrong, Susan. Please try again.

                           5 + 2 = [8]
The correct answer is 7

Press any key to continue
```

At the end of the practice, print the result of the drill on a cleared screen. Sample output:

```
Your score is  6 answer(s) correct out of  9 tries, Susan
```

Give the student three chances to answer a question correctly. If the student's answer is incorrect after the third try, display the correct answer. Use a separate subroutine to display instructions and the introductory questions. Write the subroutines described below, then print the result of the drill.

Subroutine SUBMIT QUESTION

Set up a FOR/NEXT loop in which the test value is the number of questions requested. Three counters will be needed. One counts the number of attempts, another counts the number of correct answers. The third counter counts the number of incorrect answers for each question. Initialize this latter counter to zero inside the loop.

Generate two random numbers for each question using the numbers keyed in by the student as the lowest and highest numbers in the range. Display the question using a PRINT statement that ends with a semicolon, then allow the student to type in an answer. To suppress the question mark, use the LINE INPUT statement. Store the student's answer in a string variable. Increase, by one, the counter for the number of attempts. In an IF statement, determine whether or not the answer is correct. Hint: Convert the student's answer from type string to numeric by means of the VAL function. Your IF statement must transfer control to one of the two subroutines explained below.

Subroutine CORRECT ANSWER

Increase the counter for the number of correct answers. Use the random number generator to produce the case selector of an ON . . . GOSUB statement that selects one out of three congratulatory comments. Code each of these comments in its own case block within the CORRECT ANSWER module.

Subroutine INCORRECT ANSWER

Increase the counter for the number of incorrect answers. Set up a WHILE/WEND loop that continues as long as the student's answer is incorrect and as long as the number of incorrect answers is less than or equal to 2. (The student has already answered the question once.) Use the random number generator to produce the case selector of an ON . . . GOSUB statement that selects one out of three reproving comments. Immediately following the ON . . . GOSUB statement, display the question once more and allow the student to key in another answer. Increase the counters for the number of attempts and the number of incorrect answers. End the loop.

In an IF statement, transfer control to Subroutine CORRECT ANSWER if the student's answer is correct, otherwise, display the correct answer. (This would be the student's third answer). Code each of the reproving comments in its own case block within the INCORRECT ANSWER module.

Code the subroutine that prints the result of the drill.

4. Write a program that determines the change received from the payment of an invoice. The amount of the invoice must be less than or equal to $20, the amount tendered must be $20 or lower. The change must consist of the minimum number of bills and coins. For convenience only, ignore two-dollar bills and half-dollar coins.

Sample Output:

```
                                                        (cleared screen)
This program calculates the change due from
the payment of an invoice $20.00 or less.
Do you wish to continue (y/n)? Y

                                                        (cleared screen)
          Amount of invoice? 6.87
          Amount tendered? 20.00

          Change due: $13.13
          The change is as follows:
                1 ten(s)
                0 five(s)
                3 one(s)
                0 quarter(s)
                1 dime(s)
                0 nickel(s)
                3 penny(ies)
```

Allow the user to key in the amount of the invoice and the amount tendered. Calculate the refund; that is, the change due. Since the breakdown of the change is based on cents rather than on dollars and cents, multiply, by 100, the difference between the amount of the invoice and the amount tendered when calculating the refund. Hint: Be careful of internal round off errors. Refer to page 379 for a sample statement that overcomes these errors. In your PRINT statement that prints the change due, divide the refund by 100.

In a separate subroutine, use multiple IF/THEN statements each of which calls a specific subroutine to break down the refund. The subroutine called depends on the amount of the refund. Condition checks, based on cents, are given below.

Refund:

If refund >= 1000 and refund <= 1999
If refund >= 500 and refund <= 999
If refund >= 100 and refund <= 499
If refund >= 25 and refund <= 99
If refund >= 10 and refund <= 24
If refund >= 5 and refund <= 9
If refund >= 1 and refund <= 4

To break down the refund, code a subroutine for each of the above conditions. Suppose the refund lies in the first range. Let us use $17.62 as an example. In this subroutine, we perform the following.

We divide 1762 by 1000 and use the INT function on the result. This gives us the number of ten dollar bills.

```
6010 TEN = INT(REFUND/1000)
```

We now find the number of five dollar bills by subtracting the tens (in cents) from the refund and dividing the difference by 500.

```
6020 FIVE = INT((REFUND-TEN*1000)/500)
```

We find the number of one dollar bills by subtracting the tens and the fives (both in cents) from the refund and dividing the difference by 100.

```
6030 ONE = INT((REFUND-TEN*1000-FIVE*500)/100)
```

We find the number of quarters by subtracting the tens, fives, and ones (all in cents) from the refund and dividing the difference by 25.

```
6040 QUARTER = INT((REFUND-TEN*1000-FIVE*500-ONE*100)/25)
```

This continues until the number of pennies is found. No division takes place when finding the number of pennies.

If the refund lies in the second range, the first statement in this subroutine must divide the refund by 500.

```
7010 FIVE = INT(REFUND/500)
```

The first statement for the third range must divide the refund by 100, the first statement for the fourth range must divide the refund by 25; and so on. You will need seven subroutines for the seven conditions. Other than the RETURN statement, your last subroutine should contain only xxxxx PENNY = REFUND.

In a separate subroutine, print the breakdown of the change as shown on page 402.

5. This problem reviews group printing and one-dimensional arrays. The concepts are needed in the project at the end of this book.

   Write a program that produces class lists. Each new class list must start on a new page, headed by the name of the course and the name of the instructor. The first page of each class list must be numbered 1. Data is stored in two files. Partial data files are given on page 404.

```
COURSES.DAT
100,Mathematics,Brown            — Course number, course name,
202,Data Processing,Andrews        instructor's name
205,Computer Science,Harris
...,..................,......

STUDENT2.DAT
100,167,"Smith,John"
100,1025,"Bennett,Carl"           — Course number, student number,
100,942,"Peters,Susan"             student's name
...,...,"......,....."
202,184,"Hiebert,Diane"
202,852,"Maxwell,Alan"
...,...,"........,...."
```

Note that course numbers are ordered in both files.

Partial Output:

```
COURSE: 100 Mathematics                     INSTRUCTOR: Brown

02-09-19XX              CLASS LIST                    Page 1
             ========================================
             STUDENT                      STUDENT
             NUMBER                        NAME
             ========================================
               167                   Smith,John
              1025                   Bennett,Carl
               942                   Peters,Susan
              ....                   ...............
```

```
COURSE: 100 Mathematics                     INSTRUCTOR: Brown

02-09-19XX              CLASS LIST                    Page 2
             ========================================
             STUDENT                      STUDENT
             NUMBER                        NAME
             ========================================
              ....                   ...............
              1249                   Mitchell,Karen
               688                   Olson,Douglas
               132                   Riddell,Marie
              1041                   Jennings,Joseph

Number of students in 100 Mathematics          67
```

```
COURSE: 202 Data Processing                 INSTRUCTOR: Andrews

02-09-19XX              CLASS LIST                    Page 1
             ========================================
             STUDENT                      STUDENT
             NUMBER                        NAME
             ========================================
               184                   Hiebert,Diane
               852                   Maxwell,Alan
               ...                   ...............
```

Place all items read from both files into one-dimensional arrays. For each course number in the student file, your program must search for the same number in the course file. Assume no records are missing in either file, therefore, there is no need to display a "not found" message. The search subroutine must return the position of the found course number. You will then use this position to print the number and name of the course and the name of the instructor.

Remember to find the size of each file by keeping track of the records as they are being read. This gives the sizes of all arrays. Each time a record is read from the course file, assign the course number, in string form, to local string array IN1$. This string array will be searched in Subroutine SEARCH ONE-DIMENSIONAL ARRAY for a course number in the student file.

Your main routine must call subroutines to (a) Read the course file (b) Read the student file (c) Format the report (d) Process the data. Refer to the sample program on page 219 and to the program written for Problem 3 in Chapter 9 if you need help in printing the headings and processing the data. Do not call Subroutine PRINT HEADINGS from Subroutine FORMAT REPORT. At this point the course number, the course name, and the instructor are not known since the search subroutine has not yet been called. In Subroutine FORMAT REPORT, inform the user to turn on the printer.

In the subroutine that processes the data, assign, in string form, the first course number read from the student file to local string variable IKEY$. Sample statement:

```
xxxx IKEY$ = STR$(COURSE.NO(1))
```

Call Subroutine SEARCH ONE-DIMENSIONAL ARRAY to search the course file for this course number. Following this GOSUB statement, store the position of the found course number in a program variable, say RECORD.NO, and call the subroutine that prints the headings. Use RECORD.NO as the subscript of subscripted variables in your PRINT statement to print the number and name of the course and the name of the instructor. The headings for the first page of the first class list will now be printed.

Following the GOSUB statement that called the subroutine to print the headings, set up a FOR/NEXT loop whose initial value is one and whose test value is the size of the student file. Note that the initial value must be one since the first student record has not yet been processed. You simply printed a heading.

The first statement in the FOR/NEXT loop must assign, in string form, a course number from the student file to local variable IKEY$

```
xxxx IKEY$ = STR$(COURSE.NO(I))
```

I is the control variable of the FOR statement. The remaining statements in the subroutine are similar to those in the sample program on page 219. Do not forget to count the students. Also, some of the variables that you use must be subscripted variables.

Code a subroutine that prints the one-line summary displayed at the end of a class list. In your PRINT statement, use RECORD.NO as the subscript to access the course number and course name and use your counter to print the number of students. Immediately after this PRINT, increase ROW by 2 and reset to zero the counter that counts the students in a course. Call Subroutine SEARCH ONE-DIMENSIONAL ARRAY to search for the course number assigned to IKEY$ (assigned in the FOR/NEXT loop of Subroutine PROCESS DATA). Store the position of the found course number in RECORD.NO.

To start a new class list on a new page, first compare your control variable, minus one, with the size of the student file to ensure that you have not yet reached the end of the file. If the values are not the same, reset the page number to 1, call Subroutine PRINT HEADINGS to print the headings of the next class list on a new page, and reset the number of the row. This IF statement should be placed just before RETURN in the subroutine that prints the summary.

Merge Subroutine SEARCH ONE-DIMENSIONAL ARRAY with your program.

6. Modify Accounts Receivable file AR2.DAT by placing Mr. or Ms. before each name. Also ensure that several accounts have balances over the credit limit. If you need help in modifying the file, refer to the program listed on page 144 where an Employee file is updated. You may wish to create a new file. Suggested filename: AR4.DAT.

   After modifying the file, write a program that finds each Accounts Receivable account whose balance is over the credit limit. For each account found, print the form letter created for Problem 1 and stored on disk under filename LETTER.DAT. Address the letter to the proper recipients. Display the letters on the screen, one after the other. Create address labels and display the labels on the screen following the letters. When your program is error-free, direct the letters and the labels to the printer. Each letter must be printed on a new page with a sufficient top margin so that it is centred vertically on the page. Print three labels side by side. The letter and sample labels are given on page 408.

(new page)

```
November 30, 19XX


Mr. Derek Andrews
493 Aster Bay
Anycity  ZZ
M3L 2T6

Dear Mr. Andrews:

Please be advised that the balance in your account has now exceeded
the credit limit allowed on your charge account. We assume this is
an oversight on your part and that you will remit the amount shown
on the enclosed invoice within the next few days. However, if we
do not receive payment within the date specified on the invoice,
interest at the rate of 1.5% per month will be charged.

Kindly look after this matter as soon as possible in order to
maintain your excellent credit rating.

Yours truly,

HOWARD ELECTRONICS LTD.


Mr. Kenneth Davies, Accountant
Enclosure: 1
```

(new page)

```
Mr. Derek Andrews            Ms. Jodi Morrison          Ms. Cathy Lawson
493 Aster Bay                315 Clare Blvd.            821 Devon Avenue
Anycity  ZZ                  Mytown  XX                 Anycity  ZZ
M3L 2T6                      N6Y 7C3                    M3L 7V2


Ms. Rhonda Miller            Mr. Peter Innes
912 Glenwood Avenue          169 Inkster Avenue
Mytown  XX                   Anycity  ZZ
N6Y 9D7                      M3L 8W1
```

Instructions for writing several of the modules are given below. Remember to freeze, on the screen, prompts referring to the printer in order to give the user time to turn on the printer.

The Main Routine

Code the preliminary prompts. Open the Accounts Receivable file and the file storing the form letter, then call subroutines to read both files. Call the subroutine that prints the address labels. Close the files and print the message "End of processing" on the screen.

Subroutines that Read the Data Files

Read the lines of the letter into an array using the LINE INPUT # statement within a WHILE/WEND loop. The statement is given below. K counts the lines as they are being read and is used as the subscript of variable LINES$.

```
3040 LINE INPUT #2, LINES$(K)
```

Save the size of the array (copy the value of K into variable ARRAY.SIZE.)

Before reading the Accounts Receivable file, allow the user to key in the current date, then inform the user to turn on the printer (for the printing of letters). Read the fields of a record into simple variables, not into arrays. Remember, one of the fields is a credit limit field.

Compare the balance of an account with the credit limit. If the balance is higher, increase a counter, say J, by one and call Subroutine NAME AND ADDRESS described below. The counter will later be used to access a name and the three parts of an address.

Subroutine NAME AND ADDRESS

Create arrays that store the names, street addresses, city/provinces, and postal codes of accounts with overextended balances. Arrays are needed so that the data can be reaccessed for the labels. To create the name array, copy the name of a customer whose record has just been read and whose balance is over the credit limit into a subscripted variable. The subscript must be your counter (J) from the previous subroutine. Call the subroutine that separates a name. The subroutine should be stored on your BASIC diskette under filename SEP-NAME.ASC. The subroutine places the three parts of a name into TITLE$, FIRST$, and LAST$.

Copy the address on the same record into local variable IN1$ and call the subroutine that separates an address. The subroutine should be stored on your BASIC diskette under filename SEPARATE.ASC. Create a street address array, a city/province array, and a postal code array by copying each part of the address into a subscripted variable. The subscript must be the same as that used for the name array. Examples of these statements are given below.

```
5050 STREET$(J) = OUT1$
5060 CITY.PROVINCE$(J) = OUT2$
5070 POSTAL$(J) = OUT3$
```

Call the subroutine that prints the letter.

Subroutine PRINT LETTER

Code PRINT statements that instruct BASIC to skip to a new page and to leave a sufficient top margin so that the letter is centred vertically. Hint: CHR$(12) instructs BASIC to skip to a new page, CHR$(10) instructs BASIC to proceed to the next line. On a cleared screen, inform the user that letters are being processed. Print the keyed-in date, the name and address, and the salutation as shown on page 406. To print the name, use variables TITLE$, FIRST$, and LAST$. To print the address, use subscripted variables STREET$, CITY.PROVINCE$, and POSTAL$. Use a FOR/NEXT loop to print the lines of the letter. The test value of the FOR statement must be ARRAY.SIZE.

Subroutine PRINT LABELS

Code a PRINT statement that informs the user to leave the printer on. Instruct BASIC to skip to a new page and to leave a one-inch top margin. Create a FOR/NEXT loop in which the initial value is one, the test value is your counter (J) minus one, and the step value is three. To print the labels side by side, use your control variable, say I, as the subscript of the variables for the left-most label, I+1 as the subscript of the variables for the centre label, and I+2 as the subscript of the variables for the right-most label. Refer to the program written for Problem 2 in Chapter 12 if you need help.

Merged ASCII Files

Merge the following ASCII files with your program. Subroutine SEPARATE. ASC needs to be customized.

FREEZE.ASC — Freezes a display on the screen.

SEPARATE.ASC — Separates an address into three parts. Hint: To separate an address, find the starting position of two consecutive spaces. Find two such positions: the position of the two spaces between the street and the city and the position of the two spaces between the province and the postal code.

SEP-NAME.ASC — Two subroutines. The first separates a name into three parts. The second converts letters to upper case or lower case. Hint: To separate a name, find the position of one space. Find two such positions.

Project

Rewrite the program for the project in Chapter 12. This time, write a menu-driven program that displays a menu listing the following options:

1. Display instructions.
2. Update accounts.
3. Group print all accounts by department.
4. Group print accounts with balances below the minimum.
5. End the program.

Update the accounts in data file INVENT2.DAT. Rather than updating just those accounts whose balances are below a particular minimum, as you did in Chapter 12, allow a user to INPUT the number of the account that must be updated. This means your program must search for the keyed-in account number. Refer to page 315 where modules are listed that INPUT a key and update an account.

When testing your program, increase the balances in some accounts and decrease the balances in at least four other accounts to a quantity below the minimum specified on the record. Use codes to denote an order and a sale. A "1" means an order has been filled, therefore, the balance must be increased. A "2" means a sale has been made, therefore, the balance must be decreased. As in the project for Chapter 12, display an account on the screen with prompts beneath the account where a user can key in the date, the code, and the amount of the transaction. Your program must calculate the new balance.

Write the records (some of which will be updated) first to a new file, say, INVENT3.DAT. When your program is error-free, rename the file INVENT2.DAT. After the necessary accounts have been updated, group print (on the printer) all accounts by department with each department's listing printed on a new page. Beneath each listing print the number of accounts whose balances are below the minimum in that department. In the same report, but on a separate page, print the total number of accounts whose balances are below the minimums for all departments.

The report that lists only those accounts whose balances are less than the minimum must list the accounts by department with each department's listing printed on a new page. Refer to your program written for the project in Chapter Nine.

For your current program:

1. Open and close your files in the case blocks.
2. Call a subroutine from another subroutine (with the exception of the Subroutines FREEZE DISPLAY and DISPLAY MENU both of which must be called from the main routine). After an option has been chosen, much of the communication should occur within the option.
3. When printing reports on the printer, assume the paper is adjusted to the top of a new page at the start of options 3 and 4. Each option must instruct BASIC to skip to a new page for a new listing. Sample outputs are given on pages 409 and 410.

An Account

```
        Stock number H001
        *****************************************************************
        * DEPARTMENT: Housewares                                        *
        * ITEM: Flatware (stainless steel)                 Minimum: 3   *
        *---------------------------------------------------------------*
        * DATE                         ORDERED       SOLD     BALANCE   *
        *---------------------------------------------------------------*
        * Jan. 8                                                  0     *
        *                                                               *
        *                                                               *
        *                                                               *
        *                                                               *
        *                                                               *
        *                                                               *
        *                                                               *
        *****************************************************************
Date, code, quantity? Jan. 10,1,10
Are the entries correct (y/n)? y

        Stock number H001
        *****************************************************************
        * DEPARTMENT: Housewares                                        *
        * ITEM: Flatware (stainless steel)                 Minimum: 3   *
        *---------------------------------------------------------------*
        * DATE                         ORDERED       SOLD     BALANCE   *
        *---------------------------------------------------------------*
        * Jan. 8                                                  0     *
        * Jan. 10                         10                     10     *
        *                                                               *
        *                                                               *
        *                                                               *
        *                                                               *
        *                                                               *
        *                                                               *
        *****************************************************************
Another transaction for stock number H001 (y/n)?
```

Inventory Report by Department

```
Department: Housewares             01-30-19XX            Page  1

                         INVENTORY REPORT
=================================================================
STOCK NO.                 ITEM                  MINIMUM   BALANCE
=================================================================
  H001       Flatware (stainless steel)            3         10
  H002       Flatware (silver plate)               3          7
  H003       Flatware (silver)                     3          1

Number of accounts under the minimum               1
```

Summary Page (last page of the above report)

```
         NUMBER OF ACCOUNTS UNDER THE MINIMUM   Page  4
                      01-30-19XX

   Total number of accounts under the minimum  5
```

Inventory Report of Accounts with Balances Below the Minimum

```
Department: Appliances          01-30-19XX          Page  3

                       INVENTORY REPORT
==========================================================
STOCK NO.                ITEM               MINIMUM   BALANCE
==========================================================
  A002       Microwave Oven                    6          4
  A004       Dryer                             3          2
```

Solutions for Exercises

14.1 Rounding Off Numbers

1. (a)
```
3010 NUMBER = 45.16
3020 ROUNDED = INT(NUMBER*10+.5)/10
```
(b)
```
3010 NUMBER = 45.164
3020 ROUNDED = INT(NUMBER*100+.5)/100
```
(c)
```
3010 NUMBER = 45.6879
3020 ROUNDED = INT(NUMBER*1000+.5)/1000
```
(d)
```
3010 NUMBER = 24.68
3020 ROUNDED = INT(NUMBER+.5)
```

2. (a) INT(42.15*10+.5)/10
INT(421.5+.5)/10
INT(422.0)/10
422/10
42.2

(b) INT(3.1578*100+.5)/100
INT(315.78+.5)/100
INT(316.28)/100
316/100
3.16

(c) INT(26.3941*1000+.5)/1000
INT(26394.1+.5)/1000
INT(26394.6)/1000
26394/1000
26.394

(d) INT(823.694+.5)
INT(824.194)
824

14.2 Generating a Random Number

1. (a)
```
3000 RANDOMIZE TIMER
3010 PRINT
3020 R = RND(1)
3030 PRINT R
3040 END
```
(b)
```
3000 RANDOMIZE TIMER
3010 PRINT
3020 R = INT(10*RND(1)+1)
3030 PRINT R
3040 END
```
(c)
```
3000 RANDOMIZE TIMER
3010 LOW = 20
3020 HIGH = 36
3030 N = (HIGH-LOW)+1
3040 R = INT(N*RND(1)+LOW)
3050 PRINT
3060 PRINT R
3070 END
```

2.
```
3000 RANDOMIZE TIMER
3010 FOR ROLL = 1 TO 3
3020   DIE1 = INT(6*RND(1)+1)
3030   DIE2 = INT(6*RND(1)+1)
3040   TOTAL = DIE1+DIE2
3050   PRINT
3060   PRINT "Die 1:";DIE1,"Die 2:";DIE2
3070   PRINT "Total:";TOTAL
3080 NEXT ROLL
3090 END
```

3.
```
3000 RANDOMIZE TIMER
3010 FOR TOSS = 1 TO 10
3020   R = INT(2*RND(1)+1)
3030   IF R = 1 THEN HEADS = HEADS+1 ELSE TAILS = TAILS+1
3040 NEXT TOSS
3050 PRINT
3060 PRINT "Heads:";HEADS
3070 PRINT "Tails:";TAILS
3080 END
```

14.3 User-defined Functions

```
2010 DEF FNINTEREST(PRINCIPAL,RATE) = PRINCIPAL*TIME*RATE/100
```

1. (a) Function — PRINCPAL*TIME*RATE/100
   (b) Function name — FNINTEREST
   (c) Dummy arguments — PRINCIPAL,RATE
   (d) Local variables — PRINCIPAL,RATE
   (e) Global variable — TIME

2. (a)
```
2010 DEF FNKILOMETRES(MILES) = MILES*1.609
3040 KILOMETRES = FNKILOMETRES(NO.MILES)
```
   (b)
```
2010 DEF FNCOMMISSION(SALES,RATE) = SALES*RATE/100
3040 PRINT TAB(7) USING "Sales:_$####,.##____Commission:_$###.##";
     SALES.AMOUNT,FNCOMMISSION(SALES.AMOUNT,COMM.RATE)
```
   (c)
```
2010 DEF FNAVERAGE(TOTAL,NUMBER) = TOTAL/NUMBER
3040 PRINT TAB(7) USING "The average of 4 test scores is:_###";
     FNAVERAGE(TOTAL.SCORE,NUMBER.TESTS)
```

3.
```
1000 'WEEKLY WAGES
2000 'MAIN ROUTINE
2010   DEF FNWAGES(HRS,RATE,DEDUCT) = RATE*40+(HRS-40)*RATE*1.5-DEDUCT
2020   GOSUB 3000               'Read data and print result
2030   END
3000 'SUBROUTINE READ DATA AND PRINT RESULT
3010   READ HOURS,RATE.OF.PAY,DEDUCTIONS
3020   PRINT
3030   PRINT TAB(2) USING "Hours:_##_____Weekly wages:_$###.##";
       HOURS,FNWAGES(HOURS,RATE.OF.PAY,DEDUCTIONS)
3040   DATA 44,9.15,63.85
3050   RETURN
65529 'End of program listing
```

14.4 Multiple Alternatives—The Case Structure

1. (a) The value of the case selector is negative. BASIC will print **Illegal function call in xxxx** where xxxx is the line number of the ON . . . GOSUB statement.
   (b) Nothing is wrong.
   (c) Nothing is wrong.
   (d) The value of the case selector is greater than the number of line numbers listed in the ON . . . GOSUB statement. BASIC will drop through to the statement following the ON . . . GOSUB.
   (e) The value of the case selector is zero. BASIC will drop through to the statement following the ON . . . GOSUB.

Exercise 2.

```
1000 'GRADES                            M. MCRITCHIE                          DEC 14
1002 '*********************************************************************************
1004 '          THIS PROGRAM CONVERTS SCORES TO GRADES AND PRINTS THE
1006 '                         GRADES ALONG WITH COMMENTS
1008 '*********************************************************************************
1010 'TEST       - CONTROL VARIABLE OF A FOR STATEMENT
1020 'SCORE      - SCORE
1030 'RESPONSE$  - USER'S RESPONSE (y/n)
1040 'GRADE$     - GRADE
2000 '*********************************************************************************
2002 '                                 MAIN ROUTINE
2004 '*********************************************************************************
2010  FOR TEST = 1 TO 10
2020    PRINT
2030    INPUT "Score";SCORE
2040    INPUT "Is the score correct (y/n)";RESPONSE$
2050    IF RESPONSE$ <> "y" AND RESPONSE$ <> "Y"
          THEN INPUT "Re-enter the score--",SCORE : GOTO 2040
```

```
2060     ON INT(SCORE/10+1) GOSUB 3000,3000,3000,3000,3000,3200,3400,3600,3800,
         4000,4000
2070   NEXT TEST
2080   END
3000   'SUBROUTINE CASE 1      Score >= 00 and score <= 49
3010    GRADE$ = "F"
3020    PRINT "Grade:_";GRADE$;"_____More work required"
3030    RETURN
3200   'SUBROUTINE CASE 2      Score >= 50 and score <= 59
3210    GRADE$ = "D"
3220    PRINT "Grade:_";GRADE$;"_____More work required"
3230    RETURN
3400   'SUBROUTINE CASE 3      Score >= 60 and score <= 69
3410    GRADE$ = "C"
3420    PRINT "Grade:_";GRADE$;"_____Doing average work"
3430    RETURN
3600   'SUBROUTINE CASE 4      Score >= 70 and score <= 79
3610    GRADE$ = "B"
3620    PRINT "Grade:_";GRADE$;"_____Good work"
3630    RETURN
3800   'SUBROUTINE CASE 5      Score >= 80 and score <= 89
3810    GRADE$ = "A"
3820    PRINT "Grade:_";GRADE$;"_____Excellent"
3830    RETURN
4000   'SUBROUTINE CASE 6      Score >= 90 and score <= 100
4010    GRADE$ = "A+"
4020    PRINT "Grade:_";GRADE$;"_____Excellent"
4030    RETURN
65529 'End of program listing
```

15

RANDOM ACCESS FILES

Objectives

Until now, values stored on disk have been read and processed sequentially. The first record was read, processed, and the results printed. The next record was then read and processed in a similar manner. The search for a specific item was also handled sequentially; that is, records were examined in sequence until a desired item was found.

Many applications require the direct retrieval of a specific record. Asking a customer to wait for his account to be found as the computer searches through all the preceding accounts is hardly considered practical. Random access files solve this dilemma. The computer retrieves any desired record without having to read all the preceding ones. To implement this feature in our programs, we must be familiar with the following statements and functions.

1. The FIELD statement which allows us to organize an internal storage area into fields. The storage area is called a buffer.
2. The LSET and RSET statements which move data in string form from the program into the buffer.
3. The PUT statement which moves a record from the buffer to the file.
4. The GET statement which reads a record from the random access file and places the record in the buffer
5. The LOC function which returns the number of the last record referenced in a random access file.
6. The MK functions which convert numeric values to strings before they are placed in the buffer.
7. The CV functions which convert numeric values in string form to numeric form after they have been read from the file and placed in the buffer.

Contents

15.1 Basic Concepts of Data Files

Buffers

To provide access to a data file, sequential or random access, the computer sets aside within its memory an area called a buffer. The buffer, created when a file is opened, serves as a temporary storage area for the transfer of data to and from a data file. Each opened file has its own buffer. For a sequential file the buffer is 128 bytes in length. The length of a random access buffer depends on the length allocated to a record (all records in a random access file have the same length). If no length is specified, the size of the buffer is 128 bytes. The length of a record may range from 1 to 32767 bytes. When the number of bytes in a record is greater than 128, BASIC must be loaded with the /S: option. For example, BASICA/S:512 instructs the computer to set aside a 512-byte buffer.

Sequential and Random Access Files

Records in a sequential file must be read in the order in which they were written to the file. Even if only a few records need to be updated, all records must be retrieved, the necessary records updated, then all records must be written to an output file. In a random access file, records can be written to and retrieved from the file in any order. Thus, we can retrieve any desired record, update it by changing one or more of its fields, and store the record in its former position. All records need not be retrieved and then written to an output file.

Programs using random access files are more complex to write than programs using sequential files. In a sequential file, DOS does most of the work for us. For example, DOS controls the interactions between the buffer and the data file. In a random access file, we have control over the structure of the buffer, over the transfer of data between program variables and the buffer, and over the transfer of data between the buffer and the data file. BASIC supports statements that allow us to control these operations. A program using random access files involves more tasks, on the other hand, our control over the movement of data gives us direct access to any record.

Remember, the terms transfer, move, and send do not mean that data items literally move from one storage area to another. Copies of the items are placed in the storage areas specified. When an item is transferred from a program variable to a data file, the item remains in the memory location designated by the variable. A copy of the item is placed in the buffer and another copy is placed in the data file.

Let us now find out how to create a random access file. We will explain the file-handling statements after they have been introduced in the program.

15.2 Creating a Random Access File

The program on page 417 creates an inventory file. The four records listed below will be written to data file INVENTR1.DAT. The "R" in INVENTR1.DAT signifies random access. Each record consists of an item's stock number, description, and the quantity on hand. The program produces no output other than prompts. We leave the printing of output to our next example.

Stock Number	*Description*	*Quantity*
100R9	Ribbons	8
101D5	Diskettes (5 1/4")	9
102D3	Diskettes (3 1/2")	10
103P7	Printer Paper (Box)	4

```
1000 'CREATE INVENTORY FILE                    M. MCRITCHIE                    JAN 3
1002 '*******************************************************************************
1004 '       THIS PROGRAM CREATES AN INVENTORY FILE NAMED INVENTR1.DAT
1006 '*******************************************************************************
1010 'RESPONSE$                - USER'S RESPONSE (y/n)
1020 'STOCK.NO1$, STOCK.NO$ - STOCK NUMBER
1030 'ITEM1$,ITEM$            - ITEM IN STOCK
1040 'QTY1$,QTY                - QUANTITY
1050 'NO.ITEMS                 - NUMBER OF ITEMS
1060 'RECORD.NUM               - RECORD NUMBER AND CONTROL VARIABLE
2000 '*******************************************************************************
2002 '                            MAIN ROUTINE
2004 '*******************************************************************************
2010  CLS
2020  LOCATE 12
2030  PRINT TAB(15) "This program allows you to create an inventory file"
2040  INPUT "_______________Do you wish to continue (y/n)";RESPONSE$
2050  IF RESPONSE$ <> "y" AND RESPONSE$ <> "Y" AND RESPONSE$ <> "n" AND
        RESPONSE$ <> "N" THEN PRINT : PRINT "Invalid response. Enter y or n."
        : PRINT : GOTO 2040
2060  IF RESPONSE$ = "n" OR RESPONSE$ = "N" THEN END
2070  OPEN "B:INVENTR1.DAT" AS #1 LEN = 29
2080  FIELD #1, 5 AS STOCK.NO1$, 20 AS ITEM1$, 4 AS QTY1$
2090  GOSUB 3000                    'INPUT records and write to data file
2100  CLOSE #1
2110  END
3000 '*******************************************************************************
3002 '       INPUT RECORDS. WRITE THE RECORDS TO DATA FILE INVENTR1.DAT
3004 '*******************************************************************************
3010  CLS
3020  LOCATE 3
3030  INPUT "_______________________Number of items to store";NO.ITEMS
3040  PRINT
3050  INPUT "Is the number correct (y/n)";RESPONSE$
3060  IF RESPONSE$ <> "y" AND RESPONSE$ <> "Y"
        THEN INPUT "Re-enter the number of items--",NO.ITEMS : GOTO 3050
3070  PRINT
3080  PRINT TAB(16) "Enter the stock number, description, and quantity"
3090  PRINT TAB(16) "separated by commas"
3100  FOR RECORD.NUM = 1 TO NO.ITEMS
3110    PRINT
3120    INPUT "_______________Stock number,item,quantity";STOCK.NO$,ITEM$,QTY
3130    PRINT
3140    INPUT "Are the entries correct (y/n)";RESPONSE$
3150    IF RESPONSE$ <> "y" AND RESPONSE$ <> "Y"
          THEN INPUT "Re-enter the stock number, item, quantity--",
          STOCK.NO$,ITEM$,QTY : GOTO 3140
3160    LSET STOCK.NO1$ = STOCK.NO$
3170    LSET ITEM1$ = ITEM$
3180    RSET QTY1$ = MKS$(QTY)
3190    PUT #1,RECORD.NUM
3200  NEXT RECORD.NUM
3210  RETURN
65529 'End of program listing
RUN
```

```
                                                                                  (cleared screen)
         10        20        30        40        50        60        70        80
12345678901234567890123456789012345678901234567890123456789012345678901234567890

                 This program allows you to create an inventory file
                 Do you wish to continue (y/n)? y

                                                                                  (cleared screen)
                              Number of items to store? 4

Is the number correct (y/n)? y

                  Enter the stock number, description, and quantity
                  separated by commas

                  Stock number,item,quantity? 100R9,Ribbons,8

Are the entries correct (y/n)? y
```

The remaining items are entered in a similar manner.

Recall that the OPEN statement for a sequential file specifies whether the file is opened for an INPUT, an OUTPUT, or an APPEND. If the file is opened for a particular mode, it must be closed before it can be reopened for a different mode. For a random access file, we need not specify a mode. If the file does not exist, OPEN creates a new file; if the file does exist, OPEN opens the file for a read. Therefore, a random access file is usually opened once and closed once in a program. The opening and closing of a file should be performed in the main routine with the OPEN statement near the beginning of the routine and the CLOSE statement near the end. All file operations; that is, the writing and retrieval of data must be performed between the OPEN and CLOSE statements.

Line 2070 — The OPEN statement

Line 2070 opens a random access file named INVENTR1.DAT. The OPEN statement must specify the following:

1. The drive in which our BASIC diskette resides. (Remember, we called the diskette on which we store programs and data our BASIC diskette.) If no drive is specified, the computer assumes the default drive; that is, the drive out of which the computer is currently operating.
2. The name of the file. The filename must conform with the rules for naming files. The drive and the name must be separated by a colon and enclosed in quotation marks.
3. The file number. In this OPEN statement, #1 is associated with data file INVENTR1.DAT. Subsequent file-handling statements must reference the data file by its number rather than by its name. As with sequential files, the maximum number of files that may be open by default is 3. We can change the number by using the /F: option when loading BASICA. For example, BASICA/F:6 allows six files to be open at any one time. The maximum number is 15.
4. The record length parameter. The parameter allocates the same number of bytes to each record in the file. As a result, the length of each record is fixed. This is unlike the lengths of records in sequential files. Refer to pages 419 to 422 where a comparison is made between records stored in a random access file and those stored in a sequential file. In our current program, 29 bytes are allocated to each record of data file INVENTR1.DAT. The maximum number of bytes that can be allocated to a record is 32767.

Line 2080 — The FIELD statement

BASIC allows us to structure the buffer of a random access file by letting us allocate a specific number of bytes to each field in the buffer. We do this by means of a FIELD statement. The statement first identifies the file for which the buffer was created. In line 2080, the FIELD statement identifies data file INVENTR1.DAT by specifying its file number which is #1.

Each field in the buffer will hold a string that is referenced by a unique string variable referred to as a buffer variable. To identify a buffer variable, we have added a digit to the variable name. The digit associates the variable with a data file. In the above program, STOCK.NO1$ is the buffer variable used to reference the stock number field of data file INVENTR1.DAT. (Digit "1" is used in both names.) STOCK.NO$ is a program variable. You may wish to use some other convention.

Our FIELD statement sets aside 5 bytes for the stock number, 20 bytes for the item's description, and 4 bytes for the quantity; a total of 29 bytes. We allocate 29 bytes to a record by using 29 as the record length parameter in the OPEN statement. We may allocate more bytes to each record, however, this would waste disk space. If we allocate an insufficient number of bytes to each record, BASIC displays **FIELD overflow in xxxx** where xxxx is the line number of the FIELD statement.

The fields in the buffer of a random access file and the fields in the file are not separated. The system knows where one field ends and where the next field starts since we allocated a specific number of bytes to each field. Figure 15-1 illustrates how the buffer is organized for data file INVENTR1.DAT.

FIGURE 15-1 BUFFER IDENTIFIED WITH DATA FILE INVENTR1.DAT

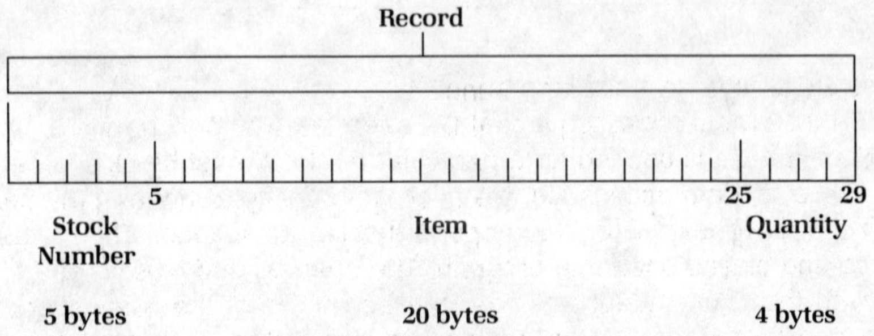

The quantity stored in the buffer must be stored as a string. Therefore, we must convert all numbers to strings before we place them in the buffer. The conversion for the quantity takes place in line 3180 and is explained later on in this section.

Figures 15-2 and 15-3 illustrate the differences between the storage of records in a sequential file and the storage of records in a random access file. Suppose each file stores the data given below.

Stock Number	*Description*	*Quantity*
100R9	Ribbons	8
101D5	Diskettes (5 1/4")	9
102D3	Diskettes (3 1/2")	10
103P7	Printer Paper (Box)	4

FIGURE 15-2 SEQUENTIAL DATA FILE

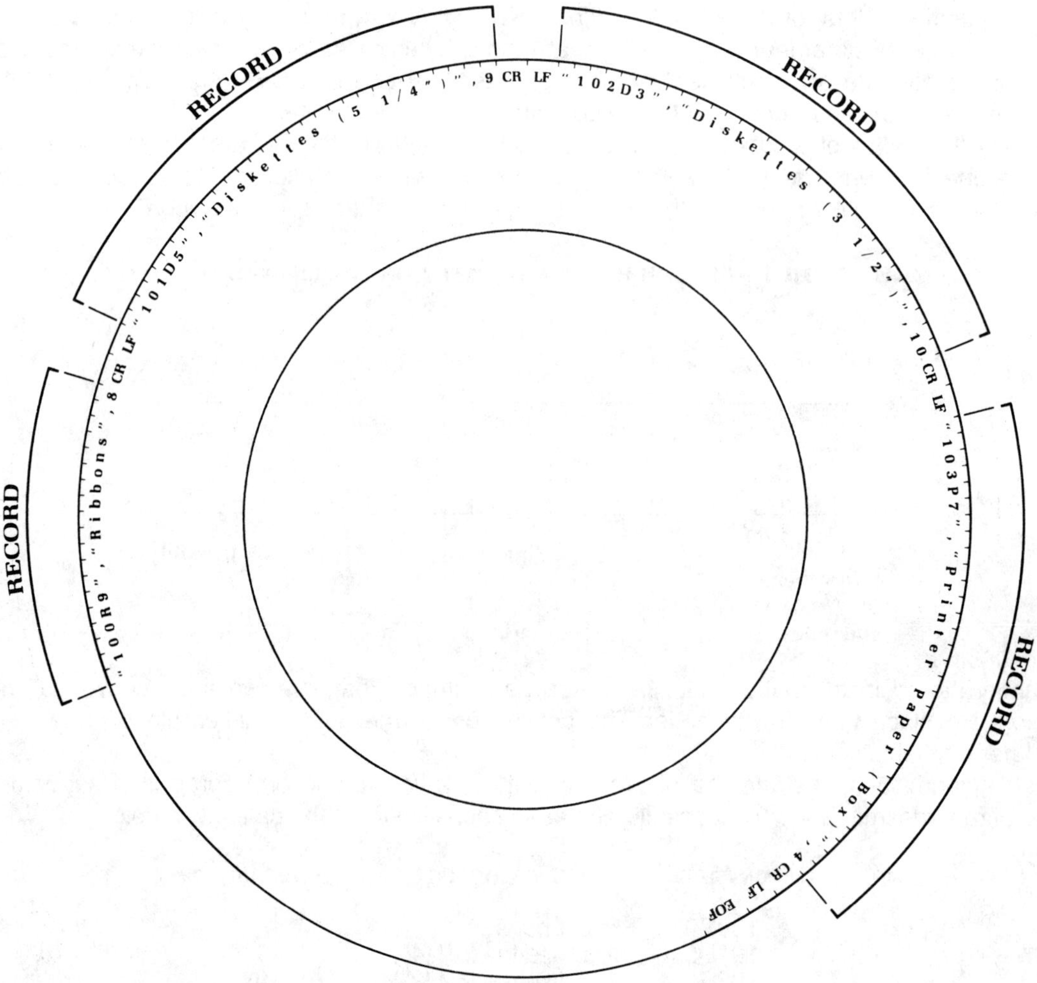

FIGURE 15-3 RANDOM ACCESS FILE

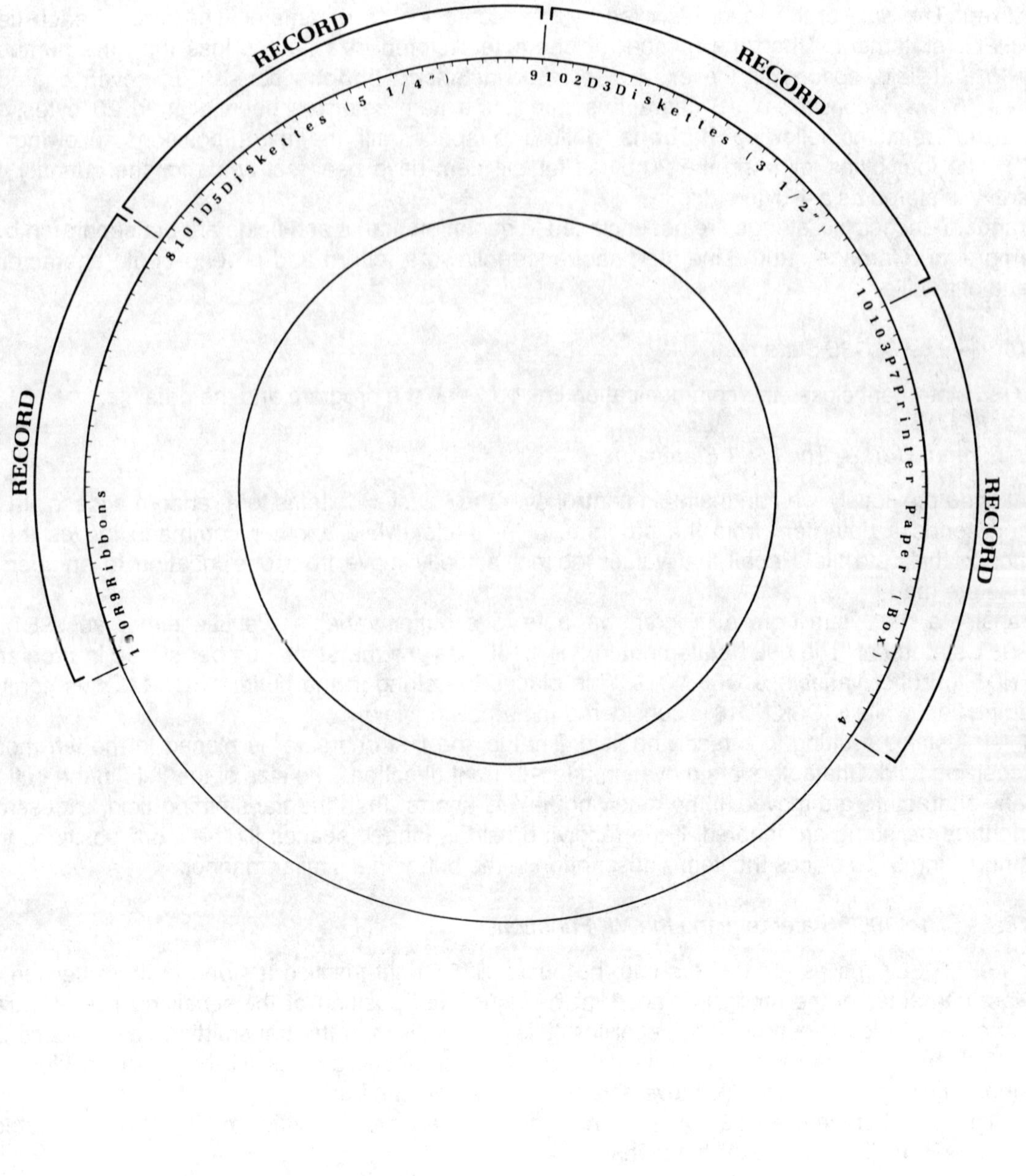

Let us first examine the sequential file. The WRITE # statement, which writes a record to a sequential file, encloses strings in quotation marks and separates fields with commas. DOS ends each record just written to the file with a Carriage return/Line feed sequence and places an end-of-file character at the end of the file. Note, particularly, that records vary in length. The first record in Figure 15-2 consists of 19 bytes, the second record consists of 30 bytes. The length of a record depends on the size of each of its fields.

Figure 15-3 shows that the size of each record in a random access file is fixed and that the size of each field is fixed. The size of the record is fixed by the record length parameter. The size of each field is fixed by the FIELD statement. When the number of characters stored in a field is less than the number of bytes allotted to that field, spaces fill the extra bytes. For instance, **Ribbons** consists of seven characters while **Diskettes (5 1/4")** consists of 18 characters. Since the item field has been allotted 20 bytes, 13 spaces fill the extra positions following **Ribbons** while two spaces fill the extra positions following **Diskettes (5 1/4")**. The four bytes following the 20 bytes for the item have been set aside for the quantity. In this file, the quantity is stored as a 4-byte string.

In a random access file, strings are not enclosed in quotation marks and fields are not separated by commas. Furthermore, no Carriage return/Line feed sequence follows a record and no end-of-file character is placed at the end of the file.

Line 2100 — The CLOSE Statement

The CLOSE statement closes the communication link between the program and the data file.

Lines 3160 and 3170 — The LSET Statement

As mentioned previously, we can maintain control over the transfer of items to a random access file. A specific command sends a data item from the program to the buffer while another command moves the record in the buffer to the data file. Recall that values do not actually move from one location to another; copies of the values are made.

To transfer a data item from a program variable to a buffer variable, we use either an LSET statement or an RSET statement. The LSET statement in line 3160 assigns the stock number stored in program variable STOCK.NO$ to buffer variable STOCK.NO1$. This places the string in the buffer. STOCK.NO$ is considered the transmitting field while STOCK.NO1$ is considered the receiving field.

LSET left-justifies a string in a receiving field. That is, the first character is placed in the left-most position of the receiving field. Characters are moved in a left-to-right direction. The size of the field in the buffer governs how many characters are moved. If the receiving field is shorter than the transmitting field, excess characters to the right of the string are ignored. If the receiving field is longer, spaces fill the extra positions to the right of the string. Line 3170 places the item's description in the buffer in a similar manner.

Line 3180 — The RSET Statement and the MK Functions

As with LSET, RSET moves a data item into the buffer. RSET right-justifies a string in the receiving field. That is, the last character of the string is placed in the right-most position of the receiving field. Characters are moved in a right-to-left direction. If the receiving field is shorter than the transmitting field, excess characters to the left of the string are ignored. If the receiving field is longer, spaces fill the extra positions to the left of the string. RSET is usually used to move a numeric value into the buffer.

Regardless whether we use LSET or RSET, a number moved into the buffer must first be converted to string form by one of the following "make" functions.

(a) MKI$ converts an integer to a string of two bytes.

(b) MKS$ converts a single-precision number to a string of four bytes.

(c) MKD$ converts a double-precision number to a string of eight bytes.

In Line 3180, we convert the single-precision number stored in QTY to a four-byte string and assign the string to QTY1$. (Four bytes is the number of bytes allotted to a single-precision number.) Thus, the quantity is stored in the buffer as a four-byte string. If we use RSET to move the quantity to the buffer, the number of bytes allocated to QTY1$ in the FIELD statement must be four. If we use LSET, we may allocate more than four bytes to QTY1$ but not less.

General Comments — The LSET and RSET Statements

The only way we can place a value into a buffer is by means of an assignment statement using LSET or RSET. It is not possible to READ or INPUT a value into a buffer. We can, however, use an explicit string or number in the assignment statement. Compare the following.

Using a program variable	Using an explicit value
`3010 ENAME$ = "Laura"` `3020 LSET ENAME1$ = ENAME$`	`3010 LSET ENAME1$ = "Laura"`
`3010 AMOUNT = 250` `3020 RSET AMOUNT1$ = MKS$(AMOUNT)`	`3010 RSET AMOUNT1$ = MKS$(250)`

Line 3190 — The PUT Statement

The computer references a record in a random access file by its position in the file. The first record is considered record 1, the second record is considered record 2, etc. Therefore, we reference a record by its number. The PUT statement moves a record in the buffer to a random access file. The statement must specify the file number and a record number. If no record by that number resides in the data file, the buffer's record will occupy a new position in the file. If a record by that number already resides in the file, the buffer's record replaces the contents of the record in the file.

The PUT statement gives us control over the movement of data from the buffer to the data file by allowing us to choose a storage position in the file. The PUT statement is one of the features that makes the file a random access file. The storage position is specified by a record number. The record number may be represented by a variable, a number, or an expression. In the statement **3190 PUT** #1,**RECORD.NUM**, #1 specifies the file number while the value of RECORD.NUM specifies the position where the buffer's contents will be stored in the file.

Subroutine 3000 accepts keyed-in data and writes the data to our data file. The statements are placed within a FOR/NEXT loop. The INPUT statement in line 3120 assigns the data items, which are keyed in as one record, to three program variables. The LSET and RSET statements transfer the data from the program variables to buffer variables. The PUT statement sends the record from the buffer to the data file. Each time the loop is executed, data for a new record is entered into the computer, placed in the buffer, and sent to the data file. Since RECORD.NUM, our control variable, varies from 1 to 4, the first record sent to the file is considered record 1, the second record sent to the file is considered record 2, etc.

15.3 Reading a Random Access File

Creating and Reading a File

The program on page 417 simply created data file INVENTR1.DAT. The program listed below not only creates the file but reads and prints its contents. The EOF function, used to signal the end of a sequential file, cannot be used in a random access file as no EOF character is placed at the end of the file. BASIC does, however, provide us with a LOC function that returns the number of the last record referenced. When the last record referenced is the last record in the file, LOC gives us the number of records in the file. This value is often needed to terminate loops, thus it is wise to store the number as a special record in the data file. In the program below, we store the number of records in the file in location one (record #1) of data file INVENTR1.DAT.

```
1000 'CREATE INVENTORY FILE                     M. MCRITCHIE                    JAN 5
1002 '**********************************************************************
1004 '  THIS PROGRAM WRITES RECORDS TO AN INVENTORY FILE NAMED INVENTR1.DAT
1006 '                    THEN RETRIEVES AND PRINTS THE RECORDS
1008 '**********************************************************************
1010 'RESPONSE$                   - USER'S RESPONSE (y/n)
1020 'NO.RECORDS1$,NO.RECORDS%  - NUMBER OF RECORDS IN THE FILE
1030 'STOCK.NO1$,STOCK.NO$       - STOCK NUMBER
1040 'ITEM1$,ITEM$               - ITEM IN STOCK
1050 'QTY1$,QTY                  - QUANTITY
1060 'NO.ITEMS                   - NUMBER OF ITEMS
1070 'RECORD.NUM                 - RECORD NUMBER AND CONTROL VARIABLE
1080 'S$                         - EQUAL SIGNS
1090 'F$                         - IMAGE OF A DETAIL LINE
1100 'HEADING$                   - HEADING
```

```
2000 '**************************************************************************
2002 '                                MAIN ROUTINE
2004 '**************************************************************************
2010  CLS
2020  LOCATE 12
2030  PRINT TAB(15) "This program allows you to create an inventory file"
2040  INPUT "______________Do you wish to continue (y/n)";RESPONSE$
2050  IF RESPONSE$ <> "y" AND RESPONSE$ <> "Y" AND RESPONSE$ <> "n" AND
         RESPONSE$ <> "N" THEN PRINT : PRINT "Invalid response. Enter y or n."
         : PRINT : GOTO 2040
2060  IF RESPONSE$ = "n" OR RESPONSE$ = "N" THEN END
2070  OPEN "B:INVENTR1.DAT" AS #1 LEN = 29
2080  FIELD #1, 2 AS NO.RECORDS1$
2090  FIELD #1, 5 AS STOCK.NO1$, 20 AS ITEM1$, 4 AS QTY1$
2100  GOSUB 3000                    'INPUT records and write to data file
2110  CLS
2120  LOCATE 12
2130  INPUT "___Writing is complete. Do you wish to see the contents of the file
(y/n)";RESPONSE$
2140  IF RESPONSE$ <> "y" AND RESPONSE$ <> "Y" AND RESPONSE$ <> "n" AND
         RESPONSE$ <> "N" THEN PRINT : PRINT "Invalid response. Enter y or n."
         : PRINT : GOTO 2130
2150  IF RESPONSE$ = "y" OR RESPONSE$ = "Y" THEN GOSUB 23000   'Read data file
2160  CLOSE #1
2170  END
3000 '**************************************************************************
3002 '  INPUT RECORDS AND WRITE THE RECORDS TO DATA FILE INVENTR1.DAT. STORE
3004 '  THE NUMBER OF THE LAST RECORD IN RECORD #1 OF THE DATA FILE.
3006 '**************************************************************************
3010  CLS
3020  LOCATE 2
3030  INPUT "_________________________Number of items to store";NO.ITEMS
3040  PRINT
3050  INPUT "Is the number correct (y/n)";RESPONSE$
3060  IF RESPONSE$ <> "y" AND RESPONSE$ <> "Y"
        THEN INPUT "Re-enter the number of items--",NO.ITEMS : GOTO 3050
3070  PRINT
3080  PRINT TAB(16) "Enter the stock number, description, and quantity"
3090  PRINT TAB(16) "separated by commas"
3100  FOR RECORD.NUM = 2 TO NO.ITEMS+1
3110    PRINT
3120    INPUT "_________________Stock number,item,quantity";STOCK.NO$,ITEM$,QTY
3130    PRINT
3140    INPUT "Are the entries correct (y/n)";RESPONSE$
3150    IF RESPONSE$ <> "y" AND RESPONSE$ <> "Y"
          THEN INPUT "Re-enter the stock number, item, quantity--",
          STOCK.NO$,ITEM$,QTY : GOTO 3140
3160    LSET STOCK.NO1$ = STOCK.NO$
3170    LSET ITEM1$ = ITEM$
3180    RSET QTY1$ = MKS$(QTY)
3190    PUT #1,RECORD.NUM
3200  NEXT RECORD.NUM
3210  NO.RECORDS% = LOC(1)
3220  RSET NO.RECORDS1$ = MKI$(NO.RECORDS%)
3230  PUT #1,1
3240  RETURN
5000 '**************************************************************************
5002 '                       FORMAT REPORT AND PRINT HEADINGS
5004 '**************************************************************************
5010  CLS
5020  LOCATE 9
5030  S$ = STRING$(47,"=")
5040  F$ = "_____________________\___\________\_________________\_______##"
5050  HEADING$ = "PHYSICAL INVENTORY"
5060  PRINT TAB((80-LEN(HEADING$))/2+.5); HEADING$
5070  PRINT TAB(17) S$
5080  PRINT TAB(17) "STOCK NUMBER"; TAB(37) "DESCRIPTION"; TAB(56) "QUANTITY"
```

```
5090   PRINT TAB(17) S$
5100   RETURN
23000 '**********************************************************************
23002 '                      READ AND PRINT DATA FILE
23004 '**********************************************************************
23010  GOSUB 5000                  'Format report and print headings
23020  FOR RECORD.NUM = 2 TO NO.RECORDS%
23030     GET #1,RECORD.NUM
23040     PRINT USING F$; STOCK.NO1$,ITEM1$,CVS(QTY1$)
23050  NEXT RECORD.NUM
23060  RETURN
65529 'End of program listing
```

In addition to the prompts shown on page 418, the program produces the following output:

(cleared screen)

```
         10        20        30        40        50        60        70        80
12345678901234567890123456789012345678901234567890123456789012345678901234567890

   Writing is complete. Do you wish to see the contents of the file (y/n)? y
```

(cleared screen)

```
                       PHYSICAL INVENTORY
           ==========================================
           STOCK NUMBER       DESCRIPTION       QUANTITY
           ==========================================
               100R9          Ribbons                  8
               101D5          Diskettes (5 1/4")       9
               102D3          Diskettes (3 1/2")      10
               103P7          Printer Paper (Box)      4
```

Lines 2080 and 2090 — The FIELD Statements

The program stores the number of the last record in the first record of data file INVENTR1.DAT. This first record in the file is referred to as the header record. The remaining records, which we will call data records, are considered records 2, 3, 4 and 5. Thus, the program creates a file of five records.

When a data file contains a header record, the buffer must be structured two ways: one structure for the header record, the other structure for a data record. The FIELD statement in line 2080 structures the header record, the FIELD statement in line 2090 structures a data record. Note that both FIELD statements communicate with the same data file; that is, with data file #1.

The number of the last record is stored in the buffer as a two-byte string identified as NO.RECORDS1$. Since each record in file INVENTR1.DAT consists of 29 bytes, the header record contains a two-byte string and 27 "empty bytes."

Line 3100 — The FOR Statement

The first data record moved from the buffer to the data file must be numbered record 2 since the first record in the file is the header record. The last data record moved from the buffer to the file must be numbered record 5. Therefore, the initial value in the FOR statement must be 2 and the test value must be 5 (NO.ITEMS+1 = 4+1 = 5).

Line 3210 — The LOC Function

As mentioned previously, the LOC function returns the number of the last record referenced in a random access file. Since the last record referenced in the above program is the last one written to the file, the LOC function returns the number 5. The number 5 also represents the total number of records in the file. This number is assigned to variable NO.RECORDS%. Note that the variable is an integer variable so that its contents can be converted to a two-byte string in a subsequent statement.

Line 3220 — The MKI$ Function

MKI$ converts the contents of integer variable NO.RECORDS% to a string of two bytes. RSET places the string in the buffer (structured by the FIELD statement in line 2080) by assigning the string to buffer variable NO.RECORDS1$.

Line 3230 — The PUT Statement

The PUT statement in line 3230 moves the value representing the number of records in the file from the buffer associated with file #1 to record #1 of the data file. Record #1 is the header record.

Line 23020 — The FOR Statement

Subroutine 23000 reads and prints the data records stored in file INVENTR1.DAT. Since Subroutine 3000 numbered these records 2, 3, 4, and 5, the initial value in the FOR statement must be 2 and the test value must be 5. As we may not be aware of the number of records in the file, variable NO.RECORDS% should be used as the test value. Recall that NO.RECORDS% stores the number 5.

Line 23030 — The GET Statement

The GET statement retrieves a record from a random access file and places the record in the buffer communicating with the file. The first value in the statement specifies the file number, the second value specifies a record number. The record number may be represented by a variable, a number, or an expression. In line 23030, the GET statement retrieves a record from data file INVENTR1.DAT, whose file number is #1, and places the record in the buffer associated with the file. Since the value of RECORD.NUM varies from 2 to 5, records 2, 3, 4, and 5 are retrieved.

The GET statement gives us control over the movement of data from the data file to the buffer by allowing us to retrieve any record residing in the file. As with the PUT statement, the GET statement is one of the features that makes the file a random access file.

Line 23040 — The CV Functions and the PRINT USING Statement

Before we can use a numeric value that has been moved from a random access file to the buffer, we must convert the value from string form to numeric form by one of the following "convert" functions.

(a) CVI converts a two-byte string (a numeric value) to an integer.

(b) CVS converts a four-byte string (a numeric value) to a single-precision number.

(c) CVD converts an eight-byte string (a numeric value) to a double-precision number.

The CVS function in line 23040 converts the four-byte string in QTY1$ to a single-precision number.

Our PRINT USING statement references the buffer's variables, thus it prints values directly from the buffer. There is no need to transfer the values from the buffer to program variables unless, for example, values must be stored in one or several arrays. Buffer variables can also be used in other BASIC statements as in the following assignment statement:

```
3060 DEDUCTIONS = CVS(TAX1$) + CVS(UNION1$) + CVS(PENSION1$)
```

Examining a Random Access File

The program on page 423 created a random access file and subsequently read and printed the records in the file. There may be times when we would like to examine the contents of a random access file. The DOS command TYPE cannot be used to examine a random access file. Therefore, we must write our own program. Listed below is a program that reads and prints the contents of data file INVENTR1.DAT.

It is important to realize that Subroutine 23000 in the previous program cannot be used as a stand-alone routine to read a data file, since it does not open and close the file, organize the buffer, nor retrieve the value that represents the number of records in the file. Although the program at the top of page 427 may require customizing, you will find it useful when you wish to examine a random access file. Suggested filename: READ-RA.BAS

```
24000 '********************************************************************
24002 '  THIS PROGRAM READS AND PRINTS THE CONTENTS OF A RANDOM ACCESS FILE
24004 '********************************************************************
24010  OPEN "B:INVENTR1.DAT" AS #1 LEN = 29
24020  FIELD #1, 2 AS NO.RECORDS1$
24030  FIELD #1, 5 AS STOCK.NO1$, 20 AS ITEM1$, 4 AS QTY1$
24040  GET #1,1
24050  NO.RECORDS% = CVI(NO.RECORDS1$)
24060  PRINT
24070  FOR RECORD.NUM = 2 TO NO.RECORDS%
24080    GET #1,RECORD.NUM
24090    PRINT STOCK.NO1$,ITEM1$,CVS(QTY1$)
24100  NEXT RECORD.NUM
24110  CLOSE #1
24120  END
RUN
```

```
100R9        Ribbons                  8
101D5        Diskettes (5 1/4")       9
102D3        Diskettes (3 1/2")       10
103P7        Printer Paper (Box)      4
```

The GET statement in line 24040 moves the contents of record #1, the header record in our file, into the file's buffer. Recall that record #1 holds the number that tells us how many records are in the file. Before we can use the number, we must first convert the value from string form to numeric form. We assign the converted number to integer variable NO.RECORDS% and use this variable as the test value in our FOR statement. We could have performed the conversion directly in the FOR statement as follows:

```
24070 FOR RECORD.NUM = 2 TO CVI(NO.RECORDS1$)
```

However, if the value is needed several times in a program, as it is in many of our programs, it is best to assign the converted value to a variable, then reference the variable. We used this latter method in the above program merely to illustrate its application.

Inside the loop, the GET statement retrieves data records 2, 3, 4, etc. The PRINT statement prints the values held in the buffer. Note that we must convert the string stored in QTY1$ to a single-precision number before the number is printed. The loop terminates when the control variable, RECORD.NUM, exceeds the number stored in NO.RECORDS%.

15.4 Adding Records to a File

Suppose we wish to add the two records listed below to our file INVENTR1.DAT. The following program performs this operation.

Stock Number	*Description*	*Quantity*
104Q8	Pens	6
105Q7	Pencils	18

```
1000 'ADD RECORDS TO A FILE                    M. MCRITCHIE                  JAN 7
1002 '********************************************************************
1004 '           THIS PROGRAM ADDS RECORDS TO DATA FILE INVENTR1.DAT
1006 '********************************************************************
1010 'RESPONSE$                  - USER'S RESPONSE (y/n)
1020 'NO.RECORDS1$,NO.RECORDS%   - NUMBER OF RECORDS IN THE FILE
1030 'STOCK.NO1$,STOCK.NO$       - STOCK NUMBER
1040 'ITEM1$,ITEM$               - ITEM IN STOCK
1050 'QTY1$,QTY                  - QUANTITY
1060 'NO.ITEMS.ADDED             - NUMBER OF ITEMS ADDED TO THE FILE
1070 'RECORD.NUM                 - RECORD NUMBER AND CONTROL VARIABLE
1080 'S$                         - EQUAL SIGNS
1090 'F$                         - IMAGE OF A DETAIL LINE
1100 'HEADING$                   - HEADING
```

```
2000 '***********************************************************************
2002 '                              MAIN ROUTINE
2004 '***********************************************************************
2010  CLS
2020  LOCATE 12
2030  PRINT TAB (12)"This program allows you to add items to the inventory file"
2040  INPUT "___________Do you wish to continue (y/n)";RESPONSE$
2050  IF RESPONSE$ <> "y" AND RESPONSE$ <> "Y" AND RESPONSE$ <> "n" AND
         RESPONSE$ <> "N" THEN PRINT : PRINT "Invalid response. Enter y or n."
         : PRINT : GOTO 2040
2060  IF RESPONSE$ = "n" OR RESPONSE$ = "N" THEN END
2070  OPEN "B:INVENTR1.DAT" AS #1 LEN = 29
2080  FIELD #1, 2 AS NO.RECORDS1$
2090  FIELD #1, 5 AS STOCK.NO1$, 20 AS ITEM1$, 4 AS QTY1$
2100  GOSUB 3000                   'Retrieve number of last record
2110  GOSUB 4000                   'INPUT and add records
2120  CLS
2130  LOCATE 12
2140  PRINT TAB(15) "The additional items have been added. Do you wish to"
2150  INPUT "_______________see the contents of the inventory file (y/n)";
      RESPONSE$
2160  IF RESPONSE$ <> "y" AND RESPONSE$ <> "Y" AND RESPONSE$ <> "n" AND
         RESPONSE$ <> "N" THEN PRINT : PRINT "Invalid response. Enter y or n."
         : PRINT : GOTO 2140
2170  IF RESPONSE$ = "y" OR RESPONSE$ = "Y" THEN GOSUB 23000  'Read data file
2180  CLOSE #1
2190  END
3000 '***********************************************************************
3002 '         RETRIEVE NUMBER OF LAST RECORD IN DATA FILE INVENTR1.DAT
3004 '***********************************************************************
3010  GET #1,1
3020  NO.RECORDS% = CVI(NO.RECORDS1$)
3030  RETURN
4000 '***********************************************************************
4002 '      INPUT ADDITIONAL RECORDS AND WRITE TO DATA FILE INVENTR1.DAT
4004 '***********************************************************************
4010  CLS
4020  LOCATE 2
4030  INPUT "_______________Number of items to add to the inventory file";
      NO.ITEMS.ADDED
4040  PRINT
4050  INPUT "Is the number correct (y/n)";RESPONSE$
4060  IF RESPONSE$ <> "y" AND RESPONSE$ <> "Y"
         THEN INPUT "Re-enter the number of items--",NO.ITEMS.ADDED : GOTO 4050
4070  PRINT
4080  PRINT TAB(16) "Enter the stock number, description, and quantity"
4090  PRINT TAB(16) "separated by commas"
4100  FOR RECORD.NUM = NO.RECORDS%+1 TO NO.RECORDS%+NO.ITEMS.ADDED
4110    PRINT
4120    INPUT "_______________Stock number,item,quantity";STOCK.NO$,ITEM$,QTY
4130    PRINT
4140    INPUT "Are the entries correct (y/n)";RESPONSE$
4150    IF RESPONSE$ <> "y" AND RESPONSE$ <> "Y"
           THEN INPUT "Re-enter the stock number, item, quantity--",
           STOCK.NO$,ITEM$,QTY : GOTO 4140
4160    LSET STOCK.NO1$ = STOCK.NO$
4170    LSET ITEM1$ = ITEM$
4180    RSET QTY1$ = MKS$(QTY)
4190    PUT #1,RECORD.NUM
4200  NEXT RECORD.NUM
4210  NO.RECORDS% = LOC(1)
4220  RSET NO.RECORDS1$ = MKI$(NO.RECORDS%)
4230  PUT #1,1
4240  RETURN
```

```
5000 '**********************************************************************
5002 '                      FORMAT REPORT AND PRINT HEADINGS
5004 '**********************************************************************
5010  CLS
5020  LOCATE 8
5030  S$ = STRING$(47,"=")
5040  F$ = "________________________\__\______________\_____________##"
5050  HEADING$ = "PHYSICAL INVENTORY"
5060  PRINT TAB((80-LEN(HEADING$))/2+.5); HEADING$
5070  PRINT TAB(17) S$
5080  PRINT TAB(17) "STOCK NUMBER"; TAB(37) "DESCRIPTION"; TAB(56) "QUANTITY"
5090  PRINT TAB(17) S$
5100  RETURN
23000 '**********************************************************************
23002 '                         READ AND PRINT DATA FILE
23004 '**********************************************************************
23010  GOSUB 5000                'Format report and print headings
23020  FOR RECORD.NUM = 2 TO NO.RECORDS%
23030    GET #1,RECORD.NUM
23040    PRINT USING F$; STOCK.NO1$,ITEM1$,CVS(QTY1$)
23050  NEXT RECORD.NUM
23060  RETURN
65529 'End of program listing
RUN
```

(cleared screen)

```
         10        20        30        40        50        60        70        80
12345678901234567890123456789012345678901234567890123456789012345678901234567890
```

```
          This program allows you to add items to the inventory file
          Do you wish to continue (y/n)? y

(cleared screen)
              Number of items to add to the inventory file? 2

Is the number correct (y/n)? y

              Enter the stock number, description, and quantity
              separated by commas
```

After you key in the two additional records, the computer displays:

```
(cleared screen)
          The additional items have been added. Do you wish to
          see the contents of the inventory file (y/n)? y

(cleared screen)
                          PHYSICAL INVENTORY
                ===============================================
                STOCK NUMBER        DESCRIPTION        QUANTITY
                ===============================================
                   100R9        Ribbons                      8
                   101D5        Diskettes (5 1/4")           9
                   102D3        Diskettes (3 1/2")          10
                   103P7        Printer Paper (Box)          4
                   104Q8        Pens                         6
                   105Q7        Pencils                     18
```

Before the records are added to data file INVENTR1.DAT, we retrieve, from the header record, the value representing the number of records in the file, convert the number from a two-byte string to an integer and assign the integer to NO.RECORDS%. This is performed in Subroutine 3000.

We also modified Subroutine INPUT RECORDS listed on page 424 in the following manner:

1. We changed the INPUT statement that asks for the number of items (line 4030).
2. In the FOR statement (line 4100), we changed the initial value to NO.RECORDS%+1 and the test value to NO.RECORDS%+NO.ITEMS.ADDED. Since our data file contains five records, the first record added to the file must be numbered 6. Therefore, the initial value in the FOR statement must be 6. NO.RECORDS% holds the number 5, thus, NO.RECORDS%+1 = 5+1 = 6. The second and last record added to the file must be numbered 7 which means that the test value must be 7. Since NO.ITEMS.ADDED = 2, NO.RECORDS%+NO.ITEMS.ADDED = 5+2 = 7.

The last record in the file is now numbered 7. This new number must replace the number 5 currently stored in the header record. The process of obtaining the number 7 by the LOC function and moving the number into the header record is performed by the same routine coded in lines 3210 to 3230 on page 424. In the above program, the statements can be found in lines 4210 to 4230. In Subroutine READ AND PRINT DATA FILE, the test value is 7 since the value of NO.RECORDS% is now 7, obtained by the LOC function in line 4210.

15.5 Retrieving a Record

Recall that the GET statement retrieves a record from a random access file and places the record in the buffer communicating with the file. The statement requires the number of the file and the number of the record. For example, in the statement **xxxx GET 1,4**, #1 is the file number, 4 is the record number. The file number is the number assigned to the file in the OPEN statement. Determining the record number poses more of a problem. If we knew where each record were stored, we would simply use a record's location in the file as the record number. For example, if Smith,John were the 215th record in the file, we would use 215 as the record number in the GET statement to retrieve this record.

Knowing the number of each record in a file is unrealistic, particularly when the number of records is large. Instead, we let BASIC compute the record number. We use one of the fields in the record as the base. The values of the chosen field must vary in a uniform manner among the records. In data file INVENTR1.DAT, we would use the stock number field as the base since the first three digits of the stock numbers increase by one from one stock number to the next; **100R9, 101D5, 102D3**. The same formula would be used on any desired record. Choosing the field and the formula would be the subject of much study. The examples in this chapter are very simple. The primary purpose here is to illustrate random access techniques.

The following program allows a user to retrieve one or several records from data file INVENTR1.DAT. Let us first examine the program, then discuss how a record is retrieved.

```
1000 'RETRIEVE A RECORD                    M. MCRITCHIE                    JAN 9
1002 '***********************************************************************
1004 '      THIS PROGRAM RETRIEVES A RECORD FROM RANDOM ACCESS FILE
1006 '      INVENTR1.DAT AND PRINTS THE ITEM'S DESCRIPTION AND QUANTITY
1008 '***********************************************************************
1010 'RESPONSE$                  - USER'S RESPONSE (y/n)
1020 'NO.RECORDS1$,NO.RECORDS%   - NUMBER OF RECORDS IN THE FILE
1030 'STOCK.NO1$,STOCK.NO$       - STOCK NUMBER
1040 'ITEM1$                     - ITEM IN STOCK
1050 'QTY1$                      - QUANTITY
1060 'RECORD.NUM                 - RECORD NUMBER
2000 '***********************************************************************
2002 '                          MAIN ROUTINE
2004 '***********************************************************************
2010  CLS
2020  LOCATE 12
2030  PRINT TAB(8) "This program retrieves a desired item from data file INVENTR
1.DAT"
2040  INPUT "_______Do you wish to continue (y/n)";RESPONSE$
2050  IF RESPONSE$ <> "y" AND RESPONSE$ <> "Y" AND RESPONSE$ <> "n" AND
        RESPONSE$ <> "N" THEN PRINT : PRINT "Invalid response. Enter y or n."
        : PRINT : GOTO 2040
2060  IF RESPONSE$ = "n" OR RESPONSE$ = "N" THEN END
2070  OPEN "B:INVENTR1.DAT" AS #1 LEN = 29
2080  FIELD #1, 2 AS NO.RECORDS1$
2090  FIELD #1, 5 AS STOCK.NO1$, 20 AS ITEM1$, 4 AS QTY1$
```

```
2100  GOSUB 3000                  'Retrieve number of last record
2110  WHILE RESPONSE$ = "y" OR RESPONSE$ = "Y"
2120    GOSUB 4000                'Retrieve record
2130    GOSUB 11000               'Freeze display
2140    CLS
2150    LOCATE 12
2160    INPUT "_________________Do you wish to retrieve another item (y/n)";
        RESPONSE$
2170    IF RESPONSE$ <> "y" AND RESPONSE$ <> "Y" AND RESPONSE$ <> "n" AND
           RESPONSE$ <> "N" THEN PRINT:PRINT "Invalid response. Enter y or n."
           : PRINT : GOTO 2160
2180  WEND
2190  CLOSE #1
2200  END
3000 '*******************************************************************
3002 '          RETRIEVE NUMBER OF LAST RECORD IN DATA FILE INVENTR1.DAT
3004 '*******************************************************************
3010  GET #1,1
3020  NO.RECORDS% = CVI(NO.RECORDS1$)
3030  RETURN
4000 '*******************************************************************
4002 '                              RETRIEVE RECORD
4004 '*******************************************************************
4010  CLS
4020  LOCATE 7
4030  INPUT "______________________________Stock number";STOCK.NO$
4040  PRINT
4050  INPUT "Is the stock number correct (y/n)";RESPONSE$
4060  IF RESPONSE$ <> "y" AND RESPONSE$ <> "Y"
         THEN INPUT "Re-enter the stock number--",STOCK.NO$ : GOTO 4050
4070  RECORD.NUM = VAL(LEFT$(STOCK.NO$,3)) - 98
4080  IF RECORD.NUM < 2 OR RECORD.NUM > NO.RECORDS% THEN PRINT : PRINT TAB(26)
        "Stock number ";STOCK.NO$;" is invalid" : PRINT :
         INPUT "Re-enter the stock number--",STOCK.NO$ : GOTO 4050
4090  GET #1,RECORD.NUM
4100  IF STOCK.NO1$ <> STOCK.NO$
         THEN PRINT : PRINT TAB(27) "Stock number ";STOCK.NO$;" not found" :
         RETURN
4110  PRINT
4120  PRINT TAB(31) USING "Item:_____\________________\";ITEM1$
4130  PRINT TAB(31) USING "Quantity: ##";CVS(QTY1$)
4140  RETURN
65529 'End of program listing
RUN
```

(cleared screen)

```
         10        20        30        40        50        60        70        80
12345678901234567890123456789012345678901234567890123456789012345678901234567890

      This program retrieves a desired item from data file INVENTR1.DAT
      Do you wish to continue (y/n)? [y]
```

(cleared screen)

```
                              Stock number? [103P7]

Is the stock number correct (y/n)? [y]

                              Item:     Printer Paper (Box)
                              Quantity:  4

Press any key to continue
```

(cleared screen)

```
                 Do you wish to retrieve another item (y/n)?
```

We use the keyed-in stock number to find a record. The INPUT statement in line 4030 allows the user to type in the stock number of the item desired. In line 4070, BASIC computes the record number using the keyed-in stock number as the base. This record number, called the key or pointer, is the location where the desired item is stored in the data file. Let us use stock number 100R9, our first data record, as an example. The records are listed on page 429. The expression in line 4070 is evaluated as follows:

```
RECORD.NUM = VAL(LEFT$(STOCK.NO$,3)) - 98
           = VAL(LEFT$(100R9,3)) - 98
           = VAL(100) - 98
           = 100 - 98
           = 2
```

Thus, the record with a stock number field of 100R9 is record number two in data file INVENTR1.DAT. Remember, the first record in the file is our header record. Stock number 103P7, in the output on page 431, is record number five.

```
RECORD.NUM = VAL(LEFT$(STOCK.NO$,3)) - 98
           = VAL(LEFT$(103P7,3)) - 98
           = VAL(103) - 98
           = 103 - 98
           = 5
```

Line 4080 checks the calculated record number to determine whether or not it lies within the range 2 to 5. The number 5, which represents the number of records in the file, was retrieved from the header record and assigned to NO.RECORDS% in Subroutine 3000. If the record number just calculated is less than 2 or greater than NO.RECORDS%, an invalid stock number has been keyed in and line 4080 displays **Stock number xxxxx is invalid** where xxxxx is the keyed-in stock number. The statement also gives the user the opportunity to re-enter the stock number. When a valid stock number is entered, the GET statement in line 4090 retrieves the desired record.

Because of the manner in which our stock is numbered, the stock number requires a second check. The first three characters of a stock number yield the record number (the pointer). The last two characters have no relationship with the pointer. For instance, stock number 103P7, which is stored in the file, and stock number 103P8, which is not, yield the same record number. If a user keys in 103P8, the GET statement would retrieve the record with stock number 103P7. The stock numbers are compared in line 4100. If the stock number keyed in is not the same as the stock number on the retrieved record, line 4100 displays **Stock number xxxxx not found** where xxxxx is the keyed-in stock number. If the numbers are the same, lines 4120 and 4130 display the description of the item and the quantity on hand.

It is important to realize that a pointer must be checked to determine whether or not it lies within a required range. However, comparing the field in the record with the keyed-in item is not always necessary. Suppose our stock numbers were numbered 100 to 103. Since no other characters follow the three digits of each stock number, no comparison is necessary. (A different formula would be required to calculate the pointer).

One last comment. Note that we use PRINT TAB rather than PRINT USING in lines 4080 and 4100. With the TAB function, the keyed-in stock number will fit exactly between the printed comments regardless of its size.

15.6 Deleting Records from a File

The following program allows a user to delete one or more records from a random access file. The program keeps the original file intact by transferring records from the original file to a new file and deleting records from the new file. The original file serves as an archives or backup file.

```
1000 'DELETE RECORDS                    M. MCRITCHIE                    JAN 12
1002 '************************************************************************
1004 '           THIS PROGRAM DELETES RECORDS FROM AN INVENTORY FILE
1006 '************************************************************************
1010 'RESPONSE$                - USER'S RESPONSE (y/n)
1020 'NO.RECORDS1$,NO.RECORDS2$,NO.RECORDS%
1030 '                          - NUMBER OF RECORDS IN A FILE
1040 'STOCK.NO1$,STOCK.NO2$,STOCK.NO$
1050 '                          - STOCK NUMBER
```

```
1060 'ITEM1$,ITEM2$              - ITEM IN STOCK
1070 'QTY1$,QTY2$                - QUANTITY
1080 'RECORD.NUM                 - RECORD NUMBER AND CONTROL VARIABLE
1090 'S$                         - EQUAL SIGNS
1100 'F1$                        - IMAGE OF A RECORD IN THE REPORT
1110 'F2$                        - IMAGE OF A "DELETED" RECORD IN THE REPORT
1120 'HEADING$                   - HEADING
2000 '*******************************************************************
2002 '                           MAIN ROUTINE
2004 '*******************************************************************
2010  CLS
2020  LOCATE 12
2030  PRINT TAB(9) "This program allows you to delete items from the inventory f
ile"
2040  INPUT "________Do you wish to continue (y/n)";RESPONSE$
2050  IF RESPONSE$ <> "y" AND RESPONSE$ <> "Y" AND RESPONSE$ <> "n" AND
        RESPONSE$ <> "N" THEN PRINT : PRINT "Invalid response. Enter y or n."
        : PRINT : GOTO 2040
2060  IF RESPONSE$ = "n" OR RESPONSE$ = "N" THEN END
2070  OPEN "B:INVENTR1.DAT" AS #1 LEN = 29
2080  FIELD #1, 2 AS NO.RECORDS1$
2090  FIELD #1, 5 AS STOCK.NO1$, 20 AS ITEM1$, 4 AS QTY1$
2100  OPEN "B:INVENTR2.DAT" AS #2 LEN = 29
2110  FIELD #2, 2 AS NO.RECORDS2$
2120  FIELD #2, 5 AS STOCK.NO2$, 20 AS ITEM2$, 4 AS QTY2$
2130  GOSUB 3000             'Retrieve number of last record
2140  GOSUB 24000            'Transfer records from original file to new file
2150  WHILE RESPONSE$ = "y" OR RESPONSE$ = "Y"
2160    GOSUB 4000           'INPUT key and delete record
2170    GOSUB 11000          'Freeze display
2180    CLS
2190    LOCATE 12
2200    INPUT "_______________Do you wish to delete another item (y/n)";
        RESPONSE$
2210    IF RESPONSE$ <> "y" AND RESPONSE$ <> "Y" AND RESPONSE$ <> "n" AND
          RESPONSE$ <> "N" THEN PRINT:PRINT "Invalid response. Enter y or n."
          : PRINT : GOTO 2200
2220  WEND
2230  CLS
2240  LOCATE 12
2250  INPUT "____________Do you wish to see the contents of the new file (y/n)";
      RESPONSE$
2260  IF RESPONSE$ <> "y" AND RESPONSE$ <> "Y" AND RESPONSE$ <> "n" AND
        RESPONSE$ <> "N" THEN PRINT : PRINT "Invalid response. Enter y or n."
        : PRINT: GOTO 2250
2270  IF RESPONSE$ = "y" OR RESPONSE$ = "Y" THEN GOSUB 23000  'Read new file
2280  CLOSE #1,#2
2290  END
3000 '*******************************************************************
3002 '          RETRIEVE NUMBER OF LAST RECORD IN DATA FILE INVENTR1.DAT
3004 '*******************************************************************
3010  GET #1,1
3020  NO.RECORDS% = CVI(NO.RECORDS1$)
3030  RETURN
4000 '*******************************************************************
4002 '                    INPUT KEY AND DELETE RECORD
4004 '*******************************************************************
4010  CLS
4020  LOCATE 8
4030  INPUT "____________________Stock number of the item to delete";STOCK.NO$
4040  PRINT
4050  INPUT "Is the stock number correct (y/n)";RESPONSE$
4060  IF RESPONSE$ <> "y" AND RESPONSE$ <> "Y"
        THEN INPUT "Re-enter the stock number--",STOCK.NO$ : GOTO 4050
4070  RECORD.NUM = VAL(LEFT$(STOCK.NO$,3)) - 98
4080  IF RECORD.NUM < 2 OR RECORD.NUM > NO.RECORDS% THEN PRINT : PRINT TAB(26)
        "Stock number ";STOCK.NO$;" is invalid" : PRINT :
        INPUT "Re-enter the stock number--",STOCK.NO$ : GOTO 4050
```

```
4090  GET #2,RECORD.NUM
4100  IF STOCK.NO2$ <> STOCK.NO$
         THEN PRINT : PRINT TAB(27) "Stock number ";STOCK.NO$;" not found" :
         RETURN
4110  PRINT
4120  PRINT TAB(20) STOCK.NO2$;"  ";ITEM2$;"  ";CVS(QTY2$)
4130  PRINT
4140  INPUT "______________________Delete above item (y/n)";RESPONSE$
4150  IF RESPONSE$ <> "y" AND RESPONSE$ <> "Y" AND RESPONSE$ <> "n" AND
         RESPONSE$ <> "N" THEN PRINT : PRINT "Invalid response. Enter y or n."
         : PRINT : GOTO 4140
4160  IF RESPONSE$ = "n" OR RESPONSE$ = "N" THEN PRINT TAB(20)
         "Deletion aborted" : RETURN
4170  LSET STOCK.NO2$ = ""
4180  LSET ITEM2$ = ""
4190  LSET QTY2$ = ""
4200  PUT #2,RECORD.NUM
4210  RETURN
5000 '************************************************************************
5002 '                          FORMAT REPORT AND PRINT HEADINGS
5004 '************************************************************************
5010  CLS
5020  LOCATE 8
5030  S$ = STRING$(47,"=")
5040  F1$ = "__________________\___\_________\_________________\_______##"
5050  F2$ = "__________________\___\_________\_________________\_______\__\"
5060  HEADING$ = "PHYSICAL INVENTORY"
5070  PRINT TAB((80-LEN(HEADING$))/2+.5); HEADING$
5080  PRINT TAB(17) S$
5090  PRINT TAB(17) "STOCK NUMBER"; TAB(37) "DESCRIPTION"; TAB(56) "QUANTITY"
5100  PRINT TAB(17) S$
5110  RETURN
23000 '************************************************************************
23002 '                            READ AND PRINT NEW DATA FILE
23004 '************************************************************************
23010  GOSUB 5000          'Format report and print headings
23020  FOR RECORD.NUM = 2 TO NO.RECORDS%
23030    GET #2,RECORD.NUM
23040    IF STOCK.NO2$ <> "_____"
            THEN PRINT USING F1$; STOCK.NO2$,ITEM2$,CVS(QTY2$)
            ELSE PRINT USING F2$; STOCK.NO2$,ITEM2$,QTY2$
23050  NEXT RECORD.NUM
23060  RETURN
24000 '************************************************************************
24002 '                  TRANSFER RECORDS FROM ORIGINAL FILE TO NEW FILE
24004 '************************************************************************
24010  RSET NO.RECORDS2$ = MKI$(NO.RECORDS%)
24020  PUT #2,1
24030  FOR RECORD.NUM = 2 TO NO.RECORDS%
24040    GET #1,RECORD.NUM
24050    LSET STOCK.NO2$ = STOCK.NO1$
24060    LSET ITEM2$ = ITEM1$
24070    RSET QTY2$ = QTY1$
24080    PUT #2,RECORD.NUM
24090  NEXT RECORD.NUM
24100  RETURN
65529 'End of program listing
RUN
```

```
                                                                  (cleared screen)
         10        20        30        40        50        60        70        80
12345678901234567890123456789012345678901234567890123456789012345678901234567890

          This program allows you to delete items from the inventory file
          Do you wish to continue (y/n)? [y]
                                                                  (cleared screen)
                    Stock number of the item to delete? [101D5]

Is the stock number correct (y/n)? [y]

                    101D5  Diskettes (5 1/4")      9

                    Delete above item (y/n)? [y]

Press any key to continue
                                                                  (cleared screen)
                    Do you wish to delete another item (y/n)? [n]
                                                                  (cleared screen)
               Do you wish to see the contents of the new file (y/n)? [y]
                                                                  (cleared screen)
                              PHYSICAL INVENTORY
                 =========================================
                 STOCK NUMBER       DESCRIPTION       QUANTITY
                 =========================================
                    100R9           Ribbons               8

                    102D3           Diskettes (3 1/2")   10
                    103P7           Printer Paper (Box)   4
                    104Q8           Pens                  6
                    105Q7           Pencils              18
```

Note that the second record has been deleted by replacing each of its fields with spaces. Some business firms prefer to retain one of the fields and to delete the remaining fields. You will be performing this type of delete in one of the programming problems.

Since the program creates a new file, we need two OPEN statements. One statement opens the original file and the other opens the new file. We named our new file INVENTR2.DAT. The OPEN statements set aside two buffers to provide access to the files. Each buffer is structured two ways: one structure for the header record, the other structure for a data record. Thus, two FIELD statements are required to structure each buffer.

The first OPEN statement opens data file INVENTR1.DAT which will be identified as file #1 in subsequent file handling statements. The second OPEN statement opens data file INVENTR2.DAT which will be identified as file #2. We differentiate the variables between the two buffers by inserting different digits in the variable names. Remember, we use a digit in a buffer variable to identify the file associated with the buffer. Buffer variables for file INVENTR1.DAT contain the digit 1 as in ITEM1$, buffer variables for file INVENTR2.DAT contain the digit 2 as in ITEM2$.

First, we retrieve the value representing the number of records in data file INVENTR1.DAT from the file's header record. This is performed in Subroutine 3000. Since we wish to keep our original file intact, we transfer all of its records to file INVENTR2.DAT. The records are transferred in Subroutine 24000. This subroutine must be called before we delete any records, therefore, we place the GOSUB statement before the WHILE/WEND loop in the main routine.

The first two statements in Subroutine 24000 place the value representing the number of records in file INVENTR1.DAT in the header record of file INVENTR2.DAT. In a FOR/NEXT loop, we GET a record from our original file, place each of its fields in the new file's buffer and send the buffer's contents to file INVENTR2.DAT. After all the records from the original file have been moved to the new file, a record can be deleted.

Subroutine 4000 allows the user to enter the stock number of the record to be deleted and deletes this record from the new file. The process of calculating the pointer, checking its validity, GETing the record, and comparing stock numbers is the same as in the routine on page 431. Notice that we GET the record from the new file. Line 4120 displays the record to be deleted and line 4140 asks the user to confirm its deletion. It is a good idea to display a record and confirm its deletion before the record is deleted. If the user decides not to delete the record, the program displays **Deletion aborted**. If the user decides to delete the record, statements 4170 to 4190 assign null strings to the buffer variables of the new file. Each buffer variable now holds spaces, the number of spaces depending on the variable's field length. Since five bytes were allotted to STOCK.NO2$, five spaces are stored in STOCK.NO2$. Similarly, 20 spaces are stored in ITEM2$ and four spaces are stored in QTY2$. In line 4200, the "blanked-out" record is sent to file INVENTR2.DAT.

A record in the new file will consist of a stock number, a description, and a quantity or it will be "blanked out" with spaces. Thus, the field for the quantity contains either a number or four spaces. If the quantity field contains a number, the number must be converted from string form to numeric form before it can be printed (refer to the THEN part of line 23040) and the edit field in the image must be numeric. If the quantity field contains spaces, no conversion takes place in line 23040 and the edit field in the image must be type string. Therefore, we need two images in Subroutine FORMAT REPORT AND PRINT HEADINGS (lines 5040 and 5050.)

In Subroutine READ AND PRINT NEW DATA FILE, we must check the record for spaces. We do this by examining one of its fields. We chose the stock number field. Note that we check for five spaces and not for the null string. (The size of the field is five bytes.) If the stock number field does not contain spaces, we print the record using the image stored in F1$ where the edit field for the quantity is numeric. If the stock number field contains spaces, we print the "blanked out" record using the image stored in F2$ where the edit field for the quantity is type string.

15.7 Updating a Random Access File

Updating a random access file means changing one or several records in the file. The desired record must be retrieved, one or more of its fields changed, and the record moved back to its original position in the file.

Suppose we wish to change the quantity of the stock numbered 102D3. The record is stored in file INVENTR1.DAT. The FIELD statement for this file is as follows:

```
2090 FIELD #1, 5 AS STOCK.NO1$, 20 AS ITEM1$, 4 AS QTY1$
```

We would like to change the quantity from 10 to 5. Assume we have entered the new quantity in variable QTY. After the record is retrieved from the file, the buffer will look as follows:

```
102D3Diskettes (3 1/2")      10
```

The following statement changes the quantity in the buffer.

```
xxxx RSET QTY1$ = MKS$(QTY)
```

The contents of the buffer will now be:

```
102D3Diskettes (3 1/2")       5
```

We PUT this record back to its original position by using the same file number and record number in the PUT statement that we used in the GET statement. If another record must be updated, we GET this record, change one or more of its fields and move the record back to its original position in the data file.

Updating a data file is left as a programming problem at the end of this chapter.

Summary of BASIC Statements

FIELD Organizes a random file buffer by defining fields in the buffer.

```
2090 FIELD #1, 5 AS STOCK.NO1$, 20 AS ITEM1$, 4 AS QTY1$
```

GET #n,r — Reads a record from a random access file and places the record in the random file buffer. The symbol n represents a file number, r represents a record number.

```
23030 GET #1,RECORD.NUM
```

LSET — Moves a value, in string form, from a program variable into a buffer variable. The string is left-justified in its field.

```
3120 LSET STOCK.NO1$ = STOCK.NO$
```

OPEN — Opens a data file by creating a communication link between the file and the program.

```
2070 OPEN "B:INVENTR1.DAT" AS #1 LEN = 29
```

PUT #n,r — Moves the contents of a random file buffer to a random access file. The symbol n represents a file number, r represents a record number.

```
3150 PUT #1,RECORD.NUM
```

RSET — Moves a value (usually a number converted to string form) from a program variable into a buffer variable. The string is right-justified in its field.

```
3140 RSET QTY1$ = MKS$(QTY)
```

Summary of BASIC Functions

CVI(S$),CVS(S$),CVD(S$) — Converts a value stored in a random file buffer from string form to numeric form. CVI converts a 2-byte string to an integer, CVS converts a 4-byte string to a single-precision number, CVD converts an 8-byte string to a double-precision number.

```
23040 PRINT STOCK.NO1$,ITEM1$,CVS(QTY1$)
```

LOC(n) — Returns the number of the last record referenced in a random access file. Argument n represents a file number.

```
3170 NO.RECORDS% = LOC(1)
```

MKI$(N),MKS$(N),MKD$(N) — Converts a numeric value to be moved into a random file buffer to string form. MKI$ converts an integer to a string of 2 bytes, MKS$ converts a single-precision number to a string of 4 bytes, MKD$ converts a double-precision number to a string of 8 bytes.

```
3180 RSET NO.RECORDS1$ = MKI$(NO.RECORDS%)
```

Summary of Library Files

READ-RA.BAS — A program that reads and prints the contents of a random access file.

Chapter Summary

1. To provide access to a data file, the computer sets aside within its memory an area called a buffer. Each data file has its own buffer.
2. In a sequential file, data is stored and retrieved sequentially. In a random access file, data can be stored and retrieved in any order.
3. Programs using random access files give the programmer control over the structure of the buffer and over the transfer of data between the buffer and the data file.
4. The OPEN statement that opens a random access file must specify the drive, the name of the file, the file number, and the record length.
5. If a random access file does not exist, OPEN creates a new file; if the file does exist, OPEN opens the file for a read.
6. Values in a buffer are stored in string variables referred to as buffer variables.
7. A specific number of bytes must be allocated to each field of a random access buffer.
8. A number must be stored in the buffer as a string.
9. The length of a record in a sequential file varies, the length of a record in a random access file is fixed.
10. Values written to a random access file are first moved from program variables to buffer variables, then moved from the buffer (as a record) to the data file. The variable from which a value is sent is called the transmitting field, the variable to which the value is sent is called the receiving field.
11. The number of characters moved to a field in the buffer is governed by the length of the receiving field. If the receiving field is shorter than the transmitting field, excess characters are ignored. If the receiving field is longer, spaces fill the extra positions.
12. A record stored in a data file is referenced by its position in the file; that is, by its record number.
13. The LOC function returns the number of the last record referenced in a random access file. When the last record referenced is the last record in the file, the value represents the number of records in the file.
14. The value representing the number of records in a random access file should be saved as the first record in the file. This record is referred to as the header record.
15. The remaining records in the file are called data records. Since the data records follow the header record, they are considered records 2, 3, 4, etc.
16. When a data file contains a header record, two FIELD statements must structure the same buffer: a FIELD statement for the header record and a FIELD statement for a data record.
17. After a numeric value has been moved from a data file to the buffer, the value must be converted from string form to numeric form before it can be used.
18. Data retrieved from a data file can be used directly from the buffer. Values need not be assigned to program variables unless, for example, values must be stored in one or several arrays.
19. To add records to a random access file, the program must first retrieve, from the header record, the number of the last record in the file. The number is then used to position the appended records.
20. After records have been added to a data file, the LOC function should be used to obtain the number of records now in the file. The new number must replace the one currently residing in the header record.
21. To retrieve a specific record from a random access file, BASIC must know the location of the record in the file. To obtain the location; that is, the record number referred to as the key or pointer, a formula is used on one of the fields of the record. The formula used depends on the contents of the chosen field.

22. The pointer must be checked for validity to ensure that it lies within the range of record numbers.
23. When one or more records must be deleted from a random access file, the original file should be kept intact by transferring its records to a new file. A record can then be deleted from the new file by placing null strings in each of its fields.

Programming Problems

Write programs for the following problems. Display the purpose of each program and allow the user early exit from the program. Prompts are given for the first two problems. Use them as guides for the remaining problems. The first five problems apply to an academic environment. Save all programs. Most produce data files that are needed in subsequent programs.

Devise formulas to retrieve desired records. The formulas to be used are relatively simple. Use the student ID as the base in Problems 2 through 5, the account number in Problem 7, and the stock number in Problem 8. You may wish to save (in ASCII format) often-used modules. For example, you could save the subroutine that reads and prints a data file and the subroutine that formats the output and prints the headings required by the programs written for Problems 1 through 5. The modules may need customizing in some programs. Suggested filenames: READS.ASC and FORMAT.ASC.

1. Use the program on page 423 as a guide to create a student file. Name your file STDENTS1.DAT. Each data record contains the following fields:

ID	A 4-digit single-precision number
Name	Maximum 15 characters
Address	Maximum 15 characters
Telephone number	8 characters
A flag	1 character (type string)

Data is given in the report shown on page 440. The field for the flag will eventually hold an asterisk for a student who has withdrawn. In this program, simply move a space into the field.

```
                                                        (cleared screen)
              This program allows you to create a student file
              Do you wish to continue (y/n)? y

                                                        (cleared screen)
                         Number of students? 4

Is the number correct (y/n)? y

           Enter a student's ID, name, address and telephone number
           separated by commas. To enter a name, type the last name
           and first name separated by a comma. Enclose both names
           in quotation marks.

ID,name,address,telephone number? 1000,"Thorpe,James",984 Arundal St.,394-1827
Are the entries correct (y/n)? y
```

After three more records have been keyed in, your program should display:

```
                                                          (cleared screen)
          Writing is complete. Do you wish to see the contents
          of the student file (y/n)? [y]

                                                          (cleared screen)
                          STUDENT FILE
=========================================================
 ID           NAME                ADDRESS         TELEPHONE
=========================================================
1000     Thorpe,James        984 Arundal St.      394-1827
1001     Corbett,Donna       637 Haines Rd.       267-3912
1002     Hunt,Gary           153 Norquay St.      418-9431
1003     Matheson,Bryan      942 Oxford Ave.      589-2416
```

2. Suppose James Thorpe and Bryan Matheson have moved. Their new addresses and telephone numbers are as follows:

Thorpe,James	849 Oakview Bay	649-2642
Matheson,Bryan	834 River Ave.	913-4657

Update data file STDENTS1.DAT to reflect the changes. A partial output is given below. Verify the address and telephone number by the screenful.

```
                                                          (cleared screen)
          This program allows you to update a student file
          Do you wish to continue (y/n)? [y]

                 Enter the student's ID
                 Enter the new street address
                 Enter the new telephone number

Press any key to continue

                                                          (cleared screen)
                        Student's ID? [1000]

Is the ID correct (y/n)? [y]

                 New address? [849 Oakview Bay]
                 New telephone number? [649-2642]

The student's new address is 849 Oakview Bay
Is the address correct (y/n)? [y]

The student's new telephone number is 649-2642
Is the telephone number correct (y/n)? [y]

Press any key to continue

                                                          (cleared screen)
        Do you wish to update another student's record (y/n)? [y]
```

After the record for Matheson has been updated, your program should display:

```
                                                        (cleared screen)
   Do you wish to see the contents of the updated data file (y/n)? y

                                                        (cleared screen)
                               STUDENT FILE
       ================================================================
        ID          NAME                 ADDRESS              TELEPHONE
       ================================================================
       1000      Thorpe,James         849 Oakview Bay          649-2642
       1001      Corbett,Donna        637 Haines Rd.           267-3912
       1002      Hunt,Gary            153 Norquay St.          418-9431
       1003      Matheson,Bryan       834 River Ave.           913-4657
```

Although your program will be similar to Program DELETE RECORDS listed on page 432, there are two major differences. The original file must not be transferred to a new file and the retrieved record must be updated rather than deleted. Furthermore, since instructions are displayed stating what must be keyed in (see the output on page 440), your program must call a subroutine that produces this display.

Many of the statements in the subroutine that updates a record should be similar to those in Subroutine INPUT KEY AND DELETE RECORD on page 433. Determine the formula that calculates the pointer. Use the student ID as the base. Your formula should return a 2 for ID 1000, a 3 for ID 1001, etc. In this program, as well as in the programs written for problems 3, 4, and 5, there is no need to compare an ID in the record with the ID keyed in.

Following verification of the keyed-in ID and validation of the pointer, GET the desired record. Code statements that allow a user to key in the new address and telephone number. Move the new address and telephone number into the buffer and transfer the updated record from the buffer to your data file.

Your program must display the updated file on the screen if the user wishes to see the file.

3. Write a program that deletes data from student records for students who have withdrawn. Use the DELETE program on page 432 as a guide. Flag the records of withdrawn students using an asterisk to flag a record. Flag records only in the original file. Do not create a flag field in your new file. Although your current data file does not have any flagged records, assume some are already flagged. Save the original file by transferring each of its records (without the flag field) to a new file. Call the new file STDENTS2.DAT. For a student who has withdrawn, delete the name, the address, and the telephone number from the new file. Do not delete the ID. Should the user key in the ID of a former student, your program must inform the user that the student has already been withdrawn. A user must be able to examine both the original file and the new file. Write subroutines that read and print these files. Call the subroutines from the main routine.

In the subroutine that transfers records from the original file to the new file (the subroutine must be called before a student's data is deleted), move the number of the last record in the original file to the header record of the new file. In a FOR/NEXT loop, get a record from the original file and check the flag field for an asterisk. If the field contains an asterisk, call a subroutine that moves the ID from the original file to the new file's buffer and places spaces in the remaining fields of the buffer. Remember, the buffer of the new file does not have a flag field. This is the record of a student who has already been withdrawn. Move this record from the buffer to the new file. If the flag field does not contain an asterisk, call a subroutine that moves the record from the original file to the new file. Code each of these subroutines.

Code the subroutine that deletes a student's data from the new file. After an ID has been INPUTed, and verified, the pointer calculated and validated, GET the desired record from both the original file and the new file. Check the flag field of the original file. If the field contains an asterisk, display

```
Student already withdrawn
```

and return to the calling module. If the field contains no asterisk, display the record from the original file and the record from the new file and confirm the deletion. Sample output lines are given on page 442.

```
Record from original file: 1000   Thorpe,James      849 Oakview Bay  649-2642
Record from new file:      1000   Thorpe,James      849 Oakview Bay  649-2642

                        Withdraw student (y/n)?
```

If the response to the above prompt is "n", display "Deletion aborted" and return to the calling module. Otherwise, LSET an asterisk in the flag field of the original file's buffer and PUT the record to the original file. Remember, the other fields of the record are already in the buffer, you are merely changing the flag from a space to an asterisk. Delete the student's data from STDENTS2.DAT by placing null strings in the name, address, and telephone number fields of the file's buffer. Leave the ID field as is. PUT this record to STDENTS2.DAT.

In the subroutine that reads and prints the original file, assign the number 1 to a variable, say SWITCH. In the subroutine that reads and prints the new file, assign the number 2 to the same variable. The variable will be used in Subroutine FORMAT REPORT AND PRINT HEADINGS to determine which heading to print. (See the headings below.) Furthermore, you need two images: one to edit a detail line for the original file, the other to edit a detail line for the new file. Your image for an "original" detail line must reserve a position for an asterisk. Recall that an exclamation mark reserves one position.

Following the prompts, the reports may look as follows:

```
                                                            (cleared screen)
                     ORIGINAL STUDENT FILE
        ===================================================================
         ID         NAME                  ADDRESS              TELEPHONE
        ===================================================================
        1000    Thorpe,James          849 Oakview Bay        649-2642
        1001    Corbett,Donna         637 Haines Rd.         267-3912 *
        1002    Hunt,Gary             153 Norquay St.        418-9431
        1003    Matheson,Bryan        834 River Ave.         913-4657 *

Press any key to continue
                                                            (cleared screen)
                        NEW STUDENT FILE
        ===================================================================
         ID         NAME                  ADDRESS              TELEPHONE
        ===================================================================
        1000    Thorpe,James          849 Oakview Bay        649-2642
        1001
        1002    Hunt,Gary             153 Norquay St.        418-9431
        1003
```

4. The unassigned ID numbers left in a student file are usually assigned to new students when they register. A file of unassigned ID numbers may prove to be useful. The ideal time to create the file would be at the time students' data are deleted. A separate program can then print the list of unassigned ID numbers.

   Write two programs. One creates the ID file, the other prints it.

(a) To create the ID file, modify the program for Problem 3 as follows:

Open a third file to store the unassigned ID numbers. Call the new file ID.DAT. As with the other files' buffers, two FIELD statements are needed. One is needed for the header record and the other is needed for an ID number. Recall that the ID number is a single-precision number. You must, therefore, allocate four bytes to its field and, in the OPEN statement, set the record length parameter at four. Call Subroutine CREATE AN ID FILE immediately following the WHILE/WEND loop in the main routine.

In Subroutine CREATE AN ID FILE, initialize a variable, say NUM, to 1. NUM represents the number of a record storing an unassigned ID. Set up a FOR/NEXT loop. Inside the loop, GET a data record from file STDENTS2.DAT. Check the name field of the record just retrieved for spaces. If the field contains spaces, increase NUM by 1, move the ID from the buffer for file STDENTS2.DAT to the buffer for file ID.DAT and transfer the record to data file ID.DAT. NUM must be increased immediately so that the first unassigned ID will be stored in record 2 of ID.DAT. Perform no tasks if the name field contains a name. Following the FOR/NEXT loop, transfer the value stored in NUM to the header record of ID.DAT.

(b) Produce a hard copy of the unassigned ID numbers. A sample list is given below.

```
UNASSIGNED ID NUMBERS

        1001
        1003

  End of the ID list
```

Remember to retrieve, from the header record, the value representing the number of records in data file ID.DAT. Also, remind the user to turn on the printer. Subroutine FREEZE DISPLAY must be executed to give the user time to turn on the printer. Modify Subroutine FORMAT REPORT AND PRINT HEADINGS.

5. Write a program that assigns the above unassigned ID numbers to the following newly registered students. Store the records of the new students in data file STDENTS2.DAT.

Shaw, Andrea	261 Wilton Rd.	462-5817
Poole, Kevin	314 Henley Ave.	637-2189

A user must key in an unassigned ID number, the new student's name, address, and telephone number. Your program must allow the user to enter data for more than one student and must give the user the opportunity to examine the contents of the updated file. The contents of STDENTS2.DAT should now look as follows:

```
                          STUDENT FILE
=================================================================
 ID              NAME                    ADDRESS          TELEPHONE
=================================================================
1000     Thorpe,James           849 Oakview Bay         649-2642
1001     Shaw,Andrea            261 Wilton Rd.          462-5817
1002     Hunt,Gary              153 Norquay St.         418-9431
1003     Poole,Kevin            314 Henley Ave.         637-2189
```

Your program must consider the following keyed-in ID's:

— An invalid ID.

— An ID that is already assigned to a student.

— An ID that is unassigned.

Allow a user to type in an unassigned ID. Verify the ID, then calculate and validate the pointer. GET the record from file STDENTS2.DAT. Determine whether or not the name field contains spaces. If the field contains a name, display **ID number xxxx already assigned** where xxxx is an ID number. It is wise to perform this check just in case the user types in an ID that is already assigned. If this happens and no check is performed, the new data will overwrite the old. If the name field contains spaces, call a subroutine that assigns the ID to a new student.

In the subroutine that assigns an ID to a student, ask the user for the new student's name, address, and telephone number. Verify these three items of data by the screenful. Place the items in the buffer for file STDENTS2.DAT and move the record to the file.

6. The Accounts Receivable programs written in previous chapters read accounts from a sequential data file. In this problem, store accounts in a random access file. Write two programs: one program creates the Accounts Receivable file given at the top of page 444, and the second program sorts the accounts by account number. Name the unsorted data file ACC-REC1.DAT.

Account Number	Name	Address	Telephone	Date	Balance
303	Fisher,Karen	468 Greene St. Anycity ZZ M3L 9T4	342-1953	Jan. 14	$316.97
301	Erickson,Brent	194 Young St. Anycity ZZ M3L 5W8	334-2854	Jan. 6	426.32
304	Sinclair,Edward	285 Oakdale Rd. Mytown XX N6Y 2A4	839-4526	Jan. 18	249.54
302	Miller,Tonia	641 River Rd. Mytown XX N6Y 7E5	998-6731	Jan. 26	157.93

Consider the account number as a string. Enter the address as two parts: the street address as one part and the city/province/postal code as the second part. Suggested FIELD statement for a data record:

```
2090 FIELD #1, 3 AS ACCOUNT.NO1$, 15 AS NAME1$, 15 AS STREET1$,
     20 AS CITY.PROVINCE1$, 8 AS TELEPHONE1$, 8 AS DATE1$, 4 AS BALANCE1$
```

Your program that sorts the accounts must display the preliminary prompts, then produce the output given below on a cleared screen. The sorted accounts should be stored in a new data file, say ACC-REC2.DAT.

```
                         ACCOUNTS RECEIVABLE
=================================================================================
ACCOUNT      NAME                 ADDRESS               TELEPHONE    DATE     BALANCE
=================================================================================
  301    Erickson,Brent     194 Young St.              334-2854     Jan. 6    $426.32
                            Anycity  ZZ   M3L 5W8
  302    Miller,Tonia       641 River Rd.              998-6731     Jan. 26   $157.93
                            Mytown  XX   N6Y 7E5
  303    Fisher,Karen       468 Greene St.             342-1953     Jan. 14   $316.97
                            Anycity  ZZ   M3L 9T4
  304    Sinclair,Edward    285 Oakdale Rd.            839-4526     Jan. 18   $249.54
                            Mytown  XX   N6Y 2A4
```

From the main routine, call subroutines to perform the following:

(a) Retrieve the value representing the number of records in data file ACC-REC1.DAT. Assign the number to ARRAY.SIZE as well as to NO.RECORDS%. ARRAY.SIZE is needed in the subroutine that sorts.
(b) Read file ACC-REC1.DAT. Read the fields of each record into arrays and make a duplicate copy of the account number array as the records are being read. As with ARRAY.SIZE, the copy is needed in the subroutine that sorts.
(c) Sort the records by account number using Subroutine SELECTION SORT WITH POINTERS.
(d) Copy the sorted numbers from the local "out" array into your account number array. Use a FOR/NEXT loop.
(e) Write the sorted records to file ACC-REC2.DAT.
(f) Read and print the sorted records stored in file ACC-REC2.DAT only if the user wishes to see them. Call Subroutine FORMAT REPORT AND PRINT HEADINGS from this subroutine.

I the subroutine that writes the sorted records to file ACC-REC2.DAT, store the value representing the number of records in ACC-REC1.DAT in the header record of ACC-REC2.DAT. Inside a FOR/NEXT loop, move an account number, name, street, city/province/postal code, telephone number, date, and balance from their respective arrays to the buffer for file ACC-REC2.DAT. To move an account number, merely move its string from the account number array to the account number field in the buffer. Use the pointer obtained from the sort subroutine to move the remaining items from their arrays to the corresponding fields in the buffer. The following statements place an account number, a name, and a balance in the buffer for file ACC-REC2.DAT.

```
24040 LSET ACCOUNT.NO2$ = ACCOUNT.NO$(RECORD.NUM)
24050 LSET NAME2$ = CNAME$(P(RECORD.NUM))
24100 RSET BALANCE2$ = MKS$(BALANCE(P(RECORD.NUM)))
```

RECORD.NUM is the control variable of a FOR statement whose initial value is 2 and whose test value is NO.RECORDS%. After all items have been moved into the buffer, PUT the record to data file ACC-REC2.DAT.

7. Write a program that updates the Accounts Receivable file sorted for Problem 6. If you did not write the "sort" program, create data file ACC-REC2.DAT. Enter the records given on page 444 in ascending order by account number.

Produce an account similar to the Accounts Receivable account shown on page 314 in Chapter 12. It was suggested on page 331 that a hard copy of the program for Problem 6 be made. Use this copy as a guide since many of its statements will be used in your current program. An Accounts Receivable account is shown below.

```
Account number 301
*******************************************************************
* NAME: Erickson,Brent                                  TELEPHONE *
* ADDRESS: 194 Young St.      Anycity  ZZ  M3L 5W8      334-2854  *
*-----------------------------------------------------------------*
* DATE              ITEM              DEBIT      CREDIT    BALANCE  *
*-----------------------------------------------------------------*
* Jan. 6            Balance                                $426.32  *
* Jan. 21                             $152.16              $578.48  *
* Jan. 30                                        $300.00   $278.48  *
*                                                                 *
*                                                                 *
*                                                                 *
*                                                                 *
*                                                                 *
*******************************************************************
```

The Main Routine

After coding the preliminary prompts and opening data file ACC-REC2.DAT, perform the following:

(a) Call a subroutine that displays the instructions given below. The subroutine must inform the user that a code of 1 denotes a sale, a code of 2 denotes a payment.

(b) Call the subroutine that retrieves the value representing the number of records in the file.

(c) Inside a WHILE/WEND loop, call the subroutine that allows the user to key in the number of the account to be updated. Also, display a prompt that asks the user if another account is to be updated.

Preliminary prompts and instructions, which should be displayed on a cleared screen, could be as follows:

```
                  This program updates Accounts Receivable accounts
                  Do you wish to continue (y/n)? [y]

                  Enter a code of 1 if the transaction is a sale
                  Enter a code of 2 if the transaction is a payment


Press any key to continue
```

Subroutine INPUT KEY (ACCOUNT NUMBER)

Allow a user to key in the number of the account to be updated. Verify the account number and calculate the pointer. Hint: Your formula must convert the account number from string form to numeric form. Validate the pointer. Print an "invalid" message if the keyed-in account number is invalid. GET the desired record and call a subroutine to update the account.

Subroutine UPDATE ACCOUNT

The subroutine that updates the account should be similar to the one coded for Problem 6 in Chapter 12. The main difference is that the date must be assigned to a simple variable, not to a subscripted variable. This is because the account can be accessed directly. In the sequential file, the fields had to be stored in arrays, then the account number array searched for the account number. Your subroutine should print one of the following prompts beneath the account. The prompt printed depends on whether or not the transaction is the first one. We have included the "Re-enter" prompt in the first display on page 448.

```
        *                                                                   *
        *                                                                   *
        *********************************************************************
Date, code, amount? [Jan. 21,1,152.00]
Are the entries correct (y/n)? [n]
Re-enter the date, code, amount--[Jan. 21,1,152.16]
Are the entries correct (y/n)? [y]

        *                                                                   *
        *                                                                   *
        *********************************************************************
Another transaction for account number 301 (y/n)? [y]
Date, code, amount? [Jan. 30,2,300.00]
Are the entries correct (y/n)? [y]
```

Subroutine PRINT ACCOUNT

Print the values of the buffer variables throughout the subroutine.

Subroutine PROCESS DATA

Check the code. If the code is one, call a subroutine that increases the current balance by the amount of the transaction. Sample statement that increases the balance:

```
9210 BALANCE = CVS(BALANCE2$)+AMOUNT
```

Increase the row by one and LOCATE ROW. Place the new date and new balance in the buffer and move the buffer's contents to the data file. Print the date of the transaction, the amount of the transaction and the new balance from program variables. Display these values within the account on the screen.

If the code is 2, decrease the current balance by the amount of the transaction. Write statements similar to those required for a code of one.

8. The data listed below is currently stored in data file INVENTR1.DAT. Write a program that allows a sales clerk to find the quantity in stock of a particular item, that updates the inventory after a sale has been made, and that prints a customer's bill.

Stock Number	*Description*	*Quantity*
100R9	Ribbons	8
101D5	Diskettes (5 1/4")	9
102D3	Diskettes (3 1/2")	10
103P7	Printer Paper (Box)	4
104Q8	Pens	6
105Q7	Pencils	18

Rough Layout of the Output:

```
                                                            (cleared screen)
            This program updates inventory, prints a customer's bill.
            Do you wish to continue (y/n)? [y]

                               Quantity check (y/n)? [y]

                               Stock number? [102D3]

Is the stock number correct (y/n)? [y]

                               Quantity of Diskettes (3 1/2")  10
```

```
Press any key to continue
                                                              (cleared screen)
                     Quantity check another item (y/n)? [n]
                                                              (cleared screen)
                     Record a sale (y/n)? [y]

                     Stock number? [102D3]

Is the stock number correct (y/n)? [y]

                     Quantity sold? [1]
                     Clerk number? [12]
                     Charge account number? [25367]
                     Date (mm/dd/yy)? [04/10/XX]
                     Unit price? [2.98]

Are the entries correct (y/n)? [y]
                                                              (cleared screen)
         ====================================================
                             MICROMEDIA
         ====================================================
         Clerk: 12                            Sales Slip 19804
         Date: 04/10/XX

                          Item: Diskettes (3 1/2")

                          Amount: 1 x $ 2.98             $ 2.98
                          Tax:                           $ 0.18

                          Total:                         $ 3.16



         Charge Account No. 25367
         ----------------------------------------------------
         Signature ______________________
         ====================================================
Press any key to continue
                                                              (cleared screen)
                     Record another sale (y/n)?
```

The Main Routine

Your main routine must contain two WHILE/WEND loops. Before the first loop, allow the user to respond to a prompt that asks for a quantity check. Inside the loop, call a subroutine that INPUTs a stock number, call the subroutine that prints the quantity of the item, then ask if another quantity check is desired. End the loop.

Before the second WHILE/WEND loop, ask if a sale is to be recorded. Within the loop, call the subroutine that INPUTs a stock number, call the subroutine that records the sale, then ask if another sale is to be recorded.

Subroutine INPUT KEY (STOCK NUMBER)

Modify subroutine RETRIEVE RECORD listed on page 431. Rather than clear the screen, leave a blank line. Do not compare the stock number keyed in with the one on the retrieved record. This is performed in the next two subroutines. Also, do not display the record retrieved.

Subroutine PRINT QUANTITY

Determine whether or not the stock number keyed in is the same as the stock number on the retrieved record. If they are the same, print the quantity of the item as shown in the output on page 446. If they are not the same, display a "not found" message.

Subroutine RECORD A SALE

Perform the same comparison as the one in subroutine PRINT QUANTITY. If the stock numbers are not the same, display a "not found" message. If they are the same, INPUT the quantity sold, the salesclerk's number, the customer's charge account number, the date, and the unit price. Calculate the quantity now in stock and move the updated quantity to the data file. Assign the rate of sales tax to a variable and call the subroutine that prints the bill.

Subroutine PRINT BILL

Calculate the cost of the item, the sales tax, and the total cost. Print the customer's bill. Use the sales slip shown on page 447 as a guide. Hint: Print the item from the buffer variable.

9. Write a program that merges two random access files. First, create the following two data files. The files store the account numbers, the names, and the account balances of customers who have deposits in two types of savings accounts in a bank. A new type of savings account has been created and the accounts are to be merged to create a new data file.

SAVINGS1.DAT

Account Number	*Customer Name*	*Balance*
2S19	Peters,William	$3,592.51
3S64	Moore,Samuel	1,469.85
5S31	Reimer,Jean	2,942.63
6S85	Cameron,Ralph	4,819.42
8S42	Lee,Barbara	3,127.36

SAVINGS2.DAT

Account Number	*Customer Name*	*Balance*
1S28	Harrison,Carl	$5,142.15
4S15	Dyck,Marion	6,093.21
7S36	Lindsay,Allan	4,228.67

Note that the records in each file are already sorted by account number and that the files are of unequal length. Your program must print the contents of the new file in the following manner:

```
              PERSONAL SAVINGS ACCOUNTS
================================================
ACCOUNT NUMBER      CUSTOMER NAME         BALANCE
================================================
     1S28          Harrison,Carl        $5,142.15
     2S19          Peters,William       $3,592.51
     3S64          Moore,Samuel         $1,469.85
     4S15          Dyck,Marion          $6,093.21
     5S31          Reimer,Jean          $2,942.63
     6S85          Cameron,Ralph        $4,819.42
     7S36          Lindsay,Allan        $4,228.67
     8S42          Lee,Barbara          $3,127.36
```

The Main Routine

Open three files: SAVINGS1.DAT, SAVINGS2.DAT, and SAVINGS3.DAT. The buffer for each file requires two FIELD statements: one for the header record and the other for a data record. Call a subroutine that retrieves the values representing the number of records in each of the files SAVINGS1.DAT and SAVINGS2.DAT, then call the subroutine that merges the two files. Give the user the opportunity to examine the merged file.

Subroutine that Retrieves Values Stored in Header Records

Assign the value representing the number of records in file SAVINGS1.DAT to NO.RECORDS1% and the value representing the number of records in SAVINGS2.DAT to NO.RECORDS2%.

Subroutine MERGE FILES

Your program must transfer a record from either SAVINGS1.DAT or SAVINGS2.DAT to SAVINGS3.DAT. The record transferred depends on the account number (whichever is lower). These transfers continue until the last record has been moved from the shorter file. The program must then transfer the records remaining in the longer file to SAVINGS3.DAT. Here are some of the tasks involved in merging the two files.

Assign 2 to record counters RECORD.NUM1, RECORD.NUM2, and RECORD.NUM3. GET the first data record from each of files SAVINGS1.DAT and SAVINGS2.DAT. Set up a WHILE/WEND loop which continues as long as RECORD.NUM1 is less than or equal to NO.RECORDS1% and RECORD.NUM2 is less than or equal to NO.RECORDS2%. Inside the loop, use an IF/THEN/ELSE statement to determine whether or not an account number in SAVINGS1.DAT is less than an account number in SAVINGS2.DAT. Call a subroutine for each alternative. Increase record counter RECORD.NUM3 by one and end the loop.

If an account number in SAVINGS1.DAT is less than an account number in SAVINGS2.DAT:

(a) Move the account number, customer name, and balance from SAVINGS1.DAT to SAVINGS3.DAT. Sample statements:

```
6210 LSET ACCOUNT.NO3$ = ACCOUNT.NO1$
6220 LSET NAME3$ = NAME1$
6230 RSET BALANCE3$ = BALANCE1$
6240 PUT #3,RECORD.NUM3
```

(b) Increase RECORD.NUM1 by 1 and GET another record from SAVINGS1.DAT.

If an account number in SAVINGS1.DAT is not less than an account number in SAVINGS2.DAT:

(a) Move the account number, customer name, and balance from SAVINGS2.DAT to SAVINGS3.DAT using statements similar to those above.

(b) Increase RECORD.NUM2 by 1 and GET another record from SAVINGS2.DAT.

Following the WHILE/WEND loop, determine which file contains records that have not yet been moved to SAVINGS3.DAT. This would be the longer file. If RECORD.NUM1 is less than or equal to NO.RECORDS1%, call Subroutine COMPLETE DATA FILE SAVINGS1.DAT, otherwise, call Subroutine COMPLETE DATA FILE SAVINGS2.DAT.

Subroutine COMPLETE DATA FILE SAVINGS1.DAT

Set up a WHILE/WEND loop which continues as long as RECORD.NUM1 is less than or equal to NO.RECORDS1%. Inside the loop:

(a) Move an account number, customer name, and balance from SAVINGS1.DAT to SAVINGS3.DAT.

(b) Increase RECORD.NUM1 by 1 and GET another record from SAVINGS1.DAT.

(c) Increase RECORD.NUM3 by 1.

Following the loop, use the LOC function to determine the number of records in file SAVINGS3.DAT, assign this value to NO.RECORDS3% and store the value in the header record of SAVINGS3.DAT.

Subroutine COMPLETE DATA FILE SAVINGS2.DAT

This subroutine is similar to the subroutine described above. The only difference is that you will be using variables for file SAVINGS2.DAT rather than variables for file SAVINGS1.DAT.

Remaining Subroutines

Write a subroutine that reads and prints the contents of data file SAVINGS3.DAT and another subroutine that formats the report.

16

PROJECT

Objectives

The project presented here is a relatively large project, incorporating much of the material covered in this book. It requires hundreds of lines of code and a number of people to design and write the programs. The project offers valuable experience in group work.

Contents

Introduction

In any large programming assignment, a project director is usually in charge of the overall job. It is the director's responsibility to ensure that the software package includes all the functions requested by the customer, that the final product is free of errors, and that it is delivered on time. The project director usually deals with more than one customer and is, therefore, usually in charge of more than one project.

The tasks are assigned to teams of programmers. One programmer on each team is delegated team leader. The team leader assigns tasks to the members on the team, coordinates the work of the team, offers suggestions, and helps with the programming.

The team leaders are responsible for the interfacing (the linking) of the major blocks of tasks. They must define global variables and ensure that local variables do not cause adverse reactions in other modules. The leaders consult with each other regularly and, periodically, report to the project director.

The Problem

The programs to be developed here will form a payroll software package. Payroll accounting differs greatly from business firm to business firm. The software to be developed for this project will be simplified to a certain extent.

A furniture manufacturer employing 40 people has asked a software firm to computerize its payroll. The furniture company has two departments: framework and upholstery. Employees are paid by the number of pieces produced. The software package must perform the following functions:

A. Create files.

1. Create a master data file (employee name, employee number, address, telephone number, rate of pay, quota, deduction rates, etc.)
2 Create an employee data file (employee number, pieces produced, gross pay, deductions, net pay, totals to date, etc.)
3. Create a text file (a form letter).

B. Maintain files.

1. Change the master data file and the employee data file. This includes the addition of new employees.
2. Delete employees from the master data file and from the employee data file.

C. Calculate wages and totals, print checks and letters.

1. Calculate wages, calculate totals to date for each employee.
2. Print checks.
3. Print the form letter.

D. Print reports and data files.

1. Print a production report.
2. Print a wage report.
3. Print the master data file.
4. Print the employee data file.

Data Specifications

The customer has requested that the following information be stored on disk for each employee and has provided the project director with the necessary data.

1. Employee number. Employees in the Framework department are numbered 1 through 20, employees in the Upholstery department are numbered 26 through 45. Numbers 21 to 25 inclusive will be assigned to new employees in the Framework department, numbers 46 to 50 inclusive will be assigned to new employees in the Upholstery department. The plant can accommodate a maximum of 50 employees after renovations; five new employees in each department.
2. Department. Framework or Upholstery.
3. Employee name. Maximum 20 characters. The title Mr. or Ms. is included.
4. Address. Maximum 25 characters. City, province, and postal code are included.
5. Telephone number. Eight characters. Example: 664-1234
6. Social insurance number. Eleven characters. Example: 431-268-513
7. Date of employment. Ten characters. Example: 02/10/19XX
8. Quota (per week). Two digits.
9. Regular rate of pay. Range: $7.48 to $10.15 inclusive.
10. Rate of income tax withheld. A percentage. Example: 25%
11. Rate of pension withheld. A percentage. Example: 6%
12. Rate of health insurance withheld. A percentage. Example: 4%
13. Date of current work week (week ending). Ten characters. Example: 10/12/19XX
14. Pieces produced each day. Two digits. Example: 12
15. Pieces produced in one week. Two digits.

16. Gross pay. Five digits. Example: 468.52
17. Income tax deducted. Five digits. Example: 117.13
18. Pension deducted, health insurance deduction. Each 4 digits. Example: 28.11
19. Net pay. Five digits. Example: 304.54
20. Total gross pay to date. Seven digits. Example: 23139.71
21. Total income tax deductions to date. Six digits. Example: 5784.93
22. Total pension deductions to date. Six digits. Example: 1388.38
23. Total health insurance deductions to date. Five digits. Example: 925.59
24. Total net pay to date. Seven digits. Example: 15040.81

The customer would like the following form letter stored on disk.

> Starting January 9, extensive renovations will be made in your department. New equipment will replace the machines currently in use. To create a more pleasant atmosphere, we will provide more floor space by the construction of an additional room at the rear of the building. We also intend to improve the lighting in your area by installing several skylights.
>
> Most of the work will be done in the new section of the plant. When renovations must occur in your area of work, you will be informed well in advance. We hope these renovations do not inconvenience you too greatly. They should be completed in approximately three months.
>
> Yours truly,
> MODERN FURNITURE COMPANY LIMITED
>
> Kenneth Williamson
> President

Organization of Teams

The project director assigns the job to four teams, distributing the work as shown in Figure 16-1.

FIGURE 16-1 ORGANIZATION OF TEAMS

Team 1	Team 2	Team 3	Team 4
Create files	Maintain files	Calculate wages,totals Print checks, letters	Produce reports Print files

Data Organization

The team leaders decide to organize the data into three files in the following manner. The 12 fields in the master data file form one record, the 14 fields in the employee data file form one record.

Master data file

1. Employee number
2. Department (e.g. framework)
3. Employee name

Employee data file

1. Employee number
2. Date of current work week (week ending)
3. Pieces produced each day (5 fields)

4. Address
5. Telephone number
6. Social insurance number
7. Date of employment
8. Quota (per week)
9. Regular rate of pay
10. Rate of income tax withheld
11. Rate of pension withheld
12. Rate of health insurance withheld

4. Pieces produced in one week
5. Gross pay
6. Income tax deducted
7. Pension deducted
8. Health insurance deduction
9. Net pay
10. Total gross pay to date
11. Total income tax deductions to date
12. Total pension deductions to date
13. Total health insurance deductions to date
14. Total net pay to date

Text File

The form letter

Breaking Down the Problem

The team leaders decide to use random access files but to transfer some of the data from the master data file and some from the employee data file into one-dimensional arrays. In this way, records can be retrieved immediately from all files yet frequently used data need not be retrieved from disk each time calculations must be performed.

Three programs must be written to create the above three files. The writing of these programs is assigned to Team One. The remaining tasks will be incorporated into one large program. These tasks, assigned to the remaining three teams, are as follows:

1. Maintain the master data file and the employee data file.
2. Calculate the wages, calculate the totals to date, print the checks and the form letter.
3. Produce the reports, print the data files.

The three team leaders in charge of the tasks listed above agree that this large program should be a menu-driven program. They decide that the program should include one main menu and several sub-menus. The main menu should list the following options:

MAIN MENU

1. Maintain files
2. Calculate wages, totals to date, print checks and form letter
3. Print reports and files
4. End the program

Each of the first three options will have sub-menus. For example, the menu for maintaining files could be:

MAINTAIN FILES

1. Add employees to or change master data file
2. Add employees to or change employee data file
3. Delete employees from master data file
4. Delete employees from employee data file
5. Return to the main menu

Sub-menus must also be displayed for options two and three shown in the main menu above. The three team leaders now break down this large program into four major blocks. Each block will be comprised of several modules.

1. The main block that interfaces with the other blocks.

2. The block of modules that maintains the master data file and the employee data file.
3. The block of modules that calculates the wages and the totals, prints the checks and the form letter.
4. The block of modules that produces the reports and prints the data files.

The three leaders design the overall program listing modules rather than detailed instructions. Suppose they choose the design shown below. (We have illustrated just the first two major blocks. The leaders must complete the design.) As the team leaders design the program, they assign a block of line numbers to each module. For instance, the 8000 block of numbers will be assigned to the subroutine that deletes data from the master data file.

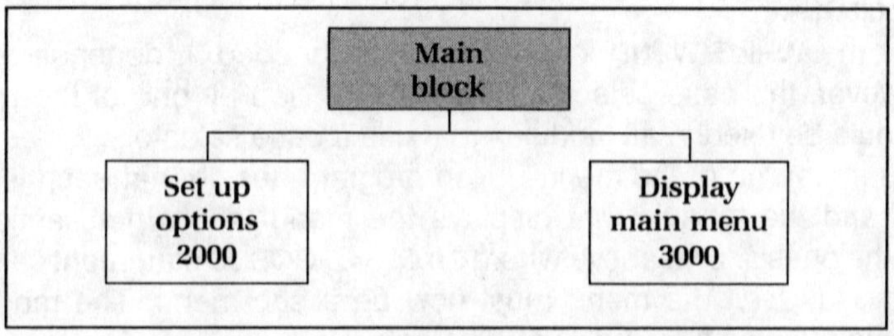

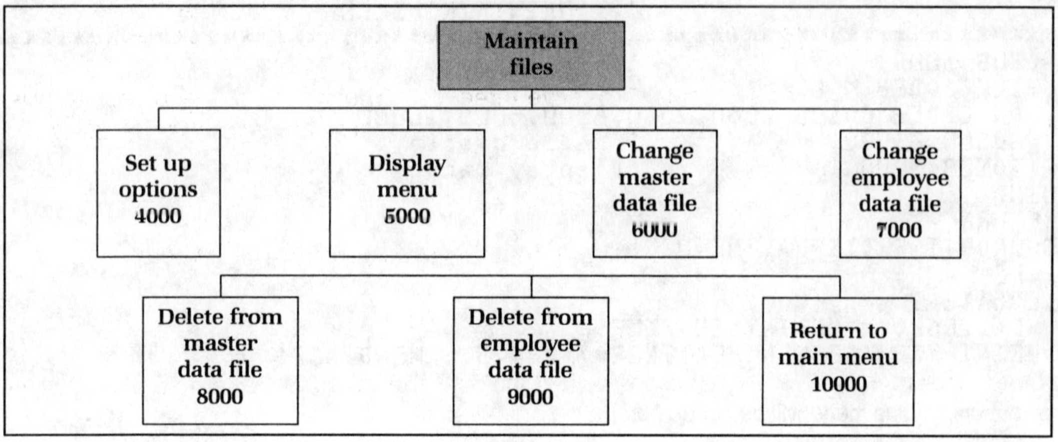

The team leaders must complete the design by breaking down major blocks 3 and 4 listed above. To ensure correct interfacing, the leaders decide to code the main block themselves. They decide on the following code. (The block will be be styled and documented later.)

```
1000 'PAYROLL
2000 'MAIN ROUTINE
2010   GOSUB 3000                    'Display main menu
2020   WHILE CODE1 < 5
2030     ON CODE1 GOSUB 4000,11000,17000,24000
2040     GOSUB 3000                  'Display main menu
2050   WEND
2060   END
3000 'SUBROUTINE DISPLAY MAIN MENU
3010   CLS
3020   LOCATE 8
3030   PRINT TAB(13) "Select one of the options shown below, then press Enter"
3040   PRINT
3050   HEADING1$ = "MAIN MENU"
3060   PRINT TAB((80-LEN(HEADING1$))/2+.5); HEADING1$
3070   PRINT
3080   PRINT TAB(23) "1.  Maintain files"
3090   PRINT TAB(23) "2.  Calculate wages, totals to date,"
3100   PRINT TAB(23) "    print checks and form letter"
3110   PRINT TAB(23) "3.  Print reports and files"
```

```
3120    PRINT TAB(23) "4.  End the program"
3130    PRINT
3140    INPUT "------------Enter an option:  1,2,3, or 4--",CODE1
3150    RETURN
```

Each of the four line numbers listed in the ON ... GOSUB statement represents the first statement of a major block of modules. Statement 4000 would be the first statement in the block of modules that maintains the files, statement 11000 would be the first statement in the block of modules that calculates the wages, prints the checks and the form letter. The two remaining line numbers in the ON ... GOSUB statement reference blocks that print reports and data files and that end the program. The line numbers we have listed are examples. A different list may be required.

It should be noted that the WHILE/WEND loop may not be needed. It depends on how control is returned to the main module. However, the case selector should be verified by one of the methods shown in chapter 14. The same method should be used in all modules that use a case selector.

The three team leaders in charge of the menu-driven program decide that each leader will write the module that sets up the options and the module that displays the menu for his/her section of the program. These modules will be similar to the ones shown above where an ON ... GOSUB statement calls the required subroutines and a menu is displayed. However, the menu must now be a sub-menu. The modules to be written by the team leader in charge of maintaining files are illustrated below.

```
4000 '*******************************************************************
4002 '                              MAINTAIN FILES
4004 '*******************************************************************
4010   GOSUB 5000                      'Display menu
4020   WHILE CODE2 < 6
4030     ON CODE2 GOSUB 6000,7000,8000,9000,10000
4040     GOSUB 25000                   'Freeze display
4050     GOSUB 5000                    'Display menu
4060   WEND
4070   RETURN
5000 'SUBROUTINE DISPLAY MENU
5010    CLS
5020    LOCATE 7
5030    HEADING2$ = "MAINTAIN FILES"
5040    PRINT TAB((80-LEN(HEADING2$))/2+.5); HEADING2$
```

(Statements that display the menu will be coded here)

```
5120    INPUT "---------------Enter an option:  1,2,3,4, or 5--",CODE2
5130    RETURN
```

Members on the team will now complete this block by writing subroutines that change (or add) records in the master and employee data files and that delete records from both files. Subroutine 10000 merely returns control to the main module. A subroutine similar to Subroutine 10000 must be coded at the end of each major block of modules.

Tasks Assigned to Each Team

Team One

Team one must write programs that create the following three files:

1. The master data file.
2. The employee data file.
3. The text file (the form letter).

To reserve positions in the files for prospective employees (a maximum of five employees may be added in each department), records must be created for employees 21 to 25 inclusive in the Framework department and for employees 46 to 50 inclusive in the Upholstery department. The employee number must be placed in the employee number field but the null string or zero may be placed in each of the other fields.

Team Two

Modules written by Team Two must perform the following functions:

1. Add employees to or change records in the master data file.
2. Add employees to or change records in the employee data file.
3. Delete employees from the master data file.
4. Delete employees from the employee data file.

Note: To add an employee, one of the fields (other than the employee number field) must be checked. If the field contains spaces or a zero, data can be moved to the record; if the field does not contain spaces or a zero, an appropriate message should be displayed.

Team Three

Three modules must be written by team three.

Module One

For each employee, this module must (a) allow the user to key in the date and the number of pieces produced each day (b) calculate the net pay, (c) calculate totals to date. The quota and the various rates needed to calculate the net pay for each employee must be obtained from the master data file. (Remember, it was suggested that some of this data be transferred from the master data file into arrays.) Any employee who produces more pieces than the quota allotted receives, on the excess pieces, a rate of pay that is one and one-half times the regular rate of pay. The following formulas must be used:

No Excess Pieces Produced:

Gross pay = Pieces produced × Regular rate of pay

Excess Pieces Produced:

Gross pay = Regular rate × Quota + (Pieces produced − Quota) × Regular rate × 1.5

Formulas for all employees:
Income tax deduction = Gross pay × Rate of income tax withheld/100

Pension deduction = Gross pay × Rate of pension withheld/100

Health insurance deduction = Gross pay × Rate of health insurance withheld/100

Total deductions = Income tax deduction + Pension deduction + Health insurance deduction
Net pay = Gross pay − Total deductions

For each employee, the module must add the gross pay, the income tax deduction, the pension deduction, the health insurance deduction, and the net pay to a respective accumulated total stored on disk to obtain totals to date. The following must be written to the employee data file for each employee. These values will replace the values of the previous week.

1. Date of current work week (week ending)
2. Pieces produced per day
3. Total pieces produced during the week
4. Gross pay
5. Income tax deducted
6. Pension deducted

7. Health insurance deduction
8. Net pay
9. Total gross pay to date
10. Total income tax deductions to date
11. Total pension deductions to date
12. Total health insurance deductions to date
13. Total net pay to date

Module Two

This module must print checks for each employee. Specific output must be sent to the printer; such as the date, the name of the payee, the amount of the check. On the check stub, each deduction, the accumulated income tax deduction, the accumulated pension deduction, and the accumulated gross pay should be printed. Assume check forms are pre-printed.

Module Three

The form letter, stored on disk, must be sent to all employees in the Framework department. Each letter must be addressed to an employee in the following manner:

October 15, 19XX

Mr. John Smith
123 Main Street
Anycity ZZ
M3L 6S7

Dear Mr. Smith:

(The form letter is typed here.)

The module must call the ASCII file that separates a name and converts, if necessary, letters in the name to upper case or lower case. The module must also call the ASCII file that separates an address. These subroutines must be renumbered before they are merged with the program so that statements in the file do not replace statements in the program. Labels must be printed for the envelopes.

Team Four

Team Four must write modules that produce a wage report and a production report and modules that print the data files. The hard copy of the master data file is required when the file is changed, the hard copy of the employee file is needed periodically for totals. Samples of the wage report and the production report are shown below. Both must be centred.

```
                           WAGE REPORT

                For Week Ending October 12, 19XX
=====================================================================
NAME                   NUMBER   PIECES   GROSS PAY   DEDUCTIONS   NET PAY
=====================================================================
Mr. James Morrison      01       10      $562.19     $169.67     $392.52
Ms. Ellen Kerr          02       13      $531.25     $148.18     $383.07
Mr. Kevin Taylor        03       12      $579.32     $181.23     $398.09
Mr. Len Dunsmore        04       13      $600.84     $196.54     $404.30
Ms. Laureen Toews       05       11      $587.58     $187.42     $400.16
Mr. Chris Bodnar        06       10      $546.93     $158.39     $388.54
..................      ..       ..      .......     .......     .......
```

The production report must be group printed by department. Each department's listing must start on a new page.

```
Department:  Framework              10-12-19XX           Page 1

                         PRODUCTION REPORT
        ==================================================
        NAME                             NUMBER        PIECES
        ==================================================
        Mr. James Morrison               01            10
        Ms. Ellen Kerr                   02            13
        Mr. Kevin Taylor                 03            12
        Mr. Len Dunsmore                 04            13
        ....................             ..            ..

Total number of pieces produced                        584
```

```
Department:  Upholstery             10-12-19XX           Page 2

                         PRODUCTION REPORT
        ==================================================
        NAME                             NUMBER        PIECES
        ==================================================
        Mr. Paul Ginter                  26            10
        Mr. Gary Hillier                 27            12
        Ms. Karen Baxter                 28            15
        ....................             ..            ..

Total number of pieces produced                        623
```

The four team leaders must decide on the number of members on each team. To determine the number, they must keep in mind the amount of work assigned to each team. Work should be distributed as evenly as possible. Team leaders meet regularly to establish global and local variables. The team leaders meet periodically with the project director to report progress and to resolve any major problems.

After all programs have been written and individually tested, the entire software must be tested to ensure that it is error-free and that it meets the customer's requests. When no further work needs to be done on the programs, external documentation must be written. This task is usually performed by the team leaders using input received from the members on their teams. Hard copies of the programs, their outputs (using sample data), the disk or disks on which the programs are stored, and the external documentation can now be delivered to the customer.

APPENDIX A

ASCII Character Codes

The following table lists the 7-bit ASCII codes most frequently used. The codes are in decimal notation. The list includes the use of or the character of each code.

ASCII Code	Use or Character	ASCII Code	Character	ASCII Code	Character
009	tab	058	:	093	]
010	line feed	059	;	094	^
011	home	060	<	095	_
012	form feed	061	=	096	grave accent
013	carriage return	062	>	097	a
028	cursor right	063	?	098	b
029	cursor left	064	@	099	c
030	cursor up	065	A	100	d
031	cursor down	066	B	101	e
032	space	067	C	102	f
033	!	068	D	103	g
034	"	069	E	104	h
035	#	070	F	105	i
036	$	071	G	106	j
037	%	072	H	107	k
038	&	073	I	108	l
039	'	074	J	109	m
040	(	075	K	110	n
041	)	076	L	111	o
042	*	077	M	112	p
043	+	078	N	113	q
044	,	079	O	114	r
045	−	080	P	115	s
046	.	081	Q	116	t
047	/	082	R	117	u
048	Ø	083	S	118	v
049	1	084	T	119	w
050	2	085	U	120	x
051	3	086	V	121	y
052	4	087	W	122	z
053	5	088	X	123	{
054	6	089	Y	124	¦
055	7	090	Z	125	}
056	8	091	[		
057	9	092	\		

APPENDIX B

Summary of Library Files

A number of modules were developed throughout the book to assist in the writing of programs. It was suggested that the subroutines be saved in ASCII format so that they can be merged with a resident program.

Two lists of these files are given below. The first displays the files alphabetically by module name, the second displays the files numerically by block number. Each list gives the names of the modules, the filenames, the line numbers used, and the page numbers in the book where the modules were given or where they were assigned as problems. Modified modules are saved as new files. An asterisk before a filename indicates that the module (or modules) was assigned as a programming problem. In the first list, a short description of each file is given as well.

LISTED BY NAME

Name of Module	Filename	Block Number	Page
CONVERT TEXT TO UPPER CASE	*CONVERT.ASC	14000	292
Converts each lowercase letter in a word (or words) to upper case. Uppercase letters remain upper case.			
CREATE A SEQUENTIAL DATA FILE	CREATE1.BAS	2000	139
A program that creates a sequential data file. All records are alike.			
CREATE A SEQUENTIAL DATA FILE	CREATE2.BAS	2000	143
A program that creates a sequential data file. One record differs from the others in the file.			
CREATE ACCOUNTS RECEIVABLE FILE	*CREATEAR.BAS	2000	157
A program that creates an Accounts Receivable file.			
FREEZE DISPLAY	FREEZE.ASC	11000	181
Causes a pause to enable a user to read instructions displayed on the screen, to examine a report on the screen, to turn on the printer, etc.			
READ RANDOM ACCESS FILE	READ-RA.BAS	24000	427
A program that reads and prints the contents of a random access file.			
REPLACE TEXT	REPLACE.ASC	13000	282
Used in a simple text editor to replace text.			
RETRIEVE A SEQUENTIAL DATA FILE	RETRIEV1.BAS	2000	141
Retrieves data from a sequential data file. All records are alike.			
RETRIEVE A SEQUENTIAL DATA FILE	*RETRIEV2.BAS	2000	144
Retrieves data from a sequential data file. One record differs from the others in the file.			
SEARCH ONE-DIMENSIONAL ARRAY	SEARCH1.ASC	17000	308
Searches a one-dimensional array.			
SEARCH TWO-DIMENSIONAL ARRAY	SEARCH2.ASC	20000	354
Searches a two-dimensional array.			
SELECTION SORT	SEL-SORT.ASC	18000	311
Performs the selection sort on a one-dimensional array.			
SELECTION SORT WITH POINTERS	SORT-P.ASC	19000	321
Incorporates pointers in the selection sort.			

SEPARATE DATA — SEPARATE.ASC — 12000 — 273

Separates data into three parts; for example, separates an address into number and street, city and province, postal code.

SEPARATE A NAME — *SEP-NAME.ASC — 15000, 16000 — 293

Merged subroutines. Subroutine 15000 separates the name into title, first name, last name. Subroutine 16000 converts the first letter of each part to upper case and the remaining letters of each part to lower case.

VERIFY DATA — VERIFY.ASC — 10000 — 179

Verifies keyed-in data by the screenful.

LISTED BY BLOCK NUMBER

Block Number	Name of Module	Filename	Page
2000	CREATE A SEQUENTIAL DATA FILE	CREATE1.BAS CREATE2.BAS	139 143
2000	CREATE ACCOUNTS RECEIVABLE FILE	*CREATEAR.BAS	157
2000	RETRIEVE A SEQUENTIAL DATA FILE	RETRIEV1.BAS *RETRIEV2.BAS	141 144
10000	VERIFY DATA	VERIFY.ASC	179
11000	FREEZE DISPLAY	FREEZE.ASC	181
12000	SEPARATE DATA	SEPARATE.ASC	273
13000	REPLACE TEXT	REPLACE.ASC	282
14000	CONVERT TEXT TO UPPER CASE	*CONVERT.ASC	292
15000 16000	SEPARATE A NAME	*SEP-NAME.ASC	293
17000	SEARCH ONE-DIMENSIONAL ARRAY	SEARCH1.ASC	308
18000	SELECTION SORT	SEL-SORT.ASC	311
19000	SELECTION SORT WITH POINTERS	SORT-P.ASC	321
20000	SEARCH TWO-DIMENSIONAL ARRAY	SEARCH2.ASC	354
24000	READ RANDOM ACCESS FILE	READ-RA.BAS	427

APPENDIX C

Files Stored on a Diskette

A diskette is available on which are stored the following program files, ASCII files, and data files. An asterisk before a filename indicates that the module (or modules) was assigned as a programming problem in the book and may be deleted from the diskette by your instructor.

PROGRAM FILES

Filename	Chapter	Page
CREATE1.BAS	7	139
CREATE2.BAS	7	143
*CREATEAR.BAS	7	157
RETRIEV1.BAS	7	141
*RETRIEV2.BAS	7	144
READ-RA.BAS	15	427

ASCII FILES

Filename	Chapter	Page
VERIFY.ASC	8	179
FREEZE.ASC	8	181
SEPARATE.ASC	11	273
REPLACE.ASC	11	282
*CONVERT.ASC	11	292
*SEP-NAME.ASC	11	293
SEARCH1.ASC	12	308
SEL-SORT.ASC	12	311
SORT-P.ASC	12	321
SEARCH2.ASC	13	354

DATA FILES

Filename	Purpose	Chapter	Page(s)
PARTS1.DAT	Exercise	8	184
HOUSE.DAT	Problem 1	8	198
SALES5.DAT	Problem 2	8	199
PHONE.DAT	Problem 3	8	200
BILL.DAT	Problem 4	8	201
TICKETS.DAT	Problem 5	8	202
APPLIANC.DAT	Problem 6	8	202
PIECES.DAT	Problem 7	8	203
PARTS.DAT	Sample Programs	9	213
AR2.DAT	Problem 4	9	230
	Problem 6	12	330
	Problem 7	12	331
SALES6.DAT	Problems 1,2,3	9	227
DEPREC.DAT	Problem 3	10	256
STORSALE.DAT	Problem 5	10	259

ADDRESS.DAT	Problem 2	11	289
	Problem 2	12	326
TEST.DAT	Problem 3	11	290
NAMES1.DAT	Exercise 12	12	325
	Problem 1	12	326
NAMES2.DAT	Problem 1	12	326
DRIVERS1.DAT	Problem 3	12	327
DEPART.DAT	Problem 4	12	327
MASTER.DAT	Problem 5	12	329
SCORES3.DAT	Problem 5	12	329
STUDENT1.DAT	Problem 6	13	370
KEY1.DAT	Problem 6	13	370
*LETTER.DAT	Problem 1	14	396
COURSES.DAT	Problem 5	14	404
STUDENT2.DAT	Problem 5	14	404
AR4.DAT	Problem 6	14	405
*STDENTS1.DAT	Problems 1 to 5	15	439
*ACC-REC1.DAT	Problem 6	15	443
*ACC-REC2.DAT	Problem 7	15	445
INVENTR1.DAT	Problem 8	15	446
SAVINGS1.DAT	Problem 9	15	448
SAVINGS2.DAT	Problem 9	15	448

APPENDIX D

DOS Commands

CAUTION: To execute the following commands, DOS must first be loaded into the computer. **Loading DOS destroys a program in memory; therefore, you must save your program before you load DOS.** The dialogue below is based on a computer system with two disk drives and with the standard keyboard. For each of the following commands, insert the DOS diskette in drive A and load DOS into the computer. Following the DOS prompt A>, type the required command, then press Enter. DOS commands, as well as responses Y and N, may be typed in either uppercase or lowercase letters.

Some of the DOS messages given in this Appendix may differ slighty from the ones that appear on your screen. The difference depends on the version of DOS being used. It should also be noted that a source diskette is the original diskette, a target diskette is a backup diskette that contains (or will contain) some or all of the contents of the original diskette.

Formatting a Diskette (FORMAT)

A new diskette is blank and must be changed to a format that is acceptable by DOS. This is performed by the FORMAT command. FORMAT analyzes the diskette for defects and initializes a directory making the diskette ready for use. **If you format a diskette on which information is stored, FORMAT destroys all this information.**

1. Type the FORMAT command as follows:

```
A>format b: ←—— Press ENTER
```

2. The symbol "b" is the drive. The computer displays:

```
Insert new diskette for drive B:
and strike ENTER when ready
```

3. Follow the above instructions.
4. The computer displays the following:

```
Formatting...
```

5. The light in drive B goes on and remains on as the diskette is being formatted.
6. The computer lets you know when formatting is complete, then displays:

```
xxxxxx bytes total disk space
xxxxxx bytes available on disk

Format another (Y/N)?
```

7. Type Y if you have another diskette to format and press ENTER. Repeat Step 3.
8. Type N if you do not wish to format another diskette. Press ENTER. The DOS prompt will appear on the screen. Remove the diskettes from the drives.

Examining a Diskette (DIR)

The FILES command lists the names of files stored on a diskette while the computer is under the control of BASIC. It is also possible to list the filenames while the computer is under the control of DOS. Use the DIR command as explained below.

1. Write protect the diskette to be examined and insert the diskette in drive B.
2. Type the DIR command as follows:

```
A>dir b:/p ←—— Press ENTER
```

   The symbol "b" is the drive. The /p parameter stops the directory listing when the screen is full. To resume the listing, press any key. When the parameter /p is not included in the DIR command, files are listed without a screen break.

3. The names of your files are displayed on the screen in the following manner:

```
PROGRAM1 BAS       4608   12-01-90     9:15a
FREEZE   ASC        360    3-26-90    12:40p
           2 File(s)    357528 bytes free
```

   DIR displays a filename with its extension, the size of the file in bytes, and the date and time the file was saved. At the end of the listing, the number of files and the number of bytes free are displayed.

4. To obtain a hard copy of the directory, turn on the printer then hold down the Ctrl key as you press the PrtSc key. Enter the following DIR command.

```
A>dir b: ←—— Press ENTER
```

   To stop the printing, press the Ctrl and PrtSc keys once more. The remaining filenames will be listed on the screen but not printed. If you allow the computer to print the entire directory, you must press the Ctrl and PrtSc keys at the end of the listing to disengage the printer from the screen.

5. After the DOS prompt appears, remove the diskettes from the drives.

Copying a Diskette (DISKCOPY)

DISKCOPY copies the contents of one diskette to a second diskette. **If the second diskette contains information, the information on the second diskette will be destroyed.**

1. Type the DISKCOPY command as follows:

```
A>diskcopy a: b: ←—— Press ENTER
```

2. The computer displays:

```
Insert SOURCE diskette in drive A:

Insert TARGET diskette in drive B:

Press any key when ready . . .
```

3. Remove the DOS diskette from drive A. Write protect your source diskette and insert the source diskette in drive A. Insert the target diskette in drive B and press any key.
4. The lights on drives A and B alternately go on and off.
5. When copying is complete, the computer displays:

```
Copy another diskette (Y/N)?
```

6. Type Y if you have another diskette to copy. Do not press ENTER. The computer displays the instructions shown in Step 2 above. Repeat the process.

7. Type N if you do not wish to copy another diskette. Do not press ENTER. The computer displays:

```
Insert disk with \COMMAND.COM  in drive A
and strike any key when ready
```

8. Remove the diskettes from the drives. On the index label (your label) of the backup diskette, write "BACKUP", the contents of the diskette, and the date. Use a felt-tip pen.

9. If you wish to load DOS, insert the DOS diskette in drive A and strike any key. The DOS prompt A> should appear on your screen.

Copying One File (COPY)

You should use the COPY command when you wish to copy a file from one diskette to another diskette. You will find this command useful when you wish to copy one of the library files, such as FREEZE.ASC, to your BASIC diskette.

1. Remove the DOS diskette from drive A. Write protect your source diskette and insert the diskette in drive A. Insert the target diskette in drive B.

2. Read the dialogue below on the COPY command then type in the command which could be as follows:

```
A>copy freeze.asc b: ←—— Press ENTER
```

   Freeze.asc is the name of the file to be copied, b is the drive to which the copy will be sent. The extension must be included in the filename of the original file. The name of the copy will be the same as that of the original file. If you wish to name the copy differently, include a filename for the copy. A sample command is shown below.

```
A>copy freeze.asc b:freeze1.asc ←—— Press ENTER
```

   The copy stored on the diskette in drive b will be named freeze1.asc. Now, type one of the COPY commands shown above and press ENTER.

3. The lights on drives A and B alternately go on.

4. When copying is complete, the computer displays:

```
        1 File(s) copied
A>
```

   Note that the DOS prompt appears. If you wish to copy another file, key in the copy command once more.

5. After all desired files have been copied, remove both diskettes from their drives. On the index label (your label) of the backup diskette, write "BACKUP", the contents of the diskette, and the date. Use a felt-tip pen.

Erasing a File (ERASE)

The KILL command deletes a file from disk while the computer is under the control of BASIC. You can also delete a file from disk while the computer is under the control of DOS. Use the ERASE command.

1. Insert, in drive B, the diskette which stores the file to be deleted.
2. Type the ERASE command.

```
A>erase b:program1.bas ←— Press ENTER
```

The symbol b is the drive, program1.bas is the name of the file to be deleted. Note that you must include the extension.

3. When the DOS prompt reappears on the screen, the file has been deleted.
4. Remove the diskette from drive B.

Renaming a File (RENAME)

1. Insert, in drive B, the diskette which stores the file to be renamed.
2. Type the RENAME command.

```
A>rename b:program1.bas program2.bas ←— Press ENTER
```

The symbol b is the drive, program1.bas is the current filename, program2.bas is the new filename. The extension must be included in the current filename. If a file by the second filename already exists or if the original file is not found, the computer displays:

```
Duplicate file name or File not found
```

3. When the DOS prompt reappears on the screen, the file has been renamed.
4. Remove the diskette from drive B.

Examining the Contents of a Sequential Data File (TYPE)

To examine the contents of a sequential data file, use the TYPE command. Suppose you wish to examine data file EMPLOYE1.DAT. Perform the following tasks.

1. Write protect the diskette on which the data file resides and insert the diskette in drive B.
2. Type the TYPE command.

```
A>type b:employe1.dat ←— Press ENTER
```

3. The computer displays the contents of the file in the following manner:

```
"Darryl Brown",9.54,38,74.57,2.25,3.67
"Ellen Miller",8.87,39,72.14,2.25,3.42
"Lorne Hayes",9.88,42,79.84,2.25,4.15
"Andrea Jones",10.04,47,85.26,2.25,6.31
```

4. To obtain a hard copy, turn on the printer then hold down the Ctrl key as you press the PrtSc key. Enter the above TYPE command. The computer directs the list to the printer as it displays the list on the screen. After the file has been printed, press the Ctrl and PrtSc keys once more to disengage the printer from the screen.
5. After the DOS prompt appears on the screen, remove the diskette from drive B.

APPENDIX E

A BASIC Command

Renaming a File (NAME)

This command performs the same function as the DOS command RENAME; that is, it renames a file.

1. Load BASICA and ensure that the BASIC prompt OK is displayed.
2. Insert, in drive B, the diskette which stores the file to be renamed.
3. Type the NAME command.

```
name "b:program1.bas" as "b:program2.bas" ←— Press ENTER
```

The symbol b is the drive, program1.bas is the current filename, program2.bas is the new filename. The extension must be included in the current filename. If a file by the second filename already exists, the computer displays:

```
File already exists
```

4. When the BASIC prompt reappears on the screen, the file has been renamed.
5. Remove the diskette from drive B.

INDEX

To the Owner of this Book:

We are interested in your reaction to *Structured Basic and Program Design* by Margaret McRitchie. Through feedback from you, we can improve this book in future editions.

1. What was your reason for using this book?
   _____University Course   _____Continuing Education
   _____College Course   _____Other (specify__________________)

2. If you used this book for a course, what is the name of the school you attend?

   ____

3. Approximately how much of the book did you use?
   _____¼   _____½   _____¾   _____all

4. Which chapters or sections were omitted from your course?

5. Have you any suggestions for improvement?

Fold here

Business Reply Mail

No Postage Stamp
Necessary if mailed
in Canada

Canada Post Postes Canada
43652

POSTAGE WILL BE PAID BY

SCOTT DUNCAN
Publisher
College Editorial Department
HOLT, RINEHART AND WINSTON
OF CANADA, LIMITED
55 HORNER AVENUE
TORONTO, ONTARIO
M8Z 9Z9

Tape shut